Language Arts

Language Arts

Extending the Possibilities

Marjorie R. Hancock
Kansas State University

Upper Saddle River, New Jersey
Columbus, Ohio

Library of Congress Cataloging-in-Publication Data

Hancock, Marjorie R.
Language arts : extending the possibilities / Marjorie R. Hancock.—1st ed.
p. cm.
Includes index.
ISBN 0-13-018990-1
1. Language arts. 2. Visual literacy. 3. Children's literature. 4.
English language—Study and teaching—Computer-assisted instruction. I. Title.
LB1576.H23319 2007
372.6—dc22

2006013904

Vice President and Executive Publisher: Jeffery W. Johnston
Senior Editor: Linda Ashe Bishop
Senior Development Editor: Hope Madden
Senior Production Editor: Mary M. Irvin
Design Coordinator: Diane C. Lorenzo
Senior Editorial Assistant: Laura Weaver
Production Coordination and Text Design: Techbooks
Cover Designer: Ali Mohrman
Cover Images: Images.com
Production Manager: Pamela D. Bennett
Director of Marketing: David Gesell
Marketing Manager: Darcy Betts Prybella
Marketing Coordinator: Brian Mounts

This book was set in Garamond by Techbooks. It was printed and bound by Von Hoffman Press, Inc. The cover was printed by The Lehigh Press, Inc. Photo on page 396 is supplied by Patrick White/Merrill. All other photos are supplied by author.

Pearson Education Ltd.
Pearson Education Singapore, Pte. Ltd.
Pearson Education Canada, Ltd.
Pearson Education—Japan
Pearson Education Australia PTY, Limited
Pearson Education North Asia Ltd.
Pearson Educación de Mexico, S.A. de C.V.
Pearson Education Malaysia, Pte. Ltd.

10 9 8 7 6 5 4 3 2 1
ISBN: 0-13-018990-1

Preface

Language Arts: Extending the Possibilities presents an insightful, developmental view of today's language arts instruction. As children's literature, visual literacy, and technology expand the dimensions of language arts classrooms, teachers need guidance in the best ways to embrace the changing landscape of education. In addition to reading, writing, listening, and speaking, the National Council of Teachers of English and the International Reading Association extended the realm of instructional possibilities by recognizing the role of viewing and visual representation in the language arts. Since technology encompasses both of these language arts, it also becomes a means of receiving and communicating information in a rapidly changing global perspective. Brimming with classroom-based lesson plans, new technology features, authentic children's work samples, interdisciplinary connections, and assessment choices, this visually appealing and content-rich textbook projects an innovative view of teaching and learning the language arts in today's classrooms.

In addition to up-to-date coverage of the language arts, this book focuses on four areas of effective, creative instruction that affect the literacy curriculum:

- ***Children's literature.*** A major focus of this text, children's literature provides a model, springboard, and inspiration for teaching the language arts across the curriculum. Readers will learn how quality literature selections can affect and enhance their instruction.
- ***Viewing and visual representation.*** The addition of viewing and visual representation to the list of the language arts invites instruction that responds to our dynamically changing world. Art, music, drama, performance, and the graphic arts become viable options for visual reception within the language arts and across an interdisciplinary framework.
- ***Technology.*** The incorporation of technology, from e-mail to the Internet, changes the way learners both send and receive information to and from their audiences. Technology can exist in harmony with the language arts as it serves a role in instructional planning, student information access, and student sharing of projects while reinvigorating both teaching and learning.
- ***Interdisciplinary focus.*** The importance of the language arts from an interdisciplinary standpoint is critical in school systems in which ever-increasing accountability demands pervade instructional time. Language arts applications in authentic contexts across all disciplines provide a key for teachers to unlock and disseminate content area knowledge through literacy practice across the entire academic day.

About the Organization of This Book

Part 1, "An Extended Vision of the Language Arts," builds on the current *Standards for the English Language Arts,* published in 1996 by the International Reading Association and the National Council of Teachers of English. Developmental, sociolinguistic, reader response, and constructivist theories provide a theoretical foundation for every teacher. Seven Principles of Language Arts Instruction form the framework for the book and weave their way throughout the philosophical strands of the text. Extending a vision of the language arts also includes a fresh vision for the literacy environment by connecting a new philosophy of language arts instruction to the classroom's physical surroundings and providing new ideas for organizing the classroom to inspire both teaching and learning. Specific guidelines and a template for lesson planning guide the creation of meaningful language arts lessons. A chapter addressing the needs of diverse learners prepares teachers for the changing face of America's classrooms.

Part 2, "The Beginnings of Language Connections," focuses on the wonders of natural language development and the beginnings of reading and writing. This section celebrates the emerging capabilities of young children as they internalize and synthesize the complexities of language. Language development in the home environment transfers to the school setting as language acquisition, modeling, and engagement in listening and speaking pervade early language development. As children embark on their journeys toward literacy in K–2 classrooms, immersion in and intensive practice with language provide mandatory steps toward conventional literacy. Shared reading, guided reading, word study, interactive writing, retellings, and visual response and representation supply the foundations of literacy in the early grades.

Part 3, "Developing, Expanding, and Refining Literacy," presents both an apprenticeship model and a workshop approach to literacy learning to assist in the ongoing development of the language arts. Chapters on listening and speaking, the reading apprenticeship, and the writing apprenticeship focus on collaborative efforts at exploring and expanding the language arts. The most recent findings of the National Reading Panel and a meaning-centered approach to reading frame the discussion here.

Three chapters provide comprehensive discussion of the power of writing in the language arts classroom. Chapter 8 explores the writing process, writing traits, writing workshop, and writing strategies. Chapter 9 highlights narrative and poetic writing, and Chapter 10 features expository writing. Each chapter is enhanced by authentic student writing samples to reflect the instructional concepts shared within each chapter. Part 3 also contains an innovative chapter on viewing and visual representation, introducing new ideas for incorporating these perspectives into the language arts instructional model. The six chapters in Part 3 form the heartbeat of the textbook and provide conceptual understandings of a variety of language arts methodologies for the preservice or inservice teacher.

Part 4, "Tools to Enhance Communication and Access Information," begins with a focus on language arts conventions. The skills and strategies of spelling, handwriting and word processing, grammar and usage, and mechanics continue to play an important role in clear communication. The key feature of this part is a chapter that focuses on technology. The role of the Internet in planning instruction and accessing information, the potential of e-mail as a communication mode, and the role of cyber inquiry across disciplines emphasize the potential of connecting technology and the language arts. Ideas to create meaningful connections to reading and writing workshop, to access information on authors and illustrators, and to research topics of interdisciplinary interest abound throughout the technology chapter.

Part 5, "Extending the Boundaries of the Language Arts," reaches into the realm of interdisciplinary instruction. With an overwhelming amount of knowledge to convey to students, teachers must efficiently and effectively cross boundaries and coordinate disciplines for instruction. Weaving language arts through an interdisciplinary theme forms the ultimate example of practicing and refining the language arts in meaningful topical contexts. This part also includes an essential chapter on assessment to monitor continuous progress in the language arts. Beyond the boundary of standardized tests lies the dynamic domain of authentic assessment. Portfolios, checklists, and rubrics inspire reflective evaluation and goal setting. Individual progress, placement, and projection serve high expectations for lifelong language arts learning. In a climate of accountability, the assessment chapter balances teaching beliefs with the reality of testing.

Enriching Features

A number of features illustrate, clarify, and extend chapter concepts to model classroom teaching and to provide the tools needed to embark on language arts teaching.

- Classroom-based language arts ***lesson plans*** built on standards, technology, and literature are found in every chapter. These lesson plans contain essential components of planning and preparation for instruction and become a template and a model for the language arts lesson plans to be created for this course. Visit the lesson plan module in Meeting the Standards on the Companion Website to this book to adapt these lessons to meet your own state's standards.
- ***Children's literature*** is integrated throughout the text—from the chapter openings to the Literature Clusters that provide quality titles across genres for use in literature-based language arts lessons. The CD-ROM *A Database of Children's Literature* that accompanies this book provides you with easily accessible information on thousands of excellent titles worth sharing with children and adolescents in an intuitive, user-friendly format.
- Each chapter presents a feature called ***Tech Tips,*** a recurring element that showcases meaningful ways to bring literacy and technology together. Chapter 13 focuses on technology and provides language arts links through Internet access, quality software, and technology devices to facilitate the presentation of language arts lessons.
- Authentic ***student samples,*** from writing assignments to visual representations, in each chapter serve to transport the reader into the real world of language arts learners. Readers can view and analyze authentic products, which reveal developmental accomplishments and perspectives.
- A ***standards-based perspective,*** including the *Standards for the English Language Arts* and the *NETS Teacher and Student Technology Standards,* pervades the chapters and provides the basis for chapter lesson plans.

Supplements

For the Student

CD-ROM. *A Database of Children's Literature* accompanies every copy of this book. This resource contains valuable information on thousands of children's literature titles at a glance. The easily navigated database helps you find titles for a lesson, unit, or read-aloud, or for one specific reader. Search by topic, author, genre, or title, and see what awards each title has received.

Companion Website. Providing more ways to use technology effectively as a teaching tool, the Companion Website, available at www.prenhall.com/hancock, offers opportunities for self-assessment; analysis, synthesis and application of concepts; regularly updated links to Web addresses; and special information for teachers required to pass state tests in language arts teaching in order to obtain credentials. The site features several components essential for the ongoing development of preservice teachers.

- *Meeting the Standards* modules provide standards-driven lessons online, which you can download onto your computer and adapt to meet your own state's standards, providing you with lessons that align with both national and state standards to take right into your own classroom.
- *Praxis practice questions* help prepare preservice teachers for the Praxis II exam.
- *Self-Assessments* help users gauge their understanding of text concepts.
- *Web Links* provide useful connections to all standards and many other invaluable online literacy sources.
- *Chapter Objectives* provide a useful advance organizer for each chapter's online companion.

For the Instructor

Instructor Resource Center. The Instructor Resource Center at **www.prenhall.com** has a variety of print and media resources available in digital format—all in one location. As a registered faculty member, you can access and download passcode-protected resource files, course management content, and other premium online content directly to your computer.

The following digital resources are available for *Language Arts: Extending the Possibilities:*

- A test bank that includes multiple choice and essay tests.
- PowerPoint presentations specifically designed for each chapter.
- Chapter-by-chapter materials, including chapter objectives, suggested readings, discussion questions, and in-class activities.

To access these items online, go to www.prenhall.com, click on Instructor Support and then go to the Download Supplements section. Here you will be able to log in or complete a one-time registration for a user name and password. If you have any questions regarding this process or the materials available online, please contact your local Prentice Hall sales representative.

Acknowledgments

This textbook is the culmination of fifteen years of college-level language arts methods instruction, preservice teacher supervision, and literature-based research at Kansas State University. Authentic classrooms, enthusiastic children, and dedicated teachers make this book trustworthy, credible, and meaningful. The success of the preservice and inservice teachers of Kansas State University's College of Education in the teaching field confirms the importance and results of implementing the instructional philosophy and the principles of language arts instruction that pervade this text as they influence student learning in their own classrooms.

Special appreciation is due to the following teachers in the North Central Kansas school districts who opened their classroom doors to my needs in collecting student work samples, photographs, and examples of quality instruction: Ginger Becker, Michelle Benoit, Melissa Brown, Karla Fisher, Lynelle Frazier, Wynette Hardy, Mary Hessenflow, Janet Jorgensen, Karol Kadel, Lotta Larson, Danny Munsell, Lori Munsell, Kimberly Oakley, Kaylee Myers, Lisa Seirer, and Stacy Wullschlager. The pages of this book reflect their instruction, their students' writing, their incorporation of quality literature, and their dynamic enthusiasm as teachers of K–8 literacy learners.

My sincere appreciation is extended to Lotta Larson, my former B.S., M.S., and current Ph.D. student. Through Lotta's years of professional development, she has inspired me with her creative thinking, forward visions of teaching, endless energy, and technology prowess. I credit Lotta with my own continued professional development as she pushes me forward with my thinking, my writing, and the conceptual changes surrounding the new literacies. Lotta Larson is responsible for the lesson plans, technology tips, and student/teacher supplements that accompany this text.

I'd also like to thank the editorial staff at Merrill/Prentice Hall. Linda Bishop helped create a vision for this book and patiently believed in my writing and supported the content as it developed over time. My development editor, Hope Madden, provided the weekly spark and helpful direction I needed whenever I became bogged down and thought I might never complete this project. Mary Irvin and the countless people who oversaw production were instrumental in creating a final product of high professional and instructional quality. Stephanie Magean, my copyeditor, graciously provided wordsmithing, polishing, and organizing that improved the clarity and accuracy of this textbook. Vijay Kataria added his special touches to the appealing presentation of the text, features, figures, and student work samples. The finished textbook stands as a tribute to this admirable team effort.

My sincere thanks goes to the professional reviewers who provided informed perspectives and opinions: Helen Abadiano, Central Connecticut State University; Gail Bauman, Florida A & M University; Ward A. Cockrum, Northern Arizona University; Judith H. Cohen, Adelphi University; Patricia DeMay, University of West Alabama; Stacey A. Dudley, Bowling Green State University; Patricia P. Fritchie, Professor Emeritus, Troy University System; David Hayes, University of Pittsburgh; Anna L. Heatherly, retired from the University of Arkansas, Little Rock; Carolyn Jaynes, California State University, Sacramento; Leanna Manna, Villa Maria College; Susan McCloskey, California State University of Fresno; Darlene Michener, California State University, Los Angeles; Laurie Elish-Piper, Northern Illinois University; Debera Price, Sam Houston State University; and Patrice Werner, Southwest Texas State University. This first edition is far better because of their suggestions and contributions.

My deepest thanks is given to my family for listening, waiting, wondering, and supporting me during this arduous process. Their understanding of my need to share my successful language arts methods teaching with the larger language arts community provided me the drive to complete this task.

I fondly dedicate this book to my grandson, Nathaniel Hancock, whose emergence into literacy has inspired me to applaud his language arts accomplishments, cherish his writing, value his love of reading, and treasure my weekly visits with him. Nathaniel, may you always be as proud as I am of your ability to read, write, listen, speak, view, and visually represent your creative thoughts and ideas.

Teacher Preparation Classroom

See a demo at
www.prenhall.com/teacherprep/demo

Your Class. Their Careers. Our Future. Will your students be prepared?

We invite you to explore our new, innovative and engaging website and all that it has to offer you, your course, and tomorrow's educators! Organized around the major courses pre-service teachers take, the Teacher Preparation site provides media, student/teacher artifacts, strategies, research articles, and other resources to equip your students with the quality tools needed to excel in their courses and prepare them for their first classroom.

This ultimate on-line education resource is available at no cost, when packaged with a Merrill text, and will provide you and your students access to:

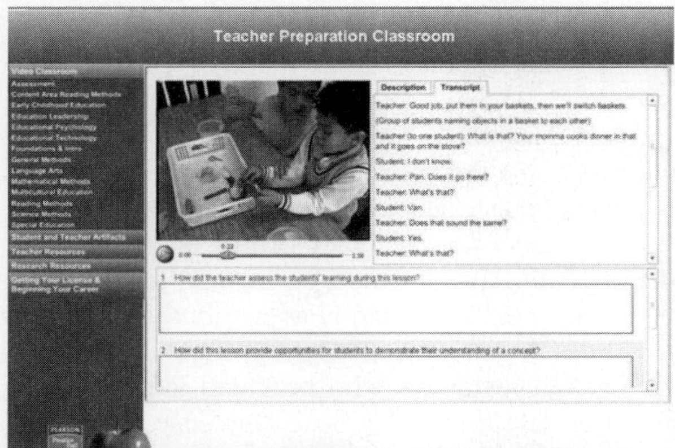

Online Video Library. More than 150 video clips—each tied to a course topic and framed by learning goals and Praxis-type questions—capture real teachers and students working in real classrooms, as well as in-depth interviews with both students and educators.

Student and Teacher Artifacts. More than 200 student and teacher classroom artifacts—each tied to a course topic and framed by learning goals and application questions—provide a wealth of materials and experiences to help make your study to become a professional teacher more concrete and hands-on.

Research Articles. Over 500 articles from ASCD's renowned journal *Educational Leadership*. The site also includes Research Navigator, a searchable database of additional educational journals.

Teaching Strategies. Over 500 strategies and lesson plans for you to use when you become a practicing professional.

Licensure and Career Tools. Resources devoted to helping you pass your licensure exam; learn standards, law, and public policies; plan a teaching portfolio; and succeed in your first year of teaching.

How to ORDER *Teacher Prep* for you and your students:
For students to receive a *Teacher Prep* Access Code with this text, instructors **must** provide a special value pack ISBN number on their textbook order form. To receive this special ISBN, please email Merrill.marketing@pearsoned.com and provide the following information:

- Name and Affiliation
- Author/Title/Edition of Merrill text

Upon ordering *Teacher Prep* for their students, instructors will be given a lifetime *Teacher Prep* Access Code.

Contents

Note: Every effort has been made to provide accurate and current Internet information in this book. However, the Internet and information posted on it are constantly changing, and it is inevitable that some of the Internet addresses listed in this textbook will change.

Chapter 1

A NEW VISION FOR THE LANGUAGE ARTS

Exploring the Possibilities

From time to time, as the world turns, something different happens, something mysterious and astonishing: a kind of brightening, a quickening, a leap beyond, when ideas brush against one another and sparks fly and ignite other ideas. It can happen anywhere, anytime.

From *The House of Wisdom* by Florence Parry Heide & Judith Heide Gilliland

This eloquently written opening paragraph from *The House of Wisdom* describes an incident in Baghdad 1,000 years ago. Young Ishaq discovers the power of words to ignite the human imagination and to connect knowledge between one faraway time and place to another.

Today, this passage reflects the dawning of a new age in the language arts as current beliefs about language and literacy merge with future possibilities that extend the power of language into unexplored realms. While *something different happens*—No Child Left Behind mandates, standards, assessments, technology—it is evident that *sparks can fly and ignite other ideas* as teachers accept new challenges by blending fresh methodologies, best practices, and heartfelt beliefs about literacy to create a renewed enthusiasm for teaching the language arts in a changing world.

The dynamic nature of literacy is a phenomenon that reflects ongoing changes and needs in our society. Centuries ago, literacy was simply defined and measured by one's ability to affix a signature to a document as evidence of rudimentary reading and writing abilities. A century ago, the ability to navigate and produce print reflected a literate citizen. In the past 30 years, literacy expanded beyond reading and writing to include aspects of speaking and listening, ultimately acknowledging the natural interrelationship of both the communicative and receptive language arts. Literacy instruction became synonymous with language arts instruction.

With the approach of the new millennium, literacy began to encompass the ability to function competitively in the visual and communicative arts (Flood & Lapp, 1997/1998), which include the basic language arts (reading, writing, listening, speaking), the visual arts (drama, art, film, video, television), and, most recently, technology (electronic communication and information retrieval). Visual media permeate almost every aspect of our students' lives. As a proliferation of communicative technological techniques such as the Internet and e-mail become integral parts of our daily lives, the conceptualization of literacy once again bears revision (Flood & Lapp, 1995).

The terms *visual literacy, media literacy,* and *computer literacy* pervade our language as the roles of images, media, and Web sites supplement the role of traditional printed text and increasingly support learning and knowing. Accessing and communicating have become as important as the higher level skills of analyzing, synthesizing, interpreting, and evaluating. Several positive consequences have resulted from expanding the concept of literacy to include media and technology:

- ***Motivating and engaging students.*** Both unconventional print and nonprint materials help students gain interest in reading and writing. Children's literature, *Reading Rainbow* videotapes, audiobooks, and Internet Web sites have stimulated student desire to read and write.
- ***Linking classrooms and communities.*** The broadened view of literacy restores a critical connection as the use of film, illustrated books, and technology bridge the gap between school and home culture. Digital media carry global images and cultures to often isolated classrooms. Web sites connect with students and ongoing events around the world, as does e-mail, which allows students across the globe to interact, sharing data, reacting to world events, and responding to children's books.
- ***Reaching ESL and bilingual students.*** The most effective instructional techniques for ESL and bilingual learners involve drama, music, and visual experiences to help convey meaning and content. An increasing proportion of our school population thrives on an expanded view of literacy that includes a respect for diverse culture and language within and beyond our boundaries—a global learning community that finds value in differences.
- ***Strengthening parent-school connections.*** A fresh notion of literacy may serve as a natural invitation for more parents to become involved in visual and technological aspects of their children's literacy. The inclusion of visual arts and technology

redefines who can be involved in the "literacy club" and proposes new roles for parents, teachers, and students in the classroom.

- ***Student-centered learning.*** Expanding the definition of literacy to include visual arts, media, and technology shifts students further toward self-directing their own lifelong learning by knowing *how* to learn, not simply *what* to learn. Recognition of varied learning styles and communicative products further individualizes language arts learning.

A dynamic definition of language arts–based literacy pervades this book. ***Literacy*** *implies many things; an individual's ability to read and write, to listen and speak, to view or visually represent thoughts and ideas through communication, understanding, and interpretation of both print and nonprint media as generated by a dynamic society.*

This new era of literacy is strongly accompanied by a new era of classroom accountability. More than ever before, the measure of student learning provides the benchmark for the effectiveness of literacy instruction. Teachers must match their literacy learning objectives to state standards and show, through test score data, that their instruction matters. Teachers as professionals know that literacy instruction must be guided by standards, but it must also be balanced with their own philosophical beliefs about how best to create literate citizens who carry the power of literacy into their own futures.

Objectives

- To introduce the current view of language arts through the *Standards for the English Language Arts* as an overview of the literacy realm.
- To define the language arts of reading, writing, listening, speaking, viewing, and visual representation.
- To formulate a theoretical framework for the language arts by including cognitive/developmental, sociocultural, response-based, and constructivist perspectives.
- To present the Seven Principles of Language Arts Instruction supported by their related research base providing the underlying philosophy and framework for this textbook.

The Standards for the English Language Arts

Teacher Prep

The Teacher Prep Web site will help you become a better teacher by linking you to classroom videos, student artifacts, teaching strategies, lesson plans, relevant education leadership articles, and practical information on licensing, creating a portfolio, implementing standards, and being successful in field experiences. Visit this resource at www.prenhall.com/teacherprep.

Much of the learning that occurs in elementary and middle-level classrooms in the next decade may be guided by the standards movement, which began as a reform movement in the 1990s that included the writing of standards to articulate expectations in literacy and content area instruction. Professional organizations in academic disciplines have prepared documents that enumerate the expectations for each child in each area of competence. The International Reading Association and the National Council of Teachers of English (1996) have published *Standards for the English Language Arts,* a document that shares a fresh, professional vision for students to develop the language skills and strategies that will make them active, informed members of society. IRA/NCTE designates three reasons for the articulation of these standards in the English language arts:

- To prepare students for the literacy requirements of the present and the future that reflect technological advances and a changing society.
- To present a shared vision of the expectations of teachers, researchers, teacher educators, and parents for student proficiency in the language arts.

- To promote high educational expectations for *all* students and to create equity in instruction, ensuring that *all* children become informed citizens and contributing members of society.

Figure 1.1 presents the IRA/NCTE standards, which articulate goals in broad terms to allow for the diverse philosophy and teaching styles of language arts teachers. Such standards provide room for the talents of individual language arts teachers yet standardize the broad outcomes for the teaching and learning of language arts across the nation. Standards provide a framework—not a formula—around which to build quality language arts instruction.

The *Standards for the English Language Arts* build upon four perspectives that help in understanding the broad overall outcomes they represent:

1. What students *should know* and what they *should be able to do* with the language arts (Content Perspective)
2. *Why we use language* and the desired outcomes to which we direct literacy practices (Purpose Perspective)
3. *How learners develop competencies* in the language arts by building knowledge and gaining a repertoire of literacy strategies (Development Perspective)
4. *How social and cultural contexts* shape language patterns, meaning, and use (Context Perspective)

Viewing this list of standards through these four lenses clarifies what students should know, why each standard is included, what each standard means, and, through inference and discussion, how each standard may be achieved.

Take the time to read and discuss the 12 standards in terms of your own past, present, and future teaching context. Think of concrete examples and visualize what might occur in an elementary middle-level classroom that reflects the spirit of each standard. Try to internalize—not memorize—the tone of the standards so you might begin to observe how they naturally infuse the sound language instruction supported throughout this book. Note the strong infusion of technology, culture, print and nonprint media, visual literacy, and informational resources that pervade the document. You will read about these standards throughout the chapters of this book as you plan lessons, evaluate teaching and learning, and visit authentic classrooms.

In addition to national standards, most states have their own set of standards in the language arts based on these 12 foundational principles. You can access these on your state board of education Web site, where they can be printed, reviewed, utilized in lesson planning, and revisited throughout this course and in conjunction with this textbook. Notice the links between the language, content, and intent of the national standards and your own state document. Observe the overlap in terminology and the overall goal of reaching *all* children. Your state document will likely be more specific and list individual skills and strategies within the language arts and may be organized by developmental and/or grade levels. Use your state document in defining your own lesson outcomes and clarifying your philosophical reasons for teaching specific lessons in the realm of the language arts domain.

Standards signal high expectations and direction for the language arts curriculum. They do not, however, mandate the philosophy or control the belief system of a language arts teacher. While providing a framework for instruction, standards allow the teacher to select appropriate materials, create a literacy environment, determine effective methodologies, and plan individual lessons that assist in reaching the outcomes for literate citizens in a dynamic society.

FIGURE 1.1

IRA/NCTE

Standards for the English Language Arts

The vision guiding these standards is that all students must have the opportunities and resources to develop the language skills they need to pursue life's goals and to participate fully as informed, productive members of society. These standards assume that literacy growth begins before children enter school as they experience and experiment with literacy activities—reading and writing, and associating spoken words with their graphic representations. Recognizing this fact, these standards encourage the development of curriculum and instruction that make productive use of the emerging literacy abilities that children bring to school. Furthermore, the standards provide ample room for the innovation and creativity essential to teaching and learning. They are not prescriptions for particular curriculum or instruction.

Although we present these standards as a list, we want to emphasize that they are not distinct and separable; they are, in fact, interrelated and should be considered as a whole.

1. Students read a wide range of print and nonprint texts to build an understanding of texts, of themselves, and of the cultures of the United States and the world; to acquire new information; to respond to the needs and demands of society and the workplace; and for personal fulfillment. Among these texts are fiction and nonfiction, classic and contemporary works.
2. Students read a wide range of literature from many periods in many genres to build an understanding of the many dimensions (e.g., philosophical, ethical, aesthetic) of human experience.
3. Students apply a wide range of strategies to comprehend, interpret, evaluate, and appreciate texts. They draw on their prior experience, their interactions with other readers and writers, their knowledge of word meaning and of other texts, their word identification strategies, and their understanding of textual features (e.g., sound-letter correspondence, sentence structure, context, graphics).
4. Students adjust their use of spoken, written, and visual language (e.g., conventions, style, vocabulary) to communicate effectively with a variety of audiences and for different purposes.
5. Students employ a wide range of strategies as they write and use different writing process elements appropriately to communicate with different audiences for a variety of purposes.
6. Students apply knowledge of language structure, language conventions (e.g., spelling and punctuation), media techniques, figurative language, and genre to create, critique, and discuss print and nonprint texts.
7. Students conduct research on issues and interests by generating ideas and questions, and by posing problems. They gather, evaluate, and synthesize data from a variety of sources (e.g., print and nonprint texts, artifacts, people) to communicate their discoveries in ways that suit their purpose and audience.
8. Students use a variety of technological and informational resources (e.g., libraries, databases, computer networks, video) to gather and synthesize information and to create and communicate knowledge.
9. Students develop an understanding of and respect for diversity in language use, patterns, and dialects across cultures, ethnic groups, geographic regions, and social roles.
10. Students whose first language is not English make use of their first language to develop competency in the English language arts and to develop understanding of content across the curriculum.
11. Students participate as knowledgeable, reflective, creative, and critical members of a variety of literacy communities.
12. Students use spoken, written, and visual language to accomplish their own purposes (e.g., for learning enjoyment, persuasion, and the exchange of information).

Source: International Reading Association & National Council of Teachers of English (1996). Standards for the English Language Arts, *Newark, DE/Urbana, IL: IRA/NCTE, p. 12. Copyright 1996 by the International Reading Association and the National Council of Teachers of English. Reprinted with permission.*

Closely related to the *Standards for the English Language Arts* are the *National Educational Technology Standards for Teachers and Students,* which have been issued by the International Society for Technology in Education (ISTE). These standards fall into six categories:

1. Basic operations and concepts
2. Social, ethical, and human issues
3. Technology productivity tools
4. Technology communications tools
5. Technology research tools
6. Technology problem-solving and decision-making tools.

Detailed benchmarks and performance indicators can be accessed at www.iste.org and are also included in Chapter 13.

The development of standards exists under a controversial aura. Some believe standards restrict learning, narrow teaching decisions, ignore differences in students, and disempower teachers. Others see standards as common goals for learning that encourage professionalism for teachers and allow for local (both district and classroom) interpretation. Standards constitute the reality of teaching today, so both sides must be weighed, discussed, and considered in teaching the language arts. The purpose of this textbook is to provide a holistic philosophy, suggest quality literature as teaching material, and model methodologies that reflect the best practices and effective learning outcomes in the educational field.

Defining Today's Language Arts

For several decades, the language arts included reading, writing, listening, and speaking. Recently, because of the increased importance of technology and visual literacy to our world, professional organizations (IRA/NCTE, 1996) extended the possibilities by expanding the language arts to include viewing and visual representation. Simple definitions of each language art lead toward an understanding of the complexity of the literate individual.

Reading includes the skills, strategies, and individual meaning-making that blend into the act of deciphering, processing, and interpreting printed text. Whether reading the morning message on the overhead, enjoying J. K. Rowling's *Harry Potter and the Sorcerer's Stone,* or anticipating delectable items on the lunch menu, reading enables each individual to make sense of his or her world through print. Although reading progresses through several developmental refinements, the reading process at any level includes the obtaining of meaning through the ongoing skills of word identification and comprehension. Reading is a highly complex, personal activity involving reader, text, and context.

Writing describes the process of recording language graphically to transmit or preserve a thought or a series of thoughts through print. Writing can be informal—a journal entry, a pen pal letter, or a limerick—or it can be formal—a published short story, a letter to the editor, or a free verse poem. Written communication involves a complex process as it moves through stages from inception to publication. Writing, too, is developmental in nature, but always includes the transmission of a message as a permanent thought that may be read and interpreted by an audience of potential readers.

Listening includes the processing of oral sounds from the environment and the interpretation of language for information or emotional pleasure. Listening involves a broad knowledge of oral language that enables the listener to process an endless variety of messages: a teacher reading aloud E. B. White's *Charlotte's Web,* a student presenting research on dinosaurs, a literature circle discussing the philosophical aspects of Lois Lowry's *The Giver*. Each listener must possess the ability to identify sounds, process them into language, and interpret them into a meaningful message.

Speaking involves the transmission of a message through the use of oral language. It typically requires an audience who in turn must listen, distinguish sounds, intercept words, and interpret the message of the speaker. Speaking requires the articulation of sounds, a knowledge of words, and the ability to structure the message in a decodable fashion for the listener. Speaking covers a wide range—from simple kindergarten show-and-tell to the articulation of a role in a dramatic production to the presentation of a commercial for an improvised product on videotape. Parallel with the varied stages of language acquisition, speaking requires a clear message accurately and articulately transmitted through oral language and individually processed and interpreted by members of a culture.

Viewing includes the observation and interpretation of a visual, nonprint form or format that results in personal meaning-making. Viewing encompasses, but is not limited to, perusing the illustrations of a children's book, watching a videotape on the Antarctic, observing a work of art, navigating a graphic organizer, or interacting with an Internet site. The possibilities for viewing are endless in the elementary and middle-level settings as visual media pervade the classroom.

Visual representation involves the use of physical symbols, lines, and shapes to communicate thoughts, messages, interpretations, information, and story. Such representation may include drawing a character web for Willy in John Gardiner's *Stone Fox,* illustrating a journal entry in response to the vast prairie as portrayed in Patricia MacLachlan's *Sarah, Plain and Tall,* making a graph of most-liked and least-liked literary characters, or creating an image or symbol to respond to a self-selected book. Visual representation—whether in the form of art, graphics, or computer-generated formats—always contains the transmission of a personal thought, message, understanding, or interpretation to be viewed by another person. As examples of the relatively new language art of visual representation continue to evolve in the classroom setting, we will see technology, art, and graphic interpretation gain access and acceptance in the school environment.

A multitude of resources are available to assist the teacher in envisioning quality instruction across the integrated language arts (see Tech Tip). These Web-based resources will guide and inspire creative possibilities in language arts instruction and assist in accessing standards-based lesson plans.

A graphic representation of the six language arts indicates their alignment as either *receptive* language or *communicative* language (Figure 1.2) as well as their integration as they support each other in conveying meaning, both through comprehension and communication.

Receptive language involves messages taken in, received, processed, comprehended, and interpreted by the learner. Reading this textbook, listening to a lecture, and viewing an illustration from a children's book exemplify the concept of receptive language. **Communicative language** involves messages formulated, constructed, symbolized, and relayed to a potential audience. Writing an autobiography, role-playing a dramatic event, or drawing a chronological mural of main events in Phyllis Reynolds Naylor's *Shiloh* trilogy constitute communicative language.

Note that reading, listening, and viewing assume the "taking in" or comprehension of oral, written, and visual messages while writing, speaking, and visual representation assume the "sending forth" or intention of oral, written, and visual thoughts to a broader audience for a variety of purposes. The language arts underlie an ongoing cycle of receiving, processing, and conveying language for meaningful purposes.

Key Internet Resources for Language Arts Educators

The International Reading Association addresses a broad range of issues in literacy education, including research, print-based reading and writing, and the "new literacies" of the Internet age. The site includes a "Web Resources" section with links to Web-based teaching tools, articles, and resources concerning current issues in literacy, and a literacy community where members can participate in online discussions. Limited access for nonmembers. **www.reading.org**

The National Council of Teachers of English provides resources that promote teaching, research, and student achievement in English language arts at all scholastic levels. The site contains myriad resources for teachers and researchers of language arts. The NCTE Listserv Subscription Page provides access to e-mail discussion lists (listservs) where users engage in online discussions with educators throughout the world. Limited access for nonmembers. **www.ncte.org**

The American Library Association offers professional services and publications to members and nonmembers. **www.ala.org/**

The Reading Zone (Internet Public Library) operates much like the fiction section at a public library. This user-friendly site offers links to online stories and magazines, resources for teachers and parents, magazines, and information about children's favorite authors. **www.ipl.org/kidspace/browse/rzn0000**

Reading Online (International Reading Association) is a free electronic journal offering hundreds of articles on a range of topics in reading education. **www.readingonline.org/**

ReadWriteThink offers a wide selection of free standards-based lesson plans and Internet resources that will help teachers and students integrate technology into the language arts curriculum. This reliable site is a partnership between the International Reading Association (IRA), the National Council of Teachers of English (NCTE), and the MarcoPolo Education Foundation. **www.readwritethink.org/**

To look more closely at these materials and others related to "A New Vision for the Language Arts," visit the Companion Website at **www.prenhall.com/hancock**.

The language arts, however, do not exist independently of each other. In almost all teaching and learning scenarios, the language arts blend together as interactive communication and reception in the larger context of authentic learning. For example, a student independently reads Kate DiCamillo's *Because of Winn-Dixie* and writes an extended journal entry that includes a visual representation of the precious dog in the story. As the learning experience shifts to a literature circle, a peer listens as the journal entry is shared aloud, speaks as a participant and shares his or her reaction to the journal entry, and views and appreciates the emotional drawing of Winn Dixie. Although there are separate definitions for each of the language arts, it is important never to forget the natural

FIGURE 1.2
The Integrated Language Arts.

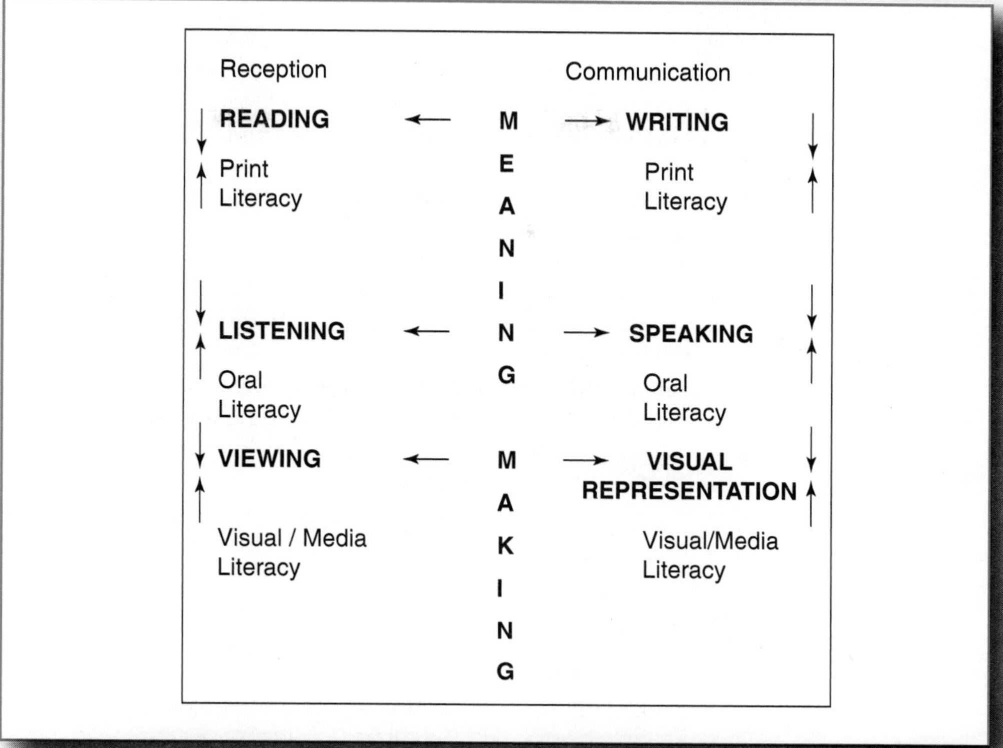

integration of these six components. In the authentic classroom setting, all of the language arts blend naturally into an engaged learning situation that highlights the interactive nature of the reception and communication of ideas through the language arts.

A Theoretical Framework for the Language Arts

Every teacher is confronted with the task of formulating a theoretical foundation for teaching the language arts, a process that provides the underpinnings from which a teacher's belief system grows. Such theories explain how children learn, how they develop language, how they make meaning, and how they respond as individuals. In this section, we look at four theories that underlie much of the content of this textbook. Although the term *theory* may be somewhat threatening to the novice teacher, we can all look upon these theories as invitations to become effective language arts teachers. Theories provide respected permission to operate under a given belief system that reflects itself in the daily choices, materials, structure, activities, and culture of the classroom. Consider each of the following four theoretical perspectives as they relate to your experiences in classroom settings and with children.

From Theory to Practice: A Cognitive Developmental Perspective

The cognitive theory of learning development, developed by Swiss psychologist Jean Piaget, impacts the foundational groundwork for language arts instruction. According to Piaget, the child is an active, engaged participant in the learning process in which the learner continuously constructs meaning (Piaget, 1952, 1955/1973). Children are able to construct a view of reality through careful observation, learning, and experience as they mature. Discovery and exploration add new information and new learning to their lives. As Piaget supports learning as an active process, he also identifies four stages of intellectual or cognitive development through which all children progress. Although the ages at which all children experience these stages vary, Piaget believed that each child developed higher reasoning abilities in the same sequence while exemplifying the following general characteristics:

Sensorimotor stage (birth to about age 2)

- Exploration of the world through the senses and through motor activity
- Inability to differentiate between themselves and their environment. (If they can't see it, it doesn't exist)

Preoperational stage (from about ages 2 to 7)

- Greater ability to communicate through speech and to engage in activities such as drawing objects and playing by pretending and imagining
- Development of numerical abilities such as the skill of assigning a number to each object in a group as it is counted
- Increased level of self-control and delay gratification, but still fairly egocentric in nature
- Inability to do conservation tasks, (which recognize that a substance remains the same even though its appearance changes)

Concrete operational stage (from about ages 7 to 11)

- Increase in abstract reasoning ability and ability to generalize from concrete experiences
- Ability to do conservation tasks

Formal operations stage (from about ages 12 to 15)

- Ability to form and test hypotheses, organize information, and reason scientifically
- Ability to show results of abstract thinking in the form of symbolic materials (e.g., writing, drama)

These stages should be interpreted not as limitations but as celebrations as each new stage is reached. The ages represent averages and provide only an overview of child development—from birth through age fifteen. Development is continuous and children readily move from one stage to the next, building an increasingly complex set of cognitive structures as they gradually progress from the concrete toward the abstract.

Piaget believed that a child's development from one stage to another takes place through a gradual process of interacting with the environment. Children develop as they confront new and unfamiliar features of their environment (e.g., language) that do not fit in with their current views of the world. When this happens, a disequilibrium occurs that the child seeks to resolve through one of two processes. The first is a process called *assimilation,* where the child may try to fit the new experiences into his or her existing view of the world. For example, a child may see a shaggy, curly-haired animal at a petting zoo and refer to it as a "dog" since it reminds him of a pet at home. The second process is called *accomodation.* In this case, a child may change his schema or view of the world to incorporate the new experience. For example, a parent might tell the child this animal is a "goat" and point out its horns, beard, and hooves, thus helping the child create a new name and accompanying characteristics for this new animal. Equilibration is the process by which balance is achieved between assimilation and accommodation. As these processes continuously interact, children construct elaborate understandings of their environments (and of their language) and continually add new information to their cognitive structure. Knowledge and language to represent that knowledge provides cognitive learning.

In some sense, this developmental process continues into the classroom and even into adulthood as we continue as lifelong learners. For example, second graders learn to identify and differentiate between illustrated picture books as "Jan Brett books"or "Patricia Polacco books" as teachers lead them through author studies. As adults, "mutual funds" might be an initial assimilated category for investment opportunities, but experienced investors eventually begin to accommodate the differences between aggressive growth funds, growth and interest funds, and growth funds. As preservice teachers make their way through this textbook, language arts provides a broad schema for instruction. Soon, however, they will find themselves differentiating between drama and readers theatre, between response prompts and comprehension questions, and between directors and vocabulary enhancers within a literature circle.

Piaget's theory of cognitive development has sound implications for the classroom. As teachers plan "developmentally appropriate" lessons, they must be aware of the average capabilities of learners. The implications for teaching includes some overall generalizations that move Piaget's theory into instructional practice during the elementary and middle level years, particularly in the area of language arts. This developmental perspective provides the foundation for effective language-based teaching and learning in the language arts classroom. Instructional insights gained from a developmental perspective include the following:

- Children have different interests and learn at different rates so different learning choices and experiences must be child-centered.
- A language-rich classroom encouraging conversation and discussion as well as a wide variety of books—read aloud to children or just made available to them—provides essential experiences for oral language development.
- The classroom environment must foster experimentation with concrete materials, encourage risk taking, and support active engagement in learning.
- Children's talk, questions, and comments offer insights into their thinking and reveal much about perceived errors in learning.

Flavell (1985) observed that "Piaget's contributions to our knowledge of cognitive development have been nothing short of stupendous" (p. 4). Educators do not always agree on the implications of Piaget's theories for classroom instruction, but his work has guided teachers in the need for concrete examples (e.g., writing models, pictures, manipulatives) and in cautiously providing concrete experiences when teaching abstract concepts to young children who may not have yet reached a formal operational stage.

From Theory to Practice: A Sociocultural Perspective

A second theoretical perspective that informs the teaching of language arts was first developed by Lev Vygotsky, a Soviet psychologist. According to Vygotsky's sociocultural theory, literacy can be viewed as a complex interactive process whose development is determined by the social and cultural contexts in which it occurs (Vygotsky, 1978, 1986). The most appropriate setting for studying how children's thinking develops was in schools and classrooms within the context of instruction (Moll, 1990). Vygotsky examined how children learn to use language as a tool to share cultural meaning as well as how using language affects the child's learning and cognitive development. The Vygotskian idea that children's thinking emerges in the context of activities that are embedded in specific social and cultural settings continues to have a profound effect on language arts instruction (Dixon-Krauss, 1996; Lee & Smagorinsky, 2000).

Vygotsky's concept of the *zone of proximal development* provides the overarching theoretical framework for understanding the role of the adult (expert)/child (novice) relationship in literacy learning. The zone of proximal development is best described as the distance between the independent, problem-solving abilities of children and their potential abilities under adult guidance or in collaboration with more capable peers (Wertsch, 1984). A child fulfills this potential by means of a *scaffold* supplied through verbal interactions with an adult.

The task of a teacher, therefore, is to support and scaffold children within this zone until they can function independently, enabling them to move to a higher level of cognitive functioning. What they were able to accomplish with assistance yesterday becomes the independent level today, leading them toward a higher level of intellectual development. These small but significant steps toward independent learning cannot be understated. Observant teachers collect important data for making informed decisions that keep children working at the cutting edge of their development.

Instruction must proceed a step ahead of development, providing temporary and adjustable support (just as a scaffold precedes the construction of a building). In the classroom, it is crucial for the teacher to be the knowledgeable adult or to identify other students who can assume such a critical role. The child benefits from the role of the more knowledgeable other who understands the learner's current capabilities, the final outcome, and the means to help the learner reach it.

A second-grade guided reading group provides a clear example of how this theory can be applied to classroom practice. The teacher has strategically placed five children in a group based on their instructional ability level in reading. That level is a bit above their ability to read independently, so higher learning can actually take place. As children read Arnold Lobel's *Frog and Toad Are Friends* silently, the teacher is available to provide useful strategies for word solving, use of context clues, or cueing from illustrations. With additional practice the next day, children gain confidence with their reading of the piece, independently applying the new strategies and moving to a higher level of reading competence. Later in the reading block, the teacher assigns peer reading, intentionally placing a struggling reader with a more able reader. As partners alternate the reading of pages, the more able reader provides a personal scaffold for the less capable reader by modeling reading strategies, skill application, and comprehension monitoring.

Vygotsky's theory is important for language arts teaching because it emphasizes the interaction between teacher and student as integral to the independent use of language—oral, written, or visual—while recognizing the role able peers can play in the language learning process. Activities that are child-centered, activity-based, and inquiry-driven support the Vygotskian principle. The social learning opportunities generated by the shared book experience, the writing process, literature circles, and many other language arts scenarios provide evidence of the link between this theory and effective classroom instruction across the language arts.

From Theory to Practice: A Response-Based Perspective

The third theoretical perspective that informs language arts instruction is the transactional theory of reader response (Rosenblatt, 1938/1995, 1978, 2004). Louise Rosenblatt spent a lifetime articulating and applying her theory to readers of all ages. Reader response to literature describes the unique, reciprocal relationship between readers and their unique responses to the text during and following engaged reading of literature. The interaction of the reader and the text is central to this theory and occurs as the reader brings life experiences to the literary text, culminating in a response (oral, written, visual) that distinguishes the literature as a truly personal experience for the reader.

Rosenblatt clearly differentiates between efferent and aesthetic reading, with the distinction lying in the primary direction or focus of the reader's attention. In *efferent reading,* the reader's attention is primarily focused on acquiring information. This might be associated with reading Diane Stanley's *Michelangelo* to obtain specific facts about the artist's life, reading J. K. Rowling's *Harry Potter and the Sorcerer's Stone* to gain familiarity with the huge cast of characters and a multitude of fantastical terms, or reading Jim Murphy's *Blizzard*! to take away historical names, places, and dates. This type of reading is termed efferent because it views reading as an information-gathering event.

In contrast, *aesthetic* reading is primarily concerned with the lived-through experience that occurs during interaction with a literary text. Aesthetic reading focuses on feelings and thoughts that flow through the reader's mind and heart during reading. Such reading might be associated with an appreciation for the creative inventiveness and persistence of Michelangelo, the touch of humor and imagination that fills the reader during a Harry Potter book, or the feeling of desperation and isolation during an uncontrolled blizzard. Aesthetic reading focuses more on the ongoing process of reading, the personal interaction rather than the product of comprehension. Equate this with literature-based reading in which personal interaction with the text is encouraged through open-ended response prompts, response journals, or literature conversations. All interactions are encouraged and valued as a targeted outcome of the active art of reading.

While the efferent stance pays more attention to the cognitive, the factual, the public, and the quantitative aspects of text, the aesthetic focuses on the affective, the emotional, the private, and the qualitative aspects of personal meaning. Most reading, however, actually incorporates a continuous, unconscious fluctuation between the efferent and aesthetic extremes. Readers are constantly moving back and forth along a continuum as they read, blending information and sentiment, knowledge and connections to their own experiences (Rosenblatt, 2004).

Three assumptions help summarize the response-based perspective (Chase & Hynd, 1987):

- Meaning is not contained in the text but is derived from a blend of the author's message and the experiences and prior knowledge of the reader.
- Readers comprehend differently because each reader is culturally and individually unique.
- Examining reader response is a more valid indication of comprehension than establishing one correct meaning for the text.

Rosenblatt's theory is effectively linked to instruction in literature-based classrooms. Applications of reader response theory have resulted in the use of aesthetic response prompts (Kelly, 1990), literature response journals (Hancock, 1993; Wollman-Bonilla & Werchadlo, 1995), grand conversations (Peterson & Eeds, 1990), and artistic response to literature (Hubbard, 1996). Entering a literature-based classroom, an astute visitor is likely to observe talk about books, independent reading of books, book clubs, response projects, aesthetic response to nonfiction across the disciplines, and literature journals—all activities grounded in Rosenblatt's theory. The impact of reader response theory, especially in the elementary setting, remains as one of the greatest contributions of the literature-based movement of the 1990s to education.

From Theory to Practice: A Constructivist Perspective

The theories of Piaget, Vygotsky, Rosenblatt, and others provide a basis for constructivism—a psychological theory of learning that implies that human beings are constantly constructing personal visions of reality while transforming it and themselves as individuals. Constructivism construes learning as an interpretive, recursive, building process by active learners interacting with a physical and social world (Fosnot, 1996). Describing how structures and deeper conceptual understandings come about, it is a theory of learning, not a description of teaching. Some general principles of learning derived from constructivism might be helpful to keep in mind before describing language arts practices grounded on this theoretical framework:

- Learning is developmental and requires invention and self-organization on the part of the learner. Learners must be encouraged to raise their own questions, to generate their own predictions and models as possibilities, and to test them.
- "Errors" must be perceived as a result of concept formation and not minimized or avoided. Challenging, open-ended exploration in meaningful contexts need to be offered, allowing learners to explore and generate many possibilities.
- Reflection is a driving force of learning. As meaning-makers, learners seek to organize and generalize across experiences. Allowing reflection time through journal writing, visual representation, and discussion of connections across experiences may facilitate complex learning.
- Dialogue within a community engenders further thinking. The classroom needs to be viewed as a learning community engaged in activity, reflection, and talk. Learners are responsible for justifying and communicating ideas within the classroom community.
- Learners proceed toward the development of meaning. These "big ideas" are learner constructed, centrally organized principles that often require the undoing or reorganizing of earlier conceptions (Fosnot, 1996).

With these learning principles in mind, envision classroom connections and their application in the context of effective teaching and learning in the language arts (Gould, 1996). The workshop approach to reading and writing allows students to try ideas on for size. Working under the guidance of a teacher and accompanied by peers, they question, brainstorm, speculate, and generate meaning. Risk taking is encouraged in both reading and writing as perfection is secondary to meaning. The transmitted message foreshadows its accuracy and comprehension takes priority over mispronunciation "miscues" that do not distort meaning. Reflection is encouraged through daily response journals and writing notebooks. Vocal sharing of ideas plays out through literature circles in response to reading and writing conferences in response to first drafts. The child-centered focus of the classroom allows for individual expression as students make learning personally meaningful as they negotiate connections between language arts and life experiences. Teachers informed by constructivist theory seek to support learning, not control it. They become planners, models, guides, observers, facilitators, and challengers for language learners. These professionals know that the development of reading and writing, listening and speaking, viewing and visual representation are never-ending processes of meaning-making.

Throughout this book, you will notice that constructivism, the cognitive theory of Piaget, the sociocultural theory of Vygotsky, and Rosenblatt's transactional theory of reader response underlie the many language-based learning activities for children. Realizing activities are grounded in theory, scrutinized through research, and eventually orchestrated

TABLE 1.1 From Theory to Principle to Language Arts Practice

Primary Theory	Principle	Practice
Cognitive developmental Sociocultural Transactional/Reader response Constructivism	Integration of reading, writing, listening, speaking, viewing, visual representation both within lessons and across the disciplines.	Chapters 1, 14* Chapters 4, 5, 6 All chapters
Transactional/Reader response Constructivism	Children's literature as an effective resource respecting diversity and culture.	Chapter 2* Chapters 3, 4 All chapters
Cognitive developmental Sociocultural Constructivism	Developmental acquisition; active engagement; apprenticeship model; workshop approach.	Chapters 4, 5* Chapters 7, 12* All chapters
Transactional/Reader response Constructivism	Meaning-centered comprehension and communication of understanding.	Chapters 3, 4, 5, 6* All chapters
Cognitive developmental Sociocultural	Skills becoming strategies when applied in authentic language arts contexts.	Chapters 7, 8, 9, 10* All chapters
Cognitive developmental Constructivism	Process orientation to the language arts; ongoing assessment and reflection	Chapter 15* Chapters 7, 8, 9, 10, 12 All chapters
Cognitive developmental Sociocultural Transactional/Reader response Constructivism	Language arts and visual literacy harmonizing with new technologies inviting creative literacy possibilities	Chapters 11, 13* All chapters

**Indicates primary emphasis*

as classroom practices is part of becoming a teaching professional. Look for these links between theory and practice throughout this book and appreciate the effectiveness of a theoretically based philosophy of teaching.

Table 1.1 illustrates possible links between the four theoretical perspectives on language learning and the Principles of Language Arts instruction presented in the upcoming section. As an emerging professional, it is important to realize the foundations of your belief system so you can explain why you teach the way you do and what underlies your instructional decisions. Linking theory to a principled belief system reflecting your own language arts practice will serve you well and continue to emerge as you move on a continuum from novice to practicing teacher.

Principles of Language Arts Instruction

Understanding, articulating, modeling, and translating a teaching philosophy into practice provides a critical goal for both preservice and practicing teachers. Knowing your own beliefs about children, learning, and the language arts, and linking them to instruction through appropriate lessons and engaged activities provide vital steps in becoming a success as an elementary or middle-level language arts teacher. The purpose of this discussion is to articulate the philosophy and principles of quality language arts instruction supported in this textbook. The accompanying photographs in Figure 1.3 clearly illustrate the application of these principles in real elementary settings so visual connections

FIGURE 1.3 Seven Principles for Language Arts Instruction.

PRINCIPLE 1. The language arts naturally integrate reading, writing, listening, speaking, viewing, and visual representation both within literacy lessons and across the disciplines.

PRINCIPLE 2. Children's literature provides an effective foundation for language arts instruction while respecting diversity in students' prior knowledge, language, culture, and literacy potentials.

PRINCIPLE 3. Language arts acquisition is developmental and demands active engagement by the emergent literacy learner through an apprenticeship model and encourages continued collaborative, interactive nurturing within a workshop approach.

FIGURE 1.3 (Continued)

PRINCIPLE 4. The primary goal of the language arts focuses on meaning-centered comprehension and communication of understanding both through the reception of ideas and communication of thought.

PRINCIPLE 5. Language arts skills grow into independent lifelong literacy strategies when applied in authentic contexts in daily reading, writing, listening, speaking, viewing, and visual representation.

PRINCIPLE 6. A process orientation to the language arts requires ongoing assessment and student reflection to provide continuous documentation of literacy growth.

FIGURE 1.3 Seven Principles for Language Arts Instruction. (Continued)

PRINCIPLE 7. The language arts harmonize with the visual nature of the learning while new technologies serve as a teaching/learning/presentation tool and invite creative possibilities in literacy.

between philosophy and practice further clarify these principles. These seven principles do not represent one educational program or even a single philosophy of teaching the language arts. They represent the best of effective language arts instruction built on a balance of philosophies and best teaching practices. They provide a window into literacy as you begin to formulate and articulate your own philosophy of the language arts. Not meant to sway you to become a single type of teacher, they should make you think, consider, challenge, and question. You are invited and challenged to try these principles on for size, as "one-size-fits-all" does not apply in the teaching profession. The sections that follow describe each principle while exemplifying some concrete ways in which each principle could be applied in an authentic elementary classroom or teaching scenario. As you read through these classroom connections, realize that many of the strategies and concepts used as examples may seem unfamiliar to you, but they will be revisited throughout the chapters of this book. The primary purpose of presenting these principles is to link educational philosophy to the real world of teaching through concrete examples for discussion and reflection.

Principle 1: The Integrated Language Arts

The language arts *naturally integrate* reading, writing, listening, speaking, viewing, and visual representation both *within literacy lessons* and *across the disciplines*. This fresh, comprehensive view of the language arts expands language reception and transmission into the area of visual language. Viewing and visual representation challenge teachers to rethink ways in which children can express their ideas, especially through art and technology. Needless to say, a teacher who functions in the abbreviated realm of the four basic language arts might be shortchanging students in their choice of options for creative expression. Earlier in this chapter, we defined each of the six language arts but emphasized their naturally integrated nature.

A teacher who activates this principle of inclusion of the six language arts in the classroom is likely to immerse students in literacy learning opportunities. The classroom will be "littered with literacy" as poems, chart paper, morning messages, and student writing fills the walls. From the moment children enter the classroom each day, language plays a primary role in the school day. Opportunities for practicing language abound through silent reading, read-alouds, daily journal writing, listening centers, writing workshop, Web site exploration, puppetry, role playing, literature circles, and artistic response to literature. Scheduled at consistent, predictable blocks of time, children learn through all venues of the language arts through continuous practice with language. Chapter 2 contains a clear portrait of the literacy environment that addresses all the language arts in the meaningful context of authentic learning. The entire textbook, however, is devoted to sharing reading, writing, listening, speaking, viewing, and visual representation across grade levels and through varied instructional methods.

In the authentic world of teaching, the language arts do not exist in isolation—they exist as an integrated network of language processes within the context of meaningfully constructed language-based activities. It is not realistic to think that any language art functions in its own realm without the other language arts. The following classroom examples will help explain the concept of the integrated language arts within a literacy lesson.

Integrating the Language Arts Within a Language Arts Lesson. Enter a first-grade classroom in which guided reading groups provide the basis of reading instruction. The class begins with a whole class read-aloud of Peggy Rathmann's *Officer Buckle and Gloria* (listening) and spontaneous responses to safety issues (speaking). As each student in the group silently reads a story (reading), the teacher suggests personal reading strategies to assist in their independent reading (listening). At the same time, other students are adding entries to their daily journals (writing) or placing safety rules on precut stars (writing/visual representation) that will later be shared (speaking/viewing) with the whole group, which will reconvene at the end of the literacy block. A Web site focusing on fire safety has been bookmarked for navigation at the classroom computer center to provide additional ideas. The natural blending of the language arts within a literacy lesson epitomizes meaningful integration and instruction. Intentionally isolating a language art removes it from its natural tendency to blend with its counterparts.

Imagine that you have entered a fourth-grade classroom during a reading workshop. Students are silently reading Chapter 4 of Jerry Spinelli's *Wringer,* both for enjoyment as well as in preparation for a choice of activities that will follow this 20-minute reading assignment. As students finish the assigned reading, they automatically take out their journals. Some write entries, some draw their responses, some list pages of story quotes, while others choose to list difficult vocabulary words. As soon as the "reading" is over, students are asked to talk in their literature circles about what they have just read. For 20 minutes, groups discuss their views of Palmer La Rue and his impending decision, while each group member pays attention so he or she can build on the conversation that is occurring (speaking/listening). The discussion turns to a picture of Palmer's anguish depicted in a face drawn in a student journal (viewing/visual representation). Another student shares her journal entry (writing/speaking) while still another reads a quote from the author while the others pay close attention to see how effectively it supports his point (reading/listening). As the discussion closes, students have the remaining 20 minutes to work on their group's response to *Wringer*. One group produces a character mural, while another creates wanted posters for each of the characters (visual representation/writing). Another group formulates and writes a sequel (speaking/writing), while still another casts a timeline of events through a story circle (visual representation/viewing). These group responses will be shared through presentations (listening/speaking/viewing) at *Wringer*'s conclusion.

These two examples at the primary and intermediate level show how all six language arts exist as an integrated whole within the context of meaningfully constructed language-based lessons and how they can be authentically represented within a single literacy lesson. We see how language works in authentic lessons. In fact, it is difficult to plan and implement a language-based lesson without naturally including most of the language arts. We would be unlikely to prepare for a performance of *Cinderella* without creating or refining a script (writing/reading) and constructing scenery (visual representation) prior to the presentation (speaking/listening/viewing). We would be unlikely to include a rhymed poem in reading class without incorporating choral reading (reading/listening), a new, adapted version (writing), and a drawing to interpret a new stanza (visual representation). Although it is obvious that every lesson need not include all the language arts, we can see that many of the language arts will surface naturally during the planning and teaching of a well-planned lesson.

A technology-based language arts lesson can also enhance the integrative aspects of instruction for students (see Lesson Plan 1.1). *Hey, Little Ant* by Phillip and Hannah Hoose combines a listening and viewing experience when accessing a Web site and a reading and visual representation read aloud with a writing extension inspired by the book itself. Teachers are encouraged to utilize accessible resources, both technology and literature, to extend the creative possibilities of their language arts integration.

LESSON PLAN 1.1

TITLE: **Points of View—What Will Happen to the Ant?**

Grade Level: 3–5

Time Frame: 1 hour

Standards:

IRA/NCTE Standards: 1, 4

NETS for Students: 3

Objective

- The writer will choose a position and present persuasive ideas to support a story ending.

Materials

- Hoose, Phillip, & Hoose, Hannah (1998). *Hey, Little Ant*. Berkeley, CA: Tricycle Press.
- Pencil, paper
- Chart paper (or board)
- Teacher model of possible story ending
- Computer (with speakers), projector, Internet access, large screen.

Motivation

- Using a projector, screen, and computer, show the official Web site of *Hey, Little Ant* (http://www.heylittleant.com) to the class. Discuss the features of the Web site and information about the authors. Listen to the song (a musical conversation between an ant about to get flattened and the child about to squish it) on which the book is based.

Procedures

- Read aloud *Hey, Little Ant.* Point out that story has no definite ending and is told from two points of views (ant and child).
- Create a T-chart to present views of both characters. Encourage discussion.
- Ask students to choose the position of one of the characters and write a story ending favoring the character of their chosen position.
- Use teacher model and persuasive writing rubric (focusing on ideas and content) to share performance expectations.
- Have students share their finished story endings from the author's chair.

Assessment

- Use a persuasive writing rubric focusing primarily on ideas and content.

Accommodation/Modification

- Remind students that they may revisit the song presented on the official Web site of *Hey, Little Ant* to recall facts or events from the story.
- To accommodate needs of English language learners, translate the *Hey, Little Ant* Web site by using Google's Language Tools (as explained in Chapter 3).

Visit the Meeting the Standards module in Chapter 1 of the Companion Website at www.prenhall.com/hancock to adapt this lesson to meet your state's standards.

Integrating the Language Arts Across the Curriculum. A broader perspective on the integrated language arts focuses on the natural inclusion of the language arts across the curriculum. This perspective emphasizes that the language arts are not isolated within the daily language arts lesson and that they can enhance instruction across all disciplines. Reading, writing, listening, speaking, viewing, and visual representation lend themselves to all content areas. A few examples illustrate the valid, effective connections that make learning and teaching even more meaningful and relevant.

The language arts enhance mathematics and science instruction in a variety of ways. Writing about a real-world numerical problem and using drawings (visual representation) to explain the problem-solving process makes learning mathematical concepts concrete and meaningful. When students write their own problems or definitions or record their steps in the problem-solving process, they make visible what otherwise might be without meaning. When students graph data that they have collected in their own classrooms, they interpret and verbally articulate their findings. Writing and visual representations become key elements in science laboratory reports. Step-by-step procedures, predictions, and outcomes require precise writing and visual representation to indicate process skills in hypothesizing, observing, and drawing conclusions. Reading informational books in the sciences, such as Laurence Pringle's *An Extraordinary Life: The Story of a Monarch Butterfly,* personalize and enhance understanding of this annual migratory journey.

The language arts also bring life to social studies as fact is blended with fiction to increase understanding and create personal relevance. Blending the reading of text and viewing of reenacted photographs in Kate Waters's *Samuel Eaton's Day* and *Sarah Morton's Day* alongside a study of pilgrims enhances a primary student's understanding of Thanksgiving in the United States. Independent reading of Karen Hesse's fictional *Out of the Dust* alongside a teacher reading aloud Jerry Stanley's factual *Children of the Dust Bowl* blends an emotional experience with an informational context for the outcomes of the Depression of the 1930s. Journal responses to fact and fiction allow students to understand the personal stakes in trying times. Social studies naturally invites the use of quality literature, plays and readers theatre, and journal entries and role playing. The natural integration of the language arts into the vast discipline of the social studies provides for enhanced learning in both domains.

The language arts become a vehicle to enhance the fine arts—drama, music, and art. A study of the Civil War invites numerous ways to incorporate the language arts: viewing of art and photography from this historical period on a Library of Congress Web site, listening to song lyrics that reflect the emotions of these conflicting times, and role playing of the dramatic surrender of Lee to Grant. These few examples illustrate the innate qualities of all the language arts to stretch across the curriculum for motivation, understanding, and personal meaning. Chapter 14, in particular, discusses the blending of the language arts across the curriculum. The lesson plans throughout this book present specific examples of how language arts naturally combine into meaningful learning experiences.

Principle 2: The Role of Children's Literature

Children's literature provides an effective foundation for language arts instruction while respecting _diversity_ in students' prior knowledge, language, culture, and literacy potentials. Children's literature can be defined as literature that appeals to the interests, needs, and reading preferences of children and captivates children as its major audience. Children's literature may be fiction, poetry, or nonfiction, or a combination of any of these. The format that houses children's literature may be a picture book in which text blends with compelling illustrations or photographs for a visual and verbal adventure through story or factual content. Or the format may be a book written in a sequence of chapters that carry the story through a sequential unfolding of fictional plot or informational descriptions. Children's literature spans classic titles—from Robert McCloskey's *Make Way for Ducklings* to Mildred Taylor's *Roll of Thunder, Hear My Cry*—as well as contemporary favorites such Lois Lowry's *Number the Stars* and Eve Bunting's *Smoky Night*, and the newest award-winning titles such as Judith St. George's *So You Want to Be President* and Louis Sachar's *Holes*, which still must undergo the true test of time. Children's literature unlocks the wonder of language, sparking imaginations, finding magic in everyday experiences, revisiting the past, and sharing lives and information (Hancock, 2004). With its many wonders, it is no question that literature serves as a powerful resource for language-based activities in the elementary classroom.

Establishing a Rationale for Literature. Teachers make countless instructional decisions based on the premise that children's books provide effective instructional resources. Plentiful research affirms the benefits of using literature as a foundation for literacy instruction (Galda & Cullinan, 2003; Morrow & Gambrell, 2000; Tunnell & Jacobs, 1998). These benefits take many forms:

- ***Literature enhances language development.*** The language of literature feeds children's linguistic word choices from encounters with story as well as influencing motivation to learn to read (Blachowicz & Fisher, 2000). Literature-based language leads to a wider oral and written vocabulary that enriches the entire literacy domain (Baumann, Kame'enui, & Ash, 2003).
- ***Literature aids comprehension.*** Stories provide a way for children to make sense of their world. Knowledge about narrative, expository, and poetic structure provide a visual framework of how reading and writing work (Pressley, 2000).

Literacy instruction surrounded by book talk also opens varied windows into deeper understanding (Raphael, Florio-Ruane, & George, 2001). Research-based evidence (Ayra et al., 2005) supports literature-based programs in providing effective learning in phonics, accuracy, and comprehension.

- ***Literature provides a writing model.*** Reading literature as a model of quality writing is linked to success in writing proficiency (Calkins, 1994; Lancia, 1997). Reading and discussing literature as the author's craft makes children more aware of their own authorship (Hansen, 2001).
- ***Literature inspires inquiry within and across disciplines.*** Many teachers enhance instruction by including related children's books as motivation for the prescribed curriculum. Inquiry-based learning often begins with the exposure to a single book but continues on an adventure through expanded literacy (Berghoff, Egawa, Harste, & Hoonan, 2000).
- ***Literature creates readers, writers, listeners, speakers, viewers, and visual representers.*** Availability and time spent with books in the company of a supportive, enthusiastic teacher are essential elements for creating language arts talent. Reading books, writing books, listening to books, adapting choral reading and readers theatre from books, viewing illustrations in books, and responding to books through a visual image puts children a step closer to becoming well-rounded, lifelong members of the universal literacy club (Smith, 2003).

Literature serves as a motivating means to learn strategies and acquire fluency, while creating excitement and enjoyment about the process of incorporating the language arts in learning. Literature creates readers, provides a springboard and model for writing, allows for read alouds and aesthetic listening, and encourages reader response to literature. The practice with language that results in interaction with books supports their inclusion as the basis of language arts instruction. Throughout this book, bibliographies of children's literature are coordinated with specific language arts activities as strong evidence of the power of literature.

Honoring the Diversity of the Learner Through Literature. Beyond the literature itself lies its extraordinary ability to reach the individual students whom we teach—students with differing backgrounds, a wide range of interests, diverse language and cultural experiences, and varied levels of literacy potential. Literature encompasses every reading level, beginning with predictable pattern books such as Eric Carle's *The Very Hungry Caterpillar* and Bill Martin Jr. and John Archambault's *Chicka Chicka Boom Boom*. Literature appeases our appetite for human emotions—from the humorous anecdotes in Richard Peck's *A Year Down Under* to the serious loss portrayed in Sharon Creech's *Walk Two Moons*. Literature reflects the diversity of our classrooms as children see their faces and experience their cultures in Allen Say's *Tea with Milk*, Gary Soto's *Snapshots from the Wedding*, Joseph Bruchac's *Crazy Horse's Vision* or Javatka Steptoe's *In Daddy's Arms I Am Tall*. Literature reflects the endless variety of language—from the authentic dialect of the South in Alan Schroeder's *Carolina Shout!* to the Spanish spoken in Carmen Lomas Garza's *In My Family/En Mi Familia*. Literature possesses the unique ability to reach each child at his or her level to inspire reading, writing, listening, speaking, viewing, and visual representation.

Teachers must honor the diversity and individuality of the learner and adjust instruction to accommodate a wide range of language and cultural needs. All children in American schools should be guaranteed a successful literacy experience through a multicultural curriculum (Fox & Short, 2003). Our goal as educators is to provide the most effective instruction to reach all learners and to meet the challenges of diversity with professional zeal. American education achieved some historical stature because of an influx of diversity into the lifeblood of the system. Respecting and meeting that diversity is a continuing challenge for teachers.

Envisioning the Role of Literature in Classrooms. Literature-based classrooms are characterized by a classroom library, author studies, big books, and student reading lists. Read-aloud time for literature, literature as a model for writing, and literature as a springboard for reader responses through speaking, writing, and artistic expression weave their way across the entire school day. Literature is used not only for reading instruction but in all areas of the curriculum to inspire learning and inquiry. Literature across all genres and the best of newly published as well as classic books reflect a teacher's professional knowledge of children's literature, a foundation for instruction that will result in a classroom filled with engaged readers who will connect books and language with their own lives.

Reader response to literature (Rosenblatt, 1978) plays a major role in literature-based instruction. Students will read not only for information but also for aesthetic enjoyment as they become lifelong readers. Reader response takes the form of oral response to prompts, written journal entries, literature circles involved in small group discussion, and even artistic dimensions that provide a meaningful response to a piece of literature. If literature is the basis of instruction, then reader response to that literature is a natural extension of the role of children's books in the classroom. Outcomes of using real literature as the basis of instruction include motivation to read books beyond ability, quality oral and written language in daily work, the desire to express feelings and opinions about books, and the promise of a future as a lifelong reader. The Literature Cluster included here provides an extensive list of picture and chapter books in which characters discover the joys of reading.

Chapter 2 provides a promising view of a literature-based classroom. Throughout the entire text, lists of children's books related to instructional ideas abound and provide countless possibilities for creating quality literature-based language arts instruction for diverse learners. Chapter 3 addresses the diversity of learners and connects literature to an appreciation of that diversity including literacy ability, cultural differences, and language needs.

Principle 3: A Developmental Apprenticeship and Workshop Model

Language arts acquisition is *developmental* and demands active engagement by the emergent literacy learner through an *apprenticeship model* and encourages continued collaborative, interactive nurturing within a *workshop approach*. Acquiring, developing, and nurturing the language arts requires continuous practice through active engagement in becoming a literacy learner. While direct instruction may assist learners in acquiring literacy, it is the teacher modeling and learner application that internalizes the language arts. This principle begins with a supportive apprenticeship model for emergent learners (Grades K–2), moving toward collaborative independence through a workshop approach with the maturing of the literacy learner (Grades 3–8).

Acquiring the Language Arts Through the Apprenticeship Model. This principle begins with a belief that emergent literacy learners should be exposed to an apprenticeship model that encourages them to become active participants in the language arts in the early primary grades (Grades K–2). Teachers who view early literacy as an

Literature Cluster

LITERACY IN LITERATURE: CHARACTERS AS READERS

Picture Books

Bradby, Marie (1995). *More than anything else.* Illus. by Chris Soentpiet. New York: Orchard.

Hest, Amy (2004). *Mr. George Baker.* Illus. by Jon J. Muth. Cambridge, MA: Candlewick.

Johnson, D. B. (2004). *Henry works.* Boston: Houghton Mifflin.

Johnston, Tony (1994). *Amber on the mountain.* Illus. by Robert Duncan. New York: Dial.

Miller, William (1997). *Richard Wright and the library card.* Illus. by Gregory Christie. New York: Lee & Low.

Mora, Pat (1997). *Tomas and the library lady.* Illus. by Raul Colon. New York: Knopf.

Parr, Todd (2005). *Reading makes you feel good.* New York: Little, Brown.

Polacco, Patricia (1993). *The bee tree.* New York: Philomel.

Polacco, Patricia (1996). *Aunt Chip and the great Triple Creek Dam affair.* New York: Philomel.

Polacco, Patricia (1998). *Thank you, Mr. Falker.* New York: Philomel.

Rahaman, Vashanti (1997). *Read for me, Mama.* Illus. by Lori McElrath-Eslick. Honesdale, PA: Boyds Mills Press.

Sierra, Judy (2004). *Wild about books.* Illus. by Marc Brown. New York: Knopf.

Smothers, Ethel F. (2003). *The hard times jar.* Illus. by John Holyfield. New York: Farrar, Straus & Giroux.

Stewart, Sarah (1996). *The library.* Illus. by David Small. New York: Farrar, Straus & Giroux.

Winters, Kay (2003). *Abe Lincoln: A boy who loved books.* Illus. by Nancy Carpenter. New York: Simon & Schuster.

Chapter Books

Cushman, Karen (1996). *The ballad of Lucy Whipple.* New York: Clarion.

Funke, Cornelia (2003). *Inkheart.* Translated from German by Anthea Bell. New York: Scholastic.

Funke, Cornelia (2005). *Inkspell.* Translated from German by Anthea Bell. New York: Scholastic.

Hesse, Karen (1998). *Just juice.* New York: Scholastic.

Kinsey-Warnock, Natalie (2002). *Lumber camp library.* New York: HarperCollins.

Lasky, Kathryn (1994). *Memoirs of a bookbat.* San Diego, CA: Harcourt Brace.

Paulsen, Gary (1993). *Nightjohn.* New York: Delacorte.

Paulsen, Gary (2003). *Shelf life: Stories by the book.* New York: Simon & Schuster.

Spinelli, Jerry (1997). *The library card.* New York: Scholastic.

Wersba, Barbara (2005). *Walter: The story of a rat.* Asheville, NC: Front Street.

apprenticeship focus on the language of instruction as they teach the art of reading and writing to young learners. Dorn, French, and Jones (1998) describe the seven principles involved in an apprenticeship approach to literacy:

- ***Observation and responsive teaching.*** Teachers observe children's literacy behavior and design instructional experiences based on children's strengths and needs. Kindergartners who chant the refrain to *Miss Mary Mack* by Mary Ann Hoberman might be ready to write a class version of this rhymed book. First graders' journals might reflect emerging knowledge of sound and symbol relationships and the need for a word wall for the common words used in daily journals. Teachers observe real children in authentic contexts; teachers respond with instruction that moves the child one small step on the path toward literacy.

- ***Modeling and coaching.*** Teachers use modeling and coaching techniques with clear demonstrations and explicit language. A first-grade teacher models writing through the morning message by means of clear handwriting and proper language structure. Eventually, students are encouraged to write their own morning messages in their journals. The teacher models a "picture walk" through a new book as children apply this comprehension strategy to independent reading time.
- ***Clear and relevant language for problem solving.*** Teachers use language prompts that enable children to plan and initiate cognitive actions for resolving problems during authentic literacy activities. Language prompts such as "Does that make sense?" "Does it look right and sound right to you?" and "Read it again and see if you can figure out what is wrong" all help move children toward solving literacy challenges on their own. In response to "How do I spell _____?" teachers can reply, "Where did you see that word this week?" or "Check the word wall" as the language of strategies pervade the apprenticeship classroom.
- ***Adjustable and self-destructing scaffolds.*** Teachers provide adjustable scaffolds that are removed when they are no longer needed. Scaffolds are various means of support that enable children to accomplish specific tasks. As children gain competence and confidence, the scaffolds are removed as children take over more responsibility. This "gradual release of responsibility model" (Pearson & Gallagher, 1983) assures the movement of responsibility for language learning to the learner.
- ***Structured routines.*** Teachers provide routine interactions with organizational structures that enable independence. Most children thrive on a predictable schedule on a daily basis, especially for independent reading and journal writing. Knowing they are responsible for locating a book after lunch for sustained silent reading time, or being prepared to share an idea in a journal at the end of the day places responsibility in the hands of the learner.
- ***Assisted and independent work.*** Teachers provide balanced opportunities for children to work at assisted and independent levels. Writing topics may be brainstormed as a group activity, and the teacher is available as everyone begins their story. Gradually, the teacher moves out of the picture as children work on their own to put their thoughts on paper. Guided reading provides initial introduction and strategy lessons to a new book. Gradually, growing confidence and familiarity provides status as an independent, successful reader.
- ***Transfer.*** Teachers teach for the transfer of knowledge, skills, and strategies across shifting circumstances and for varying purposes. Teachers constantly link what has already been learned to what is currently being learned. The application of knowledge to new learning situations provides additional practice and leads toward the continuous development of literacy.

This continuous modeling and gradual release of responsibility can be witnessed across the school day as teachers show how literacy happens but keep high expectations as students take on the responsibility for their own literacy skills, strategies, and outcomes. "I'll show you how" becomes "Now you try it" as independence in literacy emerges as the ultimate goal of the apprenticeship.

Children move from apprenticeships through practice across the language arts and across the curriculum. Only in the application and practice of modeled literacy skills and strategies can children learn how to become independent readers, writers, listeners, speakers, viewers, and visual representers. Chapters 4 and 5 provide specific guidelines for implementing the apprenticeship approach to early literacy instruction in primary classrooms.

Acquiring the Language Arts Through the Workshop Approach. As children acquire and develop their use of the language arts, the collaborative, interactive nature of literacy becomes a focus through a **workshop approach** (Atwell, 1998; Graves, 1983/2003). As they develop within the literacy learner, the language arts become enriched when they are negotiated through participation with other learners. The cooperative spirit of the present elementary classroom versus the competitive, isolated spirit of the past indicates that children can learn from each other as well as learning from their teacher. Reading buddies, literature circles, peer writing conferences, and the author's chair reflect the many ways in which this principle decentralizes the classroom and, thereby, individualizes the curriculum.

Choice plays a major role in the upper primary, intermediate, and middle-level classroom that abides by this philosophic principle. Students often retain the choices of what to read, what format their writing will take, how to respond to literature, and what topic to research. Students rely not only on the teacher for knowledge, guidance, and facilitation but on each other for locating resources, sharing opinions, and conversing about books. Peers become important partners in the learning process without diminishing the role of the teacher in the classroom as a facilitator of learning.

The reading workshop and writing workshop formats of upper primary (Grade 3), intermediate (Grades 4–5), and middle-level (Grades 6–8) classrooms provide the structure and opportunity to learn from each other. Reading workshop implies the selection of one of three related books to read. Groups of five to six students form literature circles to discuss the literature and often determine a project through which to respond to their book. While all students read the literature, group members divide tasks for discussion purposes and volunteer for duties related to the response project. Although each workshop group retains its independence, the groups do eventually come together as a community of diverse literacy learners to share projects and discuss commonalities among their books.

During a writing workshop, students often work with a peer to brainstorm topics. Peer or writing group conferences provide support and suggestions for improvement of a writing piece during revision. Sharing work in progress in the author's chair opens dialogues between all members of the class. No longer is the teacher the only audience for the product as peer acceptance or rejection restructure ownership in the piece. Children become authors subject to public scrutiny, peer suggestions, and audience praise. As newly learned skills of collaboration take hold, working with others becomes comfortable and accepted instead of awkward and defensive.

Collaborative research groups in a writing workshop also contribute toward a common goal. Individual tasks merge into a single project, as pride and ownership emerge and students learn to share materials, ideas, talents, and learning styles. For example, a classroom working on Civil War projects learned in depth about uniforms, battlegrounds, generals, and the economy of the North and South as a result of collaborative research and sharing. Collaboration tends to result in group sharing and typically incorporates all the language arts. While reading and writing remain implicit in research, listening and speaking take precedence in the sharing format. In addition, viewing and visual representation gain prominence as reports are shared through technology such as PowerPoint presentations, or authentic photographs or diaries are shared as scanned documentation.

The collaborative spirit that pervades Grades 3–8 classrooms extends beyond instructional outcomes and includes the building of a community of learners. Students care about each other within and outside the academic arena, leading to a spirit of cooperation throughout the entire school day. Children can and do learn from each other while internalizing literacy and collaborative skills that will move with them into the workplace setting. Chapters 5, 7, and 12 focus on the reading, writing, and research workshops that encourage collaborative planning and thinking as students learn from each others' experiences and performances.

Principle 4: Meaning-Centered Comprehension and Communication

The primary goal of the language arts focuses on meaning-centered *comprehension* and the *communication* of understanding both through the reception of ideas and communication of thought. The primary goal of the language arts is the comprehension and transmission of ideas. If children primarily focus on pronunciation accuracy and language arts conventions, they are likely to distort the message to fit their language ability. Children must be encouraged to be risk takers as they attempt to process words for meaning in reading and as they use their own written words to convey thoughts. Only through individual miscues can children truly learn that reading and writing must make sense. Ongoing self-corrections indicate this growth in understanding. Emphasis on the meaning and message is primary. While accuracy does play an important role in receiving and communicating, the processing of words for meaning and the attempts at sharing the exact words in a child's head and heart take precedence, particularly in early literacy development.

Proficient readers recognize their level of text comprehension, identify their purposes for reading, and adjust to the demands placed on them by a particular text. They realize when and why the meaning of a text is unclear and they elicit strategies to solve comprehension problems or to deepen their understanding of a text (Keene & Zimmerman, 1997). Proficient writers, on the other hand, have a story or information to share, focus a first draft on content rather than conventions, reread their drafts to clarify meaning through revision, and know how to employ editing conventions to further clarify their message to their audience.

In reading, a meaning-centered philosophy exhibits itself by freeing a child to process words for the sake of meaning and the sense they make. While decoding is a skill that can be strategically applied as meaning is sought, it too can often become the single focus of a child's reading. Miscue analysis has taught teachers that some inaccuracies do not affect meaning, while others do indeed distort comprehension. In a guided reading group, a teacher will use appropriate skills and strategies to assist children in their pursuit of meaning. Comprehension, however, remains the ultimate outcome. With continued rereading, the pronunciation and recognition of words will promote fluency, but it is the meaning-making process that supports comprehension.

During draft writing, emphasis remains on the fluid transmission of thought and the content of the message. Children feel free to use any word to convey a thought, especially in drafting. Less emphasis on conventions at this stage does not mean that accuracy will not be addressed. Revision and editing provide the opportunity to polish the writing piece for a public audience. Teachers who support a writing workshop model for teaching writing provide the opportunity to get personal ideas into print before addressing revision and conventions. Children are more likely to use the words inside their heads if they are allowed the freedom of fluent thought. The writing process supports revisiting the piece in gradual preparation for public scrutiny on the way to final publication. In fact, three of the five stages of writing rework the original message so it will be accurately comprehended by its public audience.

Finding the correct balance between meaning and accuracy remains critical to this principle. While society seeks and demands conventional English in spelling, punctuation, and grammar, teachers should initially focus students on the meaning in words and then move toward conventions. Striking this balance remains a challenge but can make the difference between a child who fears failure and a child who takes a risk toward literacy success. Chapters 3 through 6 and Chapter 12 reflect this philosophy in operational terms, presenting examples of both teaching and learning across all the language arts. The developmental aspects of learning to read, listen, and view parallel the emerging pathway toward comprehending a print or nonprint message. The developmental aspects of learning to write, speak, and visually represent information parallel the emerging pathway toward a process approach to learning as oral, visual, and written communication gradually lead to the most accurate communication of information.

Principle 5: From Skills to Strategies in Authentic Contexts

Language arts *skills* grow into independent lifelong literacy *strategies* when applied in *authentic contexts* in daily reading, writing, listening, speaking, viewing, and visual representation. Skills taught in the context of real reading (literature) and real writing (a child's own) are more likely to become internalized and transfer to lifelong literacy needs. Skills taught in the context of authentic speaking and listening scenarios (presentations, drama) are most likely to take hold. Skills taught in the authentic context of viewing and visual representation (films, graphs, charts, maps) are more likely to become a part of the student. However, skills taught in isolation through drill and practice worksheets detached from real literacy contexts are likely to be temporarily learned but unlikely to be transferred to other learning situations.

Consider an assignment in which you ask students to copy ten sentences from a textbook and capitalize the first word and put a period at the end of each sentence. Compare that exercise with asking them to write their own draft of a story and then to reenter it later to correct capitalization and punctuation. Skills practiced in the context of students' own writing are likely to be learned.

Consider also the rules of spelling that are taught through weekly lessons throughout the school year—the "*i* before *e* rule," for example. Students can chant it, practice it, and memorize it, and it can even help them get a perfect score on a Friday spelling test. Unfortunately, the rule is often not applied in the context of their own writing, even during the following week. It cannot be assumed that all children are ready for rules at the same time or that isolated drill and practice ensures proficiency.

Consider the word recognition skills typically taught in isolation. Students may have memorized a pack of sight word cards, but the real test of reading is the placement and recognition of those sight words in real reading contexts. Children can accurately chant through a pile of cards and still the same words go unrecognized within the context of a basal reader story or during their reappearance in an authentic literature context. Although phonics and word identification are critical to reading, true learning takes place within flexible real learning contexts rather than in drill and practice formats.

This fifth principle assumes that teachers are empowered to teach both skills and strategies in the context of student work (as they need it), not necessarily when the teacher's manual dictates that they be taught. However, it is critical that teachers know what those skills and strategies are at their own grade level and document that they have been taught within the context of children's real reading and real writing. A scope and sequence checklist enhanced by "minilessons" ascertain that a teacher is covering the grade-level requirements to learn particular skills and strategies. In addition, the application of these skills and strategies within the context of real reading and real writing better ensures their transferability to lifelong literacy competencies. Chapters 6, 7, and 8, in particular, showcase the meaningful inclusion of skill instruction in reading, writing, listening, and speaking while Chapter 11 provides the supportive skills for visual literacy. Only as skills become internalized in a meaningful context do they become strategies that will be applied during a lifetime of literacy learning.

Principle 6: Ongoing Assessment and Self-Reflection

A *process* orientation to the language arts requires ongoing *assessment* and student *reflection* to provide continuous documentation of literacy growth. A process approach to the language arts equates the process and the product and celebrates small steps in learning rather than absolute perfection in final product. A variety of authentic assessment tools reflect this principle as checklists, anecdotal records, narrative evaluation, self-evaluation and portfolios provide a focus on individual growth (Barrentine & Stokes, 2005). Although tests, both teacher-made and standardized, capture a comparative dimension of a child's language arts ability, alternative assessments showcase individual growth and accomplishments. Schools should demand both types of assessment to provide a dimensional view of student learning. Where a traditional classroom focused on averaging grades for a report card, authentic assessment-based classrooms provide student documentation through work samples and indicators that point to individual growth over time.

Entering a classroom that follows the process approach, the observer notices student language arts portfolios, which contain far more than the traditional work folder. The pieces included here are selected by the student, and each one contains a written reflection of what the piece shows about him or her as a reader, writer, listener, speaker, viewer, or visual representer. These portfolios may be shared at student-led parent conferences during the school year. While a traditional report card of subject area grades may appear alongside the portfolio, the evaluation is enhanced by the individual pieces of student work and the literacy accomplishments articulated by the child. The teacher also presents a folder that contains standardized test scores, weekly skills and strategies checklists, and anecdotal observational records. Together each student and his or her parents set literacy goals for the next quarter with specific teacher reflections on how these goals may be reached—the theory being that children are more likely to achieve target goals if they set them themselves. A reminder card is placed on each student's desk to prod performance toward the stated goals.

As the current tide of national and state standards is used as a means of assessment, teachers should not lose sight of the true progress of each student. Viewing student strengths, rather than focusing on deficits, provides a positive perspective on literacy learning and authentic documentation provides evidence of continuous growth. This principle broadens the evaluative lens to include the student, the parent, and, finally, the teacher. Self-assessment, learner reflection, and parent-student goal setting provide the impetus for a broader view of the language learner. Chapter 15 focuses on monitoring individual growth and progress in the language arts and provides numerous samples of authentic assessment tools that identify and build on the success of each learner.

Principle 7: The New Literacies and Technology

The language arts harmonize with the *visual* nature of learning while *new technologies* serve as a teaching/learning/presentation tool and invite creative possibilities in literacy. In just a short time, technology has proved its potential to provide new options for gathering information and expressing ideas. Simultaneously, technology has breathed new life into the language arts. Accessing the World Wide Web for information, communicating through e-mail, and utilizing graphic capabilities for presenting information open endless possibilities in investigating, comprehending, communicating, and sharing information through technology and the language arts (Carroll, 2004). Most schools are equipped with computers, Internet access, and software programs—from Kid Pix to PowerPoint—that provide electronic means for drawing and writing stories as well as presenting information.

Enter a classroom that epitomizes the harmonious relationship between technology and language arts. Students have written a rough draft of a paragraph describing what they want to be when they grow up. Following a draft revision, they will enter their final draft into a PowerPoint format in the computer lab. They can add pictures of themselves taken with a digital camera, choose a background color and template for their slide, and select quiet, background music for their PowerPoint slide show. This fusion of reading, writing, listening, speaking, viewing, and creating visual representation throughout the activity showcases the harmonious relationship between language arts and technology that is just beginning to be explored. The teacher retains a copy of each student's goals for the future on a CD and proudly presents this technological performance at parent night.

A second-grade class has just returned from a trip to the Pumpkin Patch in October. Their task is to compose a class language experience story about their field trip. As children dictate their sentences to the teacher, she types them on her computer keyboard and a word processing program that is linked to a projector. Children instantly see their oral language become enlarged printed words on an overhead screen. Rereading is easy for them as the clarity and size of the words facilitates the activity. The class decides an appropriate title (Small Pumpkins, Medium Pumpkins, Large Pumpkins) and expresses excitement as the teacher prints the first copy of the story. Copies are made after school and each child delights as the language experience story appears in print on each desk the next morning.

The contribution of technology may initially be the motivation it provides for literacy learners, but the endless possibilities for both literacy instruction and learning have yet to be explored. Chapter 13 focuses on the new role of technology in the language arts classroom and technological connections across all the language arts are shared as examples throughout the book.

These Principles of Language Arts Instruction provide a philosophical framework about how the language arts are best taught, practiced, developed, and learned in authentic classroom contexts. The natural integration of the language arts, the supportive power of children's literature, the effectiveness of an apprenticeship and workshop approach, the focus on comprehension and meaning, the lifelong implications of a strategies-based authentic context, a process orientation toward assessment, and meaningful integration through technology form the backbone of this instructional model.

Visit the Companion Website at www.prenhall.com/hancock and gauge your understanding of Chapter 1 concepts with the self-assessments.

Closing Thoughts

This chapter has served as an introduction to reenvisioning the traditional language arts (reading, writing, listening, speaking) to include the newer language arts (viewing and visual representation). The national standards play an important role in expanding the language arts into the realm of visual, media, and technological literacy. Although defining each of the language arts serves to delineate and separate them from each other, they are in reality naturally integrated within a language arts lesson and across the entire curriculum.

To acquire a deeper understanding of the language arts, you have been challenged to make connections between theories of language development and meaning-making with the Principles of Language Arts Instruction. As you journey through this book, keep these theoretical underpinnings and beliefs in mind as they reflect the instructional methodologies supported here. This entire textbook serves to connect seven key principles to effective language arts instruction and learning. Over time and with more authentic classroom experiences, these will provide a meaningful foundation as you develop your own philosophy of teaching the language arts and carry it with you into your own classroom.

References

Atwell, N. (1998). *In the middle: New understandings about writing, reading, and learning* (2nd ed.). Portsmouth, NH: Heinemann.

Ayra, P., Martens, P., Wilson, G. P., Altwerger, B., Jin, L., Laster, B., & Lang, D. (2005). Reclaiming literacy instruction: Evidence in support of literature-based programs. *Language Arts, 83,* 63–72.

Barrentine, S. J., & Stokes, S. M. (2005). *Reading assessment: Principles and practices for elementary teachers* (2nd ed.). Newark, DE: International Reading Association.

Baumann, J. F., Kame'enui, E. J., & Ash, G. E. (2003). Research on vocabulary instruction: Voltare redux. In J. Flood, D. Lapp, J. R. Squire, & J. M. Jensen (Eds.), *Handbook of research on teaching the English language arts* (2nd ed., pp. 752–785). Mahwah, NJ: Erlbaum.

Berghoff, B., Egawa, K. A., Harste, J. C., & Hoonan, B. T. (2000). *Beyond reading and writing: Inquiry, curriculum, and multiple ways of knowing.* Urbana, IL: National Council of Teachers of English.

Blachowicz, C. L. Z., & Fisher, P. (2000). Vocabulary instruction. In M. L. Kamil, P. B. Mosenthal, P. D. Pearson, & R. Barr (Eds.), *Handbook of reading research* (Vol. 3, pp. 503–523). Mahwah, NJ: Erlbaum.

Calkins, L. M. (1994). *The art of teaching writing.* Portsmouth, NH: Heinemann.

Carroll, M. (2004). *Cartwheels on the keyboard: Computer-based literacy instruction in an elementary classroom.* Newark, DE: International Reading Association.

Chase, N. D., & Hynd, C. R. (1987). Reader response: An alternative way to teach students to think about text. *Journal of Reading, 30,* 530–540.

Dixon-Krauss, L. (1996). *Vygotsky in the classroom: Mediated literacy instruction and assessment.* White Plains, NY: Longman.

Dorn, L. J., French, C., & Jones, T. (1998). *Apprenticeship in literacy: Transitions across reading and writing.* York, ME: Stenhouse.

Flavell, J. H. (1985). *Cognitive development* (2nd ed.). Upper Saddle River, NJ: Prentice Hall.

Flood, J., & Lapp, D. (1995). Broadening the lens: Toward an expanded conceptualization of literacy. In K. A. Hinchman, D. J. Leu, & C. K. Kinzer (Eds.), *Perspectives on literacy research and practice* (pp. 1–16). Chicago: National Reading Conference.

Flood, J., & Lapp, D. (1997/1998). Broadening conceptualizations of literacy: The visual and communicative arts. *The Reading Teacher, 51,* 342–344.

Fosnot, C. T. (1996). Constructivism: A psychological theory of learning. In C. T. Fosnot (Ed.), *Constructivism: Theory, perspective, and practice* (pp. 8–33). New York: Teachers College Press.

Fox, D. L., & Short, K. G. (Eds.). (2003). *Stories matter: The complexity of cultural authenticity in children's literature.* Urbana, IL: National Council of Teachers of English.

Galda, , L., & Cullinan, B. E. (2003). Literature for literacy: What research says about the benefits of using trade books in the classroom. In J. Flood, D. Lapp, J. R. Squire, & J. M. Jensen (Eds.), *Handbook of research on teaching the language arts* (2nd ed., pp. 640–648). Mahwah, NJ: Erlbaum.

Gould, J. S. (1996). A constructivist perspective on teaching and learning in the language arts. In C. T. Fosnot (Ed.), *Constructivism: Theory, perspective, and practice* (pp. 92–102). New York: Teachers College Press.

Graves, D. H. (1983/2003). *Writing: Teachers and children at work: Twentieth anniversary edition.* Portsmouth, NH: Heinemann.

Hancock, M. R. (1993). Exploring the meaning-making process through the content of literature response journals. *Research in the Teaching of English, 27,* 335–368.

Hancock, M. R. (2004). *A celebration of literature and response: Children, books, and teachers in K–8 classrooms* (2nd ed.). Upper Saddle River, NJ: Merrill/Prentice Hall.

Hansen, J. (2001). *When writers read* (2nd ed.). Portsmouth, NH: Heinemann.

Hubbard, R. S. (1996). Visual responses to literature: Imagination through images. *The New Advocate, 9,* 309–323.

International Reading Association & the National Council of Teachers of English (1996). *Standards for the English language arts.* Newark, DE/Urbana, IL: International Reading Association and the National Council of Teachers of English.

Keene, E. O., & Zimmerman, S. (1997). *Mosaic of thought: Teaching comprehension in a reader's workshop.* Portsmouth, NH: Heinemann.

Kelly, P. R. (1990). Guiding young students' response to literature. *The Reading Teacher, 43,* 464–470.

Lancia, P. J. (1997). Literary borrowing: The effects of literature on children's writing. *The Reading Teacher, 50,* 470–475.

Lee, C. D., & Smagorinsky, P. (Eds.). (2000). *Vygotskian perspectives on literacy research.* Cambridge, England/Urbana, IL: Cambridge University Press and National Council of Teachers of English.

Moll, L. C. (1990). Introduction. In L. C. Moll (Ed.), *Vygotsky and education: Instructional implications and applications of sociohistorical psychology* (pp. 59–88). New York: Cambridge University Press.

Morrow, L. M., & Gambrell, L. B. (2000). Literature-based reading instruction. In M. L. Kamil, P. B. Mosenthal, P. D. Pearson, & R. Barr (Eds.), *Handbook of reading research* (Vol. 3, pp. 563–586). Mahwah, NJ: Erlbaum.

Pearson, P. D., & Gallagher, M. C. (1983). The instruction of reading comprehension. *Contemporary Educational Psychology, 8,* 317–344.

Peterson, R., & Eeds, M. (1990). *Grand conversations: Literature groups in action.* New York: Scholastic.

Piaget, J. (1952). *The origins of intelligence in children.* New York: Norton.

Piaget, J. (1955/1973). *The language and thought of the child.* New York: World Book Company.

Pressley, M. (2000). What should comprehension instruction be the comprehension of? In M. L. Kamil, P. B. Mosenthal, P. D. Pearson, & R. Barr (Eds.) *Handbook of reading research* (Vol. 3, pp. 545–561). Mahwah, NJ: Erlbaum.

Raphael, T. E., Florio-Ruane, S., & George, M. (2001). Book club plus: A conceptual framework to organize literacy instruction. *Language Arts, 79,* 159–168.

Rosenblatt, L. M. (1938/1995). *Literature as exploration* (5th ed.). New York: Appleton-Century-Crofts and Modern Language Association.

Rosenblatt, L. M. (1978). *The reader, the text, the poem: The transactional theory of the literary work.* Carbondale: Southern Illinois University.

Rosenblatt, L. M. (2004). The transactional theory of reading and writing. In R. Ruddell & N. Unrau (Eds.), *Theoretical models and processes of reading* (5th ed., pp. 1363–1398). Newark, DE: International Reading Association.

Smith, F. (2003). *Unspeakable acts, unnatural practices: Flaws and fallacies in "scientific" reading instruction.* Portsmouth, NH: Heinemann.

Tunnell, M. O., & Jacobs, J. S. (1998). Using "real" books: Research findings on literature-based reading instruction. In C. Weaver (Ed.), *Reconsidering a balanced approach to reading* (pp. 373–386). Urbana, IL: National Council of Teachers of English.

Vygotsky, L. S. (1978). *Mind in society: The development of higher psychological processes.* Cambridge, MA: Harvard University Press.

Vygotsky, L. S. (1986). *Thought and language.* Cambridge, MA: MIT Press.

Wertsch, J. V. (1984). The zone of proximal development: Some conceptual issues. In B. Rogoff & J. V. Wetsch (Eds.), *Children's learning in the zone of proximal development* (pp. 7-18). San Francisco: Jossey-Bass.

Wollman-Bonilla, J. E., & Werchadlo, B. (1995). Literature response journals in a first-grade classroom. *Language Arts, 72,* 562-570.

Children's Books Cited

Bruchac, Joseph (2000). *Crazy Horse's vision.* Illus. by S. D. Nelson. New York: Lee & Low.

Bunting, Eve (1994). *Smoky night.* Illus. by David Diaz. San Diego: Harcourt Brace.

Carle, Eric (1968). *The very hungry caterpillar.* New York: Philomel.

Creech, Sharon (1994). *Walk two moons.* New York: HarperCollins.

DiCamillo, Kate (2000). *Because of Winn-Dixie.* Cambridge, MA: Candlewick.

Gardiner, John (1980). *Stone fox.* Illus. by Marcia Sewall. New York: Crowell.

Garza, Carmen Lomas (1996). *In my family/En mi familia.* New York: Children's Press.

Heide, Florence Parry, & Gilliland, Judith Heide (1999). *The house of wisdom.* Illus. by Mary Grandpre. New York: DK Publishing.

Hesse, Karen (1997). *Out of the dust.* New York: Scholastic.

Hoberman, Mary Ann (1998). *Miss Mary Mack: A hand-clapping rhyme.* Illus. by Nadine Bernard Westcott. San Diego: Harcourt Brace.

Hoose, Phillip, & Hoose, Hannah (1998). *Hey, little ant.* Berkeley, CA: Tricycle Press.

Lobel, Arnold (1970). *Frog and Toad are friends.* New York: Harper & Row.

Lowry, Lois (1993). *The giver.* Boston: Houghton Mifflin.

Lowry, Lois (1989). *Number the stars.* Boston: Houghton Mifflin.

MacLachlan, Patricia (1985). *Sarah, plain and tall.* New York: Harper & Row.

Martin, Jr. Bill, & Archambault, John (1989). *Chicka chicka boom boom.* Illus. By Lois Ehlert. New York: Simon & Schuster.

McCloskey, Robert (1941). *Make way for ducklings.* New York: Viking.

Murphy, Jim (2000). *Blizzard! The storm that changed America.* New York: Scholastic.

Naylor, Phyllis Reynolds (1991). *Shiloh.* New York: Atheneum.

Naylor, Phyllis Reynolds (1996). *Shiloh Season.* New York: Atheneum.

Naylor, Phyllis Reynolds (1997). *Saving Shiloh.* New York: Atheneum.

Peck, Richard (2000). *A year down under.* New York: Dial.

Pringle, Laurence (1997). *An extraordinary life: The story of a monarch butterfly.* Illus. by Bob Marstall. New York: Orchard.

Rathmann Peggy (1995). *Officer Buckle and Gloria.* New York: Putnam.

Rowling, J. K. (1997). *Harry Potter and the sorcerer's stone.* Illus. by Mary GrandPré. New York: Scholastic.

Sachar, Louis (1998). *Holes.* New York: Farrar, Straus & Giroux.

Say, Allen (1998). *Tea with milk.* Boston: Houghton Mifflin.

Schroeder, Alan (1995). *Carolina shout!* Illus. by Bernie Fuchs. New York: Dial.

Soto, Gary (1997). *Snapshots from the wedding.* Illus. by Stephanie Garcia. New York: Putnam.

Spinelli, Jerry (1997). *Wringer.* New York: HarperCollins.

St. George, Judith (2000). *So you want to be president.* Illus. by David Small. New York: Philomel.

Stanley, Diane (2000). *Michelangelo.* New York: HarperCollins.

Stanley, Jerry (1992). *Children of the dust bowl: The true story of the school at Weedpatch Camp.* New York: Random.

Steptoe, Javatka (Selector). (1997). *In daddy's arms I am tall: African Americans celebrating fathers.* Illus. by Javatka Steptoe. New York: Lee & Low.

Taylor, Mildred (1976). *Roll of thunder, hear my cry.* Illus. by Jerry Pinkney. New York: Dial.

Waters, Kate (1989). *Sarah Morton's day.* New York: Scholastic.

Waters, Kate (1993). *Samuel Eaton's day.* New York: Scholastic.

White, E. B. (1952). *Charlotte's web.* Illus by Garth Williams. New York: Harper & Row.

Chapter 2

TEACHING IN THE LANGUAGE ARTS CLASSROOM

Creating a Learning Community

"I want to be a teacher when I grow up," said Lilly. "Excellent choice," said Mr. Slinger.

FROM *LILLY'S PURPLE PLASTIC PURSE* BY KEVIN HENKES

Dressed in shiny red boots and sparkling, new clothes, Lilly, a diminutive, yet confident mouse, gleefully rushes off to a well-anticipated day of school. Her expressive teacher, Mr. Slinger, garbed in a colorful shirt and possessing a nontraditional teaching philosophy, enhances the physical environment of his classroom with a semicircle of desks, a Lightbulb Lab for freetime activities, and a predictable Sharing Time. Mr. Slinger encourages risk taking, shares cheese doodles during recess, and builds self-esteem in all of his student mice. Lilly quickly decides that she wants to be a teacher when she grows up.

Lilly's Purple Plastic Purse by Kevin Henkes portrays the memorable, cherished teacher who inspires confidence and learning in Lilly, his eager and articulate student. Somewhere in your memory may be a special teacher who served as a perfect role model and guided your career choice toward the teaching profession. Mr. Slinger, with his "artistic shirts" and "sunglasses on a chain around his neck," may make it look easy, but creating an environment for meaningful learning is a challenge. Enthusiastic students like Lilly may fulfill your teaching fantasies, but teaching is also filled with planning, instruction, and assessment within a well-designed learning environment.

Teaching literacy and the language arts to children is an art, a craft, and a complex talent based on some fundamental planning and instructional methods that continue to blossom and grow as you enhance your professional practice through years of teaching experience. There is no magic formula to define quality teaching, but most teachers know that professionals do get better, become more efficient, and experience continuous growth as they continue on in their teaching careers. Teachers also know that language arts teaching is a combination of the optimal physical environment, the knowledge base for literacy instruction, and the caring attitude of a teacher with high expectations for literacy learning (Routman, 2003, 2005). Within this professional environment, literacy can develop and thrive in a well-organized, efficiently manifested classroom with a knowledgeable, caring teacher who respects the individuality and celebrates the growth of each literacy learner.

The purpose of this chapter is to introduce the qualities and best practices of the teacher and teaching in a literacy-rich classroom. As you measure these traits against your own teaching personality and beliefs, you will be challenged to think critically about the importance of the what, how, and why of the blending of the classroom environment and the teacher to create optimal conditions for literacy learning.

Objectives

- To introduce a framework for creating an effective language arts classroom through environment, planning, and instruction.
- To consider the multiple dimensions of designing an optimal classroom environment, a community of learners, for language arts instruction and learning.
- To distinguish the characteristics of literacy-rich environments and schedules in primary (Grades K–2) classrooms.
- To share the characteristics of literacy-rich environments and schedules in intermediate (Grades 3–5) and middle school (Grades 6–8) classrooms.
- To enumerate the traditional and technological tools of language arts instruction.
- To provide a lesson plan template that contains ten elements for designing coherent, effective language arts lessons.

The Art of Language Arts Teaching

The art of teaching has been defined, categorized, articulated, and packaged most efficiently and effectively in Charlotte Danielson's *Enhancing Professional Practice: A Framework for Teaching* (1996). This model provides a thorough and complete template for viewing the teaching process in terms of learning outcomes and teaching evaluation purposes. In many states, it has become the model for evaluation for licensure and certification as well as the evaluative tool in teacher preparation programs. Figure 2.1

FIGURE 2.1 Charlotte Danielson's Framework for Teaching.

DOMAIN 1
PLANNING AND PREPARATION

1a: Demonstrating Knowledge of Content and Pedagogy
- Knowledge of content
- Knowledge of prerequisite relationships
- Knowledge of content-related pedagogy

1b: Demonstrating Knowledge of Students
- Knowledge of characteristics of age group
- Knowledge of students' varied approaches to learning
- Knowledge of students' skills and knowledge
- Knowledge of students' interests and cultural heritage

1c: Selecting Instructional Goals
- Value
- Clarity
- Suitability for diverse students
- Balance

1d: Demonstrating Knowledge of Resources
- Resources for teaching
- Resources of students

1e: Designing Coherent Instruction
- Learning activities
- Instructional materials and resources
- Instructional groups
- Lesson and unit structure

1f: Assessing Student Learning
- Congruence with instructional goals
- Criteria and standards
- Use for planning

DOMAIN 2
THE CLASSROOM ENVIRONMENT

2a: Creating an Environment of Respect and Rapport
- Teacher interaction with students
- Student interaction

2b: Establishing a Culture for Learning
- Importance of content
- Student pride in work
- Expectations for teaming and achievement

2c: Managing Classroom Procedures
- Management of instructional groups
- Management of transitions
- Management of materials and supplies
- Performance of noninstructional duties
- Supervision of volunteers and paraprofessionals

2d: Managing Student Behavior
- Expectations
- Monitoring of student behavior
- Response to student misbehavior

2e: Organizing Physical Space
- Safety and arrangement of furniture
- Accessibility to learning and use of physical resources

DOMAIN 4
PROFESSIONAL RESPONSIBILITIES

4a: Reflecting on Teaching
- Accuracy
- Use in future teaching

4b: Maintaining Accurate Records
- Student completion of assignments
- Student progress in learning
- Noninstructional records

4c: Communicating with Families
- Information about the instructional program
- Information about individual students
- Engagement of families in the instructional program

4d: Contributing to the School and District
- Relationships with colleagues
- Service to the school
- Participation in school and district projects

4e: Growing and Developing Professionally
- Enhancement of content knowledge and pedagogical skill
- Service to the profession

4f: Showing Professionalism
- Service to students
- Advocacy
- Decision making

DOMAIN 3
INSTRUCTION

3a: Communicating Clearly and Accurately
- Directions and procedures
- Oral and written language

3b: Using Questioning and Discussion Techniques
- Quality of questions
- Discussion techniques
- Student participation

3c: Engaging Students In Learning
- Representation of content
- Activities and assignments
- Groupings of students
- Instructional materials and resources
- Structure and pacing

3d: Providing Feedback to Students
- Quality: accurate, substantive, constructive and specific
- Timeliness

3e: Demonstrating Flexibility and Responsiveness
- Lesson adjustment
- Response to students
- Persistence

Source: Charlotte Danielson, (1996). Enhancing professional practice: A framework for teaching. *Alexandria, VA: Association for Supervision and Curriculum Development. Reprinted with permission.*

Teacher Prep

The Teacher Prep Web site will help you become a better teacher by linking you to classroom videos, student artifacts, teaching strategies, lesson plans, relevant education leadership articles, and practical information on licensing, creating a portfolio, implementing standards, and being successful in field experiences. Visit this resource at www.prenhall.com/teacherprep.

delineates the four domains of teaching that Danielson identifies: (1) planning and preparation, (2) the classroom environment, (3) instruction, and (4) professional responsibilities. Domains 1 and 2 are the focus of this chapter, as planning language arts lessons and creating the classroom environment take center stage. Domain 3, instruction, is addressed in the many chapters in this book on teaching the language arts as new methodologies are introduced. Domain 4, professionalism, weaves its way throughout the entire book as teacher reflection and professional growth and behavior provide an assumed level of participation in the language arts classroom. New teachers may seem particularly focused on the classroom environment and planning and preparation, while experienced teachers may choose to reflect on their current classrooms in light of all the domain elements. In both cases teachers are seeking the fundamentals needed to prepare a classroom for quality instruction—the most critical domain. An informative look into the planning and preparation and the classroom environment domains provides inspiring insights for both novice and experienced teachers as they develop the art of teaching in their classrooms.

The art of teaching the language arts (Calkins, 1994, 2001) flourishes within these four domains in a language-focused classroom. Planning and preparation emphasizes knowing the individual learner, designing meaningful language-based instruction, and utilizing ongoing assessment to inform instruction. The language arts classroom environment highlights teacher-student interactions, high expectations for the learner, effective literacy groupings, student confidence-building, and efficient use of time and materials. Instruction in the language arts optimizes oral and written communication, quality, open-ended questioning, engaged learning experiences, and quality individual feedback to students. Professional responsibilities within language arts instruction include continuous reflection on language arts instruction, ongoing documentation of literacy growth, service on district language arts curriculum committees, and professional membership in state and national organizations.

The Language Arts Classroom

Envision entering the ideal literacy classroom as described by contributors to *The Reading Teacher* ("Characteristics of an Ideal Reading Classroom," 1999) and synthesized for this description. The classroom walls are covered with visuals and multilingual words displayed through alluring posters of book adventures, lists of literacy strategies, and student writing and artwork. Desks arranged in groups imply a collaborative community in which curiosity, discovery, and classroom conversations abound. An open area at the rear of the room serves as a stage for acting out stories, readers theatre, and response performances. A soft area rug, colorful beanbag chairs, a thronelike author's chair, and plush pillows invite and encourage the comfortable, relaxing qualities of home. While the room exudes life and enthusiasm for learning, several quiet areas exist where children can escape and relax with a book or utilize a writing center to publish self-selected pieces. Technology infuses but does not overwhelm the classroom as Internet access, PowerPoint software, and word processing programs are readily available.

The most readily apparent feature in the room is literature—baskets of books, crates of books, displays of books, and shelves of books. Some are themed to content study, others are grouped by reading level, and still others with inviting front covers are displayed on ledges and window counters. The sunlight streaming through the large windows showcases multicultural books about the Day of the Dead and fairy tales from Spanish cultures. Literary genres from poetry to biography, literature to stir the imagination, and books that provide seeds for inquiry provide the heartbeat of this classroom.

The literacy classroom is also filled with children—children who have been invited to imagine, wonder, and reflect by using all their literacy skills in a warm, caring context. A tall, gangly boy curled in a soft, puffy chair engages with Jean Craighead George's *My Side of the Mountain*. A straggly-haired girl seems mesmerized by the photographs in Diane Swanson's *Safari Beneath the Sea*. Two classmates sketch scenes from this month's read aloud of Wilson Rawl's classic *Where the Red Fern Grows* on a bulletin board mural. An intent child composes an acrostic poem on a glowing iMac screen while another e-mails the office to report today's attendance. There is no doubt that literacy learning is taking place; this is unquestionably a literacy classroom. Children have fallen in love with literacy, and learning is as natural as breathing in this oral, reading, writing, and visual literacy environment.

There is ample evidence that the teacher loves to read and write. Her desk contains a read-aloud, a book for silent reading, lists of student self-selected projects, a to-do list for her next visit to the library, and a personal journal. A weekly parent newsletter duplicated on bright yellow paper establishes a sound home–school connection. A large three-ring binder contains an academic profile of each child including both formal and informal evaluation—standardized test scores, state assessment results, skills checklists, and anecdotal records. Behind the desk are shelves filled with three-inch ring binder literacy portfolios. These contain student self-selected literacy documentation accompanied by reflections on how their work samples reflect their abilities as literate members of the classroom community. It is clear that this is the kind of teacher who models and values literacy in all aspects of her life and helps children see that literacy provides many venues to share their experiences, feelings, and opinions. Both students and literacy are valued and the classroom is both an invitation to learn and a celebration of literacy learning. Her goal reaches far beyond the current year as she hopes to empower each student with a lifelong love of literacy.

Reflecting a Teaching Philosophy in a Classroom Environment

The ideal classroom environment reflects a well-defined teaching philosophy and a dedication to literature-based literacy instruction. The teacher's classroom that we described might not have looked like this during her first year of teaching, but time and a confirmation of teaching values have clarified the connection between the setting for learning and the philosophy of this literacy teacher. This environment becomes the goal of almost every new teacher.

Take a few minutes to review the seven principles for guiding language arts instruction presented earlier in Figure 1.3. Try to match elements of teaching philosophy with the physical, social, and cognitive elements evidenced in this classroom. For example, what aspects of the environment address diversity? What evidence of ongoing assessment exist? How does the teacher integrate the language arts both within a lesson and across the curriculum in this setting? While you will be speculating rather than genuinely confirming the connections, you will see the important match between what the teacher believes about language arts instruction and the environment that she establishes in which language learning will take place.

Five Aspects of the Classroom Environment

Danielson (1996) focuses on five aspects of the classroom environment that clarify the importance of the language arts classroom in setting the tone for learning and self-esteem:

- ***An environment of respect and rapport.*** Children cannot learn until they know that you care about them. As a new teacher, find out everything about each child before he or she enters the classroom. Access school photos to be sure you know your students' names the first day of school. Greet them by name and ask them to tell you something about themselves. Speak to each child personally each day, ending with a positive comment. Show them you care by following up on personal interests, weekend activities, special academic achievements. Look for something positive within each child and build a strong personal and professional relationship with him or her. Be yourself, be kind, be caring, be demanding yet gentle, and make each child feel like a special participant in literacy learning.
- ***A culture for learning.*** Model and articulate high expectations for learning in your classroom. Becoming a literate student is hard work, but you are there to pave the way and ease the journey. Build student pride in a job well done and recognize achievements for each student. Make language learning a priority and surround children with articulate oral language, conventional writing, quality reading, and effective visual modes of learning. If you model high expectations, your students will stretch to meet those expectations and view the classroom as a safe environment for individual learning.
- ***Classroom procedures.*** An effective literacy classroom provides children with an established set of rules and procedures for all aspects of language arts learning. Children thrive on predictability, routines, and established procedures throughout the school day. Your role in selecting and managing instructional groups sets the tone for learning. Orchestrating smooth transitions within and between areas of the daily schedule makes for effective time on task learning. Organizing the distribution, collection, and storage of materials and supplies makes for efficient use of student help in accessing and keeping track of learning. Within these efficient routines, try to be flexible and to adjust and adapt procedures to meet the needs of both the students and the planned activities.
- ***Student behavior.*** Setting high behavioral expectations for students is a necessity that provides a challenge for you as a new teacher. In a well-managed classroom, little time may be spent on behavioral concerns. High expectations and a minimum number of rules set a positive climate for learning. Yet your response to misbehavior must be consistent and fair. Explain rules clearly, clarify them through examples, and apply them consistently. Children must know your expectations, those expectation must stay constant, and the rules must be applied to all individuals at all times. Students must know when quiet talking is permitted and when quiet time is expected. Being a genuine, caring, concerned teacher who holds high behavioral and academic expectations for students and applies a few important rules consistently and fairly seems to the best rule for managing student behavior and creating a "community of learners" who care about each other and strive to do their best. Deliberately planning, orchestrating, and modeling expectations at the beginning of the school year is critical to the overall success of the language arts program across the entire year.
- ***Physical space.*** The arrangement of your classroom reflects your philosophy of teaching. Desk arrangements, student access to materials, supplies in the classroom,

and content of bulletin boards all reflect what you believe in about teaching, learning, and children. Arrangement of desks for guided reading, collaborative writing circles, or literature conversations reflects a philosophy of teaching. Provide access to technology, to the library or media center, and to writing and drawing materials. Allow the environment to reflect the needs of the students and the instructional methods. Let the room be "littered with literacy" as literature, word walls, labels, charts, and posters encourage the use and appreciation of language.

When these components of the classroom environment fall into place, magical things happen in the classroom. Student leaders emerge naturally and learning partners find their own comfort level with each other. Predictability of schedule and expectations eventually drives a well-orchestrated classroom as most children thrive on knowing what comes next, what they are expected to accomplish, and with whom they will work. The community of learners that emerges from high expectations for respect and cooperation provides a collaborative, motivating, and challenging environment for learning in which individual needs are met, individual interests are honored, and individuals are valued for their unique contributions to the entire community. As children feel safe, secure, valued, and challenged at their level, they are more willing to take risks, challenge their own learning, and motivate themselves beyond the expectations set by the teacher. This is the magic of establishing a community of learners—this is the joy of teaching in an elementary classroom.

Fundamentals of Literacy-Rich Environments

Literacy-rich environments are classroom settings that promote language and literacy learning. Morrow (1997b) suggests four perspectives that contribute to the foundations of knowledge regarding the relationship and children's literacy development: (a) language arts, (b) engagement, (c) motivation, and (d) social collaboration. The *language arts perspective* suggests that the language arts result from a concerted effort of authentic, meaningful, and functional experiences that use varied genres of children's literature as a primary source and some basic skill instruction as a secondary source for actively involving children in reading, writing, listening, speaking, viewing and visual representation. Terms such as integrated language arts, whole language, language experience, literacy apprenticeship, and reading/writing workshop apply to this perspective. The *engagement perspective* implies that children need to be actively involved with literacy materials in their environment to achieve optimal literacy success. Readers theatre, music, art, film, and creative movement have been added to the more traditional modes of storytelling and retellings, audiocassettes, puppetry, photographs, computers, and videos (Morrow, 1997b). The *motivation perspective* implies that simply initiating a literacy activity is not enough; it must be practiced, sustained, and self-selected if a feeling of success is to be achieved. Students, therefore, must be provided with literacy challenges but not frustrations; they must be given opportunities to make choices, but guided in their selections; they must feel empowered and responsible for learning, yet channeled in their intrinsic motivation by a knowledgeable teacher. The *social collaboration perspective* indicates children learn from peers as well as from the teacher, and they are often challenged to greater success through peer talk, discussion, sharing, and cooperative projects. These four perspectives should guide the efforts to design environments and should reflect the philosophical stance of teachers dedicated to leading their students toward lifelong literacy success.

Preparing the physical environment of a classroom is often underestimated or overlooked by teachers in their professional zeal to plan and instruct. As preservice teachers learn to concentrate on pedagogical and interpersonal factors, they often give little initial consideration to the critical nature of the context in which both teaching and learning occur. When they visit a classroom, an environment is already in place. Often filled with lively children, the connection between the physical setting, the culture for learning, and the teaching philosophy becomes secondary to the life of the classroom. To prepare an environment responsive to the needs of children, however, the teacher must be certain the classroom environment supports his or her philosophy of the language arts, related language-based and literature-based activities, and ultimately, the needs of children.

The Primary Literacy-Rich Environment (Kindergarten–Grade 2)

Characteristics of literacy-rich homes in which children have learned to "read and write" on their own before coming to school or who have become successful readers and writers in school have direct application to literacy-rich classrooms (McGee & Richgels, 2000). By identifying factors in the home that contribute to children's literacy success, teachers can provide classroom environments that support literacy learning. Based on the work of a multitude of literacy researchers (Neuman & Roskos, 1990; Morrow, 1989; Teale & Sulzby, 1986) and veteran practitioners (Bickart, Jablon, & Dodge, 1999), the following list provides a general overview of the content, persona, and disposition of literacy-rich classrooms.

- A variety and abundance of reading and writing materials readily available and accessible to children at appropriate age and interest levels
- A physical setting supportive of literacy, including a comfortable reading or library center in which children can browse and read, an active writing center in which children can talk and write, and numerous displays of children's literacy products and activities
- Daily literacy routines that include reading aloud, writing together, and self-selected reading and writing activities
- Children who interact with the teacher and each other through questions and comments as they read and write
- Children who are made to believe in themselves as readers and writers and thus build self-esteem, which plays a critical role in literacy learning
- Teachers who are readers and writers themselves who plan activities for both instructional and functional purposes
- Teachers who are knowledgeable about the individual and unique needs of each child, encourage risk-taking in both reading (pronunciation) and writing (constructed spelling), and respond in flexible ways to several approaches to literacy learning

For these characteristics to become a part of the primary classroom, the physical aspects must first be considered.

The environment of the primary classroom introduces young learners to the joys and importance of literacy (Cambourne, 2000; Fisher, 1996). Because the premise of primary literacy instruction focuses on the apprenticeship model, the environment of the primary classroom will reflect teaching a small group of children while other small groups focus on literacy-related centers. The responsibility of the teacher lies in creating a motivating, comfortable environment through which these children will successfully begin their journey on the road to literacy (Gambrell, 1996).

Components of a Literacy-Rich Primary Learning Environment

Seven components will assist you in imagining and creating just this type of environment in the K–2 classroom: (a) children's literature, (b) functional print, (c) library and reading center, (d) viewing and listening center, (e) writing and drawing center, (f) literacy displays, and (g) content area centers. The first two provide an overall atmosphere for the classroom, while the final five rely on literacy centers (Morrow, 1997a) as a means of managing literacy instruction and independent learning.

Children's Literature. The most obvious materials in the primary classroom are quality children's trade books across genres at both picture book and early reader levels. There are several types of children's books that are particularly enjoyable to young children and assist in literacy discoveries:

- Predictable/pattern books (Jane Yolen's *Off We Go!*)
- Participation books (Phyllis Root's *Rattletrap Car*)
- Wordless picture books (David Weisner's *Sector 7*)
- Language play books (Doreen Cronin's *Click, Clack, Moo: Cows that Type*)
- Concept books (Tana Hoban's *White on Black*)
- Alphabet books (Mike Lester's *A Is for Salad*)
- Counting books (Carol Saul's *Barn Cat*)

Each of these types and related literacy activities will be discussed in Chapter 4 on emergent literacy learning.

Functional Print. Functional print items include print that is written by the teacher and/or children such as directions, names, and reminders and are a natural part of the literacy environment. Lists kept as a record of information are also considered functional—sign-in sheets, morning messages, notes, or letters. Sign-in sheets can be expanded and used for attendance, behavior, library cards, lunch or milk count, lost teeth, or graphs (yes/no) and surveys. The class schedule, daily calendar, class rules, center groups, helper charts, weather charts, and counting tools are also functional print that visually support daily activities. Labels include both pictures and words, such as clock, pencil sharpener, "Pledge of Allegiance," directions (north, south, east, west), and the alphabet. Student name labels should be located on coathooks, cubicles, mailboxes, or center assignments. Teachers can color-code language labels (red for Spanish, blue for English) in multilingual classrooms.

Other kinds of functional print include telephone books, restaurant menus, maps, cookbooks, TV guides, newspapers, catalogs, magazines, and reference materials (e.g., pictionaries, bilingual dictionaries). Every classroom should have a word wall, on which five words are introduced every week, as they are examined for meaning, configuration, and length.

Library and Reading Center. Library and reading center designs vary greatly, but typically they are partitioned areas of arranged shelving that contain crates, baskets, and boxes that store books. Books can be organized by level (colored dots on spine), subjects (animals, countries, holidays) or author, but keeping the organization useful to young children is important. Changing displays and objects should motivate children to visit the center often. The library center might also contain literature props such as puppets, stuffed animals, or objects that bring to mind a featured story. Flannel boards encourage retellings or storytellings. Display books should be changed periodically to reflect children's interests, holidays, seasons, or current events. Multicultural titles and dual language texts should be included. Soft carpets and fluffy pillows invite children to linger, browse, and read. Books written by the class or by individual children are some of the most frequently "read" materials.

Viewing and Listening Center. Audiotapes and CDs of children's books, videotapes and DVDs of *Reading Rainbow* books, or interactive multimedia storybooks might be part of an active viewing and listening center. A key connection to children's literature, the center should provide an opportunity for seeing and hearing repetitions of familiar stories and assist the child toward independent reading of trade books. A computer with Internet access, CD, DVD, and audiotape players, and VCRs with monitors should be readily available. Headsets are imperative as many activities may be taking place at the same time.

Writing and Drawing Center. The writing and drawing center should include a table large enough to accommodate several children as well as displaying a variety of greeting cards, index cards, messages, signs, and words to motivate children to write. The center should be adjacent to the class word wall that displays familiar words formally introduced each week. Writing materials used in the center are stored on easily accessible labeled shelves, and they are changed frequently so that new materials may be explored. Journals are bound and conveniently accessible, and word processing programs at the developmental level and language of young children are available, modeled, and encouraged. A parent volunteer is often asked to help at the writing center. Nearby a special author's chair becomes a vehicle for proudly sharing writing.

Literacy-rich classrooms contain many types of writing implements and materials on which to write. Colored markers, letter stamps, letter cookie cutters, and colored chalk are just a few examples of implements, while colored paper, lined paper, computers, and lapboards illustrate a variety of writing surfaces. A walk through an office supply store can lead to the acquisition of inspiring writing materials.

Literacy Displays. Bulletin boards, wall space, counter space, chart paper, and windows can be used to display student literacy artifacts, including writing, drawing, and other visual representations of learning. A classroom littered with literacy provides models, inspirations, and ideas for further literacy. Self-esteem and seeing growth over time are two factors that encourage literacy progress. Children should be encouraged to share their reading, writing, and drawings as oral language begins to match the printed, written, or visual image. Student-generated stories, grocery lists, collages, group poems, language experience stories, and artistic response to literature are wonderful indicators of literacy learning.

Content Area Centers. An integrated approach to literacy learning includes the use of content area centers focused on topics or themes under current study. Materials are usually manipulative and activity-centered, and they should include the use of one or more of the language arts—things to read, something to write, data to record, something to graph, things to talk about, something to listen to. Centers should be designed so they can be visited independently or in small groups providing space for exploration, self-direction, or social learning. They should be set apart from the classroom by movable partitions or shelving that houses related materials. Centers are arranged so that they provide quiet academic areas as well as a place for more active play. Centers may begin with just a few materials, but new objects should be introduced and explained for purpose, use, and placement as they are added. Key materials and concepts should be labeled, often in two languages, for optimal learning. Centers can span curricular areas (e.g., art and music, science, math), enhance learning through technology (e.g., computers, Internet access) or provide imaginative play opportunities (e.g., blocks, dramatic play), but all should incorporate literature and language-related materials for effective literacy connections.

In summary, the physical features of the primary classroom reflect active, involved learning focused on exploration and discovery of oral, written, and visual literacy. The following criteria have been suggested for optimal primary (Grades K–2) classrooms (Mayfield, 1992; Mercer, 1999).

- Well-defined spaces or learning centers
- Developmentally appropriate materials for literacy learning
- Attractive and comfortable environment
- Flexible space
- Environment reflecting both the curriculum and children's interests and needs
- Readily available and abundant materials and resources
- Human resources to assist with environmental design
- Technological resources provided, modeled, and accessible
- Architectural factors (climate control, lighting, acoustics, size)

Ideal primary classroom settings parallel real-life situations and materials are selected to provide opportunities to explore, experiment, and discover the relationship between school literacy and the real world. By purposefully arranging the environment, the teacher acknowledges the physical setting as an active and pervasive influence on activities and attitudes (Morrow, 1997a; Turner, 1995).

The Primary Literacy Block Schedule

The early primary schedule should be designed around a literacy block that permits the natural integration of the language arts into a meaningful whole. A morning block of 2 hours provides an ideal time period to focus on integrating all the language arts. The entire day, however, contains elements of the language arts as reading, writing, listening, speaking, viewing, visual representation weave their way across the entire primary curriculum.

Because an apprenticeship approach to reading provides the framework for primary literacy instruction in this textbook, teacher-led small guided-reading and guided-writing groups provide leveled instruction while other children independently engage in literacy center activities. An apprenticeship implies that the teacher functions as both model and facilitator as a gradual release to independent literacy takes place. Figure 2.2 provides an example of the time, varied literacy activities, and group configurations for a 2-hour literacy block.

This type of guided reading and writing instruction interspersed with literacy center independent assignments can work only because of the way activities are structured and

FIGURE 2.2
Sample Literacy Block Schedule for Grades 1 and 2.

Time	Literacy Component	Configuration
15 minutes	Shared reading (Big Book) Read-aloud literature	Whole class.
20 minutes	Guided reading M/W Group 1 T/Th Group 2 F Book share	Small group at instructional level with teacher. Small groups assigned to independent literacy centers. Small groups selected by reading interests.
20 minutes	Phonics, working with words, spelling	Whole class.
20 minutes	Guided reading M/W Group 3 T/Th Group 4 F Book share	Small group at instructional level with teacher. Small groups assigned to independent literacy centers. Small groups selected by reading interests.
15 minutes	Journal writing	Whole class while teacher monitors.
15 minutes	Assisted writing M/W Group 2 T/Th Group 1 F Author's chair	Small group with similar writing strengths/needs with teacher. Small groups assigned to independent literacy centers. Small groups share week's published writing.
15 minutes	Assisted writing M/W Group 4 T/Th Group 3 F Author's chair	Small group with similar writing strengths/needs with teacher. Small groups assigned to independent literacy centers. Small groups share week's published writing.

Source: Adapted from Apprenticeship in literacy: Transitions across reading and writing *by Linda Dorn, Cathy French, and Tammy Jones, copyright © 1998, with permission of Stenhouse Publishers.*

organized. The teacher must spend a great deal of time showing primary children how to be independent learners at these literacy centers, modeling how to do the tasks in each center and providing supervision for them early on (through parent volunteers, teacher aides) until they are gradually able to engage in these activities without being fully supervised. Teachers report organizing and facilitating literacy centers while working with a guided reading group as one of the foremost challenges of primary teaching. Assignment boards of center icons and children's names on velcro assist in ever-changing groups as students develop their reading and writing skills. Chapter 5 will provide detailed information on the methods behind these literacy activities.

You are now invited to enter Mrs. Lisa Seirer's first-grade classroom for a morning of literacy activities. Figure 2.3 describes the world of a well-orchestrated primary classroom,

FIGURE 2.3 **Mrs. Seirer's First Grade: A Primary Literacy Classroom Experience.**

Lisa Seirer's first-grade classroom overflows with the joys of becoming emergent readers and writers. The sounds of language follow "The Busy Bees" through the school day as the wonder of rhyme, words, and literature fill the classroom. The activity-packed day begins with the traditional "Pledge of Allegiance" as the enthusiastic voices of young patriots fill the room and break into the "Red, White, and Blue" song. The announcement of pizza for lunch brings forth children's connections to literature previously read—*The Lady with the Alligator Purse* and Eric Carle's *The Very Hungry Caterpillar*. As children line up to meet their fourth-grade partnership buddies in the gym, they respond to the daily question "Are you wearing green?" with clothespins as tallies.

Mrs. Seirer has duplicated a story called "Slam Dunk Sanchez" from an educational Web site (www.learningpage.com) for this partnership reading activity that occurs once per month. After reading the story together, first- and fourth-grade readers and writers are to create a basketball word web. A leadership experience for the fourth graders and a learning experience for the first graders evolves as brainstorming, spelling, and word awareness emerge. Wakefield Elementary School houses K–8 classrooms inviting much cross grade level interaction among classrooms.

Energetically returning to the classroom, the first graders prepare for Calendar Time. Dates, counting, time, days of the week, weather, and tallying reponses to the Question of the Day ensue. In the midst of this activity, a high school Spanish student stops by to teach the children a Spanish phrase. Today it is "Happy Saint Patrick's Day" (*Feliz Dia Je San Patricio*). Share time immerses children in oral language practice as Mrs. Seirer guides, encourages, inquires, and inspires the use of language in the context of familiar objects. Oral language continues as familiar rhymes are recited to celebrate class birthdays and a morning ritual promising to "do my best" today.

The Daily Message stands at attention on chart paper for curious young eyes to read and scrutinize for errors. Children receive simple minilessons on grammar, capitalization, and spelling strategies in the context of this daily communication lesson. Children mention words from their Word Books and recognize "spelling chunks" that they have been learning. With new learning behind them, Mrs. Seirer plays the harpsichord as the children join in on a language-rich song.

As the children return to their desks, they are already dreaming of their responses to write in their Daily Message Journals—What would you do if you found the leprechaun's gold? Some children begin by drawing, others by writing, but most stay right on task. While their styles vary, their enthusiasm for journal writing is apparent. Some write stories while others write sentences and a few struggle with a short phrase. No right answers, no penalty for incorrect spelling. All ideas are valued, and all efforts are encouraged.

The children revisit yesterday's paired reading of Leo Lionni's *A Color of His Own*. They eagerly color and cut out the color of their own chameleon ranging from solid reds to polka-dotted blues. All the children accept the invitation to the carpet area where a huge sheet of chart paper awaits them. The challenge is to create a graph of "our favorite chameleons." Mrs. Seirer wisely steps back as she allows the students to problem solve how to categorize, group, and share the eighteen chameleons they have lovingly created. With her able assistance, children discuss the few chameleons that do not fit in clear-cut colored categories. Selecting a few children to paste them down, Mrs. Seirer guides the project toward completion. Students eagerly make oral statements about the visual display before them: "There are more blue chameleons than red chameleons," "There is only one polka-dotted and one striped chameleon," "There are more orange chameleons than any other color."

The afternoon descends on the classroom far too quickly as the accomplishments of the morning inspire even more language and literature-based learning. The computer lab showcases student projects related to Eric Carle's *The Very Hungry Caterpillar*. Pairs of students use Kid Pix to create five slides of this popular book

FIGURE 2.3 (Continued)

including both self-illustration and text to accompany them. Attention and pride reign apparent as the children work hard and long to complete their projects.

Upon our classroom return, children choose to share oral presentations from favorite books. For example, Sarah shares *Little Red Riding Hood* with a handmade puppet while Brad shares *Frog and Toad Are Friends* with stick puppets. These literature-based, language-rich puppet presentations stretch expectations of what first graders can accomplish. They swell with pride and ooze with the rhyme and patterns of the literary texts.

As the day draws to a reluctant close, Mrs. Seirer requests that all the children write a birthday note to Tanner, who has been beaming all day. At the same time, Tanner fills in a sheet all about himself on his birthday. These authentic notes reflect the sense of community that pervades this classroom. "The Busy Bees" have not only had a productive day, they have respected each others talents and work, they have experienced the exhilaration of reading and writing, and each of them has generously contributed to a learning and literacy community.

and the classroom diagram in Figure 2.4 illustrates the philosophy and the activities of this learning environment. The configurations of desks, types of materials, bulletin board displays, and evidence of instruction and learning clearly reflect all the language arts. How do these elements reflect the teaching philosophy of this teacher? How does this classroom reflect the Principles of Language Arts Instruction?

The Intermediate and Middle-Level Literacy-Rich Environment

A workshop approach provides the scenario for language arts learning in the intermediate (Grades 3–5) and middle level (Grades 6–8). Built on reading, writing, listening, speaking, viewing, and visual representation, the workshop approach incorporates whole group, small group, and individual learning scenarios. The classroom must have flexible seating to accommodate varied configurations, and the spirit of a community of learners is critical to optimal learning.

Reading workshop requires an abundance of literature for teacher-selected and student-selected reading. Class sets (same title for each student) or text sets (six titles for each group) provide adequate literature for whole class reading or small group related literature (theme sets, genre sets, character sets, author sets). In addition, attractive reading posters, reading folders listing books read, and displays of response projects should be visible on walls, counterspace, and bulletin boards. Author studies should be displayed, and rotated new literature should be available for check out for silent reading throughout the school day.

Reading and Writing Workshop Schedule and Procedures

The reading workshop schedule is built around at least one hour devoted to reading of, responding to, and talking about literature. Each session begins with a whole class

FIGURE 2.4 Mrs. Seirer's First-Grade Classroom's Physical Environment.

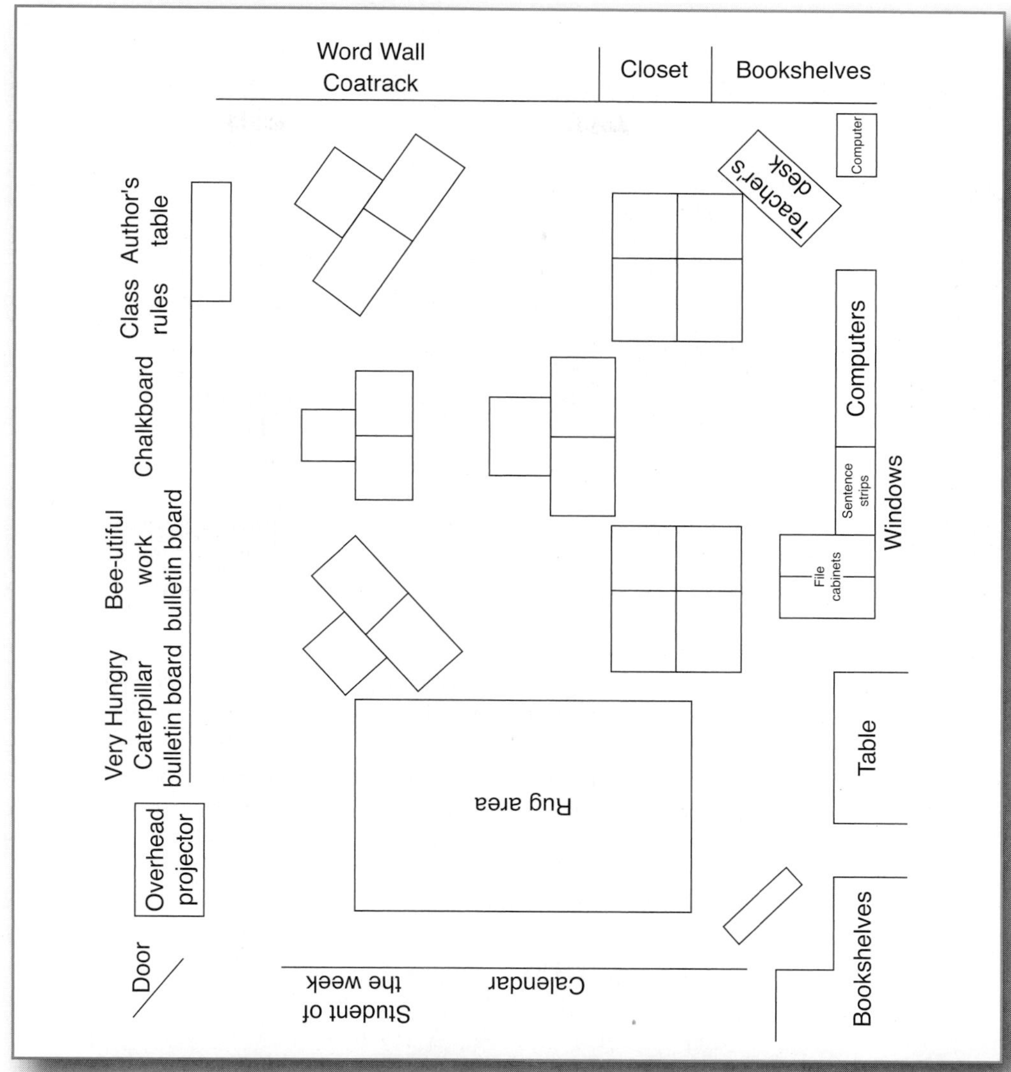

minilesson (10 minutes) on reading strategies or skills, workshop procedures, or literary concepts. Modeling and direct instruction facilitate introduction of a concept or practice with a skill or strategy. Students then spend 20 minutes in real reading in which the newly taught concepts, strategies, and skills are applied in an authentic reading setting. Reading is followed by response to the literature. The response session requires another 20 minutes and can vary from individual journal responses to paired dramatic rereading to small group performance skits or literature circles for discussion. The final 10 minutes of reading workshop is reserved for sharing literature, personal responses, and progress on response projects. The teacher floats among groups and individuals providing directions and suggestions during the primary workshop time, but always teaches in the opening portion and assesses progress during the closing portion of each workshop. Although the time configuration may vary within classrooms, the roles, responsibilities, and expectations of the teacher and learners are well-established.

Similarly, the writing workshop consists of a one-hour time block in which students pursue varied writing interests. The first 15 minutes are devoted to a teacher minilesson on writing skills or strategies or to a read-aloud demonstrating a writing concept or genre. Thirty minutes are devoted to actual on-task writing. During that time, students may sign up for teacher conferences or conduct writing conferences with a peer, edit each other's work, or communicate with their writing group. Some teachers keep students on similar stages of the writing process, while others have students working at various stages and on a variety of pieces. The expertise and comfort level of the teacher determines the flexibility within the workshop approach. The final 15 minutes is devoted to sharing, either in the author's chair or during a question and answer session during which students share writing problems, challenges, and successes.

In many classrooms today, reading and writing are being conducted in adjacent technology labs or in classroom computer centers in which assessing of reading skills and word processing as a mode of writing are facilitated through appropriate software. Even so, the format of reading and writing workshops begins in and returns to the home classroom at both ends of the workshop hour. Figure 2.5 visually demonstrates the reading and writing workshop schedules for the intermediate grades (Grades 3–5). It can be assumed that middle-level students will keep a similar schedule, but that reading and writing workshops might occur on alternate days in regular or block scheduling.

To facilitate a workshop approach, students must be seated in a collaborative configuration so that response groups and writing groups can function effectively. The classroom needs posters that remind students of stages of the writing process, response options, literature posters, and displays of student work. Opportunities to separate oneself for independent reading or writing is effective, but the group setting is mandatory for much of the workshop hour. Resources for reading and writing (e.g., dictionaries, thesaurus) should be conveniently located in the classroom and Internet access should be provided for research writing.

Particularly with intermediate and middle-level students, a common factor in establishing a literacy learning environment is setting the tone of the classroom for the entire year. The first few weeks of school prove critical in establishing the demeanor, routines, and tone of the classroom for the remainder of the year. Establishing a classroom with meaningful activities and actively engaged learners who cooperate with each other begins the first day of school. The goal is to establish a community of learners who support each other in learning, social interactions, and class spirit. This does not occur automatically; it happens only through the guidance of a teacher who knows that valuing children as individuals within the larger social unit of the classroom is necessary to build the helping, caring relationships that result in optimal individual, small group, and whole group learning. A learning community requires the gradual, consistent, and ongoing teacher assurance that all learners are valued and contribute to the cohesiveness of the classroom unit.

Teachers must establish routines, expectations, and appropriate social interactions for a reading and writing workshop within the first weeks of the school year. Students do not automatically come to the upper-level classroom as responsible, cooperative, and respectful individuals. These traits must be modeled and expected during the first few weeks. Consistent modeling of appropriate behavior, actions, and interactions provides sound guidelines for daily learning. Literacy procedures might include modeling how to select a book to read, how to check out literature, or how to discuss a book within a literature circle. Ways of responding to literature, interacting in a group project, and respecting each other's ideas and statements set the tone for the entire school year. While

FIGURE 2.5
Reading and Writing Workshop Schedules for the Intermediate Grades.

Reading Workshop

Time	Literacy Activity	Configuration
10 minutes	Minilesson on reading skill/strategy	Whole class
20 minutes	Independent reading	Whole class, but small groups may be reading varied reading selections
20 minutes	Reader response Literature circle *or* Group response project M Group 1 T Group 2 W Group 3 Th By group request F Sharing projects *or* Whole group discussion	Small groups formed by same reading selection, either interest-based or instructional level
10 minutes		Whole class

Writing Workshop

Time	Literacy Activity	Configuration
15 minutes	Minilesson (traits of writing; examples of effective literature writing)	Whole class
30 minutes	Writing groups M Group 1 T Group 2 W Group 3 Th Individual appointments F Author's chair	Heterogeneous groups blending students with varied writing strengths and needs. Teacher meets with groups and individuals. Peers within groups provide suggestions.
15 minutes	Sharing writing	Whole class. Students share writing problems, ask for help, and share good writing related to minilesson.

the role of teacher as facilitator dominates the intermediate and middle-level classroom, the teacher sets the tone for cooperating, time on task, valuing literacy, and creating lifelong readers and writers in a workshop format.

You are now invited into the sixth-grade classroom of Mrs. Mary Hessenflow. As part of a K–6 building, her literature-based classroom centers on a reading and writing workshop and social studies, while her partner teacher covers reading and writing workshop and mathematics and science instruction. Figure 2.6 describes instructional tendencies from the Principles of Language Arts Instruction that reflect the philosophy of this teacher.

FIGURE 2.6 Mrs. Hessenflow's Sixth Grade Classroom: An Intermediate Literacy Classroom Experience.

Entering Mary Hessenflow's classroom, the visitor experiences an integrated focus on reading, writing, and social studies. A well-organized, veteran teacher, Mrs. Hessenflow holds high expectations and accountability for her students. Reading and writing folders house the process approach to writing, lists of books read, and daily response journals. A literature-based teacher, Mrs. Hessenflow's room overflows with literature that reflects strong reading, writing, and social studies connections.

The classroom is arranged around tables rather than desks so students can interact and work together in both literature and writing circles. Mobiles hanging from the ceiling reflect an "I Have a Dream" project as students share dreams for their community, their country, and their world. Displayed on the ceiling are well-known authors who have already been studied this year—Jane Yolen, Jean Craighead George, and Gary Paulsen. More will be added as the year progresses. The walls abound with response prompts to inspire journal writing and with literary elements to direct the focus of reading. Bookcases overflow with literature for reading while a special display of literature themed to the current social studies topic provides resources for related projects.

Mrs. Hessenflow can best be described as an orchestrator of learning. While she makes announcements, instructs, and models from her podium, she spends most of her time circulating among reading and writing groups and giving individual assistance and ideas to her sixth graders. A sense of responsibility abounds as students stay on-task and dedicated to their assigned reading and writing projects. As with all sixth grades, the day is often interrupted by band practice and other activities, but the independent nature of this classroom allows learning to continue even when some students leave for other commitments.

Students go to other classrooms for part of the sixth-grade curriculum while other students come to Mrs. Hessenflow for social studies. Her literacy commitment flows into her world history curriculum as she incorporates literature related to early civilizations of the Sumerians and Egyptians, Greek and Roman cultures, and the medieval European world. Projects integrate great literature with visual representations of pyramids, ancient Greek and Roman antiquities, and castles of the Middle Ages. This blending of literature across genres keeps interest alive and knowledge growing.

As Mrs. Hessenflow prepares her students for their impending entry into middle school (Grades 7 and 8), she has most certainly given them authentic practice in literature-based reading and writing and left them with an avid interest in social studies. Her authentic integrated assignments extend literacy into the visual representation realm. Her enthusiasm for teaching, high expectations for students, and love of literature result in a respectful community of learners genuinely dedicated to learning and literacy.

Figure 2.7 illustrates the design of this collaborative classroom. Look for aspects of increasing responsibility on the part of the student as more freedom with accountability dominates the intermediate and middle-level literacy classroom.

The Role of Literature in the Language Arts Classroom

Children's literature plays a critical role in the language arts classroom. As you recall the Principles of Language Arts Instruction, one principle applauds the power of children's literature as the foundation of language arts teaching. While basic instruction may be mandated by textbooks, literature trade books provide the creative balance that inspires and motivates children to learn. Teachers who embrace children's literature, respond to it with their mind and heart, make it an instrument of their teaching, and share it with children in their classrooms balance the best of both worlds in teaching the language arts (Metsala, 1997). Children's

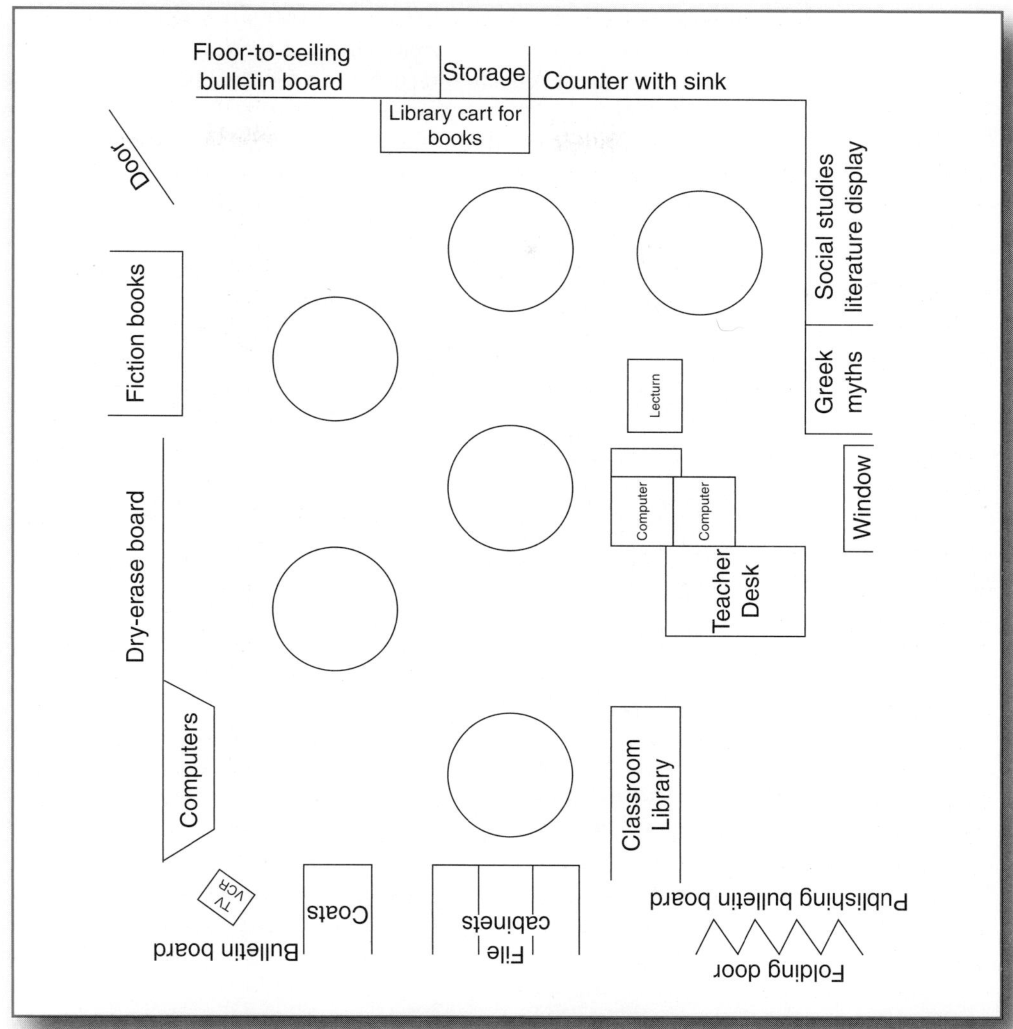

FIGURE 2.7 Mrs. Hessenflow's Sixth-Grade Classroom's Physical Environment.

literature has the ability to touch children's lives, turn them into avid readers and writers, and motivate them to respond to what they read through talk, writing, and visual representation. Children's literature transcends curricular areas and breathes life and light into content areas. Used as reading material or a response initiative, or for viewing information in unique formats, children's books provide sound connections between effective teaching and lifelong learning. Children's books transcend, transform, transport, and translate the printed word into avenues for response through additional reading, writing, listening, speaking, viewing, and visual representation (McClure & Kristo, 1994, 1996).

A brief review of the values of children's literature in the classroom matched to the array of literary genres provide a wide range of reasons why literature must be an integral part of an elementary classroom (Hancock, 2004).

- ***Children's literature crafts words, creates images, and describes everyday objects in special ways.*** Children's books capture and share the wonder of the written word and the appeal of well-chosen language. Rhyme, rhythm, and repetition are the hallmark of books with appeal for the very young. Typically captured in poetic voice, young children can celebrate familiar Mother Goose characters or identify with everyday experiences through a language-based adventure. **Poetry collections** (Joan Bransfield Graham's *Flicker Flash*) and poem picture books (S. D. Sindler's visual interpretation of Rosemary and Stephen Vincent Benet's *Johnny Appleseed*) contain words that roll off the tongue, create visual interpretations, and applaud the sounds of language. **Picture storybooks** (Karen Hesse's *Come on Rain*) eloquently select words and phrases that hold the interest of the listener on an enjoyable adventure through a book. Older readers focus on the use of word choice and literary devices as authors weave their stories through creative use of language. Vocabulary and language motifs eventually make their way into children's own speaking and writing.

- ***Children's literature challenges creativity and ignites inventiveness in children.*** All children enjoy books that whet their imaginative powers and allow them to venture into the realm of the impossible. A beautiful princess, a wizard with a magic quidditch, and a talking lion can transport a child into a special place where the unbelievable seems real. **Traditional folk and fairy tales** typically have strong appeal to young readers as versions of *Rapunzel* by Paul Zelinsky and *The Gingerbread Boy* by Jim Aylesworth become a part of early childhood literacy experiences. Literary tales of **fantasy** spark the imaginations of older readers as well and transport them to worlds of talking animals, or to a kingdom called Narnia (C. S. Lewis's *The Lion, the Witch, and the Wardrobe*), or to a wizard school named Hogwarts (J. K. Rowling's *Harry Potter and the Sorcerer's Stone*) that stretch their beliefs beyond reality. Imagination can result in creative writing, sketches of visualized castles, and access to a world of playful fantasy that is a part of childhood.
- ***Children's literature affirms real life and offers vicarious experiences from authentic situations while fostering empathy for the human condition.*** From going to bed to going to school, from gaining a sense of family to struggling to find acceptance, children's literature honestly portrays the life of children and preadolescents during those important years of growing up. **Realistic fiction** reveals experiences common to childhood and impending adulthood, including those that challenge and define the nature of the individual (Kate DiCamillo's *The Tiger Rising*). Reading and responding to these books through conversations, writing, or drawings can help focus an understanding of others and provide a sense of security in knowing you are not alone.
- ***Children's literature transports readers and transcends time while encouraging valid connections between the past and present.*** Books transport readers to historical places and settings or introduce characters in historical contexts. **Historical fiction** reveals the realities of historical circumstances, introduces flesh and blood characters, and shares unique perspectives about significant historical events that impact contemporary life (Harry Mazer's *A Boy at War: A Novel of Pearl Harbor*). Literature connections to social studies inspire integration of language arts across content lines as children write simulated journals, build replicas of medieval castles, or perform Shakespeare.
- ***Children's literature replays the triumphs and determination of reknown figures and shares an explosion of information and facts about the world in which we live.*** Children's books share the lives of historical and contemporary heroes and the feats and triumphs of everyday people through **biography**. From sports heroes (*Lou Gehrig: The Luckiest Man* by David Adler) to leadership models (*Eleanor Roosevelt* by Russell Freedman), character and determination provide inspiration and direction in children's own lives. Dressing up as a subject of a

Self-selecting quality children's literature across genres motivates readers.

biography and speaking in his or her own voice showcase character. **Nonfiction informational books** extend the growing body of information about our world. Quality factual representations introduce the learner to the facts behind science (Meredith Hooper's *The Drop in My Drink*), a retrospective journey into history (Aliki's *William Shakespeare and the Globe*), or an introduction to the arts (Lucy Micklethwait's *A Child's Book of Play in Art*). Books provide the momentum to access further information through technological resources and to organize and share new learning with others.

- ***Children's literature celebrates cultural diversity and inspires the reader to appreciate both similarities and differences between and among cultures.*** **Multicultural literature** across genres provides the opportunity to visit new places, become acquainted with new people, experience new customs, holidays, and traditions, and learn more about our world. George Ancona, for example, transports us into the spirit of Mexican tradition through *Mayeros: A Yucatec Maya Family,* while Gary Soto's *Snapshots from the Wedding* points out the many ways in which ceremonies are alike as well as different.

The content and format of current children's literature across all literary genres is both impressive and readily adaptable to existing curriculum. The Literature Cluster included here shares quality titles across all genres. The visual appeal of books, the linguistic value of well-written text, and the motivational aspect of children's literature make them a necessary and contributory element in the language arts classroom.

Traditional and New Technology Tools for Instruction

An important component of the literacy-rich classroom includes the tools with which the teacher presents information and directs instruction. This discussion begins with simple traditional tools and moves toward those that have been enhanced through technology (Reinking, Labbo, & McKenna, 1997).

Transparencies and Projection Visuals. Overhead projectors, while a part of the old technology, are underused in the classroom. Instructional transparencies can be used

Literature Cluster

QUALITY LITERATURE ACROSS LITERARY GENRES

Picture Storybooks

Juster, Norton (2005). *The hello, goodbye window,* Illus. by Chris Raschka. New York: Michael di Capua Books/Hyperion.

Lear, Edward (2005). *A was once an apple pie.* Illus. by Suse McDonald. New York: Orchard.

Priceman, Marjorie (2005). *Hot air: The (mostly) true story of the first hot-air balloon ride.* New York: Anne Schwartz/Atheneum.

Traditional Tales

Gerstein, Mordicai (2005). *Carolinda Clatter!* New York: Roaring Book Press.

Mora, Pat (2005). *Dona Flor: A tall tale about a giant woman with a big heart.* Illus. by Raul Colon. New York: Knopf.

Stanley, Diane (2006). *Bella at midnight.* Illus. by Bagram Ibatoulline. New York: HarperCollins.

Fantasy

Di Camillo, Kate (2006). *The miraculous journey of Edward Tulane.* Illus. by Bagram Ibatoulline. Cambridge, MA: Candlewick Press.

Hale, Shannon (2005). *The princess academy.* New York: Bloomsbury Children's Books.

Pullman, Philip (2005). *The scarecrow and his servant.* Illus. by Peter Bailey. New York: Knopf.

Poetry

Cheng, Andrea (2005). *Shanghai messenger.* Illus. by Ed Young. New York; Lee & Low.

Janeczko, Paul (Ed.) (2005). *A kick in the head: An everyday guide to poetic forms.* Illus. by Chris Rasczka. Cambridge, MA: Candlewick Press.

Sidman, Joyce (2005). *Song of the water boatman and other pond poems.* Illus. by Beckie Prange. Boston: Houghton Mifflin.

Realistic Fiction

Bridsall, Jeanne (2005). *The Penderwicks: A summer tale of four sisters, two rabbits, and a very interesting boy.* New York: Knopf.

Perkins, Lynne Rae (2005). *Criss cross.* New York: Greenwillow/HarperCollins.

Weeks, Sarah (2004). *So B. it.* New York: HarperCollins/Laura Geringer Books.

Historical Fiction

Armstrong, Alan (2005). *Whittington.* Illus. by S. D. Schindler. New York: Random House.

Bruchac, Joseph (2006). *Geronimo: A novel.* New York: Scholastic.

Erdrich, Louise (2005). *The game of silence.* New York: HarperCollins.

Biography

Bolden, Tonya (2005). *Maritcha: A nineteenth-century American girl.* New York: Harry N. Abrams.

Giovanni, Nikki (2005). *Rosa.* Illus. by Bryan Collier. New York: Holt.

White, Linda Arms (2005). *I could do that! Esther Morris gets women the vote.* Illus. by Nancy Carpenter. New York: Farrar/Melanie Kroupa.

Nonfiction/Informational

Bartoletti, Susan Campbell (2005). *Hitler youth: Growing up in Hitler's shadow.* New York: Scholastic Nonfiction.

Freedman, Russell (2005). *Children of the Great Depression.* New York: Clarion.

Walker, Sally M. (2005). *Secrets of a Civil War submarine: Solving the mysteries of the H. L Hunley.* Minneapolis, MN: Carolrhoda Books.

Multicultural

Canales, Viola (2005). *The tequila worm.* New York: Wendy Lamb/Random House.

Muth, Jon (2005). *Zen shorts.* New York: Scholastic.

Woodson, Jacqueline (2005). *Show way.* Illus. by Hudson Talbot. New York: Putnam.

to share outlines, webs, or graphic organizers of new lesson material, to provide visual cues to new vocabulary, or to present labeled diagrams for topics under study. Transparencies can be used for modeling writing or for sharing student writing. They provide a vehicle for morning message or daily oral or written language practice. Do not underestimate the continued importance of this simple, but effective technology. For those fortunate to have a projection system in their classrooms, visual information can readily be placed on something like the Elmo document camera to enhance the quality and importance of both visual and textual material.

Audiotapes. Recorders and audiotapes are readily available in most classrooms but often underused with new teaching demands. Audiobooks (books on tape) assist struggling readers when they attempt to read quality literature. Parents, adults, or good readers can prepare additional audiotapes for content area reading materials. Audiotapes can be used for class literature conversation groups. Audiotaped interviews of local or visiting authors can later be transcribed and distributed. Oral presentations can be audiotaped for evaluative purposes. Moving old technology toward new classroom needs makes what is old quite new again.

Videotapes. Videotape recorders and camcorders are generally available in elementary and middle schools. They add a visual dimension to the presentation and recording of reports or language-based events such as readers theatre, book character reports, author studies, and content-related presentations.

Digital Video Discs. A digital video disc (DVD) is a disc that is the same size as a CD, delivers outstanding video and audio, and holds more data than other media. DVD-ROM players are becoming more readily available on computers.

Electronic Databases. Electronic databases provide the categorization and storage of data as well as searches for retrieving that data. Electronic encyclopedia (on CD-ROMs, DVD-ROMs, or the Internet) provide multimedia connections allowing students to read about a topic, click on a word or icon, and link to related articles, pictures, animation, video clips, or audio clips. Electronic atlases are useful reference tools in content area instruction with zoom-in views.

Word Processing and Desktop Publishing Software. Word processing software (e.g., Microsoft Word, AppleWorks) allows students to write stories, poems, and reports and revise them with a minimum of frustration by inserting, deleting, and moving material with the click of a mouse. Desktop publishing software (e.g., Microsoft Publisher, Kid Pix) allows the integration of text and graphics into a document. Chapter 13 provides many more details for both teacher use and student use of this technology.

Presentation Software. Multimedia presentation software (e.g., HyperStudio, PowerPoint) makes informative, eye-catching presentations possible for both teachers and students. Print, graphics, images, sound effects, and speech assist in presenting information.

The Internet. The Internet provides an international linking of computer networks that can communicate with one another through the World Wide Web, providing unlimited potential for teaching and learning in the elementary setting. It allows users to access multimedia materials through the use of a Web browser (e.g., Internet Explorer, Netscape Navigator). Sites on the Web are useful as teacher instructional resources and for student learning in any content area discipline. Other valuable resources such as electronic texts and books and myriad Web sites support basic literacy and can also be found on the Internet.

New Technologies for the Language Arts Classroom

Digital Cameras

A digital camera works like a traditional camera except that it does not use film, and images are digitally stored on a memory card or disk. The storage capacities of memory cards and disks vary, as do picture quality and camera features. There are many camera models available to suit a range of needs. Images are easily transferred to a computer by connecting the camera to a special cable or camera cradle. Digital cameras have many uses in the language arts classroom as students may add digital photographs to essays, nonfiction reports, or author notes. To recapture special events or field trips, students may create a display of colorful images and detailed captions.

Document Cameras and Visual Presenters

More advanced than a traditional overhead projector, document cameras and visual presenters allow teachers to show three-dimensional objects or texts and colorful images from literature or sheets of paper to large audiences. In contrast to a traditional overhead projector, they must be connected to a separate projector or TV monitor. Teachers in the language arts classroom use such devices to present literature during a shared reading experience or to teach writing lessons while projecting students' writing samples on a large screen.

Interactive Whiteboards

The interactive whiteboard looks and functions much like a traditional whiteboard on which students and teachers can write with dry-erase markers and erase their scribbles with a cloth or eraser. By connecting the electronic whiteboard to a classroom computer and projector it becomes an interactive computer screen from which favorite software or Internet applications can be launched. Most interactive whiteboard software include capabilities to annotate, highlight, or make notes over any computer application such as word processing or publishing programs. Teachers can even save, print, or e-mail lessons and all notations to students who are away from class.

To look more closely at these materials and others related to "Teaching in the Language Arts Classroom," visit the Companion Website at www.prenhall.com/hancock.

The Tech Tip included here highlights and defines new technologies for the language arts classroom. Chapter 13 details language arts–related sites and instructional configurations for utilizing the wonders of the Internet for navigating, study and research, and electronic mail and mailing lists related to literacy as well as additional information on the use of multimedia environments for primary, intermediate, and middle-level students.

Planning and Preparation of Language Arts Instruction

Planning and preparing for language arts instruction may be the most time consuming aspect of teaching, yet the one that influentially determines the kind and amount of learning that will actually take place. Much time in teacher preparation programs goes into modeling lesson planning and writing lesson plans for the language arts classroom. In her book *Enhancing Professional Practice: Framework for Teaching* (see again Figure 2.1), Danielson (1996) delineates several important considerations that provide the foundation for the planning phase of teaching complimented by some examples from the realm of language arts:

- ***Knowledge of content and pedagogy.*** Teachers must have knowledge of what is to be taught and match it to an effective methodology for teaching. For example, reading fluency (intonation, pace, comprehension) may be best practiced through readers theatre. Editing skills (punctuation, spelling, grammar) may best be practiced in the context of authentic student writing through peer review and self-editing.
- ***Knowledge of students.*** Teachers must know developmentally appropriate practices to match with the abilities of the students they teach. Knowing the interests and cultural background of individuals, the varied skills they bring to a complex task, and their different approaches to learning provide targets for lesson plans. For example, teaching a picture cue strategy to visual learners in a primary classroom typically provides a comprehension strategy at the emergent reader level. On the other hand, drawing inferences from text provides further reading strategy instruction within a lesson that is more appropriate at an intermediate reader developmental level.
- ***Selecting instructional goals.*** Teachers must always identify what it is that they want children to learn. What are the learning outcomes of the lesson? What do they want children to produce as documentation of learning? Teachers select these goals from district, state, or national standards but typically articulate them in specific terms of authentic learning. For example, Students will retell Jim Aylesworth's (1998) traditional tale, *The Gingerbread Boy,* as a sequential comprehension check on character, setting, problem, and resolution.
- ***Knowledge of resources.*** Teachers must gather textbooks, trade books, Internet sites, and a variety of materials to plan for effective instruction. Teachers need to know where to go, whom to ask, and how to locate and access information on a topic. For example, gathering information for an expository writing project on sea animals yields teacher-gathered materials about sea creatures on a laser disk, dozens of nonfiction trade books, an *Encarta* online encyclopedia CD-ROM, a science textbook chapter, and numerous Web sites on the ocean accessed during computer lab time. The teacher as facilitator of learning must gather and present knowledge from a wide range of resources.
- ***Designing coherent instruction.*** Instruction must be planned step-by-step using clear explanations, teacher modeling, setting high expectations, effective grouping, and engaged learning activities. Planning for the gradual release of responsibility from the teacher to the student provides sound instruction. For example, student brainstorming for a narrative essay on "My Favorite Place" asks each student to list five favorite places, circle a choice, and discuss the selected topic with a peer. The articulation of ideas through talk provides a scaffold and rehearsal for the impending drafting stage.
- ***Assessing student learning.*** The planning stage does indeed demand the preparation for the assessment of student learning preceding lesson implementation. Checklists, rubrics, models, and assessment criteria reflecting instructional goals provide expectations for students. While more specifics will be provided in Chapter 15 of this text, it cannot be overemphasized that assessment must parallel the instructional objectives. The teacher must monitor the learning outcome that matches their instructional objective. Therefore, if the goal is for students to improve the element of word choice in their writing, the assessment instrument must reflect that, indeed, word

choice selection shows improvement (e.g., the student's writing reflects the use of quality word choice through a minimum of five descriptive adjectives and five powerful verbs). Assessment becomes a reflective part of teaching as attainment (or nonattainment) of a goal determines the next stage or topic for planning and instruction.

Learning to plan language arts lessons takes time, attention to detail, and patience, but preparation does become easier and more efficient with practice. Preservice teachers need to clearly articulate step-by-step plans, whereas experienced teachers often internalize the steps of the planning process and fit those plans in abbreviated codes into a small section of their weekly plan book. Much of what preservice teachers actually write into a plan gradually becomes internalized planning as they become more experienced. Yet the process of planning and the varied steps do not become ready for instruction without specific attention to each stage of the planning process. For the benefit of new teachers and as an organizer for experienced teachers, Figure 2.8 illustrates the 10 essential components for a language arts lesson plan. Each step provides ongoing practice in realizing the small steps that build toward effective instruction as a teacher implements instruction in an authentic classroom setting. The components of a language arts lesson plan contain consistent elements to assist the novice or in-service teacher in implementing quality instruction. Although your university teacher education program or your school district may use a variation of this form (e.g., different terminology, fewer elements, more elements), this format parallels essential thinking that is included in effective lesson plans.

This suggested template can be used in conjunction with Lesson Plan 2.1, which illustrates how a literature base and a technology base become components of a well-written (and eventually well-implemented) lesson plan. The plan focuses on word choice in picture captions and blends visual literacy, word choice, and technology presentation within a language arts lesson. Use this model to develop your own language arts lessons. Take the time to notice those details that blend literature, language arts, and technology through visual representation and writing.

LESSON PLAN 2.1

TITLE: **Word Choice in Picture Captions**

Grade Level: 4–6

Time Frame: Two 45-minute classes

Standards

IRA/NCTE Standards: 4, 10

NETS for Students: 2, 3, 5

Objectives

- The students will select quality word choice to reflect the visual image of a photograph.
- The writer will use a scanner and a printer to reproduce a photographed image and word processing to publish a picture caption.

Materials/Setting/Groups

- Locker, Thomas (1997). *Water Dance.* Harcourt Brace.
- Paper, pencils
- Selection of photographs
- Teacher-created model of a picture caption

Procedures

- Read aloud *Water Dance* and revisit the text for word choice. As a class, generate a list of words that visually depict book illustrations.
- Share project expectations through selection of photos and teacher model. Emphasize the importance of using descriptive language and appropriate word choice.
- Distribute photographs to pairs or small groups of students. Ask students to brainstorm a list of descriptive words and phrases to capture the mood and content of the photograph.
- Using their brainstormed ideas, students should compose a brief caption (2–3 sentences) to accompany their photograph.
- Working through the steps of the writing process, the students revise and improve the quality of word choice and peer edit for conventions.
- Scan photos and word process the final caption in selected font.
- Print and present to class.

Assessment

- Teacher-created checklist reflecting lesson outcomes.

Accommodation/Modification

- Some students may use a digital camera to take their own photographs, print them, and write a quality word choice caption.
- The group will support members who may struggle with word choice or technology.

Visit the Meeting the Standards module in Chapter 2 of the Companion Website at www.prenhall.com/hancock to adapt this lesson to meet your state's standards.

Effective Language Arts Teaching and Learning

Effective literacy teaching and learning in the elementary and middle-level grades becomes evident in a variety of sound teaching contexts. The teacher is ultimately responsible for a learning environment that produces children who read, write, listen, speak, view, and visually represent. A literacy classroom must become the type of environment in which all children can succeed as literacy learners (Gambrell, Morrow, Neuman, & Pressley, 1999). The following characteristics, followed by an italicized statement of good advice for both the novice teacher and the teacher seeking professional growth, reflect the key elements in a successful literacy program:

- ***Time on task.*** Classrooms in which much time is spent on learning to read and write are classrooms in which children become readers and writers. Well-established routines and schedules reflect more time spent learning and less time spent transitioning from one activity to the next. Structure with freedom blends high expectations with respect for individuals as learners. The more time spent on authentic literacy activities, the more opportunity to practice skills and strategies in the context of literacy. *Provide a well-organized, well-orchestrated classroom that encourages children to be on the task of literacy learning.*
- ***Goal-orientation.*** Classrooms in which children succeed as literacy learners are those in which the teacher holds high expectations and articulates them in terms

FIGURE 2.8 Language Arts Lesson Plan Template.

Title: *What am I going to teach?*
Your first step is to articulate the focus of the lesson, the skill to be taught, the language arts emphasis, the process, product, or unique element of the lesson.

Grade Level: *Who is my audience?*
You must learn to target the developmental appropriateness of the topic or skill of the lesson. Since literacy classrooms typically contain more than one level of learner, this becomes critical in designing instruction to meet the needs of a range of learners.

Time Frame: *How much time will it take me to teach the lesson and for children to achieve the outcome?*
Planning the length of a lesson will help you determine the content that can effectively be taught. State this time frame in minutes, hours, or days, depending on the scope of the lesson.

Standards: *What national, state, or district standards in the language arts do I address in the lesson? What national, state, or district technology standards do I address?*
Refer to national or state standards (benchmarks and indicators) to find your purpose for teaching the lesson and which language arts to highlight. This statement will be reflected in the assessment portion of your lesson plan, as a match will exist between learning outcome and type of assessment selected.

Objectives: *What do I want students to learn and be able to do?*
Your lesson plan should contain two to three measurable objectives related to the content. Determine how each student will reach these objectives. Check to be certain that the objectives match the selected standards, benchmarks, or indicators.

Materials, Setting, and Groups: *What will I need to teach this lesson and where will I teach it? If groups are incorporated, how will they be selected and utilized?*
Make an exhaustive list of all materials needed for your teaching, student engagement, and final outcome documentation. Include children's literature, textbook resources, and supplies to complete the lesson outcome. Determine the location of instruction and the physical arrangements needed. Consider transitions necessary between parts of the lesson. If the lesson involves the teaching or facilitating of small groups, include details of who, what, and where.

Motivation: *How do I increase students' interest in the lesson and activate prior knowledge? How do I set a purpose for the lesson?*
Determine what format you will use to compel students to engage in the activity and achieve the language arts objectives. List guiding questions that might impact this developing interest.

Procedure: *How will my students become engaged in the learning process? What is the best way to use technology to enhance instruction or student presentation of their work?*
If you follow a step-by-step sequence of teaching, your students will become engaged as you deliver the lesson. Include grouping, modeling, demonstration, engagement, and a clearly articulated assignment, as well as indicating the gradual release of your teaching to their practice, and ultimately to their achievement of the objectives. Be specific and detailed and reread the procedures section to make certain that no instructional gaps exist.

You may use technology for planning a lesson from online resources. Include those Web sites in this section of your plan. However, you may more substantially use technology for your own instructional presentation of the lesson. This may include PowerPoint or the use of a projection system or white board to enhance the lesson delivery. Your students may also be assigned a technology component for the final presentation of their work product through word processing or PowerPoint.

FIGURE 2.8 (Continued)

Assessment: *How will I know if the students have achieved my objectives and standards?*
Prior to teaching, you must construct a means to formally or informally document learning. Rubrics, checklists, narratives, self-reflections, anecdotal records, and tests provide a tentative match between the objectives and standards listed earlier in the plan and the documented evidence that learning has taken place. Plan how you will use the assessment to guide future lessons and how you will assist those students who do not meet the stated objectives or standards. After the lesson, reflect on what changes might make this an even more effective learning experience.

Accommodation and Modification: *How will I adapt the lesson to meet the requirements of all students (including special needs learners and culturally and linguistically diverse learners)?*
Since all students need to succeed, try to differentiate the abilities of learners. While most of your target learners will accomplish a task, you must find the means for which intervention and enrichment will meet the needs of struggling or gifted learners, special needs students, and English language learners. Less (or more) of the same is not an option.

of specific literacy goals. For example, a teacher who is aware of district, state, and national standards for literacy instruction holds the key to the knowledge that each child must learn. Planning and implementing developmentally appropriate literacy instruction based on such goals and standards will guide this teacher in a positive direction. New teachers, especially, need a learning map to follow to make certain that all components of literacy are introduced, practiced, and applied in authentic literacy lessons and activities. *Be aware of documents that specifically discuss your district, state, and national guidelines for the language arts.*

- ***Rigorously paced, predictable schedule.*** The momentum of the classroom must carry children from one literacy task to another without interruption. Creating a flow of instruction is critical in providing the best use of time in the classroom. Children who internalize a daily schedule are better prepared for learning. Teachers who expect attention to a new task accelerate the pace of learning and make efficient use of teaching time. *Model and expect sound management and discipline so a daily schedule becomes routine, procedures are expected, and transitions between activities are efficient and effective.*
- ***Optimal time spent planning.*** Teachers who spend time planning for daily lessons, collecting materials to enhance instruction, and building individual lessons toward broader goals provide strong instruction for literacy learners. This implies that quality time—not an excessive amount of time spent planning—should be spent thinking through why we are teaching what we are teaching. *Become an effective conveyor of literacy instruction by spending adequate time planning what to teach, how best to teach it, what materials will be required, and how to adapt lessons to individual learner needs.*
- ***Curriculum coverage.*** Teachers who know the expectations of the language arts curriculum at the district and state level make more efficient use of time spent teaching. Knowing what language arts skills and strategies were learned the previous year and what language arts skills and strategies will be learned the following year help a teacher target language arts goals for the current year. This premise still allows teachers the flexibility of when to teach the expected curriculum, but it

ensures that the curriculum will be covered. Teachers often spend time on skills and strategies children already know when those skills and strategies might best be practiced and applied in the context of authentic reading and writing activities. *Know language arts curricular expectations, know your students' language arts abilities and capabilities, and teach what is expected of children.*

- ***Variety in instruction.*** Children function as literacy learners in an environment that provides variety in instruction. Many well-researched methods for literacy instruction provide various ways to instruct children. Experienced teachers know that each child learns differently. Staying with one particular mode of instruction may reach some children but leave others at the fringes of learning. *Provide a variety of instructional methods for teaching reading and writing in order to reach all children and their varities of learning styles.*
- ***Release of responsibility to students.*** The best teachers provide sound direct instruction and sufficient guided practice, and then gradually release responsibility of learning to students. Teachers model lessons, provide coaching to individuals as needed, and ensure that all children fulfill literacy tasks. Although some children will need more guidance and practice and some will need less, the teacher is available to adapt instruction and performance to ensure success. *Know when to teach, when to guide, and when to provide students the responsibility to apply learning on their own.*
- ***Academically focused programs.*** Teachers who hold high but realistic expectations for academic literacy learning evidence high levels of literacy learning in their classrooms. Teachers who follow programs that expect learners to evidence achievement over periods of time are likely to guide children toward more academic learning. Teachers who document learning through a variety of authentic means (e.g., tests, portfolios, checklists, continuum) are more likely to bring about real learning. *Document ongoing student learning so that daily and long-term literacy learning can be readily evidenced through a blend of standardized and authentic assessment means.*
- ***Libraries and media centers used to full potential.*** Classrooms in which children grow in literacy learning appear to be those that use libraries frequently and effectively. The library that functions as a constant literacy resource rather than being limited to a single weekly visit is one that continuously supports classroom learning. Librarians and media specialists who allow children to pursue unfolding interests, to select books for daily independent reading, and to spend time browsing through literacy materials are those who envision learning as a lifelong, not a once-a-week, process. Teachers who use libraries as resources for more effective teaching and as sources of new books for classroom display and motivation model the functional uses of literacy. *Utilize the library and media center for effective instruction and encourage your students to visit it frequently to pursue individual interests and literacy needs.*
- ***Focus on the larger community.*** Classrooms in which literacy learning succeeds typically look beyond the classroom walls to invite parents and community to be a part of the literacy journey. From parent volunteers who listen to children read aloud to guest speakers who teach about the history and occupational opportunities in the community, the world outside the classroom can contribute to literacy growth. *Reach beyond the classroom door to make literacy relevant through real-life connections between home, school, and community.*

Once again, connect these examples of effective instruction to the seven Principles of Language Arts Instruction. You will note that each effective instructional trait aligns with one or more of the principles. A knowledgeable, internalized belief in the effective teaching of the language arts reflects itself both in classroom design and also in language arts teaching methodology.

Visit the Companion Website at www.prenhall.com/hancock and gauge your understanding of Chapter 2 concepts with the self-assessments.

Closing Thoughts

This chapter contains many elements of the wisdom of teaching the English language arts as well as the broader wisdom of the general teaching profession. Be sure to read "between the lines" as you develop a broader perspective on becoming an effective teacher of the language arts and blending the language arts across the curriculum. Use visual imagery as you envision your literacy classroom and align your teaching philosophy with the varied aspects of your classroom. Consider the importance of creative planning that aligns student outcomes with assessment, details the step-by-step procedure to disseminating skills and knowledge, while addressing the needs and ensuring the success of all learners. Contemplate the wisdom of "best practices" as you consider the elements of effective literacy instruction. Carry these ideas with you throughout this textbook as it moves beyond the classroom environment and planning and preparation to the actual literacy methodologies with which you will build your language arts teaching repertoire of methods to deliver instruction.

References

Bickart, T. S., Jablon, J. R., & Dodge, D. T. (1999). *Building the primary classroom: A complete guide to teaching and learning.* Portsmouth, NH: Heinemann.

Calkins, L. M. (1994). *The art of teaching writing.* Portsmouth, NH: Heinemann.

Calkins, L. M. (2001). *The art of teaching reading.* New York: Longman.

Cambourne, B. (2000). Conditions for literacy learning—Observing literacy learning in the elementary classroom: Nine years of classroom anthropology. *The Reading Teacher, 53,* 512–515.

Characteristics of an ideal reading classroom (1999). *The Reading Teacher, 52,* 904–906.

Danielson, Charlotte (1996). *Enhancing professional practice: A framework for teaching.* Alexandria, VA: Association for Supervision and Curriculum Development.

Fisher, Bobbi (1996). *Inside the classroom: Teaching kindergarten and first grade.* Portsmouth, NH: Heinemann.

Gambrell, L. B. (1996). Creating classroom cultures that foster reading motivation. *The Reading Teacher, 50,* 14–25.

Gambrell, L. B., Morrow, L. M., Neuman, S. B., & Pressley, M. (Eds.) (1999). *Best practices in literacy instruction.* New York: Guilford Press.

Hancock, M. R. (2004). *A celebration of literature and response: Children, books, and teachers in K–8 classrooms* (2nd ed.). Upper Saddle River, NJ: Merrill/Prentice Hall.

Mayfield, M. I. (1992). The classroom environment: A living-in and learning-in space. In L. O. Ollila & M. I. Mayfield (Eds.), *Emerging literacy: Preschool, kindergarten, and primary grades* (pp. 166–195). Boston: Allyn & Bacon.

McClure, A. A., & Kristo, J. V. (Eds.) (1994). *Inviting children's responses to literature.* Urbana, IL: National Council of Teachers of English.

McClure, A. A., & Kristo, J. V. (Eds.) (1996). *Books that invite talk, wonder, and play.* Urbana, IL: National Council of Teachers of English.

McGee, L. M., & Richgels, D. J. (2000). *Literacy's beginnings: Supporting young readers and writers* (3rd ed.). Boston: Allyn & Bacon.

Mercer, D. K. (1999). *Teachers' perceptions of a primary literacy environment for culturally and linguistically diverse students.* Doctoral dissertation, Kansas State University, Manhattan, KS.

Metsala, J. L. (1997). Effective primary-grade literacy instruction = Balanced literacy instruction. *The Reading Teacher, 50,* 518–521.

Morrow, L. M. (1989). Designing the classroom to promote literacy development. In D. S. Strickland & L. M. Morrow (Eds.), *Emerging literacy: Young children learn to read and write.* Newark, DE: International Reading Association.

Morrow, L. M. (1997a). *The literacy center: Contexts for reading and writing.* York, ME: Stenhouse.

Morrow, L. M. (1997b). *Literacy development in the early years: Helping children read and write* (3rd ed.). Boston: Allyn & Bacon.

Neuman, S. B., & Roskos, K. (1990). Play, print, and purpose: Enriching play environments for literacy development. *The Reading Teacher, 44,* 214–221.

Ostrow, J. (1995). *A room with a different view: First through third graders build community and create curriculum.* York, ME: Stenhouse.

Reinking, D., Labbo, D., & McKenna, M. (1997). Navigating the changing landscape of literacy: Current theory and research in computer-based reading and writing. In J. Flood, S. B. Heath, & D. Lapp (Eds.), *Handbook of research on teaching literacy through the communicative and visual arts* (pp. 77–92). New York: Macmillan.

Routman, R. (2003). *Reading essentials: The specifics you need to teach reading well.* Portsmouth, NH: Heinemann.

Routman, R. (2005). *Writing essentials: Raising expectations and results while simplifying teaching.* Portsmouth, NH: Heinemann.

Teale, W. H., & Sulzby, E. (1986). *Emergent literacy: Writing and reading.* Norwood, NJ: Ablex.

Turner, J. C. (1995). The influence of classroom contexts on young children's motivation for literacy. *Reading Research Quarterly, 30,* 410–441.

Wolk, S. (1998). *A democratic classroom.* Portsmouth, NH: Heinemann.

Children's Books Cited

Adler, David (1999). *Lou Gehrig: The luckiest man.* Illus. by Terry Widener. San Diego: Harcourt Brace.

Aliki (1999). *William Shakespeare and the Globe.* New York: HarperCollins.

Ancona, George (1997). *Mayeros: A Yucatec Maya family,* New York: Lothrop, Lee & Shepard.

Aylesworth, Jim (1998). *The gingerbread boy.* New York: Simon & Schuster.

Benet, Rosemary, & Benet, Stephen Vincent (1933/2001). *Johnny Appleseed.* Illus. by S. D. Sindler. New York: McElderry.

Carle, Eric (1968). *The very hungry caterpillar.* New York: Philomel.

Cronin, Doreen (2000). *Click, clack, moo: Cows that type.* Illus. by Betsy Lewin. New York: Simon & Schuster.

DiCamillo, Kate (2001). *The tiger rising.* Cambridge, MA: Candlewick Press.

Freedman, Russell (1993). *Eleanor Roosevelt: A life of discovery.* Boston: Clarion.

George, Jean Craighead (1959/1988). *My side of the mountain.* New York: Dutton.

Graham, Joan Bransfield (1999). *Flicker flash.* Illus. by Nancy Davis. Boston: Houghton Mifflin.

Henkes, Kevin (1996). *Lilly's purple plastic purse.* New York: Greenwillow.

Hesse, Karen (1999). *Come on rain.* Illus. by Jon J. Muth. New York: Scholastic.

Hoban, Tana (1993). *White on black.* New York: Greenwillow.

Hooper, Meredith (1998). *The drop in my drink: The story of water on our planet.* Illus. by Chris Coady. New York: Viking.

Lester, Mike (2000). *A is for salad.* New York: Putnam.

Lewis, C. S. (1951). *The lion, the witch, and the wardrobe.* New York: Macmillan.

Lionni, Leo (1975). *A color of his own.* New York: Random House.

Locker, Thomas (1997). *Water dance.* San Diego: Harcourt Brace.

Mazer, Harry (2001). *A boy at war: A novel of Pearl Harbor.* New York: Simon & Schuster.

Micklethwait, Lucy (1996). *A child's book of play in art.* New York: Dorling Kindersley.

Rawls, Wilson (1961). *Where the red fern grows.* New York: Doubleday.

Root, Phyllis (2001). *Rattletrap car.* Illus. by Jill Barton. Cambridge, MA: Candlewick Press.

Rowling, J. K. (1998). *Harry Potter and the sorcerer's stone.* Illus. by Mary GrandPré. New York: Scholastic.

Saul, Carol (1998). *Barn cat.* Illus. by Mary Azarian. Boston: Little, Brown.

Soto, Gary (1997). *Snapshots from the wedding.* Illus. by Stephanie Garcia. New York: Putnam.

Swanson, Diane (1994). *Safari beneath the sea: The wonder world of the North Pacific coast.* Photographs by the Royal British Columbia Museum. San Francisco: Sierra Club.

Weisner, David (1999). *Sector 7.* New York: Clarion Books.

Westcott, Nadine (1998). *The lady with the alligator purse.* New York: Little, Brown.

Yolen, Jane (2000). *Off we go!* Illus. by Laurel Molk. New York: Little, Brown.

Zelinsky, Paul O. (1997). *Rapunzel.* New York: Dutton.

Chapter 3

LANGUAGE AS THE FOCUS OF DIVERSITY

Portraits of Language Learners

Joys are the same and love is the same. Pain is the same, and blood is the same. Smiles are the same, and hearts are just the same . . .

FROM *WHOEVER YOU ARE* BY MEM FOX

Who are the children that we teach? Mem Fox's *Whoever You Are* joyfully celebrates the emotional bonds that unite all children, all humanity. Our students come in all sizes, all colors, all abilities. They speak different languages, have different family backgrounds, possess different capacities for learning, and bring different experiences to learning. Some thrive on literacy, while others struggle to keep up. Some show proficiency in spoken and written English, while others find comfort and confidence in their first language. But our students are all children who feel, love, and care. They are children who want to please their parents, their teachers, and themselves. But they are children who learn through different styles, at different paces, and through different means.

In *Kids Come in All Languages*, Cortes (1994) reminds teachers that students come to school speaking varied languages. With them come home and behavioral problems, diverse learning styles, varied prior knowledge, and differing emotional experiences. "Many have little vision of future careers or awareness of what educational steps they must take in order to transform dreams into possibilities" (p. 31).

The language arts professional, in particular, faces the demanding challenge and responsibility of addressing the diverse language needs of all children. The fastest growing school age population in the United States is that of linguistically diverse learners. According to the U.S. Department of Education (2002) the enrollment of linguistically diverse learners has grown from 2.1 million to 4.4 million over the last decade. The U.S. Census Bureau (2000) projects that this trend in culturally and linguistically diverse student population growth will continue. Schoolchildren whose first language is not English will constitute an estimated 40 percent of the K–12 population in the United States by the year 2030. Garcia (2000) reminds educators that in the next few decades it will be almost impossible for a teacher to serve in a public school setting, or even in a private school context, in which the students are not racially, culturally, or linguistically diverse. The International Reading Association and the National Association for the Education of Young Children (1998) in a joint position statement assert that educators must understand second language acquisition while respecting and celebrating the home language

We can begin sharpening our awareness of linguistic diversity by reflecting on our own exposure to this diversity through the people, places, and texts in our own lives (Barnitz, 1997). As a child, I grew up in a Chicago suburb in a home with immigrant ties to Germany and Czechoslovakia. References to these languages occurred infrequently but were mostly in a food context or a holiday setting, or during visits with relatives. My best friend down the street was part of an intergenerational household in which an Italian-speaking grandfather often scolded us proficiently in his native tongue. As a child, I recall attending Catholic mass that was printed in English text in my missal, but spoken by the priest in Latin. These were my first exposures to second languages.

The linguistic texture of my life was enriched as an adult and teacher when children whose first language was Spanish trickled into my classroom in the 1980s. I treated them as children first, then as children who spoke only Spanish as a second consideration. Although they were pulled out to a bilingual program daily, I believe the time I spent with them in my classroom immersing them in English was most valuable. My final stage of language awareness came from my own travels as I experienced British dialects and Irish brogues as well as the expressiveness of Italian, the differences between Scandinavian languages, the challenges of Hungarian, and the forcefulness of German. As a second language learner in these international contexts, I realized how easily a foundational knowledge in one language can facilitate connections to another. Think of your own exposure to linguistic variation and literacy and realize how many encounters with diverse languages you have already experienced. Your personal awareness and experiences will never fail to positively affect your literacy instruction.

While this chapter focuses mostly on children with Spanish as their first language, teachers are well aware that language differences transcend the globe. Within the Hispanic domain lie Puerto Rican, Chicano, Mexican, Salvadoran, Cuban, and other distinct cultures. Children from Taiwan to the Ukraine to Indonesia bring their own languages to the classroom setting as well. Language learners experience either success or failure in their English literacy acquisition, depending on what occurs in their homes and classrooms. If teachers make linguistically informed decisions about curriculum and instruction, children can learn to read and write English in the context of linguistically diverse classrooms. Current literacy instructional practices view reading and writing as cognitive, linguistic, cultural, and social processes in which learners actively construct meaning by using their prior experiences and linguistic knowledge. To ensure that *all* language learners succeed in acquiring both language and literacy, a balanced approach to language instruction and the activation of prior knowledge must surround the comprehending and composing processes supported by natural conversations within the classroom.

Throughout the chapter, you will encounter a variety of children's writing and visual representation (Student Samples 3.1–3.6) that reflect second- and third-grade reflections and interpretations of diversity. As you read and view them, realize how accepting and celebratory children are of differences in our diverse world.

Objectives

- To examine the theoretical foundation of second language acquisition.
- To define linguistic diversity and understand its prevalence in our current classrooms and communities.
- To differentiate between different types of English language learners.
- To understand basic principles of literacy development that can be applied to all language learners.
- To implement effective instructional strategies for English learners.
- To consider selection of materials for English language learners.
- To appreciate the power of multicultural literature to greet and reach children of varied cultures.

Theories Supporting Second-Language Acquisition

In determining whether a second language is acquired the same as the first language and the implications for instruction, it is necessary to examine some basic theoretical foundations that support how children acquire a second language. Stephen Krashen (1981) proposed five hypotheses of second-language acquisition that support the innate learning process within the learner: (a) the acquisition versus learning hypothesis, (b) the natural order hypothesis, (c) the monitor hypothesis, (d) the input hypothesis, and (e) the affective filter hypothesis. A brief description of each will assist in learning more about all language learners in classrooms.

Teacher Prep

The Teacher Prep Web site will help you become a better teacher by linking you to classroom videos, student artifacts, teaching strategies, lesson plans, relevant education leadership articles, and practical information on licensing, creating a portfolio, implementing standards, and being successful in field experiences. Visit this resource at www.prenhall.com/teacherprep.

Krashen first identifies the *acquisition versus learning hypothesis,* in which he describes acquisition as a natural process such as acquiring one's first language and learning as a more formal, classroom-centered process. Teachers know most about language learning since their own language acquisition occurred at a very early age. Some learners acquire a second language through immersion, by living in another country and having to use the language to deal with daily needs.

In the *natural order hypothesis,* Krashen states that grammar structures are acquired in a fairly predictable order. The order of acquisition for a first and

STUDENT SAMPLE 3.1 Morgan's Second-Grade Poem on Diversity.

second language is similar, although not exactly the same. Certain simple grammar structures, such as plurals, are acquired early while other more complex structures, such as irregular verbs, are acquired later.

According to the *monitor hypothesis,* we have an internal monitor that falls into place in conscious learning situations. However, before this monitor can be put into place, a consciousness of rules and an awareness of correctness must be activated.

In the *input hypothesis,* Krashen emphasizes the need for comprehensible input, or a match to the learner's level of proficiency. Students understand more than they can produce. Teachers should provide abundant comprehensible input through meaningful activities and reduce worksheets and drill. Comprehensible input should include language in authentic context that is just a bit above students' competence levels, thus nudging their language ability forward in an ongoing manner.

The *affective filter hypothesis* examines attitudinal variables. Krashen notes that if the learning situation is tense, there is a high affective filter and learners are anxious and less open to input. If the classroom is relaxed, however, there is a low affective filter and learners are more receptive to input, thus resulting in greater language acquisition.

Krashen's five hypotheses translate from theory to practice in an instructional method called the "natural approach" (Krashen & Terrel, 1983). Lessons designed according to theory advocate relaxed acquisition situations with rich input provided by using authentic materials, contextualized vocabulary, visuals, and hands-on activities. Hadaway, Vardell, and Young (2002) suggest a simple natural approach lesson that uses picture books or poems about families. Holding up photographed illustrations of families of different sizes and with a variety of family members, the teacher describes the picture, points to the family members, and then hands the book to a student. After key vocabulary has been introduced through several visual examples, the teacher begins a series of questions. Who has a family with five members? Who has a picture with a grandfather? Students hold up book pictures as a nonverbal response. Next, the teacher can diagram his or her own family tree and display key terms denoting family relationships. The students can then draw a family tree and label their family relationships. The teacher may write a sentence or paragraph describing his or her family. Beginning English language learners can simply draw a family illustration and label members or write short sentences. The teacher's speech and modeling provide the support needed to encourage understanding and to interact with the language. Such interactions are readily seen to be critical to learning language.

Another way to celebrate and enhance diversity in the classroom includes the use of picture dictionaries. Lesson Plan 3.1 shows how children can increase word meaning and quality word choice by accessing Web-based picture dictionaries and viewing related books.

LESSON PLAN 3.1

TITLE: Celebrate Diversity with Picture Dictionaries

Grade Level: 1–2

Time Frame: 45 minutes (ongoing throughout the school year)

Standards

IRA/NCTE Standards: 4, 10

NETS for Students: 2, 3, 5

Objective

- Students will create a picture dictionary to increase word meaning and quality word choice.

Materials/Setting/Groups

- Variety of children's picture dictionaries in various languages (to suit the diverse needs of your students)
  - *My Very Own Big Spanish Dictionary* (2005). Houghton Mifflin.
  - *The Firefly Five Language Visual Dictionary: English, Spanish, French, German, Italian* (2004). Firefly Books.
  - *The American Heritage Picture Dictionary* (2003). Houghton Mifflin.
- Blank teacher-created dictionary for each student (one page for each letter of the alphabet).
- Computer, projector, Internet access, large screen.
- Teacher-created model of a picture dictionary.

Motivation

- Using a projector, screen, and computer, introduce the *Little Explorers Picture Dictionary* Web site (http://www.enchantedlearning.com/Dictionary.html) to the class. Discuss the features of the Web site, including the many language versions.
- Browse through the picture dictionary, translate words, and complete selected activities as a class.

Procedures

- Introduce several picture dictionaries (books) to the students, possibly in several languages.

- Discuss the purpose for using a dictionary (to translate words and/or to find the meaning or spelling of words). Explain how dictionaries help student writers.
- Ask students to create their own picture dictionaries. Selected words may include high-frequency words or content-related vocabulary. Use a teacher model to communicate expectations and guidelines.
- Encourage students to add words to their dictionaries throughout the school year and use their dictionaries to increase their word choice while writing.

Assessment

- Teacher-created rubric or checklist reflecting lesson outcomes.

Accommodation/Modification

- For the English language learner, encourage students to include translations in their dictionaries.

Visit the Meeting the Standards module in Chapter 3 of the Companion Website at www.prenhall.com/hancock to adapt this lesson to meet your state's standards.

Linguistic Diversity and the Language Learner

Linguistic diversity includes the range of structures and functions of languages and dialects found in our schools and wider communities. Such diversity is a way of life in an increasing number of classrooms and communities across the United States and throughout the English-speaking and non–English-speaking world. Learners experience success or failure in their English acquisition depending on what occurs in their homes and classrooms. If teachers consider linguistically informed decisions about literacy instruction, children can learn to read and write English in the context of linguistically diverse classrooms.

All language learners experience practical instructional principles from teachers as they facilitate literacy development for *all* learners. The following list is based on several effective principles for literacy instruction in linguistically diverse classrooms (Barnitz, 1997):

- ***Recognize linguistic variety.*** A starting point is to acknowledge that linguistic diversity exists naturally. Although there are some universal similarities across all languages, variations across basic linguistic systems should be recognized. Linguistic awareness allows teachers an understanding of which linguistic forms and functions should develop naturally and which need to be taught directly. Understanding linguistic diversity leads to greater appreciation for the linguistic strengths that children bring to learning to read and write. All students come to school with a great deal of experience with oral and written language communication. It is important for teachers to discern the literacy knowledge that they have in both English and their first language and to find ways to draw on and validate this knowledge in the classroom.
- ***Build self-esteem in the second-language learner.*** Language, culture, and knowledge must be accepted and affirmed as children feel a sense of dignity and self-worth. Teachers who strive for the success of each of their students, including those learning English as a second language, must be certain all students participate fully in academic endeavors by establishing a social and political classroom context that builds dignity and self-worth. It is critical that the teacher accept and support interpretations and approximations of meaning and provide an environment rich in

STUDENT SAMPLE 3.2 Nico's Third-Grade Acrostic Poem on Diversity.

UNITED STATES OF AMERICA
THE MELTING POT

Meeting new freinds
Ethnic groups
Looking forward
To be a good citizen
Interested in other religions
Not being disrespectful to others
Generosity

People into United groups
Others to respect
Think about others

NAME Nico

models of proficient language use. As students gain access to meaningful and purposeful literacy events throughout the school day, develop a sense of power over written language, build confidence to take risks, and show willingness to construct their own meanings, ESL students' self-esteem develops and prospers.

- ***Facilitate authentic discourse.*** Encouraging talk and allowing for cultural varieties of talk provides for socially constructed discourse communities in classrooms. The language experience approach, for example, incorporates authentic talk to support the acquisition of the reading and writing process. Authentic texts and literacy artifacts from a culture, such as menus or newspapers, as well as cultural children's literature provide rich input for literacy acquisition. Language develops through authentic language use, not language exercises. Language learners play active, collaborative roles in the social learning context. The value of each student's contribution must be acknowledged and appreciated.
- ***Teach language in the context of authentic, meaningful reading and writing.*** Children acquire literacy best when classroom literacy events are functional and meaningful (Freeman & Freeman, 1992). As readers and writers compose and comprehend whole texts, they acquire oral and written language skills in the context of real reading and real writing. Text mapping and context-based strategies take priority over teaching skills in isolation.
- ***Design literature-based lessons with linguistic benefits.*** Reading to and with children in homes and classrooms yields literacy benefits. Children with more

> literature experiences in any language are further advanced in their acquisition of linguistic structures in oral and written language. Using literature is a powerful way to encourage children's acquisition of standard English. Second-language learners benefit from literature-based instruction because it provides authentic, natural text with contextual support from illustrations (Allen, 1989).

Whatever language or dialect students bring to learning English at school, diversity need not interfere with their literacy. Diversity can actually be a linguistic asset.

Types of English Language Learners

Olsen and Jaramillo (1999) are among the researchers who have identified three types of English language learners: (a) long-term English language learners, (b) recent arrivals with limited or interrupted schooling, and (c) recent arrivals with adequate schooling. Teachers who recognize that differences exist between educational backgrounds of learners can better address their different needs in learning oral and written English and building knowledge in content area instruction.

Long-Term English Language Learners

Long-term English language learners have been in the United States for several years. Although they may have been placed in bilingual or ESL classrooms, they have not had a consistent, well-articulated English instruction program. They speak English, but often struggle academically with reading and writing English. They turn in assignments, earn Bs and Cs, and often "fall through the cracks" of our system. They usually do poorly on standardized tests and have trouble with state-mandated exams as well. This may cause them to be discouraged, and many will eventually drop out of school (Freeman & Freeman, 2004).

Olga is an example of a student who has developed conversational proficiency in English. She can talk to her native English-speaking friends, but she struggles with school because she lacks academic language proficiency in either of her languages. Because she lacks the language of mathematics, science, and social studies, she struggles in the content areas as well. Even though Olga seems to speak English well, she lacks the formal register of English demanded for school success.

Recent Arrivals with Limited or Interrupted Schooling

Students who are recent arrivals often have limited formal schooling and no preschool experiences. These children may have interrupted schooling because their parents follow agricultural opportunities. They often speak little English, have low grades, and score poorly on tests. Although they have oral proficiency in a native language, they lack academic language and have not developed content area concepts expected for the age level.

Jose, a Spanish-speaker from Mexico, travels with his family on their yearly journey from Texas to pick crops in Illinois. He spends April and May as well as August through October in one school before returning to his home school in Texas. Jose seems able to draw on the background from his Texas school and strives to catch up with classmates. He faces the challenge of developing conversational English to function socially in and out of school as well as developing academic English and subject matter to succeed in school. This challenge is influenced by the fact that he will move from school to school and state to state each year.

STUDENT SAMPLE 3.3 Second Grader's Visual Representation of Diversity.

Recent Arrivals with Adequate Schooling

Children who arrive in the United States after attending a bilingual school in another country often have a chance to catch up with classmates. Although not fully prepared to speak English, such children at least have a start. A good school in another country can provide the academic language and content knowledge needed to succeed in the school setting.

Hsin-Rong, a Chinese-speaker from Taiwan, learned English in her homeland school beginning in the third grade. When she arrived in the United States, she had a strong academic background and a basic knowledge of how English works. She is more likely to succeed in language skills as her parents value English, although they do not speak it at home, and she brings success in content areas from a credible school setting. She excels in mathematics without having to even speak English. Although she has a huge challenge ahead of her, she can transfer academic language and concepts into English because there is a common underlying proficiency (Cummins, 2000). What students learn in one language, they can access and express in a second language once they have developed sufficient proficiency in the second language (Freeman & Freeman, 2004). Hsin-Rong needs new words to express concepts she already knows. This is a far easier task than having to develop both the concepts and the academic English terms.

Too often, school programs in English language are based on the assumption that all English language learners are like Hsin-Rong. Often the students or their backgrounds are blamed for lack of success. However, because these students are not alike, it is understandable why their school performances differ. This is an important starting point for teachers who are striving to understand language differences.

Instructional Strategies for the English Language Learner

Language develops naturally in situations that are meaningful to the learner (Cummins, 1989; Krashen, 1985). All children come to school with a wealth of experiences with their first language. Since literacy is developmental, educators must consider where children are on a literacy continuum, regardless of their first language. A positive view of literacy requires us to view all children as language learners and to determine what they know and can do and build on those foundations. This principle rings just as true for the English language learner. Schools must be literacy-rich environments in which children work and play with language to actively construct meaning and new understandings. Teachers must provide rich environments with stimulating opportunities through integrated reading, writing, listening, speaking, viewing, and visual representation.

As teachers design instruction for ESL learners, they must keep the same basic literacy principles in mind as for emergent learners in English:

- Literacy develops in a variety of language-rich contexts.
- Language learning takes place in risk-free environments in which learner experiences and contributions are valued.
- Language is learned best when it is used for real and meaningful purposes.
- Reading and writing are mutual literacy processes through which children construct meaning, using prior knowledge and strategies to build comprehension.

STUDENT SAMPLE 3.4 Brooke's Third-Grade Acrostic Poem on Diversity.

UNITED STATES OF AMERICA
THE MELTING POT

M any people
E thnic groups
L iving human beings
T reat others kindly
I n different countries
N o More violence
G o visit other countries

P eople from all over the world
O ther religions
T heir lives

NAME Brooke

Several instructional strategies build from theses literacy principles and support the language learner, and, in particular, the English language learner.

Real World Print

Even before they enter a classroom, all children have experiences with environmental print—from traffic signs to product logos and labels. Just as English-speaking children can read "Stop," "McDonald's," and "Coca Cola," so too can nonnative speakers. Language acquisition comes through the use of language in context (Krashen, 1981). The teacher can build upon students' ability to recognize words in context by integrating print into the classroom:

- Label items, locations, and activities in the classroom, on bulletin boards, and on display tables.
- Write directions, schedules, calendar information, names, and work duties on the board and refer to them as information is discussed orally.
- Include simple reading and writing activities as reinforcement for language practice, including penmanship, labeling, vocabulary, word wall words, matching activities, word puzzles, and simple directions.
- Identify and display key words that children want to know in print.
- Provide a notebook or note cards where children can keep track of important words by using English words with a picture cue or English words and a native language definition.

Teachers may also use magazines, newspapers, brochures, catalogs, posters, menus, and job applications in the native language of the learner as powerful resources in ESL children's literacy acquisition.

Utilizing Children's Own Writing

The language experience approach (Stauffer, 1976) allows beginning readers to draw on their own experiences and language as they make connections to written text. Dictated stories recorded by a teacher allow a child to read a story aloud to the class as oral language becomes written text. The same relevancy can be gained through word charts related to theme study or class books following field trips. Children see written language used for an authentic purpose. Cultural background and prior knowledge are respected, while children's native languages may be used in the context of English text. Such materials develop a strong, supportive print environment upon which ESL students can continue to draw.

Reading as Preparation for Writing

Second-language learners need multiple opportunities to become familiar with language. They need to practice not only listening to and speaking English but also using reading as a rehearsal for writing. Once again, patterned and predictable text invites simple whole class construction of similar narratives on chart paper. Teachers need to be certain that students have appropriate prior knowledge by helping them bring what they know to the reading and writing experience. For example, discussion based on story elements (e.g., plot, setting, character, conflict, resolution) provides a grammar framework to operate during reading and writing. Students can begin writing by rewriting simple story endings or by retelling familiar stories. Children must experience reading across genres as they begin to see themselves as writers.

Writing with a partner prior to reading assists in accessing prior knowledge.

Writing as Preparation for Reading

Brainstorming before reading helps display ideas to assist with understanding. Writing words or phrases on an overhead transparency ignites prior knowledge. Writing before reading helps students access ideas to facilitate understanding. The prior knowledge that both native and nonnative speakers bring to a literacy task exerts a powerful influence on their ability to comprehend and communicate. For English language learners, drawing before reading can identify prior knowledge and key vocabulary needed for upcoming comprehension.

Webbing/Concept Mapping

Webbing provides a framework through which students can access and organize information and ideas. A vehicle for enhancing comprehension and learning (Bromley, 1996), webbing becomes a literacy scaffold or network of ideas to highlight vocabulary and concrete representation of information in a way that connects concepts.

Retelling and Summarizing

To help children with the simple concept of retelling or the more complex task of summarizing, the teacher should model each process using a variety of materials. Simply retelling the events in Verna Aardema's *Why Mosquitoes Buzz in People's Ears* in sequential form can model text structure and order. Moving beyond chronology, students need to see summarizing modeled through a teacher "think aloud" as small ideas are organized into a written short summary.

The Morning Message

Classroom practices should foster a need to become a literate individual. The morning message is a simple, deliberately structured activity to demonstrate the importance of reading and writing in the classroom. Simple messages contain practical information and an item of interest to the children. The teacher, asking children to read along, reads the message while pointing to the words. Following a second reading, children engage in a discussion of the written text. A daily routine becomes an instructional event as capital letters, contractions, days of the week, and word endings are noticed and discussed. As the school year progresses, the complexity of the message increases and grows into multiple sentences.

Student and Teacher Journals

Journals for language learners should be structured to motivate children to interact with both reading and writing. These dialogue journals serve as communication between teacher and learner with responses written in the first language of the learner. As students learn English, they can incorporate some English into their writing with assistance. The teacher supports literacy development with personal comments or questions. The intent is to involve language learners in processes that promote both communication and motivation.

ESL Friendly Web Sites for Students and Teachers

Teachers of diverse students may access additional ideas and assistance in designing their lessons. The Tech Tip included here highlights several outstanding ESL Web sites to support both teachers and second-language learners.

ESL Friendly Web Sites for Students and Teachers

The Internet search engine Google provides many special features, including *Google Language Tools*. Using machine translation technology, Google gives English speakers access to a variety of non-English Web pages (currently available in Italian, French, Spanish, German, Japanese, Chinese, and Portuguese). Language Tools also translates texts entered by the user. For example, an English-speaking student may type in a passage from his or her favorite book and opt to have the passage translated into German or Spanish, to be shared with second-language learners in the classroom. The Google Language Tools further allows users to search Web pages written in a specific language (over 30 choices) or to locate web pages published in a certain country. **http://www.google.com/language_tools?h=en**

Little Explorers Picture Dictionary provides students with over 2,000 illustrated dictionary entries with links to related Web sites. Versions in several languages are available, including Dutch, French, German, Italian, Japanese, Portuguese, Spanish, and Swedish. **http://www.enchantedlearning. com/Dictionary.html**

For older students, Purdue University's *Online Writing Lab* includes links to resources that assist ESL students by answering general questions about the English language, grammar problems, idioms, and academic conventions. Free materials are available for teachers and students, including printer-friendly resource pages and handouts. **http://owl.english.purdue.edu/handouts/esl/index.html**

The Internet TESL Journal site hosts extensive links of interest to students and teachers of English as a second language. The site is noncommercial with few frames or pictures but the links are frequently updated. **http://iteslj.org/links/TESL/**

Activities for ESL Students contains quizzes, tests, exercises, and puzzles for students learning English as a second language. A project of *The Internet TESL Journal,* this site has thousands of contributions by teachers. **http://a4esl.org/**

(Continued)

Maintained by experienced ESL teachers, authors, and researchers, *EverythingESL.net* features a myriad of ESL-related lesson plans, teaching tips, Web links, discussion topics, and resource picks for teachers of English language learners. **http://www.everythingesl.net/**

Dave's ESL Cafe is a fun and popular site (with over a million hits a month) for ESL students and teachers. Although the site contains some commercial elements, the resources, including chats, bulletin boards, and Web links, are free for students and teachers. **http://eslcafe.com/**

To look more closely at these materials and others related to "Language as the Focus of Diversity," visit the Companion Website at www.prenhall.com/hancock.

These simple, but effective instructional strategies pave the way toward literacy for both native English and non-English learners. Engaging all learners in activities that promote authentic interactions and meaningful communications will guide all children as they become emergent readers and writers.

Materials for Instruction of English Language Learners

All children on their journey toward literacy must make the connection between oral language and written language. A major issue continues to focus on whether ELL students should be taught to read and write in their own language or whether they should begin the process in English. Common sense suggests that if children begin to learn about reading and writing in a language they already control, they can draw upon knowledge of sounds, structures, and meaning of that language as they move into print (Hudelson, 1987). However, a rich array of materials may be available in Spanish, but not in a language such as Hmong or Arabic. Therefore, many ELL students may be learning to read and write at the same time they are acquiring spoken English. When possible, however, books and materials in the child's native language should be a part of the literacy program.

Allen (1994) identifies criteria for selecting reading materials for the ELL student. Such materials should do the following:

- Encourage children to want to read.
- Help children discover the functions of written language.
- Permit children to use written language for a variety of purposes.
- Be appropriate for the age and interest level of the children.
- Consider the children's cultural background.
- Use the children's native language when possible.
- Support the children's English acquisition.
- Offer a rich array of genres.
- Utilize text structure that supports children's understanding.
- Consider the children's prior knowledge and background experience.

With these criteria in mind, children's literature provides a showcase for English language learning.

STUDENT SAMPLE 3.5 Second Grader's Visual Representation of Diversity.

Children's Literature: A Linguistically Rich World

Children's literature is viewed by many researchers as the most effective material for reading instruction (Huck & Kiefer, 2004). Children's books provide rich and patterned language, predictable structure, and supportive illustrations. They also provide invitations for talk and frameworks for simple writing tasks. Quality children's literature assists in making the move for second language learners into their new language and the world of literacy (Allen, 1989).

A variety of books for the beginning ELL student provide effective print material for instruction. Remember that the "beginning" ELL student can be of any age, not simply a kindergarten or primary-age child. Hadaway, Vardell, and Young (2002) suggest that the following questions be answered when selecting children's books for the ELL learner:

- Is the story or topic familiar or helpful?
- Are there abundant illustrations?
- Do the illustrations help convey the story or relay information?
- Is the language simple and direct?
- Is the book culturally relevant?

Various types of simple texts provide materials with which to introduce new learners to English in a relevant manner.

Concept Books. Children acquiring a second language need to learn labels for both familiar and new experiences. Concept books describe simple objects, categorize knowledge, or give concrete meaning to abstract ideas. Anne and Harlow Rockwell's *The Toolbox,* for example, features clear and simple pictures of a hammer, wrench, and screwdriver. Tana Hoban's skill as a photographer helps children focus on simple concepts in *Circles, Triangles, and Squares* and *Push Pull, Empty Full: A Book of Opposites*. The bold, colorful illustrations in Lois Ehlert's *Growing Vegetable Soup* let children observe the growth of seeds into plants while discovering categories and names of vegetables as they are picked and dug up. See the extensive list in Chapter 4 to locate other books appropriate to this type.

Predictable and Pattern Books. Predictable books relate to background experiences of children, reflect language patterns, repeat vocabulary, and incorporate illustrations as they support text meaning. *Brown Bear, Brown Bear, What do you See?* by Bill Martin Jr. contains repetitive language patterns for English language learners. Chunks of language invite children to join in and read along. Repetition is particularly inviting and encouraging for English speakers and English learners. See the extensive list in Chapter 4 to locate other appropriate books of this type.

Books with Meaning-Centered Illustrations. Books that extend ESL students' understanding of a story and draw them more deeply into the world of the book provide powerful learning materials. Because reading is comprehension-based, books need to be selected that promote both fluency and understanding. Books with photographs or meaning-centered illustrations provide support for both the first and second language learner. For example, Sandra Markle's *Spiders: Biggest! Littlest!* or Steve Jenkins's *Actual Size* can assist the language learner in understanding the concept of size in the insect and animal worlds.

Books that Invite Talk. The opportunity to respond to the personal relevance of a book is central to becoming an invested reader. Children's responses to books provide an opportunity to make a personal connection to a book. For young children, Leo Lionni's *Frederick* as a read-aloud can explore the theme of being oneself. Gary Soto's *Snapshots from the Wedding* and *Too Many Tamales* introduce common values and common experiences between cultures. These titles provide real reasons to talk in the first language of a child, even if not English, to show acceptance and support.

Books that Provide a Framework for Writing. Children's books can provide a simple framework for meaningful writing tasks. An alphabet book, for example, provides a framework for a book in any language. Although a few letters may vary, children are quick to catch on to the pattern of an alphabet book on animals, on landforms, or on weather. Christopher Wormell's *Teeth, Tails, and Tentacles: An Animal Counting Book* provides simple structure and rich language to support writing one's own alphabet and counting book.

Books that Support the Curriculum. In the intermediate elementary classroom, the content of curriculum provides a challenge to ESL learners. The task shifts from reading books to helping them use books to find information. Textbooks are far too difficult for ESL children, but all children in class can benefit from informational nonfiction trade books. Books by Gail Gibbons (*The Honeymakers* and *Thanksgiving*) and Seymour Simon (*Crocodiles and Alligators* and *Mars*) cover social studies and science topics as drawings and photography aid understanding. All children should have access to a large number of books that deal with a curricular topic. These books should have a wide range of reading levels and offer children rich resources through photographs, maps, diagrams, and drawings to support the selected content.

Cultural Literary Connections

Books that include authentic images of different cultures and language users present an excellent opportunity for honoring the culture of ESL children while exposing children of other cultures to new knowledge and understandings. English and Spanish language trade books represent the largest number of published books flowing between two cultures and languages. Although cultural portrayal has shown improvement, these books must still be scrutinized for cultural authenticity (Nilsson, 2005). Multicultural books that celebrate language diversity must have authentic authors and illustrators, must respectfully portray a culture and its history, must be carefully researched, and must employ language or symbols of the culture in a culturally distinct fashion. The power of language used to varying degrees in these books gives personal voice and respect to individuals and communities (Crowell, 1998). Already, Latino children's literature is being used with preservice teachers to help those in teacher education programs gain background knowledge of the Latino elementary school children they will serve (Nathenson-Majia & Escamilla, 2003).

Codeswitching as Authentic Language. Unfortunately, some trade books are considered multicultural if they simply insert children of color into illustrations of a story about a mainstream culture. In contrast, quality multicultural titles celebrate the richness of daily life among people of different cultures and use the language of people in authentic ways. Codeswitching alternates the use of two languages at the word, phrase, clause, or sentence level as dual languages help to tell stories, identify speakers, and define social roles. Gary Soto's *The Old Man and His Door* is the story of an old man who does not listen carefully to his wife's wishes. Instead of bringing a *puerco* (pig) to a barbeque, he brings a *puera* (door). A glossary defines the Spanish words that Soto weaves into the text, but children can readily figure out the meaning within the context of the story and in the humorous illustrations by Joe Cepeda.

Mama Provi, a Puerto Rican grandmother, uses food to comfort her ailing granddaughter in *Mama Provi and the Pot of Rice* by Sylvia Rosa-Casanova. When Lucy gets chicken pox, Mama Provi decides to make *arroz con pollo,* a traditional Puerto Rican recipe of chicken and rice. As grandmother climbs the steps to the top floor apartment, she knocks at ethnic neighbors' doors offering to exchange some *arroz con pollo* for some bread, some *frijoles negros,* and Chinese tea. Spanish words and phrases are embedded in the text within the bilingual conversations of Lucy and Mama Provi. Other examples of codeswitching texts across cultures can be found in the Literature Cluster included here.

Dual-Language Texts. In these English/Spanish books, translations of the full text are found in page-by-page formats or in separate editions released simultaneously. *Gathering the Sun* by Alma Flor Ada is an alphabet book written in Spanish with an English translation by Rosa Zubizaretta. Each letter of the Spanish language reflects a poem celebrating the pride and honor of farmworker families in the Southwest. While some words begin with the same letter in English and Spanish (e.g., lettuce/*lechuga*), not all letters match. Yet the book, enhanced by vibrant, sun-drenched illustrations of Simon Silva, invites readers into the lives, homes, hearts, and cultures of these hardworking people.

Ginger F. Guy's *¡Fiesta!* (1996), a bilingual counting book, finds three children strolling through a marketplace, filling their basket with items to fill a pinata. Young children of both cultures will enjoy learning numbers in Spanish and English. Other examples of dual-language text featuring side-by-side English and Spanish text are found in the Literature Cluster.

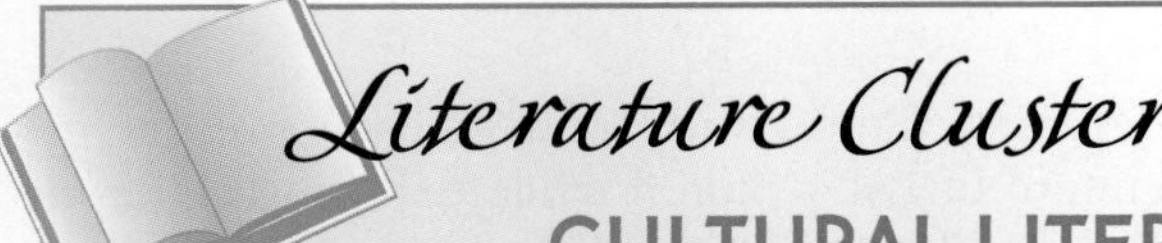

Literature Cluster

CULTURAL LITERATURE CONNECTIONS

Codeswitching Texts

Ada, Alma Flor (2002). *I love Saturday y domingos*. Illus. by Elivia Savadier. New York: Simon & Schuster.

Ancona, George (1998). *Charro: The Mexican cowboy*. San Diego: Harcourt.

Carling, Amelia Lau (1998). *Mama and Papa have a store*. New York: Dial.

Elya, S. M. (1996). *Say hola to Spanish*. Illus. by Loretta Lopez. New York: Lee & Low.

Garay, L. (1997). *Pedrito's day*. New York: Orchard.

Johnston, Tony (1997). *The day of the dead*. Illus. by Jeanette Winter. San Diego: Harcourt.

London, J. (1997). *Ali: Child of the desert*. Illus. by Ted Lewin. New York: Lothrop, Lee & Shepard.

Lopez, L. (1997). *The birthday swap*. New York: Lee & Low.

Mora, Pat (1996). *Confetti: Poems for children*. New York: Lee & Low.

Soto, Gary (1995). *Canto familiar*. Illus. by Annika Nelson. San Diego: Harcourt.

Dual-Language Texts

Alarcon, F. X. (1997). *Laughing tomatoes/Jitomates riseuenos*. Illus. by Maya C. Gonzales. San Francisco: Children's Book Press.

Dominguez, Kelli Kyle (2002). *The perfect piñata/ La piñata perfecta*. Illus. by Diane Paterson. Morton Grove, IL: Albert Whitman.

Garza, Carmen L. (1990). *Family pictures/Cuadros de familia*. San Francisco: Children's Book Press.

Garza, Carmen L. (1996). *In my family/En mi familia*. San Francisco: Children's Book Press.

Garza, Carmen L. (1999). *Magic windows/Ventanas magicas*. San Francisco: Children's Book Press.

Stevens, J. R. (1993). *Carlos and the squash plant/ Carlos y la planta de calabaza*. Illus. by J. Arnold. Flagstaff, AZ: Northland.

Stevens, J. R. (1995). *Carlos and the cornfield/Carlos y la milpa de maiz*. Illus. by J. Arnold. Flagstaff, AZ: Northland.

Stevens, J. R. (1997). *Carlos and the skunk/Carlos y el zorrillo*. Illus. by J. Arnold. Flagstaff, AZ: Northland.

Winter, Jonah (2006). *Diego*. Illus. by Jeanette Winter. New York: Knopf.

Language and Cultural Traditions

Aldana, P. (1996). *Jade and iron: Latin American tales from two cultures* (H. Hazelton, Trans.) Illus. by L. Garay. Toronto, Canada: Groundswood.

Anaya, R. (1997). *Maya's children: The story of La Llorona*. Illus. by M. Baca. New York: Hyperion.

Andrews-Goebel, Nancy (2002). *The pot that Juan built*. Illus. by David Diaz. New York: Lee & Low.

Jaffe, N. (1996). *The golden flower: A Taino myth from Puerto Rico*. Illus. by E. O. Sanchez. New York: Simon & Schuster.

Cross-Cultural Experiences

Ancona, George (2001). *Harvest*. New York: Marshall Cavendish.

Bernhard, E. (1996). *Happy New Year!* New York: Dutton.

Hopkins, L. B. (1994). *Weather: Poems for all seasons*. New York: Harper Trophy.

Jenkins, Steve (1995). *Biggest, strongest, fastest*. New York: Houghton Mifflin.

Jenness, A. (1990). *Families: A celebration of diversity, commitment, and Love*. Boston: Houghton Mifflin.

Wong, Janet (2000). *This next New Year*. Illus. by Yangsook Choi. New York: Farrar/Frances Foster.

Language and Cultural Traditions. Although it is difficult to locate books in languages from all cultures in today's classrooms, a wealth of traditional tales become pathways to diverse cultures. Most of these titles contain embedded words indigenous to the culture. *Señor Cat's Romance and Other Favorite Stories from Latin America* by Lucia Gonzalez contains a Caribbean connection to the author's childhood in Cuba. Clever characters like Cucarachita Martina, Don Gato, and Juan Bobo fill the pages with silly but clever tales. In contrast to this Latino tale collection, Jane Kurtz brings life to an authentic Eritrean tale from her childhood in Ethiopia. *Trouble* crosses cultural barriers as it tells the universal story about unintentionally causing problems as it sprinkles a few native words into the context of this amusing story. See the Literature Cluster for other books that feature language and cultural traditions.

Cross-Cultural Experiences. No matter what language we speak, universal experiences exist that provide common activities around the world. Norah Dooley's *Everybody Bakes Bread* and *Everybody Cooks Rice* ignite our prior knowledge about eating bread and rice yet differentiate the various means for preparing them according to our cultural background. The Literature Cluster list several cross-cultural experience books that capture the universal human experience of family, weather, and celebration.

All of these types of books provide ways to respect the linguistic abilities of children from all language communities. Children need access to these books and other materials written in their own and other languages. Including books in as many languages as possible in our classrooms reminds us that no one language has priority on telling a good story.

Multicultural Gateways Through Literature

Multicultural literature transports the reader to many lands and surveys many cultures as it attempts to share differences among peoples of the world. Yet in its showcase of diversity, it encourages the recognition of commonalities among cultures. Although cultural connections change, people retain their sameness, revealing similarities in emotions, commitments, dreams, and expectations. Literature of a parallel culture—African American, Asian Pacific American, Hispanic American, Native American—opens the culture's heart to the reading audience, showing the culture's joy and grief, love and hatred, hope and despair, expectations and frustrations, and the effects of living in a society where differences are not always readily accepted (Cai & Bishop, 1994). Language provides the connection between the common cultures of humanity as it serves as the means to transmit history and ideals through quality literature.

Multicultural literature serves a dual purpose in the lives of children. When children see themselves—their own color, heritage, traditions—in a text, they feel pride, acceptance, and belonging. The other purpose of multicultural literature involves mainstream or "ethnically encapsulated" children (Banks, 1988) who remain isolated in their own world and lack exposure to the richness of diverse color and cultures. Exposure to multicultural literature provides both a mirror into one's own world and a door into the culture and lives of others (Hancock, 2004).

Selection Criteria

Many teachers and librarians lack confidence in their ability to make informed decisions about multicultural titles, believing they lack the cultural knowledge to select titles that do

STUDENT SAMPLE 3.6 Sharon's Second-Grade Poem on Diversity.

not foster stereotypes of a particular group. A reputable identification of quality multicultural literature comes from book award winners that have been carefully scrutinized by children's literature experts across cultures. The Coretta Scott King Award honors outstanding African American authors and illustrators for children and young adults. The Pura Belpré Award honors Latino writers and illustrators whose work best portrays, affirms, and celebrates the Latino cultural experience in children's literature. The Notable Books for a Global Society provides an annual list of outstanding trade books for enhancing student understanding of people and cultures throughout the world.

All multicultural literature, however, must first fulfill the same standards for literary traits that are used to evaluate all quality children's books. Figure 3.1 delineates specific criteria for multicultural literature gleaned from the high standards maintained by researchers and children's literature experts (Diamond & Moore, 1995; Finazzo, 1997; Glazer, 1997; Huck & Kiefer, 2004; Tunnell, Jacobs, & Darigan, 2002).

Relevance of Multicultural Literature in the Language Arts Curriculum

Banks (1989) describes a hierarchy of four curricular models for integrating multicultural and multiethnic content into the existing school curriculum: (1) the contributions approach, (2) the ethnic additive approach, (3) the transformation approach, and (4) the social action approach. These models have been explored in relation to literature connections by Rasinski & Padak (1990) and Bieger (1996). They provide a meaningful framework

FIGURE 3.1 Criteria for Notable Multicultural Books.

1. Portray cultural accuracy and authenticity of characters in terms of the following:
   - Physical characteristics
   - Intellectual abilities and problem-solving capabilities
   - Leadership and cooperative dimensions
   - Social and economic status
2. Be rich in cultural details.
3. Honor and celebrate diversity as well as common bonds in humanity.
4. Provide in-depth treatment of cultural issues.
5. Include characters with a cultural group or between two or more cultural groups who interact substantively and authentically.
6. Include members of a "minority" group for a purpose other than filling a "quota."
7. Invite reflection, critical analysis, and response.
8. Demonstrate unique language or style.
9. Meet generally accepted criteria of quality for the genre in which it is written.
10. Have an appealing format and be of endearing quality.

Specific Criteria for Cultural Character

- Characters should authentically reflect the distinct cultural experience of a specific cultural group.
- Names of characters should be culturally authentic and their personalities should reflect believable attributes.
- Characterization should be true to life and balanced, representing both positive and negative behaviors and traits.
- Perpetuation of cultural stereotypes must be avoided.
- Gender roles within the culture should be portrayed authentically, reflecting the changing roles and status of women and men in cultures.

Specific Criteria for Cultural Settings

- Setting should be representative of and consistent with historical or contemporary time, place, or situation of a particular culture.
- Factual information describing a historical setting must be accurate in detail.
- Contemporary settings must align with current situations of a cultural group.

Specific Criteria for Themes

- Themes should be consistent with the values, beliefs, customs, traditions, and conflicts of the specific cultural group.
- Social issues and conflicts related to cultural groups should be treated honestly, accurately, and openly.

Specific Criteria for Diverse Language

- Language should reflect distinctive vocabulary, style, and patterns of speech of the cultural group.
- Dialect should be natural and blend with plot and characterization while not being perceived as substandard language.
- Language should represent sensitivity to a people; derogatory terms should be excluded unless essential to a conflict or used in a historical context.

Source: From M. R. Hancock (2004). A celebration of literature and response: Children, books, and teachers in K–8 classrooms *(pp. 186–187). Upper Saddle River, NJ: Merrill/Prentice Hall.*

FIGURE 3.1 (continued)

Specific Criteria for Illustrations

- Physical characteristics of a people of a diverse culture should replicate natural appearance and avoid stereotypes.
- Illustrations should reflect accurate cultural setting.
- Characters should be portrayed as unique individuals within a culture.
- Illustrations should complement and enhance imagery of the story.

through which to address response-based connections between the reader and multicultural literature.

Contributions Approach. The contributions approach functions at the lowest level of the multicultural hierarchy, where students read about or discuss ethnic holidays, heroes, and customs. The teacher may read Doreen Rappaport's *Martin's Big Words* to commemorate the birthday of Martin Luther King Jr. or share Louise Borden and Mary Kay Kroege's *Fly High! The Story of Bessie Coleman* during Black History Month. Unfortunately, this is the single level at which most classrooms currently function, yet it serves as a possible springboard to higher level connections. Biographies seem to fit well into this approach, as do bio-poems and reader response prompts that address character traits from quality language connections.

Ethnic Additive Approach. The ethnic additive approach adds content and themes that reflect other cultures to the existing curriculum, maintaining its purpose and structure. This approach adds multicultural literature to the curriculum but not necessarily from a cultural perspective. A kindergarten teacher, for example, might read Debbi Chocolate's *Kente Colors* because recognizing colors is a learning outcome. The teacher emphasizes the colors described rather than discussing the culturally distinctive *kente* cloth. Folktales abound within this approach as they carry the reader to a variety of cultures that share similar stories. Multicultural versions of Cinderella range from John Steptoe's *Mufaro's Beautiful Daughters* from Zimbabwe to Ai-Ling Louie's *Yeh-Shen,* which is embedded in Chinese lore. In such books, compare and contrast exercises can serve as a higher level of interpretive response.

Transformation Approach. The transformation approach actually changes the structure of the curriculum to enable readers to view problems and themes from the [Rhoda Blumberg's *York's Adventures with Lewis and Clark*], perspective of different ethnic and cultural groups. An example is found in a study of Lewis and Clark, the Louisiana Purchase, and Westward Expansion through the unlikely point of view of York, a Black slave who accompanied the explorers on their journey and dared to dream of freedom as he gazed at the vastness of the unexplored wilderness. Carolyn Reeder's *Across the Lines* reveals the contrasting human sides of the Civil War as Edward, a plantation owner's son, and Simon, his Black companion and servant, share their close friendship, different choices, and the demands of newly attained freedom from two points of view. This approach challenges the creative teacher to locate books that invigorate thinking and highlight multiple perspectives on an event.

Social Action Approach. The social action approach challenges readers to identify social problems, make decisions, and take action to resolve problems. For example, the issue of racial discrimination can be presented in Evelyn Coleman's *White Socks Only*. This picture book highlights places children could not go and things they could not do because of color. Ruby Bridges's *Through My Eyes* brings fact to the reality of 1960 as the voice of a 6-year-old girl shares her isolation in spite of an effort to desegregate Southern schools. Response takes the form of a discussion of ways in which discrimination still exists and what can be done to alleviate prejudice in our schools, our community, and our nation.

The four levels of multicultural involvement through literature identified by Banks (1989) set high standards as teachers strive to climb this hierarchy. Teachers can gain confidence to move beyond the first level through the identification of quality literature that will result in effective lessons. Banks's categories, supported by a growing knowledge of multicultural titles, provide the sense of direction all teachers need for gradual but committed growth to multicultural education.

Visit the Companion Website at www.prenhall.com/hancock and gauge your understanding of Chapter 3 concepts with the self-assessments.

Closing Thoughts

As children of culturally and linguistically diverse backgrounds continue to be a growing segment of our country's population, the need and desire for quality multicultural literature remains strong. Every child needs to feel secure in a classroom by developing his or her own confidence and sense of place within the school community of learners. Strong literature-based language arts programs demand that children of color have access to literature that is relevant to their own lives and that portrays all children, not merely those of the dominant culture. Teachers' growing consciousness of a global society requires that they expose all children to a multicultural perspective, and multicultural literature provides a means for accomplishing this end.

Resources for locating quality multicultural literature have become more extensive in the past few years. The editors of *Kaleidoscope: A Multicultural Booklist for Grades K–8* (Barrera, Thompson, & Dressman, 1997) contend that "the transformation of children's literature into a mirror that reflects the diversity of America's children, and the application of that literature toward the advancement of our multicultural society, has hardly begun" (p. xii). Educators must use titles to broaden the curricular base to include multiple cultural references, develop cultural and visual literacy, and encourage children to make connections between personal experiences, other books, and knowledge of the global society. The discussion of culture, of sameness and difference, can be part of a general unit on community or meet specific social studies standards.

Throughout this chapter, you have witnessed second- and third-graders' drawings and structured poems relating to the differences between and among each other in their classrooms. Children readily recognize differences, but they tend to focus on similarities—that children need friends, that they need to succeed, that they need to help each other. While adults can balk at the differences among themselves, children seem ready and willing to accept and celebrate those differences and then to move beyond them within their classroom communities. The more a teacher knows and focuses on diversity in language and culture, the more today's children—tomorrow's adults—will be prepared to accept and celebrate diversity within the global community.

References

Allen, V. G. (1989). Literature as support to language acquisition. In P. Rigg & V. G. Allen (Eds.), *When they don't all speak English: Integrating the ESL student into the regular classroom* (pp. 55–64). Urbana, IL: National Council of Teachers of English.

Banks, J. A. (1988). *Multicultural education: Issues and prospectives.* Boston: Allyn & Bacon.

Banks, J. A. (1989). Multicultural education: Characteristics and goals. In J. A. Banks & C. A. M. Banks (Eds.), *Multicultural education: Issues and perspectives* (pp. 2–26). Needham Heights, MA: Allyn & Bacon.

Barnitz, J. G. (1997). Emerging awareness of linguistic diversity for literacy instruction. *The Reading Teacher, 51,* 264–266.

Barrera, R. B., Thompson, V. D., & Dressman, M. (Eds.) (1997). *Kaleidoscope: A multicultural booklist for grades K–8* (2nd ed.). Urbana, IL: National Council of Teachers of English.

Bieger, E. M. (1996). Promoting multicultural education through a literature-based approach. *The Reading Teacher, 49,* 308–312.

Bromley, K. D. (1996). *Webbing with literature: Creating story maps with children's books.* Boston: Allyn & Bacon.

Cai, M., & Bishop, R. (1994). Multicultural literature for children: Towards a clarification of the concept. In A. Dyson & C. Genishi (Eds.). *The need for story: Cultural diversity in classroom and community* (pp. 57–71). Urbana, IL: National Council of Teachers of English.

Cortes, C. E. (1994). Multiculturalism: An educational model for a culturally and linguistically diverse society. In K. Spangenberg-Urbschat & R. Pritchard (Eds.), *Kids come in all languages: Reading instruction for ESL students* (pp. 22–35). Newark, DE: International Reading Association.

Crowell, C. G. (1998). Celebrating linguistic diversity. *Language Arts, 75,* 228–235.

Cummins, J. (1989). *Empowering minority students.* Sacramento: California Association for Bilingual Education.

Cummins, J. (2000). *Language, power, and pedagogy: Bilingual children in the crossfire.* Tonawanda, NY: Multilingual Matters.

Diamond, B. J., & Moore, M. A. (1995). *Multicultural literacy: Mirroring the reality of the classroom.* White Plains, NY: Longman.

Finazzo, D. A. (1997). *All for the children: Multicultural essentials of literature.* Albany, NY: Delmar.

Freeman, D., & Freeman, Y. (2004). Three types of English language learners. *School Talk, 9,* 1–3.

Freeman, Y. S., & Freeman, D. E. (1992). *Whole language for second language learners.* Portsmouth, NH: Heinemann.

Garcia, G. E. (2000). Bilingual children's reading. In M. L. Kamil, P. B. Mosenthal, P. D. Pearson, & R. Barr (Eds.), *Handbook of reading research* (Vol. 3, pp. 813–834). Mahwah, NJ: Erlbaum.

Glazer, J. I. (1997). *Introduction to children's literature* (2nd ed.). Upper Saddle River, NJ: Merrill/Prentice Hall.

Hadaway, N., Vardell, S., & Young, T. (2002). *Literature-based teaching with English language learners.* New York: Allyn & Bacon/Longman.

Hancock, M. R. (2004). *A celebration of literature and response: Children, books, and teachers in K–8 classrooms* (2nd ed). Upper Saddle River, NJ: Merrill/Prentice Hall.

Huck, C. S., & Kiefer, B. Z. (2004). *Children's literature in the elementary school* (8th ed.). Boston: McGraw Hill.

Hudelson, S. (1987). The role of native language literacy in the education of language minority children. *Language Arts, 64,* 827–841.

International Reading Association & the National Association for the Education of Young Children (1998). Learning to read and write: Developmentally appropriate practices for young children. *The Reading Teacher, 52,* 193–214.

Krashen, S. D. (1981). *Second language acquisition and second language learning.* Oxford, England: Pergamon.

Krashen, S. D. (1985). *The input hypothesis: Issues and implications.* New York: Longman.

Krashen, S. D., & Terrell, T. D. (1983). *The natural approach.* San Francisco: Alemany Press.

Nathenson-Majia, S., & Escamilla, K. (2003). Connecting with Latino children: Bridging cultural gaps with children's literature. *Billingual Research Journal, 27,* 101–116.

Nilsson, N. L. (2005). How does Hispanic portrayal in children's books measure up after 40 years? The answer is "It depends." *The Reading Teacher, 58,* 534–548.

Olsen, L., & Jaramillo, A. (1999). *Turning the tides of exclusion: A guide for educators and advocates for immigrant students.* Oakland, CA: California Tomorrow.

Rasinski, T. V., & Padak, N. (1990). Multicultural learning through children's literature. *Language Arts, 67,* 576–580.

Stauffer, R. G. (1976). *The language experience approach to the teaching of reading.* New York: Harper & Row.

Tunnell, M. O., Jacobs, J. S., & Darigan, D. L. (2002). *Children's literature: Engaging teachers and children in good books*. Upper Saddle River, NJ: Merrill/Prentice Hall.

U. S. Census Bureau (2000). Census 2000, summary file 3 from the World Wide Web. Retrieved December 27, 2004, from http://www.census.gov/population/cen2000/phc-t20/tab02.pdf.

U.S. Department of Education (2002). Survey of the states' limited English proficient students and available educational programs and services 1999–2000 summary report. Washington, DC: National Clearinghouse for English Language Acquisition and Language Instruction Educational Programs.

Children's Books Cited

Aardema, Verna (1975). *Why mosquitoes buzz in people's ears*. Illus. by Leo & Diane Dillon. New York: Dial.

Ada, Alma Flor (1997). *Gathering the sun*. Illus. by Simon Silva. New York: Lothrop, Lee & Shepard.

Blumberg, Rhoda (2004). *York's adventures with Lewis and Clark*. New York: HarperCollins.

Borden, Louise, & Kroeger, Mary Kay. (2001). *Fly high! The story of Bessie Coleman*. Illus. by Teresa Flavin. New York: McElderry.

Bridges, Ruby (1999). *Through my eyes*. Illus. with photographs. New York: Scholastic.

Chocolate, Debbi (1996). *Kente colors*. Illus. by John Ward. New York: Walker.

Coleman, Evelyn (1996). *White socks only*. Illus. by Tyrone Geter. Morton Grove, IL: Albert Whitman.

Dooley, Norah (1992). *Everybody cooks rice*. Illus. by Peter J. Thornton. Minneapolis, MN: Carolrhoda.

Dooley, Norah (1996). *Everybody takes bread*. Illus. by Peter J. Thornton. Minneapolis, MN: Carolrhoda.

Ehlert, Lois (1987). *Growing vegetable soup*. San Diego: Harcourt Brace.

Fox, Mem (1997). *Whoever you are*. Illus. by Leslie Staub. San Diego: Harcourt Brace.

Gibbons, Gail (1997). *The honeymakers*. New York: Morrow.

Gibbons, Gail (2004). *Thanksgiving*. New York: Morrow.

Gonzalez, Lucia M. (1997). *Señor Cat's romance and other favorite stories from Latin America*. Illus. by Lulu Delacre. New York: Scholastic.

Guy, Ginger Fogelsong (1996). *¡Fiesta!* Illus. by Rene King Moreno. New York: Greenwillow.

Hoban, Tana (1974). *Circles, triangles, and squares*. New York: Simon & Schuster.

Hoban, Tana (1976). *Push pull, empty full: A book of opposites*. New York: Macmillan.

Jenkins, Steve (2004). *Actual size*. New York: Scholastic.

Kurtz, Jane (1997). *Trouble*. Illus. by Durga Bernhard. San Diego, CA: Harcourt Brace.

Lionni, Leo (1967) *Frederick*. New York: Pantheon.

Louie, Ai-Ling (1982). *Yeh-shen: A Cinderella storg from China*. Illus. by Ed Young. New York: Philomel.

Markle, Sandra (2004). *Spiders: Biggest! Littlest!* Honesdale, PA: Boyds Mills Press.

Martin, Bill, Jr. (1983). *Brown bear, brown bear, what do you see?* Illus. by Eric Carle. New York: Holt.

Rappaport, Doreen (2001). *Martin's big words: The life of Dr. Martin Luther King, Jr.* Illus. by Bryan Collier. New York: Jump at the Sun/Hyperion.

Reeder, Carolyn (1997). *Across the lines*. New York: Atheneum.

Rockwell, Anne & Harlow (2004). *The toolbox*. New York: Walker.

Rosa-Casanova, Sylvia (1997). *Mama Provi and the pot of rice*. Illus. by Robert Roth. New York: Atheneum.

Simon, Seymour (1987). *Mars*. New York: Morrow.

Simon, Seymour (1999). *Crocodiles and alligators*. New York: HarperCollins.

Soto, Gary (1997). *Snapshots from the wedding*. Illus. by S. Garcia. New York: Putnam.

Soto, Gary (1993). *Too many tamales*. Illus. by J. Martinez. New York: Putnam.

Soto, Gary (1996). *The old man and his door*. Illus. by Joe Cepeda. New York: Putnam.

Steptoe, John (1987). *Mufaro's beautiful daughters: An African tale*. New York: Lothrop, Lee & Shepard.

Wormell, Christopher (2004). *Teeth, tails, and tentacles: An animal counting book*. Philadephia: Running Press.

Chapter 4

EMERGENT LITERACY

Transitioning from Home to School

Well, let's hear you spell your name," said the teacher.
*"F-e-*fe, *l-e-*le, *p-o-k,* pok*!" said Philipok.*
Everyone laughed.
But the teacher said, "Good boy! . . ."
Then, feeling bolder, he went on. "I'm really clever. I learn very quickly. You see, I'm very smart!"

FROM *PHILIPOK* BY ANN BENEDUCE

The powerful text of Ann Beneduce and the breathtaking illustrations of Gennady Spirin combine to retell a Leo Tolstoy tale of early literacy from Russia. Philipok, an inspired emergent learner, slips out of his grandmother's attentive care because his desire to learn to read and write is so intense. Braving wintry winds and a pack of fierce dogs, he makes his way to the village schoolhouse. The teacher allows him to stay for the day, but tells Philipok he must know the alphabet before learning to read. In his academic innocence and with personal stature and confidence, Philipok spells his name with phonemic cues. While initially questioning his presence, the teacher accepts Philipok's early literacy strategy and belief in himself and invites him to begin attending school. After that, Philipok goes merrily to school every day with his brother, Peter, and all the other village children.

Almost all children come to school believing in themselves. The challenging task of a caring, knowledgeable teacher of young children is to make the dream of literacy not only a possibility but a reality. Yet much precedes the opening of the schoolhouse door on the first day of school as home and family play a critical role in the initial development of the emergent literacy learner.

Research and practice on early literacy in the past several years has witnessed a shift in emphasis toward investigating the literacy competence of children before entering school. Children's first experiences with literacy are mediated by the ways in which parents and caregivers use reading and writing in their lives (Purcell-Gates, 1996). The nature and importance of emergent literacy has reawakened a realization that a significant, fundamental development in oral language, reading, writing, and drawing/viewing occurs in the child prior to entering school. The foundation of literacy "neither begins at five years of age nor at nine o'clock in the morning" (Clark, 1976, p. 106). Understanding the literacy achievements or background of children before entering kindergarten in a formal school setting are essential to understanding the literacy development of children as they transition into kindergarten and the primary grades.

The home environment of children is a powerful force on their success with literacy. Children who have been encouraged to express and reflect on ideas, who have shared in many different experiences, and who talk and delight in language understand the power of reading and writing. Children who see parents or caregivers read and write with pleasure as a matter of course, who are surrounded by books of all kinds, whose attention is drawn to the words that surround them in their everyday life are emerging as readers and writers long before they begin school.

For those who have not experienced this love affair with language and literature, all is not lost. Children today have opportunities through Even Start and Head Start programs to experience some of the literacy opportunities that should be available to all children. Responsible, knowledgeable teachers can provide a replication of the home environment in early school settings to ensure the valuing of oral and printed language in a safe, enjoyable atmosphere for exploring and sharing.

For many children today, the "home" environment looks different than the traditional concept, perhaps including the home of a relative, an adult caregiver, a day care facility, or a preschool program for a part of the child's day. In this chapter, the term *home* is a broad concept that is distinct from the term *school,* which formally begins with kindergarten. The assumption is that the home environment, whatever its location or title during the day, still places children in the care of their parents for the major portion of a day. Although a 3- to 6-hour learning setting does truly impact children, parents remain the first and foremost teachers of their children. The responsibility for literacy lies in the home with caring parents, warm parent-child interactions, and unconditional love and value for each child. Although educators envision this scenario for young children, it is not always the case. For some emergent learners, the home literacy environment must be replicated in their first school setting as an introduction to literacy.

Objectives

- To define emergent literacy.
- To understand language acquisition and its power in early literacy development.
- To differentiate between Halliday's functions of language.
- To understand Cambourne's conditions of natural learning and be able to link them to primary classroom literacy learning.
- To appreciate the importance of the role of literature in beginning literacy.

Emergent Literacy

Teacher Prep

The Teacher Prep Web site will help you become a better teacher by linking you to classroom videos, student artifacts, teaching strategies, lesson plans, relevant education leadership articles, and practical information on licensing, creating a portfolio, implementing standards, and being successful in field experiences. Visit this resource at www.prenhall.com/teacherprep.

The term "emergent literacy" describes the period between birth and the time when children write and read in conventional ways (Teale & Sulzby, 1986). Literacy implies that not only reading and writing but oral language development should be considered in conjunction with each other. The term *emergent literacy* reflects a positive view of child development, implying gradual, but continual growth as a literate individual. The term reflects many realistic aspects of the process:

- At any point in his or her development, the child is in the process of becoming literate.
- Continuity in literacy development is ensured, no matter how rapid or slow the rate of that development.
- Literacy growth can and does take place both inside and outside a school setting as both home and school environments contribute to literacy development.
- Literacy is like a seed inside of each child, waiting to bloom with the proper nurturing, care, and encouragement.

Emergent literacy actually implies a developmental miracle that takes place within each child, but at the appropriate time and rate designed for each individual. Examples of parental behaviors and attitudes that have a positive effect on children's literacy prior to entering kindergarten are provided in Figure 4.1. While literacy is influenced greatly by a literacy-rich home environment, the early school setting should replicate characteristics of the home literacy environment to transition children on their formal literacy journey. As more children seemingly lack the optimal literate home environment before coming to school, it is mandatory for the school to create a home literacy scenario in the early primary classroom.

Six principles help both primary educators and parents to understand and appreciate the related literacy events that influence children long before they enter school (Teale & Sulzby, 1986):

1. **Children in a literate society actually begin to read and write very early in life.** Case studies of very young children give evidence of the importance of initial encounters with books and writing events (Baghban, 1984; Bissex, 1980; Martens, 1996). Early literacy has been characterized by intelligence, persistence, and curiosity (Durkin, 1966) as well as engagement by the child and the academic achievement orientation of the parents (Briggs & Elkind, 1977). More recent research indicates that children develop early literacy skills in the context of everyday living through environmental

FIGURE 4.1 **Parental and Family Influences on Literacy.**

- Parental beliefs and attitudes regarding literacy influence children's literacy development (Spiegel, 1994).
- Mealtime conversations foster knowledge about the importance of oral language as communication (Snow & Tabors, 1993).
- Parents who believe literacy is a source of enjoyment have children with a more positive view about literacy than those who emphasize the skills aspect of literacy development (Baker, Scher, & Mackler, 1997).
- Asking and responding to children's questions during parent–child reading has an important influence on emergent literacy ability (Teale, 1978).
- Parents who believe their children are interested in literacy tend to provide abundant print-related experiences to their child (Hiebert, 1981).
- Print-rich home environments (magnet letters, writing materials, newspapers, books) and parent attention to print are linked to a child's print acquistion (Goodman, 1986).
- Children learn the purposes of literacy in the family setting as parents utilize literacy in everyday life (Taylor & Dorsey-Gaines, 1988).
- Parents who exhibit enthusiasm, enjoyment, and engagement in literacy transfer literacy skills to their child (Snow & Tabors, 1996).
- Children are more likely to persist in learning to read if parents view reading as a story event (rather than a decoding lesson) and encourage questions and risk taking and exhibit a sense of humor during the reading event (Baker, Serpell, & Sonnenschein, 1995).

Source: Adapted from C. E. Snow, S. Burns, & P. Griffin (Eds.) (1998). Preventing reading difficulties in young children. *Washington, DC: National Academies Press.*

print—those items of print from outside the home or originating outside the home to which there is public access. Examples include the McDonald's golden arch, the Burger King crown, the Pepsi symbol and colors, and the *Sesame Street* logo. Environmental print is usually considered contextualized, implying that the meaning of the print is, to a large extent, self-evident from the context that surrounds it. When children are shown environmental print or logos, many can identify them in an isolated context (Harste, Woodward, & Burke, 1984) and they are also sensitive to graphic cues when attending to environmental print. Obviously, children ask countless questions early on (What does that say?) and become aware that the environment carries a message. The knowledge accumulated about environmental print can foster an understanding of written language. Literacy is initially facilitated by a rich world of and response to environmental print.

2. **The young child's reading, writing, and oral language mutually reinforce each other, developing concurrently and interrelatedly.** Dividing literacy into isolated skills (reading, writing, speaking) creates unnatural boundaries between related language processes. It is in learning oral language that a child gains the background vocabulary to later read and write. Attempting to isolate reading and writing from the natural speaking tendencies of a child should be discouraged. Let them talk and talk and talk. For within language itself lie the foundations of complete literacy (Holdaway, 1979). As language surrounds the child, aspects of reading and writing begin to take hold. For example, "once upon a time" at the beginning of a story will eventually bridge to the printed word on the first page of a fairy tale or the opening of the child's own story. Language weaves within and between reading and writing as continuous practice leads to application in further literacy events.

3. **Literacy develops out of real life settings where reading, writing, speaking, and drawing are used to get things done.** Simple acts like writing a shopping list, paying bills, signing greeting cards, and reading the newspaper or *TV Guide* are models of literacy. We do them not for the sake of doing them but for the outcome they bring. A grocery list is used at the store to bring home items (e.g., cereal, cookies, juice) that play an important role in the child's life. Reading the schedule for television programs results in the viewing of *Sesame Street, Blues Clues,* or *Barney and Friends.* Literacy is used to solve everyday problems (a manual to put together a new bicycle) and to maintain social relationships (a birthday card to/from Grandma).
4. **Literacy demands that children be actively involved in their literate development.** This will include social interactions with parents and teachers in activities that involve reading, writing, listening, speaking, viewing, and visual representation. The social and related language interactions between a child and adult contribute greatly to a child's literacy development. Baking cookies results in a conversation about directions and ingredients, whereas shopping implies naming products, identifying concept words, and recognizing environmental print. Creative play with an adult can lead to the creation of a situation that inspires language, sequence of events, characters, and other story elements. The parent or adult who initiates and encourages language-based social interactions builds foundations toward the creation of a literate individual.
5. **Being read to plays a crucial role in literacy development of the young child.** Success in beginning to read in school is first and foremost associated with being read to at home (Anderson, Hiebert, Scott, & Wilkinson, 1985). Eagerness to learn to read is spurred on by being read to by an adult. Children begin to "talk like a book" (Clay, 1992) and evolve through stages of mumble reading, echo reading, cooperative reading, and completion reading as they "pretend" to read (Doake, 1985). Building self-esteem as a reader and writer emerges during these initial interactive book sessions in which children begin to believe in themselves as literate beings. Even Huey as early as 1908 stated that "the secret to it all lies in the parents' reading aloud to and with the child" (p. 332). Now, almost a century and countless research studies later, we know what is instinctively true—reading aloud to a child is the foremost contributor to reading success and achievement in school.
6. **Literacy is a developmental process for young children, and they pass through its stages in a variety of ways at different rates.** As a teacher of young children, it is critical to realize that not all learners will be at the same place in their literacy development when they enter your classroom. Some will actually be reading, some will recognize a few words, and others may not recognize the letters of the alphabet. A key example of literacy as a developmental process is *constructed spelling*—writing perceived sound and symbol relationships on paper. Some kindergartners might use random scribbles on the page to tell their story. Others might show evidence of letters, although no sound-symbol relationship exists. But in the work of some children, there may be a relationship between the *M* on the page and the glass of milk in their drawing or between the *BK* on the page and the book that they portray in their illustration. Since literacy is a developmental process, oral, written, and visual literacy will progress at differing rates among children. As long as there is evidence of progress over time, teachers and parents should celebrate these small steps toward literacy development.

The Tech Tip included here suggests many Web sites where parents, caregivers, and educators can find materials to encourage early literacy development and the home–school connection. Use of these resources can provide breadth and depth in offering optimal literacy environments for young children.

Tech TIP

Enhancing the Connection Between Home and School

The Public Library Association (a division of the American Library Association) offers, free of charge, a wealth of handouts, brochures, and PowerPoint presentations, ready to be downloaded at no cost to help inform parents of young children of their critical role as their children's first teacher. This is an excellent resource that teachers may want to share with parents during parent–teacher conferences or through newsletters. **http://www.pla.org/ala/pla/plaissues/earlylit/earlyliteracy.htm**

The Buddy Family Backpack project encourages teachers and library/media specialists to work collaboratively to promote family literacy (reading, viewing, and the integrated use of home-based technologies) by making theme-based backpacks filled with materials, resources, and activities for use in the homes of elementary school students. The site contains instructions and hints for creating the backpacks and an extensive list of ideas for themes. **http://www.buddyproject.org/backpack/default.asp**

Using the Internet to communicate with parents

To ease the transition from home to school, consider communicating with parents via the Internet.

- E-mail parents on a regular basis with news and updates. (To save time, set up an e-mail group or listserv of all your parents.)
- Create a class Web site with information about your daily activities, schedules, upcoming events, etc. With parental permission, you may even consider posting student work or digital photographs from the classroom. Teachers may create a Web page using software such as Microsoft FrontPage. There are also several Internet sites available where teachers may create and post a home page. (Although many provide this service for free, some sites require an annual membership fee.)

  http://teacherweb.com/
  http://teacher.scholastic.com/homepagebuilder/index.htm
  http://www.schoolnotes.com/
  http://teachers.net/sampler/

To look more closely at these materials and others related to "Emergent Literacy," visit the Companion Website at www.prenhall.com/hancock.

Language Acquisition

Language is a complex system of verbal and graphic symbols associated with ideas and objects that are produced in systematic patterns to communicate meaning from one person to another. Language development and literacy processes are linked as children become skilled users of their native language before entering school (Ruddell & Ruddell, 1994). As teachers attempt to further understand the complex nature of language, however, language deserves a closer and careful overview.

Language is symbolic as it represents concrete and abstract objects with specific symbols. A two-legged, web-footed, feathered creature that quacks, for example, is a "duck." Language symbols are applied arbitrarily as words randomly represent something. While many English words are based on words from other languages, many have nothing to do with the word meaning. Language is systematically created as needed. Technology alone has been responsible for the creation of dozens of new words—from *Internet, e-mail,* and *videodisc,* to *information superhighway.* Language also serves as a social instrument that facilitates communication between people within a culture. *First down, quarterback,* and *touchdown* may be used to discuss American football, while *gelato, prosciutto,* and *polenta* describe well-loved foods to Italians. Language is ever-evolving and changing. New words spring up overnight to describe new products, concepts, and trends, including *sports utility vehicle, money market account, cellular phone,* and *broadband communication.*

Language assumes another level of complexity in considering the "language of language." *Syntax* is the meaningful arrangement of order of words in sentences. "Arthur hit D. W." certainly has different meaning than "D. W. hit Arthur." *Semantics* is the study of word meaning. Young children actually acquire order before meaning as they often automatically repeat words without knowing what they mean or represent. *Pragmatics* refers to the socially acceptable use of language in a particular situation. School often provides the first opportunity to distinguish language heard at home from language used in school. Yet the roots for the understanding of this complex system lie in the first few years of life through continuous exposure in the home environment.

A Continuum of Language Development

The act of discovering and exploring language is perhaps the greatest intellectual achievement each of us makes within our lifetimes. The amazing fact is that children master language between the ages of 2 and 5—a feat that attests to the magnificent curiosity and intellectual capability of young children. Children acquire language through listening and observing how those around them use language in meaningful ways, and by practicing, imitating, and inventing language as they make it their own. This impressive accomplishment takes place in the absence of formal instruction and results in an oral vocabulary of 2,500 words and a listening vocabulary of 5,000 words by age 5. By the time children enter school, they have mastered most aspects of oral language. Regardless of the socioeconomic status or level of literacy in the home, children know much about the language that they learn between birth and the day they come to school.

Language progresses through various stages within the home setting. In the first year of life, infants cry, coo, and babble as the first signs of language. The *da-da/ma-ma* consonant and vowel combinations at 3 to 6 months lead toward their first words at 9 to 12 months (*bye-bye*). Between the ages of 1 and 2 years, toddlers begin producing language to express a need or fulfill a desire. Language progresses from single words (*ball*) to telegraphic speech (*Want juice, Daddy*) that contains no function words but communicates a definite message. Between the ages of 2 and 4, language expands by filling in detailed function words (*a, the, an, of*), mastering syntax, and increasing precision.

From 4 to 5 years of age, children internalize the rules of language but tend to overapply them in their attempts to understand those rules. For example, they learn that the addition of an "s" sound creates more than one with *houses, toys,* and *cars* and then conclude that *sheeps* must mean more than one sheep. Similarly, they are likely to overapply the "-ed" ending for past tense as "Mommy buyed me a new bike" is tried on for size. By age 5 to 6, however, most children internalize grammar, articulate most sounds, and form concepts. Inventing and playing with language is characteristic of children entering school. Finally, metalinguistic awareness occurs as children enter school and an understanding of "letter," "sound," "word," and "sentence" allow them to fully participate in the literacy experience in the classroom.

Certainly there are many more tiny steps and celebrations of language along the way, but this achievement emphasizes the importance of language in the home environment. Children need to talk, listen to talk, practice talk, and internalize word meanings in the home setting as they build a foundation for further emergent literacy growth in the school setting. One of the greatest literacy milestones is a child's desire and ability to actively interact with his or her environment through language.

Halliday's Functions of Language

Children learn early and practice often just how language works. Not only do they learn language in those early years at home and at school, but they learn to actually do things with language as well. Michael Halliday's (1973) *Explorations in the Functions of Language* describes the connections children make between the types of language they use and the fulfillment of their intentions. While these are learned in the home, they are practiced socially in preschool, and nurtured in the school setting. Figure 4.2 provides a condensed model of these seven categories.

The *instrumental function* is used to get something the child wants. "I want . . ." can be practiced in the kitchen, a play situation, or a retail store. Children learn early and often how productive this use of language can be, so they usually achieve a high level of proficiency as they seek to fulfill their needs.

The *regulatory function* is used to control behavior and is typically applied in a play or social situation. "Stop that" is often heard from the backyard, but children also practice this function by giving directions to their peers for playing a game, making cookies, or taking a walk in their neighborhood.

The *heuristic function* is used to find things out through questioning. Children love to ask questions and never seem to tire of them. A visitor, an encounter with a new animal, or a vacation to a new setting all provide the incentive to ask questions. This basis for later inquiry not only helps phrase questions (What is it? Why does it have those scales?), but actually raises the level of inquiry as a child strives to learn more. The art of asking questions becomes one of the survival skills of the classroom.

FIGURE 4.2 Halliday's Functions of Language.

Instrumental	"I want . . ."	Fulfilling needs
Regulatory	"Don't do that!"	Controlling
Heuristic	"What's that?"	Finding out
Interactional	"I love you."	Relating to others
Personal	"This is me."	Defining self
Imaginative	"Let's pretend."	Making believe
Informative	"This is how it is."	Communicating content

Source: M. A. K. Halliday (1973). Explorations in the function of language. *London, England: Edward Arnold.*

The *interactional function* is used to create and maintain social relationships. Most children seem comfortable with meeting new children as they learn to ask, "How are you?" or "What did you do over the weekend?" This social language builds toward the cooperative, community spirit exhibited in many classrooms.

The *personal function* is used to explore and communicate individual feelings. During and following an adult read-aloud, children like to share personal connections to a storybook. Talking about the things that make them afraid or the places that seem the most special are ways to communicate innermost feelings in a safe context. Literature provides the impetus for this type of discussion as the aesthetic response to children's books is natural and spontaneous.

The *imaginative function* allows children to play with language and create their own world. They love to invent their own stories, retell some of their favorites, and make up their own games and playing scenarios. The use of language abounds in these situations as new words, imaginary characters, and fantasy worlds are created. Puppets are an especially useful way for children to create and verbalize new adventures.

The *informative function* is used to convey information. A "show and tell" type atmosphere encourages children to talk about the things they value, where they got them, and what is special about them. Children like to talk about a day at the amusement park, about the kitten they found in the backyard, or about the dinosaur they saw at the museum. All that is required is an interested adult listener who provides an outlet for this type of language enhancement.

Because language requires constant practice in young children, a knowledge of Halliday's functions affects adults whether they are parents or teachers. A realization of the seven functions and the need for children to practice them can encourage role-playing, interviews, show and tell, and responses to books. All of these provide meaningful opportunities to sort through the powerful things language can do for the young language learner.

Cambourne's Conditions of Natural Learning

As children acquire oral language, the path to literacy naturally leads toward reading and writing. Brian Cambourne (1988) has identified eight conditions of natural learning. Figure 4.3 provides a summary of these conditions as they apply to language acquisition and critical links to effective literacy acquisition in the classroom setting. Cambourne also shares two axioms upon which these conditions are built:

- ***Learning to become literate ought to be as uncomplicated and barrier-free as possible.*** However, learning must include effort and challenge, and struggle is indeed an essential part of learning. A sense of accomplishment or achievement needs to accompany the literacy learning experience. Genuine pleasure can result from a struggle, but, if the struggle turns to suffering, unpleasant, and joyless learning occurs.
- ***Once learned, the skills of literacy should be durable.*** This means that the end product of literacy is so worthwhile, children will continue to use it outside of the classroom for the rest of their lives. Children will continue to turn to books for both pleasure and learning. Children will continue to write to identify and solve problems, to clarify thinking, to help them learn, and to communicate with others.

While these conditions originated with language acquisition, connections are readily linked to literacy in both the home and the early school environment. Learning to use and control the oral language of the culture into which we are born is a successful, painless, taken-for-granted task. Learning to control the written form of language, therefore, should not be

FIGURE 4.3 Cambourne's Conditions of Natural Learning in the Emergent Learner Environment.

CONDITION	CLASSROOM CHARACTERISTICS
Immersion	Print displays located at eye-level (labels, charts, books, dictated stories) Useful, meaningful print for the learner (rules, schedule, date, lunch, morning message) Print displays at learner's literacy level
Demonstration	Teacher-modeled literacy lessons (read-alouds, journal writing, morning message, signing in) Lessons at learner's literacy level Small group or individual modeling as needed
Engagement	Literacy learners see themselves as readers, writers, listeners, speakers, viewers, and visual representers (i.e. doers of literacy) Taking risks with literacy encouraged in a safe continuous learning environment
Expectations	Teacher-conveyed high expectations for literacy learning Expectations realistic for developmental level Learner holds individual, positive, realistic expectations
Responsibility	Abundant choice opportunities Learner treated as a reader/writer and given responsibilities with textual material Learner actively engages in literacy activities rather than merely observing (interactive read alouds, choral reading, journal writing)
Approximation	Approximations in reading/writing encouraged and celebrated as a natural part of learning Approximations linked to further teacher modeling to ensure literacy growth (word wall, environmental print)
Use	Adequate time and practice to connect the learner with authentic reading and writing events Literacy experiences relevant and meaningful Literacy practices continue at home
Response	Timely, specific, and frequent feedback (verbal comments, individual help) Feedback recognizes the developmental level of the learner Feedback positive, yet honestly assists the learner in moving one step ahead in literacy

any more difficult, complex, or painful than learning to talk. With children's amazing potential for language learning, the conditions that prevail for oral language acquisition should be present and applied to literacy learning. Understanding these eight conditions and linking them to classroom literacy learning are critical for primary literacy teachers.

Immersion. When children acquire language, they are saturated in the language model from parents and elders. Infants recognize language in the form of voices shortly after birth. Being constantly surrounded by language during infancy leads to internalization and eventually the acquisition of sounds, words, and eventually sentences. Language is always shared in a holistic context that makes sense. Children use the adult model to figure out how language works and to apply it to their own needs.

If immersion in language assists children in language acquisition, then oral and visual immersion in other forms of literacy can lead them to become readers and writers. A classroom displaying meaningful print in any form (labels, charts, posters, books, dictated stories) provides an immersion in print that leads to familiarity, comfort, and eventual recognition. Teachers reading aloud to children are saturating them with the rhythms, sounds, and repetitions of oral language. Even "reading" of self-selected texts gives the literacy learner control through immersion. Immersion that is "long and deep is more effective than that which is shallow and quick" (Cambourne, 1988, p. 46). Therefore, children need teachers who provide opportunities, plenty of books, and fair amounts of time to immerse themselves in literacy.

Demonstration. Parents melt as they see their child smile for the first time. The next step they await is the first word and they demonstrate or model "mama" and "dada" until the baby, of its own accord, finally verbalizes that long-awaited sound. This first demonstration of language leads the way toward acquisition of other first sounds and first words. The adult model of language serves to inspire and to demonstrate how to "do" oral language. Demonstrations can include an action (throwing a ball) or an artifact (a book), but Cambourne (1988) views demonstrations as the "raw data" that children use to learn how the language they must acquire works. Gradually, children learn to express ideas ("I can talk!") Similarly, demonstration of reading and writing by a teacher provides the model, the incentive, and the belief that "I can read!" and "I can write!" Demonstrations are necessary conditions for literacy learning to occur.

The classroom should be filled with relevant and functional literacy demonstrations. The shared book experience with big books, choral reading of nursery rhymes and poems, language experience stories, and interactive writing provide opportunities for teachers to model the reading and writing connection. Associating the spoken word with printed or handwritten text provides a key component in linking oral language to reading and writing. The modeling of the morning message or a journal entry demonstrates how reading and writing "work" and provides another potential link toward literacy. Demonstrations need to be continually repeated, with variation in materials, until skills and strategies become a natural part of the learner's repertoire.

Engagement. Probably one of the reasons that children learn language so naturally at home is that they are actively involved with it in daily contexts of the authentic experience. They talk while they bathe, they talk while they eat, and they talk while they play. Parents model and attempt to move children's talk toward conventions, but children seem to have a level of confidence that propels them at their own speed in learning. Immersion and demonstration may not take hold if engagement is not fostered (Cambourne, 2002). Engagement is maximized when learners are able to do the following:

- See themselves as potential doers of the demonstration (*I can learn to do this myself*).
- See the engagement as furthering a purpose in their lives (*I want to learn to read and write by myself*).
- See that engagement will not lead to discomfort or humiliation (*I will be safe if I take a risk and become involved*).
- See demonstrations conducted by those significant in their lives (*I want to get involved because my parent/teacher is a part of it*).

The same confidence developed in the home must travel with a child in the literacy classroom. Believing in oneself as a "doer" of literacy brings the self-esteem necessary to become a reader and a writer. If a teacher or other children keep "doing" it (pronouncing and spelling words correctly) for the child, literacy learning is slowed. Building confidence through predictable or patterned text and communicating thought through risk taking result in children viewing themselves as "doers" of literacy. To do this, teachers must

Engagement in authentic literacy experiences expands the use of language.

convince children that they genuinely care about them and believe in their potential as readers and writers. Teachers must also be conscious of inviting student participation in literacy activities and responding with respect and celebration.

Expectations. All parents expect that their baby will one day smile, get a first tooth, roll over, crawl, and talk. Although the question of when these events occur varies for each child, these accomplishments eventually happen. Expectations are high with little discouragement and much anticipation. As young as they are, babies sense the pleasure of their parents as each of these milestones is reached in succession. Young learners actually believe they can learn anything until convinced otherwise. Expectations are subtle but powerful indicators of potential learner behavior (Cambourne, 2002).

As children enter school, high expectations for reading and writing should be held by teachers who must believe that each child will blossom into a reader and writer when the time is right. Positive expectations for literacy should be held for each child who enters the classroom. Reality leads us to know that literacy weaves its own path within each child, but that each child will reach his or her potential as a reader and a writer. Teachers must convey to each child that they are confident in his or her ability to master the skills leading to literacy. Each child must be made to feel like a likeable, worthy, valued individual and that he or she is a special person in the classroom. Teachers must also convince learners that reading and writing are worthwhile activities that will become valuable and functional in their lives. Expectations are closely related to self-esteem and are part of a genuine, trusting relationship tailored to the realistic potential of each child.

Responsibility. A child's learning of language in the home environment is a result of his or her own efforts. The desire and need to communicate love and needs require that language take hold. So too is independence indicated through play as children decide between toys or create their own imaginative play. If parents gave lessons in language, distributed worksheet practice, or orchestrated play, language learning would be decontextualized and fragmented from its authentic use. The same independence and responsibility of learning present in the home should guide children in the literacy classroom.

If children are to take responsibility for their own learning, several actions are implied in the school setting. While it takes time to gradually release this responsibility to the learner, teachers provide options for thinking and acting within this realm. Children should be given decision-making opportunities related to what they want to "read," what they want to "write," or what they want to "draw." Structured choice within the classroom literacy environment places responsibility for literacy learning on the child. Teachers, on the other hand, must realize that a preplanned program of literacy activities for all children at the same time is almost an impossibility with so many different learners. The teacher gradually structures the learning environment around choice and provides instruction when needed, and the children act as responsible individuals at their own locations on the road toward literacy. Rather than "spoon-feed" correctness, the teacher guides and encourages risk taking that inches the learner toward conventional literacy.

Approximation. The infant who says "mama" is not corrected or prompted into saying "Mommy." Likewise, the amusing mispronunciation of "pasketti" for "spaghetti" brings a smile to parent's faces. Adults know that the immature form will eventually move toward correctness. Instead of demanding correctness in the classroom, teachers can celebrate the attempt that is leading toward conventional literacy. The willingness to accept approximations is essential to the processes that accompany language learning. Yet, when the child enters school, the risk taking of early oral language is often replaced by unrealistic expectations of a society that advocates correctness and error avoidance. Within natural development, however, a child acquires language by taking small steps toward correctness.

Since literacy is a developmental process, teachers must realize and treat approximations of learning as critical steps on the literacy journey. Accepting, celebrating, and evaluating for growth over time constitute approximation in the early literacy classroom. Avoiding errors forces a child to abandon natural development and place conventional reading and writing on a pedestal. Prioritizing conventions produces safe behavior in children and "get-it-right-the-first-time" teaching in teachers. Teachers seem forced to break language down into small parts so children can indeed get it right. Freedom to approximate must be considered an essential ingredient of the literacy process if natural learning is to occur.

Use. The only way that a baby learns language is to play with it through practice. It is through continuous use, especially during play, that language learning takes place. Children feel accomplishment in repeating *Mother Goose* rhymes or *The Itsy Bitsy Spider* finger play over and over again. The opportunity to talk seems to be a given in a child's life and children learn to talk as they negotiate the rules of language on their own.

Practice makes perfect in the literacy classroom as well. It is only through multiple reading and writing opportunities across the school day that a child learns to read and write. Beyond the language arts block, children need to hear read-alouds, create stories, write journals, and draw representations of learning across the entire curriculum. Children learn to read by reading and they learn to write by writing. Literacy moments must surround them throughout the school day. Learners must experience activities that go beyond learning language, filling in time, or practicing a skill. Teachers must create settings in which language can be used to achieve ends beyond learning to read and write (for example, designing a book cover for a library display, locating a favorite poem for a class anthology).

Response. All children respond to pleasing an adult. From the parent's smile and warm embrace when a first word is spoken, children live to please an adult and gain that same warm response. Gradually response turns to positive oral statements that spur the child forward not only in language but in life.

That same positiveness has a place in a primary literacy classroom. Nonthreatening feedback has far-reaching effects in assisting the literacy process. The mutual exchange between an expert (teacher) and the novice (student) can become relevant, functional, and meaningful as the next literacy step occurs. Cambourne (1988) characterizes four types of response and feedback: (a) acceptance, (b) celebration, (c) evaluation, and (d) demonstration. This cycle, repeated in literacy events, leads the teacher to keep a finger on the pulse of the child's literacy development providing responses that offer a bridge to new learning. All children respond to positive input, suggestions, and praise. Teachers who retain a positive view of learning and children, who acknowledge small steps in the learning process, and who lead as well as nudge provide the positive response children need to work toward successful literacy.

Although based in language development, Cambourne's conditions of natural learning are applicable to natural literacy acquisition in the primary classroom. They speak to no single philosophy of the language arts but contain principles that support teachers who believe in the literacy potential of learners. The heart of these conditions lies in the strength of demonstration as a key to effective instruction.

The Role of Literature in Beginning Reading

Literature remains a primary vehicle for parents to share in the home as children learn language, develop a sense of story, and learn to appreciate the value of reading and the meaning that lies in print. This section is intended to serve as a guideline for the types of books that are available for young children and the manner in which they may be most effectively shared by parents.

Baby/Board Books. First books for babies receive increasing importance as research continues to point out the connections between early reading to children and later academic success (Teale, 1986). These books are manufactured of thick cardboard, plastic, or cloth to stand the wear and tear of eager, little hands. Many classic titles including Margaret Wise Brown's *Goodnight Moon* and new favorites like Rosemary Wells's *Max's Birthday* have assumed the board book format as the popularity of these books have increased. They serve as important lap-sitting experiences as young hands begin to turn the pages, eager fingers point to bright colors, and a sense of story begins to take hold. Independent exploration with these books fulfills a need to discover the wonder of books.

Mother Goose and Nursery Rhymes. The rhythm, rhyme, and predictability of *Mother Goose* and traditional nursery rhymes cause these books to be read over and over again as children value and appreciate the sound of language. Rosemary Wells's *Max's Birthday* and Iona Opie's dual set of *My Very First Mother Goose* books serves as an outstanding language model for children as they begin to experiment with language by attempting to join in or repeat these well-loved rhymes. The illustrations in the books often have strong appeal to young children as characters like Old King Cole, Little Boy Blue, and Peter Peter Pumpkin Eater come to life on the page. Language repetition and physical delight (e.g., clapping, pointing, smiles) result as children recognize familiar characters and related language as valued friends.

Participation Books. Participation books beg active involvement through instant pop-up devices, tracing shapes or textures with fingers, sliding pages to uncover colorful images, or lifting-the-flap to reveal exciting surprises. These titles are meant for exploration by young children and serve as an opportunity to answer questions by moving parts of the book, taking an active role in storytelling, or discovering facts about the natural world. Many of these titles, however, are delicately constructed and are not meant for young children. Choose those that are sturdily contructed, invite exploration, and encourage (not discourage) interaction, such as Dorothy Kunhardt's classic *Pat the Bunny,* Robert Crowther's *Colors,* or Eric Carle's *The Very Hungry Caterpillar.*

LITERATURE FOR EARLY LITERACY EXPERIENCES

Baby/Board Books

Hague, Michael (1993). *Teddy bear, teddy bear: A classic action rhyme.* New York: Morrow.

Hoban, Tana (1993). *Black on white.* New York: Greenwillow.

Martin, Bill, Jr. & Archambault, John (1993). *Chicka Chicka ABC.* Illus. by Lois Ehlert. New York: Simon & Schuster.

Miller, Margaret (1996). *At the seashore.* New York: Simon & Schuster.

Oxenbury, Helen (1995). *I see.* Cambridge, MA: Candlewick Press.

Wells, Rosemary (1985). *Max's breakfast.* New York: Dial.

Yorinks, Arthur (1996). *Frank and Joey eat lunch.* Illus. by Maurice Sendak. New York: HarperCollins.

MotherGoose/Nursery Rhymes

Anholt, Catherine, et al. (1996). *The Candlewick book of first rhymes.* Cambridge, MA: Candlewick.

dePaola, Tomie (1985). *Tomie dePaola's Mother Goose.* New York: Putnam.

dePaola, Tomie (1993). *Mother Goose's nursery rhymes.* New York: Random House.

Dyer, Jane (1996). *Animal crackers: A delectable collection of pictures, poems, and lullabies for the very young.* Boston: Little, Brown.

Lobel, Arnold (1997). *The Arnold Lobel book of Mother Goose.* New York: Knopf/Random House.

Opie, Iona A. (1996). *My very first Mother Goose.* Illus. by Rosemary Wells. Cambridge, MA: Candlewick.

Rosenburg, Liz (1994). *Mama Goose: A new Mother Goose.* Illus. by Janet Street. New York: Philomel.

Zemach, Mrgot (2001). *Some from the moon, some from the sun: Poems and songs for everyone.* New York: Farrar, Straus and Giroux.

Participation Books

Carle, Eric (1968). *The very hungry caterpillar.* New York: Philomel.

Carle, Eric (1984). *The very busy spider.* New York: Philomel.

Carle, Eric (1990). *The very quiet cricket.* New York: Philomel.

Carle, Eric (1995). *The very lonely firefly.* New York: Philomel.

Crowthers, Robert (2001). *Colors.* Cambridge, MA: Candlewick.

Ehlert, Lois (1997). *Hands.* San Diego: Harcourt Brace.

Predictable/Pattern Books

Appelt, Kathi (1993). *Elephants aloft.* Illus. by Keith Baker. San Diego: Harcourt Brace.

Aylesworth, Jim (1994). *My son John.* Illus. by David Frampton. New York: Holt.

Blos, Joan (1992). *A seed, a flower, a minute, an hour.* New York: Simon & Schuster.

Charlip, Remy (1964). *Fortunately.* New York: Parents Magazine Press.

Fleming, Denise (1992). *Lunch.* New York: Holt.

Predictable/Pattern Books. Books with predictable text and repetitive language foster interactive storybook reading. While parents read such books aloud, a child quickly joins in on predictable words, phrases, or sentences. After several readings, children begin to "read" the book independently. Classic examples include Bill Martin Jr.'s version of *Brown Bear, Brown Bear, What Do You See?* and Sue Williams's *I Went Walking.* The Literature Cluster included here lists many classic and contemporary titles that contain predictable text and make children feel like they can read.

Fleming, Denise (1993). *In the small, small pond.* New York: Holt.

Fleming, Denise (1998). *Mama cat has three kittens.* New York: Holt.

Gag, Wanda (1929). *Millions of cats.* New York: Coward-McCann.

Martin, Bill, Jr. (1991). *Polar bear, polar bear, what do you hear?* Illus. by Eric Carle. New York: Holt.

Peek, Merle (1985). *Mary wore her red dress.* Boston: Clarion.

Root, Phyllis (2001). *Rattletrap car.* Illus. by Jill Barton. Cambridge, MA: Candlewick.

Scheer, J., & Bileck, M. (1964). *Rain makes applesauce.* New York: Holiday House.

Van Lann, Nancy (1998). *So say the little monkeys.* Illus. by Yami Heo. New York: Atheneum.

Williams, Sue (1990). *I went walking.* Illus. by Julie Vivas. San Diego: Harcourt Brace.

Williams, Sue (1998). *Let's go visiting.* Illus. by Julie Vivas. San Diego: Harcourt Brace.

Wordless Picture Books

Baker, Jeannie (1991). *Windows.* New York: Greenwillow.

Blake, Quentin (1995). *Clown.* New York: Holt.

dePaola, Tomie (1978). *Pancakes for breakfast.* San Diego: Harcourt Brace.

Rohmann, Eric (1994). *Time flies.* New York: Crown.

Wiesner, David (1991). *Tuesday.* Boston: Clarion.

Concept Books

Grover, Max (1996). *Circles and squares everywhere!* San Diego: Harcourt Brace.

Hoban, Tana (1992). *Spirals, curves, fanshapes, and lines.* New York: Greenwillow.

Hoban, Tana (1995). *Animal, vegetable, or mineral?* New York: Greenwillow.

Hoban, Tana (1996). *Just look.* New York: Greenwillow.

Rotner, Shelley (1997). *Close, closer, closest.* Photos by Richard Olivo. New York: Atheneum.

ABC Books

Aylesworth, Jim (1992). *Old black fly.* Illus. by S. Gammell. New York: Holt.

Darling, Kathy (1996). *The Amazon ABC.* New York: Lothrop, Lee & Shepard.

Lobel, Anita (1990). *Allison's zinnea.* New York: Greenwillow.

McDonnell, Flora (1997). *Flora McDonald's ABC.* Cambridge, MA: Candlewick.

Shannon, George (1996). *Tomorrow's alphabet.* Illus. by Donald Crews. New York: Greenwillow.

Slate, Joseph (1996). *Miss Bindergarten gets ready for kindergarten.* New York: Dutton.

Counting Books

Bang, Molly (1997/1993). *Diez, neuve, ocho.* Trans. by Clarita Kohen. New York: Greenwillow.

Hoberman, Mary Ann (1997). *One of each.* Illus. by Marjorie Priceman. Boston: Little, Brown.

Moss, Lloyd (1995). *Zin! Zin! Zin!: A violin.* Illus. by Marjorie Priceman. New York: Simon & Schuster.

Pomeroy, Diane (1996). *One potato: A counting book of potato prints.* San Diego: Harcourt Brace.

Roth, Susan (1997). *My love for you.* New York: Dial.

Wordless Picture Books. Picture books without words let the illustrations tell the story on their own. They provide the opportunity for language development as children attempt to impose their developing sense of story on the illustrations. Parents can interactively guide children through the story with questioning and prediction techniques. Emily Arnold McCully's *Picnic* and *First Snow* invite active detail-filled voices to be added to common childhood experiences. Children's voices and imaginations create the story as self-generated story language is valued. Lesson Plan 4.1 demonstrates a creative viewing and oral language interpretation of a wordless picture book experience.

LESSON PLAN 4.1

TITLE: **Creating Stories with Wordless Picture Books**

Grade Level: K–1

Time Frame: 45-minute sessions

Standards

IRA/NCTE Standards: 1, 3, 12
NETS for Students: 1, 3

Objectives

- Students will use their imaginations to create story lines for wordless picture books.
- Students will orally share their imaginative stories with an audience (peers).

Materials

- An assortment of wordless picture books such as the following:
  - Lehman, Barbara (2004). *The Red Book*. Houghton Mifflin.
  - Carle, Eric (1988). *Do You Want to Be My Friend?* Philomel.
  - McCully, Emily Arnold (1984). *Picnic*. Harper & Row.
- Document camera (Elmo), projector, and large screen

Motivation

- Use a document camera (Elmo) to display a wordless picture book on a large screen. Show book illustrations and discuss what students notice. Ask students to create a story in their mind that goes with the pictures.
- "Read" the book by sharing your imagined version of the story. Ask students how their imagined stories were similar/different from the your version. Discuss how the same wordless picture book can tell many different stories.

Procedures

- After copies of wordless picture books have been distributed to pairs of students, students will preview their books by looking at the pictures.
- With a partner, students will create a story to accompany the text.
- Working with their partner, students will practice telling their imagined story.
- Using the document camera, students will share their wordless books and accompanying stories with an audience (peers).

Assessment

- Teacher-created checklist reflecting lesson objectives (Do story lines and illustrations match?).

Accommodation/Modification

- Select wordless picture books that suit needs and abilities of individual learners.

Visit the Meeting the Standards module in Chapter 4 of the Companion Website at www.prenhall.com/hancock to adapt this lesson to meet your state's standards.

Concept Books. Concept books are among the first informational books that teach children about various aspects of their world. Tana Hoban is synonymous with bold, clear concept books on shapes, sizes, and other aspects of the world that engage children in early book encounters while building the parental bond during a lap reading experience. Concept book interactions may lead to greater observation of details, predictions, and heightened inquiry as indicated by the questions that children ask.

Alphabet books are specific types of concept books, but a bit of caution is offered. Today's alphabet books with unique designs and minimal text are intended to teach far more than the ABCs. Parents should focus on those ABC books that present familiar objects, names, or places with alphabet letters in creative ways. Bill Martin and John Archambault's brightly colored and rhymed *Chicka Chicka Boom Boom* shares letters in the context of a story but does not overwhelm the reader with unknown objects. Young children should respond to alphabet books through predictable, familiar content or through ties to phonemic awareness. (See the Literature Cluster for a list of uncomplicated, satisfying alphabet books for young children.)

Counting books in their simplest form present material in a predictable, sequenced format that appeals to the young child. Numbers are teamed with photographs or illustrations and the corresponding number of objects. Children count aloud, point to objects, make number-print associations, and generate talk as part of the interactive nature of counting books. Caution is again offered as many number books are intended for establishing mathematical concepts beyond counting. Choose those that exhibit simple one-on-one correspondence between familiar or related objects and the numbers.

Concepts of Literacy Learned in Beginning Reading

Early experiences with children's books result in many literate behaviors that are common to literacy novices (McGee & Richgels, 2000). Holding a book upright, turning pages, recognizing books by names, and participating with an adult in book sharing result in the following literacy-related concepts:

- *Books are pleasurable.* Children learn early that reading is a pleasurable activity, and they often choose books as a preferred activity. Book reading is one of the physically and emotionally closest activities parent and child share, generating warm feelings for the adult, the book, and the book reading experience.
- *Books are handled in specific ways.* Children learn book handling skills to assist them in looking at books. Holding the book right-side-up, turning pages, and discovering that books are a means for viewing and reading provide initial concepts that lead toward literacy.
- *Book sharing involves familiar language and routines.* Familiar, expected language, action, and routines surround book sharing. Selecting a book, climbing on a lap, pointing and naming objects, making comments, asking questions, and answering questions help children realize there are certain roles they play in book sharing. Parents give children opportunities to use these new skills as the child's role increases and the parent's role decreases in the book-reading experience.
- *Pictures in books are symbols.* Children soon learn that the shapes and colors represent objects and actions. Although they are not real things, they do represent things and provide symbols of real things. As a child touches a picture of a kitten, he knows that it is not a real kitten but that it is representative of a real kitten.
- *Books and print communicate meaning.* Through many exposures to books, children learn that print materials communicate meaning and share a message.

> Communicating understanding is a major outcome of literacy activities. When an adult reads print aloud, tells a story, or talks about pictures, children learn to make sense of what is going on. The young child understands a situation, the talk surrounding it, and the visual symbols that represent it.

Children who acquire these literate behaviors prior to the formal school experience are more likely to succeed in literacy experiences when they enter school (Burns, Griffin, & Snow, 1999).

The Beginnings of Writing

Long before children enter kindergarten, they draw wiggly, wavy lines or tiny shapes that resemble letters. Writing begins long before children compose a readable message through conventional print. Attempted signatures on birthday cards, early drawings with letterlike shapes, and "pretend" writing gradually lead to writing their own name or even combining pictures and writing into a "story." Before children come to school, many consider themselves writers, although in a developmental rather than a conventional sense.

Continuing interest in a child's early writing has resulted in fresh views relating language competence (Clay, 1991; Morrow, 1993) and children's ideas about written language (Harste, Woodward, & Burke, 1984). A large body of research indicates that starting with picture representations and scribbling, children attempt to connect their oral language with written language and understand the relationship of graphic symbols and sounds (Clay, 1975; Dyson, 1982, 1984). Whether they use conventional symbols or not, beginning writers produce contextually appropriate writing—itemized shopping lists, letters to grandma, lists of words they can write (Temple et al., 1988).

Beginning writers progress through stages from drawing or scribbling marks on paper to printing with conventional or constructed spelling, thus creating permanent printed evidence of meaningful events (Harste, Woodward, & Burke, 1984). Other researchers have referred to these beginning writing stages as patterns that children use in individual ways (Sulzby, Barnhart, & Hieshima, 1989). Certain conclusions can be drawn from this core of emergent writing research:

- Written language, like oral language, is learned naturally.
- Children in literate societies are involved at an early age in understanding and controlling print.
- Children's perceptions of print are organized, systematic, and identifiable (Harste, Woodward, & Burke, 1984).

Parents and primary teachers can foster confidence and development in early writing if they are aware of and understand the "precursors of writing" (Temple et al., 1988). Children appear to go through a process of sorting and classifying as they make sense of their world. Learning to write, it might seem, is nothing more than learning to make letters and combine them into words. Yet it appears that children actually learn to write by mastering the whole (written lines) before preceeding to the parts (letters).

Common Principles in Early Writing

Marie Clay (1975) outlined a set of features, or graphic principles, that are common in young children's early writing, before they can produce the recognizable letters of the alphabet. All of these principles—recurring, generative, flexibility, and directionality—must be learned by children before they can "write," but many of them are discernible in children's emerging scribbles before adults notice they are really trying to produce writing. All the student samples included in the following discussion are derived from kindergarten journals.

The Recurring Principle. Children's early attempts to imitate writing often show a characteristic repetition of movement, loops, sticks, and circles. Clay (1975) applied the label *recurring principle* to the idea that writing consists of the same move repeated over and over again. Children actually delight in filling whole lines or even whole pages by repeating the same moves over and over and over again. Jessica's "writing" (Student Sample 4.1) consists of repeated movements "written" in her journal. It appears that the movement flowing across the page imitates the writing that she has seen modeled by an adult. Grayson's journal (Student Sample 4.2) reflects the repeated use of an X, O, $, 1, and 3 repeated over and over in the context of a drawing.

The Generative Principle. Children learn early on that the same character repeated over and over is not really writing. To qualify as writing, they sense there must be vari-

STUDENT SAMPLE 4.1 Jessica's Early Writing. (Recurring Principle).

STUDENT SAMPLE 4.2 Grayson's Journal. (Recurring Principle).

ety in the arrangement of marks. Although it is possible to create writing with just a few characters, those characters must be repeated in different combinations, a process referred to as the generative principle. Student Sample 4.3 shows how Cody used a small set of letters but combined them in different ways to produce writing. Note how 3, A, O, B, and U are scattered randomly across the page. Student Sample 4.4 shows Daniel's attempt to place letters on the page, although it is obvious that making those letters proved a difficult task. The generative principle does not include a sound-symbol relationship between the letters on the page and the phonemic sound of those letters, but it does provide the next necessary developmental step toward eventual conventional writing.

The Flexibility Principle. Once children begin to experiment with writing, a long period of months or years may go by before they know all letter forms. During that

STUDENT SAMPLE 4.3 Cody's Letters and Numbers. (Generative Principle).

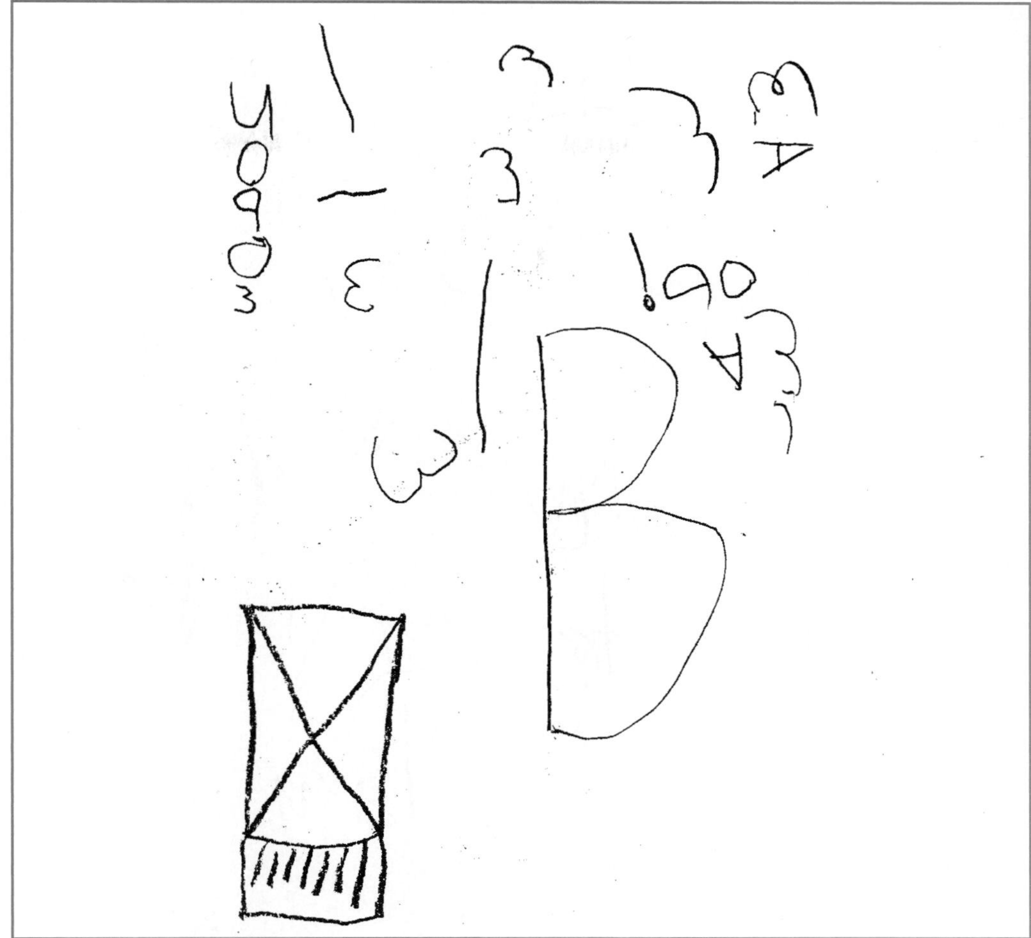

time, they begin to focus on distinct features of letters that can be varied to produce new letters. For example, the letter *d* can be turned upside down to produce a *p*, or flipped to the right to create a *b*. An *L* can become an *E* with the addition of two horizontal lines and an *E* can become an *F* with the removal of the lower horizontal line. While children are discovering ways to make these letters, they also tend to invent letters that do not exist. Clay (1975) refers to this ongoing discovery as the flexibility principle. By varying letter forms that they know, children can produce letters they did not know how to make. However, not all letter forms are acceptable in conventional writing. Children exploring this principle should be viewed as positive as they gain control over the features of print and help them attend to the distinguishing features of letters. Notice Jaira's attempt to "copy" the alphabet in Student Sample 4.5 Her list includes many letters that have been reversed, but provides a valiant attempt at making letters. Note that she completed her journal entry by writing "CAT CAT" to affirm the letters that she can write conventionally.

The Directionality Principle. The arrangement of print on the page in English begins on the left-hand side of the page at the top, proceeds across to the right side, returns

STUDENT SAMPLE 4.4 Daniel's Letters. (Generative Principle)

to the left side again, drops down a single line, and proceeds to the right and on and on to the bottom of the page. Clay (1975) found that although children read from right to left, from top to bottom, they still struggled with directionality in writing. If children draw a picture and then write, their print is often arranged as a matter of remaining space as in Student Samples 4.6 and 4.7. Jacob's first day of school entry (August 24) reveals letters added to a drawing in available enclosed spaces—the body and the sun—as well as in open areas. In a later entry (October 12), Jacob writes letters across the top of the page as if to label his drawing. There is no evidence of sound and symbol relationships here, but Jacob did write left to right on this entry.

These four principles help both the parent and the teacher of young children understand and appreciate the intricate experimentation that leads to conventional writing. This developmental process is gradual, but each phase is filled with new learning to celebrate as the child becomes a writer. Parents should treasure these examples of early writing by displaying them and storing them away. As time progresses, the developmental aspects of writing become apparent through this dated documentation and the art of writing is appreciated as the complex process and symbolic system that it is.

STUDENT SAMPLE 4.5 Jaira's Alphabet. (Flexibility Principle).

Children should be encouraged to "write," especially when a parent or teacher is writing. Most children prefer to generate letters of their own rather than copying. Children's names are typically the first objects of print to be traced, copied, and eventually generated. But before that occurs, children need to explore, discover, take risks, and celebrate their many attempts at writing.

Concepts of Literacy Learned in Early Writing

As children interact with adults and with a variety of markers, crayons, and writing materials, they learn several concepts about drawing and writing (McGee & Richgels, 2000). These initial concepts continue to build the literacy foundation that will encourage them on their journeys toward literacy. These drawing and writing concepts make several assumptions:

- ***Drawing and writing are pleasurable.*** Children enjoy drawing and writing, and they concentrate as they hold tightly to a writing tool and create shapes. Children often choose writing and drawing as a preferred activity. A new box of crayons or a new pad of fresh paper create excitement and provide pleasurable hours of drawing and writing.

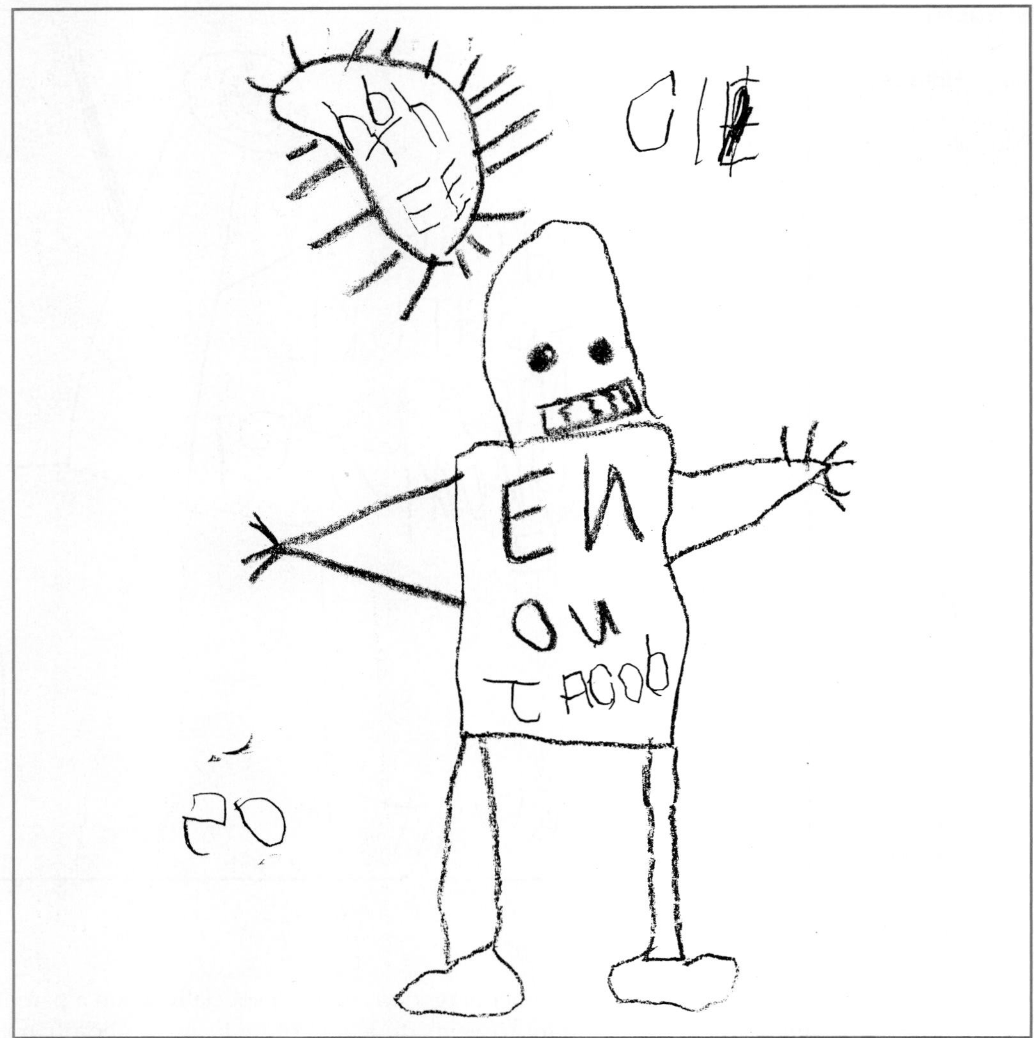

STUDENT SAMPLE 4.6 Jacob's Early Writing. (Directionality Principle).

- ***Movements are controlled.*** Children learn that they can control their movements to create shapes and lines. To create dots or circles, children must learn how to control those movements. Children begin with back-and-forth movements and progress to circlelike shapes. These movements become the building blocks of drawing and writing.
- ***Writing and drawing involve familiar routines and language.*** Young children draw to gain adult attention and involve others in social interaction. Routine language such as "Let's draw," "You draw," and "Draw a circle" engage others in the process. Children often name a word, letter, or object, and parents draw it or write it.
- ***Writing and drawing can be named.*** Children often draw with no intention to create a specific object. Yet they often name or label the object in an attempt to make it meaningful. Parents lead them in this direction when they say, "Tell me about your picture." This becomes a meaningful step toward creating symbols in representational drawings. As parents question intentionality, they actually move children toward actual representation in drawing or writing.

STUDENT SAMPLE 4.7 Directionality in Jacob's Writing. (Directionality Principle).

- ***Drawings are symbols.*** Children eventually learn not only that their drawings can be named but also that they become representative of things. For example, dots and lines became symbols of "rain" for young children. Early representational drawings often depict humans in a circle with vertical lines.

Not all children, unfortunately, have these literacy concepts formed before entering school. Literacy concept development depends on the nature of interactions with parents as they share books and write and draw together.

This discussion was limited to the early emergent stages of writing. As children enter kindergarten, they often progress beyond these stages and begin the journey toward both conventional writing and spelling. Chapter 5 will discuss and demonstrate the stages of constructed spelling and the developmental road toward becoming a conventional writer as evidenced in ongoing journal entries.

Visit the Companion Website at www.prenhall.com/hancock and gauge your understanding of Chapter 4 concepts with the self-assessments.

Closing Thoughts

Children come from home environments that support literacy development to different degrees. Ideal development occurs through interactions with adults who are physically, emotionally, socially, and cognitively suited to the dynamic needs of children. During the transition from the home to the school environment, children are "hard at work as scholars of language" yet "playful and exploratory" in the accomplishment of most of their language-based activities (Snow, Burns, Griffin, 1998, p. 60).

The dynamic emergent literacy perspective discussed in this chapter should provide useful information to parents, caregivers, preschool teachers, and early primary teachers. This new paradigm suggests that children come to school with a great deal of knowledge about language and literacy. The role of early literacy models in a child's life is to provide conditions that support self-generated, self-motivated, and self-regulated learning (Stickland & Morrow, 1989). How then should this valuable literacy information affect you as a parent or teacher?

- ***Knowledge.*** You now have a sense of the developmental processes of reading and writing and the scope of literacy behaviors you can expect from a wide range of young children. All children progress in language development and in early reading and writing as unique individuals. Do not expect to find a chart that defines exactly when these literacy moments will occur. There is no right time or definitive formula, but there is the concept of continuous development over time as the small steps gradually become giant steps toward literacy.
- ***Observation.*** You now are equipped with some understanding of the acquisition of oral language, reading, and writing in children. Close observation combined with this knowledge should result in tracking a child's development over time. The ability to respond to or understand a child's desire to read along or scribble strings of letters on a page allows adults to celebrate these small, but critical steps in literacy alongside the child.
- ***The well-balanced child.*** No matter how important literacy development is to an adult, the child's social, emotional, and physical development must be considered foremost as you keep total child development in mind. Forcing children to sit for long periods of time engaged in literacy activities may be detrimental. Engaging children in reading and writing process activities is preferred to pencil and paper drill and practice. No matter how important reading and writing exploration is, it must be offered in ways congruent with the natural learning development of the child.
- ***A natural literacy.*** Oral language, reading, and writing not only develop in concert but also reinforce each other in these early stages of literacy learning. Setting literacy in real-life contexts from a trip to the library to nature discovery in the backyard make learning more natural. Segmenting oral language, reading, and writing is not consistent with what we know about language learning. Real-life experiences lend themselves to well-rounded literacy events as children talk about a trip to the zoo, read a book on lions, and draw and write about their favorite zoo animal. Focusing on the total literacy package in contrast to emphasizing its separate elements provides a more meaningful approach and celebrates the natural connectedness between language, reading, and writing. As you interact with young children, remember the importance of this natural, authentic approach to the development of literacy in the emergent learner. Nurture children's literacy growth from an inherent seed to a blossoming flower surrounded by books, language, and love.

As this chapter concludes, savor and reflect on the words of Bill Martin Jr. (1972):

Learning to read
is not something that happens
after a stereotyped readiness period
in first grade or in kindergarten.
Learning to read
is the job of a lifetime.
Two-and-three-year-old children who are read to a lot
begin their reading careers early.
The day a child gets hold of a sentence pattern that works for him
and reads it into the telephone directory
or the Montgomery Ward catalog
or his daddy's newspaper at night,
he is launching himself as a successful reader.
The day a child reads a book from memory,
he is furthering his reading career.

He, in truth, is finding joy and power
in the pages of a book,
a psychological posture that every successful reader
continuously brings to each reading encounter,
knowing, subconsciously if not consciously,
that he can make a go of print.
This is the first and foremost reading skill.

Written more than 30 years ago as an essay printed in the teacher's edition of his language-based basal series, *The Sounds of Language,* these words express the essence of emergent readers (and writers) as they transition from home to school. The magic of Martin's words provide teacher inspiration to carefully nurture and intentionally continue the joy and wonder of language and literacy that begins at home and continues into the K–2 classroom setting.

References

Anderson, R. C., Hiebert, E. H., Scott, J. A., & Wilkinson, I. A. G. (1985). *Becoming a nation of readers: The report of the Commission on Reading.* Washington, DC: National Institute of Education, U.S. Department of Education.

Baghban, M. J. M. (1984). *Our daughter learns to read and write: A case study from birth to age three.* Newark, DE: International Reading Association.

Baker, L., Scher, D., & Mackler, K. (1997). Home and family influences on motivation for reading. *Educational Psychologist, 32,* 69–82.

Baker, L, Serpell, L. R., & Sonnenschein, S. (1995). Opportunities for literacy learning in the homes of urban preschoolers. In L. M. Morrow (Ed.), *Family literacy: Connections in schools and communities* (pp. 236–252). Newark, DE: International Reading Association.

Bissex, G. L. (1980). *GNYS AT WRK: A child learns to read and write.* Cambridge, MA: Harvard University Press.

Briggs, C., & Elkind, D. (1977). Characteristics of early readers. *Perceptual and Motor Skills, 44,* 1231–1237.

Burns, S., Griffin, P., & Snow, C. E. (1999). *Starting out right: A guide to promoting children's reading success.* Washington, DC: National Academy Press.

Cambourne, B. (1988). *The whole story: Natural learning and the acquistion of literacy in the classroom.* Auckland, NZ: Ashton Scholastic.

Cambourne, B. (2002). Holistic, integrated approaches to reading and language arts instruction: The constructivist framework of an instructional theory. In A. E. Farstrup, & S. Samuels (Eds.), *What research has to say about reading instruction* (pp. 25–47). Newark, DE: International Reading Association.

Clark, M. (1976). *Young fluent readers: What can they teach us?* Exeter, NH: Heinemann.

Clay, M. M. (1975). *What did I write? Beginning writing behavior.* Exeter, NH: Heinemann.

Clay, M. M. (1991). *Becoming literate: The construction of inner control.* Portsmouth, NH: Heinemann.

Clay, M. M. (1992). Introducing a new storybook to young readers. *The Reading Teacher, 45,* 264–273.

Doake, D. B. (1985). Reading-like behavior: Its role in learning to read. In A. Jagger & M. T. Burke-Smith (Eds.), *Observing the language learner* (pp. 82–98). Newark, DE: International Reading Association.

Durkin, D. (1966). *Children who read early: Two longitudinal studies.* New York: Teachers College Press.

Dyson, A. H. (1982). Reading, writing, and language: Young children solving the written language puzzle. *Language Arts, 59,* 829–839.

Dyson, A. H. (1984). Learning to write/learning to do school: Emergent writers' Interpretations of school literacy tasks. *Research in the Teaching of English, 18,* 233–264.

Goodman, Y. M. (1986). Children coming to know literacy. In W. H. Teale & E. Sulzby (Eds.), *Emergent literacy: Writing and reading.* Norwood, NJ: Ablex.

Halliday, M. A. K. (1973). *Explorations in the function of language.* London: Edward Arnold.

Hancock, M. R. (2004). *A celebration of literature and response: Children, books, and teachers in K–8 classrooms* (2nd ed.). Upper Saddle River, NJ: Merrill/Prentice Hall.

Harste, J. C., Woodward, V. A., & Burke, C. L. (1984). *Language stories and literacy lessons.* Portsmouth, NH: Heinemann.

Hiebert, E. (1981). Developmental patterns and interrelationships of pre-school children's point awareness. *Reading Research Quarterly, 16,* 236–260.

Holdaway, D. (1979). *Foundations of literacy.* Sydney, Australia: Ashton Scholastic.

Huey, E. B. (1908). *The psychology and pedagogy of reading.* New York: Macmillan.

Martens, P. (1996). *I already know how to read: A child's view of literacy.* Portsmouth, NH: Heinemann.

Martin, Bill, Jr. (In collaboration with Peggy Bronan) (1972). *The Sounds of Home* (*Sounds of Language* Series). New York: Holt.

McGee, L. M., & Richgels, D. J. (2000). *Literacy's beginnings: Supporting young readers and writers* (3rd ed.). Boston: Allyn & Bacon.

Morrow, L. M. (1993). *Literacy development in the early years: Helping children read and write* (3rd ed.). Boston: Allyn & Bacon.

Purcell-Gates, V. (1996). Stories, coupons, and the "TV Guide": Relationships between home literacy experiences and emergent literacy knowledge. *Reading Research Quarterly, 31,* 406–428.

Ruddell, R. B., & Ruddell, M. R. (1994). Language acquisition and the literacy processes. In R. B. Ruddell, M. R. Ruddell, & H. Singer (Eds.), *Theoretical models and processes of reading* (4th ed., pp. 83–103). Newark, DE: International Reading Association.

Snow, C. E., Burns, M. S., & Griffin, P. (Eds.) (1998). *Preventing reading difficulties in young children.* Washington, DC: National Academy Press.

Snow, C. E., & Tabors, P. O. (1993). Language skills that relate to literacy development. In B. Spodek, & O. N. Saracho (Eds.), *Language and literacy in early childhood education* (pp. 1–20). New York: Teachers College Press.

Snow, C. E., & Tabors, P. O. (1996). Intergenerational transfer of literacy. In L. A. Benjamin & J. Lord (Eds.), *Family literacy: Directions in research and implications for practice.* Washington, DC: Office of Educational Research and Improvement, U.S. Department of Education.

Spiegel, D. L. (1994). A portrait of parents of successful readers. In E. H. Cramer & M. Castle (Eds.), *Fostering the love of reading: The affective domain in reading education.* Newark, DE: International Reading Association.

Stickland, D., & Morrow, L. M. (Eds.) (1989). *Emerging literacy: Young children learn to read and write.* Newark, DE: International Reading Association.

Sulzby, E. (1985). Children's emergent reading of favorite storybooks: A developmental study. *Reading Research Quarterly, 20,* 458–481.

Sulzby, E., Barnhart, J., & Hieshima, J. (1989). Forms of writing and rereading from writing: A preliminary report. In J. Mason (Ed.), *Reading and writing connections* (pp. 31–63). Needham Heights, MA: Allyn & Bacon.

Taylor, D., & Dorsey-Gaines, C. (1988). *Growing up literate: Learning from inner-city families.* Portsmouth, NH: Heinemann.

Teale, W. H. (1978). Positive environments for learning to read: What studies of early readers tell us. *Language Arts, 55,* 922–932.

Teale, W. H. (1986). Home background and young children's literacy development. In W. H. Teale & E. Sulzby (Eds.), *Emergent literacy: Writing and reading* (pp. 158–188). Norwood, NJ: Ablex.

Teale, W. H., & Sulzby, E. (1986). *Emergent literacy: Writing and reading.* Norwood, NJ: Ablex.

Temple, C., Nathan, R., Burris, N., & Temple, F. (1993). *The beginnings of writing* (3rd ed.). Boston: Allyn & Bacon.

Children's Books Cited

Beneduce, Ann Keay (Reteller) (2000). *Philipok.* Retold from Leo Tolstoy. Illus. by Gennady Spirin. New York: Philomel.

Brown, Margaret Wise (1947). *Goodnight moon.* Illus. by Clement Hurd. New York: Harper & Row.

Carle, Eric (1968). *The very hungry caterpillar.* New York: Philomel.

Crowther, Robert (2001). *Colors.* Cambridge, MA: Candlewick.

Ehlert, Lois (1989). *Color zoo.* New York: Lippincott.

Fleming, Denise (1992). *Count!* New York: Holt.

Geisert, Arnold (1992). *Pigs from 1 to 10.* Boston: Houghton Mifflin.

Hoban, Tana (1986). *Shapes, shapes, shapes.* New York: Greenwillow.

Kunhardt, Dorothy (1940). *Pat the bunny.* Racine, WI: Western Publishing.

Martin, Bill, Jr. (1983). *Brown bear, brown bear, what do you see?* Illus. by Eric Carle. New York: Holt.

Martin, Bill, Jr., & Archambault, John (1989). *Chicka chicka boom boom.* Illus. by Lois Ehlert. New York: Simon & Schuster.

McCully, Emily Arnold (1984). *Picnic.* New York: Harper & Row.

McCully, Emily Arnold (1985). *First snow.* New York: Harper & Row.

Opie, Iona (Ed.) (1996). *My very first Mother Goose.* Illus. by Rosemary Wells. Cambridge, MA: Candlewick Press.

Opie, Iona (Ed.) (1999). *Here comes Mother Goose.* Illus. by Rosemary Wells. Cambridge, MA: Candlewick Press.

Wells, Rosemary (1985). *Max's birthday.* New York: Dial.

Zelinsky, Paul O. (1990). *The wheels on the bus.* New York: Dutton.

Chapter 5

EMBARKING ON THE JOURNEY TOWARD LITERACY (GRADES K–2)

The Literacy Apprenticeship

You can be most anything
in dreams or wide awake
If you agree that juice is tea . . .
If you believe that mud is cake.
FROM *MUD IS CAKE* BY PAM MUÑOZ RYAN

At the 19th World Congress on Reading of the International Reading Association in Edinburgh, Scotland, Margaret Meek Spencer (2002), keynote speaker and literacy icon, read aloud *Mud Is Cake* by Pam Muñoz Ryan to illustrate the conference theme: "Imagination is at the heart of learning to read." Her premise focused on the fact that imagination has "the capacity to enrich thinking" and that "imagination is the ultimate freedom as it helps us see how things could be otherwise."

Mud Is Cake encourages you to think back to your childhood and those magical moments built on your imagination. Performing on the front porch to an imaginary audience, selling shoes from a sofa shoe store, digging a hole to China, or using juice cans and string to communicate across the next door neighbor's yard—all these incidents nurture our imaginations as future readers and writers. At the heart and soul of literacy is a child who dreams, who visualizes, who pretends, and who brings those experiences to the art of reading and writing.

ne of the most exciting moments for children is the first day of school. Bright-eyed, crisply dressed boys and girls beam with confidence as they dream of learning to read and write. Filled with this natural curiosity and energy for learning, children embark on the journey toward literacy. For some, it will be an easy journey filled with personal fulfillment, unlocked doors, and inviting opportunities. For others, it will be a slower journey filled with eternal optimism, belief in oneself, and staunch determination to succeed. Unfortunately, for a few children, the road toward literacy may be strewn with challenges, frustrations, and bitter complexities. The teacher of literacy greets *all* of these children at the classroom door on the first day of school, playing a critical role in planning appropriate instruction, maintaining motivation, and nurturing the seed of belief that *all* children will become readers and writers. The challenging task of a caring, knowledgeable teacher of young children is to make the dream of literacy a possibility.

Recapturing, encouraging, and retaining the "imagination" of children should be the ultimate goal of early literacy instruction, both in reading and writing. Although the challenge of addressing the needs of diverse learners requires a balance of teaching methodologies, teachers should not lose sight of the role of imagination as the pulse of literacy achievement. Rather than being drenched by the dearth of expectations for teachers of early readers, primary teachers should be energized and build on the natural enticement that reading and writing present to children. Master teachers serving as guides in a literacy apprenticeship (Dorn, French, & Jones, 1998) model the step-by-step, developmental aspects of emergent literacy that gradually and confidently lead children toward future success as readers and writers. Although the balanced approach to literacy requires some direct instruction, teachers should never forget that *enjoyment* of literacy is the motivation for its continued development, growth, and maintenance during lifelong literacy.

Overall, this chapter defines balanced literacy at the primary level through several different lenses. Literature study encompasses a study of shared reading, interactive storybook reading, read-alouds, and reader response to literature. The five building blocks of reading (National Reading Panel, 2000) provide a framework for teachers to explore methods and strategies of phonemic awareness, phonics, fluency, vocabulary, and comprehension. Guided reading and guided writing provide teachers with numerous reading and writing strategies to be taught within authentic contexts of leveled texts and meaningful writing situations. Independent reading and writing encourage ongoing practice providing effective application of strategies in the context of personal reading and writing. All of these lenses combine to provide a broad perspective on teaching reading and writing in the primary grades with a child-centered, strategies-based, and literature-focused foundation.

Objectives

- To understand the benefits of all aspects of a balanced language arts program in motivating children in their early journey toward literacy.
- To support the use of literature study as a gateway into the realm of literacy and language arts.
- To apply the findings of the National Reading Panel through explicit instruction of phonemic awareness, phonics, vocabulary, fluency, and comprehension in the early stages of literacy development.
- To envision a guided reading lesson as it serves the apprenticeship goal of modeling strategy development within the context of authentic literature.
- To envision a guided writing lesson as it moves novice writers from oral language to printed text through teacher modeling and interactive involvement in early writing.
- To understand the need for time for independent reading and writing as practice builds confidence, word knowledge, sense of story, and comprehension.
- To appreciate the expertise of an early literacy professional who serves as a model and guide in a literacy apprenticeship that moves learners toward independence in reading and writing.

A Balanced Language Arts Program

Teacher Prep

The Teacher Prep Web site will help you become a better teacher by linking you to classroom videos, student artifacts, teaching strategies, lesson plans, relevant education leadership articles, and practical information on licensing, creating a portfolio, implementing standards, and being successful in field experiences. Visit this resource at www.prenhall.com/teacherprep.

As primary teachers plan and prepare the literacy journey for their students, they may choose from a variety of published programs, a wide range of materials, assorted self-selected activities, and tried-and-true learning experiences. There is no magical formula that turns all children into readers and writers. A balanced approach to teaching reading arises from a philosophical perspective, a set of beliefs about what children should know about reading, who has the knowledge, and how the different kinds of knowledge can be learned (Fitzgerald, 1999). Balanced literacy does not imply a single approach, a right or wrong way, or the single manifestation of a particular approach. Aspects of literacy that must be included as ingredients in a balanced literacy program include comprehension, skills and strategies, and the enjoyment of reading. What the teacher does to plan, set up, and conduct the program is paramount. Balancing these components within a literacy program assists in providing sound, well-rounded instruction for the primary student (Blair-Larsen & Williams, 1999). Children's active engagement and processing as apprentices in reading and writing supports the goal of gradually taking over the learning process while discovering new things both under the guidance of the teacher and ultimately through independent work (Askew & Fountas, 1998).

Consider the following philosophical aspects of a balanced language approach in the primary grades:

- ***Reading to children.*** Reading aloud to children each day is an essential prerequisite of an effective literacy program. Reading across genres, styles of writing, and topics of interest assists in building background knowledge, a framework for story structure, and an appreciation for the language of literature.
- ***Writing to children.*** The teacher who writes daily for or to students is demonstrating that writing serves a functional purpose. Recording the class schedule,

creating a morning message, and writing about classroom procedures help children see why we learn to read and write.

- ***Reading with children.*** Shared reading and guided reading provide the opportunity to model reading while teaching reading strategies. Shared reading with big books includes pointing to words, revisiting text, joining in repeated phrases, making predictions, and talking about books. Guided reading with a small group matches text with the abilities of readers while children practice the reading skills and strategies they have learned.
- ***Writing with children.*** Writing with children is a process of shared or interactive writing. Writing ideas or messages on chart paper as the teacher thinks aloud both models and guides students through the composing process. As students join in, the teacher continues to ask questions to clarify the intended message, the audience, and the purpose. Children are invited to share the pen and write whatever they can.
- ***Reading by children.*** Time for independent, self-selected reading and rereading of texts provides essential daily practice of authentic reading. Reading literature or "reading the room" (charts, poems, messages, songs, student-written stories) provide materials for an established, scheduled independent reading time each day.
- ***Writing by children.*** Writing independently each day within a predictable structure and routine provides time to become a writer. Students have choices about what to write, and share that writing through conferences and the author's chair. Direct instruction of a writing skill or strategy often begins each session. Students are encouraged to experiment with journals, stories, news, letters, and a variety of forms across the curriculum.

As you consider the gradual release of the language arts to children, you can sense the shift through modeling by the teacher, guided practice alongside the literacy apprentices, and eventual independent incorporation of the language arts in the daily literacy repertoire of the classroom. Teacher modeling, learner hand-holding, and the ultimate release of responsibility to the child characterizes the language arts apprenticeship model of early literacy development.

Literature Study

A balanced literacy approach begins by building on the strengths of the lap-reading experience in the home environment. All children come to school believing that they can be readers. The big book/shared reading experience reinforces a personal desire and belief in potential literacy success in the emergent reader. Teacher read-alouds continue the immersion in literature to which children can respond through their observations, feelings, and connections to their own lives. Reading aloud across genres of literature reinforces the innate desire to want to read independently. The teacher's expressive voice models the language of literature, creates a sense of story across genres, and invites the child into the enjoyable world of reading.

Shared Reading

One of the first steps children take on the path to literacy is to participate in a shared reading experience, even on the first day of school. In shared reading, the teacher reads with the children from a big book—an enlarged copy of authentic literature—and the children actively contribute to the reading with the teacher's guidance by pointing to the text and encouraging predictions along the journey. Shared reading enables the child to begin reading successfully from predictable text from early in the school year. Nonthreatening and enjoyable, shared reading strengthens the language skills of even struggling readers. Reading a familiar text over and over builds the literacy skills needed to become a reader. Shared reading activities provide the practice needed for young learners who will soon be announcing to all that they can read.

The shared book experience (Holdaway, 1979; Slaughter, 1993) incorporates the use of big books to replicate the lap-reading experience of the home literacy environment. Imagine a copy of *I Went Walking* by Sue Williams in a 24″ × 30″ format. The exact words from the text and the precise illustrations from the book are enlarged so all children can see both words and illustrations as part of the reading experience. Enlarged texts offer teachers opportunities to help children develop concepts about print and understanding about the reading process (Strickland, 1988).

Before Reading. The teacher begins the lesson by explaining the concept of author, illustrator, and title, and reads the title of the book to the children. After discussing the background of the story, the teacher asks the children to predict what the book might be about. The children participate by talking and listening as the teacher directs the discussion. They begin to note the meaning of the words on the book cover.

During Reading. As the primary reader on the first read through, the teacher exhibits anticipation and eagerness toward reading. Delight in both language and story are evident as children pick up on the excitement of reading. As the teacher tracks the print with a hand or a pointer, children begin to see the connection between the teacher's voice and the printed word as print carries meaning. As the child follows the movement of the hand or pointer, the directionality of reading (left to right) is modeled as speech is matched to print. Throughout the reading, the teacher stops periodically to think aloud about understanding the story, making further predictions, or drawing conclusions. At appropriate parts, the teacher even asks children what might happen next. The read-aloud voice of the teacher hesitates at predictable parts of the text as children begin to fill in possible repeated words or phrases.

After Reading. As the teacher guides a brief discussion, children realize that reflecting on and personalizing a text is part of the reading process. As children recall parts of the text, they use print to confirm their thoughts. Children are then invited to a rereading of the book and asked to join in the reading at parts in which they feel confident. Along with confidence comes beginning reading fluency. The teacher might even cover words with adhesive notes or flaps to encourage word or phrase predictions. Children use both memory and semantic (meaning) and syntactic (order) clues to fill in the words.

Repeated Readings. On repeated readings in the coming days, the teacher focuses on repeated words, beginning patterns, and even punctuation marks, always using proper terminology to discuss these features of print. For example, the teacher revisits the text to note capital letters that distinguish character names or to recognize the repeated phrases that arise during predictable sections of the text. Children begin to internalize the features of print and develop an initial understanding of decoding within the meaningful context of a story. Finally, the teacher makes the big book and "little book" paperback copies of the big book available for independent practice and reading. Children begin to read at their own pace, increase their confidence with print, and begin to understand the reading process by practicing it independently. Gradually, the children celebrate and take the paperback versions of the books home to show their parents that they can read.

Although the big book shared reading experience seems simple, there is a wide range of reading concepts that are explored with such books:

- Book conventions (author, illustrator, title)
- Directionality (left-to-right, top-to-bottom)
- One-to-one matching of printed text to spoken word
- Locating known words and letters
- Beginning letter/sound correspondence
- Predicting and cross-checking predictions
- Rereading favorite books

These concepts align with specific tasks of a scope-and-sequenced early literacy curriculum as well. While repeated reading is the key to reading confidence, teachers should not underestimate the power of this early reading modeling to motivate children to believe in themselves as readers. They can use pointers, framing cards, post-its, and sentence strips to assist in their students "learning to read."

Besides authentic literature made into a big book format, several other reading materials may be utilized with the shared reading experience. Poems on chart paper or transparencies, nursery rhyme charts, favorite songs, finger plays, and class-composed language experience stories also become text for shared reading. With a small group, a trade book in picture book format becomes the source of an interactive reading session.

Beyond the pages of a big book lies a technological version of this type of learning experience shown in Lesson Plan 5.1. Children may access the *Beyond the Lions* website, read an online story, or read a printed version that is their own to keep. The value of repeated readings in an electronic form resides in the repetitive exposure to the same text in varied formats.

LESSON PLAN 5.1

TITLE: **Repeated Reading**

Grade Level: K–2

Time Frame: Two 30-minute sessions (Day 1: introduction of literature; Day 2: responding to literature)

Standards

IRA/NCTE Standards: 1, 12

NETS for Students: 1, 3

Objectives

- Students will read and reread texts to gain fluency in oral reading.

Materials

- Printed copy of a *Between the Lions* story for each student (available from http://pbskids.org/lions)
- Selection of *Between the Lions* trade books (Golden Books)

- Computer, projector, Internet access, large screen
- Teacher-created model of response to literature

Technology

- Students use a variety of media and technology resources for directed and independent learning activities.

Motivation

- Using a projector, screen, and computer, introduce the *Between the Lions* Web site (http://pbskids.org/lions) to the class. Discuss the features of this site.
- Read one of the online stories to the class. Click on hyperlinked vocabulary words. Discuss.

Procedures

Day 1

- Explain to students that the *Between the Lions* stories come in many different formats. They can watch the stories on television, read the online stories, read a book (hold up a book from your selection), or read a printed version that is their very own to keep (hold up a printed story).
- Distribute copies to students. Choral read as a class a few times. Discuss vocabulary and emphasize fluency. Students may continue to practice in smaller groups or with a partner.
- Send books home to read to family members for further fluency practice.

Day 2

- As a class, discuss the experience of sharing the book with family members at home.
- Discuss how students felt about the story: How did the story make you feel? What was your favorite part? What did the story make you think of?
- Using the teacher model, instruct students to write and illustrate a response to the story (based on any of the above questions).
- While students are writing, listen to individual students reread the story and assess them for fluency.
- When finished, ask students to share their responses from the author's chair.

Assessment

- Teacher assesses fluency by listening to students read individually.
- Teacher looks for evidence of comprehension and/or personal meaning making in students' written and illustrated responses.

Accommodation/Modification

- The levels of the stories presented on the *Between the Lions* Web site vary greatly. Select stories suitable for each child's reading level.
- For English language learners, translate the *Between the Lions* Web site (including printable stories) by using Google Language Tools (as explained in Chapter 3).

Visit the Meeting the Standards module in Chapter 5 of the Companion Website at www.prenhall.com/hancock to adapt this lesson to meet your state's standards.

Interactive Storybook Reading

All children, but especially those who enter school with limited storybook reading experience, benefit from interactive storybook reading (Klesius & Griffith, 1996). Intended to build language and literacy understanding with young children, interactive read-alouds also encourage oral responses to literature. As teachers read stories interactively, they encourage children to interact orally with texts, their peers, and the teacher during, rather than following, the read-aloud. During interactive reading, teachers pose questions that lead readers to make sense of the text while eliciting aesthetic, personal responses (Koblitz, 2002).

The process of using ongoing conversation during a read-aloud without distracting from the story is more challenging than it may appear. Barrentine (1996) has suggested the following steps when planning an interactive read-aloud:

- Select a high-interest picture book with rich language, absorbing plots, lively characters, and multiple layers of meaning.
- Read the book several times to yourself.
- Think about the type of read-aloud and plan goals for the listeners.
- Identify those places where children should predict, join in, discuss, reflect, or connect.
- Anticipate if or where you may need to build students' background knowledge.
- Think through how you might invite children to participate in the read-aloud.
- Be prepared to allow for spontaneous response by maintaining flexibility in your reading style.
- After reading, plan a means for children to revisit the story by reading it a second time or through an invitation to connect in a personal way.

Karma Wilson's *Bear Snores On,* well-suited for a light-hearted interactive read-aloud, is a story in rhyme, a predictable book, and an adventure into hibernation. The bright, spirited illustrations by Jane Chapman assist in inviting children into the story. The predictability of the story and the repetition of phrases guide the interactive framework of the read-aloud. The story begins: "In a cave in the woods, in a deep dark lair, / through the long, cold winter / sleeps a great brown bear . . . The cold winds howl / and the night sounds growl / But the bear snores on. . . ." The pattern set by the text quickly allows children to note the various types of animals and the repeated phrase "But the bear snores on. . . ." Teacher prompts can help students predict the next animals to attempt to wake up Bear. Children can join in on well-chosen alliterative language ("Chew—Chomp—Crunch") and on the repeated phrase that marks the turning of the page. Small groups can take time to count the forest inhabitants featured on each page. Words and phrases describing the wintry cave (*blustery, dank*) can be discussed for vocabulary building. Predicting the ending means listening to the text and observing the illustrations for clues to the book's conclusion.

Not every read-aloud justifies an interactive approach, but the ideal one will consistently engage students in response throughout the process rather than limiting response to that of a retrospective nature (Hancock, 2004). The Literature Cluster on page 130 provides a list of classic and contemporary picture books of an interactive nature. Categorized by their unique quality (e.g., pattern, love of language, text-to-life connection), these books will assist the teacher in choosing a stance for planning the read-aloud.

Beyond the library shelf exists a wealth of Web sites featuring interactive storybooks. The Tech Tip included here shares three quality sites that motivate and engage the early literacy learner with visual representation, listening, and reading. Access these sites to discover the contribution of technology to emergent literacy while participating in an interactive storybook experience.

Literature Cluster
INTERACTIVE READ-ALOUD PICTURE BOOKS

Axtell, David (1999). *We're going on a lion hunt.* New York: Holt.

Aylesworth, Jim (1994). *My son John.* Illus. by David Frampton. New York: Holt.

Brown, Margaret Wise (2002). *My world of color,* Illus. by Loretta Krupinski. New York: Hyperion.

Charlip, Remy (1964). *Fortunately.* New York: Parents Magazine Press.

Falwell, Cathryn (1998). *Word wizard.* New York: Clarion.

Fleming, Denise (1993). *In the small, small pond.* New York: Holt.

Gag, Wanda (1929). *Millions of cats.* New York: Coward-McCann.

Martin, Bill, Jr. (1999). *A beasty story.* Illus. by Steven Kellogg. San Diego: Harcourt Brace.

Rockwell, Anne (1999). *Bumblebee, bumblebee, do you know me?* New York: HarperCollins.

Root, Phyllis (2001). *Rattletrap car.* Illus. by Jill Barton. Cambridge, MA: Candlewick.

Taback, Simms (1999). *Joseph had a little overcoat.* New York: Viking.

Van Laan, Nancy (1998). *Little fish, lost.* Illus. by Jane Conteh-Morgan. New York: Atheneum.

Van Laan, Nancy (1998). *So say the little monkeys.* Illus. by Yami Heo. New York: Atheneum.

Waite, Judy (1998). *Mouse, look out!* Illus. by Norma Burgin. New York: Dutton.

Williams, Sue (1990). *I went walking.* Illus. by Julie Vivas. San Diego: Harcourt Brace.

Williams, Sue (1998). *Let's go visiting.* Illus. by Julie Vivas. San Diego: Harcourt Brace.

Yolen, Jane (2000). *Off we go!* Illus. by Laurel Molk. New York: Little, Brown.

Reading Aloud and Reader Response

Beyond the shared book experience, the balanced reading approach supports the reading aloud of quality literature by a teacher serving as a reading model who then invites children to spontaneously talk about the literature that has been read aloud. Inviting children as listeners to share thoughts, feelings, and connections in response to read-aloud literature prepares them for the personal interactions they will experience as they eventually read literature in groups or independently.

Many teachers of young children assume that talking about books in a whole class or small group format is beyond the scope of primary-level students. Although adjustments must be made for developmental levels and reading capabilities in the lower primary grades, the task of exploring meaning and engaging in conversations about literature are still paramount. Although a facilitator (e.g., parent, intern, upper-grade student) is necessary if using small groups of young children, the teacher can momentarily step back and allow personal thoughts to provide the script for a literature conversation.

An important facet of primary-level literature conversations is book selection. Because most kindergarten and first-grade students cannot read substantive picture books on their own, the literature conversation typically begins with a teacher read-aloud. The book selected should meet the following criteria:

- Well-crafted story with a meaningful theme
- Sufficient depth to elicit discussion
- Inclusion of memorable language
- Diverse characters in real-world situations

Web Sites for Early Readers

PBS Between the Lions is an outstanding Companion Website to the popular television series. Intended as a way for parents or teachers and their kids to surf together, the site contains a myriad of interactive games, printable coloring sheets, video clips, and a 200-word illustrated speaking glossary. Children can enjoy over 70 interactive online stories, each including a printable version, as well as templates for creating their own storybooks and bookmarks. **http://pbskids.org/lions/**

The *Starfall* learn-to-read Web site is a free service where children have fun while learning to read. Designed primarily with first graders in mind, Starfall contains talking storybooks, interactive games, systematic phonics instruction, and a variety of activities designed to support beginning readers of all levels. This exceptional site is sure to inspire a love of reading and writing. **http://www.starfall.com/**

Clifford Interactive Storybooks (Scholastic) offers phonics fun for beginning readers. In addition to interactive Clifford stories, the free site offers many types of learning games. Links to additional Clifford reading and writing activities are readily available. **http://teacher.scholastic.com/clifford1/**

To look more closely at these materials and others related to "Embarking on the Journey Toward Literacy (Grades K–2)," visit the Companion Website at www.prenhall.com/hancock.

The book should be read at least two times so the children can absorb its content and establish a personal response. With repeated readings, many children will even be able to read the book independently by the day of the scheduled conversation. Some children may want to draw their artistic response to the book or bookmark a favorite part with an adhesive note in preparation for their small group discussion. The Literature Cluster on page 132 presents an age-appropriate list of picture books and transitional chapter books that provide substantive themes for thoughtful response.

The importance of rereading or revisiting old favorites for literature conversations with young children cannot be stressed enough. Understandings are difficult to articulate on a first reading and multiple readings improve the quality of the conversation. A "whole class" literature conversation can serve as a model and conceptual foundation before moving to small groups. Three generic but powerful literature response prompts should be continuously presented across several months of the school year.

- What did you notice in the story?
- How did the story make you feel?
- How does the story relate to your own life?

With repeated exposure to these prompts, the length, depth, and detail of children's oral responses show growth (Kelly, 1990). Over time, children internalize the focus of these predictable prompts, thus preparing themselves to respond to them following each read-aloud. This whole class approach then builds toward small group literature conversations.

Literature Cluster

READ-ALOUDS FOR THOUGHTFUL RESPONSE

Picture Books

Arnold, Marsha Diane (2000). *The bravest of us all.* Illus. by Brad Sneed. New York: Dial.

Bradby, Marie (2000). *Momma, where are you from?* Illus. by Chris K. Soentpiet. New York: Orchard.

Bunting, Eve (1991). *Fly away home.* Illus. by R. Himler. Boston: Clarion.

Bunting, Eve (1994). *Smoky night* Illus. by David Diaz. San Diego: Harcourt Brace.

Bunting, Eve (1996). *Train to somewhere.* San Diego: Harcourt Brace.

Curtis, Gavin (1998). *The bat boy and his violin.* Illus. by E. B. Lewis. New York: Simon & Schuster.

Fox, Mem (1985). *Wilfred Gordon McDonald Partridge.* Illus. by Julie Vivas. La Jolla, CA: Kane Miller.

Grimes, Nikki (2002). *Talkin' about Bessie: The story of aviator Elizabeth Coleman.* Illus. by E. B. Lewis. New York: Orchard.

Henkes, Kevin (2000). *Wemberly worried.* New York: Greenwillow.

Howe, James (1999). *Horace and Morris but mostly Dolores.* Illus. by Amy Walrod. New York: Atheneum.

Howard, Elizabeth Fitzgerald (2000). *Virgie goes to school with us boys.* Illus. by E. B. Lewis. New York: Simon & Schuster.

LaMarche, Jim (2000). *The raft.* New York: HarperCollins.

MacLachlan, Patricia (1994). *All the places to love.* Illus. by M. Wimmer. New York: HarperCollins.

McCully, Emily Arnold (1992). *Mirette on the high wire.* New York: Putnam.

McKissack, Patricia (2000). *The honest to goodness truth.* Illus. by Giselle Potter. New York: Atheneum.

Mochizuki, Ken (1997). *Passage to freedom: The Sugihara story.* Illus. by Dom Lee. New York: Lee & Low Books.

Napoli, Donna Jo (2001). *Albert.* Illus. by Jim LaMarche. San Diego: Harcourt Brace.

Nivola, Claire A. (2002). *The forest.* New York: Farrar, Straus and Giroux.

Polacco, Patricia (2000). *The butterfly.* New York: Philomel.

Polacco, Patricia (2001). *Mr. Lincoln's way.* New York: Philomel.

Rappaport, Doreen (2001). *Martin's big words: The life of Dr. Martin Luther King, Jr.* Illus. by Bryan Collier. New York: Hyperion.

Say, Allen (1993). *Grandfather's journey.* Boston: Houghton Mifflin.

Stewart, Sarah (2001). *The journey.* Illus. by David Small. New York: Farrar, Straus and Giroux.

Turner, Ann (1997). *Mississippi mud: Three prairie journals.* Illus. by Robert Blake. New York: HarperCollins.

Turner, Ann (2001). *Abe Lincoln remembers.* Illus. by Wendell Minor New York: HarperCollins.

Woodson, Jacqueline (2001). *The other side.* Illus. by E. B. Lewis. New York: Putnam.

Yangsook, Choi (2001). *The name jar.* New York: Knopf.

Transitional Chapter Books

Gardiner, John (1980). *Stone fox.* New York: HarperCollins.

Haas, Jessie (2001). *Runaway radish.* Illus. by Margot Apple. New York: Greenwillow.

Hesse, Karen (1994). *Sable.* Illus. by Marcia Sewall. New York: Holt.

Hesse, Karen (1999). *Just juice.* Illus. by Robert Andrew Parker. New York: Scholastic.

MacLachlan, Patricia (1985). *Sarah, plain and tall.* New York: HarperCollins.

MacLachlan, Patricia (2001). *Caleb's story.* New York: HarperCollins.

Wells, Rosemary (1998). *Mary on horseback: Three mountain stories.* New York: Dial.

Wells, Rosemary (2002). *Wingwalker.* Illus. by Brian Selznick. New York: Hyperion.

The optimal size for a primary-level literature conversation seems to be four children. With short attention spans but a strong desire to talk, young children in small groups can begin conversations by talking about favorite parts of the book and relating the story to experiences from their own lives. From there they move on to articulation and elaboration of their own drawings in response to the story. A teacher, student intern, or adult facilitator is necessary to assist young conversationalists in focusing on specific issues and building the framework of the decision.

What kinds of responses can teachers expect young children to produce when encouraged to share personal thoughts without the use of prompts? Wollman-Bonilla and Werchaldo (1995) and Dekker (1991) provide response data on which to build a possible framework to assist in anticipating oral response potential with young children:

- Text-Centered Responses (What is happening in the book?)

  Retelling; recounting story events.

  Understanding characters; expressing understanding of character thoughts and feelings, either stated or implied in the text.

  Questioning; expressing curiosity about plot or character actions and vocalizing questions about the book itself or ideas it explored.

  Predicting; speculating on plot or character actions.

- Reader-Centered Responses (What is happening inside the reader?)

  Personally reacting; expressing one's own feelings about the text.

  Relating to experience; relating text to events or people in one's own life.

  Putting self in story; expressing sense of being or desire to participate in the story.

  Evaluating story/characters; telling what they liked or disliked about the book/characters, often with specific examples from the text.

Teachers should not be limited by these oral response possibilities. Knowledge of potential types of response can help children articulate richer and more varied responses. These text-centered and reader-centered categories serve as a catalyst for teachers who value talk about books. Building an awareness of response potential is a way to begin and to set expectations for themselves in facilitating quality literature conversations.

With significant modeling and the selection of appropriate titles to discuss, young children can succeed in talking about literature in a small group format. Literature-based teachers report the success of literature conversations in their primary classrooms (Roller & Beed, 1994; Schlick-Noe, 1995) and strongly encourage their peers to venture into this oral response realm with children. Making talk about literature a natural by-product of reading sets a future reader's focus on meaning-making as comprehension becomes the main focus of reading a book.

While shared reading builds reader confidence, reading aloud and reader response prompts showcase personal interactions with literature. Both literature study activities provide adult models for reading, focus on the importance of reading comprehension, create a means of expressing reactions to reading, and build self-esteem and belief in oneself as a reader. Combined with other aspects of a balanced reading approach, children confidently and competently begin their journey toward literacy.

The Five Building Blocks of Reading

Identifying and learning more about the building blocks of reading has gained recent attention in the literacy arena. Beyond the importance of the desire to become a reader lie the tools of reading that enable emergent readers to reach their goals. The National Reading

Panel (2000) issued a report that responded to a congressional mandate to help parents, teachers, and policymakers identify key skills and methods essential to reading achievement. Based on scientifically based research, the panel focused on five areas essential for reading instruction:

- Phonemic awareness
- Phonics
- Fluency
- Vocabulary
- Comprehension

This section provides a brief overview of these five building blocks while focusing on these areas for well-planned, explicit instruction. While these areas may be taught through isolated practice, they ultimately blend into an instructional program that uses them as building blocks in the complex process of reading authentic texts.

Additional information and implications for teaching may be accessed through the publication, *Put Reading First: The Research Building Blocks for Teaching Children to Read* (Armbruster & Osborn, 2001). This booklet is recommended as an additional source for learning more about these key areas for reading instruction. The publication can be downloaded at the National Institute for Literacy Web site at www.nifl.gov.

What then are these key areas that some readers need to break the code and move toward independence in reading? As you read about each of these five identified areas for instruction, be sure you understand their role as part of a balanced approach to reading.

Phonemic Awareness

Phonemic awareness is the understanding that the sounds of spoken language work together to make words. It involves the ability of a child to hear, identify, and manipulate individual sounds in spoken words. Phonemic awareness instruction may help most children learn to read and learn to spell, but is *not* a complete early literacy program. In fact, an entire phonemic program should take no more than 20 hours over an entire school year. Phonemic awareness is typically presented in an early literacy program for preschoolers, kindergartners, or first graders who are first learning to read, and older, less able readers.

Teachers may incorporate phonemic awareness activities as follows:

- Recognizing individual sounds in a word (phoneme isolation—e.g., *pan* = */p/*)
- Recognizing the same sound in different words (phoneme identity, e.g., *mix, mall, mop, /m/*)
- Recognizing a word in a set of three similar words (phoneme categorization—e.g., *bus, bun, rug*)
- Combining phonemes to form a word (phoneme blending—e.g., */b/ /i/ /g/* = *big*)
- Breaking a word into separate sounds (phoneme segmentation—e.g., How many sounds are in *crab*? */c/ /r/ /a/ /b/*. Write *crab*)
- Recognizing a word when a phoneme is removed from a word (phoneme deletion—e.g., *smile* – */s/* = *mile*)
- Making a new word by adding a phoneme to a word (phoneme addition—e.g., add */s/* to *park* = *spark*)
- Substituting one phoneme for another to make a new word (phoneme substitution—e.g., change */b/* to */f/* in *bun* = *fun*)

The most effective reason for the explicit teaching of phonemic awareness lies in its future application not only in comprehension but also in learning to write and spell words. As an isolated reading skill, phonemic awareness does not ensure success as a reader or writer. Many teachers suggest the context of specific oral language activities (Ericson & Juliebo, 1998a; Yopp, 1992) and literature-based reading (Opitz, 1998a; Yopp, 1995) as vehicles for developing phonemic awareness in young children.

Phonics

Instruction in **phonics** teaches children the relationships between the letters of written language and the individual sounds of spoken language. Phonics may help children read and write words. Systematic phonics is the direct teaching of a set of letter-sound relationships in a clearly defined sequence. While systematic phonics instruction may improve word recognition, spelling, and reading comprehension, it is *not* an entire reading program for beginning readers. Approximately two years of phonics instruction (K–Grade 1 or Grades 1–2) is sufficient for most students (Stahl, 1992).

The goal of phonics is to help children learn the alphabetic principle—the fact that there are systematic and predictable relationships between written letters and spoken sounds. Knowing these relationships can help emerging readers "decode" new words. Perhaps the most effective outcome of direct phonics instruction is the application of embedded phonics in which children are taught letter-sound relationships during the reading of connected text (Dahl & Scharer, 2000). Application of knowledge of phonics as children read words, sentences, and texts is the ultimate outcome of this direct instruction.

All children, regardless of their reading program, learn about letter-sound correspondence as part of learning to read. Building on a valued literacy study of the early 1990s (Adams, 1990), Stahl (1992) suggested nine guidelines for teaching phonics meaningfully. Exemplary phonics instruction

- builds on a child's rich concepts about how print functions;
- builds on a foundation of phonemic awareness;
- is clear and direct;
- is integrated into a total reading program;
- focuses on reading words, not learning rules;
- may include onsets (part of a syllable before a vowel) and rimes (the part from the vowel onward);
- may include constructed spelling practice;
- develops independent word recognition strategies, focusing attention on the internal structure of words; and
- develops automatic word recognition skills so that students can devote their attention to comprehension, not words.

The word wall—an ongoing alphabetized list of frequently used words in the context of reading and writing that is displayed in a prominent place in the classroom—addresses practical, ongoing knowledge of sound-symbol correspondence (Wagstaff, 1997/1998; 1999). The application of alphabetic principles through early writing is evidenced as young writers consult the word wall during journal writing. The introduction of five words per week with an emphasis on the sounds, the letters, and the forms of words, assist in building a classroom resource for repeated exposure to phonetic words. Making words through the manipulation of letters and word families (Cunningham & Hall, 1994) and word solving strategies (Pinnell & Fountas, 1998) confirm the need to practice applying the phonetic principles in authentic reading and writing experiences.

Fluency

Fluency is the ability to read a text accurately and effortlessly with expression, providing an opportunity to focus on comprehension. Less fluent readers focus their attention on decoding individual words, thus giving little attention to comprehending the text. The fluency of readers will vary, depending on what they are reading, their familiarity with words, and the amount of practice in reading the text. Fluency develops gradually over time and through substantial practice. Even when young children recognize many words automatically, their reading may still lack expression.

Modeling fluent reading, practicing repeated reading of familiar text (Samuels, 1997), and monitoring oral reading may improve reading fluency, even in emergent readers. Studies have found a close relationship between fluency and comprehension (Rasinski, 2000; Richards, 2000). However, just because a child reads fluently does not necessarily mean comprehension is in place. Since fluency has been a neglected skill in many classrooms, its reintroduction into the balanced early literacy program provides a rationale for the use of repeated readings, with teacher or adult guidance and feedback. There are several ways emergent readers can practice orally rereading text:

- ***Student-adult reading.*** This one-on-one reading can assume the adult is the teacher, a parent, an aide, or a volunteer tutor. The adult provides a model of oral fluency and the student then reads the same passage with adult assistance and encouragement.
- ***Choral reading.*** Children read along in a group led by a teacher. Patterned or predictable books and poetry seem particularly well-suited to fluency practice.
- ***Tape-reading.*** As an audio tape of a book read by a fluent reader is played, the child follows along, pointing to each word. The child then reads aloud along with the reader. The goal is to have the child eventually read the book independently, without the tape.
- ***Partner reading.*** More fluent readers may be paired with less fluent ones as they take turns reading aloud to each other. Another option is for two readers of equal ability to practice rereading after hearing an adult read the text.
- ***Readers theatre.*** Students rehearse and perform from a script derived from a book. Students take character or narrator lines and improve fluency through rereading of text in preparation for a performance (Martinez, Roser, & Strecker, 1998/1999).

The topic of reading fluency will be also be revisited at greater length in Chapter 6.

Vocabulary

Vocabulary refers to the words the reader must know to communicate effectively and includes both oral/speaking vocabulary and reading/print vocabulary. Vocabulary contributes to making sense of words in print to aid in comprehension. Children learn the meaning of most words indirectly when they engage in oral language, listen to adults read to them, and read extensively on their own. Although they may be directly taught individual words or word learning strategies, they should always include the use of context clues to predict word meaning. The vocabulary in authentic literature provides a meaningful context for recognizing and understanding new words.

Although students learn most vocabulary indirectly through listening to read-alouds and reading on their own, there are word learning strategies that should be directly taught to them (Rupley, Logan, & Nichols, 1998/1999; Winters, 2001).

- ***Using dictionaries and other reference aids.*** Glossaries in nonfiction literature and picture dictionaries provide definitions for unfamiliar words for young learners. Sentences that provide the word in context seem to be the most useful part of this strategy.
- ***Using word parts.*** Knowing some common prefixes and suffixes, base words, and root words can provide a springboard for defining and learning related words.
- ***Using context clues.*** Hints about the meaning of an unknown word can be perceived through the words, phrases, and sentences that surround the word. While not all contexts are helpful for learning new word meanings, this is a critical means of word-solving as one internalizes new vocabulary.

More discussion on the application of these word strategies in older readers will be discussed in Chapter 7.

Comprehension

Comprehension is the ultimate reason for reading—the understanding and meaning that comes from interacting with print. Effective readers read with purpose while actively engaged with the text. Eight comprehension strategies have been identified as a means of improving reader comprehension:

- ***Activating prior knowledge.*** Good readers draw on prior experience to help them understand what they are reading. Ask readers what they know about the content, author, time period, topic, or text structure. Take a picture walk through the text by leading them to predict possible events by looking at the illustrations. Discuss key vocabulary. Prepare the reader for the journey through the text.
- ***Monitoring comprehension (metacognition).*** Readers know when they do and do not understand. With this knowledge, they apply fix-up strategies (e.g., reread, slow down, read ahead) to resolve their comprehension problems.
- ***Using graphic organizers.*** In story frames, readers define and see the relationship between the literary elements of a fictional story. Through concept mapping, readers can help identify how informational concepts are related to each other. Graphic organizers assist in development of knowledge of text structure, visual representation of information, and summarization of text (Merkley & Jefferies, 2000/2001).
- ***Answering questions.*** Questions give readers a purpose for reading and focus attention on what they are reading. They also allow readers to think actively during reading and to relate what they read to what they know. Instruction focuses on sample questions and answers that can be text explicit (stated directly in a single sentence), text implicit (implied in information in two or more sentences), or a reader-response connection (part of the reader's prior knowledge).
- ***Generating questions.*** Students who ask their own questions actively engage in the text and aid their comprehension. Ability to answer one's own questions implies integrating information during the reading process.
- ***Recognizing story structure.*** Recognizing setting, goals, attempts, and outcomes may assist in comprehension. Instruction in the content and organization of a story genre improves both comprehension and memory of story structure.

- ***Summarizing.*** Determining what is important in text helps readers condense and put information in their own words. In summarizing, readers can identify or generate main ideas, connect ideas, eliminate unnecessary information, and recall what they have read.
- ***Using mental imagery.*** Good readers form pictures or images in their minds as they read. Young readers who visualize characters, settings, and events remember what they read. During reading, activating all senses (i.e., smelling, tasting, touching, seeing, hearing) keeps the reader actively engaged in the text.

Teaching these eight strategies in isolation is merely the beginning of improving comprehension for young readers. Helping readers to use these strategies flexibly and in combination with one another is essential to eventual application in independent reading. Direct instruction of these strategies provides varied means for focusing on meaning, but independent application of blended strategies ensures ongoing development as a lifelong reader.

A balanced approach to reading justifies the use of purposeful, direct instruction for some aspects in the five areas of reading instruction discussed earlier (phonemic awareness, phonics, fluency, vocabulary, and comprehension). Not all aspects of these areas can be taught and applied in the K–2 primary grades. Reading instruction is ongoing, with a scope and sequence approach to revisiting, revitalizing, reinforcing, and reapplying these areas to increasingly challenging text as the reader develops. In all cases of direct instruction, the teacher should note the importance of moving instruction from isolated presentation to meaningful application in the context of authentic literature texts. Figure 5.1 provides ideas for parents and teachers to link language and literacy in authentic home and school literacy contexts. This extensive list of activities parallels and extends National Reading Panel findings through an early literacy lens.

Guided Reading

As children gain an initial confidence in reading, begin to develop sound and symbol relationships that assist with decoding words, and have a significant number of sight words in their repertoire, teachers can begin the process of guided reading, a teaching approach designed to help individual students learn how to read a variety of increasingly challenging texts with understanding and fluency. Guided reading is a part of a well-balanced approach to teaching three levels of reading: (a) independent reading, (b) guided reading, and (c) literature study.

To be able to deliver effective guided reading instruction, a teacher needs to acquire an understanding of its basic techniques. Fountas and Pinnell (1996) have identified the essential components of guided reading:

- A teacher works with a small group.
- Children in the group are similar in their development of the reading process and are able to read the same level of text.
- The teacher introduces the story and assists students in ways that help them develop independent reading strategies.
- Each child reads the whole text.
- The goal is for each child to read independently and silently.
- The emphasis is on slowly developing independent reading by gradually introducing increasingly challenging books over time.
- Children are grouped and regrouped in a dynamic process that involves ongoing teacher observation and assessment.

FIGURE 5.1 Linking Language and Literacy: Suggested Activities for Young Children.

Vocabulary and Language Development

Children who are exposed to a wide vocabulary through books and conversations learn the words they will later need to recognize, write, and understand.

- Provide oral labels for objects, pictures, and events in books, magazines, and real life.
- Talk with children during daily routines, watch children's TV programs together, and spend time talking about your lives.
- Enjoy outings to new places through language by surrounding the experience with talk before, during, and after the event.
- Select literature that connects to a child's own life and talk about that connection.
- Encourage children to "read" a familiar book to you by telling the story in their own or remembered words. Provide help rephrasing and asking questions, and encourage expanding with each "reading."

Phonological Awareness

Children become gradually aware of the sounds of words as they notice rhymes, make up words, clap syllables, or note the beginning sounds of words.

- Spark children's awareness of the sounds of language through songs, rhyming games, language play, and nursery rhymes.
- Talk about words and beginning sounds in the context of daily activities.
- Select children's books that focus on sounds and language play that will lead to chanting and modeling a pattern.

Speech Discrimination

Children can accurately perceive the differences between similar sounding words, which helps in phonological awareness.

- Make a game of pointing to pictures of objects with similar names (*tie/pie, socks/fox*) that the child already knows.

Concept of Story

Children should be comfortable with the elements of a story, including character, sequence of events, and dialogue.

- Select, read, and enjoy good storybooks throughout the day and at bedtime.
- Share the magic of oral storytelling by retelling favorite fairy tales or encouraging children to retell favorites in their own words.
- Encourage children to make up their own stories, act them out, or share them with puppets.

Book and Print Awareness

Children gradually begin to understand that print surrounds them and that reading and writing are means to get ideas, information, and knowledge.

- Provide a print-rich environment with high-quality books, writing materials, and letter toys/blocks.
- Point out and read print in everyday life from labels and menus to posters and signs.
- Label some of the important things in a child's world such as "Tommy's Room" or "Sylvia's Toys" and let the child decorate the signs.

Adapted from M. Susan Burns, Peg Griffin, and Catherine E. Snow (Eds.) (1999). Starting out right: A guide to promoting children's reading success. *Washington, DC: National Academies Press. Copyright 1999 by the National Academy of Sciences, courtesy of the National Academies Press, Washington, DC. Reprinted with permission.*

FIGURE 5.1 (Continued)

Functions of Print

Children begin to understand the meaning and value of print in their daily lives.

- Point out the purpose of bills, checks, menus, mail, and greeting cards.
- Suggest that students write a shopping list or note when you do.
- Use print resources to look up answers to children's questions and show them where you found the answer.

Print Concepts

Children gradually understand conventions of print, including directionality (left-right/top-bottom), spacing, and punctuation.

- Point to the name of a book and the name of its author/illustrator and run a finger along the text while you read.
- Stop to talk about a book at the end of a sentence, paragraph, or page so the child realizes there are natural breaks in print.

Letter and Early Word Recognition

Children begin to recognize some printed alphabet letters and words, especially those in their names.

- Help children locate and identify the initial letters in their own names and then ask them to find these letters in other words and signs.
- Write and display the child's name often until gradual recognition occurs. Do this with other familiar words.
- Watch *Sesame Street* and learn letter songs as a parent and child team.

Comprehension

Children increasingly grasp the meaning of language in everyday conversation and books and indicate that understanding through questions and comments.

- Listen to an audiobook alongside the real book and have the child draw and talk about their favorite part.
- Ask children questions to help them think during the reading of a book.

Literacy as a Source of Enjoyment

Children need to feel positive about literacy by celebrating personal reading and writing events.

- Create a warm atmosphere around storytime, reading, writing, and play activities.
- Take children to the library regularly and let them self-select some titles.
- Connect the visual representation of CD-ROMs, videos, and educational television programs to reading and books.

Guided reading in kindergarten may look more like an excursion into simple sight words and the early concepts of print. Children might learn a core of 20 to 30 words and be able to read simple text. The main goal of guided reading at this early level would be for children to become comfortable with print.

The Guided Reading Group Lesson

A guided reading group lesson (Grades 1–2) involves the following framework:

- An introduction to the text
- Individual reading

- Explicit instruction for processing strategies for both fiction and nonfiction
- Extension through talk and writing

Examining the sequence of a guided reading lesson exemplifies the gradual release of the reading process from the teacher to the student. The master reader (teacher) models the strategies of reading in an authentic context with the apprentice reader (student) in an attempt to gradually shift the application of strategies into the reader's control.

Before Reading. One of the critical components of success in guided reading is that the teacher selects an appropriate text—one that is at a sustainable level but still contains a few challenges to be confronted. The teacher must know the reader and text and must understand the reading process. Selecting a text that is "just right" means that book and print features, content and theme, text structure, and language and literacy features must be considered (Rog & Burton, 2001/2002). These books must provide the proper mix of support and challenge by drawing on skills readers already know while expanding processing strategies beyond their current level. The goal of the "just right" text is to nudge readers beyond their current development by engaging in successful reader problem solving (Fountas & Pinnell, 1996). Teachers need to ask, "What does the text demand of the reader?" and choices must nudge students to a higher level by challenging them in a new way. Even published basal programs can be targeted and leveled as guided reading materials if properly matched to the instructional level of the emergent reader (Fawson & Reutzel, 2000).

When the "just right" book is selected, the teacher introduces the story, blending the language and visual information in the text with the knowledge, prior experience, and strategies of the readers. Children engage in a conversation about the story while raising questions, predicting events, and noticing how the text is presented.

During Reading. The teacher listens in as each child reads the entire text or a part to themselves using a soft voice. Children request help in solving words or making meaning

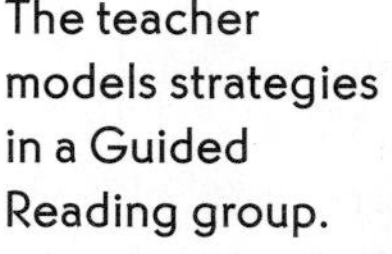

The teacher models strategies in a Guided Reading group.

when needed. The teacher continuously observes and keeps track of the use of varied reading strategies. While confirming the positive use of strategies and successes, the teacher also interacts with a child to model and assist with the reading process.

After Reading. The teacher initiates a conversation about the book and invites personal responses from each reader while informally assessing student comprehension. Children talk about the story while checking and reacting to their predictions. Strategically, the teacher reverts to the text for one or two teachable opportunities such as modeling of a strategy or finding evidence of related words. Although children may occasionally be invited to extend the story through other language arts activities, the story is often simply reread with confidence and application of new strategies to a reading partner or independently.

This model may remind teachers of the traditional reading groups of which they were a part during their own elementary classroom days, but there are major differences in the guided reading model from traditional grouping:

- Changing of group members takes place on a continual basis based on the ability to apply strategies in the context of reading, rather than general reading ability (Opitz, 1998b).
- Dynamic groupings are based on reading strengths and level of text difficulty or interest (rather than on deficits and predetermined reading level text).
- Skills and strategies are taught within the context of reading (rather than in isolation through drill and practice worksheets).
- Selections are read and reread for fluency (rather than visited only a single time).

Inexperienced teachers are often overwhelmed when they feel they do not know what should be taught during a guided reading session. Decoding skills, new vocabulary, comprehension strategies, response to literature, self-monitoring of understanding, and oral and silent reading fluency are only a few of the reading strategies that help children develop into readers. Figure 5.2 provides an overview of reading skills and strategies that require explicit instruction, repeated practice, and application in both guided and independent reading. While these strategies can become the focus of planned lessons, they also prove effective when taught within the context of daily reading materials. For example, retelling lends itself to folktales or fairy tales, while creating visual images might be incorporated into a text with minimal illustrations.

In order for guided reading to truly be effective, teachers need to "keep track" of both the skills and strategies they teach and the skills and strategies students apply during guided reading lessons. Focusing on a small number of children allows the teacher the opportunity to individualize instruction as occasions arise and need is indicated. Yet documentation of these learning opportunities and applications must be recorded. Quantitative assessments, such as running records, miscue analysis, and informal reading inventories, provide the needed data to detect ongoing growth in reading. Informal comprehension checks or checklists of use of reading strategies provide an additional dimension in monitoring continuous progress. At the primary level, a reading continuum (see Chapter 15) provides dated occurrences of individual reading characteristics.

Guided reading teachers believe that children learn to read by authentic reading. Children need to build a massive amount of reading throughout the entire day, not just during the guided reading block of time. The most effective indicator of guided reading success is a supportive team approach in which both the teacher and students interact to provide authentic reading practice in a safe, confidence-building learning environment. Another indication of facilitative success in guided reading is the teacher's ability to create and simultaneously manage literacy centers for writing, word study, literature study, or independent reading.

FIGURE 5.2
What to Teach Students During Guided Reading Lessons.

- Figuring out unknown words: decoding/vocabulary
  - Phonics
  - Context
  - Structure/syntax
  - Rereading
  - Self-correcting
- Understanding text/comprehension
  - Activating prior knowledge
  - Reciprocal teaching (predicting, asking questions, summarizing)
  - Determining important ideas
  - Creating mental and visual images
  - Making inferences
  - Retelling
  - Skimming and scanning
  - Thinking aloud
  - Reading nonfiction and other genres
  - Understanding story through graphic organizers
  - Writing and sharing responses or summaries
- Responding to or interpreting text
  - Identifying story structure and literary elements
  - Comparing texts by theme
  - Connecting text to life and other texts
  - Using response logs
  - Incorporating readers theatre
- Self-Monitoring and self-evaluation
  - Choosing books to be read independently
  - Applying skills and strategies independently
  - Maintaining a reading record
  - Knowing when understanding is taking place
  - Seeking help when comprehension breaks down
- Reading orally (should be kept to a minimum)
  - Reading for pleasure
  - Determining level of text
  - Demonstrating oral fluency
  - Reading a well-written passage

Literacy Centers

Even the most experienced teacher wonders what other children do while the teacher is working with a guided reading group (Cambourne, 2001). The effective management of work groups has been and always will be one of the greatest challenges of teaching reading. In order to focus on a small group of children, it is necessary to plan and provide precisely for meaningful literacy-related centers for the rest of the students. How can children have meaningful practice in the language arts while the teacher is working with another group? Instruction away from the teacher needs to be as powerful as instruction with the teacher

FIGURE 5.3
Primary Literacy Centers.

Listening post	Independent project center
Readers theatre	Computer workstations
Reading and writing the room	Retelling center
Pocket charts	Content area centers
Poems/story packs	Language games
Big books	Dramatic play center
Responding through art	Overhead project center
Journal writing	Whiteboard activities
Independent reading	Newspaper/magazine center
Word scavenger hunts	Buddy reading center

(Ford & Opitz, 2002; Opitz & Ford, 2001). Literacy centers set up children for success as they see themselves evolve as independent readers—the goal of guided reading.

Effective organization, high expectations, and student responsibility are the keys to work group success. Teachers need to plan a variety of small work group activities, model them effectively, and provide a daily procedure that maximizes on-task behavior. The following guidelines can be used to form the infrastructure of literacy centers:

- Facilitate independent use by students.
- Operate with minimum transition time and management.
- Encourage equitable use of activities among learners.
- Include a built-in accountability system.
- Allow for efficient use of teacher preparation time.
- Build around classroom routines.

Figure 5.3 lists several types of primary literacy centers that can meaningfully utilize the time when students are not working in a guided reading group with a teacher. All planned options, however, must focus on some aspect of the six language arts (i.e., reading, writing, listening, speaking, viewing and visual representation) and be purposeful. For example, a writing center provides the opportunity to write about a book that was read earlier in the week or a favorite character. A listening center provides an audiotape of a book by the same author as last week's guided reading lesson. Technology provides visual representation of favorite books. A pocket chart allows exploration with sounds, words, or sentences.

A chart or bulletin board matches groups and activities on a rotating daily basis. Yet all of this requires planning ahead, assembling materials, assigning activities, modeling expectations, and facilitating on-task behavior. Many teachers choose to incorporate a paraprofessional in the classroom or prepare a parent volunteer to assist with work groups during guided reading time. While this multiple group configuration requires advance planning and fluid orchestration, the time the teacher spends with the guided reading group is well worth the inclusion of this model as an effective one for early literacy instruction and practice.

Guided Writing

The reading and writing connection provides a strong literacy link in the primary grades. Children capably "read" their own "writing" as a first step toward conventional reading. The opportunity to see their oral language replicated in written symbols creates a springboard to making the connection between oral and written language. Referring to this gradual process as *guided writing* allows the child to move slowly from teacher-generated to student-generated writing under teacher guidance, and, ultimately, to independent writing by the student. This gradual release of responsibility follows the same philosophy as the guided reading model. These transitional writing opportunities facilitate students' gradual acquisition of writing skills.

Language Experience Approach

Children delight in the experience of seeing their own words and thoughts recorded on paper come to life as authentic writing. According to the language experience approach (LEA), the teacher records the words of students on chart paper following a lived-through common experience (Stauffer, 1970). A trip to the zoo, a walk through the autumn leaves, a visit with an author or illustrator, or an interview with a World War II veteran may provide the opportunity to motivate writing. The teacher engages children in the composing process through oral language as she demonstrates the writing process through the printed word. The complexity or simplicity of the text is related to the language used by the children. Because the teacher does the writing, spelling, punctuation, capitalization, and other conventions are standard. Letter formation and spacing are neat and provide a worthy model of conventional print.

Not only do children see how conventional written language works, but the language experience story provides a source of reading material throughout the school year. Visual art may even accompany the story. Used in a small or large group setting, the strengths of the LEA lie in children composing the authentic text while the teacher acts as recorder of oral language. The teacher's thinking aloud during the demonstration process provides a link between the spoken and the written word. The text serves as a record of children's experience and language and can be transcribed and/or duplicated for individual reading copies. Children readily reread their own words and repeated reading allows them to read all the authentic language from a treasured, self-generated class story. Student Sample 5.1 presents an authentic language experience story created after first graders returned from the grand opening of a Wal-Mart superstore in their community. The teacher has retyped the story from the original chart paper and distributed it for rereading the following day.

Shared Writing

Shared writing also requires the teacher to demonstrate the writing process while children engage in the mental composing process. Unlike the LEA, which is focused on authentic experience, shared writing focuses on providing demonstrations of how to construct words using sound and letter relationships, to understand the patterns of written language, and to see the conventions of writing in print. The teacher and children compose the text together while focusing on how thoughts become print. Children engage in planning the text so it can be accessed by the intended readers.

STUDENT SAMPLE 5.1
Kindergarten Language Experience Story.

We woke up early and our parents drove us to the new Wal-Mart.
Wal-Mart people gave us new blue vests to wear.
We said the Pledge of Allegiance at the opening ceremony.
We ate donuts and drank orange juice.
We took a tour of the new Super Center.
We were tired when we returned to school.
We felt special today.

STUDENT SAMPLE 5.2 First-Grade Morning Message.

Good morning, first graders!
Today is Friday, October 8th.
Today is Jason's birthday.
We will walk to the park to see the pretty autumn leaves this afternoon at 2:00.

Skills Taught within the Context of this Morning Message

Writing shares a message.
Writers can begin different ways.
Spaces.
Consonant blends.
Left-to right directionality.
What does the exclamation mark tell the reader?
What other marks did I use today?
If I didn't know how to write "park" what could I do?
What other way could I start this message?

Compound words.
How do we know how to spell "October"? (calendar)
How do we know how to spell "autumn"?
Word endings.
High-frequency word wall word.
What kind of letter do we use to begin sentences?
Writing shares information.
Break words into parts to figure out how to write them.

Imagine a first-grade teacher eliciting the text to an invitation for an author tea that will be sent to fifth-grade book buddies. Gathered on the carpet near the chart paper, the group orally composes the invitation for information, but the teacher guides and records the words for format and conventions. Creating readable text that can be used and read again is the outcome of shared writing. Often the shared writing stays on display to be used as a resource for locating known and new words in children's independent writing.

The morning message is another effective medium for a shared writing lesson. Teacher talk generates and guides the composition of three to four conventionally correct sentences, each containing multiple literacy lessons. Student Sample 5.2 illustrates a typical first-grade morning message and the aspects of teacher talk that make it a well-rounded learning experience. Throughout the day, the morning message can be related to a topic for journal writing, linked to a problem-solving situation, or used as a writing resource. The demonstration of sharing a meaningful message through conventional print provides a model and inspiration during independent writing.

Interactive Writing

Interactive writing involves both the teacher and the children composing the text together and mutually sharing in the physical writing of the text (McCarrier, Pinnell, & Fountas, 2000). Children activate prior knowledge through brainstorming, set a purpose for writing, compose the text verbally, and construct the text through conventional print while "sharing the pen" with the teacher. Throughout the process, children reread, revise, and proofread the text and apply word-solving skills and conventions to the written product. Upon completion, children think about all they have learned and extend the writing through display and continued classroom reading (Button, Johnson, & Furguson, 1996).

Figure 5.4 reveals the eight elements of interactive writing (McCarrier, Pinnell, & Fountas, 2000). Although complex and time consuming, this joint effort at composition of ideas and construction of text places children in direct context with the skills and strategies of the

FIGURE 5.4
Essential Elements of Interactive Writing.

- *Provide an active learning experience* through children's home experience, shared classroom experiences, and class read-aloud experience.
- *Establish a writing purpose through talk,* which serves as an oral language rehearsal for the writing topic.
- *Compose the text* while jointly thinking about topic, audience, language, text structure, and organization.
- *Construct the text* by sharing the pen as children apply phonemic awareness and phonics in creating the visual aspects of print.
- *Reread, revise, and proofread the text* to familiarize children with the text, to provide opportunities for revisions, and to check their work for accuracy.
- *Revisit the text to support word solving* by noting parts of words and similar sounds in words, and by visually connecting words.
- *Summarize the learning* by helping children to realize the steps involved in verbalizing their own knowledge.
- *Extend the learning* by posting the writing on the wall for independent reading, by using it for shared reading, or by using it as a resource for future writing.

Source: Adapted from A. McCarrier, G. S. Pinnell, & I. C. Fountas (2000). Interactive writing: How language and literacy come together, K–2. *Portsmouth, NH: Heinemann.*

writing process. Each child's contribution is a literacy lesson learned that is likely to be applied in independent writing. The real strength of interactive writing lies in teaching writing skills and strategies within the context of an authentic writing experience. Children talk, compose, construct, and reread as they learn about the writing process. They enjoy the results of their contributions by being able to read, reread, display, and consult their student-generated writing again and again. The text may be easily reproduced or used in a functional way in the classroom (e.g., recipes, story mural, author display, character webs). Children surrounded by their own interactive writing may become inspired writers as they move toward independence.

Student Sample 5.3 presents a simple interactive writing lesson with a single child from a small group of first graders. Imagine the teacher inviting individuals from a small group of four students to respond to the prompt, "What exciting thing did you see or do this weekend?" Brianna eagerly volunteers to participate. The teacher clears a fresh sheet of chart paper and asks Brianna for her response. Brianna states, "I saw a fire in my grandma's back yard." Now it is her task, with teacher guidance, to get that thought down on the chart paper. The teacher must slow down the composing process by encouraging Brianna to place the words she knows on the chart paper and by prompting her about how to write an uppercase "I." Brianna writes "saw" as on the word wall, then breezes through "a," but hesitates on "fire." The teacher reminds her of the location of the word on a safety poster and another child locates and spells the word accurately. Brianna once again masters "in my" but needs teacher guidance to work on the next word. The teacher helps Brianna and group members to sound out "g – r – a – n – d" but notes the other children getting fidgety. The teacher shares the pen and add's "ma's" to the word. Brianna sounds out "back" by herself, but the teacher assists with the beginning and ending consonants of "y" and "d." Once again, the teacher shares the pen and writes the "ar" sound in the word as Brianna adds a period at the end of the sentence. Pride surrounds Brianna while reading aloud the sentence she has composed with the interactive help of her teacher.

STUDENT SAMPLE 5.3 Brianna's First-Grade Interactive Writing.

Note the insertion of difficult letters by the teacher as she assisted the student in completion of a brief statement. During the lesson, all the students are learning about letters, spaces between words, the concept of first and last, letter formation, the names of letters, punctuation, sound concepts, high frequency words, and the reading of self-created text. This interactive writing lesson took 10 minutes, but the literacy strategies learned within its context, for both Brianna and her classmates, make it well worth the time invested.

The teacher continuously turns each word into a learning experience by pointing out sight words, sound and symbol relationships, punctuation marks, capitalization, and legibility. Several class days of 15-minute writing sessions may accompany the interactive writing. The pattern of talk, composition, construction, and rereading repeats itself with each new sentence. The strength of the process, however, lies with the teaching of writing skills in the context of children's own compositions. Skills and strategies are more likely to take hold within the personal context of meaningful writing with the assistance of a knowledgeable teacher.

Interactive writing can be used in a whole class or small group setting. Creating simple, readable texts that can be achieved with conventional spelling and punctuation as well as letter formation and capitalization at the level of the children is the goal. While children contribute aspects of words they know, the teacher supports the process by controlling what the children do not yet know.

Independent Reading

Another essential aspect of a balanced reading approach is independent reading, a time during which students use self-selected literature to engage in the reading process and apply reading strategies learned during guided reading. To create engaged readers, teachers must help children find books that they can enjoy, books that make them believe that they are readers and books that will build confidence in their reading ability (Calkins, 2002). Finding the perfect match between books and children is a worthy challenge.

While teachers should be well-versed in the best of children's literature, there are several sources to help in making the perfect match between the readers and books. Fountas & Pinnel (2005) have both a book (*The Fountas and Pinnell Leveled Book List, K–8*) and a Web site (www.FountasandPinnellLeveledBooks.com) that list over 16,000 book titles by author, level, and genre, blending classic and contemporary literature. Rona Flippo (2005) provides key strategies for focusing on the importance of student interests and incorporates forms that help teachers survey children's favorite topics, curiosities, and purposes.

Some teachers use color-coded stickers to mark the reading levels of books to be selected by students for independent reading. Others ask students to conduct a simple test for selection criteria—"If you stumble over five words on the first page, the book may be too difficult for you." Of course, books of high interest to children, particularly nonfiction (e.g., snakes, dinosaurs, butterflies), often provide the momentum to read above their level because of prior knowledge or expertise on the topic. Wutz and Wedwick (2005) provide a classroom poster that identifies criteria for guiding young readers toward the book that best matches reading level, interest areas, and genre appeal (Figure 5.5).

A predictable time slot (10 minutes in kindergarten to 20 minutes in Grade 2) should be designated for independent reading each day. Sustained silent reading (SSR) or drop everything and read (DEAR) provide scheduled time to practice independent reading. Although this reading does not substitute for quality guided reading group instruction, it does provide the practice needed for independent application of learned literacy strategies.

Keeping track of independent reading through an ongoing reading log or a list of books read provides the feeling of success needed by emerging readers. Such activities generate feelings of confidence and accomplishment in early readers who feel empowerment with each independent reading they complete.

Independent Writing

Independent writing provides the opportunity for children to both compose and construct written text on their own with occasional support from the teacher. The process of independent writing challenges children to use their current knowledge of how print works to produce "readable" text. Typically, the text includes some words spelled conventionally and some word-spelling attempts. While this practice may look different in a kindergarten, first-grade, and second-grade classroom, the results document the growth of writing over time. Many teachers utilize writing portfolios to showcase this growth during conferences.

Working individually, children are encouraged to construct words using current knowledge of sound and letter relationships, sight words, word wall words, and other strategies and to apply all they know about reading and writing. Independent writing may take the form of a daily journal, a continuing story, or any form or genre in which the child has interest. The emphasis in independent writing is not on correctness but on the willingness to take risks and to apply new skills and knowledge to the writing process. The teacher as facilitator provides the support needed to slowly transition students toward conventional writing.

In some writing workshop classrooms, independent writing may be moved toward class publication through editing. Spelling becomes conventional, while other conventions vary with the growing skills of the writer. Children's independent writing

FIGURE 5.5
BOOKMATCH Classroom Poster.

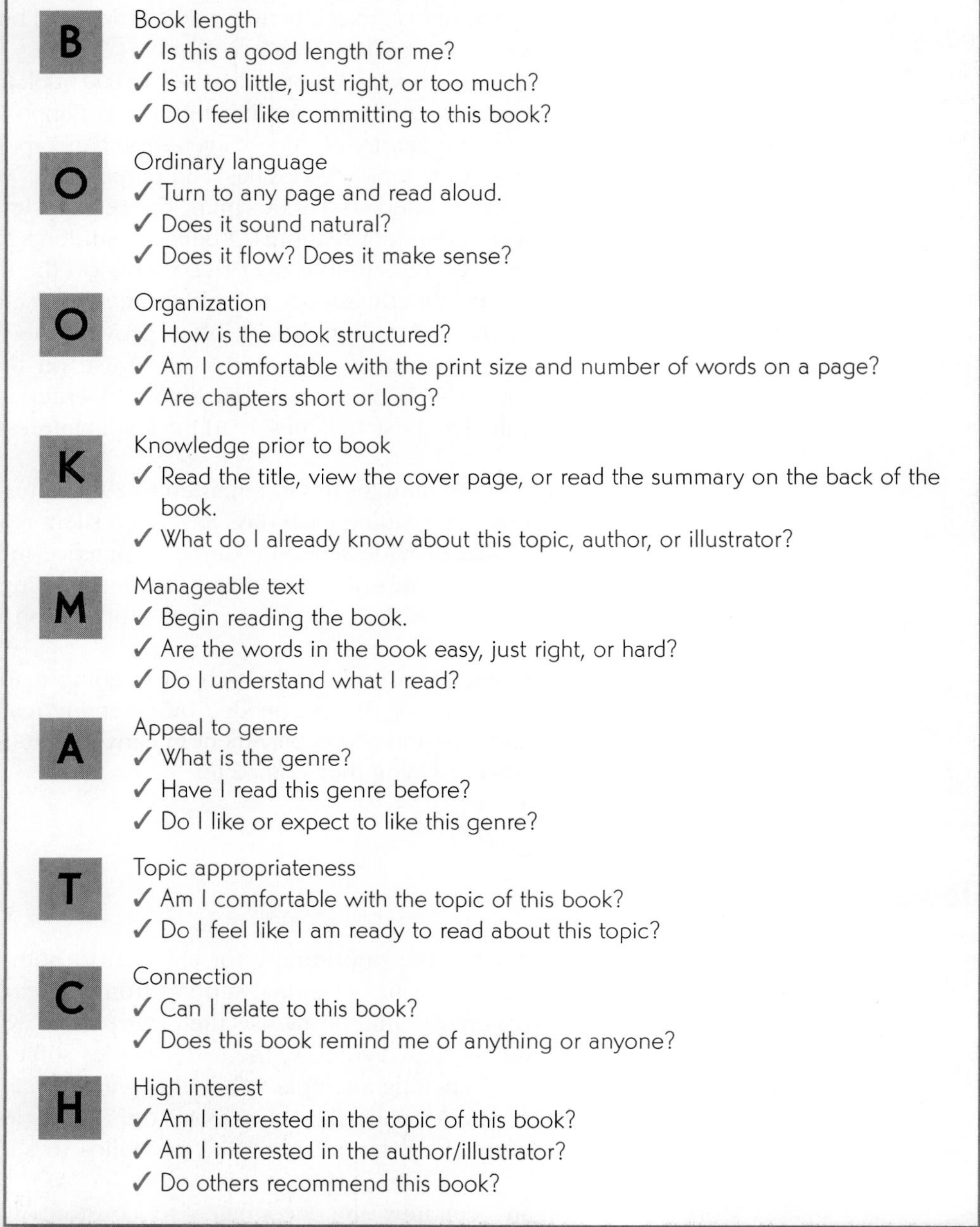
B Book length
✓ Is this a good length for me?
✓ Is it too little, just right, or too much?
✓ Do I feel like committing to this book?

O Ordinary language
✓ Turn to any page and read aloud.
✓ Does it sound natural?
✓ Does it flow? Does it make sense?

O Organization
✓ How is the book structured?
✓ Am I comfortable with the print size and number of words on a page?
✓ Are chapters short or long?

K Knowledge prior to book
✓ Read the title, view the cover page, or read the summary on the back of the book.
✓ What do I already know about this topic, author, or illustrator?

M Manageable text
✓ Begin reading the book.
✓ Are the words in the book easy, just right, or hard?
✓ Do I understand what I read?

A Appeal to genre
✓ What is the genre?
✓ Have I read this genre before?
✓ Do I like or expect to like this genre?

T Topic appropriateness
✓ Am I comfortable with the topic of this book?
✓ Do I feel like I am ready to read about this topic?

C Connection
✓ Can I relate to this book?
✓ Does this book remind me of anything or anyone?

H High interest
✓ Am I interested in the topic of this book?
✓ Am I interested in the author/illustrator?
✓ Do others recommend this book?

Source: From Jessica Ann Wutz and Linda Wedwick (2005). BOOKMATCH: Scaffolding book selection for independent reading. The Reading Teacher, *59 (1), 16–32. Reprinted with permission.*

can be displayed, published through computer word processing, collected in a writing folder, or stored in a portfolio. Children often enhance their personal writing with art to accompany their finished pieces. Student Sample 5.4 showcases the independent writing of four first graders. Note the developmental differences, yet celebrated attempts, to become literate writers within the context of their own authentic experiences.

STUDENT SAMPLE 5.4A Four Examples of First-Grade Independent Writing.

Closing Thoughts

The balanced literacy approach presented in this chapter cannot take place without the expertise of an informed, caring, professional who believes, articulates, and practices this philosophy of literacy learning in a comfortable learning environment. A continuum of expertise of early literacy teachers (Block, Oakar, & Hurt, 2002) showcases noteworthy, appropriate terminology to eloquently describe the special, talented teacher who judiciously guides the literacy journey of K–2 emergent learners. This research demonstrates that teaching expertise makes a significant difference in the rate and depth of literacy growth and that highly effective teachers share similar characteristics.

According to Block's continuum (Block et al., 2002, p. 188), the kindergarten teacher assumes the role as *guardian* of children's discoveries about print in a print-rich and homelike classroom reinforcing positive emotions to print and written messages. As teachers relate to children, they praise correct portions in a celebration of learning. Throughout the day, individual learners are praised for their individual pace of literacy learning. Songs, drama, and objects reignite interests in reading as adult role models repeat the literacy experience using the same text and context as a primary support to emergent literacy.

STUDENT SAMPLE 5.4B

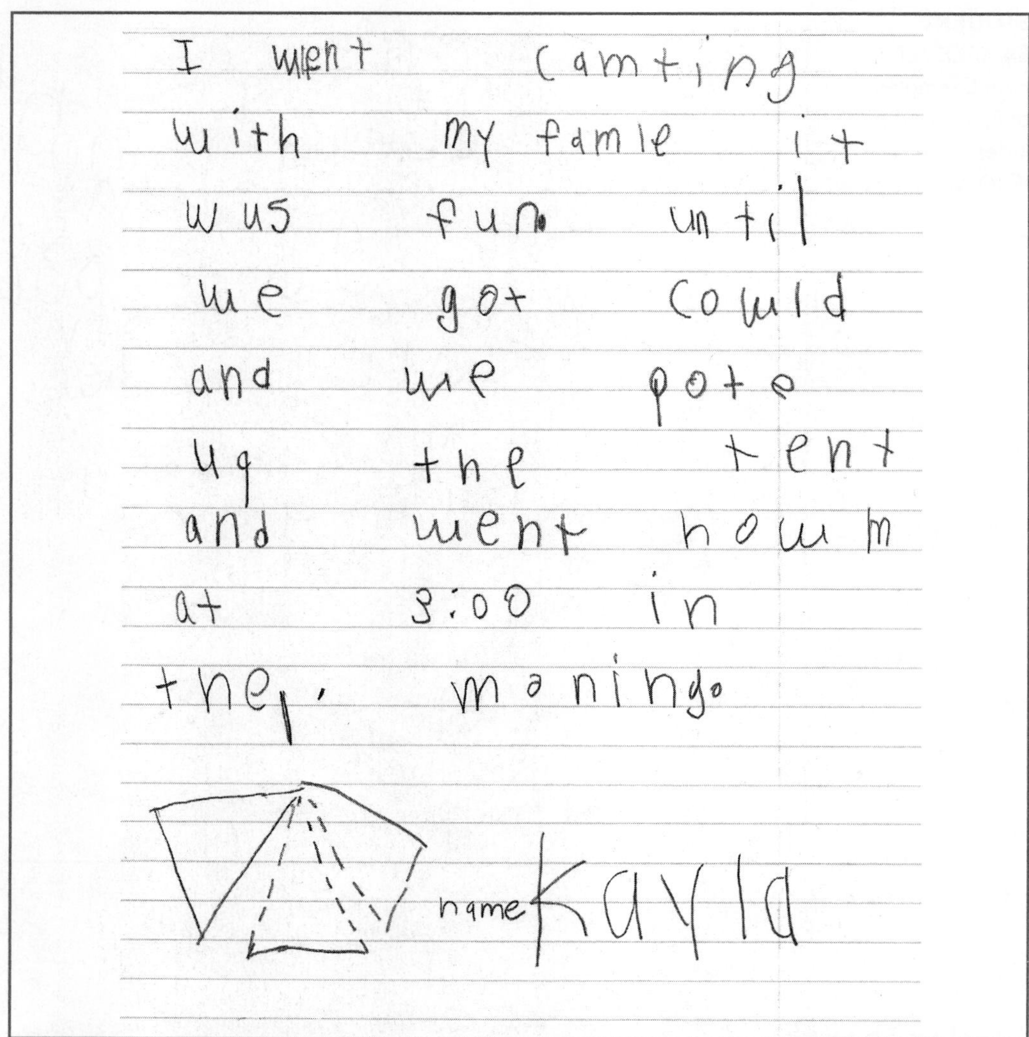

Block goes on to say that first-grade teachers are viewed as *encouragers and supporters* who teach literacy throughout the entire school day. Their agile ability to teach up to twenty different skills in an hour reflects the rapid-paced, play-filled environment in which they set the stage for literacy fun with students. Their ability to praise learning in progress as they move students toward using print-rich space independently is applauded. Reviewing concepts using varied content, books, methods, and contexts moves learners toward becoming self-regulated learners.

Block's continuum suggests that second-grade teachers showcase themselves as *demonstrators* who provide masterful think-alouds to provide the modeling needed for ongoing literacy learning. Observing how much adults enjoy and value literacy motivates the young learner toward a literacy future. The teacher's role is to hold students' hands as they find answers to their own questions about literacy as well as to listen appreciatively

STUDENT SAMPLE 5.4C

and reflectively in their tie to individual learners. New resources and print are used to challenge students to think deeply while lessons are differentiated and creative as students are guided forward to new learning experiences.

The road to literacy in the primary grades must be paved with individualization of literacy instruction, time for guided and practice reading and writing, and dedicated confidence building as the child emerges as a real reader and writer. A balanced approach to early literacy instruction blends teacher modeling, direct instruction, guided literacy instruction, and independent practice of both reading and writing. Perhaps the most important component of early literacy learning is the qualified teacher who cares deeply about each student and is in a position to determine whether a child will succeed as a reader and a writer.

STUDENT SAMPLE 5.4D

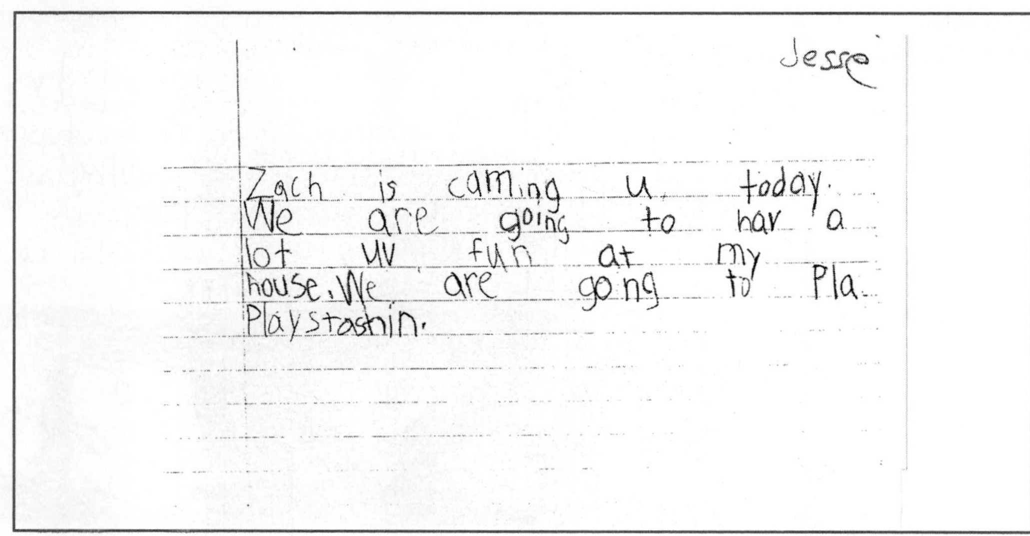

In the midst of the scientifically based study of literacy, it is easy to forget the joy of literacy itself. If teachers are to create a desire in emergent learners to become readers and writers, the component of literacy purpose and enjoyment must pervade the classroom. As advocates for our students, teachers must celebrate small steps in literacy learning, cheer students on daily, and become constant supporters for their success. Teachers need to make certain not only that students can read and write well but that they also enjoy the art and presence of reading and writing in their daily lives. The attitude young learners develop toward early literacy instruction and literacy production may impact choices throughout their lifetimes.

Visit the Companion Website at www.prenhall.com/hancock and gauge your understanding of Chapter 5 concepts with the self-assessments.

References

Adams, M. J. (1990). *Beginning to read: Thinking and learning about print.* Cambridge, MA: MIT Press.

Armbruster, B. B., & Osborn, J. (2001). *Put reading first: The research building blocks for teaching children to read.* Jessup, MD: National Institute for Literacy.

Askew, B. J., & Fountas, I. C. (1998). Building an early reading process: Active from the start! *The Reading Teacher, 52,* 126–134.

Barrentine, S. J. (1996). Engaging in reading through interactive read alouds. *The Reading Teacher, 50,* 36–43.

Blair-Larsen, S. M., & Williams, K. (1999). *The balanced reading program: Helping all students achieve success.* Newark, DE: International Reading Association.

Block, C. C., Oakar, M., & Hurt, N. (2002). The expertise of literacy teachers: A continuum from preschool to grade 5. *Reading Research Quarterly, 37,* 178–206.

Button, K., Johnson, M. J., & Furguson, P. (1996). Interactive writing in a primary classroom. *The Reading Teacher, 49,* 446–454.

Calkins, L. M. (2002). *The art of teaching reading.* New York: Longman.

Cambourne, B. (2001). What do I do with the rest of the class? The nature of teaching-learning activities. *Language Arts, 79,* 124–135.

Cunningham , P. M., & Hall, D. P. (1994). *Making words.* Torrance, CA: Good Apple.

Dahl, K. L., & Scharer, P. L. (2000). Phonics teaching in whole language classrooms: New evidence from research. *The Reading Teacher, 53,* 584–594.

Dekker, M. M. (1991). Books, reading, and response: A teacher-researcher tells a story. *The New Advocate, 4,* 37–46.

Dorn, L, J., French, C., & Jones, T. (1998). *Apprenticeship in literacy: Transitions across reading and writing.* York, ME: Stenhouse.

Ericson, L., & Juliebo, M. F. (1998). *The phonological awareness handbook for kindergarten and primary teachers.* Newark, DE: International Reading Association.

Fawson, P. C., & Reutzel, D. R. (2000). But I only have a basal: Implementing guided reading in the early grades. *The Reading Teacher, 54,* 84–89.

Fitzgerald, J. (1999). What is this thing called "balance?" *The Reading Teacher, 53,* 100–107.

Flippo, R. (2005). *Personal reading: How to match children to books.* Portsmouth, NH: Heinemann.

Ford, M. P., & Opitz, M. F. (2002). Using centers to engage children during guided reading time: Intensifying learning experiences away from the teacher. *The Reading Teacher, 55,* 710–717.

Fountas, I. C., & Pinnell, G. S. (1996). *Guided reading: Good first teaching for all children.* Portsmouth, NH: Heinemann.

Fountas, I. C., & Pinnell, G. S. (2005). *The Fountas and Pinnell leveled book list, K–8.* Portsmouth, NH: Heinemann.

Hancock, M. R. (2004). *A celebration of literature and response: Children, books, and teachers in K–8 classrooms* (2nd ed.). Upper Saddle River, NJ: Merrill/Prentice Hall.

Holdaway, D. (1979). *Foundations of literacy.* Sydney, Australia: Ashton Scholastic; distributed by Heinemann.

Kelly, P. R. (1990). Guiding young students' responses to literature. *The Reading Teacher, 43,* 464–470.

Klesius, J, & Griffith, P. (1996). Interactive storybook reading for at-risk learners. *The Reading Teacher, 49,* 552–560.

Koblitz, D. (2002). Reading to students as part of genre study. *School Life, 7,* 1–2.

Martinez, M., Roser, N. L., & Strecker, S. (1998/1999). "I never thought I could be a star": A Readers Theatre ticket to fluency. *The Reading Teacher, 52,* 326–334.

McCarrier, A., Pinnell, G. S., & Fountas, I. C. (2000). *Interactive writing: How language and literacy come together, K–2.* Portsmouth, NH: Heinemann.

Merkley, D. M., & Jefferies, D. (2000/2001). Guidelines for implementing a graphic organizer. *The Reading Teacher, 54,* 350–357.

National Reading Panel, National Institute of Child Health and Human Development. (2000). *Teaching children to read: An evidence-based assessment of the scientific research literature on reading and its implications for reading instruction* (NIH Publication No. 00-4769). Washington, DC: U.S. Government Printing Office.

Opitz, M. F. (1998a). Children's books to develop phonemic awareness—for you and parents, too! *The Reading Teacher, 51,* 526–528.

Opitz, M. F. (1998b). *Flexible grouping in reading: Practical ways to help all students become better readers.* New York: Scholastic Professional Books.

Opitz, M. F., & Ford, M. P. (2001). *Reaching readers: Innovative and flexible strategies for guided reading.* Portsmouth, NH: Heinemann.

Pinnell, G. S., & Fountas, I. C. (1998). *Word matters: Teaching phonics and spelling in the reading/writing classroom.* Portsmouth, NH: Heinemann.

Rasinski, T. V. (2000). Speed does matter in reading. *The Reading Teacher, 54,* 146–151.

Richards, M. (2000). Be a good detective: Solve the case of oral reading fluency. *The Reading Teacher, 53,* 534–539.

Roe, L. J., & Burton, W. (2001/2002). Matching texts and readers: Leveling early reading materials for assessment and instruction. *The Reading Teacher, 55,* 348–356.

Roller, C. M., & Beed, P. L. (1994). Sometimes the conversations were grand and sometimes. . . . *Language Arts, 71,* 509–515.

Rupley, W. H., Logan, J. W., & Nichols, W. D. (1998/1999). Vocabulary instruction in a balanced reading program. *The Reading Teacher, 52,* 336–346.

Samuels, S. J. (1997). The method of repeated readings. *The Reading Teacher, 50,* 376–381.

Schlick-Noe, K. L. (1995). Nurturing response with emergent readers. In B. Campbell Hill, N. J. Johnson, & K. L. Schlick-Noe (Eds.), *Literature circles and response* (pp. 41–54). Norwood, MA: Christopher-Gordon.

Slaughter, J. P. (1993). *Beyond storybooks: Young children and the shared book experience.* Newark, DE: International Reading Association.

Spencer, M. M. (2002). *What more needs saying about imagination?* Paper presented at the meeting of the International Reading Association World Congress, Edinburgh, Scotland. (See *The Reading Teacher, 57,* 105–111 for full text.)

Stahl, S. A. (1992). Saying the "p" word: Nine guidelines for exemplary phonics instruction. *The Reading Teacher, 45,* 618–625.

Stauffer, R. G. (1970). *The language experience approach to teaching reading.* New York: Harper & Row.

Strickland, D. S. (1988). Some tips for using big books. *The Reading Teacher, 42,* 966–967.

Wagstaff, J. M. (1997/1998). Building practical knowledge of letter-sound correspondence: A beginner's word wall and beyond. *The Reading Teacher, 51,* 298–304.

Wagstaff, J. M. (1999). *Teaching reading and writing with word walls.* New York: Scholastic.

Winters, R. (2001). Vocabulary anchors: Building conceptual connections with young readers. *The Reading Teacher, 54,* 659–662.

Wollman-Bonilla, J. E., & Werchaldo, (1995). Literature response journals in a first-grade classroom. *Language Arts, 72,* 562–570.

Wutz, J. A., & Wedwick, L. (2005). BOOKMATCH: Scaffolding book selection for independent reading. *The Reading Teacher, 59,* 16–32.

Yopp, H. K. (1992). Developing phonemic awareness in young children. *The Reading Teacher, 45,* 696–703.

Yopp, H. K. (1995). Read-aloud books for developing phonemic awareness: An annotated bibliography. *The Reading Teacher, 48,* 538–542.

Yopp, H. K., & Yopp, R. H. (2000). Supporting phonemic awareness development in the classroom. *The Reading Teacher, 54,* 130–143.

Children's Books Cited

Ryan, Pam Munoz (2002). *Mud is cake.* Illus. by David McPhail. New York: Hyperion.

Williams, Sue (1990). *I went walking.* Illus. by Julie Vivas. San Diego: Harcourt Brace.

Wilson, Karma (2002). *Bear snores on.* Illus. by Jane Chapman. New York: McElderry.

Chapter 6

LISTENING AND SPEAKING

Talk in a Community of Learners

ACT THREE

The old gray rat was quick to her door
and Frog was the dandy he was before.
"Charmed," said Rat and gave his consent.
Next you'll hear how the wedding went.

FROM *FROG WENT A-COURTING: A MUSICAL PLAY IN SIX ACTS* BY DOMINIC CATALANO

Dominic Catalano provides a familiar tale that may rekindle rich memories of an oral language performance from elementary school. A brilliant cast of characters, including Frog, Miss Mouse, Reverend Bug, and Madam Moth, and brief, easily memorized lines are accompanied with music to this familiar song. As the opening script continues, the listener learns that Miss Mole made the wedding gown from the finest silks in town. Miss Mouse then walked down the aisle to face Reverend Bug. As the saga continues, the marriage and aftermath of the wedding of Frog and Miss Mouse unfold through delightful rhymed language.

The combination of music and drama readily lends itself to an enjoyable parent night performance. This short scripted book includes a chapter that emphasizes the importance of speaking, listening, oral language expression, and the value of talk in the classroom. Communication provides the key to establishing a community of learners who appreciate each other's unique personalities, voices, and talents as a natural support for mutual learning experiences.

Listening and speaking play mutually reinforcing roles in a literate classroom community of learners. Children and teachers who talk to each other about literature, writing, presentations, research, or performances are also likely to listen to each other as they share plans, emotions, ideas, and information. As a learning community redefines the classroom setting, the role of listening and speaking expands beyond the traditional dominant voice of the teacher. The voices of children speaking and being listened to play a vital role in the learning that takes place in a community setting. Talk goes on so implicitly in the classroom that its daily role and contribution to learning are often underestimated. Yet discourse supplies the language of teaching and learning that pervades the classroom (Cazden, 1988). The purpose of this chapter is to reawaken in teachers as well as students the value of talk in both formal language arts activities and in the natural social contexts of the classroom.

The value of listening and speaking in a classroom community is grounded in several beliefs (Lundsteen, 1971). The word "talk" will be used in this chapter to imply the mutual relationship between listening and speaking:

- *Talk* is the vehicle that creates a safe learning environment conducive to taking risks, thus building a learning community in the classroom.
- *Talk* implies ownership as students participate in curriculum planning and make choices involving their own learning.
- *Talk* is the vehicle for sharing language arts strategies that assist in learning, assessing, and revaluing the curriculum.
- *Talk* is the means through which students build on their ideas and the ideas of others, carrying students to higher level thinking and learning.
- *Talk* is the way students bring meaning to their world.

This refreshing view of talk in the classroom holds high regard for the ability of children to learn not only from the teacher but from each other. Education, for the most part, has come a long way from the days of equating student talk with a lack of classroom discipline. Talk is now valued as a means for students to learn from each other, an opportunity to share ideas about reading and writing, and also a way to assess and evaluate each other's work.

A community of learners requires support, negotiated guidelines, and clearly articulated expectations. If we want children to talk, we must give them something worthwhile to talk about. Literature circles, research project groups, discussions following read-alouds, brainstorming sessions, and peer writing conferences represent means for talk to facilitate learning in the classroom. Understanding the kinds of talk that are appropriate and constructive to learning is key to an effective literacy community.

Objectives

- To provide a framework for the five types of listening and to introduce structured listening activities.

- To encourage read-alouds, interactive read-alouds, retellings, readers theatre, puppetry, storytelling, choral reading, and oral presentations as the focus of formal, structured listening and speaking lessons.
- To explore the potential of talk in learning communities, both through formal structured listening and speaking activities and informally in structured conversational groups, and to foster an understanding of the "cycles of meaning" (Pierce & Gilles, 1993) that lead to authentic learning.

Listening: The Neglected Language Art

Teacher Prep

The Teacher Prep Web site will help you become a better teacher by linking you to classroom videos, student artifacts, teaching strategies, lesson plans, relevant education leadership articles, and practical information on licensing, creating a portfolio, implementing standards, and being successful in field experiences. Visit this resource at www.prenhall.com/teacherprep.

Listening has long been referred to as the "neglected" language art (Landry, 1969). Although teachers often assume listening ability is in place when children come to school, they soon discover the "art of listening" must be addressed through specific instruction and through an abundance of practical learning situations. Regardless of age or grade level, listening skills must be developed, nurtured, and practiced for a variety of receptive purposes. Because we spend 53% of our time in school, in the workplace, and at leisure in the act of listening (Hunsacker, 1989), it seems critical that more attention should be given to this neglected language art. Because listening is an integral part of instruction in all content areas, it seldom has a specific time or place in the classroom. Sometimes a broad approach to incorporating listening across the curriculum often undermines the fact that listening is a learned skill that requires directed practice within the context of all learning activities. Modeling good listening, providing specific listening instruction, and creating opportunities to practice effective listening appear critical to the acquisition and development of listening strategies within and beyond classroom boundaries (Brent & Anderson, 1993).

Listening for Different Purposes

Just like reading and writing, listening is a process that involves the use of cueing systems at three distinct levels: (a) the phonological level, (b) the syntactic level, and (c) the semantic level. The *phonological* level focuses on sound bundles, or phonemes. Discriminating between different sounds eventually turns individual sounds into words, words into sentences, and sentences into a total message. At the phonological level, the listener also focuses on the intonation patterns (high/low), the variations in stress (loud/soft), and the juncture between words and sentences. At the *syntactic* level, the listener must focus on the order, arrangement, and endings of words to detect meaning. At the *semantic* level the listener must understand how words relate to each other and the way ideas are connected in order to process meaningful thoughts. All three cueing systems contribute to the receiving, processing, and comprehending of a message.

Listening can effectively be categorized by the purpose that the listener assigns to the listening task (Wolvin & Coakley, 1996). Five purposes of listening requiring skills acquired through ongoing practice have been identified: (a) discriminative listening, (b) efferent listening, (c) aesthetic listening, (d) critical listening, and (e) therapeutic listening (Tompkins, 2005). Prior knowledge and a purpose for listening direct the task and focus the listener on the reason for listening, the formality or informality of the message, and what the listener will do with the message once it is received, processed, and evaluated.

Discriminative listening is a process that distinguishes among sounds while noting the nonverbal cues of the speaker. Such discrimination may be an auditory process in which the listener recognizes sounds such as consonants, vowels, syllables, and rhyming words. The listener may also discriminate between the tone and pitch of the speaker in order to interpret the urgency and importance of the message. The listener also engages in visual discrimination, interpreting the body posture, eye contact, head movement, and facial expression of the speaker.

In the classroom setting, discriminative listening is practiced in the primary grades through phonemic awareness activities and listening to rhymed poetry. In the intermediate and middle level classroom, students learn about literary devices such as onomatopoeia, alliteration, similes, and metaphors to better understand the use of words in context. Students who are able to focus productively discriminate between the sounds, words, or images conveyed.

Efferent listening involves listening for information and comprehension. When focusing on their work, students should be able to recall the main idea as well as details and even to make inferences from the information. Oral directions, direct instruction, class presentations, and the listening that occurs in conjunction with audiotapes or videotapes require efferent listening. Lecture formats—not always the most effective instruction—often result in note-taking or filling in information on a graphic organizer in the intermediate- and middle-level classroom. The student takes away specific information, accesses it at another time, and learns information in the process.

Aesthetic listening is a process that involves relaxed attention for enjoyment, pleasure, and personal satisfaction reflecting the background experience, interest, and motivation of each listener. The dominant example in the elementary setting is the read-aloud in which children enjoy meeting new book characters, anticipating outcomes of challenging situations, and letting the momentum of the text carry them through each session. Aesthetic listening focuses on the power of language, the vivid choice of words, the flow of the sentences, and the detailed visualized images generated by well-written descriptions that carry students into the world of a book.

The elementary classroom also lends itself to aesthetic listening in a community setting through choral reading, readers theatre, poetry recitation, dramatic production, and storytelling. Listening for participation cues, for the satisfaction of rhyme and rhythm, and for the exciting ending to a well-told story also imply an aesthetic listening stance. Listening is an integral part of music, conveying messages through the lyrics of popular songs and Broadway musicals. The aesthetic listener may gradually develop an appreciation for dramatic readings, movies, theater, and musical performances. Such ongoing enjoyment of language through varied media provides pleasure beyond the classroom setting.

Critical listening requires the listener to make a judgment regarding a message based on personal values, morals, and beliefs. In everyday life, citizens are called upon to judge the content of political speeches, debates, news reports, and commercial advertising. Today's young people must critically judge the integrity of conflicting information, the varied points of view of their peers, and the validity of advertised products through the media.

Critical listening blends with critical thinking, one of the most valued skills of the workplace. Evaluating persuasive speeches in a classroom provides excellent practice for judgments made through analyzing, inferring, and evaluating. Learning to listen to the message of others forces us to broaden our own limited views of complex issues. As children grow to adulthood, the value of critical listening gives them the power to take control of the decisions they make in their own lives.

Therapeutic listening involves empathy—the ability to listen to the fears, joys, hopes, and traumatic experiences of others. In the community of learners in a classroom, listening and empathy might span a wide range of activities—from conflict resolution between peers to listening to a classmate who fears parental divorce or is experiencing the emotion of losing a loved one. Teachers often set up group sessions for discussing class issues and problems. Often, however, this type of listening is done on a one-to-one basis. Children need to learn how to give full attention to their peers and to understand the role of eye contact and receptive body language. The teacher must value the importance of establishing a setting of comfort and trust, and how to respond in an empathetic, helpful manner. Drawing from personal experiences often provides the needed tools to follow careful, sympathetic listening with sound, experienced advice and feelings. Students who practice therapeutic listening skills at a young age will build strong relationships throughout life.

Children's literature seems to provide a direct link for integrating listening skills into the existing curriculum. Teachers can build on a captive audience at read-aloud time to develop listening skills geared toward the five types of listening. Schmar (1999) suggests the following guidelines when choosing children's books to teach listening skills:

- Choose literature that best fits the precise purpose for listening—discriminative, efferent, aesthetic, critical, or therapeutic.
- Help students identify the purpose during an introduction to the read-aloud and model specific skills to be employed during the session.
- Pause and stop throughout the read-aloud to help students refocus on the listening purpose and to be certain appropriate listening skills are being applied.
- Return to the listening purpose following the read-aloud and discuss how using these skills helped students listen more effectively.

The Literature Cluster on page 162 matches picture and chapter book titles with the five purposes of listening. Students must be guided before, during, and after the read-aloud to make certain these listening purposes and related skills have taken hold and can be applied in real-world situations.

Listening and Speaking Activities

While listening and speaking occur naturally throughout the school day, formal, planned activities that address these language arts help focus on a critical area of language learning. By encouraging the art of reading aloud as well as the responses to a read-aloud—from interactive storybook reading, retellings, storytelling, choral reading to puppetry, readers theatre, dramatic performances, and oral presentations—teachers bring enduring lessons in listening and speaking into their learning communities. These activities require special literature-based selection, well-organized planning, and well-managed implementation in order to have their optimal impact on the listening and speaking of both performers and audience.

Reading Aloud

Teacher read-alouds in Grades K–8 are probably the most dominant formal listening lesson shared in classrooms. A teacher reads . . . children listen. But much planning goes on "behind the scenes" in making the read-aloud event in any classroom successful. Begin by considering the deeper purposes for reading aloud beyond the act of pure listening (Huck & Kiefer, 2004):

- To develop enjoyment and instill motivation for reading and writing
- To develop a sense of story (characters, setting, plot sequence, problem, resolution) and a sense of genre (poetry, narrative, information)
- To model and develop new vocabulary and language structures

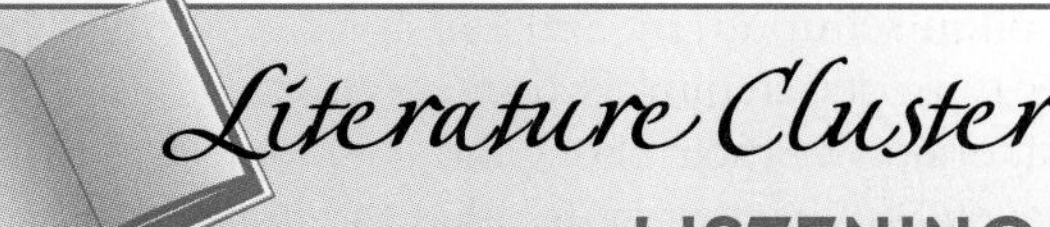

LISTENING AND LITERATURE

Discriminative Listening

Clements, A. (1997). *Double trouble in Walla Walla.* New York: Millbrook Press.

Martin, Bill, Jr. (1999). *A beasty story.* Illus. by Steven Kellogg. San Diego: Harcourt Brace.

Showers, P. (1991). *The listening walk.* New York: HarperCollins.

Waddell, M. (2001). *Webster J. Duck.* Illus. by D. Parkins. Cambridge, MA: Candlewick Press.

Wood, A. (1997). *Birdsong.* New York: Scholastic.

Comprehensive Listening

Aliki (1999). *William Shakespeare and the Globe.* New York: HarperCollins.

Banks, S. H. (1999). *Abraham's battle: A novel of Gettysburg.* New York: Atheneum.

Davies, N. (2001). *Bat loves the night.* Illus. by S. Fox-Davies. Cambridge, MA: Candlewick Press.

Fleischman, P. (1999). *Westlandia.* Illus. by Kevin Hawkes. Cambridge, MA: Candlewick Press.

Wick, W. (1997). *A drop of water.* New York: Scholastic.

Therapeutic Listening

Ernst, L. C. (1997). *Bubba and Trixie.* New York: Simon & Schuster.

Hopkinson, D. (1999). *A band of angels: A story inspired by the Jubilee Singers.* New York: Atheneum.

Palatini, M. (2001). *The Web Files.* Illus. by Richard Egielski. New York: Hyperion.

Polacco, P. (1998). *Thank you, Mr. Falker.* New York: Philomel.

Tillage, L. W. (1997). *Leon's story.* New York: Farrar, Straus & Giroux.

Critical Listening

Hesse, K. (2001). *Witness.* New York: Scholastic.

Mazer, H. (2001). *A boy at war: A novel of Pearl Harbor.* New York: Simon & Schuster.

Medina, J. (1999). *My name is Jorge: On both sides of the river (Poems in English and Spanish).* Honesdale, PA: Wordsong/Boyds Mills.

Mochizuki, K. (1997). *Passage to freedom.* New York: Lee & Low.

Myers, W. D. (1999). *At her majesty's request: An African princess in Victorian England.* New York: Scholastic.

Appreciative Listening

Esbensen, B. J. (1996). *Echoes for the eye: Poems to celebrate patterns in nature.* New York: HarperCollins.

Florian, D. (1999). *Winter eyes.* New York: Greenwillow.

King, M. L., Jr. (1997). *I have a dream.* Illus. by Coretta Scott King Award illustrators. New York: Scholastic.

Locker, T. (1997). *Water dance.* New York: Harcourt Brace.

Myers, C. (1999). *Black cat.* New York: Scholastic.

- To model and learn about the forms and conventions of writing
- To share information about other times, places, and cultures

To meet these outcomes of reading aloud, time, care, and consideration must be given to the selected book, whether a picture book that will be read in a single session or a chapter book that will be read over a period of several days. A good read-aloud should be fast-paced, allowing children's listening interest to be captured as quickly as possible (Trelease, 1985). Clear, rounded characters make for easy identification. Crisp, easy-to-read dialogue helps maintain listener attention. Long, descriptive passages, while excellent for older students, should be kept to a minimum in primary and intermediate grades. The selected book must be one about which the reader is enthusiastic—an all-time favorite, a revered classic, a recently discovered new title. Whatever the book, it is essential to find a perfect match between book and the audience. Linking selections to the personalities, ages, and interests of listeners creates a scenario for powerful reading and listening enjoyment. A good read-aloud should motivate students to want to read that book on their own or to read any book for the enjoyment it brings. The following considerations should be kept in mind when selecting the best read-aloud:

- Be judicious in your selections. Not every book in the school library makes a good read-aloud.
- Determine whether book sharing will be whole class, small group, or individual—a key factor that influences book selection.
- Select books that stretch imaginations, build on curricular interests, expose children to quality writing, and cause children to visualize the story.
- Read a variety of books across genres (poetry, biography, folk/fairy tales, nonfiction, multicultural) to capture the interests of all children over time.
- Select books through which you can communicate mood and meaning of characters and story through voice.
- Reread favorite books children have already listened to because they listen with "fresh ears" as they grow developmentally.

Although these guidelines initially seem long and cumbersome, they gradually become second nature and internalized in book selection. Remember that read-aloud time is limited and demands that the best books be shared with children. When choosing read-alouds across a variety of genres, remember to include nonfiction so that you broaden the reading interests of all children and develop tastes beyond fictional stories (Doiron, 1994).

Begin a read-aloud with a brief introduction of the author and illustrator, and link the book to others the children know. Ask them to predict what they think it will be about from the cover and title. Throughout the book, invite spontaneous comments, but do not let conversation detract from the flow of the text. After finishing the book, take time to let children share their personal connections, comments, and opinions. However, keep in mind that not all books have to be discussed or dissected to make them enjoyable read-alouds.

A list of "dos" implies a related list of "don'ts." Don't try to read aloud if you don't have sufficient time. Hurrying only detracts from the relaxed atmosphere that brings pleasure for both the reader and the listeners. Don't read too fast (the number one error for new teachers) because children's listening comprehension must follow the words and process the action in order for meaning making to occur. Slow the reading down to allow students the time to visualize characters and scenes and to savor words and creative use of language. Do not link the book with any negative experience or take away the class privilege of a read-aloud. Do not detract in any way from the major purpose of the read-aloud—to capture and create independent readers.

As you read aloud, determine the parameters for your students. In primary grades, children often sit close to the teacher and maintain eye contact with the book while not bothering other classmates. In intermediate and middle grades, students remain at their desks or tables and are often allowed to draw or work on homework. The teacher must decide how focused the listening aspect of the read-aloud should be. Setting rules, routines, and expectations early on in the school year establishes a pattern of participation and will provide a model for all subsequent read-alouds. Read-aloud time may become the most delightful time of the day for both students and teacher. Young children who ask their teacher

FIFTY QUALITY TITLES FOR READING ALOUD

Primary: Grades K–2

Cooney, Barbara (1982). *Miss Rumphius.* New York: Viking.

dePaola, Tomie (1975). *Strega Nona.* New York: Putnam.

Gag, Wanda (1928). *Millions of cats.* New York: Coward-McCann.

Henkes, Kevin (1991). *Chrysanthemum.* New York: Greenwillow.

Keats, Ezra Jack (1962). *The snowy day.* New York: Viking.

Lionni, Leo (1969). *Alexander and the wind-up mouse.* Pantheon.

Lobel, Arnold (1970). *Frog and Toad are friends.* New York: Harper & Row.

McCloskey, Robert (1941). *Make way for ducklings.* New York: Viking.

McCully, Emily Arnold (1992). *Mirette on the high wire.* New York: Putnam.

Polacco, Patricia (1990). *Thundercake.* New York: Philomel.

Rathman, Peggy (1995). *Officer Buckle and Gloria.* New York: Putnam.

Steig, William (1971). *Amos and Boris.* New York: Farrar, Straus and Giroux.

Steptoe, John (1987). *Mufaro's beautiful daughters: An African tale.* New York: Lothrop, Lee & Shepard.

Taback, Simms (1997). *There was an old lady who swallowed a fly.* New York: Viking.

White, E. B. (1952). *Charlotte's web.* Illus. by Garth Williams. New York: Harper & Row.

Wood, Audrey (1984). *The napping house.* Illus. by Don Wood. New York: Harcourt Brace.

Yolen, Jane (1987). *Owl moon.* Illus. by John Schoenherr. New York: Philomel.

Intermediate: Grades 3–5

Bunting, Eve (1991). *Fly away home.* Illus. by Ronald Himler. Boston: Clarion.

Cooper, Floyd (1994). *Coming home: From the life of Langston Hughes.* New York: Philomel.

Dahl, Roald (1961). *James and the giant peach.* Illus. by Nancy E. Burkert. New York: Knopf.

DiCamillo, Kate (2000). *Because of Winn-Dixie.* Cambridge, MA: Candlewick Press.

Fleischman, Sid (1986). *The whipping boy.* Illus. by Peter Sis. New York: Greenwillow.

to "read it again" should be heeded as revisiting the book brings new perspectives and confidence to a reader (Martinez & Roser, 1985). Older readers begging for "just one more chapter" are also exhibiting be a natural response of engaged listeners. Do not underestimate the quality of the selected literature in the success of a read-aloud. The list of books in the Literature Cluster above, have proved to be particularly successful in read-alouds.

Oral Response to a Read-Aloud

Spontaneous responses to literature before, during, and following a read-aloud provide evidence of students' prior knowledge, ongoing comprehension, and literary understanding. Reader response theory (Rosenblatt, 1978) underlies the premise that readers individually construct meaning as they transact with the text, while readers actually read themselves into the text (Bleich, 1978) as they personalize meaning and message. The construction of literary understanding in oral response to picture storybook read-alouds occurs in children as young as first and second grade (Sipe, 2000). Sipe suggests three basic literary impulses that spontaneously occurred during a study of 83 read-alouds to primary children:

Fox, Mem (1985). *Wilfred Gordon McDonald Partridge.* Illus. by Julie Vivas. New York: Kane Miller.

Gardiner, John (1980). *Stone fox.* Illus. by Marcia Sewall. New York: Crowell.

Greenfield, Eloise (1978). *Honey I love and other poems.* Illus. by Leo & Diane Dillon. New York: Crowell.

Hoffman, Mary (1991). *Amazing Grace.* Illus. by Caroline Binch. New York: Dial.

Lowry, Lois (1989). *Number the stars.* Boston: Houghton Mifflin.

MacLachlan, Patricia (1985). *Sarah, plain and tall.* New York: Harper & Row.

Martin, Bill, Jr. (1987). *Knots on a counting rope.* Illus. by Ted Rand. New York: Holt.

Naylor, Phyllis Reynolds (1991). *Shiloh.* New York: Atheneum.

Paterson, Katherine (1977). *Bridge to Terabithia.* New York: Harper & Row.

Pinkney, Andrea Davis (1998). *Duke Ellington.* Illus. by Brian Pinkney. New York: Hyperion.

Ringgold, Faith (1991). *Tar beach.* New York: Crown.

Rylant, Cynthia (1982). *When I was young in the mountains.* Illus. by Diane Goode. New York: Dutton.

Taylor, Mildred (1995). *The well.* New York: Dial.

Van Allsburg, Chris (1985). *The polar express.* Boston: Houghton Mifflin.

Wilder, Laura Ingalls (1953). *The little house in the big woods.* Illus. by Garth Williams. New York: Harper & Row.

Middle-Level: Grades 6–8

Avi (1990). *The true confessions of Charlotte Doyle.* New York: Orchard.

Blackwood, Gary (1998). *The Shakespeare stealer.* New York: Dutton.

Cushman, Karen (1994). *Catherine, called Birdy.* Boston: Clarion.

Fletcher, Susan (1998). *Shadow spinner.* New York: Atheneum.

Holt, Kimberly Willis (1998). *My Louisiana sky.* New York: Holt.

Lawrence, Iain (1998). *The wreckers.* New York: Delacorte.

Paterson, Katherine (1996). *Jip: His story.* New York: Lodestar.

Paulsen, Gary (1987). *Hatchet.* New York: Bradbury.

Peck, Richard (1999). *A long way from Chicago.* New York: Dial.

Sachar, Louis (1999). *Holes.* New York: Farrar, Straus and Giroux.

Staples, Suzanne Fisher (1989). *Shabanu: Daughter of the wind.* New York: Knopf.

Wisniewski, David (1997). *Golem.* Boston: Clarion.

- *Hermeneutic impulse:* Children are concerned with interpreting and understanding the story.
- *Personalizing impulse:* Children connect the story to themselves.
- *Aesthetic impulse:* Children are concerned with having the lived-through experience of the story or using it to express their own creativity.

Although children's spontaneous thoughts and reactions to read-aloud books constitute a highly valued oral response to literature, novice teachers can introduce a structured, open-ended approach to encourage similar thought and expand response offerings. The use of open-ended reader response prompts following a read-aloud event invites readers to focus, feel, connect, and relate literature. The power of the prompt lies in it challenging children to stretch their thinking without distorting their natural response to a book.

A response prompt is an open-ended question designed to encourage the listener (or reader) to respond following a read-aloud event. Unlike a traditional closed-end comprehension question, a response prompt has no predetermined answer. The response lies within each child and each response is expected to be unique. David Bleich (1978) improvised three prompts which provide the basis for responding orally to any piece of literature at any level:

- What did you notice in the story? (hermeneutic)
- How did the story make you feel? (aesthetic)
- What does the story remind you of from your own life? (personalizing)

While these prompts at first seem quite simple, they actually open vistas of response to children that otherwise might be left unexplored. Kelly (1990) utilized these prompts with third graders over an entire school year and documented remarkable growth in quality, quantity, and depth of oral response. At first, children responded to the prompts following read-alouds, but gradually the prompts provided an independent reading framework. Initially, respondents seemed confused by the prompts because they differed from traditional comprehension questions. With teacher modeling and listener experience over time, these prompts became internalized by the students. Teachers no longer needed to state the prompts—they automatically became the framework for oral response.

As children grow in response to these three basic prompts, teachers may choose to pose other open-ended prompts to their students.

- What special meaning or message does the story have for you?
- What did you like or dislike about the story?
- What was the most important part of the story?
- What would it feel like to be [character's name]?
- Who have you known that was like [character's name]?
- What have you experienced that was like what [character's name] experienced?
- What do you think will happen to [character's name] in the future?
- What else do you have to say about what you just read?

Such prompts continue to invite individual oral response and encourage independent thought. While prompts add unique discussion following a read-aloud, they should not become a standard routine. A knowledgeable teacher familiar with literature will realize that a few, well-selected prompts lend themselves to a particular book, but a steady diet of the same prompts, day after day, can become as inhibiting as standard comprehension questions at the end of a basal reader story. Choose prompts wisely, ascertain their connectedness to the literature, and present the prompts effectively in a nonthreatening format.

Teachers can enhance oral response by providing a consistent environment in which book talk is valued (Hepler, 1991). Not only must children be given ample time to talk during formal oral sharing, but they must be provided time for informal responses as well. In a literacy-rich classroom, children talk about books when they arrive in the morning, when they get ready to go home, and the many times in between. Response should not be built into a drill-and-practice routine, but encouraged in a natural environment of acceptance of unique thoughts in response to the literature that is being read.

Book Talks

To assist readers in selecting quality literature for reading, teachers and students may engage in book talks—brief, enticing reviews of the story and content of a prospective reading choice. Teachers will often verbalize their own delight in a book in order to entice children into reading. Such listening and speaking activities can be modeled very effectively through Lesson Plan 6.1, which features a student-initiated book talk activity. As children learn to create their own oral book talks, they make book choices and share reading recommendations with their peers.

LESSON PLAN 6.1

TITLE: Reading and Writing Book Talks

Grade Level: 3–5

Time Frame: Two days of 45–60 minutes per session

Standards

IRA/NCTE Standards: 5, 12

NETS for Students: 3, 4

Objectives

- Students will listen to audio recordings of book talks and understand the purpose and format of book talks.
- Students will write book talk manuscripts and record audio book talks.

Materials

- Computers with Internet access; headphones (optional)
- Computers with audio recording capability (including microphones) or tape recorders
- An assortment of *Reading Rainbow* books and videotapes

Motivation

- Read a *Reading Rainbow* book aloud and/or watch a *Reading Rainbow* TV/VHS segment. Discuss the purpose and goals of the *Reading Rainbow* series (available at pbskids.org/readingrainbow/).
- Explain to students that the Reading Rainbow Web site includes numerous audio recordings of book talks to get children excited about reading and to help readers select books they will enjoy.

Procedures

Day 1

- Working individually or in pairs, students listen to numerous book talks on the *Reading Rainbow* Web site. Discuss how the narrator gets the listener excited about a book.
- Read a picture book aloud to the class. Discuss what makes the book exciting and how students would entice others to read the book. As a class, write a short transcript for a book talk.

Day 2

- Working in pairs, students read picture books and write their own book talk transcript.
- Students record their book talks using tape recorders or computer technology. Consider videotaping the presentations.
- Students present to the class or to students in other classes.

Assessment

- Teacher evaluates the students' recordings based on lesson objectives.

Accommodation/Modification

- If Internet technology is unavailable, students can watch or listen to book talks included with each *Reading Rainbow* episode.

Visit the Meeting the Standards module in Chapter 6 of the Companion Website at www.prenhall.com/hancock to adapt this lesson to meet your state's standards.

Interactive Storybook Reading

Teachers differ in their read-aloud styles and in the amount of dialogue in which they engage their students during and after reading (Martinez & Teale, 1993). All children, but especially those who enter school with limited storybook reading experience, benefit from interactive read-alouds (Klesius & Griffith, 1996). As teachers read stories interactively in the early grades (K–2), they encourage children to listen accurately and to interact orally with the text, their peers, and their teacher during the read-aloud. During interactive reading, teachers pose questions that lead readers to make sense of text while eliciting personal response (Barrentine, 1996). (See Chapter 5 for a detailed discussion of the concept of interactive storybook reading as a method of promoting early literacy.)

Phyllis Root's *One Duck Stuck,* well-suited for a light interactive read-aloud, is a story in rhyme, a counting book, and a tale of a swamp adventure. The bright, spirited illustrations by Jane Chapman immediately invite children into the story. The predictability of events and the repetition of phrases guide the interactive framework of the read-aloud. The story begins with a mention of the marsh and adds words like "sleepy" and "slimy" to add to the enjoyment of descriptive language. When "one duck gets stuck in the muck," the pattern set by the text quickly allows children to predict the numbers (ranging from 1 to 10) of various types of animals along with a repeated phrase. Teacher prompts can help children predict the next number of swamp creatures (Grades K–1) or the next kind of animals or insects (Grades 1–2) by drawing on knowledge of swamp critters or the sound the creatures will make. Children can join in on well-chosen alliterative language for each critter (*splish, splish—fish; clomp, clomp—moose*) and on a repeated phrase (*Help! Help! Who can help?*) that marks the turning of a page. Small groups can take the time to count the swamp inhabitants featured on each page. Words describing the marsh (*squishy, pricky, croaky, soggy, mossy*) can be discussed for vocabulary building. Predicting the final outcome means listening carefully to the text and observing the colorful illustrations throughout the read-aloud.

Not every read-aloud justifies an interactive approach, but the interactive read-aloud does consistently engage students with literature, reading, listening, and speaking throughout the read-aloud rather than retrospectively at its conclusion. The Literature Cluster on page 169 lists several books that invite oral language during an interactive listening and reading experience.

Story Retelling

For many years, reading followed by retelling has been utilized for assessing comprehension or as an instructional tool to facilitate reader understanding of the reading process (Morrow, 1986). More recently, retelling has become a device to invite oral language

Literature Cluster

BOOKS FOR INTERACTIVE STORYBOOK READING

Peek, Merle (1985). *Mary wore her red dress and Henry wore his green sneakers*. Boston: Clarion.

Root, Phyllis (2001). *Rattletrap car*. Illus. by Jill Barton. Cambridge, MA: Candlewick Press.

Rosen, Michael (1989). *We're going on a bear hunt*. Illus. by Helen Oxenbury. New York: McElderry.

Rounds, Glen (1990). *I know an old lady who swallowed a fly*. New York: Holiday House.

Taback, Simms (1997). *There was an old lady who swallowed a fly*. New York: Viking.

Van Laan, Nancy (1990). *Possum come a-knockin'*. Illus. by George Booth. New York: Knopf.

Westcott, Nadine (1987). *Peanut butter and jelly*. New York: Dutton.

Williams, Linda (1986). *The little old lady who was not afraid of anything*. Illus. by Megan Lloyd. New York: HarperCollins.

following a listening experience. Retellings provide a powerful departure from recall questions and with teacher encouragement can reflect personal meaning making. Retellings can personalize a book by drawing on a sense of story, personal experience, and feelings and reactions. Although retellings that involve younger children may be aided by visual representations, they still depend on sharp listening enhanced by the individual voice and style of the reader.

Morrow (1986) found that repeated retellings result in a positive effect on the future oral dictation of original stories as children improve their story sense and understanding of story elements. Providing an opportunity to express understanding in a nonthreatening way, retellings challenge children to state everything they remember in their own words without the fear of being wrong. They should be offered encouragement and praise for remembering details, mentioning story elements, and describing their personal reactions. Over time, retellings become richer as growth in listening, meaning making, and oral articulation becomes the ultimate outcome.

Teachers should be aware of the following elements in considering level of performance of retellings or in modeling their own retellings.

- Setting — Begins story with an introduction. Includes time and place of story.
- Characters — Names main character. Names some secondary characters.
- Problem — States the main problem in the story.
- Episodes — Recalls episodes or segments of the story. Sequences episodes properly.
- Solution — Identifies the solution to the problem. Provides story ending.

Certain types of stories lend themselves to retellings because of structure and repetition. *Bearsie Bear and the Surprise Sleepover Party* by Bernard Waber contains the perfect elements for successful retelling. Character names like Cowsie Cow and Moosie Moose are easily remembered. Repetitive scenes of knocks on the door and requests to stay overnight form a pattern for the reteller. Repetitive dialogue (*Good night! Piggie Pie may sleep over*) also provides confidence for retellers. Remembering that Porkie Porcupine has a different fate than the rest of the visitors implies comprehension. The oral inflection of dialogue, the changing voices of characters, and the reaction to the story ending provide meaningful outlets for speaking skills. The use of retellings to improve listening and speaking also results in a deeper understanding of story elements when monitored over time.

Storytelling

Storytelling is the art of precisely retelling a story through expressive oral language and gestures to an attentive audience. A step above the previously mentioned story retelling, the typical storyteller may be the teacher or an invited guest. But the modeling of storytelling in language similar to that in the text easily motivates students to try to tell stories themselves. Storytelling helps children understand the oral tradition of literature while allowing the storyteller, unencumbered by a book, the freedom of gestures and actions to better involve listeners in the literary experience. However, the language of the storytelling attempts to stay as close to the written text as possible.

Selecting the right story for storytelling is a challenge. Folktales have several benefits that make them particularly appropriate for beginning storytelling. Look for a strong opening that brings listeners quickly into the fast-paced action and several colorful characters with whom the listener can identify. Select a plot that is not too complicated and creates a mood, whether humorous and lighthearted or serious and scary. Strong climaxes with satisfying endings are most welcome by children (Hamilton & Weiss, 1996).

Preparation for the storytelling is critical to its success:

- Read the story aloud several times to internalize the rhythm and style so it can be retold in a similar fashion.
- Consider the major actions or events of the story and conceptualize an outline to follow in telling the story.
- Develop a sense of the characters by envisioning the clothes they wear, their heights and sizes, unusual features, personality traits, speech, and mannerisms. Plan your verbal portrayal carefully so that your listeners will have a clear image.
- Draw a map of the setting with words so the listener can clearly imagine it.
- Locate repeated phrases and language patterns key to the story and incorporate them in the plan.
- Plan gestures that add to the story, and practice them in a mirror.
- Prepare an introduction and conclusion that sets the right mood, provides background information, or presents an interesting tangible artifact.
- Practice the story, being sure to note gestures, expression, intonation, and voice qualities you want to emphasize in your delivery.

The preparation is well worth the reception that a successful storytelling will receive. This special, rare treat warms students to the storyteller, the unique format, and the opportunity to be verbally drawn into a story. Set a mood for the storytelling (e.g., dim lights, lantern, shawl, rocking chair) and maintain full eye contact with the children during the presentation. Use a short step or movement or lean toward the children to indicate a change in scene, character, or action or to heighten suspense. After telling the story, pause briefly for the audience to absorb the impact of the story.

A book that lends itself to storytelling is Jan Wahl's *Tailypo,* a scary tale set in the bayou country of Louisiana. The storytelling strength of this book lies in the characters (the old man, his dogs, the monster), in the setting (cabin in the marshy woods), and in the repeated phrases ("Tailypo, tailypo, all I want is my tailypo."). Introduce the story with the background of a bayou, and provide a few props to incite interest. Create a mood by darkening the room, donning a shawl, and using a table lamp for lighting. Planned gestures can include the "scritch-scratch, scritch-scratch" sound on the chalkboard, the loud and sudden calling for the dogs ("Hey! Hey!"), and the fall of the axe on Tailypo's tail. Children will spontaneously join in on the repeated phrase. The interesting ending will require a slight pause before applause. Sharing the original book and its illustrations and discussing the visual versus illustrated image of the monster make for an effective conclusion and a reading motivation.

Literature used for storytelling often belongs to the genre of traditional tales because of the oral tradition. Verna Aardema's *Anansi Does the Impossible* revisits the beloved trickster spider as he and his wife outsmart the Sky God and win back the folktales of their people. A storytelling of Steven Kellogg's contemporary version of *The Three Little Pigs* (who are named Percy, Pete, and Prudence) will prove successful with a group of young children who have just read the original version. "Open up, Pork Chop! Or I'll huff and I'll puff and I'll flatten this dump." A multicultural storytelling of Sylvia Rosa-Casanova's *Mama Provi and the Pot of Rice* becomes a feast as a simple pot of *arroz con pollo* (chicken and rice) becomes a feast as it makes its way up eight floors of an apartment building inhabited by people of all ethnicities. The sequence of events and the various ingredients add to a structural framework for storytelling. John Bierhorst's brief retellings in *Is My Friend at Home? Pueblo Fireside Tales* weaves the theme of friendship through seven interconnected stories originally told at Native American storytelling sessions. Many picture books share stories in a sequential structure, include strong dialogue, and contain excellent descriptions that can be savored and expressed through storytelling. The Literature Cluster on page 172 provides a list of picture books that lend themselves to sharing through storytelling, either by a teacher or, eventually, by students themselves.

Oral language development is fostered in young children through the use of a feltboard or storyboard for storytelling. *Stories in My Pocket* (Hamilton & Weiss, 1996) provides an extensive offering of tales children can tell. As children develop their own storytelling skills, several intermediate-level classmates may storytell different versions of a folktale, such as the many multicultural versions of Cinderella. *Here Comes the Storyteller* (Hayes, 1996) will assist teachers in learning the secrets of successful storytelling, in this case stories of the Southwest (many with Spanish language phrases). Accompanied by photographs of the storyteller, this book models effective gestures and appropriate facial expressions as well as providing great stories from which to select a favorite. Middle-level students may choose to investigate, locate, read, and storytell folktales from a single country they may be studying. At all levels, storytelling need not be confined to the voice of a teacher or an adult. Students of all ages, with assistance, guidelines, and structure can become a part of the oral tradition that shares a story through storytelling.

Choral Reading

A simple, but effective outlet for dramatic speaking exists through the performance medium of choral reading (McCauley & McCauley, 1992). Poetry is the genre that naturally lends itself to this oral sharing of language, expression, and rhythm through dramatic, humorous, or purely enjoyable readings. Young children have a natural affinity toward verse, rhyme, riddles, and songs, while older readers revel in well-chosen language, varied moods, and the succinctness of poetry.

Literature Cluster

BOOKS FOR STORYTELLING

Aylesworth, Jim (1999). *The full belly bowl.* Illus. by Wendy A. Halperin. New York: Atheneum.

Brown, Dee (1993). *Dee Brown's folktales of the Native American retold for our times.* New York: Holt. (See "The story of the bat.")

Charlip, Remy (1969). *What good luck! What bad luck!* New York: Scholastic.

Galdone, Paul (1984). *The gingerbread boy.* Boston: Clarion.

Ginsburg, Mirra (1979). *The twelve clever brothers and other fools: Folktales from Russia.* New York: Lippincott. (See "Eight Donkeys," "The clever fool.")

Hamilton, Virginia (1985). *The people could fly: African black folktales told by Virginia Hamilton.* New York: Knopf. (See "Better wait till Martin comes.")

Hamilton, Virginia (1997). *A ring of tricksters: Animal tales from America, the West Indies, and Africa.* Illus. by Barry Moser. New York: Scholastic.

Hodges, Margaret (1997). *The true tale of Johnny Appleseed.* Illus. by Kimberly Root. New York: Holiday House.

Kellogg, Steven (1986). *Pecos Bill.* New York: Morrow.

Kimmell, Eric A. (Reteller) (1996). *Onions and garlic: An old tale.* Illus. by Katya Arnold. New York: Holiday House.

Lobel, Arnold (1980). *Fables.* New York: Harper & Row. (See "The bad kangaroo," "The hen and the apple tree," "King Lion and the beetle.")

McCaughrean, Geraldine (1995). *The golden hoard: Myths and legends of the world.* Illus. by Bee Wiley. New York: McElderry.

McCaughrean, Geraldine (1996). *The silver treasure: Myths and legends of the world.* Illus. by Bee Wiley. New York: McElderry.

McCaughrean, Geraldine (1997). *The bronze caldron: Myths and legends of the world.* Illus. by Bee Wiley. New York: McElderry Books.

McCaughrean, Geraldine (1998). *The crystal pool: Myths and legends of the world.* Illus. by Bee Wiley. New York: McElderry.

McCaughrean, Geraldine (1999). *Roman myths.* Illus. by Emma C. Clark. New York: McElderry.

McDermott, Gerald (1975). *The stonecutter: A Japanese folktale.* New York: Viking.

Muten, Burleigh (1999). *Grandmothers' stories: Wise woman tales from many cultures.* Illus. by Sian Bailey. New York: Barefoot Books.

Nolan, Dennis (1997). *Androcles and the lion.* San Diego: Harcourt Brace.

Phillip, Neil (Reteller) (1995). *The illustrated book of myths: Tales and legends of the world.* Illus. by Nilesh Mistry. New York: Dorling Kindersley.

Rockwell, Anne (1996). *The one-eyed monster and other stories from the Greek myths.* New York: Greenwillow.

Rosenthal, Paul (1998). *Yo, Aesop! Get a load of these fables.* Illus. by Marc Rosenthal. New York: Simon & Schuster.

Schwartz, Alvin (1981). *Scary stories to tell in the dark.* New York: Harper & Row. (See "The Viper.")

Schwartz, Alvin (1984). *More scary stories to tell in the dark.* New York: Harper & Row. (See "The bad news," "The bride," and "Cemetery soup.")

Schwartz, Alvin (1985). *All of our noses are here and other noodle tales.* New York: Harper & Row. (See "All of our noses are here," "The best boy in the world," "Sam and Jane go camping," and "Sam's girlfriend.")

Schwartz, Alvin (1991). *Ghosts: Ghostly tales from folklore.* New York: HarperCollins. (See "A little green bottle," and "Susie.")

Scieszka, Jon, & Smith, Lane (1992). *The stinky cheese man and other fairly stupid tales.* New York: Viking. (See "The other frog prince," "The princess and the bowling bowl," and "The stinky cheese man.")

Scieszka, Jon, & Smith, Lane (1998). *Squids will be squids: Fresh morals, beastly tales.* New York: Viking.

Seabrooke, Brenda (1995). *The swan's gift.* Illus. by Wenhai Ma. Cambridge, MA: Candlewick Press.

Sierra, Judy (Reteller) (1996). *Nursery tales around the world.* Illus. by Stefano Vitale. New York: Clarion.

Slobodkina, Esphyr (1940). *Caps for sale.* New York: Scholastic.

Young, Ed (1992). *Seven blind mice.* New York: Philomel.

Choral reading can be delivered in several formats and can be orchestrated as individual performance or partner presentations, in small groups, or as an entire class. Stewig (1981) suggests the following choral reading formats:

- ***Echo reading:*** The leader reads each line and the group repeats it. This requires a simple, quiet poem where repetition breeds reflection. Try "Forest Scenes" from Constance Levy's *A Tree Place and Other Poems.* Or try "Night Garden," the title poem from Janet Wong's *Night Garden*. The resonance of the well-read lines brings these poems to life.
- ***Paired reading:*** Paired reading provides a side-by-side delivery format for poems meant to be read aloud as dual voices. This mode of choral reading became particularly popular through Paul Fleischman's books *I Am Phoenix* and *Joyful Noise: Poems for Two Voices,* which invite side-by-side reading. Children learn to appreciate the sounds, feelings, joy, and magic of poetry through this planned vocal expression experience. Try "Whirligig Beetles" or "Book Lice" to enjoy the resounding magic of dual voices reading a single text. For a further challenge, Fleischman's *Big Talk: Poems for Four Voices* weaves spoken quartets into word music.
- ***Small group reading:*** The class divides into small groups and each group reads part of a poem. The repetition of "Can I, Can I Catch the Wind" from Pat Mora's *Confetti: Poems for Children* lends itself to this type of reading. Each group may attain ownership of a single line (or stanza) with all joining in on the first and last lines.
- ***Cumulative reading:*** One group or student reads the first line or stanza as others join in on additional lines or stanzas. An entire class presentation can emerge from Rebecca K. Dotlich's collection *Sweet Dreams of the Wild.* Each of 16 poems begins with a simple question that can be read by the whole group ("Hummingbird, hummingbird, where do you sleep?"). The answer to the question can be prepared by individual readers. The final line of each poem is the same and can be read by the entire group again. An opening and closing rhyme in this collection enclose this special blend of read-aloud poems that beg for choral performance.

The outcomes of choral reading in the classroom should include expression, intonation, voice quality, and articulation. Speaking skills can be practiced in the enjoyable context of poetry that is easy to locate, fun to arrange and rehearse, and enjoyable to present. The Literature Cluster on page 174 lists several poems that are ideal for these four types of choral reading.

Readers Theatre

An effective means to communicate the language of literature and the joy of reading is through readers theatre—a presentation of two or more persons who read from scripts and interpret a literary work in such a way that the audience senses characterization, setting, and action. While the primary purpose is reading aloud (as opposed to memorization, action, props, or costumes), the intent is for students to read expressively so that they paint an image of the events and actions in the minds of the audience (Bauer, 1987). The words typically come from literature, but the expressive response comes from inside the heart of the performers as they internalize both character and situation. A second-grade performance of Martin Waddell's *Owl Babies,* for example, yields concern, fear, and relief from a trio of baby owls as mother owl leaves the nest to seek food for her growing family.

Although intended to benefit the reader through smoother oral fluency, increased sight vocabulary, and improved comprehension, readers theatre focuses on specific oral

Literature Cluster

CLASSIC AND CONTEMPORARY POETRY FOR CHORAL READING

Adolff, Arnold (1991). *In for winter, out for spring*. Illus. by Jerry Pinkney. San Diego: Harcourt Brace.

Begay, Shonto (1995). *Navajo: Visions and voices across the mesa*. New York: Scholastic.

Cullinan, Bernice E. (Ed.) (1996). *A jar of tiny stars: Poems by NCTE award-winning poets*. Honesdale, PA: Boyds Mills Press and the National Council of Teachers of English.

de Regniers, Beatrice Schenk (Ed.) (1988). *Sing a song of popcorn*. Illus. by nine Caldecott Medal artists. New York: Scholastic.

Feelings, Tom (1993). *Soul looks back in wonder*. New York: Dial.

Florian, Douglas (1998). *Insectlopedia*. San Diego: Harcourt Brace.

George, Kristine O'Connell (1997). *The great frog race and other poems*. Illus. by Kate Kiesler. Boston: Clarion.

Greenfield, Eloise (1995). *Honey, I love*. Illus. by Jan Spivey Gilchrist. New York: HarperCollins.

Mora, Pat (1994). *The desert is my mother/El desierto es mi madre*. Illus. by Daniel Lechon. Houston, TX: Pinata Books.

O'Neill, Mary (1989/1961). *Hailstones and halibut bones*. Illus. by Leonard Weisgard. New York: Doubleday.

Prelutsky, Jack (1993). *The dragons are singing tonight*. Illus. by Peter Sis. New York: Greenwillow.

Prelutsky, Jack (1998). *A pizza the size of the sun*. Illus. by James Stevenson. New York: Greenwillow.

Silverstein, Shel (1974). *Where the sidewalk ends*. New York: Harper & Row.

Viorst, Judith (1982). *If I were in charge of the world and other worries: Poems for children and their parents*. Illus. by Lynne Cherry. New York: Atheneum.

Wong, Janet (1996). *A suitcase of seaweed and other poems*. New York: McElderry Books.

presentation outcomes as well (Laughlin & Latrobe, 1989). Expressiveness of oral reading and individual interpretation of text constitutes the core of this activity. Voice projection, appropriate inflection, accurate pronunciation, vocabulary extension, and language imagery become components of expression as the reader strives to share the emotion of the text. Personal interpretation results as the meaning derived from the text gives rise to the emotional effort behind the words (Wolf, 1993, 1994).

Aaron Shepard (1994) aptly defines readers theatre by what it is not—no memorizing, no props, no costumes, no sets. Yet he does suggest minimal equipment for readers theatre to add to its effectiveness: script binders, smocks, chairs, high stools, portable screens, and small props. Instead of constructing a set, the setting can be suggested by the location of the speakers and their movement and gestures. When action is described in the script, readers should act it out or suggest it through gestures. Common mime techniques to polish the performance include walking in place, climbing up or down stairs, lifting or pulling heavy objects, flying, or falling. Focus refers to where the readers are looking. Narrators use audience focus, but characters use on-stage focus by looking at the character to whom they are speaking. For opening polish, one reader should introduce the story with the title and author, then wait to begin until all players are frozen in place and the audience is quiet. For closing finesse, the last few words are spoken slowly and the readers freeze to break the action. They close their scripts, face the audience, and bow together.

Teacher-generated or adapted scripts provide an initial experience. A simple starting point might be Amy MacDonald's *Rachel Fister's Blister* or *Cousin Ruth's Tooth* (see Figure 6.1). These humorous stories follow the Fister family as they seek a solution to the latest family crisis. The efforts of relatives, neighbors, and friends move at a rapid pace to the solution of a wise queen. The text easily adapts into a whole class script with minimal roles for almost 20 students. The crisp, brief, and fast-paced text abounds with humorous characters and should be introduced as a read-aloud and savored several times prior to the readers theatre performance.

FIGURE 6.1
A Readers Theatre Script.

Cousin Ruth's Tooth
Amy MacDonald
Illus. by Marjorie Priceman
Houghton Mifflin, 1996
Adapted for a Readers Theatre

MRS. FISTER: Rachel Fister, get your sister!
NARRATOR: Mrs. Fister spread the word.
MRS. FISTER: Cousin Ruth has lost a tooth! O, careless youth! It's too absurd.
RACHEL: Never mind it! We shall find it!
We will search both low and high.
RUTH: Well . . . to tell the truth, I . . .
MRS. FISTER: Hush, now darling, don't you cry
MR. FISTER: Find your cousins,—several dozens—
Get your uncles and your aunts.
RACHEL: Bess! Matilda! . . . Olga! Zelda! . . . Mary Lee and Uncle Lance!
MR. FISTER: Uncle Walter! Never falter.
Search the collar, check the roof.
MRS. FISTER: Norma Jean and Aunt Bodine
Go check the attic for the tooth.
BESS: Search the yard and search the garden.
UNCLE LANCE: Check the engine of the car.
MATILDA: Check the hatbox. Check the catbox.
OLGA: Look inside the VCR!
ZELDA: Faster! Harder! Check the larder.
MARY LEE: Check the pocket of your pants!
AUNT BEA: Harder! Faster! Quelle disaster!
NARRATOR: Said Aunt Bea, who'd been to France.
NARRATOR: Though they searched in ways most ruthless, after days they still were . . .
ALL: TOOTHLESS!

Consult the original book to continue text adaptation into Readers Theatre Script.

Source: From Cousin Ruth's Tooth *by Amy MacDonald. Text copyright © 1996 by Amy MacDonald. Adapted and reprinted by permission of Houghton Mifflin Company.*

Listening/Speaking: Talk in a Community of Learners

Students of all ages may create and write their own readers theatre scripts. Whether scripts are based on authentic literature or imaginary works, producing a digital video of their performance becomes an excellent way of encouraging communication while sharing their production with others. Apple's *imovie* or Microsoft's Windows *Movie Maker* are standard features on most computers. Such user-friendly software encourages students to capture audio and video to create their own productions without too much of a software learning curve. Helpful tutorials are available on the Web.

www.microsoft.com/windowsxp/using/moviemaker/getstarted/default.mspx
www.apple.com/ilife/imovie/

To look more closely at these materials and others related to "Listening and Speaking," visit the Companion Website at www.prenhall.com/hancock.

A Beautiful Feast for a Big King Cat by John Archambault and Bill Martin Jr. provides a highly scriptable text for readers theatre. A mischievous, bold mouse shielded by his protective mother challenges an arrogant cat. Mouse finds himself in the cat's clutches, but plays on the cat's ego to get released and return home safely. The varied characters provide for individual response through oral expression. Written entirely in rhymed text, the repeated lines lend the text to small group performance. Although a readers theatre script lists character names on the left-hand side of each page, it should retain the exact words as the original text.

Success in early ventures into readers theatre are built on selection of quality literature for creating scripts or readily available scripts. In creating scripts from literature, look for books (or chapters) that are short in length so they can be shared in their entirety. The books should have an emotional appeal and three or four main characters, and they should contain ample dialogue. The Tech Tip included here offers suggestions for extending the readers theatre experience through the use of technology and preserving the dramatic performance for presenting to home or other classroom audiences.

Older children are capable of integrating writing into speaking by adapting picture books or book chapters into scripts themselves. Ann Turner's picture book, *Katie's Trunk,* takes little rewriting to attain script form about the Revolutionary War in an intermediate classroom. Narrator roles can be strategically built into the script as transitions between dialogue. The clever language and action of Sid Fleischman's *The Whipping Boy* provides several episodes for script adaptation. The Literature Cluster on page 177 lists several picture and chapter books that might be effectively adapted into readers theatre scripts.

While scripting, assignment of roles, rehearsal, and staging are important facets of readers theatre, its true success lies in the expressive nature of individuals speaking and reading fluently and adding interpretive expression to their voices. The freedom to express themselves through a character's words provides the dramatic flair that makes this such an enjoyable speaking activity.

A successful readers theatre results in a positive audience reaction, increased reading of the book that produced the script, and audience comments and suggestions for improvement. Readers theatre is an excellent way to introduce students to the world of dramatic performance. Once students have a general idea of how the process works, they

Literature Cluster
BOOKS THAT INVITE READERS THEATRE

Beatty, Patricia (1987). *Charley Skedaddle*. New York: Morrow.

Byars, Betsy (1988). *The burning questions of Bingo Brown*. New York: Viking.

Cleary, Beverly (1999). *Ramona's world*. Illus. by Alan Tiegreen. New York: Morrow Junior Books.

Cohen, Barbara (1983). *Molly's pilgrim*. Illus. by Michael J. Deraney. New York: Lothrop, Lee & Shepard.

Gardiner, John Reynolds (1980). *Stone Fox*. Illus. by Marcia Sewell. New York: Crowell.

Howard, Elizabeth Fitzgerald (2000). *Virgie goes to school with us boys*. Illus. by E. B. Lewis. New York: Simon & Schuster.

McBratney, Sam (1995). *Guess how much I love you*. Cambridge, MA: Candlewick Press.

McKissack, Patricia (2000). *The honest to goodness truth*. Illus. by Giselle Potter. New York: Atheneum.

Schroeder, Alan (1995). *Carolina shout!* Illus. by Bernie Fuchs. New York: Dial.

Taylor, Mildred (1987). *The friendship*. Illus. by Max Ginsberg. New York: Dial.

Turner, Ann (1987). *Grasshopper summer*. New York: Macmillan.

Prepared Scripts and Suggestions for Script Development

Laughlin, Mildred K., Black, Peggy T., & Loberg, Margery K. (1991). *Social studies readers theatre for children: Script and script development*. Englewood, CO: Libraries Unlimited.

Laughlin, Mildred K., & Latrobe, Kathy H. (1990). *Readers theatre for children: Scripts and script development*. Englewood, CO: Libraries Unlimited.

can take over much of the staging themselves and gain confidence in their level of professional performance.

Puppetry

Puppetry reflects dramatic improvisation in which children's voices, aided by the guise of a puppet, tell or retell stories, share information, or become a character in a improvised scenario. Puppetry requires minimal planning, spontaneous monologue or dialogue, and visual support for oral language.

Puppets must remain secondary to the oral language emphasis. A variety of puppets—finger puppets, box puppets, or shadow puppets—can be created by the children with gloves, sticks, or styrofoam balls. Puppets can take the form of masks, or they can be plush, soft, and cuddly (Flower & Fortney, 1983). However, the puppet should not be the outcome—oral language practice is the objective of puppetry.

There are several reasons why puppets are a successful speaking activity in the elementary classroom:

- Puppets provide a sense of security for the learner. Many children are shy, but when given a puppet, they find a voice within to project through the puppet.
- Puppets provide an opportunity for meaningful expression. Puppets serve as a natural tool for oral performance. They inspire oral language.
- Puppets give children the opportunity to retell or reinvent stories. Retelling provides evidence of comprehension, while switching roles and points of view provides a creative twist to known stories.

Planning and implementing puppetry is most effective when the puppet play links to quality literature. There are hundreds of books with animal characters that young children love to portray. Select books that have repetitive text to encourage comfortable participation. Consider books that will be visual and active when staged as a puppet performance as puppets come to life through movement. Be sure to select books that you and the students like. Familiar classic stories, rather than current popular books, make wonderful puppet plays. Paul Galdone's *The Little Red Hen,* for example, has repetitive text, lots of action, and a cast of animal characters that are familiar.

Stages for puppet productions do not need to be elaborate. Hand puppets can be shown through a sheet with cut holes. Puppets can appear from behind a cardboard box or a plywood theater. Placing a table on its side at a door or the front of a room can also create an effective stage. Because the emphasis is primarily on oral language, time is more effectively spent on oral language than creating props, puppets, or scenery. Working on voice projection, pronunciation, and confidence are more critical to a meaningful performance.

Keep the puppet production short since puppets have limited actions and voices can often be hard to hear. Children should improvise language rather than memorize it. While rehearsal can take place, flexibility of language is a key component during the puppet performance. Narrators should be used to move along the action, fill in the setting, or describe the passage of time. Darkening the room, introducing the players and parts, and having puppets take a curtain call all make for an enjoyable oral language experience.

Martin Waddell's *Farmer Duck* provides ample animal characters for a story reenactment. Envision a lazy farmer surrounded by a hardworking duck surrounded by a cast of a cow, hens, and a sheep. A read-aloud of the story with young children responding through puppet characters fulfills the goals of oral language enactment. Verna Aardema's *Traveling to Tondo: A Tale of the Nkundo of Zaire* is well-suited to the use of paperplate masks or stick puppets as animal travelers en route to a wedding are delayed by a series of silly circumstances. Even Barry Moser's *The Three Little Pigs,* a traditional retelling of the familiar tale, keeps characters simple and actions sequential for a puppet performance.

Older students might turn puppetry into role playing with moderately structured dramatics in which they develop a story, create characters, or plan dialogue ahead of time. Or they can create a puppet play to share with younger children.

After reading John Winch's *The Old Man Who Loved to Sing,* fourth graders prepared a parallel script to present as a puppet play (Student Sample 6.1). They designed stick puppets to represent the animals of the Australian outback, the setting of the story. After studying the structure and morals of fables, sixth graders wrote their own fables and shared them using a stick puppet as a prop to illustrate the story (Student Sample 6.2). As with all credible speaking activities, puppet-play audiences simultaneously practice optimal listening skills as they make meaning from the puppet production.

Creative Drama and Play Performance

One of the fondest memories of elementary and middle school for many children is a treasured performance in a class or school play. While taking much time and preparation, dramatic performance is the ultimate reflection of speaking ability. Not only does it require practice, drama approaches perfection as a performance nears. Making language come alive through the reading of plays provides a masterful oral language performance (Manna, 1984).

Miniperformances (Morado, Koenig, & Wilson, 1999) involve primary students in performances based on literature, verbal interactions, and imagination. Action and dialogue are formalized into a written script with the guidance of a teacher. The script incorporates the children's retelling of the story in their own words. The script is typed in a large font

STUDENT SAMPLE 6.1 Fourth-Grade Puppet Play.

THE OLD MAN WHO LOVED TO SING: GROUP TWO

Old man: Ally
Narrator: Christine
Dingoes: Dylan and Stefan
Birds: Sean and Jessica
Koala: Brooke
Mice: Christine
Wombat: Robert
Kangaroo: Ally and Robert
Platypus: Robert
Possum: Dylan

NARRATOR: This is a story about an Old Man who loves to sing. Our story begins in Sydney, Australia.
OLD MAN: [Plays his gramophone.]
CITY: [Various city noises. Banging, honking, beeping, dinging, sirens.]
OLD MAN: I can't stand all the noise here! I'm moving to the outback.
NARRATOR: So he packs up his things and moves to the Outback.
OLD MAN: This is a nice quiet place to live. It's so quiet here that I can sing and build a cabin. [Begins to sing along with the gramophone.]
DINGOES: This music is squeaky!
BIRDS: What is that terrible noise?
KOALA: Can't a koala get any sleep around here?
MICE: There is so much noise we can't even sneak to the cheese!
WOMBAT: I can't dig underground because there is too much noise.
KANGAROO: We can't hop around with all this racket!
PLATYPUS: We can't lay eggs with all this racket!
NARRATOR: Time went by and eventually the animals began to like the music.
POSSUM: [Swinging by his tail] I actually like this music!

with speakers' parts in boldface and children's names as authors of the script. Movement, music, and drama interweave into this literacy activity through modalities often not emphasized in traditional instruction, therefore working effectively with primary at-risk students. The goal of miniperformances is for children to explore, internalize, and recreate story elements. Comprehension is emphasized over memorization. Figure 6.2 lists the sequential development of a miniperformance over 6 days. This adapted story reenactment for young children provides the opportunity for small scale productions with effective results both with language and personal self-esteem.

Gary Soto's *Navajo Boy: A Play* may rejuvenate an interest in play performance for older students. This lighthearted play about the mixed joy and sorrow of young love in a Mexican American community will spark the attention of middle-school students. While teachers find dramatic performances exhausting in terms of time, anxiety, and attention, plays create memorable moments in school life and often showcase students who otherwise may be lost in pencil and paper assessment. In addition, those who struggle with reading often warm to the performance of literature as it provides motivation and needed practice (McMaster, 1998).

STUDENT SAMPLE 6.2 Sixth-Grade Stick Puppets.

FIGURE 6.2
Miniperformances at a Glance.

Day 1

- Introduce and read the story.
- Generate a list of characters.
- Decide who will play which part, balancing integrity of the story with each child's role preference.

Day 2

- Review the story, clarifying unfamiliar vocabulary.
- Decide where in the performing space each part of the action will take place and a starting location for each character.
- As the teacher reads the story and serves as narrator, children take on their chosen role and follow the action.
- Students begin to help tell the story by reciting key repetitive lines.

Days 3 and 4: Producing the script

- Narrator reads story, and children now put into their own words what their characters will say. One teacher transcribes characters' dialogue as the action progresses.
- Songs, chants, and movements are added to personalize the story.
- At the end of Day 4, teachers produce a miniperformance script, with students' original words, to be distributed to the students for reading, studying, and practicing both at school and at home.

Day 5

- During the final rehearsal, emphasis is placed on speaking with loud, clear voices while facing where the audience will be.
- Rehearse opening and closing the performance: introducing the story to the audience, bowing at the end, and introducing the cast.

Day 6: Miniperformance day

- Gather performers 10 minutes before show time, getting them into costumes and applying face paint. Warm up and focus the group by rehearsing beginnings, endings, key sections, or songs.
- Present the miniperformance to a small audience of classmates, siblings, teachers, and parents.
- Present personalized copies of the original story book to cast, classroom, and school library.

Source: From Carolyn Morado, Rosalie J. Koenig, & Alice S. Wilson (1999). Miniperformances, many stars! Playing with stories. The Reading Teacher, *53 (2), 116–123. Reprinted with permission of Carolyn Morado and the International Reading Association. All rights reserved.*

Dramatic performance provides a mode of response that involves quality speaking, internalization of character, and transmission of both words and emotions to a motivated audience.

Oral Reports and Presentations

The transmission of information from a speaker to an audience takes the form of an oral report or presentation in the intermediate and upper grades. Whether sharing the facts on a South American country, speaking in the guise of a biographical subject such as Lord

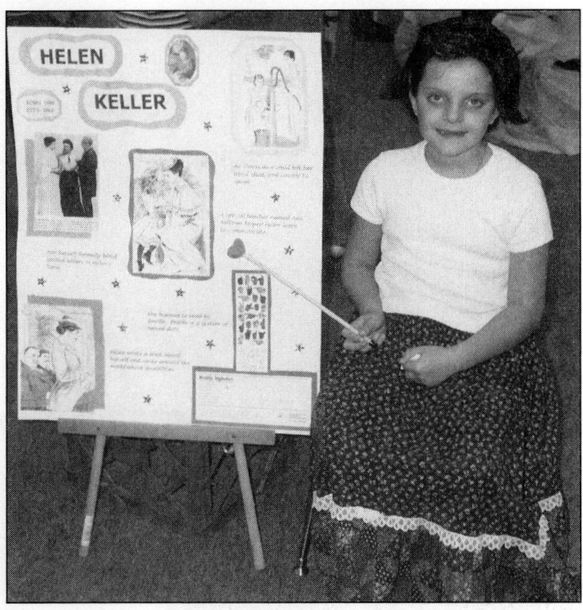

An oral report is guided and enhanced through visual representation.

Shackleton or Gertrude Ederle, or presenting a poster session on a science project, speaking becomes the focus of the presentation. Oral reports reflect language functions as they inform or persuade. To make oral reports effective teachers must model and explain their preparation. Too often, students merely copy information from a resource, thus changing the oral report into a reading exercise. The result is that students learn to dread speaking in front of a group rather than gaining confidence in sharing their own information. Tompkins (2005) suggests a six-step process for preparing information for an oral report:

- ***Choose a topic.*** While a teacher may suggest a broad topic (e.g., the human body, state reports, the Civil War), students focus in on a narrow topic which satisfies their interests (e.g., the skeletal system, Alaska, uniforms of the confederacy). Graphic organizers provide a strong overview of individual topics in the classroom. Teachers might also suggest four to five questions that must be answered about each of the narrower topics.
- ***Gather and organize information.*** Students gather information using a variety of sources, including informational books, newspapers, Web sites, and encyclopedias. Students can also access nonprint resources such as filmstrips and videotapes, or they can conduct on-site interviews. When all the information is gathered, students must decide how it will most effectively be presented to their audience. The report must be interesting and well-organized to hold listener attention. Notes and information in abbreviated form should be transferred to notecards.
- ***Develop the report.*** Students review their gathered information and determine the structure that will best present the report in an interesting and well-organized format. Students can transfer notes to note cards, but only minimal key terms should be included.
- ***Create visual representations of information.*** Students can develop charts, diagrams, timelines, maps, or models. Visuals provide not only an interesting focus for the audience but a reminder to the speaker of information to be shared. Students can also use a scanner to share visuals through a PowerPoint presentation.

- ***Rehearse the presentation.*** Students choose an attention-getting fact to capture audience interest as the opening of the presentation. Reading note cards and reviewing information helps in preparation. Repeated practice builds delivery confidence and oral expression.
- ***Share the oral presentation.*** Rehearsing and ultimately sharing the report with the class brings report preparation to its final outcome. Teacher minilessons on speaking loudly, maintaining eye contact with the audience, staying on topic, briefly referring to notecards, and using visuals effectively provide high expectations for speakers. Starting with an interesting fact or artifact and speaking from personal interest and knowledge (rather than reading the report) can ensure greater success. The audience of listeners can learn the responsibilities of being attentive, listening to the speaker, asking questions, and providing meaningful feedback to the speaker.

Oral reports and presentations provide a first step for gaining confidence in speaking in front of a large group of peers. Oral language abilities are practiced and growing confidence makes this speaking and listening activity meaningful beyond the classroom.

Figure 6.3 presents a continuum of developmentally appropriate oral listening and speaking activities for the classroom. Such activities provide the variety and practice that students need to refine their listening skills and speaking strategies.

FIGURE 6.3 **Developmental Listening and Speaking Activities.**

Listening Activities for Grades K–2

What's that sound?
I can make that sound!
What is it?
Naming activities
Repeat after me
Predicting outcomes
Following directions
Rhyming words
Recognizing sequences
Identifying consonant sounds

Speaking Activities for Grades K–2

Pantomime feelings, actions, short scenes
Simple storytelling
Introducing oneself
Introducing another person
Starting a conversation
Nonverbal behavior
Using emotional tone

Listening Activities for Grades 3–5

Reality/fantasy read-alouds
Critical thinking
Oral history guest speaker

Speaking Activities for Grades 3–5

Articulation
Extemporaneous speech
Persuasive speech
Interviewing
Group storytelling
Cultural heritage speech
Multicultural story interpretation

Listening and Speaking Activities for Grades 6–8

Oral history interview
Persuasive speech with outline
Job interviewing
Informative speech
Impromptu speech
Panel discussion

Source: Activities adapted from suggestions by A. L. Chaney & T. L. Burk (1998). Teaching oral communication in Grades K–8. *Boston: Allyn & Bacon.*

Classroom Conversations: Informal Productive Talk

In teaching the language arts, opportunities abound for whole group and small group conversations built on informal productive talk. The oral expression of personal ideas, thoughts, and response provides an interactive learning tool in the classroom. All knowledge does not come from the teacher alone as children do learn from others through on-task, focused talk. Students talking and listening to one another provide authentic communication with a real audience and a real purpose. Whether working in a writing group, responding in a literature conversation, or focusing on a group research project, small group learning focuses on student-centered learning as an approach to teaching the language arts.

Research has shown that working in cooperative groups improves students' academic achievement, social skills, and self-esteem (Slavin, 1990). In teaching the language arts, opportunities exist for working and sharing in small groups. Several cooperative learning strategies (Baloche, 1998; Kagan, 1992) have been developed that apply to language arts learning. An example of the cooperative strategy is accompanied by a language arts connection.

- ***Jigsaw.*** Students may form reading teams as each student becomes an expert on a specific picture book by Patricia Polacco during an author study on this prolific author and illustrator. The following books might be assigned:

  Member A: *Betty Doll*

  Member B: *My Rotten Redheaded Older Brother*

  Member C: *The Bee Tree*

  Member D: *Thundercake*

  Member E: *Thank you, Mr. Falker*

  All members of the same letter read and discuss together with other members assigned the same topic. When students return to their original teams, they share what they have learned about Polacco's life from their assigned book.
- ***Think—Pair—Share.*** Reading buddies can employ this cooperative learning strategy by reading an assigned trickster tale such as Gerald McDermott's *Zomo the Rabbit: A Trickster Tale from West Africa,* discussing it with a partner, and sharing the common elements of trickster tales with the entire class who have been assigned other similar tales.
- ***Pair Interviews.*** During the brainstorming stage of the writing process, students might bring a favorite object to school (e.g., stuffed animal, doll, seashell, insect) and interview a partner about it. Where did you get it? Why is it so special to you? How long have you had it? Why is it different than any other ____? Each partner then shares what he or she has learned with a small group or the whole class before the drafting stage.
- ***Cooperative projects.*** Students from a literature response group might agree to construct a mural of the main events in response to Christopher Paul Curtis's *Bud, Not Buddy.* While students are working toward a common goal, they must each make an identifiable contribution to the group task, such as prioritizing ten events, illustrating the scenarios, adding quotations to the mural, or sharing the mural orally with the class.

These provide just a few examples of how collaborative talk relates to the oral opportunities in the language arts classroom. Perhaps the literature conversation provides the most effective application of collaborative talk.

Literature Conversations

As children lean toward the early and advanced independent reading of literature, teachers strive to provide more experiences of reading wonderful books and talking about them with others. Small groups of children with similar reading interests read picture books, short chapter books, and full-length chapter books, discussing and responding to what they read. Literature conversations engage children in collaborative listening and speaking groups as interactive dialogue leads participants toward new perspectives on a book. Literature conversation groups are composed of four to six students who ideally, over time, build a dining room table style of conversation to response sessions (Atwell, 1987).

Owens (1995) suggested a sound rationale for utilizing literature conversations as a support framework for sharing oral response. Literature conversations improve oral response to books in several ways:

- Promote a love of literature and positive attitudes toward reading.
- Reflect a constructivist, child-centered model of literacy.
- Encourage extensive and intensive reading.
- Invite natural discussions that lead to higher level, critical thinking.
- Support a diverse response to literature.
- Foster interaction and collaboration.
- Encourage response to literature from multiple perspectives.
- Nurture private reflection and oral articulation of thoughts.

Many classroom-based studies highlight the potential of literature conversations to improve the ability to communicate personal thoughts about literature, to build critical listening and speaking skills, and to keep an open mind to new perspectives on a literary text (Eeds & Wells, 1989; Lehman & Scharer, 1996). Guidelines for organizing, managing, and facilitating literature conversations with young children (Chapter 5) and with intermediate and middle-level students (Chapter 7) will provide a detailed framework for this productive talk mode in the context of reading workshops in the classroom. When you revisit this topic in later chapters of the book, the impact of listening and speaking in a literature conversation will remind you of the power of classroom conversation in a community of learners.

Visit the Companion Website at www.prenhall.com/hancock and gauge your understanding of Chapter 6 concepts with the self-assessments.

Closing Thoughts

This chapter cast a spotlight on the lesser mentioned language arts of listening and speaking. Beginning with an opening focus on the "neglected" language art of listening, we have seen the importance of including formal instruction and practice in this neglected area. The varied types of listening match with literary texts that focus instruction on learning about all aspects of the art of listening.

The chapter focused on the many classic listening and speaking activities that provide memorable experiences through active listening engagement, speaking performance, and listening and speaking integration. It also showed how you can be energized by the prospect of planning and experiencing read-alouds, interactive reading, and story retelling.

The potential of readers theatre as a reading, writing, listening, speaking activity, as well as a performance mode was discussed. Puppetry was shown to combine visual representation by constructing puppets and listening and speaking to their words and stories. Choral reading was discussed as a means to achieving listening and speaking outcomes. Finally, oral presentations were shown to be comfortable and confidence-building experiences for students.

The last phase of the chapter addressed the importance of productive talk in the context of a community of learners. Collaborative learning groups in the language arts classroom provide a productive means of interactive learning through listening and speaking components. The potential of talk as a vehicle toward collaborative teaching and learning emerges clearly in this chapter, helping teachers to manage and facilitate small group activities within the classroom.

As you move on to other areas of language arts, keep listening and speaking close to your heart and your lesson delivery. While too many teachers assume that listening and speaking are already in place, they are surprised to discover that specific listening and speaking activities are needed to focus on the skills necessary for learning and sharing across the entire curriculum. With proper modeling and practice, students can succeed in both the receptive and the communicative realm of the listening and speaking domains of the language arts.

References

Atwell, N. (1987). *In the middle: Writing, reading, and learning with adolescents*. Portsmouth, NH: Heinemann.

Baloche, L. A. (1998). *The cooperative classroom: Empowering learning*. Upper Saddle River, NJ: Prentice Hall.

Barrentine, S. J. (1996). Engaging with reading through interactive read alouds. *The Reading Teacher, 50,* 36–43.

Bauer, C. (1987). *Presenting readers theatre*. New York: Wilson.

Bleich, D. (1978). *Subjective criticism*. Baltimore, MD: Johns Hopkins University Press.

Brent, R., & Anderson, P. (1993). Developing children's classroom listening strategies. *The Reading Teacher, 47,* 122–126.

Cazden, C. D. (1988). *Classroom discourse: The language of teaching and learning*. Portsmouth, NH: Heinemann.

Chaney, A. L., & Burk, T. L. (1998). *Teaching oral communication in grades K–8*. Boston: Allyn & Bacon.

Doiron, R. (1994). Using nonfiction in a real-aloud program: Letting the facts speak for themselves. *The Reading Teacher, 47,* 616–624.

Eeds, M., & Wells, D. (1989). Grand conversations: An exploration of meaning construction in literature study groups. *Research in the Teaching of English, 23,* 4–29.

Flower, C., & Fortney, A. (1983). *Puppets—methods and materials*. New York: Davis.

Hamilton, M., & Weiss, M. (1996). *Stories in my pocket: Tales kids can tell*. Golden, CO: Fulcrum Publishing.

Hayes, J. (1996). *Here comes the storyteller*. El Paso, TX: Cinco Puntos Press.

Hepler, S. (1991). Talking our way to literacy in the classroom community. *The New Advocate, 4,* 179–191.

Huck, C. S., & Kiefer, B. Z. (2004). *Children's literature in the elementary school* (8th ed.). Madison, WI: Brown & Benchmark.

Hunsacker, R. (1989). What listening skills should be taught to teachers and students? In P. Cooper and K. Galvin (Eds.), *The future of speech communication education* (pp. 27–30). Annandale, VA: Speech Communication Association.

Kagan, S. (1992). *Cooperative learning*. San Juan Capistrano, CA: Kagan Cooperative Learning.

Kelly, P. R. (1990). Guiding young students' responses to literature. *The Reading Teacher, 43,* 464–470.

Klesius, J., & Griffith, P. (1996). Interactive storybook reading for at-risk learners. *The Reading Teacher, 49,* 552–560.

Landry, D. (1969). The neglect of listening. *Elementary English, 46,* 599–605.

Laughlin, M. K., & Latrobe, K. H. (1989). *Readers theatre for children: Scripts and script development*. Englewood, CO: Libraries Unlimited.

Lehman, B. A., & Scharer, P. (1996). Reading alone, talking together: The role of discussion in developing literary awareness. *The Reading Teacher, 50,* 26–35.

Lundsteen, S. (1971). *Listening: Its impact on reading and other language arts.* Urbana IL: National Council of Teachers of English.

Manna, A. L. (1984). Making language come alive through reading plays. *The Reading Teacher, 37,* 712–717.

Martinez, M. G., & Roser, N. L. (1985). Read it again: The value of repeated readings during storytime. *The Reading Teacher, 38,* 782–786.

Martinez, M. G., & Teale, W. H. (1993). Teacher storybook reading style: A comparison of six teachers. *Research in the Teaching of English, 27,* 175–199.

McCauley, J. K., & McCauley, D. S. (1992). Using choral reading to promote language learning for ESL students. *The Reading Teacher, 45,* 526–533.

McMaster, J. C. (1998). "Doing" literature: Using drama to build literacy classrooms: The segue for a few struggling readers. *The Reading Teacher, 51,* 574–584.

Morrow, L. M. (1986). Effects of structural guidance in story retelling on children's dictation of original stories. *Journal of Reading Behavior, 2,* 135–151.

Owens, S. (1995). Treasures in the attic: Building the foundations for literature circles. In B. Campbell Hill, N. J. Johnson, & K. L. Schlick Noe (Eds.), *Literature circles and response* (pp. 1–12). Norwood, MA: Christopher-Gordon.

Pierce, K. M., & Gilles, C. (Eds.) (1993). *Cycles of meaning: Exploring the potential of talk in learning communities.* Portsmouth, NH: Heinmann.

Rosenblatt, L. M. (1978). *The reader, the text, the poem: The transactional theory of the literary work.* Carbondale, IL: Southern Illinois University Press.

Schmar, E. (1999). Listening: The forgotten language art. *Kansas Journal of Reading, 15,* 32–41.

Shepard, A. (1994). From script to stage: Tips for readers theatre. *The Reading Teacher, 48,* 184–185.

Sipe, L. (2000). The construction of literary understanding by first and second graders in oral response to picture storybook read-alouds. *Reading Research Quarterly, 35,* 252–275.

Slavin, R. (1990). *Cooperative learning: Theory, research, and practice.* Upper Saddle River, NJ: Prentice Hall.

Stewig, J. (1981). Choral speaking: Who has the time? Why take the time? *Childhood Education, 57,* 25–29.

Tompkins, G. E. (2005). *Language Arts: Patterns of practice* (6th ed.). Upper Saddle River, NJ: Merrill/Prentice Hall.

Trelease, J. (1985). *The read-aloud handbook.* New York: Viking/Penguin.

Wolf, S. A. (1993). What's in a name? Labels and literacy in readers theatre. *The Reading Teacher, 46,* 540–545.

Wolf, S. A. (1994). Learning to act/acting to learn: Children as actors, critics, and characters in classroom theatre. *Research in the Teaching of English, 28,* 7–44.

Wolvin, A. D., & Coakley, C. G. (1996). *Listening* (5th ed.). Madison, WI: Brown & Benchmark.

Children's Books Cited

Aardema, Verna (1991). *Traveling to Tondo: A tale of the Nkundo of Zaire.* Illus. by Will Hildebrand. New York: Knopf.

Aardema, Verna (1997). *Anansi does the impossible: An Ashanti tale.* Illus. by Lisa Desimini. New York: Atheneum.

Archambault, John, & Martin, Bill, Jr. (1994). *A beautiful feast for a big king cat.* Illus. by Bruce Degan. New York: HarperCollins.

Bierhorst, John (Reteller) (2001). *Is my friend at home? Pueblo fireside tales.* Illus. by Wendy Watson. New York: Farrar, Straus & Giroux.

Catalano, Dominic (1998). *Frog went a-courting: A musical play in six acts.* Honesdale, PA: Boyds Mills Press.

Curtis, Christopher Paul (1999). *Bud, not Buddy.* New York: Delacorte.

Fleischman, Paul (1985). *I am Phoenix: Poems for two voices.* Illus. by K. Nutt. New York: Harper & Row.

Fleischman, Paul (1988). *Joyful noise: Poems for two voices.* Illus. by E. Beddows. New York: Harper & Row.

Fleischman, Paul (2000). *Big talk: Poems for four voices.* Illus. by Beppe Giacobbe. Cambridge, MA: Candlewick Press.

Fleischman, Sid (1986). *The whipping boy.* Illus. by Peter Sis. New York: Greenwillow.

Galdone, Paul (1979). *The little red hen.* New York: Clarion.

Levy, Constance (1994). *A tree place and other poems.* Illus. by Robert Sabuda. New York: McElderry Books.

MacDonald, Amy (1990). *Rachel Fister's blister.* Illus. by Marjorie Priceman. Boston: Houghton Mifflin.

MacDonald, Amy (1996). *Cousin Ruth's tooth.* Illus. by Marjorie Priceman. Boston: Houghton Mifflin.

McDermott, Gerald (1992). *Zomo the rabbit: A trickster tale from West Africa.* San Diego: Harcourt Brace.

Mora, Pat (1996). *Confetti: Poems for children.* Illus. by Enrique O. Sanchez. New York: Lee & Low Books.

Moser, Barry (Reteller) (2001). *The three little pigs.* Boston: Little, Brown.

Polacco, Patricia (1990). *Thundercake.* New York: Philomel.

Polacco, Patricia (1993). *The bee tree*. New York: Philomel.

Polacco, Patricia (1994). *My rotten redheaded older brother*. New York: Philomel.

Polacco, Patricia (1998). *Thank you, Mr. Falker*. New York: Philomel.

Polacco, Patricia (2000). *Betty doll*. New York: Philomel.

Root, Phyllis (1998). *One duck stuck*. Illus. by Jane Chapman. Cambridge, MA: Candlewick Press.

Rosa-Casanova, Sylvia (1997). *Mama Provi and the pot of rise*. Illus. by Robert Roth. New York: Atheneum.

Soto, Gary (1997). *Navajo boy: A play*. San Diego: Harcourt Brace.

Turner, Ann (1992). *Katie's trunk*. Illus. by Ron Himler. New York: Macmillan.

Waber, Bernard (1997). *Bearsie Bear and the surprise sleepover party*. Boston: Houghton Mifflin.

Waddell, Martin (1991). *Farmer duck*. New York: Candlewick Press.

Waddell, Martin (1992). *Owl babies*. Illus. by Patrick Benson. New York: Candlewick Press.

Wahl, Jan (1991). *Tailypo*. Illus. by Wil Clay. New York: Holt.

Winch, John (1996). *The old man who loved to sing*. New York: Scholastic.

Wong, Janet (2000). *Night garden*. New York: McElderry.

Chapter 7

CONTINUING THE READING APPRENTICESHIP

Reading Workshop and Comprehension Strategies (Grades 3–8)

"How am I to do it all myself? How are you going to help me if you do not have a wheel of your own? And how is the wheel to be made if you do not fetch logs of considerable size? Go!" Min gestured impatiently toward the mountains.

Tree-ear had already turned to leave when the full import of Min's words reached his understanding. A wheel of your own?

Min was going to teach him to throw pots! Tree-ear glanced back over his shoulder, a foolishly wide grin on his face. . . .

How long would it be before he had skill enough to create a design worthy of such a vase? . . . One day at a time, he would journey through the years until he came upon the perfect design.

FROM *A SINGLE SHARD* BY LINDA SUE PARK*

This excerpt from Linda Sue Park's Newbery Medal winner *A Single Shard* set in 12th century Korea captures the teacher and learner relationship between a master craftsman (Min, a teacher) and the apprentice (Tree-ear, a learner). This analogy reflects the apprenticeship model throughout history. The apprentice comes under the guidance of a master teacher who teaches and guides him on a daily basis in the context of an authentic task (celadon pottery). Each day, new facets of the trade arise and new skills are taught as Tree-ear gradually becomes stronger, and more confident and independent. As practice continues over time, the apprentice builds a repertoire of skills and experiences from which to draw in solving problems. As these skills are applied over and over again, the apprentice eventually works toward the creation of a masterpiece—a celadon pottery vase that reflects Tree-ear's ability to move on to a lifetime of producing masterpieces on his own.

So, too, does the apprenticeship model apply to the art of reading. With guidance, practice, skill application, strategy internalization, an increasingly rich vocabulary, and an understanding of varied text structures and genres, a novice reader moves toward completing the reading masterpiece—the individual understanding, personal connections, and inherent pleasure of the art of reading. In order for the goal of independent, lifelong reading to come to fruition, however, time, choice, practice, and responsibility (Hanson, 2001) must be provided and expected across the elementary and middle-level grades. Without these interim developmental steps on the literacy journey, the process may not be complete. The art of lifelong reading is attained only with determined persistence, continuous growth, masterful guidance, and the promise of the lifelong satisfaction of reading.

The apprenticeship model of reading (Dorn, French, & Jones, 1998) provides a parallel vision for the way reading should be taught, nurtured, and practiced in Grades 3 through 8 as readers move along the pathway to lifelong reading. An apprenticeship model implies that the reader is embarking on a learning journey toward becoming a master of the art of reading. Along the way, the novice reader learns strategies and skills to ease the task, enhance understanding, and make reading a pleasurable experience. Nevertheless, it is a continuous process as the reader takes small steps by increasing his or her reading arsenal with increasingly complex skills, new vocabulary, applied strategies, genre understandings, and textual frameworks. Eventually, with time, practice, and choice, readers move toward independence, develop and appreciate a higher level of individual comprehension, and retain a repertoire of strategies readily applied in the context of a variety of texts. Indeed, the reader becomes a master of the art of reading.

Objectives

- To envision the organization and implementation of reading workshop as a vehicle for teacher modeling and learner practice of the art of reading.
- To conceptualize the four major components of reading workshop: literature selection, literature response journals, project response options, and literature conversations.

*Excerpt from *A Single Shard* (pp. 146–148) by Linda Sue Park. Reprinted by permission of Clarion Books, an imprint of Houghton Mifflin Company.

- To determine how to select class sets and text sets across genres.
- To differentiate between structured, unstructured, and character response journals.
- To grasp the possibilities of response options across the arts.
- To organize literature conversations by participant roles.
- To provide an overview of strategic reading within a reading workshop approach.
- To understand the seven comprehension strategies that characterize proficient readers.
- To understand the role that reading workshop fulfills within a balanced literacy program.

Reading Workshop

One of the most common literature-based configurations and methods of teaching reading in the upper primary, intermediate, and middle-level grades is the reading workshop (Atwell, 1998; Serafini, 2001). According to the reading workshop approach, students practice a common task as a collaborative community of learners under the watchful, competent, well-planned guidance of a teacher who knows how to teach reading, how to organize for instruction and practice, and how to value the unique thoughts and responses of individual readers.

Establishing Elements of a Reading Workshop

Five and Egawa (1998) provide a research-into-practice synthesis of four criteria for establishing a workshop approach to teaching reading: (a) time, (b) predictable structure and routines, (c) ownership and choice, and (d) response opportunities. Reading workshop requires large blocks of time as well as predictable structures and routines where students have opportunities for ownership, choice, and response to the books they read.

Time. Workshop time is scheduled on a frequent, regular basis (45 to 60 minutes, five times per week). Scheduling large blocks of restricted time reflects the value the teacher puts on reading. Students need plenty of time to become engaged in reading, to apply new strategies within the context of real reading, to experience the enjoyment of reading whole texts, and to grow as readers. While most teachers establish a separate reading workshop block, some teachers combine a larger block of time for both reading and writing workshops.

Predictable Structure and Routines. Students must be well-versed and accustomed to the daily routines and demands of a reading workshop. Teachers introduce workshop procedures through strategy lessons and demonstrations so that the students will understand what to do and what is expected of them each day. Responsibility and accountability play an important role in the efficiency and effectiveness of a reading workshop. Predictable routines and expectations enable students to begin work each day without confusion and to develop greater independence as they take on responsibility for their learning.

Teacher Prep

The Teacher Prep Web site will help you become a better teacher by linking you to classroom videos, student artifacts, teaching strategies, lesson plans, relevant education leadership articles, and practical information on licensing, creating a portfolio, implementing standards, and being successful in field experiences. Visit this resource at www.prenhall.com/teacherprep.

Ownership and Choice. Within a reading workshop environment, students are expected to make decisions—from choosing literature for reading and selecting ways to respond to literature to sharing ideas, thoughts, and feelings about the books they read with peers. Often, teachers guide students with these choices in order to broaden their experiences as readers. With ownership and choice comes responsibility for reading assigned chapters, completing response activities, and being prepared for and contributing to literature conversations.

Response Opportunities. In a reading workshop community, different points of view and trust between learners are valued. A respect for diverse ideas, backgrounds, and ways of learning is fostered. Teacher responses to students and student interactions with each other must highlight individual strengths and unique contributions. Even when responses might not make sense, they must be honored as meaningful. Students should feel secure in sharing their thoughts, responses, and opinions in a risk-free environment that builds on individual interests and strengths.

Structuring and Scheduling the Reading Workshop

The time configuration for a reading workshop requires that a full hour or more be set aside to address all of its opening, skills minilesson, assignments and progress, reading of text, response options, literature conversations, and closing sharing time. The predictability of the format provides efficient time-on-task learning as students ready themselves for scheduled components. Figure 7.1 provides an overview of the time structure of a daily reading workshop, and Figure 7.2 provides an example of a typical weekly schedule for this format of instruction.

Sharing Time

The first 5 to 10 minutes of a reading workshop should be used to spark interest in reading. A teacher might introduce a book by a new author or other books by the author of a book that the students are currently reading. Brief book talks by both teacher and students can open eyes to new reading possibilities for sustained silent reading. A new literary genre may

FIGURE 7.1 Time Structure of a Typical Reading Workshop.

0:00–0:10	**Sharing Time** Share book talks, read-alouds, and introduce new genres to inspire further reading among peers.
0:10–0:18	**Reading Strategy Lesson** Introduce a predetermined reading strategy and student application within the context of the reading workshop texts.
0:18–0:20	**Organizing the Workshop** Gather materials, locate group settings, and prepare for an on-task workshop atmosphere through an efficient, daily routine.
0:20–0:50	**Reading and Responding** Assign independent reading of text, guide reader response activity, set days for literature conversations, and present project response options. **Independent Reading** Encourage choice literature for those completing reading and response assignments.
0:50–0:60	**Group Sharing Time** Read aloud special passages, share responses from journals, or summarize thoughts of literature conversations by students. Jointly set goals for the next reading workshop day.

FIGURE 7.2 Weekly Schedule for Reading Workshop.

Monday	**Tuesday**	**Wednesday**
Introduce lit options through book talks	Read aloud	Read aloud
Introduce genre structure of text sets	Set expectations	Set expectations
Read-aloud	Strategy lesson	Strategy lesson
Assigned reading	Assigned reading	Assigned reading
(Teacher holds reading conferences during this time)		
Response journals	Literature conversation	Response journals
Independent reading	Independent reading	Independent reading
Sharing time	Sharing time	Sharing time
Thursday	**Friday**	
Read aloud	Read aloud	
Strategy lesson	Discuss response projects	
Assigned reading	Assigned reading	
(Teacher holds reading conferences during this time)		
Independent reading	Independent reading	
Literature conversation	Response option/project	
Sharing time	Sharing time	

be introduced, even through a picture book. Characteristics of the genre (traditional literature, biography, historical fiction) may be enumerated and illustrated through brief examples. Sharing time can be used to introduce the next literature selection(s) with background information to whet reading interests. The purpose of sharing time is to bring the whole class together to talk about the wonder of books and inspire further reading selections.

Reading Strategy Lessons

In a reading apprenticeship, ongoing learning of skills and their application as reading strategies continue to take place. Each day for 8 minutes, the teacher introduces a predetermined reading strategy that might be applied within the context of the reading workshop texts. This short, focused whole group instructional lesson can be drawn from three sources:

- ***The apparent needs of the students:*** Experienced teachers detect simple skills that need review or complex skills that require introduction.
- ***Selected skills from curriculum scope and sequence:*** The required skills and strategies of reading are often guided by a preset language arts curriculum. Teachers document instructional lessons and students' application and mastery of specific grade-level reading skills.
- ***Prereading preparation:*** Teachers design a brief minilesson related to the specific reading of the day. Examples might include a discussion of character traits, a graphic organizer of sequenced events, meanings of prefixes and suffixes, and an introduction of the omniscient point of view.

Although this lesson is brief, it ensures that the skills of reading are being introduced or revisited in challenging contexts and that they are becoming internalized as reading strategies within the context of daily reading. Minilessons serve as reminders of the building blocks of reading that must be acquired and applied appropriately if the art of reading is to be mastered over time. The last section in this chapter discusses reading strategies and their importance in the reading program.

Organizing the Workshop

Only 2 minutes should be devoted to addressing daily responsibilities, reiterating expectations, retrieving reading and response materials, recording progress, and getting students to work areas. Some teachers conduct a "status of the class" (Atwell, 1998) check by calling student names and recording plans for the workshop time. Others use pocket folders to organize skills checklists, daily reading assignments, sustained silent reading records, and response contracts so that they can be easily distributed and collected. The more time spent in real reading, authentic responding, and actual conversing about books, the more efficient the limited reading workshop time. The management of reading workshop should be minimized to allow for on-task reading instruction, reading practice, and reader response.

Reading and Responding

The reading and response portion of a reading workshop lasts about 30 minutes, depending on whether literature conversations are assigned for the day. If reading and response is the full 30 minutes, students must read the assigned pages of their book, proceed with the selected response activity, and fill in any remaining time with silent reading from a self-selected book. The teacher often uses this time to conduct two reading conferences per day. During these informal conferences, oral reading fluency, comprehension, and personal response are monitored and documented. If literature conversations are scheduled (two times per week), then reading lasts 15 minutes with the additional 15 minutes allotted for talking about the books in literature groups (see again Figs. 7.1 and 7.2).

Group Sharing

The last 5 to 10 minutes of the reading workshop provides time for student sharing of a special reading passage, new discoveries about reading, insightful conversations from literature groups, and fresh excitement and predictions about the selected literature. This brings small groups together for a whole group closure as the community of learners reestablishes itself as a learning unit. This interaction provides a critical opportunity for building and reinforcing a sense of community among learners.

Key Components of Reading Workshop

There are four major components of a reading workshop: (a) literature selection, (b) literature response journals, (c) project response options, and (d) literature conversations. Discussing each of these helps in an understanding of the value, depth, and potential of the workshop approach to teaching reading. Figure 7.3 illustrates the four main components and subcomponents of a reading workshop.

FIGURE 7.3 The Components of a Reading Workshop.

Literature Selection

- Class sets
- Text sets
  - Author studies
  - Theme studies
  - Character studies
  - Genre studies

Literature Response Journals

- Structured
- Unstructured response journals character journals

Project Response Options

- Art
- Music
- Drama
- Writing
- Visual recreation

Literature Conversations

- Conversation roles
- Response guidelines

Literature Selection

Perhaps the most important component in the facilitation of a reading workshop is the selection of the literature. Not every trade book contains the depth, emotion, characters, or plot to sustain itself through a workshop approach. The selection of a book is based on both the ability of the readers and the promise of the literature.

Most new teachers tend to choose a *class set* of books—multiple copies of the same book that can be distributed to the entire class. For example, 24 copies of Katherine Paterson's *A Bridge to Terabithia* in a fifth grade classroom would constitute a class set. The strength of a class set lies in the organizational advantage of using a single book with an entire class. The weakness of a class set, however, is that this type of selection implies that all students are reading at or about at the same reading level. If the text is chosen at the middle range of readers, a few will be challenged but may be motivated by relevant content. A few will find the reading easy but will be sustained by strong characters, a moving plot, and issues relevant to their interests. Most, however, will find the book to be a perfect match for reading and interest ability. Keeping quality in mind while sustaining interests at the grade level of the students in the reading workshop is paramount as the teacher makes the selection of a class set. The Literature Cluster on page 196 presents several examples that might work across a variety of reading levels because of the high interest of the story.

More experienced teachers and those with an abundance of available literature may choose *text sets*—sets of literature containing six to eight copies of the same book. Teachers have the option of selecting three to four different text sets for one reading workshop subdivided into three groups with some common strand woven between them. The common strand might be the author of the books that ties the workshop together. For example, three Gary Paulsen books—*Hatchet, The Haymeadow,* and *Brian's Return*—might be used by a single sixth-grade workshop. Teachers may also assign books by reading levels or, perhaps more appropriately, may allow students to select one of the three choices based on previous reading and personal interests.

Another common strand in text sets might be a genre study in which three books exemplify the best of a specific genre. For example, Mildred Taylor's *Mississippi Bridge,* Christopher Paul Curtis's *Bud, Not Buddy* and *The Watsons Go to Birmingham—1963* all

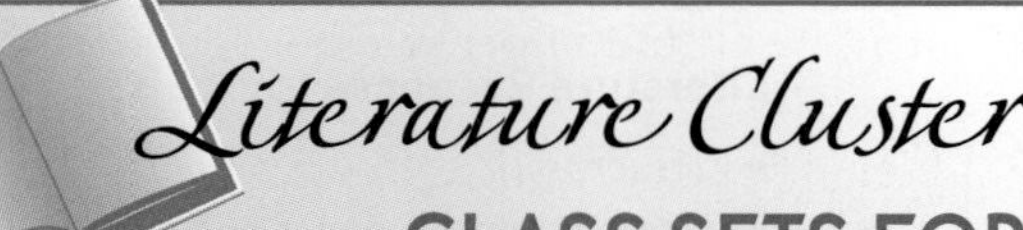

Literature Cluster

CLASS SETS FOR READING WORKSHOP

Grades 3–5

Bauer, Marion Dane (1994). *A question of trust.* Boston: Houghton Mifflin.

Clements, Andrew (2000). *The Landry news.* New York: Atheneum.

Fraustino, Lisa Rowe (2001). *The hickory chair.* Illus. by Benny Andrews. New York: Scholastic.

Giff, Patricia Reilly (2001). *All the way home.* New York: Delacorte.

Hahn, Mary Downing (2001). *Anna on the farm.* New York: Clarion.

Hesse, Karen (1998). *Just Juice.* New York: Scholastic.

Holt, Kimberly Willis (1998). *My Louisiana sky.* New York: Holt.

Lord, Bette Bao (1984). *In the year of the boar and Jackie Robinson.* New York: Harper & Row.

Lynch, Chris (2000). *Gold dust.* New York: HarperCollins.

Mikaelsen, Ben (1991). *Rescue Josh McGuire.* New York: Hyperion.

Naylor, Phyllis Reynolds (1994). *The fear place.* New York: Atheneum.

Paterson, Katherine (1994). *Flip-flop girl.* New York: Lodestar.

Smith, Robert Kimmel (1984). *The war with Grandpa.* New York: Delacorte.

Taylor, Mildred (1990). *Mississippi bridge.* New York: Bantam.

Walter, Mildred Pitt (1986). *Justin and the best biscuits in the world.* New York: Lothrop, Lee & Shepard.

Williams, Vera B. (2001). *Amber was brave, Essie was smart.* New York: Greenwillow.

Grades 6–8

Avi (1991). *Nothing but the truth.* New York: Avon.

Blackwood, Gary (1998). *The Shakespeare stealer.* New York: Dutton.

Cooney, Caroline B. (2001). *The ransom of Mercy Carter.* New York: Delacorte.

Farmer, Nancy (2002). *The house of the scorpion.* New York: Atheneum.

Hesse, Karen (2001). *Witness.* New York: Scholastic.

Jiminez, Francisco (2001). *Breaking through.* New York: Houghton Mifflin.

Johnston, Tony (2001). *Any small goodness: A novel of the barrio.* New York: Scholastic.

Lowry, Lois (1993). *The giver.* Boston: Houghton Mifflin.

MacLachlan, Patricia (1991). *Journey.* New York: Dell.

Naidoo, Beverly (2001). *The other side of truth.* New York: HarperCollins.

Peck, Richard (1998). *A long way from Chicago: A novel in stories.* New York: Dial.

Philbrick, Rodman (2000). *The last book in the universe.* New York: Scholastic.

Sachar, Louis (1998). *Holes.* New York: Farrar, Straus and Giroux.

Staples, Suzanne Fisher (1989). *Shabanu: Daughter of the wind.* New York: Knopf.

Taylor, Mildred (2001). *The land.* New York: Putnam.

have African American multicultural literature and historical fiction as a common genre. These books are written at three different reading levels, so they might suit a range of reader abilities in a fifth-grade workshop.

Selected literature might also include text sets linked by a common theme, such as growing up and belonging. Fourth graders might select from Katherine Paterson's *The Great Gilly Hopkins,* Jerry Spinelli's *Wringer,* and Sharon Creech's *Walk Two Moons* as they discuss the common theme of the role played by family in the trying times of growing up. These Newbery and Newbery Honor books contain quality writing at a variety of reading levels, have both male and female characters, and appeal to the needs and interests of fourth-grade students.

Finally, a teacher may determine literary elements to be the common factor between text sets in a middle-level setting. Strong female characters as a literary element might lead to the selection of Katherine Paterson's *Lyddie* and Karen Cushman's *The Midwife's Apprentice* or *The Ballad of Lucy Whipple*. Written across different historical periods and at a variety of reading levels, these titles contain memorable female characters who exhibit some common personality traits and decisive actions that are worthy of comparative discussion.

These authentic text options are critical in predicting the successful outcome of the reading workshop. Randomly choosing any book or books does not ensure success. The best literature written at a variety of levels for different reading interests yet woven with some common theme seems to provide the most fruitful choices for reading workshop. The Literature Cluster on page 198 lists several groupings of text sets that work together effectively in a reading workshop setting.

Literature Response Journals

The response of the individual reader to the reading itself is the second component of the reading workshop. Typically, the common mode of response is through a literature response journal (Hancock, 2004). Writing responses during the reading of the text, rather than merely at its conclusion, provides an ongoing account of thoughts, emotions, and issues throughout the reading experience. Because reader response is a developmental process that requires practice and risk taking, a series of types of response experiences is determined by grade level. A knowledgeable teacher, however, should determine the background response experiences of his or her readers and in which journal option they are prepared to respond. Flexibility should be built into the response journal options to fit the individual response experiences and desires of each student.

Structured Response Journals. For third- and fourth-grade readers, a structured response journal seems to be most effective. Teacher-constructed prompts provide guidelines for response at the end of selected but not all chapters. The term "prompt" implies an open-ended probe that allows each reader to uniquely respond through his or her own connections with the text. Well-planned and well-written prompts encourage diverse response at four levels of reader interaction with literature: (a) experiential prompts, (b) aesthetic prompts, (c) cognitive prompts, and (d) interpretive prompts (Hancock, 2004). Figure 7.4 defines and provides broad examples of each type of prompt. The power of literature, a series of thought-provoking prompts, the openness of the teacher to unique response, and the honesty of reader response combine to provide authentic testimony to capturing these emotions on paper. For prompts to be an effective vehicle for response, they must have certain characteristics:

- They must be open-ended so that no single answer is considered correct.
- They must be teacher-generated and meaningfully constructed to elicit powerful response.
- They must be sprinkled strategically throughout the text at appropriate interactive moments.
- They must connect to prior experiences and inner emotions, and have personal meaning for students to allow them to predict outcomes.

Literature Cluster

TEXT SETS FOR READING WORKSHOP (GRADES 3–6)

Genre Study

Historical Fiction

Avi (2001). *The secret school.* New York: Harcourt Brace.

Cushman, Karen (1996). *The ballad of Lucy Whipple.* Boston: Clarion.

Osborne, Mary Pope (2000). *Adaline Falling Star.* New York: Scholastic.

Realistic Fiction

Creech, Sharon (2002). *Ruby Holler.* New York: HarperCollins.

Holt, Kimberly (1998). *My Louisiana sky.* New York: Holt.

Wiles, D. (2001). *Love, Ruby Lavender.* New York: Harcourt Brace.

Biography

Freedman, Russell (1997). *Out of darkness:* The story of Louis Braille. Boston: Clarion.

Myers, Walter Dean (2001). *The greatest: Muhammed Ali* New York: Scholastic.

Warren, Andrea (2001). *Surviving Hitler: A boy in the Nazi death camps.* New York: HarperCollins.

Author Study

Clements, Andrew (1998). *Frindle.* New York: Simon & Schuster

Clements, Andrew (2000). *The janitor's boy.* New York: Simon & Schuster.

Clements, Andrew (2001). *The school story.* New York: Simon & Schuster.

MacLachlan, Patricia (1985). *Sarah, plain and tall.* New York: HarperCollins.

MacLachlin, Patricia (1994). *Skylark.* New York: HarperCollins.

MacLachlin, Patricia (2002). *Caleb's story.* New York: HarperCollins.

Naylor, Phyllis R. (1991). *Shiloh.* New York: Macmillan

Naylor, Phyllis R. (1994). *The fear place.* New York: Atheneum.

Naylor, Phyllis R. (1996). *Shiloh's season.* New York: Atheneum.

Theme Study

Disabilities

Gantos, Jack (1999). *Joey Pigza swallowed the key.* New York: Farrar, Straus & Giroux.

Holt, Kimberly (2001). *Dancing in Cadillac light.* New York: Putnam

White, Ruth (1997). *Belle Prater's boy.* New York: Scholastic.

Family

DiCamillo, Kate (2000). *Because of Winn-Dixie.* Cambridge, MA: Candlewick.

Martin, Ann (2001). *Belle Teale.* New York: Scholastic.

Park, Barbara (1995). *Mick Harte was here.* New York: Random House.

Cultural Diversity

Curtis, Christopher Paul (1999), *Bud, not Buddy.* New York: Delacorte.

Erdrich, Louise (1999). *The birchbark house.* New York: Hyperion.

Park, Linda Sue (2001). *A single shard.* New York: Clarion.

Ryan, Pam Muñoz (2001). *Esperanza rising.* New York: Scholastic.

FIGURE 7.4
The Four Types of Structured Response Journal Prompts.

- ***Experiential prompts.*** Response prompts that elicit prior knowledge, prior personal experience (text-to-life connections), prior reading experience (text-to-text connections), and prior viewing experience (text-to-media connection). They focus on what the reader brings to the reading experience.

  How do you relate this chapter to your own life?
  How does [name of character] remind you of someone you know?
  How does [name of character] remind you of someone you met in a book or through a form of media?

- ***Aesthetic prompts.*** Response prompts that elicit feelings, empathy, and character identification. They promote emotional interactions with the text, moving response beyond efferent plot summary.

  How does this chapter make you feel?
  How would you feel if you were [name of character] in this situation?
  How would you feel if you were [name another character]?

- ***Cognitive prompts.*** Response prompts that encourage solving problems, making predictions, and making inferences about characters and plot development. They require readers to think, brainstorm, create, and construct outcomes.

  What do you think will happen to [name of character]?
  If you were [name of character], what would you do in this situation?
  What advice would you give [name of character] at this point in the story?

- ***Interpretive prompts.*** Response prompts that elicit personal consideration of meaning or message, morals or values, and personal judgment of characters and situations. They call for a degree of higher level reasoning by requiring an explanation that is often difficult to put into words.

  What meaning or message does this passage have for you?
  Why do you believe [name of character] did or did not make the right choice?
  What do you think the following words mean? [Quote from text]
  What kind of person do you think [name of character] is? How do you know?

The potential of prompts to elicit written responses to literature through active reflection should not be underestimated. Prompts ask readers to think, to feel, to express, to connect, to predict, to interpret, to relate, and to become a character. Prompts compel readers to focus on characters, dilemmas, causes, outcomes, and implications. Although prompts may be seen as restrictive, they can in fact serve as facilitators of understanding, feeling, and active engagement in literature. Prompts provide a framework for response for late-primary and early-intermediate readers who still require some response direction. Note the fifth graders' prompted responses to Linda Sue Park's *A Single Shard* in Student Sample 7.1.

Unstructured Response Journals. As students become familiar with the kinds of responses that can be shared in a written format, they require fewer prompts and gain more independence and trust in sharing their thoughts, opinions, and viewpoints in a journal. The next step is to introduce the freedom of the unstructured literature response journal. Independent reading and spontaneous recording of thoughts is the developmental hallmark of a literature response journal. While a natural first step is to write responses

STUDENT SAMPLE 7.1 Fifth- and Sixth-Graders' Prompted Response to *A Single Shard* and *Bud, Not Buddy*.

Fifth-graders' prompted response to *A Single Shard* by Linda Sue Park

My favorite part was when Ajimg, Min's wife, said to Tree-ear, "Please come and make this your new home. We will change your name to Hyung-pil" That was the name of their first son who died. That is so nice of her to do that and welcome Tree-ear to their home. He will now learn to make pottery like his new father.

—EMILY

All of this book will catch someone's interest, but my favorite part was the breathtaking ending. When Tree-ear arrived back at Min's house his heart shattered like Min's pottery when he found out that Crane-man, his only friend, died. I could feel his rage and disappointment. Then his emotions changed rapidly when he finally had a new family. Tree-ear, now Hyung-pil, is no longer an orphan, but a happy boy. This story has one big lesson. If you want to accomplish something, and once you try hard enough, you should know how much effort you put into it. Even if along the way something blocks your path, or all your hard work shatters in front of you, something good comes out of it, as long as you try.

—SPENCER

Sixth-graders' open response to *Bud, Not Buddy* by Christopher Paul Curtis

One thing I notice about Bud is he's been raised well and that if he wants to do something he sure will. When he got to Grand Rapids, he was determined to find his daddy. One thing I think is that Mr. C. isn't his daddy, but might know where Bud's daddy really is. I also feel Bud is a courageous and brave young man. Oh, and my favorite part in the stop is when he poured water on Todd's p.j.'s so he'd wet his bed and get his mama all angry! This might be one of my favorite books!

—ASHLEY

Mr. C. seems to be embarrassed about Bud and will not admit to have left his wife (or some girl he met) alone with a baby. Most of the book has great words and details, except for "woop-zoop-sloop." It sounds just really annoying and dumb. I think that maybe Mr. C. will like Bud a little, but not too much. Since he knows that his demanding nature drove his daughter that died away, the last sentence may be correct.

—QUINT

I have felt like Bud in that you don't always know if someone's joking or serious. If you question them and they're joking they laugh and if they're serious they get mad. That is how this book reminds me of my life. I think Bud will make peace with Herman E. Calloway after Herman gets over Bud's mother. I think Bud will play his saxophone with the band—or should I say Sleepy LaBone!

—BRIDGET

after completing a chapter, capable students should be encouraged to respond at any point in the book in which a response enters their mind. This freedom elicits the fullest, richest range of responses. Examples of sixth-grade open responses to Christopher Paul Curtis's *Bud, Not Buddy* are shown in Student Sample 7.1.

The guidelines in Figure 7.5 provide direction, focus, and options for sharing written response through an unstructured literature journal. They reflect the openness and freedom of the journal, while encouraging risk taking, responsibility, and trust. These guidelines provide impetus, but should not limit response options.

Teachers need to be cognizant of the variety of responses that might occur within the unstructured journal. Extensive research (Hancock, 1993b) alerts teachers to the possibilities of response in Figure 7.6. Teacher knowledge of types of response provides an informative framework for encouraging students to respond. An exploration of these types of response alerts the teacher to the possibilities, not the probabilities, of response. The goal for readers should not be to include all types of response but to expand the number and kind of individual response options over time. Continuous, encouraging feedback with some suggestive, but not demanding, comments helps lead children to fulfill their own unique response potential and develop a characteristic response style.

FIGURE 7.5 Guidelines for Unstructured Literature Response Journals.

- *Feel free to write* your innermost feelings, opinions, thoughts, likes, and dislikes. This is your journal. Feel the freedom to express yourself and your personal responses to reading through it.
- *Take the time to write* down anything that you are thinking while you read. The journal is a way of recording those fleeting thoughts that pass through your mind as you interact with the book. Keep your journal close by and stop to write often, whenever a thought strikes you.
- *Don't worry* about the accuracy of spelling and mechanics in the journal. The content and expression of your personal thoughts should be your primary concern. The journal will not be evaluated for a grade. Relax and share.
- *Record the page number* on which you were reading when you wrote your response. Although it may seem unimportant, you might want to look back to verify your thoughts.
- *Write on one side only* of your spiral notebook paper, please. Expect to read occasional, interested comments from your teacher. These comments will not be intended to judge or criticize your reactions but will create an opportunity to "converse" about your thoughts.
- *Relate the book* to your own experiences and share similar moments from your life or from books you have read in the past.
- *Ask questions* while reading to help you make sense of the characters and the unraveling plot. Don't hesitate to wonder why, indicate surprise, or admit confusion. These responses often lead to an emerging understanding of the book.
- *Make predictions* about what you think will happen as the plot unfolds. Validate, invalidate, or change those predictions as you proceed in the text. Don't worry about being wrong.
- *Talk to the characters* as you begin to know them. Give them advice to help them. Put yourself in their place and share how you would act in a similar situation. Approve or disapprove of their values, actions, or behavior. Try to figure out what makes them react the way they do.
- *Praise or criticize* the book, the author, or the literary style. Your personal tastes in literature are important and need to be shared.
- *Do not limit* the types of responses you may want to write. Your honesty in capturing your thoughts throughout the book is your most valuable contribution to the journal. These guidelines are meant to trigger, not limit, the kinds of things you write. Be yourself and share your personal responses to literature through your journal.

Character Journals. Another type of journal that actively engages the reader in the reading process through a first-person writing stance is the character journal—a written diary kept by the reader as he or she assumes the role of a character as a book is read. The reader actually becomes the character and keeps an ongoing account of episodes encountered throughout the reading of the book. The reader writes in the first person sharing his or her thoughts, feelings, and trepidations throughout the unfolding events of the story. A character journal compels a reader to climb into the character's skin, to walk in the character's shoes, and to realize the character's joys and frustrations. Simultaneously, the character journal encourages reflection as the reader thinks, judges, and weighs the

FIGURE 7.6 Categories of Intermediate and Middle-Level Responses to Literature.

Immersion Responses

Reader attempts to make sense of emerging plot and character.

- ***Understanding.*** Responses indicate the reader's current understanding of both character and plot. Responses move beyond summary to reflect a personal interpretation or sudden discovery of meaning.

  [character] is having trouble . . .
  [character] doesn't want [another character] to . . .
  These past few pages show how . . .

- ***Character introspection.*** Responses indicate the reader's attempt to have insights into the feelings, thoughts, and motives for behavior of the characters. Responses reflect a sense of understanding through reasoning but indicate a degree of uncertainty on the part of the reader. They often begin with tentative statements.

  It sounds like . . .
  He must be . . .
  She probably . . .
  I think [character] . . .

- ***Predicting events.*** Responses reflect reader speculation about what will unfold as the text proceeds. Also included are statements that validate or invalidate both stated and unstated predictions, serving as a link between prediction and understanding.

  If [character] . . . then he will . . .
  I bet [character] will . . .
  I didn't think [character] would . . .

- ***Questioning.*** Responses reflect a lack of complete understanding or a questioning of text. Statements may reflect puzzlement and questions may reflect confusion. Statements may reflect doubt or disbelief in the reader's attempt to comprehend the text.

  I wonder if . . .
  This is strange. Why does [character] . . .?
  What do they mean by . . .?
  I can't believe . . .
  I didn't know . . .

Involvement Responses

Reader becomes personally involved with the character and/or the plot.

- ***Character identification.*** Responses show the reader has achieved a sense of personal identification with the character. Empathetic identification or sharing a related experience from the reader's life may also occur. Directly addressing the character or giving advice also indicates involvement.

  For Pete's sake, [character], tell him . . .
  If I were [character], I would . . .
  I experience the same . . .
  I know how [character] feels . . .
  I feel sorry for [character] because . . .

Source: Revised from Hancock (1993a) reader response categories.

FIGURE 7.6 (Continued)

- ***Character assessment.*** Responses indicate reader judgment of the actions and values of the character measured against his or her own personal standards of behavior. Evaluative terms and distinctive expression of likes or dislikes may appear. Responses may also indicate perception of growth or change.

  I like [character] because . . .
  That was a smart [dumb] thing to do because . . .
  [character] is starting to change . . .

- ***Story involvement.*** Responses reflect reader's reaction to setting, theme, actions, or sensory aspects of the story through evaluative terms. Responses may reflect personal satisfaction/dissatisfaction with the unfolding events. Active or passive anticipation of reading might be shared.

  I just lost my appetite . . .
  I would be nice to . . .
  I can't wait to get to the part where . . .
  Disgusting! Absolutely disgusting!! . . .

Literary Connections

Responses indicate the reader detaches himself or herself from the text to make a statement regarding a literary element or to connect the book to another book, one's personal experience, or other forms of media. Responses also can evaluate the book in comparison to other books read over a lifetime.

- ***Intertextual connections.*** Response reflects reader's desire to connect the book being read to another previously read text.

  This book reminds me of . . .
  I read another book like this that . . .
  This book is just like . . .

- ***Text-to-Life Connections.*** Response reflects reader's desire to connect an episode or character from the book to a personal experience or acquaintance from his or her own life.

  [character] reminds me of . . .
  I remember . . .
  This part of the book reminds me of the time I . . .

- ***Text-to-Media Connections.*** Response reflects reader's desire to connect the book being read to a previously viewed movie, television show, video game, or advertisement.

  This part reminds me of a movie I saw that . . .
  I saw something on TV that . . .
  [character] reminds me of [TV character] because . . .

- ***Literary Evaluation.*** Responses indicate the reader's evaluation of all or part of the book. They may include praise or criticism of the author, writing style, literary genre, or ability to maintain reader interest.

  This was a boring chapter because . . .
  This is the best book I've ever read . . .
  The way the author described the [character, setting] was . . .

actions, emotions, and reactions of the character against his or her own moral standards and behavior (Hancock, 1993b).

Not all book titles and genres work with the character journal format of response. Several criteria must be followed when choosing the perfect book to partner with a character journal:

- The age of the character should be similar to the age of the reader.
- The main character should be strongly portrayed and evidence growing maturity as the book unfolds.
- The plot must evolve through a series of highly emotional events compelling the reader to be involved.
- The text should be written in third person so that conversion to a first-person journal retains originality and creates a character voice.

Examples of such books include Katherine Paterson's *Lyddie* and *Jip,* Will Hobb's *Bearstone* and *Beardance,* and Ben Mikaelson's *Sparrow Hawk Red* and *Petey.*

Because the character journal is written from a character's point of view, the reader vicariously lives through the experiences and emotions of the story, which can be both hard work and emotionally draining. The character journal attains a high level of involvement, sustains a personal interest in the outcome of the story, enhances the literature experience through an insider stance, and contributes to a deeper level of understanding of characters from different cultures, genders, ages, and times. Sharing the fate of characters enables readers to challenge or clarify their own sets of beliefs and choices, which may result in new insights into themselves. This level of intensity seems best suited to upper intermediate and middle-level students. Figure 7.7 presents student guidelines for a character journal and provides examples of quality literature that meet the criteria for this specific type of response journal.

A developmental approach to response journals seems most appropriate in addressing the reading and response capabilities of grade level students. Late primary students seem to share response best through structured prompts. By the intermediate grades, a combination of structure with some freedom provides a compromise for growing independent readers. At the middle level, readers prefer the spontaneous flow of unstructured response options, but minimum expectations (number of responses, length of responses) should be clarified by the teacher.

Project Response Options

In addition to journals as a vehicle for written response to literature, the reading workshop also invites other project-based response options based on the individual talents and tastes of readers. Readers can tire of a steady diet of journals as the only response option during a reading workshop. Responses can venture beyond writing to include art, music, drama, research, displays, or interviews. The following examples are individual or group projects that can be used in the expression of responses:

- Create murals, dioramas, illustrations, paintings, collage, sculpture, or posters in response to a book.
- Perform dramatized versions of powerful book episodes.
- Visual representation of the personal meaning of powerful book episodes.
- Set up a learning center or display related to the author, setting, or theme of the book.
- Create a newpaper based on the events from a historical fiction book.

FIGURE 7.7
Student Guidelines for a Character Journal Response and Books Inviting that Response.

- Become the main character and record your thoughts, feelings, and reflections in your journal through the character's voice.
- Write the chapter number to which your journal entry refers in the left margin.
- Choose one episode from each chapter to relive in your written journal entry.
- Write on only the front side of each page in your journal. Your teacher (or partner) will comment back to you as you become the main character.
- There are no right or wrong entries for the character journal. Your journal will be unique. Find a style of first-person writing that feels comfortable to you.
- Don't be concerned about spelling and mechanics. Expressing your thoughts in the voice of the character through involvement in the book is your main objective.
- Feel free to write whatever you are thinking as you become the character. One of the unique features of the journal is the freedom it allows. You may say the things you feel in the role of the character.
- Use parentheses ( ) following your character entry to express your own personal thoughts on the actions, motives, decisions, or feelings of the character. Use this option as a means of being and expressing yourself.
- *Remember:* Write the thoughts and feelings of the character as you live through the episodes of the book with him/her. Put yourself in the mind and heart of that character and write what you, as the main character, think and feel.

Banks, Kate (2002). *Dillon Dillon.* New York: Farrar, Straus and Giroux.
Bauer, Joan (2002). *Stand tall.* New York: Putnam.
Bauer, Marion Dane (1994). *A question of trust.* New York: Scholastic.
Clements, Andrew (2002). *A week in the woods.* New York: Simon & Schuster.
DeFelice, Cynthia (1998). *The ghost of fossil glen.* New York: Farrar, Straus and Giroux.
DiCamillo, Kate (2002). *The tiger rising.* Cambridge, MA: Candlewick.
Fleischman, Sid (2001). *Bo & Mzzz Mad.* New York: Greenwillow.
Gaiman, Neil (2002). *Coraline.* New York: HarperCollins.
Hahn, Mary Downing (1991). *Stepping on the cracks.* Boston: Clarion.
Hill, Kirkpatrick (1990). *Toughboy and Sister.* New York: Macmillan.
Hobbs, Will (1989). *Bearstone.* New York: Atheneum.
Kurtz, Jane (2001). *Jakarta missing.* New York: Greenwillow.
Mikaelsen, Ben (1993). *Sparrow hawk red.* New York: Hyperion.
Paterson, Katherine (1991). *Lyddie.* New York: Dutton.
Paulsen, Gary (1992). *The haymeadow.* New York: Delacorte.
Pearsall, Shelley (2002). *Trouble don't last.* New York: Knopf.
Spinelli, Jerry (1990). *Maniac Magee.* New York: HarperCollins.
Tolan, Stephanie (2002). *Surviving the Applewhites.* New York: HarperCollins.

- Describe cooking experiences that directly relate to the book or characters.
- Simulate an interview with the author.
- Select background music for emotional or action episodes in the book.
- Research a related aspect of the book (e.g., setting, historical period) on the Internet.
- Use the Internet to create a bibliography of related books or other books by the author.
- Create a computer-generated brochure that advertises the book to prospective readers.

Reading, Literature, and the Web

The Internet provides a myriad of opportunities for students to read and respond to authentic literature. Using the Web, students can learn more about their favorite authors and award-winning literature, read and write book reviews, and engage in literature conversations or book clubs with children from around the world.

Book-Clubs-Resource.com is a comprehensive guide to online book clubs and reading groups. Use this site selectively as some of the online clubs may not be appropriate for your students. **www.book-clubs-resource.com/online/**

Nancy Keane's Children's Literature Webpage includes lists of recommended books, book reviews and booktalks written by children, and numerous links to children's literature resources on the Web. The site is updated often and students may contribute their own booktalks and reviews. **www.nancykeane.com/**

KidsReads.com is a user-friendly resource where students can learn more about their favorite books and authors. The site includes information about writing to authors, interviews with children's authors, and plenty of reviews of current titles. Students can participate in literature-related trivia games and word scrambles. **www.kidsreads.com/**

To look more closely at these materials and others related to "Continuing the Reading Apprenticeship," visit the Companion Website at www.prenhall.com/hancock.

The possibilities are endless, but the qualifying factor is that the response-based activity includes a meaningful connection to the book that reflects emotion, comprehension, and unique interaction with the text. These types of response activities are viable for readers from third through eighth grade with proper management, high expectations, sound organization, and accessible materials. Throughout the school year, the reading workshop should ensure that all readers experiment with a variety of response options rather than finding a comfortable niche with one or two. While learning styles and talents come into play, the ultimate outcome of the response portion of the reading workshop is the expression and sharing of personal interactions with literature through written, oral, artistic, musical, dramatic, technological, and visual means (see the Tech Tip above).

Literature Conversations

The fourth essential component of a reading workshop is a small-group literature conversation among four to six common readers of literature. Known by several names, including literature circles (Daniels, 2002), grand conversations (Peterson & Eeds, 1990), and book clubs (Raphael et al., 2001), such small group discussions explore "rough draft understandings" (Short & Pierce, 1990) of literature with other readers. Literature conversations are based on the belief that reading is a transactional process as students bring meaning to and take meaning from the text. Built on an aesthetic response to literature, students engage in collaborative listening, thinking, and understanding as dialogue leads

The "literary luminary" shares selected book passages during a literature conversation.

participants to new perspectives on the book. A sense of community and an acceptance of risk taking are necessary to the success of the literature conversation. The conversation must be viewed as dialogue among readers rather than the fulfillment of a teacher-generated agenda. Honesty and personal interpretations must be valued, honored, and used as a springboard for evolving discussion.

New teachers are best served by selecting group members early in the school year. As trust, responsibility, and discussion skills grow, teachers may see fit to allow students to select their own literature conversation group. In order to participate in a 20-minute literature conversation, readers must do the following:

- Complete the reading of the assigned portion or the entire book.
- Complete a literature response journal or another response-based activity and bring it to the conversation to share.
- Take on a specific discussion task to facilitate quality discussion.
- Bring questions and an open mind for individual interpretation as well as a willingness to listen to and share with the members of the group.

Proper modeling of a literature conversation sets the standards for acceptance of diverse opinions, proper conversation etiquette, and quality content. Literature conversations should model the following oral engagements:

- Personal responses to the book (favorite parts, specific passages)
- Connections to personal experiences and other book titles or video representations (text-to-text, text-to-life, text-to-film)
- Specific conversational focus (critical dialogue, considering the thoughts of others, focusing on specific textual aspects)
- Expansion of textual support and building off of participant comments
- Determination of focus for next meeting (starting point for tomorrow)

Even with proper modeling, teachers quickly discover that talking about books requires some structure and organization. Assigning roles prior to the meeting of the literature conversation group helps focus on the literature without limiting or inhibiting the freedom it demands. Daniels (2002) describes six roles that students might assume within a literature conversation:

- ***Discussion director:*** Makes certain the group has brought along questions for discussion, shares responses from journals, and keeps focused on the purpose of the conversation
- ***Literary luminary:*** Locates sections of the book that read aloud well, marks them with post-its, and shares them at appropriate times to lend deeper insight into the discussion
- ***Connector:*** Looks for connections between the book and the real-world experiences of the readers, including text-to-life, text-to-text, and text-to-film connections
- ***Illustrator:*** Creates any type of graphic or visual representation (illustrated time line, mural, series of interpretive drawings) to describe what has been read
- ***Vocabulary Enricher:*** Locates important word choices that enrich the writing and deepen the understanding of the reader
- ***Summarizer:*** Wraps up the reading for the day by assimilating the discussion and making a final closure statement

While the group consists of the same students over a period of time, the roles rotate with shared responsibility, response possibilities, and continued interest.

Another means of keeping students on track during a literature conversation is to provide response guidelines for a specific title. Figure 7.8 illustrates how such guidelines might be developed for Avi's *The True Confessions of Charlotte Doyle.* Prepared by the teacher or an advanced discussion director, the guidelines can facilitate oral responses when natural discussion diminishes. Experienced groups might never need these discussion stimuli, but novice conversationalists may depend on them to sustain talk for 20 minutes.

Related Reading Workshop Activities

Within the context of a reading workshop, students are typically reading assigned literature, responding to literature, or conversing about books. The grouping of a reading workshop allows other types of instruction to occur with the small-group framework. It is important to realize the flexibility within the reading workshop that can provide variety, attention to individual student needs, and effective instruction with a small-group configuration.

Shared Reading. Although many reading workshops require individual, silent reading, other types of reading scenarios may effectively occur. The term *shared reading* implies that all group members are in the same place in the same text and that the teacher can join a group and demonstrate how reading aloud can include predicting, intonation, and fluency. *Partner reading* allows two readers to take turns reading aloud to each other as they talk and clarify both meaning and reading strategies they employ during reading. *Books-on-tape* can provide struggling readers with an oral reading model as they follow the text. Shared reading involves all readers in the reading experience at their current level of ability. While the primary focus of a reading workshop is individual silent reading and understanding, these shared reading activities provide variety and effective modeling, instruction, and comprehension enhancement.

Guided Reading. Guided reading is ongoing, explicit reading instruction that takes place within the small-group setting. It extends skill and strategy instruction beyond the minilesson portion of reading workshop and provides individual and small-group instruction

FIGURE 7.8
Literature Conversation Guidelines for Avi's *The True Confessions of Charlotte Doyle.*

- Discuss the following characters in terms of their strengths, weaknesses, triumphs, and downfalls:

Charlotte	Zachariah	Charlotte's father
Capt. Jaggery	Mr. Hollybrass	Keetch

- If this book were to be made into a movie, who do you envision playing, these roles?
- Discuss the story setting/period in terms of the following aspect of mid–nineteenth-century sealife:

The role of women	Piracy on the high seas	A sailor's life

- Locate and respond to your favorite passage.
- How did you feel when you realized that Charlotte would defy her parents and go back to the sea?
- What meaning or message about "being true to yourself" do you gain from the book?
- What will happen to Charlotte as the book ends?
- What did you like/dislike about the book? How would you change it?
- How did you react to the following?

  Charlotte's adjustment to seasickness and her quarters
  Charlotte's early impressions of Capt. Jaggery
  The mutiny
  Charlotte's climbing of the ropes
  The trial
  The end of Capt. Jaggery
  The control Charlotte's father has over his daughter

- Read a response from your journal in which you do the following:

  Use a quote from the book
  Talk to a character
  Judge a character
  Give advice to a character
  Indicate questions or confusion
  Make a text-to-text connection
  Make a text-to-life connection
  Laughed out loud
  Felt like crying

within the context of authentic literature. In Grades 3 through 6, the guided reading lesson is organized and orchestrated by the teacher who assesses distinct needs of a group of readers or instinctively connects the literature being read to a particular reading skill or strategy (Fountas & Pinnell, 2001) .

Independent Reading. As students finish reading workshop responsibilities, they may find some available time to read independently. Students are responsible for having a self-selected book with them during the workshop. Students develop strategies for selecting books appropriate to both interests and reading levels. Although the classroom schedule includes a daily sustained, silent, independent reading time outside of the workshop time, students read self-selected books when the reading workshop allows. Reading and writing book reviews provides a means for selecting and sharing independent reading book choices with other readers. Lesson Plan 7.1 proposes a detailed framework for inviting book choices based on the online reviews of others.

LESSON PLAN 7.1

TITLE: **Discover Books Through Online Book Reviews**

Grade Level: 4–8

Time Frame: Two 45-minute sessions

Standards

IRA/NCTE Standards: 1, 4, 5

NETS for Students: 5, 6

Objectives

- Students will read and write book reviews and understand the elements/structure of and purpose for such reviews.
- Students will compare and contrast their own opinion of a book with that of the published reviewer.

Materials

- Literature selections that match students' reading levels, interests, and assigned text sets
- Computers with Internet access

Motivation

- Distribute selected literature to students. Tell students to read the title and view the cover. They should *not* open the book.
- Explain to students that before they can open their books, they will read published book reviews on the Internet to learn more about the book and the opinions of other readers of the story.
- Explain that *reading* book reviews can help us select books that we really want to read. *Writing* book reviews is a way to share a good book with others. Book reviews generally tell us what a book is about, what the reviewer likes about the book, and the book's overall theme or message.

Procedures

Day 1

- Direct students to Web sites that include reviews of the assigned literature, such as *Nancy Keane's Children's Literature Webpage* (www.nancykeane.com/), or *KidsReads.com* www.kidsreads.com/. Commercial sites such as Amazon (http://www.amazon.com) and Barnes & Noble (www.barnesandnoble.com) also contain reader reviews.
- While reading the online reviews, students should learn as much as possible about their books (title, author, publishing year, page numbers, etc.). Students should also learn what the book is about and the reviewer's opinion about the book.

- Ask students to record their findings. Students should also include a prediction on whether or not they will agree with the reviewer's opinion about the book.
- Students read their books.

Day 2

- As a class or in small groups, invite students to discuss their interpretation of the book as compared to their prediction from the previous day. Were the students' predictions correct? Did the students' opinions of the book(s) agree/disagree with the reviewer's?
- Ask students to respond to the text by writing their own book reviews revealing what the books is about, what they like about the book, and the book's theme or message.
- Students should compare and contrast their reviews with those previously read online (students may want to revisit the Web sites). Ask students to explain why and how their reviews are similar/different from the published reviews.

Assessment

- Teacher-created checklist or rubric reflecting lesson objectives (Did student include critical elements in their written reviews? Did student identify similarities/differences between his or her review and the published review?)

Accommodation/Modification

- Select books of varying lengths and reading levels that suit needs and abilities of individual learners.
- For audio recorded book reviews, visit the *Reading Rainbow* Website (pbskids.org/readingrainbow/).

Visit the Meeting the Standards module in Chapter 7 of the Companion Website at www.prenhall.com/hancock to adapt this lesson to meet your state's standards.

Reading Conferences. Reading conferences provide a teacher check on the ongoing progress and accomplishments of individual readers. The teacher should attempt to have a one-on-one reading conference with each child once per week. This means that she or he circulates during the reading workshop to monitor individual reading progress. During a reading conference of 5 to 10 minutes, students may be asked to read aloud to the teacher, discuss the book they are reading, show evidence of response projects, or discuss strategies that they use as readers. Strategy checklists, book lists, and reading records can be documented during the reading conference. Teachers often post the names of students who will conference each day and a schedule should be maintained to make certain all children spend quality time with the teacher at least once a week. Conference time also allows for children to ask questions about reading, discuss reading selections, and share independent reading choices.

Although the group configuration is the norm for reading workshop, these additional reading activities and scenarios provide options for inclusion within the Reading Workshop block. They provide opportunities to work with a partner, to read aloud, to read independently, and to meet for an individual conference with the teacher. Creating an atmosphere that encourages student interaction, reader independence, teacher accountability, and student responsibility seems to blend the best of whole class, small group, and individual reading instruction.

Reading workshop is built on the philosophical premise that literature is the best medium for motivating reading, that reader response provides a means for individual expression of comprehension, and that literature conversations among readers extend meaning. Many teachers, however, agree that a balanced reading program needs a strong focus on comprehension. The teaching of comprehension strategies at the third- through eighth-grade levels remains an important aspect of literacy instruction.

Strategic Reading

Perhaps the most effective way to help students become independent readers is to teach them reading strategies in meaningful contexts (Harvey & Goudvis, 2000). A strategies-based approach may be implemented within whole-class, small-group, or individual reading instruction.

Differentiating between a *skill* and a *strategy* is essential to an understanding of teaching strategic reading. *Skills* describe a set of helpful tools that students practice in order to become better readers. A skill becomes a *strategy* when learners can apply it independently, when they can reflect on and understand how it works and then apply it to new reading material (Robb, 1996).

By third grade, each child comes to a teacher with some individual reading strategies, based both on decoding and meaning making. Intermediate and middle-level teachers continue to demonstrate skills and strategies, both modeling them and teaching them through direct instruction. Teachers must be knowledgeable about the reading process and the following three cueing strategies:

- ***Graphophonic strategies:*** The use of sound/symbol relationships to determine words. *Does the word match what I am saying?*
- ***Syntactic strategies:*** The blending interrelationships between words, sentences, and paragraphs with knowledge of grammar and structure. *Does it sound right?*
- ***Semantic strategies:*** The use of meaning, context, and background knowledge. *Does it make sense?*

The strategies for making words, for making sense, and for making meaning align with these systems. Students must be flexible in the use of all three strategies as they strive to extract meaning from the text.

Reading strategies include cognitive and social strategies used by readers to construct meaning during reading. The purpose of teaching reading strategies is to assist learners in developing a repertoire of options from which they can choose when they encounter difficulty as they become independent readers. Strategies are not necessarily taught in any particular sequence; rather, students begin with existing strategies and build new strategies as they acquire a full range of options. Strategy learning is a lifelong process as more challenging materials, new genres, and more complex content area reading enters their academic, personal, and professional lives. Teachers serve a primary role in the scaffolding of students' comprehension of text by teaching strategies and providing flexible, adaptable support to readers (Clark & Graves, 2005).

Strategies can be learned when they are taught in the context of real reading in a reading workshop format. Some teachers, however, may prefer a more defined time for direct instruction of these strategies. They can be practiced during silent reading of easier materials or during reading of more difficult text sets in preparation for literature conversations. Rereading is an excellent way to more fluidly reapply strategies. Specific strategy lessons during the opening of the reading workshop provide a constant flow of new techniques for the growing reader. Strategy lessons help focus readers on specific cognitive and social strategies used by proficient readers. During reading conferences, teachers should ask students what strategies they used in reading a difficult page. Strategies are internalized through constant practice during engaged reading and provide a significant part of the total reading program.

Defining Comprehension

Comprehension instruction is an essential component of a balanced literacy program. Because meaning-making is the heartbeat of reading, comprehension instruction highlights several dimensions and perspectives (Barton & Sawyer, 2003/2004; Pressley, 2000).

- Exposure to different texts, text structures, and genres:
  Narrative, expository, poetic, and technical text
  Illustrations as an embellishment of the text
  Cultural voices of authors revealed through multicultural text
  Genre as a conveyor of varied writing styles of authors
- Reader/text connections:
  Text-to-text connections (character/plot to related reading)
  Text-to-life connections (student lives to characters' lives)
  Text-to-world connections (plot to broader settings and situations)
- Reader response:
  Engagement in reading to deepen comprehension
  Questioning the text to stimulate varied response
  Reflection on and extension of initial responses
- Direct instruction in comprehension strategies:
  Determination of strategies to use based on content of text
  Whole group instruction followed by small group guided practice
  Selection of specific strategies for instruction
- Visual structure to support comprehension:
  Narrative/story graphs (problem; rising or falling action; resolution)
  Expository text graphic organizers (description, sequence, cause and effect, problem and solution)
- Metacognitive awareness of comprehension:
  Declarative knowledge (what strategy to use in a situation)
  Procedural knowledge (how to successfully apply a strategy)
  Conditional knowledge (knowing the purpose of the strategy and when to employ it)
  Evaluating the difficulty of the text (regulating, monitoring, evaluating the effectiveness of the strategy, and modifying)

The complexity of the comprehension process invites ongoing guided instruction throughout elementary and middle-level literacy instruction (McLaughlin & Allen, 2003). Internalizing the varied reading strategies takes time, practice, and application in the context of both guided and independent reading. If students are to become lifelong readers, the importance of acquiring these independent strategies is unquestionable. Once teachers understand what is involved in comprehending and how the factors of reader, text, and context interact to make meaning, they can more effectively teach their students to be effective comprehenders of their reading (Pardo, 2004).

Comprehension Strategies

This complex process of comprehension is surrounded by an extensive list of comprehension strategies that lead to meaning making and understanding. Keene and Zimmerman (1997) have identified what they describe as a "mosaic" of seven categories of comprehension strategies:

- Activating prior knowledge
- Determining the essence of text
- Delving deeper through questioning
- Creating sensory images
- Adding personal meaning through inference
- Summarizing to synthesizing
- Utilizing fix-up strategies

The idea of comprehension as a mosaic evokes the image of the complexity of the comprehension process and how the engaged reader must initiate and piece together many dimensions of comprehension for optimal meaning-making to take place in the reader's mind.

Activating Prior Knowledge. Before, during, and after reading, the reader should attempt to relate unfamiliar text to prior global knowledge and personal experience. Text-to-self connections link reading to the reader's own life. Text-to-text connections remind the reader of previous books and information related to the setting, characters, or plot of the evolving book. Text-to-world connections remind the reader of broader issues or themes that have been discussed or viewed in varied academic and personal contexts.

Recognizing both adequate and inadequate background information and knowing how to build a schema before reading provides greater understanding during reading. Knowing an author's writing style also assists in predicting the upcoming text. Recognizing difficult or unfamiliar text structure can provide a heads-up to potential reading challenges.

Creating these prior knowledge connections provides adequate background to make reading richer, to enhance personal response, and to create deeper understanding of the text. Knowing about the history of orphan trains across mid-America might enhance the reading of Karen Cushman's *Rodzina,* the story of an orphan awaiting adoption by farmers as she travels across the country. Having read other books by Karen Cushman (e.g., *Catherine, Called Birdy*), the reader may be better prepared for the evolving actions of another strong, determined female character. A pervious understanding of the broader theme of a sense of belonging might better prepare the reader to comprehend the needs, desires, and actions of Rodzina as she rejects adoption in favor of a sense of permanence.

Determining the Essence of Text. What is really important in a text? The effective reader needs to sift through the mass of words, sentences, paragraphs, and chapters of books that often run more than 100 pages in an attempt to derive the main idea or theme of the work itself. Readers should start at the word level: What words in a paragraph, on a page, or in a chapter really carry the meaning of the text? They should then proceed to the sentence level—What key sentence carries the weight of the meaning for a passage or section?—and conclude with the whole text level: What are the key ideas, concepts, or themes in the text? Students can use adhesive notes to identify important words, phrases, and paragraphs directly in the book.

Linda Sue Park's *A Single Shard* provides a substantive read for sixth-grade readers. Sorting through chapters for key words, phrases, and ongoing themes will assist students in capturing the evolving essence of the book. Key words like *celadon pottery* and *master craftsman* and phrases like *under the bridge* and *half-filled dinner bowl* provide cues to the early background of the story. Emotional sentences such as *Min never indicated any satisfaction with Tree-ear's work* or *He did not ask, as Min preferred to work with as few words as possible* reflect the evolving respectful relationship of master-apprentice established throughout the book. Seeking the essence of story through key words, phrases, and sentences provides a comprehension-assisting strategy with focus and purpose.

Delving Deeper Through Questioning. The effective reader needs to be aware of questions lingering in his or her mind before, during, and after reading or listening to a book. Questions should be used to clarify meaning, to wonder about forthcoming text, to speculate on the author's intent, style, content, or format. Questions can provide predictions that can be confirmed or denied as the reading continues. Readers must be made aware of three types of questions:

- Questions occurring before reading the story
- Questions initiated during the reading of the story
- Questions lingering beyond the conclusion of the story

With this awareness comes understanding of how questioning can enhance comprehension.

In Kate DiCamillo's *Because of Winn-Dixie,* fourth-grade readers may question naming a dog Winn-Dixie. During the reading, they might wonder if Opal's mother is still alive and may be coming back to her by the end of the book. After the reading, inquiring readers might question the future impact of Gloria Dump, Fanny Block, and guitar strumming Otis on India Opal's life. Only by asking questions—of the author, of the text, and beyond the text—do readers truly delve deeper into the comprehension of quality literature.

Creating Sensory Images. The visual aspects of reading that occur in the mind's eye enhance comprehension throughout the reading process. Proficient readers spontaneously and purposefully create vivid mental images during and after the reading of a text. Mental images immerse the reader in rich details. These images also serve as rehearsals for written response or related writing following the reading event. As a book continues, mental images such as the envisionment of a character's appearance may actually adapt or alter to match ongoing descriptions and character development. Understanding that sensory images enhance comprehension serves as an invitation to the reader to draw on descriptions, sounds, smells, sights, and settings to contribute to the growing mosaic of the mind.

Christopher Paul Curtis' *Bud, Not Buddy* conjures up vivid mental images as Bud is locked in a dark shed with buzzing wasps. An auditory image of the jazz music of the thirties surrounds the adept reader as this sensory image enhances comprehension. The visual image of Bud's cherished suitcase and its contents bring reality to Bud's unfolding search for his family. Artistic response results when readers draw pictures of what they have just read. Theater corners, artist studios, and writing dens provide additional centers that encourage the visual expression of comprehension. Although many teachers think that students naturally read with the mind's eye, they may be surprised when reading comprehension indicates that it is sensory, not verbal imaging, that ultimately enhances understanding.

Adding Personal Meaning Through Inference. To infer meaning from a text is to build comprehension beyond the printed page. Whether the inference is a quick, subconscious prediction, a sense of outrage at the actions of the character, or part of an engaged literature conversation, inference makes text the reader's own. "When we read, we stretch the limits of the literal text by folding our experience and belief into the literal meanings of the text, creating a new interpretation, or inference" (Keene & Zimmerman, 1997, p. 147). This original meaning lies at the intersection of the reader's prior knowledge, the printed text, and the ability to blend the personal into an interpretation that is unique. Inference borders the realm of reader response as students lift ideas from the text and add an individual connection to them.

Drawing conclusions and making predictions become an important part of inference. Pam Muñoz Ryan's *Esperanza Rising* provides fertile opportunity for readers to speculate on outcomes. Predicting the ability or failure of the self-centered Esperanza to adapt to the demeaningly hard work of the migrant community is essential to understanding this story. Detecting Esperanza's growing relationships with new characters and speculating on her response to the striking workers and her mother's illness assists in deeper emotional involvement with the character and plot. The role of inference propels the reader to a higher level of textual connections and another level of the reading process. With understanding comes reader enjoyment that will influence lifelong choices as a reader.

Summarizing to Synthesizing. The summarizing of text often occurs through the process of retelling. The facts, ideas, and characters in a reading are listed in a sequenced manner in an attempt to recall the details of the text as it builds into a cohesive whole. Synthesis, however, is about organizing the different pieces in an attempt to understand the whole even better. The higher level act of synthesizing causes readers to revisit the text, meld it into their own experiences, and weave it into a meaningful whole—more vivid and enhanced than its separate parts. Synthesis provides an invitation to make meaning of the knowledge gained within the boundaries of the reader's own life spectrum. The pinnacle of comprehension may be the synthesis of the parts of the text into a integral whole expressing the reader's unique perspective.

Retelling of what has been read serves as a foundation for creating a personal meaning or message from the text. Karen Hesse's *Out of the Dust* may inspire a retelling of events from the tragic loss of this family compounded by the ghastly ecological conditions that cause Billie Jo to feel isolated, alone, and disconnected from the place she has called home. As retelling builds to synthesis, however, the reader attempts to make sense of this chain of events by discussing the persistence of the human spirit during desperate times. Blending events, setting, character, and theme with the broader reality of human survival of both personal and environmental experiences takes the reader to the pinnacle of synthesis—the process of drawing broader strokes in the discussion of theme, viewpoint, and analysis of the text. On the hierarchical pyramid of developmental comprehension strategies, synthesis resides at the pinnacle. Proficient readers practice to attain this level of comprehension as they strive to reach the ultimate satisfaction of reading enjoyment.

Utilizing Fix-Up Strategies. While the first six types of comprehension strategies exist to enhance understanding, there are situations in reading that require different yet equally important strategies to guide the reader toward this level. Fix-up strategies provide a well-developed arsenal of tools to solve both word identification and literal comprehension dilemmas.

For readers to uncover meaning in a text, they must transcend the surface structure—phonemic awareness, word knowledge, and language structure. Although teachers often associate these areas with primary literacy, they all apply at the intermediate and middle level. As vocabulary becomes more challenging, as content implies greater background knowledge, and as sentences build in complexity, readers fall back on strategies they learned initially. Sight word recognition, decoding, and word analysis lead toward unlocking difficult words that appear in the text. Rereading, reading ahead, or the use of context clues can help clarify meaning through these substantive yet simple fix-up strategies. The deeper structure of text includes word meaning, prior knowledge, and the purpose or intended audience of the text. Fix-up strategies to negotiate the deeper structure of text requires the application of the other six comprehension strategies to attain the deepest levels of understanding.

As readers become more proficient, they acquire comprehension strategies over time through a developmental lens as a teacher models and demonstrates them in authentic contexts. With plentiful reading experiences, readers practice these strategies by sharing derived meaning through talking and literary response. They eventually internalize these strategies over time, both consciously and subconsciously applying them on the journey toward independent reading. Using strategies simultaneously and with awareness, they develop the ability to read more critically. Strategies provide the tools to unlock the deeper treasures of text comprehension. For proficient readers, comprehension strategies become second nature to the reading process itself.

Determining Which Strategies to Teach

How do teachers make informed decisions about which strategies to teach? In what contexts are certain strategies best taught? Is there a developmental perspective to introducing strategies? Consider the following background knowledge suggested by Five and Dionisio (1998):

- ***Careful observation of students' reading:*** During individual reading conferences teachers observe what children do when they read. They listen to them read aloud, note their miscues, evaluate their retellings, and record their strategies. They note how they solve problems to make meaning, record their fluency rate, and observe how rate affects comprehension. Teachers record this ongoing information allowing them to identify what each child knows and what each child needs to know. Reading interviews also help teachers detect a child's self-concept as a reader and his or her ability to select books at an appropriate level. Teachers truly have their finger on the reading pulse of each of their students, being able to detect what strategies they have, what strategies they need, and what strategies will place them one step closer toward independence.
- ***Fundamental understanding of the development of reading:*** As professionals, teachers are constantly acquiring and refining knowledge of literacy through books and journals. New knowledge informs the methods, contexts, and sequence of teaching those strategies. In addition, developmental expectations of what readers should know and be able to do informs instructional decisions. The listings of state and local curricular scope and sequence strategy also influence the teaching of strategies. Teaching experience with children at a particular grade level perhaps provides the most effective understanding of strengths, needs, problems, and goals that lead toward expectations for readers at a particular level.
- ***Personal experiences as a reader:*** Teachers who think about their own reading and have an awareness of their personal reading strategies will be better able to model or demonstrate how and when to use particular strategies. Such demonstrations of real reading by teacher-as-reader are powerful ways to teach skills and strategies to students. Modeling these during read-alouds or discussing strategy application within personal reading provides examples of how readers cognitively determine their levels of comprehension and which strategies to apply for clarified meaning-making.

FIGURE 7.9 Examples of Reading Strategies.

Self-Monitoring Strategies

Reading on to make certain predictions make sense
Self-correcting when something does not make sense
Sensing if the sentence sounds right
Thinking about what would make sense
Rereading a difficult passage
Reading faster for momentum and fluency
Stopping at certain points to think and predict
Asking yourself questions about what is happening
Reading what you don't understand slowly and what you do quickly

Unknown Word Strategies

Predicting words using letter/sound relationships
Thinking about what word would make sense
Looking at an illustration for clues
Breaking a word into parts—beginning, middle, end
Using letters and sounds to predict the word
Looking for a little word in a bigger word
Relating the word to a familiar word
Skipping the word and going on
Reading on to get more information on what the word might be
Asking someone who knows the word
Looking up really important words in the dictionary

Meaning-Centered Strategies

Previewing a book through title, illustrations, headings, etc.
Predicting using context clues
Thinking about what you already know about a topic
Making a connection to other related stories or genres
Creating a visual image or mental picture of the story
Creating an analogy or metaphor to understand the story
Talking to someone else who has read the story (literature conversation)
Paying attention to what's new

Careful observation, developmental perspective, and personal reading experience contribute to making instructional decisions on when to teach specific strategies to the reader. There are three types of strategies that need to be taught, as shown in Figure 7.9:

- ***Self-monitoring strategies:*** These strategies imply that metacognitive readers must learn to check on themselves and that there is a correspondence between what is on the page and what each reader says. The reader who hesitates, stops, or goes back to reread is self-monitoring for meaning.
- ***Unknown word strategies:*** These strategies require the use of sound and symbol relationships in figuring out words. Looking at the first letter, locating little words in a bigger word, sounding out the word slowly, and thinking of a word that makes sense are strategies that help the reader understand words during the act of reading.

- ***Meaning-centered strategies:*** These strategies build from experiences in which readers read whole texts. The use of context clues and knowledge of story structure are best learned in the context of whole texts. Reading workshop provides opportunities to focus on meaning-centered strategies for specific literary genres. Learning that reading biography differs from reading realistic fiction provides genre strategies to clarify meaning. Using strategies that help them to focus on meaning, readers chunk text into sections, constantly making predictions and connections.

Finding Time and Place for Strategy Instruction

A balanced reading approach provides several opportunities to teach, revisit, or practice designated strategies. Focused strategy instruction may occur on a daily basis and address an entire class. For example, the teacher may directly teach a strategy for creating a visual image of a story during reading by modeling a sketch-to-stretch activity (Whitin, 1996). Sketch-to-stretch encourages the visual representation of story comprehension through drawing. Students move on to their guided reading or reading workshop groups to practice the strategy within the context of the real literature they are reading. A shared teacher read-aloud at the opening of a reading workshop might provide an opportunity for modeling a strategy by pausing to think aloud or formulate questions during reading. During the concluding shared reading portion of a reading workshop, teachers and students may utilize a reading strategy to read a single book passage. Teaching this way provides flexibility in the use of strategies in a variety of contexts.

Teachers working with guided reading groups may demonstrate a strategy for determining an unknown word. Weekly reading conferences provide an individual opportunity to introduce or reteach a particular skill or strategy or for individual readers to describe the skills and strategies they use, evaluate their progress, and set goals. Sitting in on literature conversations enables teachers to provide strategies for analyzing or interpreting text.

No matter when teachers insert strategy instruction into balanced literacy, they cannot leave these strategies to chance. Learners, especially struggling readers, rarely acquire skills and strategies on their own. Skill and strategy instruction should be a predictable part of daily literacy instruction. Such instruction is a necessary and essential part of the reading program, but not the entire reading program. The real art of becoming a reader is the spontaneous application of strategies in meaningful reading contexts with authentic text. Reading workshop provides the opportunity to blend literature-based reading with the application of reading strategies in an effort to create lifelong, independent readers.

Research supports the fact that reading comprehension performance can be significantly improved with effective teaching (Dole, Brown, & Trathen, 1996; Pressley, Johnson, Symons, McGoldrick, & Kurita, 1990). Since reading involves active thinking, this process can be improved through teacher demonstration of the strategies that proficient readers use. Moving toward modeling of a strategy in an authentic context may foster greater comprehension (Allington, 2001). Readers need repeated demonstration of effective strategy use and many opportunities to apply the strategy in authentic reading contexts over time.

Considering a Balanced Literacy Program

Unfortunately, not all teachers of reading have the administrative support to design a reading program precisely aligned with their literacy philosophies. In today's standards-based world of teaching and testing, educators are often provided a published program with all its accessories as a literacy delivery system. Both novice and experienced teachers are challenged to blend their own literacy beliefs with those of the district literacy program in an attempt to provide the most effective literacy instruction for their students. While this is challenging, many teachers have found ways to balance published programs with a literature-based philosophy.

For example, many basal reader programs are now literature-based. Utilizing the reprinted literature in the basal format provides an almost ideal reading workshop format. In delivering strategies, teachers may use the published scope and sequence guide of the basal to determine which strategies need to be taught at a designated reading level. While teachers may "balance" a program by teaching those strategies in the context of literature, they can document that these strategies were indeed taught and applied in authentic reading contexts.

One of the greatest challenges of reading instruction is addressing the needs of struggling readers (Dudley-Marling & Paugh, 2004). Considering student-centered activities that differentiate instruction and focus on each student's needs provides the new balanced reading curriculum.

Duffy-Hester (1999) reviewed six research-based classroom reading programs that have been shown to enhance the reading performance of struggling readers. The following 10 principles reflect the essence of teaching reading at the third- to eighth-grade level to support the reading growth of struggling readers and provide a framework for designing a reading program for all students:

- *A reading program should be balanced, drawing on multiple theoretical perspectives.* The balanced reading program suggested in this chapter draws from the perspectives of reader response, comprehension, and direct strategies-based instruction. Teachers should not allow a single program, theory, model, or philosophy to dominate their reading agenda. The best teachers thoughtfully draw from various sources, use many techniques, and utilize a wide variety of reading materials. A balanced approach to literacy is likely to support the reading and overall literacy growth of all children.
- *There should be a practical and theoretical justification for every component and element in the reading program.* Both research and teacher experience should determine the instructional and theoretical merit of each selected reading activity. In a classroom in which every minute counts, teachers need to be able to justify their literacy programs as they align them with national and state standards while staying true to their own literacy beliefs.
- *The explicit teaching of word identification, comprehension, and vocabulary strategies may take place in conjunction with authentic reading and writing tasks.* Strategies taught explicitly and in conjunction with authentic reading and writing events, rather than through isolated drill and practice, may result in more successful application within personal reading and writing.
- *On a daily basis, teachers should read aloud to students from a variety of genres and create opportunities for students to read instructional and independent level texts.* Within both reading workshop and guided reading, teachers make time for read-aloud modeling of literature across genres. Generous opportunities for independent reading abound each day. A balanced literacy diet ensures that each reader has an opportunity to blend instructional literacy challenges with independent literacy enjoyment.
- *Reading instruction should be informed by and based on meaningful reading assessments.* Informal reading inventories, reading records, portfolios, and anecdotal records (see Chapter 15) exist to inform instruction. Rather than basing instruction

on a prescribed scope and sequence curriculum, optimal progress requires responsiveness to reader needs. Meeting the needs of each student as close to his or her performance level as possible ensures that constant nudge toward continuous growth in literacy.

- *Teachers should be decision makers, using their practical, personal, and theoretical knowledge to inform their reading instruction.* No single program meets the needs of all readers. While teachers should design their programs on an evidence base, their implementation of these programs should be blended with their practical knowledge, experience, and beliefs about the best way to teach reading. Adapting an established program to meet a teacher's philosophical beliefs is likely to result in optimal student learning.
- *Staff development for preservice and practicing teachers of reading may include providing opportunities for teachers to reflect on their practice.* Reflective practitioners are encouraged to determine how to make a program work by planning modifications based on what they learn through self-reflection. Adjusting programs to their own teaching situations and student audiences may assist in making the critical link between research and practice.
- *Reading programs may be based on multiple goals for student success.* Programs that focus on a variety of reading goals, beyond those of a prescribed program, are more likely to produce engaged, motivated, strategic readers.
- *Reading programs may provide multiple contexts for student learning—a blend of talk structure and task structure.* The reading workshop provides an opportunity for the social talk that surrounds literacy learning. The direct strategy instruction that occurs within the workshop approach provides the modeling and perceived application of comprehension skills. Overlapping reading, talking, and strategy application provides an appropriate blend for optimal learning.
- *Reading programs should be designed to support the reading growth of all children, both struggling and nonstruggling readers.* All children need to have their literacy needs assessed and addressed within a classroom reading program. Quality reading instructional programs for struggling readers should be based on the same principles as programs for nonstruggling readers. Within these programs, instruction must be individualized to meet the specific reading needs of each child.

These characteristics of reading programs that "work" for struggling and striving readers provide guidelines in preparation for the wide range of reading abilities that teachers encounter in a typical third-grade to eighth-grade classroom. They remind teachers that their goal is to teach *all* children to become literate contributors to a community of learners in our classroom.

Visit the Companion Website at www.prenhall.com/hancock and gauge your understanding of Chapter 7 concepts with the self-assessments.

Closing Thoughts

Envisioning and encouraging the organization and implementation of a reading workshop built on authentic literature is the theme of this chapter. Blending the literature, reader response, and literature conversations provides both the motivation and enjoyment for reading literature and engaging in written responses and oral conversations. Within the authenticity of literature, the strategies of comprehension characterizing proficient readers can be taught, practiced, and applied.

The teacher, not the program, is the single most important factor in determining the success of readers in the classroom setting. Having a greater impact than any single program, method, or approach, effective teachers of reading base their instructional decisions, in part, on reading research and theory. Yet those decisions are also bound in practical applications and implications in the instructional setting. Finding the appropriate balance of theory and practice that meets the needs of all children is the ongoing challenge of teachers of reading. Acquiring and applying the strategies of reading in the context of authentic literature is the challenge of readers who seek proficiency in lifelong reading as a goal.

References

Allington, R. L. (2001). *What really matters for struggling readers: Designing research-based programs.* New York: Longman.

Atwell, N. (1998). *In the middle: Writing, reading, and learning with adolescents* (2nd ed.). Portsmouth, NH: Heinemann.

Barton, J., & Sawyer, D. M. (2003/2004). Our students are ready for this: Comprehension instruction in the elementary school. *The Reading Teacher, 57,* 334–347.

Clark, K. F., & Graves, M. F. (2005). Scaffolding students' comprehension of text. *The Reading Teacher, 58,* 570–580.

Daniels, H. (2002). *Literature circles: Voice and choice in book clubs and reading groups* (2nd ed.). York, ME: Stenhouse.

Dole, J., Brown, K. J., & Trathen, W. (1996). The effects of strategy instruction on the comprehension performance of at-risk students. *Reading Research Quarterly, 31,* 62–88.

Dorn, L. J., French, C., & Jones, T. (1998). *Apprenticeship in literacy: Transitions across reading and writing.* York, ME: Stenhouse.

Dudley-Marling, C., & Paugh, P. (2004). *A classroom teacher's guide to struggling readers.* Portsmouth, NH: Heinemann.

Duffy-Hester, A. M. (1999). Teaching struggling readers in elementary school classrooms: A review of classroom reading programs and principles for instruction. *The Reading Teacher, 52,* 480–495.

Five, C. L., & Dionisio, M. (1998). Teaching reading and writing: Organizing for sensible skills instruction. *School Talk, 4,* 1–3, 7.

Five, C. L., & Egawa, K. (1998). Reading and writing workshop: What is it, and what does it look like? *School Talk, 3,* 1–4.

Fountas, I. C., & Pinnell, G. S. (2001). *Guiding readers and writers, grades 3–6.* Portsmouth, NH: Heinemann.

Hancock, M. R. (1993a). Character journals: Initiating involvement and identification through literature journals. *Journal of Reading, 37,* 42–50.

Hancock, M. R. (1993b). Exploring the meaning-making process through the content of literature response journals: A case study investigation. *Research in the Teaching of English, 27,* 335–368.

Hancock, M. R. (2004). *A celebration of literature and response: Children, books, and teachers in K–8 classrooms.* Upper Saddle River, NJ: Merrill/Prentice Hall.

Hanson, J. (2001). *When writers read* (2nd ed.). Portsmouth, NH: Heinemann.

Harvey, S., & Goudvis, A. (2000). *Strategies that work: Teaching comprehension to enhance understanding.* York, ME: Stenhouse.

Keene, E. O., & Zimmerman, S. (1997). *Mosaic of thought: Teaching comprehension in a reader's workshop.* Portsmouth, NH: Heinemann.

McLaughlin, M., & Allen, M. B. (2003). *Guided comprehension: A teaching model for grades 3–8.* Newark, DE: International Reading Association.

Pardo, L. S. (2004). What every teacher needs to know about comprehension. *The Reading Teacher, 58,* 272–278.

Peterson, R., & Eeds, M. (1990). *Grand conversations: Literature groups in action.* New York: Scholastic.

Pressley, M. (2000). What should comprehension instruction be the instruction of? In M. L. Kamil, P. B. Mosenthal, P. D. Pearson, & R. Barr (Eds.) *Handbook of reading research* (Vol. 3, pp. 545–561). Mahwah, NJ: Erlbaum.

Pressley, M., Johnson, C. J., Symons, S., McGoldrick, J., & Kurita, J. (1990). Strategies that improve memory and comprehension of what is read. *Elementary School Journal, 90,* 303–322.

Raphael, T. E., Florio-Ruane, S., & George, M. (2001). Book club plus: A conceptual framework to organize literacy instruction. *Language Arts, 79,* 159–168.

Robb, L. (1996). *Reading strategies that work: Teaching your students to become better readers.* New York: Scholastic.

Serafini, F. (2001). *The reading workshop: Creating space for readers.* Portsmouth, NH: Heinemann.

Short, K., & Pierce, K. M. (Eds.) (1990). *Talking about books: Creating literate communities.* Portsmouth, NH: Heinemann.

Whitin, P. E. (1996). Exploring visual response to literature. *Research in the Teaching of English, 30,* 114–140.

Children's Books Cited

Avi (1991). *The true confessions of Charlotte Doyle.* New York: Orchard.

Creech, Sharon (1994). *Walk two moons.* New York: HarperCollins.

Curtis, Christopher Paul (1996). *The Watsons go to Birmingham–1963.* New York: Delacorte.

Curtis, Christopher Paul (1999). *Bud, Not Buddy.* New York: Delacorte.

Cushman, Karen (1994). *Catherine, called Birdy.* Boston: Clarion.

Cushman, Karen (1995). *The midwife's apprentice.* Boston: Clarion.

Cushman, Karen (1996). *The ballad of Lucy Whipple.* Boston: Clarion.

Cushman, Karen (2003). *Rodzina.* New York: Clarion.

DiCamillo, Kate (2000). *Because of Winn-Dixie.* Cambridge, MA: Candlewick.

Hesse, Karen (1997). *Out of the dust.* New York: Scholastic.

Hobbs, Will (1989). *Bearstone.* New York: Atheneum.

Hobbs, Will (1991). *Beardance.* New York: Atheneum.

Mikaelson, Ben (1993). *Sparrow hawk red.* New York: Hyperion.

Mikaelson, Ben (1998). *Petey.* New York: Hyperion.

Park, Linda Sue (2001). *A single shard.* New York: Clarion.

Paterson, Katherine (1977). *Bridge to Terabithia.* New York: Crowell.

Paterson, Katherine (1978). *The great Gilly Hopkins.* New York: Crowell.

Paterson, Katherine (1991). *Lyddie.* New York: Dutton.

Paterson, Katherine (1996). *Jip.* New York: Dutton.

Paulsen, Gary (1987). *Hatchet.* New York: Bradbury.

Paulsen, Gary (1992). *The haymeadow.* New York: Delacorte.

Paulsen, Gary (1999). *Brian's return.* New York: Delacorte.

Ryan, Pam Muñoz (2000). *Esperanza rising.* New York: Scholastic.

Spinelli, Jerry (1997). *Wringer.* New York: HarperCollins.

Taylor, Mildred (1990). *Mississippi bridge.* New York: Dial.

Chapter 8

THE WRITING APPRENTICESHIP

Steps Toward Literacy (Grades 3–8)

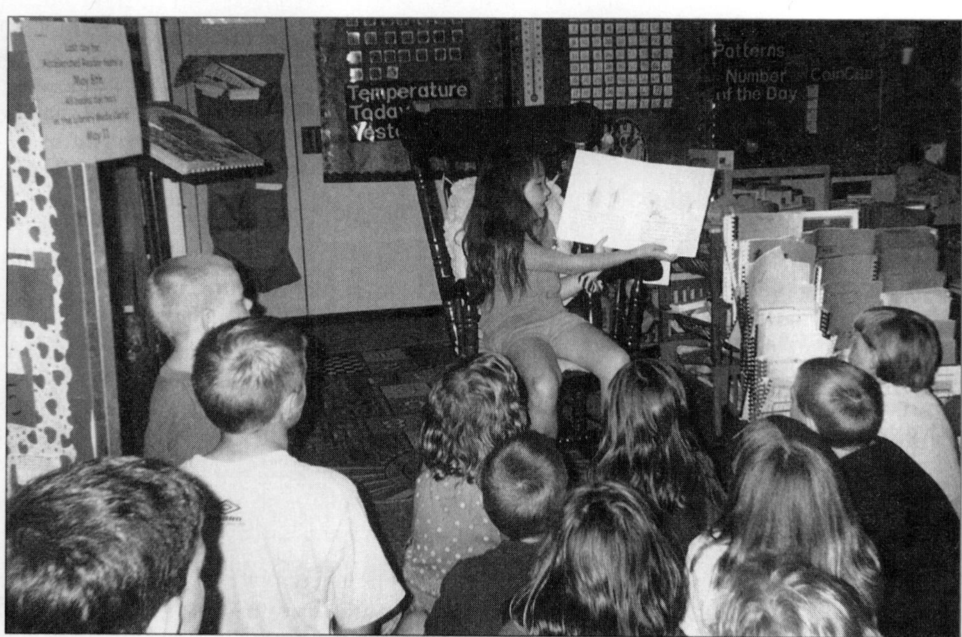

Stretch. . . . Use your imagination. If your story doesn't go the way you want it to, you can always stretch the truth. You can ask, "What if?" and make up a better story.

FROM *NOTHING EVER HAPPENS ON 90TH STREET* BY RONI SCHOTTER

In Roni Schotter's *Nothing Ever Happens on 90th Street,* Eva is faced with the challenge of a school writing assignment. Discouraged that she has nothing to write about, Eva sits on the stairs outside her apartment building while neighborhood residents from all walks of life point out the wonder of everyday life on their street. Mr. Sims convinces Eva that she need only observe the "players" carefully and tend to the details. Mr. Morley suggests finding the "poetry" through appropriate word choice. According to Mrs. Martinez, adding some action and a little "spice" will help make something happen. Peppered with writing advice, Eva is inspired to write and revise a story full of detail, dialogue, great word choice, and even a happy ending. Eva employs the writing process—from brainstorming to first draft to revision to final draft—and agrees that everyday life can be filled with the extraordinary events needed to create a story.

Writing is indeed hard work and a complex task. Authors, both emerging and accomplished, struggle with getting started, following where their writing leads them, incorporating endless revisions, and polishing a piece for audience approval. Even when ideas are at the tip of the writer's pencil or wordprocessing fingers, the challenges presented by writing continue to both frustrate and invigorate the novice and expert writer. Yet it is this uncertainty, this roller coaster excitement, that drives all authors to dream, problem solve, create unique pieces, and share their craft with others.

The research of Donald Graves (1975) and subsequent publication of his *Writing: Teachers and Children at Work* (1983/2003) marked a milestone for change and created a new instructional philosophy for the teaching of writing in the elementary and middle-level classroom. Moving from a product to a process orientation, this book instilled a fresh set of teacher beliefs about the teaching and learning of writing. These beliefs arose from teacher observation of children's writing behaviors, a growing knowledge about literacy and learning, and teachers' personal experiences with writing. Revisiting essential beliefs about the teaching of writing impact the way writing is taught, practiced, and celebrated within the classroom community.

Revisiting and rethinking writing as both a process and product has revolutionized the way writing is taught in today's classrooms (Harwayne, 2001). Perhaps you remember writing for a single audience—the teacher—and writing to a single assigned topic. Recall the "one time" aspect of writing—first copy, teacher corrections in red pen, final copy in your best handwriting. Writing was a silent time as writers worked in isolation and talk between writers was discouraged. Writing lessons focused on handwriting, spelling, grammar, and other conventions taught in the context of a language arts textbook rather than in the context of your own writing. Finally, writing was likely a once a week event rather than an ongoing daily happening.

Today's writing classroom is a socially interactive writing workshop in which talk is as critical as putting the pencil to the paper. Students function within writing groups where ideas are shared, suggestions are made, and individual styles are valued. Writing is less isolated and more supportive. The audience for writing has expanded beyond the teacher to an entire community of writers. Writing now requires committed ownership, dedicated work, and daily revisiting. No longer is a writing product completed in a one-day writing time, but a piece is brainstormed, drafted, revised, edited, and shared over a period of days or even weeks. No longer are students all writing to the assigned topic. Conventions remain a priority, but not until ideas have been clarified. Students consider themselves writers, gain confidence in their writing ability, and grow in their desire to share their writing with others. Today's young author has the opportunity to experience the genuine pleasure of the gradual unfolding of a writing piece as it grows from a simple idea to a satisfying manuscript.

Despite the pressures of national and state standards and related testing in writing, the writing process and its accompanying delivery format, the writing workshop, have endured and continue to flourish in schools across the nation (Fletcher & Portalupi, 2001). Because the process approach to writing leads toward higher quality writing products (the focus of state testing), this instructional approach lingers. With skills taught in the context of authentic writing, teachers find the balance that ensures an optimal blend of writing process, writing skills, and writing products.

Objectives

- To envision the characteristics of a writing classroom that embraces the apprenticeship philosophy.
- To articulate the five stages of the writing process and the importance of each stage in the development of a child's writing.
- To explore the craft of writing in an apprenticeship model through an honest writing mentor, an environment for risk taking, and a love of language.
- To model and instruct using the traits of writing that guide writing instruction and lead apprentices toward proficient authorship.
- To organize and implement read-aloud models, minilesson instruction, conferencing, and apprentice sharing within a writing workshop.
- To understand the role that a writing workshop fulfills within a balanced literacy program.

The Writing Apprenticeship Classroom

Over the past 20 years, research into practice supports several beliefs about the teaching of writing. These beliefs inform instructional practice through a process approach to writing, the writing workshop model, and the optimal blend of writing craft and conventions. There are several essential factors to consider about the teaching of writing in today's writing classroom (Five & Dionisi, 1998):

- ***Time.*** Large blocks of predictable, consistent time are needed to engage in the writing process. A writing block (30–60 minutes) should be included three to five times per week at all grade levels.
- ***Choice.*** Students should have the opportunity to choose the topics and format for their own writing, and to develop their own writing style. Within this framework, structured choices on assigned topics, genres, and forms are also encouraged.
- ***Modeling.*** Teachers must share their own writing with students through modeling. This writing should be drawn from both functional writing (letters, thank you notes) and personal writing (journals, poetry). Teacher writing demonstrations and the valuing of writing prove essential components in inspiring young authors.
- ***Instruction.*** Teachers must explicitly teach writing skills and strategies when they are needed through minilessons or demonstrations with the whole class, small-group activities, or individual conferences. Whether teaching about strong leads, varied sentence length, or an organized roadmap through a piece, teachers must focus on the art of teaching writing.
- ***Audience.*** Focusing on the reading audience and the reason for writing provides direction for choices of topic, form, and style. The reality of a wider audience for sharing provides impetus for revision and editing.
- ***Support.*** A supportive community of learners values student ideas and risk taking in a safe environment. Writing as a process rather than a product allows room for valuing and developing individuality as a writer. Talk with both teacher and peers is an essential part of writing both during brainstorming and revision.

The Teacher Prep Web site will help you become a better teacher by linking you to classroom videos, student artifacts, teaching strategies, lesson plans, relevant education leadership articles, and practical information on licensing, creating a portfolio, implementing standards, and being successful in field experiences. Visit this resource at www.prenhall.com/teacherprep.

- ***Feedback.*** Opportunities for constructive, supportive responses from both teacher and peers helps students consider, reconsider, question, and confirm their writing and to see it from an alternate point of view. Feedback must occur throughout the writing process in order for continuous changes and improvements to take shape.
- ***Revision.*** Students have more control and ownership over their writing when encouraged to revise throughout the writing process. Teachers must demonstrate and encourage the types of changes that constitute true revision. The process of deleting, inserting, and moving words, ideas, and phrasing requires students to rethink their work on a substantive level.
- ***Literature.*** Writers benefit from listening to, reading, and talking about the writing in quality literature. With teacher direction, the genres, styles, techniques, and conventions of writing can be modeled through quality literature.
- ***Conventions.*** Writers write so readers may read; therefore, attention must be paid to the conventions of spelling, grammar, and punctuation. Not only must conventions be taught, but students must exercise the responsibility to apply them in the context of their own writing.
- ***High expectations.*** Teachers and student writers must hold high expectations for quality writing and for the use of time spent writing. Students must be accountable and document their growth as writers through portfolios that reflect different types of writing and growth in the application of conventions.
- ***Assessment.*** Both teachers and student writers must be responsible for assessing continuous progress in writing. All stages of the writing process combine to create the final product. In addition, writing rubrics, both teacher and student-generated, set high expectations for the writing process and product.
- ***Celebration.*** Students must be offered showcased opportunities to share their final pieces of writing with both peers and adults. No longer is the teacher the sole recipient of the final product. The author's chair and varied forms of publication create a wider audience for appreciation.

These classroom characteristics reflect a new vision that has turned traditional writing upside down. With a positive attitude toward writing, mutual sharing of the writing craft, proper attention to writing skills, and a platform for improvement, today's young authors are surrounded by a risk free environment that results in individual growth and success.

In today's writing classrooms, a critical consideration involves the "why" and the "what" of writing. Figure 8.1 illustrates the authentic purposes and specific genres of writing that span the K–8 writing curriculum.

The Writing Process

Donald Graves (1983/2003) has identified five stages in the writing process that support and accompany the ongoing evolution of a finished piece of writing: (a) rehearsal, (b) drafting, (c) revision, (d) editing, and (e) publishing. Figure 8.2 clarifies and discusses each stage, illustrating how the writer conceives, composes, revisits, corrects, and shares a final piece of writing. Writing is a craft that requires skill, expertise, and the use of many

FIGURE 8.1 Why Do We Write? Purposes and Genres.

Purposes	Genre/Formats
To record events	Diaries, journals, lists, autobiographies, letters, informal notes, notetaking, reports, minutes of meetings, transcripts of discussions, reports
To explain	Recipes, charts, brochures, captions, instructions, definitions, rules, handbooks
To hypothesize	Arguments, theories
To persuade	Job applications, advertisements, invitations
To invite a response	Invitation, question, complaint, lost and found notice, note, request, wanted notice
To predict	Horoscope, weather forecast, timetable, graphs
To request	Business letters, invitations, applications
To entertain	Graffiti, jokes, riddles, bumper stickers
To narrate	Fables, stories, myths
To create	Play, commercial, poem, rhyme, lyrics, slogans
To inform	Announcements, book jackets, certificates, labels, menus, posters, pamphlets, lists, catalogs
To find out	Interviews, questionnaires, surveys, observations
To reflect	Journals, questions, quotations, personal reflections
To summarize	Postcards, reports, summaries
To express an opinion	Editorials, letters to the editor, debate notes

strategies that will help the writer craft a clear, coherent, and effective composition (Dahl & Farnan, 1998). It is important to remember, however, that not all pieces of writing developed in the elementary and middle-level classroom are ready for sharing with a larger audience. While one or two pieces may evolve through the entire writing process each quarter or grading period, other pieces are written as informal exercises with self-selected favorites developed through the entire writing process.

Focusing on each stage of the writing process provides the teacher deeper understanding of the ongoing journey of a writing product from mere idea to final publication.

1. **Rehearsal.** The rehearsal stage of the writing process involves brainstorming to find possibilities for topics for writing. Children write best from their own experiences, so generating a list of topics on which a child is an "expert" often leads in the right direction. This prewriting stage is filled with reflection, peer talk, and decision making. Interviews provide a means for limiting topics as writers seek input and opinions of peers. For younger children, drawing a picture provides rehearsal for writing that will later occur. A few teachers underestimate the importance of this prewriting stage, but research indicates the quality of final writing reflects the quality and quantity of this preparation time (Graves, 1994).
2. **Drafting.** The writer begins to express thoughts and feelings on paper during the drafting stage. Little attention is given to conventions in the first draft, since initiating

FIGURE 8.2
The Writing Process.

1. **Rehearsal**
   Brainstorm potential ideas (thinking, talking, drawing, remembering).
   What am I going to write about?
   Clarify purpose for writing.
   Choose a topic.
   Determine the audience.
   Who is my audience? What do I want them to know?
   Order information.
   What do I know about my topic? How do I organize the information?
   Select an appropriate form.
   Which form do I use to effectively share my writing?
2. **Drafting**
   Get ideas down on paper.
   What do I want to say?
   Compose
   How can I transfer the ideas in my head to my paper?
   Bring light and life to the story in your head.
   Take information from your notes to compose a report.
3. **Revision**
   Add, move, and/or delete words, sentences, paragraphs.
   How can I make my writing clear and effective?
   What word can I use to better describe an idea, an action, or a feeling?
   How can I vary the length and style of my sentences?
   How can my paragraphs lead the reader through my writing?
   What transitions can more effectively guide the reader?
4. **Editing**
   Proofread for conventions in spelling, punctuation, capitalization, and mechanics.
   How do I make my writing ready for a reader?
   What editing can I address on my own?
   How can I respond to a peer's editing?
   How can I respond to my teacher's editing?
5. **Publishing**
   Share with selected audience.
   How can I best publish my writing?
   How will my audience respond to my writing?
   Select word processing or handwriting.
   Select media, form, style.

Source: Adapted from New Zealand Ministry of Education (1992). Dancing with the Pen: The Learner as Writer. *Katonah, NY: Richard Owen.*

a flow of words is the ultimate goal. A wonderful thing about draft writing is that it often takes unexpected directions as ideas flow quickly, sometimes too quickly, from mind to pen and paper. The New Zealand Ministry of Education (1992) describes this natural flow of ideas as stories in the mind evolve into words on the printed page as "dancing with the pen."

A sixth-grade author shares ideas and feelings in the first draft of a story.

3. **Revision.** Developing writers must learn the skill of revision—the process of incorporating peer suggestions and their own ideas to improve writing as words, phrases, sentences, and paragraphs are added, deleted, or moved within the written draft. The desire to clarify, detail, exemplify, or enumerate compels authors to make changes in their original draft (Heard, 2002).

   The cornerstone of revision is the writing conference—a meeting that may occur informally within a writing group or more formally through a teacher-student conference. In a group writing conference, the students meet during the revision stage of an assigned writing piece, and peer mentors (rather than a teacher) offer comments and suggestions on the working draft. Each student reads his or her rough draft aloud, then asks for feedback (positive and negative) from peer mentors, fields peer group questions, and considers suggestions from each member of the group. The writer takes notes on his or her draft, but ultimately decides which suggestions will be incorporated in the revision. This process is repeated until all members have had an opportunity to share their work and obtain suggestions for revisions. Students then begin to write a second draft, incorporating revisions that add needed information, delete redundancies, or move sections of the writing piece for greater clarity and flow.

   Because a discussion of possible revisions is the most challenging part of the writing conference, small problems may occur. Peer mentors often have difficulty in determining what to say during a writing conference without harming the author's confidence. A discussion later in this chapter provides a sample of open-ended comments and detailed aspects of writing that could be mentioned, if appropriate. Some students tend to make simple revisions rather than substantive ones as they revise. Teachers can intervene at such points to provide examples of effective ways in which a writing piece can be revised at various developmental levels (words, phrase, sentence, paragraph), thus helping students to make meaningful changes that truly effect the quality of their written pieces.

   The teacher-student writing conference is another way to monitor the ongoing progress of student as writers. The goal of these brief, yet productive interactions is to celebrate achievements of young authors and to assist them over specific writing hurdles. More information on structuring these conferences is presented later in this chapter. Whether utilizing small group writing conferences or individual teacher-student conferences, the conference remains the heartbeat of the writing process. Within its structure lies the potential for student growth in his or her writing.

FIGURE 8.3 Editing Checklists: A Developmental Approach.

Grades 1–2

Did I put my name on my writing piece?
Did I read my draft to myself?
Did I point to every word I said with my pencil?
Did I ready my draft aloud to a friend?
Did I underline spelling words with which I need help?
Did I check for capital letters?
Did I check for end marks (. / ? / !)

Grades 3–4

Did I read my draft to myself?
Did I read my draft aloud to a friend?
Did I spell all words correctly?
Did I write each sentence as a complete thought?
Did I end each sentence with correct punctuation?
Did I begin each sentence with an uppercase letter?
Did I use uppercase letters for names, cities, states, etc?
Did I insert commas where needed?
Did I indent each paragraph?

Grades 5–8

Did I read my draft to myself?
Did I read my draft aloud to a friend?
Did I use standard editing marks to assist with my changes?
Did I delete unnecessary words or sentences?
Did I insert missing words?
Did I capitalize? Did I change to lowercase?
Did I add commas and apostrophes as needed?
Did the editing help the text appear clean and polished?
Did the editing assist the reader in processing the text without distraction or confusion?
Did the editing bring the text closer to polishing for publication?

4. **Editing.** The fourth stage of the writing process incorporates the editing of a piece to move it toward standard conventions in spelling, punctuation, capitalization, and mechanics. Only after a piece has been revised through a writing conference should it be edited. The author may actually be the first to edit the piece, followed by peer editors. Young students may focus on only a few writing skills for editing while more experienced ones may concentrate on skills within the context of the entire piece (Figure 8.3). Errors and changes can be noted with different colors of ink or pencil to more readily distinguish self-editing, peer-editing, and teacher-editing. Corrections are recorded on the second draft, but will be incorporated in the final draft.
5. **Publishing.** The publishing stage of the writing process finalizes the writing for the reading audience—to be read aloud from the author's chair, displayed on a bulletin board, or inserted as a page in a class book. This stage allows each writer to showcase the final product that has evolved through the writing process. Whether word processed or penned in a student's distinct handwriting, the final draft looks quite different than the first draft. As a work becomes ready for another reader's eyes, pride and self-esteem accompany this positive writing accomplishment and motivate the student author to move on to a new piece of writing.

During the five stages of the writing process, teachers should use modeling to show young writers how to accomplish writing goals at each stage. A teacher might draw up a list of five topics and discuss each in determining which one to select as a writing focus. Projecting a rough draft on an overhead transparency will allow teachers to describe aloud the thoughts and word choices that come to mind as changes are made and the recursive nature of revision is demonstrated during drafting. The teacher mentor may revise on the draft transparency by drawing arrows, crossing out words, and making marginal notes while thinking aloud about choices to be made. Teachers might also model a writing group, creating a blueprint of the process and steps in sharing, complimenting, questioning, and suggesting changes. An editing workshop provides the opportunity to model the editing process within a student-generated writing sample. Discussing what the writer did well, locating quality word choices, and selecting a favorite sentence start the process. The teacher then models proofreading by pointing to each word as spelling, punctuation, capitalization, and mechanical miscues are acknowledged and remedied. During publishing and sharing, a teacher may actually read a piece that he or she has been working on to demonstrate the value of revised writing in communicating ideas with a reading or listening audience.

Throughout the writing process, the teacher meets with individual students as each shares personal writing, discusses what is going well and what is going poorly, and mentions at least one writing skill that is developing or taking hold within the writing context. Although the informal conference may last only a few minutes, touching base with an adult writing mentor provides students with the needed suggestions to move the writing process ahead.

The five stages of the writing process form a sequential framework for developing apprenticeship authorship. The writing process provides a roadmap for beginning, developing, nurturing, re-envisioning, altering, and polishing a writing piece. Lesson Plan 8.1 illustrates how teachers can engage students in descriptive process writing and guides them through the five stages of the writing process. This process provides a single but critical perspective on the ongoing development of both the apprentice as confident author and the work as textual evidence of an authorship "masterpiece." Figure 8.4 presents the authentic comments of sixth-grade students who have spent a year immersed in learning the stages of the writing process.

FIGURE 8.4 **Reflections on Writing and the Writing Process by Sixth-Grade Authors.**

- What do you enjoy most about writing?

  The thing I like most is letting your imagination soar. (Andrea)
  I enjoy making it better by correcting my mistakes. (Kellyn)
  I feel good sharing my work with other people. (Ben)
  When I write something and someone says they like it. (Christian)
  I've always loved writing since I was little. To see myself progress more and more after each assignment is very enjoyable to me. (Kaylie)

- What is the most frustrating part about writing?

  What I find frustrating about writing is coming up with ideas to write. (Sarah)
  When I am writing a story, I get tired of having to go through so many steps because it takes a lot of hard work, but it's worth it. (Lindsey)
  The most frustrating part about writing is sometimes you know what you want to say, but you don't know how to put it in words. (Kaylie)
  The most frustrating part about writing is the first sentence. (Christian)
  The most frustrating part is the boundaries set by the teacher. (Andy)

LESSON PLAN 8.1

TITLE: Describing a Special Place

Grade Level: 3–6

Time Frame: Five 30-minute sessions

Standards

IRA/NCTE Standards: 2, 5

NETS for Students: 1, 3

Objectives

- Students will apply the steps of the writing process to produce a well-written descriptive paragraph about a special place.
- Students will utilize technology productivity tools to enhance learning and creativity.

Materials

- Literature:

  Siebert, Diane, (1989). *Heartland.* Illus. by Wendell Minor. HarperCollins.

  Bouchard, David, (1995). *If You're Not from the Prairie.* Illus. by Henry Ripplinger Atheneum.
- Computers with graphic organizer and/or word processing software.

Motivation

- Read *Heartland* or *If You're Not from the Prairie* to your students. Invite students to comment on what they notice about the book's illustrations and text. Point out that the author uses descriptive language to help paint a mental picture for the reader. As a class, revisit the text; generate a list or web of descriptive words that describe the prairie.

Procedures

Day 1—Rehearsal

- Encourage students to think about a place that has special meaning to them (prairie, mountains, meadow, lake, etc.). Explain that each student will write a descriptive paragraph depicting their special place.
- Using paper and pencil or graphic organizer software such as *Inspiration* or *Kidspiration,* each student generates a web with descriptive words or phrases that describe his or her special place.

Day 2—Drafting

- Ask students to refer to their webs as they draft descriptive paragraphs about their special places. Remind students of the importance of getting their ideas on paper and to skip lines to leave room for revisions and editing suggestions.

Day 3—Revising

- Using an overhead projector or visual presenter (Elmo), model how to improve a draft by making substantive revisions (ask a student for permission to use his or her first draft). Focus on word choice, sentence fluency, voice. Can readers paint a picture in their mind of the author's special place?

- Working in small groups or partners, students read their drafts aloud to each other. Encourage students to close their eyes and paint a mental picture as their partner reads his or her draft. Students should offer revision suggestions and compliments to their partner(s).

Day 4—Editing

- Using the overhead or visual presenter, model how to look for spelling and grammar mistakes and how to mark such errors (colored pens, special editing marks, etc.)
- Allow time for self-editing and peer-editing.

Day 5—Publishing

- Students will make their descriptive paragraphs accessible to readers through the use of word processing software or by neatly rewriting their final draft in their best handwriting. Consider fonts, illustrations, and other visual features as you guide students toward publishing their written pieces.

Assessment

- Writing rubric addressing the 6 + 1 traits of writing.

Accommodation/Modification

- Provide struggling writers or ESL students with additional children's literature that models vocabulary describing their special place.

Visit the Meeting the Standards module in Chapter 8 of the Companion Website at www.prenhall.com/hancock to adapt this lesson to meet your state's standards.

The Writing Craft of an Apprentice

In *What a Writer Needs,* Ralph Fletcher (1993) describes three essentials needed by apprentice writers—children or adults—to succeed in their craft: (a) an honest mentor; (b) an environment for risk taking; and (c) a love of language. These ingredients that encourage and support writing are essential if teachers expect writing to unfold in a magical, comfortable, natural way within and outside their classroom walls.

The Mentor

A teacher who values writing, struggles with the process, yet experiences the joy of completing a satisfying writing piece serves as the most effective mentor to a novice writer. Teachers serve as guides, sounding boards, nudgers, encouragers, realists, and supporters. "We must speak to our students with honesty tempered by compassion: Our words will literally define the ways they perceive themselves as writers" (Fletcher, 1993, p. 19). Teachers often fail to realize the influential role they play in the attitude and outcomes of student writers. The following traits will enable mentor writing teachers to have a positive impact on writing apprentices:

- *A mentor has high standards.* Teachers must not praise mediocre work, but they should encourage the novice writer to reach beyond simplicity to something special. A mentor's honesty is respected by students and spurs them to new heights.

- *A mentor builds on strengths.* It is best for teachers to start an informal or formal writing conference by pointing out a writing strength: "I really like the way you are using descriptive words in opening your story." They can then suggest changes that students can make to improve their writing even more.
- *A mentor values originality and diversity.* A teacher values the individual voices and unique ideas of all writers. Once in awhile, a special writer appears that shows exceptional writing talent. Instead of being threatened or competing with such talent, an effective mentor recognizes its value and gives the writer space to define himself or herself.
- *A mentor is passionate.* A teacher supplies the fire and incentive that sets the apprentice author aglow. An excited teacher provides the impetus that will allow a simple idea to become a great one. If a teacher is bored with, scared of, or tired of writing, the fire is extinguished and the students lack the desire to become writers. But when the teacher is passionate, the energy pervades the classroom, making writing a much anticipated activity across the school day.
- *A mentor sees writing as a slow, challenging process.* Patience is a virtue in being a teacher of writing. It takes time to develop the skills, focus the ideas, command the words, and ignite the spirit of a writer. Gentle encouragement has a more far-reaching effect than harsh, immediate demands. The big picture showcases writing growth over time, not within a single writing period or even a single academic year.

Think back to a teacher of writing who exemplified these characteristics. Undoubtedly it was a teacher who monitored your slow, yet steady progress, who nurtured your rich, unique ideas, and who balanced your writing strengths with honest suggestions for improvement. The teacher as mentor writer may be the most important element in the development of the apprentice.

The Risk-Taking Environment

When writing is allowed to evolve through the writing process, changes occur that shape new discoveries and uncover new ways of sharing ideas. The tendency of most writers, however, is to take the safe route, avoiding temptations to try something new, organize in a new mode, or start all over again. The best writing environments are those taught by teachers who allow children to experiment (rather than meet deadlines), to explore (rather than choose a safe format), and to expose themselves (rather than hide their inner selves) though writing. Fletcher (1993) refers to the tendency to take the safe way out as "freezing to the face of the cliff" (p. 24). When student writers find a creative tension springing up between their original writing plans and how they seem to be turning out, the teacher must encourage the new route, the unexplored, the innovative. Taking a chance on a richer writing experience rather than staying with the safe topic occurs only when risk taking is encouraged and valued.

A Love of Language

As a reader, you learn to write. As a writer, you learn to read (Hansen, 2001). And one of the most significant tools of reading and writing is a fascination with words. "Artists develop a love for the feel of their tools, the smell and texture of clay, wood, or paint . . . Writers are no different. Writers love words . . ." (Fletcher, 1993, p. 32). A fascination with words begins with a child's natural play with language. Children love the sounds of language they hear through rhyme, repetition, chanting, and alliteration. As children become readers, they grow in their desire to find "just the right word" to capture the moment. For example, Kevin Henkes' *Chrysanthemum* "wilted" when the children teased her about her name, but she "bloomed" when her music teacher praised flower names. Those "aha" moments in reading transfer to "aha" moments in writing as a powerful vocabulary allows a writer to get richness of thought on paper.

You can infuse students with this natural affinity toward language by pointing out great word choice during read-alouds (Ray, 1999). Encourage children to keep a list or writer's notebook of favorite words as they hear them. Invite them to mark and read aloud book passages that overflow with well-chosen words. Keep a class list of special vocabulary to be savored and used when a special opportunity arrives. Showcasing the wonder of words throughout the curriculum supports a most important writing tool.

If apprentices begin their writing attempts with these three essentials in place—an honest mentor, a risk-free environment, a love of language—they are more likely to be inspired to write, to explore the myriad adventures of writing, and to connect the quality written aspects of literature with the writing they undertake. Additional options for motivating students as writers can be found at a multitude of Web sites where students can exchange ideas, communicate with authors, or publish their work (see the Tech Tip included here).

Tech TIP

Using the Internet to Motivate Student Writers

Based in New Zealand, *Writers' Window* is a user-friendly site that is a great resource for student authors of all ages. The site contains information about writers' workshop, discussion boards, and a readers' cafe. Students may engage in writing continuous stories and publish their own compositions. There are also many links to support writers with their craft: tips for character development, descriptive tips, story builders, story planners, etc. **english.unitecnology.ac.nz/writers/home.html**

Writing with Writers invites students to develop their writing skills by working with authors, editors, and illustrators in exclusive workshops. This site includes mystery writing with Joan Lowery Nixon, myth writing with Jane Yolen, student work, a teacher's guide and a related book list. **teacher.scholastic.com/writewit/index.htm**

The Write Site is an interactive language arts and journalism project for middle school teachers and students. This site is easy to navigate with a plethora of links to help students explore the world of journalism. **http://www.writesite.org/default.htm**

For a small, one-time fee, student authors may publish their stories on *Kidpub,* a site that holds more than 43,0000 stories written by and for children. Students may share story ideas and talk about writing in the Author's Forum, or add the next paragraph to the continuous Never Ending Story. **http://www.kidpub.org/kidpub/**

KidsBookshelf encourages creativity and imagination in children through reading, writing, and drawing. The site publishes original book reviews, poems, and short stories of no more than 1,000 words. Teachers and parents may also post original projects, recipes, poems, and short stories written for children. Children may enjoy writing to some of the many authors and illustrators whose addresses are included. **http://www.kidsbookshelf.com/index.asp**

To look more closely at these materials and others related to "The Writing Apprenticeship," visit the Companion Website at **www.prenhall.com/hancock**.

Apprenticing the Writing Traits

Writing is hard work. Sometimes it seems impossible to come up with an idea, or a story gets stuck in the middle, or a title doesn't seem quite right. Sometimes student writers have trouble incorporating suggested revisions and they get frustrated and feel like quitting. Helen Lester's *Author: A True Story* vividly describes the memorable frustrations of being a children's book author. Yet this process of bringing the ideas of the imagination and intellect to the page as written words is well-worth the struggle encountered along the way before reaching satisfaction, delight, and pride in a job well-done. Learning the author's craft takes time, practice, and continuous modeling through both writing demonstrations and reading of literature models.

Teachers must guide young writers in an awareness of some of the common traits of the craft of writing—those characteristics that integrate focus, organization, voice, word choice, fluency, and conventions into good writing. Quality children's writing contains common elements that provide a framework for discussion, instruction, and assessment. To improve the quality of children's writing and to provide noteworthy suggestions for this improvement, teachers need to understand the traits that characterize sound writing at any level. No trait can be taught and applied at a single grade level. Traits are modeled from literature, taught through minilessons, and applied in daily writing throughout the elementary and middle-level years, thus reinforcing the apprenticeship model of writing as movement toward the creation of a writing "masterpiece" is approached.

The traits discussed in this section are derived from the 6 + 1 traits of writing (Culham, 2003; Spandell, 2001). Although several states utilize these traits for teaching and assessing children's writing, this is not the only writing model to be followed. Yet the simplicity of focused areas for instruction provide a strong framework for writing instruction. The 6 + 1 trait model includes seven categories:

- Idea and content
- Organization
- Voice
- Word choice
- Sentence fluency
- Conventions
- Presentation (the +1 trait most recently added to the list)

These seven traits provide some common ground on which to build a discussion of a developmental perspective on children's writing. These traits reflect the knowledge base of writing. Teachers who do not know what to teach during writing or as minilessons in writing workshop too often focus only on writing convention instruction rather than these authentic aspects of writing. A working knowledge of writing traits gives teachers direction, focus, and the content needed to help children grow as authors.

Ideas and Content

Ideas and content provide the message of the writing—what the author has to say about a topic of choice. In selecting topics, children should choose something that is important to them and something about which they have something to say. If their topic is too big (animals), they end up with too much to say. So they need to pare an interesting topic down to size (the snow leopard at the Sunset Zoo) so they can handle it.

Once the topic is selected, it must be enhanced with details to keep the audience's attention. Children need to write like experts, not only telling but showing through words the story they wish to convey. Being specific and surprising the reader make for great writing. "The arrogant snow leopard stalked the onlooking visitors as his glinting, focused eyes and smooth, polished coat reflected through the protective glass barrier." Clear, specific, detailed writing means careful observation by the writer and decision making about what to keep and what to leave out. Selecting a topic that is just the right size for the writer—not too broad and not too narrow—makes for an ideal idea upon which to share and develop a writing piece. Focusing on that topic and not straying from the established focus is the mark of a competent writer.

Idea development might best be presented to writing apprentices through picture books based on personal experiences. Gary Soto's *Too Many Tamales* shares a Hispanic family Christmas Eve interrupted by a missing wedding ring. Eve Bunting was inspired to write *Fly Away Home* upon witnessing the homeless in an airport. Patricia Polacco is known for sharing small fragments of her family's life through self-illustrated books such as *Betty Doll*. These small slices of real life provide focused, well-written stories that capture a single incident or idea through detailed description, distinctive characters, and a memorable message.

The teacher's goal as author/mentor is to help writing apprentices to narrow their topics to a finer slice of a larger event. Encouraging children to keep a list of writing ideas in a small notebook aids in collecting focused writing topics. Assigning a broad topic such as "A Special Place" or "A Momentous Event" models the focus and development of a single idea. The seed of an idea easily grows, but focusing on key aspects of that idea is the challenge of a writer. In "The Saddest Day of My Life" (Student Sample 8.1), a third grader reveals the power of focusing emotion and details on a single event.

Organization

A writer establishes a well-marked, ordered trail that motivates the audience to want to continue to read. Organization gives writing purpose and direction, thus providing an

STUDENT SAMPLE 8.1 A third grader exhibits idea and content development.

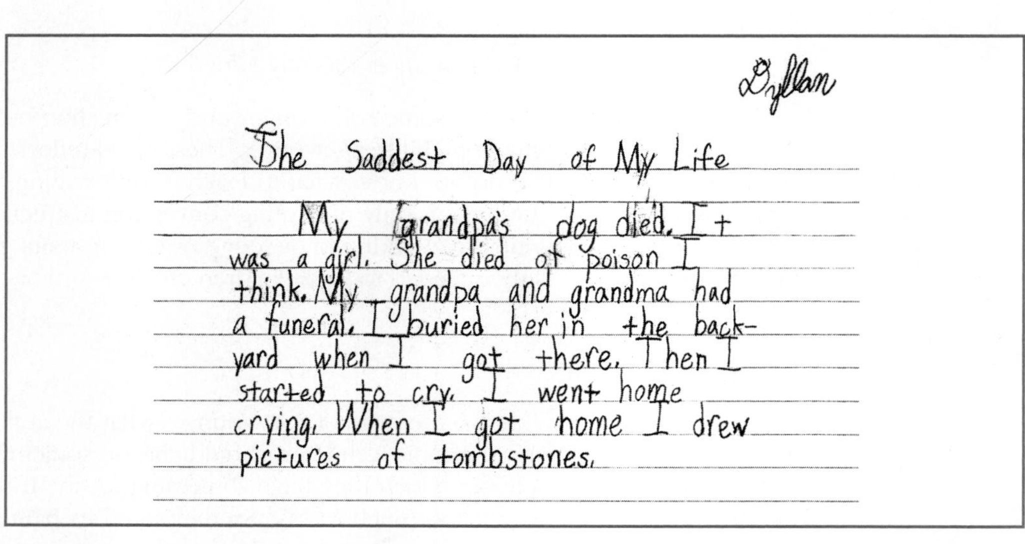

Dylan

The Saddest Day of My Life

My grandpa's dog died. It was a girl. She died of poison I think. My grandpa and grandma had a funeral. I buried her in the back-yard when I got there. Then I started to cry. I went home crying. When I got home I drew pictures of tombstones.

interior framework and an order that works well with the topic. Writing begins with a strong lead (opening sentence, paragraph, chapter) building momentum along the way. Keeping the writing moving in a logical order toward the center of the action and on to a resolution is challenging. An optimal ending leaves the audience thinking, yet feeling satisfied that the writing has reached closure.

The unraveling of a narrative story must be clear and sequential, and it must eventually mark closure. Organization implies order, but it also implies pace and the gradual dissemination of story. Spending too much time describing a character can take away time from the development of the character's dilemma. Taking too long to get a character to a climactic event can result in a hurried ending. Children often write stories that fill a page; when they get to the bottom of the page—they stop, no matter where they are in their stream of organization. Knowing how to begin, how to trickle out story, and when to stop marks the work of an organized narrative writer. Student Sample 8.2 shows how a third grader uses dialogue to guide the reader through a tale of friendship in "Elephant and Mouse."

Jean Craighead George's powerful text and Thomas Locker's outstanding oil paintings inspire the reader to follow an evolving story in *To Climb a Waterfall*. David Cunningham's *A Crow's Journey* follows melting snow on its trek to the sea surrounded by precise, poetic language that leads from a crow's inquiry to a satisfying response. Gary Blackwood's *The Shakespeare Stealer* provides an enticing lead and a memorable conclusion as creative bookends to a tale of adventure in Elizabethan England.

For young children, establishing the beginning, middle, and end of a story is an important apprenticeship springboard to the development of the organizational trait. Retellings of stories in books such as *Gator Gumbo* by Candace Fleming provide effective practice for conceptualizing organization. Using graphic organizers to reflect the structure of story elements (conflict, highpoint, roadblocks, resolutions) establishes a

STUDENT SAMPLE 8.2
A third grader exhibits writing organization.

ELEPHANT AND MOUSE
by Blair

One cloudy day, Mouse and Elephant were walking in the forest.

"Why are you Elephants so big," blurted Mouse. "Why can't you be small like us mice?"

"Well, I don't know. I guess that's just the way it is," Elephant said calmly.

"My friends always tease me because of how big you are and how small I am," mouse said angrily.

"Don't listen to them then. My friends tease me, too," snorted Elephant. "plus, what other friends do you have anyway?"

"Well, if that's the way it's going to be, I guess I won't hang out with you ever again!" shrieked Mouse.

"Fine!" yelled Elephant back. . . .

The next day, Mouse and Elephant got so lonely, that they started walking toward each other's houses. They didn't care about what one another would say.

They met up with each other halfway.

"What are you doing here?" they both stammered at the same time.

"Well, I was coming to see you," said Mouse in a small voice.

"Really?! Me too," boomed Elephant.

"I really missed you," said Mouse cheerfully.

"Me too," bursts Elephant.

"I think we should promise each other to never fight again," said Mouse.

template for writing one's own episode. Reading great lead paragraphs and outstanding final paragraphs from literature provide a further model as literary bookends for a story.

Informational writing of expository text highlights another type of organization. Categories, life cycles, chronological details, and sequential development provide the format for organized, expository writing. Effective leads and conclusions still play a vital role in informational text as they draw the reader in and bring a sense of closure to a piece. Seymour Simon's *Crocodiles and Alligators* showcases excellent examples of organized, descriptive factual text encased by strong leads and impressive conclusions. Jim Murphy encourages readers to follow the trail of key, chronicled events in *An American Plague*. Authors can thus weave varied trails of chronological or episodic order to assist readers on their way toward meaning.

Voice

As writers compose, they leave the fingerprints of voice all over their work—the imprint of the person on the piece, the personality, demeanor, and attitude of the writer. Voice gives writing a special sound, touch, and look of its own, an honest sharing of feelings that helps one write from the inside-out. A sense of audience is a part of establishing voice as authors write directly to readers, as if they were conversing with them. Being true to oneself and one's writing persona is important in creating the writer's voice. Enthusiasm and confidence exude when a writer uses his/her voice as an expert on a topic, situation, or self-created story. While voice may change somewhat between writing genres, the author's style often carries distinctive features that make voice clearly discernible across writing pieces.

Writing should sound like a real person speaking. Readers quickly lose interest in voiceless writing. They appreciate an author's voice that brings emotion, excitement, and engagement to the reading experience, begging them to laugh, cry, or feel a lump in the throat. Voice brings the writer's personal flavor and flair to a piece, allowing readers to see the world from a unique perspective. Student Sample 8.3 reveals the distinctive writing voice and imagination of Josh, the third-grade author of "Rain Games."

Authors' voices ring true in Avi's *The True Confession of Charlotte Doyle* (first-person historical narrative), Robert Burleigh's *Black Whiteness: Robert Byrd Alone in the Antarctic* (third-person narrative), and Paul Fleischman's *Bull Run* (first-person historical fiction, multiple characters). A confident, lively, honest, and powerful voice is displayed in Jim Murphy's *Blizzard! The Storm that Changed America*. Speaking directly to his readers as he gives them an eyewitness account, the author projects his voice through every word and his writing sounds different than the way anyone else would depict this tragic event.

STUDENT SAMPLE 8.3
A third grader exhibits voice.

RAIN GAMES
by Josh

There were friends named Jordan and Jack. Jordan and Jack played with each other for a long time. They came to the park day after day, but if it would rain, it would be days before they could play in the park. It kept raining so much that all you could see were the boys' ears. It kept raining and raining for days. Oh, no! Soon all you could see was the top of their head! So they stretched and stretched their legs to get their heads out of the water. They were now 10 feet tall and they saved the city by the park by warning the people about the flood.

An author's voice can best be identified through journal writing or letter writing. Dan Gutman's *Race for the Sky: The Kitty Hawk Diaries of Johnny Morris* and Nikki Grimes's *Talking About Bessie: The Story of Aviator Elizabeth Coleman* provide perfect models to replicate the power of voice to transmit both emotion and information as a means of captivating a reader.

Word Choice

A rich vocabulary of precise, distinct, colorful words provides the writer with a resource for choosing the exact word that creates a mental image. Word choice is a powerful tool in the writing craft as precise nouns, strong verbs, and descriptive adjectives add momentum to a piece. Words that are snappy, brisk, striking or fresh energize writing (Ray, 1999). Care must be taken, however, not to overwhelm the reader with such impressive vocabulary that it seems unnatural and detracts from the writing itself.

Look to literature to locate outstanding word choices. Bill Martin Jr., a master of language, uses "quietude" and "solitude" to capture the aftermath of a storm in *Listen to the Rain*. In J. K. Rowling's *Harry Potter* books, invented words such as "muggles" and "quidditch" have become favorites among readers and beg repetition. Perfect word choice does not just happen, especially in a picture book where words are at a minimum. Word choice is probably the trait that even the youngest children respect and admire as well-chosen words flow quickly into their own writing.

Always point out unforgettable language during read-alouds. Showcase the wonder of words through poetry or alphabet books. Encourage rich vocabulary development through the use of a thesaurus. Practice "snapshot writing" to focus on descriptive words to bring a focused view of an object to life for the reading audience. Student Sample 8.4 illustrates how the well-chosen words of a third-grader bring "Alligator Escape" to life.

Sentence Fluency

The best way to determine the flow of a piece of writing is to read it aloud. Listen to the rhythm of the language and the flow of the words from one sentence to the next, from

STUDENT SAMPLE 8.4
A third grader exhibits word choice.

ALLIGATOR ESCAPE
by Madison

Once upon a time a boy named Joel and a girl named Ginger lived by a swamp with alligators, piranhas, and sharks. The people and the animals actually were very good friends. They played sports and they had cappuccino or tea daily.

One day an alligator bit into the other alligators! Joel and Ginger saw what the alligator did. So they tied him up for a month. Ginger and Joel told the bad alligator not to do that ever again. So he didn't.

One day Ginger and Joel killed a snake for supper. It tasted like chicken. In the morning the bad alligator escaped, but they did not want him anymore. He was all shriveled up and had lost his teeth. So he had to eat baby food the rest of his life.

Joel and Ginger tell me that some evenings you can hear the alligator smacking his lips!

THE END

one paragraph to the next, from one section to the next. Sentence fluency describes the efficiency and effectiveness of words and sentences as they move the reader through the piece. Economizing on sentence length, varying the beginning of sentences, and combining short sentences are some examples of how the writer achieves sentence fluency. Some sentences can be short and snappy, while others can be long and stretchy. There is no one right length for a sentence, but the shorter sentence seems to hold more power and influence with the reader.

Sentence fluency also implies the use of connecting and transition words to carry the reader from one scene or fact to the next. A natural, smooth flow is the ultimate outcome of sentence fluency. Children's book read-alouds provide the best testimony to and modeling of sentence fluency. In Gloria Houston's *My Great Aunt Arizona,* sentences vary from long ones that travel the length of a page to short snappy ones that require fewer than ten words. Angela Johnson's *I Dream of Trains* balances short sounds and echoes of the train with the meandering sentences that reflect its extensive journey. Repetition of the book title in Cynthia Rylant's *When I Was Young in the Mountains* provides predictive security and melodic undertones.

Point out the quality of sentence pace and variety in read-aloud models. Make students aware of transitions between sentences, between paragraphs, and between chapters in books. Request that young authors read aloud their compositions to a peer to assess fluency and flow. Model and teach the effective use of transitions in moving the reader from sentence to sentence, paragraph to paragraph. The best evidence of sentence fluency is the genuine flow of the words as authors read aloud their writing. Student Sample 8.5 illustrates how this flow of sentences was achieved by the third-grade author of "The Indigo Snake."

Writing Conventions

Writing conventions include spelling, punctuation, capitalization, paragraphing, usage, and grammar. In fact, conventions include what many of us learned as the focus of the language arts. Today writing conventions are only one of seven writing traits, reaffirming the fact that correct conventions, in and of themselves, are not the only outcome of writing. Yet correct conventions prevent mistakes from coming between the message and the reader. Good editing polishes a piece and showcases it so all the other traits may be more appreciated.

When everything else is complete in a piece of writing, it is time to read it with a proofreader's eye, checking all aspects of conventions and correcting them for the ease and comfort of the audience. Editing is a precise skill that requires slow, careful reading and a dedicated, consistent effort to get every word ready for the reader. Typically, it takes more than the writer as editor to locate miscues, grammatical mistakes, and misspelled words, so a peer or the teacher may step in. Applying the rules and strategies of writing conventions may seem bothersome to a young writer, but the gradual acquisition of writing conventions certainly leaves an impression on the reading audience. As writing approaches publication, there must be no glaring errors that detract from the meaning or message of the author.

Examining a published page from a child's favorite book is an effective way to emphasize how important these conventions are to the reader. Chris Raschka's *Yo! Yes?* shows how end marks influence a read-aloud. Gary Paulsen's *Hatchet* illustrates the use of ellipses to indicate pauses for thought. By looking to literature to model conventions, an apprentice sees the importance of correctness, and in return responds by polishing his

STUDENT SAMPLE 8.5
A third grader exhibits sentence fluency.

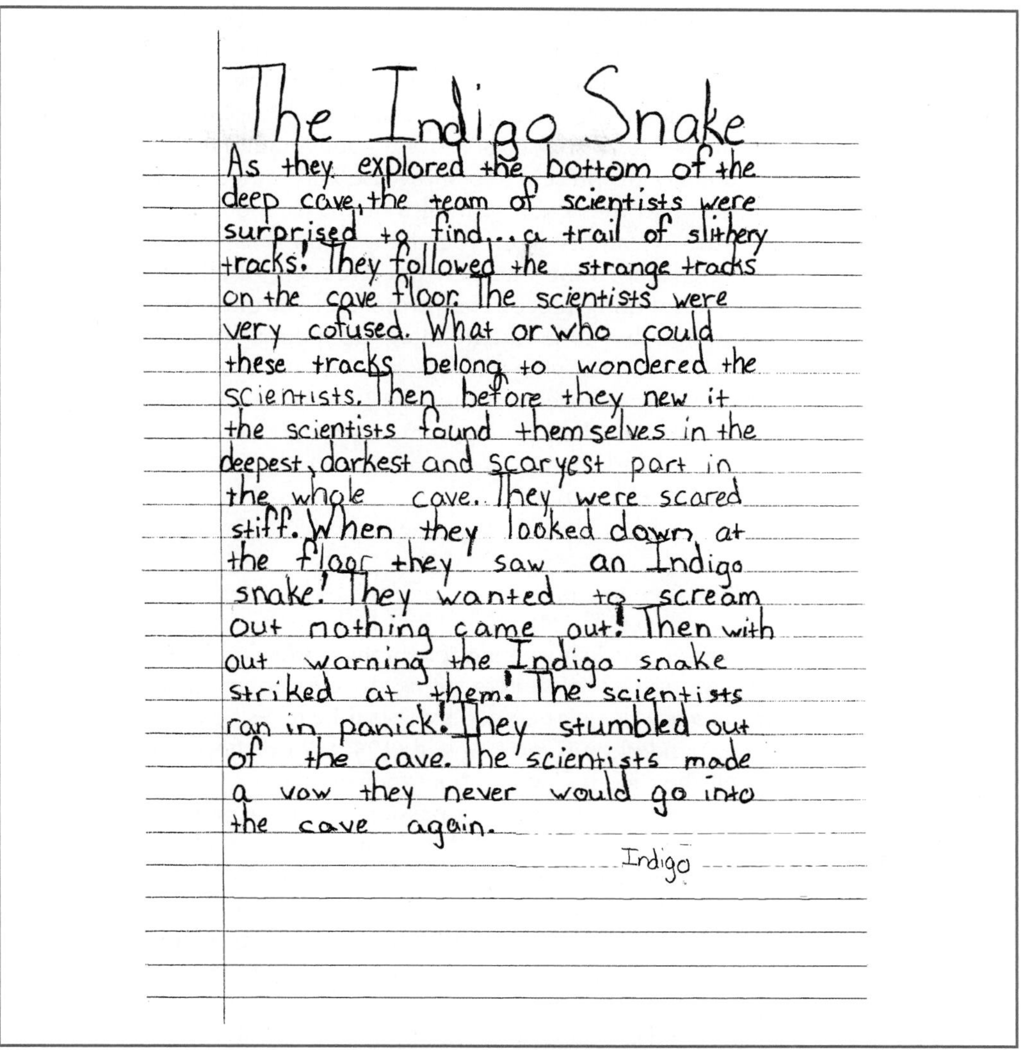

The Indigo Snake

As they explored the bottom of the deep cave, the team of scientists were surprised to find... a trail of slithery tracks! They followed the strange tracks on the cave floor. The scientists were very cofused. What or who could these tracks belong to wondered the scientists. Then before they new it the scientists found themselves in the deepest, darkest and scaryest part in the whole cave. They were scared stiff. When they looked down at the floor they saw an Indigo snake! They wanted to scream out nothing came out! Then with out warning the Indigo snake striked at them! The scientists ran in panick! They stumbled out of the cave. The scientists made a vow they never would go into the cave again.

Indigo

or her own writing in readiness for the reader. Doreen Cronin focuses on the use of commas in a series in *Giggle, Giggle, Quack* and oversized, emphasized end punctuation is featured in Judy Hindley's *Do Like a Duck Does!* The reader/writer stands to learn the importance of correct conventions to the reading audience of any written composition through the literature model.

Presentation (the +1 Trait)

The art of effective sharing of written communication with an audience involves the trait of presentation. Paragraphing, spacing, margins, readability, and uniqueness all attract the reader to a written work. Whether penned with the author's own handwriting or created through the self-selected font, style, and fomat of word processing, writing gains ease through its appearance to the perspective reader. The message or story can be lost in the midst of erasure smudges or questionable marks across the page. The clear, sharp image of a final presentation copy, however, invites the reader to relax and enjoy the writer's words. When teachers display previous final copies of student work or model choices in painting the final portrait of a story, young authors are encouraged to take the extra time and attention to present and showcase a treasured work.

Although the seven writing traits have been discussed separately, the writer must be aware that traits work together within the writing process. The holistic nature of writing envisions the interplay and weaving of all seven traits throughout the composition of a writing piece. The purpose of a working knowledge of these traits is not to isolate them but to gradually integrate them as building blocks toward more effective, aesthetic, and satisfying writing experiences. Teachers who point out the seven writing traits used by children's authors and who focus instruction on the author's craft alongside books are likely to encourage stronger writing in their own young writers. The books included in the Literature Cluster on page 245 present a variety of literature models for each trait.

The Writing Workshop

The writing workshop is an interactive, process-oriented configuration for the teaching and development of writers within the elementary and middle-level classroom. The term *writing workshop* was coined by Donald Graves (1983/2003) and Lucy Calkins (1994) and later expanded by Nancie Atwell (1987). Workshops are places where emerging authors can tell their stories, write about their memories, practice crafting their words, find their writing voices, and develop a passion for the art of writing. Writing is the primary goal of such workshops, with the tools of writing taught within the context of the real writing that is taking place. The writing workshop is a way to stop time, explore an idea, reconsider a thought, develop an idea, and share evolving text with others. It provides an extended period of time for teachers, as mentors, to write with their apprentices, to point out the joys and challenges of a developing manuscript, and to share the mental decision-making process of the emerging piece.

Within the writing workshop, children usually write on self-selected topics and across writing genres while assuming self-ownership of their pieces. The classroom becomes a community of authors who write, share, discuss, and follow the writing process in the development of final published works in a safe, secure setting. Apprentices begin to build confidence and see themselves as authors in this supportive writing community. The classroom environment must be one where trust and respect is established early in the school year, where routine and expectations are set, and where risk taking and seeking assistance is encouraged.

A writing workshop requires a teacher who is knowledgeable about the writing process and the need for ownership, choice, and time. The teacher becomes a coach, a guide, an instructor, and a facilitator. The teacher must understand the development of young writers, their need to evolve at their own pace, and the instruction that must occur to nudge them ahead in their individual development. Writing workshop teachers constantly observe, take notes, ask questions, listen, and provide encouragement in order to assist each young author in writing proficiency. The teacher is an active participant in all aspects of the workshop approach.

The students in a writing workshop keep writing folders that house all stages of the writing process for a developing work. They may also maintain writing notebooks

Literature Cluster

APPRENTICING THE AUTHOR'S CRAFT: SIX + 1 TRAIT LITERATURE MODELS

Ideas and Content Development

Blake, Robert (1993). *The perfect spot.* New York: Philomel.

Fleming, Candace (2003). *Boxes for Katje.* Illus. by Stacey Dressen-McQueen. New York: Farrar, Straus & Giroux.

Giff, Patricia Reilly (2001). *All the way home.* New York: Delacorte.

Howard, Elizabeth Fitzgerald (2001). *Virgie goes to school with us boys.* Illus. by E. B. Lewis. New York: Simon & Schuster.

McKissack, Patricia (2001). *Goin' someplace special.* Illus. by Jerry Pinkney. New York: Athenuem.

Peck, Richard (2001). *Fair weather.* New York: Dial.

Organization

Avi (2001). *The secret school.* New York: Harcourt Brace.

Coy, John (1996). *Night driving.* Illus. by Peter McCarty. New York: Holt.

Fleming, Candace (2003). *Muncha! Muncha! Muncha!* Illus. by G. Brian Karas. New York: Atheneum.

Johnson, Angela (2004). *Just like Josh Gibson.* Illus. by Beth Peck. New York: Simon & Schuster.

Osborne, Mary Pope (2002). *The brave little seamstress.* Illus. by Giselle Potter. New York: Atheneum.

Raven, Margot Theis (2004). *Circle unbroken.* Illus. by E. B. Lewis. New York: Farrar, Straus & Giroux.

Voice

Burleigh, Robert (1991). *Flight: The journey of Charles Lindberg.* Illus. by M. Wimmer. New York: Philomel.

Creech, Sharon (2001). *Love that dog.* New York: HarperCollins.

Di Camillo, Kate (2003). *The tale of Despereaux: Being the story of a mouse, a princess, some soup, and a spool of thread.* Illus. by Timothy Basil Ering. Cambridge, MA: Candlewick.

Hopkinson, Deborah (2002). *Under the quilt of night.* Illus. by James E. Ransome. New York: Atheneum.

Wells, Rosemary (2002). *Wingwalker.* Illus. by Brian Selznick. New York: Hyperion.

Word Choice

Floca, Brian (2003). *The racecar alphabet.* New York: Atheneum.

Franco, Betsy (2003). *Mathematickles!* Illus. by Steven Salerno. New York: McElderry.

Hopkins, Lee Bennett (Selector) (2004). *Wonderful words: Poems about reading, writing, speaking, and listening.* Illus. by Karen Barbour. New York: Simon & Schuster.

Rylant, Cynthia (1998). *Scarecrow.* Illus. by Lauren Stringer. San Diego: Harcourt Brace.

Steig, William (1971). *Amos & Boris.* New York: Farrar, Straus & Giroux.

Sentence Fluency

Bordon, Louise, & Marx, Trish (2003). *Touching the sky: The flying adventures of Wilbur and Orville Wright.* Illus. by Peter Fiore. New York: McElderry.

Johnson, Angela (2003). *I dream of trains.* Illus. by Loren Long. New York: Simon & Schuster.

Rockwell, Ann (1998). *One bean.* Illus. by Megan Halsey. New York: Walker.

Lyon, George Ella (2004). *Weaving the rainbow.* Illus. by Stephanie Anderson. New York: Atheneum.

Conventions

Ada, Alma Flor (2001). *With love, Little Red Hen.* Illus. by Leslie Tryon. New York: Atheneum.

Alborough, Jez (2003). *Some dogs do.* Cambridge, MA: Candlewick.

Hest, Amy (2003). *You can do it, Sam.* Illus. by Anita Jeram. Cambridge, MA: Candlewick.

Presentation

Janeczko, Paul (2001). *A poke in the I: A collection of concrete poems.* Illus. by Chris Raschka. Cambridge, MA: Candlewick.

Stockton, Frank R. (2004). *The bee-man of Orn.* Illus. by P. J. Lynch. Cambridge, MA: Candlewick.

Woodson, Jacqueline (2003). *Locomotion.* New York: Putnam.

FIGURE 8.5
The six components of a writing workshop.

1. **Literature**
   - Read aloud
   - Model of literary element
   - Springboard for writing
2. **Minilessons**
   - Procedural lessons
   - Skill lessons
   - Craft lessons
3. **Writing**
   - Ample time to work on self-selected manuscripts
   - Assistance from teacher and writing peers
4. **Conferences**
   - Teacher-student
   - Student-student
   - Writing group
5. **Sharing**
   - Author's chair
   - Celebrating successes
   - Seeking suggestions
6. **Assessment**
   - Writing record
   - Anecdotal records
   - Conference forms
   - Self-evaluation
   - Skills checklist

that contain fleeting thoughts, images, words, quotes, or personal experiences to be used as future sources for writing projects. Literature plays a critical role in the writing workshop as it provides both a writing model and a springboard of ideas for quality writing. Literature models the craft of writing as the teacher reads aloud and delineates the components and decision-making moments encountered by children's and young adult authors.

The writing workshop classroom is set up in writing groups with desks or tables accommodating four to six students. The groups may stay intact for a long period of time (quarter, semester, entire academic year) as a community, while risk taking, encouragement, and support grow through continuous interaction within a writing group.

The writing workshop can be divided into six components: (a) literature, (b) minilessons, (c) writing, (d) conferences, (e) sharing, and (f) assessment as illustrated in Figure 8.5. This configuration allows time to learn, time to talk, time to write, and time to self-evaluate. Ideally, the writing workshop should occur five days per week for an hour per day. In many cases, however, writing workshop occurs on three consecutive days for 45 to 60 minutes. Teachers work hard to carve out sufficient time to ascertain that each child has the time to develop the skills and the confidence of a writer. Figures 8.6 and 8.7 present a daily time structure and a weekly plan for implementing a writing workshop.

Literature

The writing workshop opens with the teacher reading aloud from quality literature aligned with a writing goal for the day or week. Literature serves as a model from which developing authors may discuss, learn, and apply in their own writing (Wall, 2000). Children's literature is key in teaching the literary elements of writing. Books demonstrate effective writing techniques including descriptive language, paragraph structure, dynamic chapter titles, and satisfying resolutions. For example, a kindergarten teacher may read Mirra Ginsberg's *Clay Boy* to establish beginning, middle, and

FIGURE 8.6
Time structure of the daily writing workshop.

0:00–0:10	Literature Read-Aloud Literature serves as a model from which developing authors may discuss, learn, and apply in their own writing. Books demonstrate effective writing techniques while literature models the writing craft of published authors as students attempt to try on techniques and styles in developing their own.
0:10–0:18	Minilessons Procedural, skill, and writing craft lessons focus on the emerging authorship needs of the students. Topics are revisited as needed while teacher keeps track of topics introduced, practiced, and mastered.
0:18–0:20	Organizing for the Workshop Minimal time to access writing files, materials, and settle into one's space for a productive writing session.
0:20–0:50	Writing Time/Conferencing A full 30 minutes is devoted to productive writing time. During this period, the teacher may schedule 5–10 minute writing conferences to discuss the progress, the frustrations, and the ongoing plans of each young author. On assigned days, students may conference with a writing peer or as a writing group.
0:50–0:60	Sharing A range of sharing activities from daily successes, overcoming writing barriers, plans for the next day, suggestions for writing challenges, to a full presentation of a finished work in the author's chair.

end when developing a sense of story in young readers; a third-grade teacher may focus on word choice as she reads the familiar sounds of Jane Yolen's *Owl Moon* to her students; a fifth-grade teacher wanting to focus on composing motivating leads might read the opening description of the month of August in Natalie Babbit's *Tuck Everlasting;* a seventh-grade teacher might illustrate point of view by reading aloud the powerful first-person voice from Avi's *The True Confessions of Charlotte Doyle*. Literature can thus model the writing craft of published authors as students of all ages attempt to try on techniques and styles in developing their own writing (Harwayne, 1993).

Minilesson

The minilesson is a planned instructional event based on teacher observations of the specific skills and techniques that students need at the current time to grow as a writer. Typically, the topic must be revisited through a series of lessons, but the timing of the skills to the needs of the writers is key. The teacher needs to keep a record of skills to ascertain that grade-level benchmarks are reached, yet the sequence is totally dependent on the needs of the children. Once a skill is introduced and revisited, a teacher's expectations for application of the skill in the context of writing becomes clear.

FIGURE 8.7 Weekly schedule for the writing workshop.

Monday	Tuesday	Wednesday
• Introduce literature that aligns with weekly literature writing genre or task	• Read-aloud of additional literature model	• Read-aloud of additional literature model
• Minilesson: Writing genre introduction related to expectations for the week	• Minilesson: Craft lesson related to the genre	• Minilesson: Skill lesson related to the genre
• Writing time Writing conferences assigned or sign-up Teacher monitoring	• Writing time Writing conferences assigned or sign up Teacher monitoring	• Writing time Writing conferences assigned or sign-up Teacher monitoring
• Sharing Interesting leads Problems getting started	• Sharing Inclusion of minilesson craft Suggestions/help	• Sharing Minilesson skill Suggestions/help

Thursday	Friday
• Read-aloud of additional reading model	• Student read-aloud of work or related model
• Minilesson: Skill lesson related to the genre	• Minilesson: Craft lesson related to editing, revision, publication
• Writing time Writing conferences Assigned/sign-up	• Writing time Writing conferences Teacher-determined
• Sharing Writing successes Lingering concerns	• Sharing Celebratory presentations Plans for next week

At the beginning of the school year, *procedural lessons* provide the content of minilessons. Gathering writing materials, facilitating group cooperation, scheduling writing conferences, and acknowledging teacher etiquette provide early topics for workshop organization. Review of the writing process, accountability for daily work, and daily self-evaluative records establish the consistent routine that makes writing workshop a productive time.

Skill lessons provide a second tier of minilessons. For example, emerging writers become users of conversation early, but vary in their need for the correct use of quotation marks. Planning a lesson on the use of quotation marks demonstrated within a piece of children's literature can explain how quotation marks are used to designate dialogue. A continuing lesson might focus on capitalization and punctuation placement within the conversation. Another lesson might highlight paragraphing of dialogue. Although not all children will be ready for all stages of minilesson instruction, teachers can utilize a small-group instructional approach to target those students needing specific skills. Focusing on specific children who need help without frustrating other writers is the goal of the minilessons.

Craft lessons (Fletcher & Portalupi, 1998), which are often built on the seven traits of writing, provide the third tier of writing minilessons. In optimal cases, the teacher may ask permission of a classroom author to share a well-written lead, a series of paragraph transitions, an organizational framework, effective word choices, or a variety of sentence lengths and structures to provide an authentic basis for discussion. How students make decisions and work their way through various writing dilemmas provide real contexts for improving writing.

The time set aside for minilessons should be no more than 10 minutes of the workshop schedule. Although it is important for students to learn procedures, skills, and the writing craft, it is equally important to provide them with the time for writing and applying the content of minilessons.

Writing and Writing Conferences

An important component of the writing workshop is the actual time spent on the task of writing. Because writing is hard work and requires a concerted, focused effort, this period should last for at least 30 minutes. During this time, children may converse with writing group members, but the expectation is that all students will write and move ahead with their writing goals. Practice provides the opportunity to think, apply, learn, struggle, and brainstorm solutions related to the craft of writing. Wherever students have left off from the previous writing time, they can resume working on a targeted manuscript.

During the writing phase of writing workshop, the teacher may schedule one-on-one writing conferences with individual students or students may sign up for a conference when needed. The goal is to talk to each child at least once per week to determine writing progress, struggles, roadblocks, and solutions (Robb, 1998). The teacher can ask probing questions (Figure 8.8), but it is the child's questions and personal responses that direct the conference.

The conference may begin with the young author reading aloud his or her current writing piece. The teacher may introduce probes such as "What do you like about this piece?" or "What problems are you having with your writing?" More confident students may initiate a discussion of the contents of the writing, what they like best about it, what parts may be confusing, and how they expect to proceed.

A common tension with writing conferences is that they may easily be dominated by the teacher's agenda instead of collaboration (Nickel, 2001). The ratio of teacher talk to student talk, the quality and quantity of open-ended questions, and the amount of silence (beyond wait time) provide important indicators of "who" is the focus of the conference. Even the phrasing of questions ("Why did you choose this title for your story?") may imply teacher disapproval and phrasing may need to be reconsidered.

In their zest to be helpful facilitators, teachers must be careful not to threaten student ownership of their work. Some apprentice authors may actually reject a teacher's suggestions because they have an agenda of their own, yet have not been asked to share it. The formulation of teacher-generated questions is a critical step toward student recognition of the power of revision. Nickel (2001) offers the following advice:

- ***Ask questions prudently.*** If a student begins to retreat, the teacher must move toward more student-centered queries.

FIGURE 8.8
Conference probes for teachers or peers.

- Getting the conference started

  Tell me about your piece of writing.
  Why did you choose this subject to write about?
  What surprises you most about this draft?
  What kinds of changes have you made [do you anticipate] for this draft?
  What problems are you having?
  Where is this piece of writing taking you?
  What questions do you have for me?

- Uncovering idea/content

  How many different stories do you have here?
  What is the most important thing you are trying to share?
  How does your title fit your draft?
  Underline the sentence that tells what your draft is about.
  Clarify this part for me.

- Revealing organization

  Where are you going with this draft?
  What do you think of your beginning? Your ending?
  How does the beginning grab your reader?
  How can you better tie your ending to your beginning?

- Discovering voice

  How does this draft sound when you read it aloud?
  Show me a place where I can tell you have written this piece.
  Read the most exciting part to me.

- Enhancing word choice

  What are your action words?
  What is another way you might say this?
  Is this the best word for this context?

- Creating momentum

  What do you intend to do next?
  How can you make this draft better?
  What's working well that can help you proceed?

- Providing reflective promise

  What have you learned about writing from this piece?
  How does this piece compare with others you have written?
  What did you try in this draft that you never tried before?
  How has this piece reflected your growth as a writer?

- ***Be aware of teacher power.*** Children will often incorporate a teacher's suggestions just because they want to please the teacher. Reassure the writers of the power of choice in maintaining ownership of a piece.
- ***Listen for the student's intentions.*** Children can sense when questions are authentic and when they are simply a means to stretch more writing from a struggling author. If the teacher listens, the sense of the child's attitude toward the writing

emerges. Just as we encourage readers to try a new book, a frustrated student needs to be able to abandon a story and make a fresh start.

- ***Conduct conferences at a child's request.*** Student-initiated conferences may be more valuable than teacher-scheduled conferences. Allow some time during the workshop for daily sign-ups for those who need a timely response to move their writing piece forward.
- ***Offer assistance through demonstration.*** Rather than offering suggestions in words, offer them in actions. Show students an example from your writing or from literature. Show them ways to avoid confusion rather than interrogating them endlessly. Guiding takes the form of showing rather than simply telling. Assure writers that this is an option, not a teacher mandate. Teachers walk a fine line between determining when a demonstration is useful and when it might overtake student ownership.
- ***Accept the possibility that not all your suggestions will be implemented.*** Your goals will not be realized for every child's writing. Often, a suggestion will be incorporated in a future writing project after being posed by the teacher. What might help this writer over time is more important than what will help the current writing piece (Calkins, 1994).

Conferences are probably the most important component of the writing workshop because they provide individualized writing instruction in the context of each writer's compositions. They can be conducted as a writing group activity, especially during revision (see Figure 8.9) as peers steer peers toward substantive changes to improve a first draft.

Intuition about the developmental levels of emerging authors (Glasswell, Parr, & McNaughton, 2003), recognition of student acceptance or rejection of revision suggestions, and mandatory retention of student ownership should combine and contribute to the kind and quality of the writing conference. Whether teacher-student, student-student, or group-student, the revision process is made richer through teacher and peer intervention.

Sharing

At the conclusion of each writing workshop, some students are asked to share in-process or completed pieces from the author's chair (Graves & Hansen, 1983). During this time, peers listen carefully so they may then comment, both with positive comments and useful suggestions, on the author's work. As the process of sharing continues, a genuine audience of peers will provide a social context for writing and build confidence in both writing and social interactions. Teachers serve as models of the types of comments that are both helpful and respectful of peer-authors. Teaching students how to respond to their classmates is critical as community-building takes hold in a contributory setting.

The author's chair also provides the occasion for recognition of final pieces of writing. The confidence, pride, and audience response that will be generated at the completion of each unique writing contribution will serve all students well on their journey toward good writing.

Assessment of Writing Workshop

Because much of writing workshop is spent in independent writing time, many teachers face accountability issues in documenting ongoing student progress. The following documents can assist with daily or weekly accountability:

- ***Writing record.*** This list documents daily progress by recording the date, accomplishments for the day, and plans for the next writing period.

FIGURE 8.9
Writing group tasks during revision.

1. Bring your draft and a revising pen.
2. Share your draft aloud.
3. Talk about your draft and listen to compliments, questions, and suggestions.
4. Take notes on your draft.
5. Make a plan for revising the draft.
6. Be a good listener while others share their drafts.
7. Give compliments, ask questions, and make suggestions for others' drafts.

- Conversation starters during writing group (Use these open-ended prompts to start the flow of writing conversation.)

  I like . . .
  I got confused when . . .
  Tell me more about . . .
  Your writing reminds me of . . .
  My favorite part is . . .
  Could you try to. . . .

- Conversation focus of writing group discussion (Designate two to three of these writing characteristics as the focus of the writing conversation.)

  Narrow topic/focus
  Details
  Organization (beginning/middle/end)
  Lead/conclusion
  Word choice (descriptive adjectives, active verbs, specific nouns)
  Literary elements (character, setting, problem, conflict, resolution)
  Voice
  Sentence fluency (determine by author reading aloud)

- ***Conference writing record.*** This form accompanies each student to his or her writing conference. It lists a date, "the things I can do well," "the things I'm working on," and "the things on which I need assistance."
- ***Anecdotal records.*** Teachers can record anecdotal observations during writing time when not conducting conferences. Comments may address cognitive problem-solving, knowledge of writing, affective responses to writing, social interaction with peers, and use of imagination in writing.
- ***Peer conference form.*** Once per week, each student may meet with a writing peer to discuss each other's writing progress. A peer conference summary form should contain targeted questions to guide the discussion: *What is my story about? What do you like best about it? Did I say anything confusing? Do I need to add more details? Where? How can I make my writing better?*
- ***Self-evaluation form.*** Teachers can ask students to complete a self-evaluation form that asks them to think about what they did and what they hope to accomplish during writing workshop. Used in a positive way, students work toward meeting their goals and writing deadlines.
- ***Skills checklist.*** The teacher notes whether students are understanding and applying minilesson skills into the context of their authentic writing by documenting

their progress on a checklist of grade-level writing skills. Once students have accomplished their goals, the expectations are that the skills will be consistently applied in future writing.

This listing of so many types of accountability indicates clearly that writing workshop is not an unmonitored writing event. Evaluations by students, teachers, and peers integrate the multiple perspectives needed to evaluate the ongoing growth, evolving products, and skills mastery that is the goal of successful writers.

Blending the Writing Process and Writing Traits into a Writing Workshop

As each teacher attempts to blend conceptual knowledge about the writing process, writing traits, and the configuration of a writing workshop the vision of how the "pieces fall together" is critical in determining facilitation of this model in the classroom (Ray & Laminack, 2001). To provide a clearer vision of integrating the writing process and writing traits into a writing workshop format, the following sixth grade classroom example is shared.

Mrs. Larson, a sixth-grade teacher, formulated a writing process assignment focused on personal narrative writing. She modeled each stage of the writing process during her daily openings to writing workshop. Student Samples 8.6 and 8.7 illustrate how the stages

STUDENT SAMPLE 8.6
Danielle's first draft and revision feedback.

1st Draft

Danielle #11
October 6

The hay prickled at my feet and every thing smelled of straw and wood. I stuck my ~~little~~ hand in the nearest grassy box, the first of 6. ~~Nothing~~. 1 egg. ~~[There were 6 boxes.]~~ I moved to the next box and found ~~to~~ two eggs. I pulled them out and ~~moved on~~ stepped up to the ~~next~~ third box in front of the open shed door.

Can you include this information in the above sentence?

[I peeked out and saw my grandpa waiting outside the fence, the ~~fence~~ Gate closed so as not to let the brown and gray chickens loose.] My breath caught in my throught as I saw ~~Hulio~~ Leroy the old rooster standing on a post. He was staring straight at me. I backed away quickly from the door and plunged my hand in the ~~next~~ hen box. Seeing this, he ~~jumped~~ hopped off his post and ~~started to~~ strutedover twoards me.

Reread this sentence. Does it make sense?

Can you provide more details about Hulio? I don't know his name yet.

Leroy was ~~a~~ tall ~~rooster~~ and red and brown all over. He had peircing black eyes.

Did you back away slowly, quickly? Add an adverb.

good word choice

STUDENT SAMPLE 8.7
Danielle's second draft and editing feedback.

2nd Draft

Will you help me think of a better title or maybe just some ideas thanks!

Rooster Run October 8

by DANIELLE

Everything smelled of straw and wood and the hay prickled at my bare feet. I stuck my hand in the first of six grassy boxes and found one smooth white egg. I moved to the next and found two more eggs. After taking them out I went to the 3rd (spell out) box in front of the open shed door. I peeked out and saw my grandpa wating (sp) by the fence, the gate closed so as not to let the chickens lose (loose). My (breath) caught in my throat as I saw Leroy, the old rooster, standing on a post. He was staring straight at me. His dark, beady eyes (were) peircing (sp) mine. Leroy was tall, and (was) red and brown all over. His yellow beak looked very sharp.

of writing workshop can be integrated with the writing process and the seven writing traits in Danielle's ongoing development of her "Rooster Run" narrative. In this unique scenario, Mrs. Larson encouraged students to incorporate revision and editing suggestions from preservice teachers in a Professional Development School Partnership as a part of the workshop process. Taking approximately 10 hours to complete, Mrs. Larson's assignment asked students to write a personal narrative about any experience that caused them to feel a strong emotion.

- ***Rehearsal:*** Students are required to choose a topic from their brainstorming sheet. They are cautioned to think "snapshot" rather than "video" in narrowing their individual topics. A series of questions on a prewriting sheet helps generate possible writing topics: *Who are important people in your life? Where have you traveled? What do you like to do? What are your worst memories? What are your best memories?*
- ***Drafting:*** Students are requested to develop their prewriting ideas into a first draft. They are told to skip lines on the draft to leave room for revisions and editing suggestions. Getting ideas down on paper is key at this stage. Correct spelling and

grammar will be addressed in later stages of the writing process. Mrs. Larson reminded the sixth graders to target sequential order, details, an effective introduction, and a strong resolution.

- ***Revision:*** Two preservice teachers review Danielle's first draft and write comments and suggestions on it. Many comments focus on adding details, more effective word choice, clarifying reader confusion, and creating a stronger ending. To replicate the writing conference approach, the preservice teachers generate a list of positive comments, helpful suggestions, and words of encouragement. (See again Student Sample 8.6, which shows a portion of the first draft narrative and the preservice teacher comments.)

  Upon receiving these comments, Danielle gets right to work determining which suggestions will enhance her narrative. In addition, she uses a seven-trait revision checklist that targets her incorporation of these elements of the writing craft. She uses a yellow highlighter to designate some word choice possibilities. Danielle spends several hours revising her narrative as it now moves on to the next stage of authorship support.
- ***Editing:*** Preservice teachers review and further support Danielle's revisions in her second draft (see a portion of the draft in Student Sample 8.7) and begin the process of editing for spelling, capitalization, punctuation, grammar, and usage. Inserted words, paragraphing, end punctuation, verb tense, and spelling are among the editing suggestions of preservice teachers to the sixth-grade writers.
- ***Publishing:*** Danielle incorporates the editing suggestions and types her final draft (Student Sample 8.8). She chooses a font to match her personality and incorporates clip art for audience interest. Although her project has taken time, she is satisfied with the final product and folder showing all stages of the writing process that led to this writing accomplishment.
- ***Sharing/assessment:*** Danielle's final word-processed piece is read by the preservice teachers. They make use of the six-trait writing rubric (Figure 8.10) to designate their professional impressions of Danielle's rankings in each trait. A final note from the preservice teachers (Figure 8.11) congratulates Danielle on the evolution of this process writing piece, while reminding her of continued goals toward word choice and correct conventions for the future.

This full-length presentation of the blending of process writing, writing workshop, and the 6 + 1 trait writing model clarifies and illustrates the potential of incorporating both process and product, writing traits and skills, and students and preservice teachers in a challenging sixth-grade writing workshop.

Visit the Companion Website at www.prenhall.com/hancock and gauge your understanding of Chapter 8 concepts with the self-assessments.

Closing Thoughts

Today's children are growing up in a different world from the one in which we began developing our own writing skills. Technological advances have brought new tools into the hands of our students—handheld computers, cell phones, video games, electronic mail, digital cameras. Oral and visual communication seem to have replaced writing as a traditional form of communication.

STUDENT SAMPLE 8.8 Danielle's published narrative.

Work Sample 8
Published Story
Rooster Run

Danielle #11
October 14, 2003

ROOSTER RUN

Being chased by a rooster could be any 12 or 13 year olds dream, but being chased by a rooster when you are only four years old is a whole other story.

"Come on now," my grandpa's gruff voice told me one morning. "Let's go get some eggs from the hen boxes." We had come to my grandparent's small farm in Colorado for a visit a day or two before. Now I was outside on a crisp morning following my grandpa to the chicken coop. There was a slight breeze that made me shiver as the wind seeped through my light pajamas.

"Run on in and see what you can find in those boxes." My grandpa opened the wire fence and I stumbled in through the gate. I went through a small yard and into a rusted blue shed where the chickens were kept at night.

Everything smelled of straw and wood and the hay prickled at my bear feet. I stuck my hand in the first of six grassy boxes and found one smooth white egg. I moved on to the next and found two more eggs. After taking them out I went to the third little box in front of the open shed door. I peeked out and saw my grandfather waiting outside the fence,

STUDENT SAMPLE 8.8 (Continued)

the gate closed so the chickens wouldn't get loose. My breath caught in my throat as I saw Leroy the old rooster staring straight at me. His dark beady eyes piercing into mine. Leroy was red and brown all over and his yellow beak looked very sharp.

I quickly backed away from the door and plunged my hand in the hen box. Seeing this Leroy jumped off his post and strutted towards me. I gave a little cry and headed for the door with the four eggs I had found.

Leroy gave a "COCKA DOODLE DOO!" and the chase was on. I yelped and started running in circles the brown and white chickens cackled as they dodged my stomping feet.

My grandfather gave a half sigh half chuckle and called to me as he opened the gate. I didn't hear him call, but ran along the fence trying to find my way out. Leroy was right at my heels, pecking at my toes every chance he could.

My eyes were as wide as teacups filled with fear. My mother and grandma came out of the house hearing my screams and the chickens. As soon as I saw them, I zoomed out of the gate and up to the house. I could still hear the outraged chickens and Leroy behind me.

I didn't stop running until I was safe inside. Over the years, I got used to Leroy's chasing and pecking. But one year Leroy was not there. While we had been away an old raccoon had killed and eaten Leroy in the night.

When I went out to the yard it seemed to lonely and to quiet without his screeching. It made me sad to know that I would never be chased, pecked at, or hear his call in the morning when we came, ever again.

FIGURE 8.10 The six-trait writing rubric used by the preservice teachers.

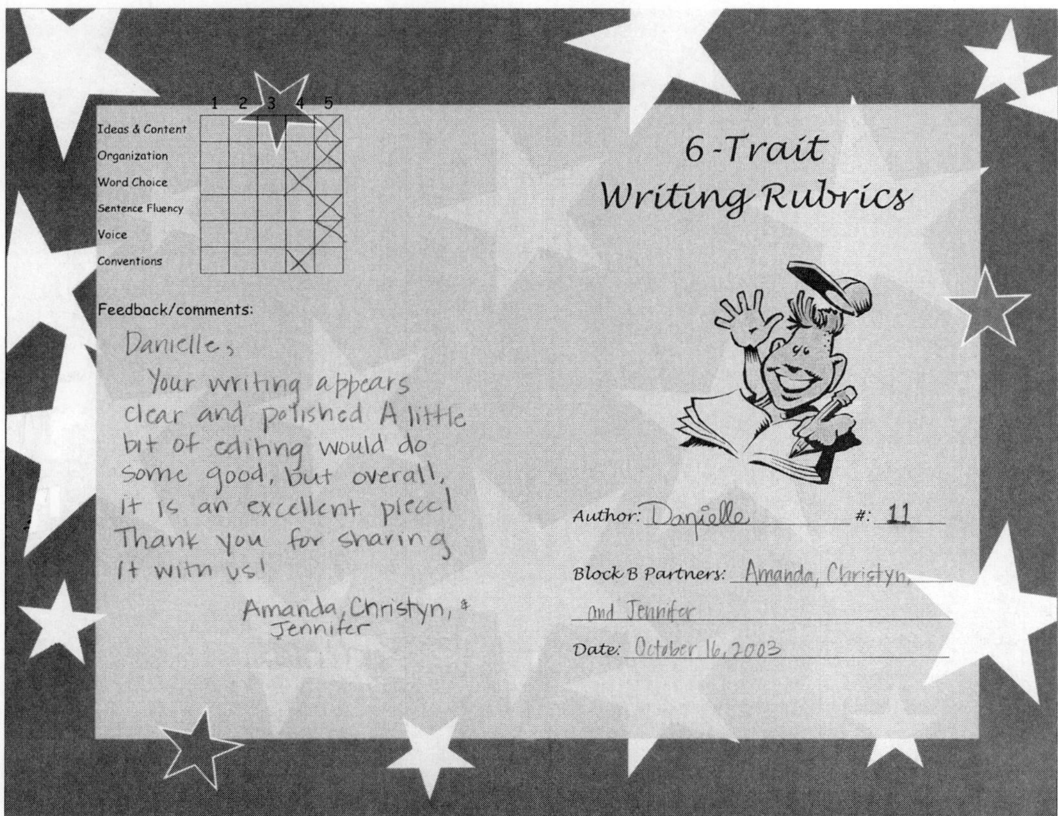

Rubric Source: From V. Spandell (2001). Creating Writers Through 6-Trait Writing Assessment and Instruction *(3rd ed.). New York: Addison-Wesley/Longman.*

Time is the scarcest resource in our schools. The writing workshop approach requires a substantial slice of an already burdened school day and requires recurring reflection—an undervalued but necessary commodity in today's fast-paced world. Writing is a thinking medium, a way to stop time and explore, a means to reconsider and revise, and an opportunity to share thoughts with others. Although many teachers rightfully ask how they can squeeze writing in on top of everything else, those who strive to infuse the joy as well as the craft of writing into their writing program discover that required writing curriculum and writing workshop work together effectively to accomplish both ends.

The No Child Left Behind legislation has refined the parameters of the school day. Federal mandates send the message that children should be good receivers of information through reading but seemingly bypass the importance of being good senders of information through writing. Writing is actually the making of reading. Unfortunately, legislators seemingly downplay the development of children's ideas through print in favor of filling in the right answer on a test sheet. Teachers are forced to make choices about what to teach, and too often writing takes a backseat to the demands of national and state test scores (Shelton & Fu, 2004).

As we move into the next two chapters on narrative and poetic writing and expository writing the focus of the writing discussion shifts to specific genres of writing. Dedicated

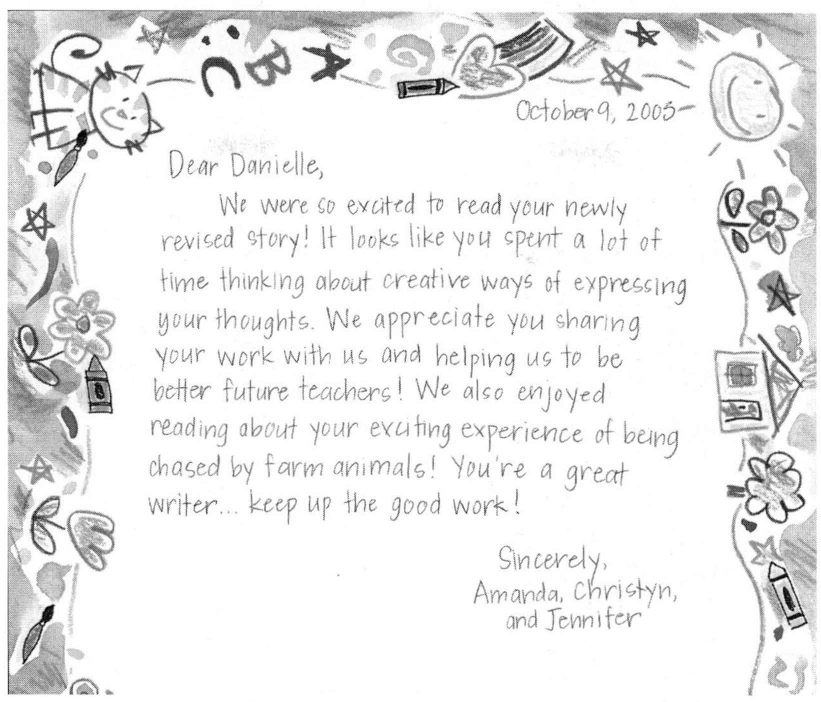
October 9, 2005

Dear Danielle,

We were so excited to read your newly revised story! It looks like you spent a lot of time thinking about creative ways of expressing your thoughts. We appreciate you sharing your work with us and helping us to be better future teachers! We also enjoyed reading about your exciting experience of being chased by farm animals! You're a great writer... keep up the good work!

Sincerely,
Amanda, Christyn,
and Jennifer

FIGURE 8.11 Preservice teacher response to Danielle's published writing.

writing teachers justify their extensive inclusion of writing workshop time on varied writing genres in our literate world. As classroom teachers we need to give the time and focus to the "essentials" in teaching writing (Routman, 2004) as well as showcasing writing genres. Teachers need to ensure that all our students have the opportunity to be guided to discover and develop the writers within themselves.

References

Atwell, N. (1987). *In the middle: Reading, writing, and learning with adolescents.* Portsmouth, NH: Heinemann.

Calkins, L. M. (1994). *The art of teaching writing.* Portsmouth, NH: Heinemann.

Culham, R. (2003). *6 + 1 traits of writing: The complete guide.* New York; Scholastic.

Dahl, K. L., & Farnan, N. (1998). *Children's writing: Perspectives from research.* Newark, DE: International Reading Association; Chicago, IL: National Reading Conference.

Five, C. L., & Dionisi (1998). Teaching reading and writing. *School Talk, 4.* 1–8.

Fletcher, R. (1993). *What a writer needs.* Portsmouth, NH: Heinemann.

Fletcher, R., & Portalupi, J. (1998). Craft lessons: *Teaching writing* K–8. Portland, ME: Stenhouse.

Fletcher, R., & Portalupi, J. (2001). *Writing workshops: The essential guide.* Portsmouth, NH: Heinemann.

Glasswell, K., Parr, J. M., & McNaughton, S. (2003). Four ways to work against yourself when conferencing with struggling writers. *Language Arts, 80,* 291–298.

Graves, D. H. (1975). An examination of the writing processes of seven-year-old children. *Research in the Teaching of English, 9,* 227–241.

Graves, D. H. (1983/2003). *Writing: Teachers and children at work* (20th anniversary edition). Portsmouth, NH: Heinemann.

Graves, D. H. (1994). *A fresh look at writing.* Portsmouth, NH: Heinemann.

Graves, D. H., & Hansen, J. (1983). The author's chair. *Language Arts, 60,* 176–183.

Hansen, J. (2001). *When writers read* (2nd ed.). Portsmouth, NH: Heinemann.

Harwayne, S. (1993). *Lasting impressions: Weaving literature into the writing workshop.* Portsmouth, NH: Heinemann.

Harwayne, S. (2001). *Writing through childhood: Rethinking process and product.* Portsmouth, NH: Heinemann.

Heard, G. (2002). *The revision toolbox.* Portsmouth, NH: Heinemann.

New Zealand Ministry of Education (1992). *Dancing with the pen: The learner as a writer.* Katonah, NY: Richard C. Owen.

Nickel, J. (2001). When writing conferences don't work: Students' retreat from teacher agenda. *Language Arts, 79,* 136–147.

Ray, K. W. (1999). *Wondrous words: Writers and writing in the elementary classroom.* Urbana, IL: National Council of Teachers of English.

Ray, K. W. (2002). *What you know by heart: How to develop curriculum for your writing workshop.* Portsmouth, NH: Heinemann.

Ray, K. W., & Laminack, L. (2001). *The writing workshop: Working through the hard parts (and they're all hard parts).* Urbana, IL: National Council of Teachers of English.

Robb, L. (1998). *Reading and writing conferences: Practical ideas for making conferences work.* New York: Scholastic Professional Books.

Routman, R. (2004). *Writing essentials.* Portsmouth, NH: Heinemann.

Shelton, N. R., & Fu, D. (2004). Creating space for teaching writing and for test preparation. *Language Arts, 82,* 120–128.

Spandell, V. (2001). *Creating writers through 6-trait writing assessment and instruction* (3rd ed.). New York: Addison Wesley/Longman.

Wall, H. (2000). How do authors do it? Using literature in a writer's workshop. *The New Advocate, 13,* 157–170.

Children's Books Cited

Avi (1990). *The true confessions of Charlotte Doyle.* New York: Orchard.

Babbitt, Natalie (1975). *Tuck everlasting.* New York: Farrar, Straus & Giroux.

Blackwood, Gary (1998). *The Shakespeare stealer.* New York: Dutton.

Bunting, Eve (1991). *Fly away home.* Illus. by Ron Himler. Boston: Clarion.

Burleigh, Robert (1998). *Black whiteness: Admiral Byrd alone in the Antarctic.* Illus. by W. L. Krudop. New York: Atheneum.

Cronin, Doreen (2002). *Giggle, giggle, quack.* Illus. by Betsy Lewin. New York: Simon & Schuster.

Cunningham, David (1996). *A crow's journey.* Morton Grove, IL: Albert Whitman.

Fleischman, Paul (1993). *Bull run.* Woodcuts by David Frampton. New York: HarperCollins.

Fleming, Candace (2004). *Gator gumbo: A spicy hot tale.* Illus. by Sally Anne Lambert. New York: Farrar, Straus & Giroux.

George, Jean Craighead (1995). *To climb a waterfall.* Illus. by Thomas Locker. New York: Philomel.

Ginsburg, Mirra (1997). *Clay boy.* Illus. by Jos. A. Smith. New York: Greenwillow.

Grimes, Nikki (2002). *Talkin' about Bessie: The story of aviator Elizabeth Coleman.* Illus. by E. B. Lewis. New York: Orchard.

Gutman, Dan (2003). *Race for the sky: The Kitty Hawk diaries of Johnny Morris.* New York: Simon & Schuster.

Henkes, Kevin (1991). *Chrysanthemum.* New York: Greenwillow.

Hindley, Judy (2002). *Do like a duck does!* Illus. by Ivan Bates. Cambridge, MA: Candlewick.

Houston, Gloria (1992). *My Great Aunt Arizona.* Illus. by Susan Condie Lamb. New York: HarperCollins.

Johnson, Angela (2003). *I dream of trains.* Illus. by Loren Long. New York: Simon & Schuster.

Lester, Helen (1997). *Author: A true story.* Boston: Houghton Mifflin.

Martin, Bill, Jr., & Archambault, John (1988). *Listen to the rain.* Illus. by J. Endicott. New York: Holt.

Murphy, Jim (2000). *Blizzard! The storm that changed America.* New York: Scholastic.

Murphy, Jim (2003). *An American plague: The true and terrifying story of the yellow fever epidemic of 1793.* New York: Clarion.

Paulsen, Gary (1987). *Hatchet.* New York: Bradbury.

Polacco, Patricia (2001). *Betty doll.* New York: Putnam.

Raschka, Chris (1993). *Yo! Yes?* New York: Orchard.

Rowling, J. K. (1998). *Harry Potter and the sorcerer's stone.* New York: Scholastic.

Rylant, Cynthia (1982). *When I was young in the mountains.* Illus. by Diane Goode. New York: Dutton.

Schotter, Roni (1997). *Nothing ever happens on 90th Street.* Illus. by Kyrsten Brooker. New York: Orchard.

Simon, Seymour (2000). *Crocodiles and alligators.* New York: HarperCollins.

Soto, Gary (1993). *Too many tamales.* Illus. by J. Martinez. New York: Putnam.

Yolen, Jane (1987). *Owl moon.* Illus. by Jon Schoenherr. New York: Philomel.

Chapter 9

NARRATIVE AND POETIC WRITING

Creating Young Authors

Make a picture
in your mind,
clear, true.
Move that picture from your mind
down to a piece of paper. . . .

FROM *YOU HAVE TO WRITE* BY JANET WONG

The text of Janet Wong's picture book, *You Have to Write,* invites young authors into the challenging but satisfying craft of writing. As prospective young authors travel through the pages of this simple yet poetic text, Wong provides a multitude of examples for changing a dreaded experience into a writing craft accomplishment. The author inspires young writers by telling them that writers and poets write best about those things they know best. Simple things from our daily lives as writing topics can change a reluctant writer into a fulfilled author.

Cool summers in the shadow of a snow-capped mountain, the antics of a pesky, younger freckled-faced brother, the aroma of a batch of chocolate chip cookies, or the warmth and emotional strength of a special grandmother provide the seeds for narrative and poetic writing. Cynthia Rylant's *When I Was Young in the Mountains,* Jerry Spinelli's *Maniac Magee,* and Patricia Polacco's *Thundercake* comprise stories based on real-life experiences of the authors. Focusing on emotional topics or personal ones—a favorite season or even an object—poets are able to share their unique vision through the medium of poetry. Georgia Heard selected poems about September 11 in *This Place I Know: Poems of Comfort* following the aftermath of the terrorist attack on the World Trade Center, while Douglas Florian wrote seasonally themed poems in *Summersaults* and Alice Schertle's *Keepers* is a series of poems about special artifacts and childhood experiences. Janet Wong offers advice to those children who may have experienced struggles with writing: "Because you have to write, and you want it to be good," even the most reluctant budding author may be inspired.

Writers and poets create their best work when their imaginations weave the elements of a story or a well-selected description into an intriguing episode that captures the unwavering attention of the reader. The frightening description of a beast living in a web-filled attic, the courageous antics of a female superhero disguised as a fifth-grade student, the mystery of the missing flag on the Fourth of July, and the discovery of a magical elf at the end of the rainbow rise from imaginative young minds. Susan Cooper's *The Boggart* and Phyllis Reynold Naylor's *The Bomb in the Bessledorf Bus Depot* spring from powerful imaginations. The poetic rhyme of Edward Lear's *The Owl and the Pussycat,* the word choice in Douglas Florian's *Insectlopedia,* and the humor of Jim Aylesworth's *The Burger and the Hot Dog* also spring from the creative imaginations of these poets.

Writers and poets also work best when their real-life experiences are enhanced by vivid imaginations and the power of exaggeration. The annual family reunion spiced with unusual relatives and unique food, the unfortunate mishaps of an ill-fated birthday celebration, the unexpected arrival of a package on the front porch, or the humorous tales of a memorable teacher blend real people, places, and episodes with the world of imagination for the creation of enjoyable stories. Jacqueline Woodson's *There Was a Picnic this Sunday Past,* Andrew Clements' *Frindle,* and Gary Soto's *Snapshots from the Wedding* blend real life with fantasy. Jack Prelutsky's *Scranimals* displays the creative genius of the author in a poetic mode. X. J. Kennedy's *Exploding Gravy* and selections from Shel Silverstein's *Falling Up* also show how humorous exaggerations can evolve into poetry.

The purpose of this chapter is to share, teach, and practice the art of narrative writing and the creative aspects of poetic writing with children. More time is likely spent on these two writing genres in the classroom than on the multiple genres that balance the writing curriculum in K–8 classrooms. Immersing, understanding, synthesizing, and implementing the writing craft through narrative and poetic text leads children toward the art of authorship while building their success and confidence.

Objectives

- To explore the narrative and poetic writing genres through exemplary literary models.
- To articulate the elements of narrative writing (plot, setting, character, theme, point of view) both as isolated elements and blended in the context of literature.

- To appreciate the language of poetry through the use of word choice and literary devices.
- To acknowledge the variety of poetic forms and formats including syllable count poems, free form poems, and rhymed verse.
- To recognize the role of the writing process in creating narrative and poetic writing.
- To explore and analyze the development levels of children's narrative and poetic writing from authentic student writing samples.
- To consider the key assessment criteria for the genres of narrative and poetic writing.

Narrative Writing

Narrative writing encompasses the world of real-life experiences as transformed by the imagination and creativity of the writer through the written word into the realm of storytelling. The language of narrative springs from the heart and mind of the author as the fine line between truth and fantasy creates the stories that capture the attention of engaged readers.

First Step into Narrative: Beginning, Middle, and End

Arthur Applebee (1978) explores the developing *sense of story* that occurs throughout childhood—from a child's emerging literacy to a young adult's proficient literacy accomplishments. Young children begin with a concept of story that has a *beginning, middle,* and *end.* They learn early that terms such as "once upon a time" or "happily ever after" denote the beginning and end of a story. All that occurs between is internalized as "middle" matter.

Mrs. Fisher's read-aloud of Vera B. Williams *A Chair for My Mother* provided the structure of beginning, middle, and ending for kindergarten students. The teacher read the story in its entirety. She then divided chart paper into three columns to designate the beginning, middle, and end of the story. "What happened at the beginning of the story?" she questioned as she wrote the word "BEGINNING" in the first column. Children recalled that a fire destroyed furniture in the family's apartment. The teacher recorded student language (as in a language experience story) and, with her talent in art, sketched the apartment with a fire. "What happened at the end of the story?" she asked as she wrote "END" in the final column. Children described the purchase of a pink chair with red roses that made the mother very happy. Once again, the teacher sketched the dynamic design and colors of this special chair and recorded student language. The teacher asked a final question, "What happened in the middle of the story?" as she wrote MIDDLE on the center column. Children remembered the long-time saving of coins in a jar that preceded the purchase of the chair as the teacher sketched a jar with coins and recorded students' words. She then called on a student to "retell the story" using cues from the chart. This model provided the impetus for story discussion throughout the early part of the school year. Children began to use the terminology of "beginning, middle, end" when they read independently, when they discussed other books, and, eventually in their own writing.

Sensing the sequence of story in the primary grades initially comes from teacher read-alouds. Gradually, children retell a story incorporating the framework of beginning, middle, and end. Eventually, they move on toward the true elements of story, at first one element at a time and eventually merging into a meaningful and complete story episode. From simple beginnings and articulated understandings come the foundations of becoming young writers.

Teacher Prep

The Teacher Prep Web site will help you become a better teacher by linking you to classroom videos, student artifacts, teaching strategies, lesson plans, relevant education leadership articles, and practical information on licensing, creating a portfolio, implementing standards, and being successful in field experiences. Visit this resource at www.prenhall.com/teacherprep.

Defining and Exploring the Elements of Story

There are five key elements in narrative writing: (a) plot, (b) setting, (c) character, (d) theme, and (e) point of view. It is best to define and discuss each element separately as children build their own concept of story. Eventually, the narrative literary elements blend in the context of an entire picture book story or chapter book. Let's explore each element separately and then move to discovering their optimal blending both an award-winning picture book and a chapter book.

Plot. **Plot** is the sequence of events that occurs through the characters of a story. Young children learn early elements of plot by determining what happened in the beginning, middle, and end of the story. As children grow developmentally in their understanding of narrative, the subelements of plot thicken and enrich understanding. *Conflict* is the tension that occurs within the plot—between a character and nature or a character and society, or between characters, or even within a single character. As conflict unfolds, it ultimately leads to *resolution* as the inner-workings and the ending of a narrative take shape. *Plot development* begins when a conflict and the resulting problem are introduced, continues as *roadblocks* are placed in the path of the character, and reaches a *high point* or *climax* when the problem is about to be solved. The *solution* of the problem and the removal of roadblocks form the *conclusion* of the story (Tompkins, 2005).

Setting. **Setting** is generally described as the place where a story occurs, but setting may also include the dimensions of *location, time or time period,* and *weather* (Tompkins, 2005). From San Francisco to Decatur, from Warsaw, Poland to Seoul, Korea . . . from the Metropolitan Museum of Art in New York City to the Boston Common or the Sears Tower in Chicago—all are examples of specific locations. Some stories have undefined backdrops or generic settings, barely sketched, while others have specific, well-described locations. The time or time period can simply refer to the time of day (daybreak, lunchtime, sunset) in realistic fiction or the historical context of the Revolutionary War or the Civil Rights Movement in historical fiction. The weather can even better place the reader in a precise situation by describing a winter snowstorm, a hot, humid August afternoon, or the first day of spring. The author's ability to utilize setting to draw the reader into the story and to paint a textual portrait of that setting in the reader's mind constitutes an important element of the narrative writing craft.

Characters. **Characters** are the individuals portrayed in a story—the vehicles through which the plot weaves. The *main character* is fully developed, while *supportive characters* are minimally portrayed in their pivotal roles. Authors develop characters through *appearance, action, dialogue,* and *monologue* (Tompkins, 2005). Appearance is the first way in which young writers learn to describe characters. Physical features and visualized image paint a portrait of the character in the reader's mind. Although *actions* are related to plot, they also characterize a person by informing the reader about what he or she does in daily life and about interests and friends as well as decision-making tendencies. What a character says to other characters constitutes *dialogue,* adding another layer in the character mix as spoken words reveal personal traits, beliefs, and intentions. Most revealing, perhaps, is the *monologue,* a dramatic speech that showcases the thoughts of the one character—the innermost workings of the mind that foreshadow upcoming decisions and actions.

Favorite characters are unforgettable because of the author's ability to build *character development*—personal growth within a situation or over time. Literary characters such as Barbara Cooney's *Miss Rumphius,* Katherine Paterson's *Lyddie,* and Avi's *Crispin* readily come to mind. Kate DiCamillo, author of *Because of Winn-Dixie* and *The Tale of*

Despereaux refers to character as the engine. "Start with a good character, and the rest will take care of itself" (DiCamillo, 2005, p. 26). "Characters, then, are a conduit through which readers enter, move through, and are affected by narratives" (Roser & Martinez, 2005, p. 7). Likewise, characters become the vehicle for action and emotion for young writers as they reveal their original story from beginning to middle to end through the mind, heart, and words of the character.

Theme. **Theme** is the underlying meaning or message of a story that encompasses the truths about human nature and society. Usually dealing with the character's emotions or values, themes are either explicitly stated or inherently implied through a character's actions. Friendship, courage, responsibility, truth, and justice are common themes in children's literature and in children's authorship (Tompkins, 2005). Since theme is more abstract, it is usually designated as a higher-level narrative writing element. While it may subconsciously weave its way through a primary student's writing, it can become the overriding feature of a middle-school author. The prompt, "What meaning or message does this story have for you?" is a way of helping children identify both theme in literature and theme in their own writing (Hancock, 2004).

Point of View. **Point of View** is the focus of the narrator determining the believability of the plot and the reader's understanding of the story. In children's literature read by intermediate and middle-level readers, the first-person point of view and the omniscient point of view are most commonly used and most frequently make their way into adolescent authorship. A story told through the eyes of the main character using the narrative "I" is *first-person* point of view. The narrator is both an eyewitness and a story participant. The *omniscient* viewpoint, on the other hand, is assumed by a narrator who knows all and sees all. The author thus informs the reader of a character's thoughts and feelings from an outside but informed perspective. The *limited omniscient* viewpoint is told in the third person and concentrates on the thoughts, emotions, and past experiences of the main character. In the *objective viewpoint,* readers experience the story firsthand with a focus on retelling events. Folktales, in particular, illustrate this point of view.

Developmentally, the elements of story must be taught individually and revisited at more specific levels as developmentally appropriate to the age, grade, and writing-level of students. For example, discussing the beginning, middle, and end of a story is the first stage of understanding plot. Creating the visual appearance of a character is more likely a first stage introduction to character. While first-person point of view is most effective for primary students, the omniscient point of view may be fine-tuned in the middle-school setting. The Literature Cluster on page 266 presents an overview of the developmental considerations of teaching all the story elements of a narrative.

Blending the Story Elements Through the Writing Craft

After establishing a sound knowledge of the definition and developmental aspects of teaching and learning story elements, the next step is to blend them into a meaningful instructional model through well-constructed literature. An example of a picture book and a chapter book provide optimal models.

Kevin Henkes won the 2005 Caldecott Medal for his illustrations in *Kitten's First Full Moon*. The simplicity of the story itself bears testament to the inclusion of all story elements. The *plot* involves a kitten's exploration of the first full moon and a misinterpretation of it as a bowl of milk in the sky. The *conflict* results when the kitten unsuccessfully attempts to get to that elusive "bowl of milk." *Roadblocks* include licking the sky (resulting in bugs on her

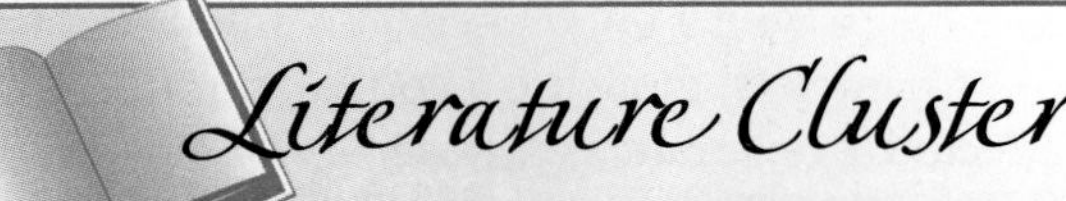

A DEVELOPMENTAL PERSPECTIVE ON THE ELEMENTS OF A STORY

Plot

Beginning, Middle, and End of Story (PreK–2)

Brett, Jan (1989). *The mitten*. New York: Putnam.

Carle, Eric (1990). *The very quiet cricket*. New York: Philomel.

Henkes, Kevin (1996). *Lily's purple plastic purse*. New York: Greenwillow.

Conflict (Grades 2–5)

Bunting, Eve (1994). *Smoky night*. San Diego, CA: Harcourt Brace.

Paulsen, Gary (1987). *Hatchet*. New York: Bradbury.

Polacco, Patricia (1990). *Thunder cake*. New York: Philomel.

Resolution (Grades 2–5)

Gardner, John (1980). *Stone Fox*. New York: Harper & Row.

Naylor, Phyllis Reynolds (1991). *Shiloh*. New York: Atheneum.

Plot Development (Grades 5–8)

Lowry, Lois (1993). *The giver*. Boston: Houghton Mifflin.

Peck, Richard (2001). *A year down under*. New York: Dial.

Setting

Location (Grades 2–3)

Johnston, Tony (1994). *Amber on the mountain*. Illus. by Robert Duncan. New York: Dial.

Ringgold, Faith (1991). *Tar beach*. New York: Crown.

Weather (Grades 4–5)

MacLachlan, Patricia (1983). *Sarah, plain and tall*. New York: Harper & Row.

Ruckman, Ivy (1984). *The night of the twisters*. New York: HarperCollins.

Time/Time Period (Grades 6–8)

Curtis, Christopher Paul (1999). *Bud, not Buddy*. New York: Delacorte.

Cushman, Karen (2003). *Rodzina*. New York: Clarion.

tongue), springing from the porch (resulting in a bumped nose and pinched tail), chasing it (but never getting closer), climbing a tree (but never reaching it), and seeing its reflection in a pond (resulting in a wet, sad kitten). The *resolution* occurs when the kitten dejectedly goes home, where there is a bowl of milk on the porch waiting for her.

The *setting* is generic—any porch, the vast sky, the full moon at night, a tree, a pond. The *character* is the unnamed kitten who may or may not have learned something from her quest for the elusive milk bowl in the sky. The character's appearance is revealed through gouache and color pencil illustrations, but the actions of the kitten are the vehicle for revealing personality and potential character development. The *theme* may be that home-sweet-home is the best place to fulfill our needs. The book is told from the omniscient *viewpoint* as Kevin Henkes observes and reveals the sequence of events in the story. This analysis shows that even in the simplest of picture books, readers can meet characters with distinctive personalities who experience a range of emotions and may even grow and change in only thirty-two precious pages (Martinez & Roser, 2005).

These story elements become more distinctive, developed, and intricate when analyzing a chapter book. Kate DiCamillo's *Because of Winn-Dixie,* a winner of the Newbery

Character

Main Character (Grades K–2)

Appearance (Grades 2–4)

Henkes, Kevin (1991). *Chrysanthemum*. New York: Greenwillow.

Mc Kissack, Patricia (2001). *Goin' someplace special*. New York: Atheneum.

Action (Grades 4–6)

Avi (1990). *The true confessions of Charlotte Doyle*. New York: Orchard

Sachar, Louie (1998). *Holes*. New York: Farrar, Straus & Giroux.

Dialogue (Grades 4–8)

Creech, Sharon (1995). *Walk two moons*. New York: HarperCollins.

Park, Linda Sue (2001). *A single shard*. New York: Clarion.

Monologue (Grades 6–8)

Cushman, Karen (1995). *The ballad of Lucy Whipple*. New York: Clarion.

Rylant, Cynthia (1992). *Missing May*. New York: Orchard.

Supporting Characters (Grades 5–8)

Konigsberg, E. L. (1997). *The view from Saturday*. New York: Atheneum.

Spinelli, Jerry (1990). *Maniac Magee*. New York: Little, Brown.

Theme

Explicit Meaning or Message (Grades 2–5)

DiCamillo, Kate (2000). *Because of Winn-Dixie*. Cambridge, MA: Candlewick.

Spinelli, Jerry (1997). *Wringer*. New York: HarperCollins.

Underlying Meaning or Message *(Grades 5–8)*

Giff, Patricia Reilly (2002). *Pictures of Hollis Woods*. New York: Random House.

Hesse, Karen (1997). *Out of the dust*. New York: Scholastic.

Point of View

First-Person (Grades 5–8)

Paterson, Katherine (1991). *Lyddie*. New York: Lodestar.

Objective (Grade 3–6)

Andersen, H. C. (2005) *The ugly duckling*. Illus. by Robert Ingpen. New York: Minedition/ Penguin.

Omniscient (Grades 5–8)

Babbitt, Natalie (1975). *Tuck everlasting*. New York: Farrar, Straus & Giroux.

Limited Omniscient (Grades 6–8)

Ryan, Pam Muñoz (2000). *Esperanza rising*. New York: Scholastic.

Honor Medal, exemplifies the blending of story elements into a memorable whole. The beginning *plot* of this realistic fiction transports the reader to the small southern town to which India Opal Baloni has just moved with her preacher father. Opal not only faces the continuing longing for her mother, but she must make new friends in yet another attempt to find a place she can call home. Adopting a ragged mutt named Winn-Dixie helps her in making friends with the eccentric characters of the town. The plot resolution occurs when Opal comes to realize that she has much for which to be grateful and is ready to move on from past memories to making a new life.

The *setting* for *Because of Winn-Dixie* is the steamy, sultry town of Naoimi, Florida, a small community showcasing a Winn-Dixie supermarket, the Herman W. Block Library, Otis' Pet Store, and a variety of eccentric inhabitants. The Open Arms Baptist Church attempts to instill a growing community spirit in this southern town while it reluctantly opens its arms to the new preacher and his daughter. The loss of Opal's mother at age three provides the reader with background of the melancholy, lonely life of the reverend and his daughter, constantly leaving friends and memories behind in their mobile life.

India Opal Baloni, the main *character,* is portrayed as a lonely ten-year-old prone to making unusual friends. After picking up a dog and naming him for the local grocery store, Opal also befriends mysterious Gloria Dump, storytelling librarian Fanny Block, and guitar-strumming Otis before coming to terms with her peers, Sweetie Pie, Stevie, and Dunlap Dewberry. Opal longs to hold on to the memories of her mother, so the preacher provides her with a list of ten things about her mama. While finding her place in her new home, Opal realizes she and the dog are instrumental in building a future with those who embrace her engaging spirit. Kate DiCamillo creatively develops supporting characters, thus allowing the reader to see the personal skills of Opal in bringing lonely but kind individuals together.

The *theme* in *Because of Winn-Dixie* focuses on the loss of a loved one, the role of inner strength, and the power of friends in building a new life. "Mama. . . . I know ten things about you, and that's not enough . . . He misses you and I miss you, but my heart doesn't feel empty anymore. It 's full all the way up" (pp. 177–178). A tender canine becomes the instrument that draws Opal to newfound friends, leading her to realize just how much for which she should be thankful.

In *Because of Winn-Dixie,* the author describes Opal's every action, feeling, and thought through a first-person viewpoint. Opal describes her early encounters with townspeople and her evolving friendships and intriguing episodes with them. Opal pours out her heart through the author's well-chosen words, thus tugging at the heartstrings of the reader. The first-person voice brings the reader even closer to the main character vicariously feeling her loss and her recovery throughout the story.

These examples of the use of the five literary elements—plot, setting, character, theme, and point of view—in *Kitten's First Full Moon* and *Because of Winn-Dixie* document literature as a literary model. This is how children should learn about literary elements before taking the leap to application within their own writing (Dressel, 1990). While many of the elements come naturally when retelling personal experiences and events, they become richer through an in-depth understanding of how each "works" within the entire framework of narrative.

Narrative and the Writing Process

The writing process—rehearsal, drafting, revision, editing, publishing—can be incorporated seamlessly into the genre of narrative writing. Brainstorming may begin with a list of possible narrative topics. Note sixth grade Alison's list (Student Sample 9.1) which presents a list generated by a sixth grader as part of her writing folder. Note the numerous personal topics with which she has first-hand experience. The use of graphic organizers is also common, allowing children in rehearse, outline, and sketch the details of their writing.

Drafting means moving those thoughts from the seed of an idea to the page in a first draft. It is at this point that teachers should encourage the fast flow of narrative from the mind and heart in an effort to capture the flow of story, setting, and characters. Knowing that the draft will be revisited allows students to focus on recording thoughts as they flow.

The second draft requires sharing narrative writing with an audience and determining the clarity, or lack of clarity, of the sequence of events. The writer must also describe characters, establish the setting, and articulate themes. Writing partners, teacher-student writing conferences, and writing groups will help facilitate the suggestions for improvement with special emphasis on the elements of story.

The editing and the final draft are often incorporated using word processing in the final presentation. Presenting the finished narrative—read aloud in the author's chair,

STUDENT SAMPLE 9.1
A sixth grader's list of writing ideas.

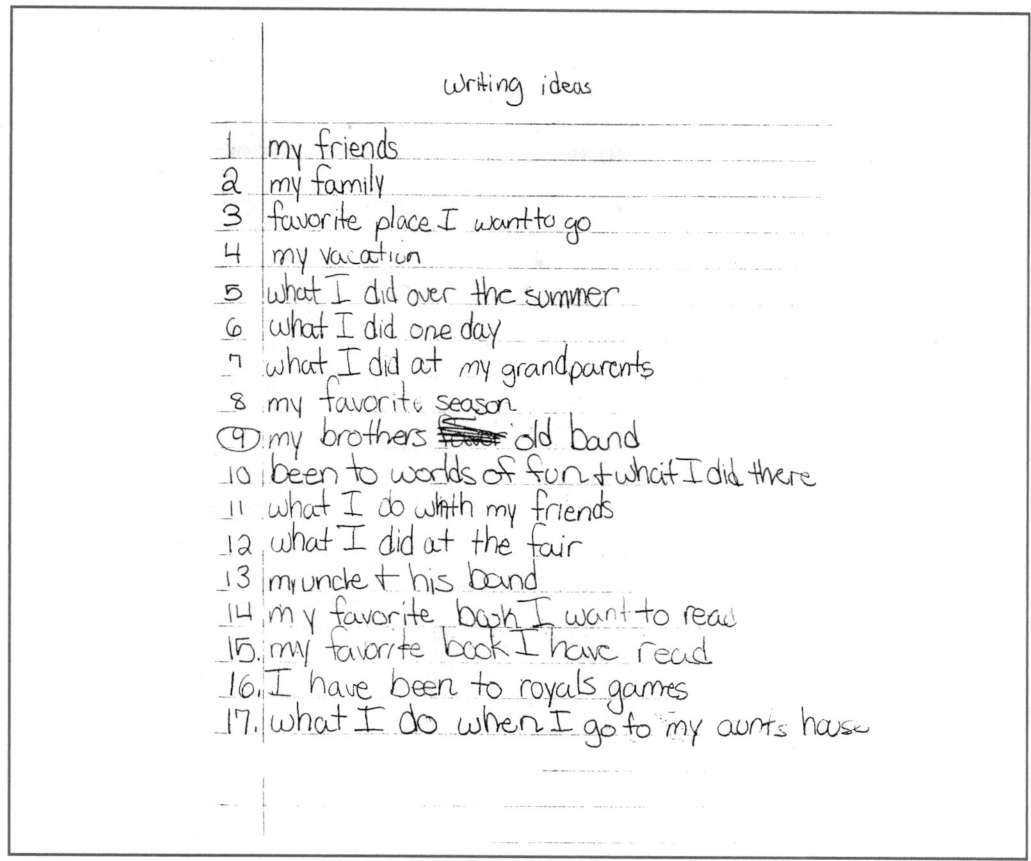
Writing ideas

1 my friends
2 my family
3 favorite place I want to go
4 my vacation
5 what I did over the summer
6 what I did one day
7 what I did at my grandparents
8 my favorite season
9 my brothers ~~~~ old band
10 been to worlds of fun + what I did there
11 what I do whith my friends
12 what I did at the fair
13 my uncle + his band
14 my favorite book I want to read
15. my favorite book I have read
16. I have been to royals games
17. what I do when I go to my aunts house

displayed on the writer's bulletin board, or incorporated into ongoing writing documentation in a writing folder—provides continuous access to a young author's growth.

Children's Narrative Writing—A Developmental Perspective

Viewing the elements of story within children's writing provides the next step in addressing instruction and developmental growth as children progress in narrative writing strategies. Sharing the writing assignments and the writing samples of a variety of authentic narrative products provide a means to plan effective instruction and monitor continuous student growth in writing.

Sharon is a second-grade student who simply loves to write, as evidenced by her story "Eddie, His Family, and a Cat!!!" (Student Sample 9.2). The blend of text and illustration is optimal at the second-grade level, where the visual nature of a illustration sparks details in writing. Sharon employs several of the narrative text elements. Her setting is simply one winter day in the Biggs' house. Her main characters are Norris, the cat, and Eddie, the mouse. The theme of friendship evolves as the plot moves from the problem of the mice living with a cat to the simple solution of friendship. Two roadblocks occur when the family fears it will have to move because of the cat's presence, and again when Norris dies; yet the new family cat shows promise of a continuing friendship at the resolution of the story.

Courtney is a second-grader in the same classroom. Her narrative, "The Enormous Radish" (Student Sample 9.3), springs from a teacher read-aloud of *The Enormous Turnip*

STUDENT SAMPLE 9.2
A second grader's writing sample.

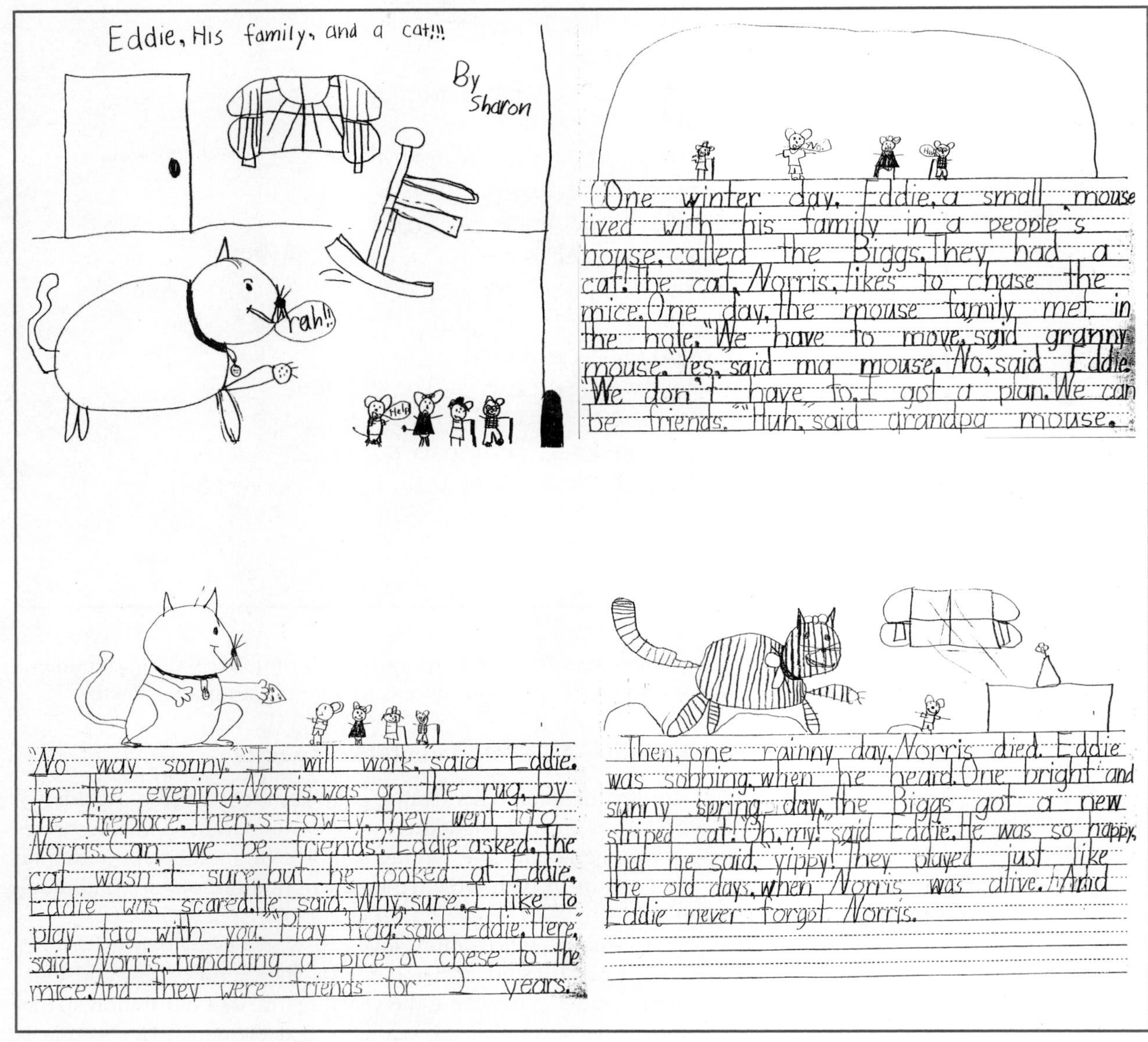

by Leo Tolstoy. Courtney incorporates "literary borrowing" as she uses the framework of the original story but employs her own literary elements to make the story her own. The setting is simply a summer day and the characters have memorable names such as Wide Mama Betty, Strong Papa Bill, and Little Lacie. The plot develops as Little Lacie dances around the radish, making it grow to an enormous size. The roadblock is presented when the overgrown radish must be removed from the soil. The resolution occurs when Little

STUDENT SAMPLE 9.3 A second grader's narrative writing sample.

THE ENORMOUS RADISH
by Courtney

One summer day, Wide Mama Betty planted a radish seed in the ground. "I'm going to have radish stew when it is big enough."

Next Little Lacie came. "I'm going to have a nice radish cake."

"Oh no you aren't."

"If we want to have this," said Little Lacie, "we should work hard." . . .

"I do not want to," said Little Lacie. "I want to make it grow faster."

"OK," said Wide Mama Betty.

"OK," said Strong Papa Bill. So Little Lacie stayed and made that radish grow. . . .

PQP! Out came the radish.

They had radish stew, radish cup cakes, and radish cake. They lived happily ever after.

STUDENT SAMPLE 9.4A
A Sixth Grader's Narrative.

The Three Little Moles

Long ago, when wishes still came true, there were three little moles named Molly, Mary, and Matthew. They lived at home with their mother, Momma Mole, and were very happy.

One day, Momma Mole announced that she thought the three little moles were old enough to move out and start out on their own.

The only thing their mom informed them about was the Big Bad Wolf. She said that he would burrow into their din and eat them up!

The moles started having second thoughts about moving out. Their mother said that if they stayed together and worked together, then everything would be just fine.

The next day, the three little moles started out on their own and decided that moving out was a good idea and thought they would have fun.

After a while, molly started on her dugout. When she finished, her brother and sister inspected it and found out that it was in poor condition, like their momma's old apron. They hoped that they wouldn't have to depend on her den.

The day after, Mary started on her dugout. When she finished, her brother took a look at it and found out that it wasn't first class, but wasn't as bad as Molly's.

Matthew started on his dugout. It was by far the best of the three dugouts.

STUDENT SAMPLE 9.4B

Molly whined, "Why does yours always have to be the best?"

Mary agreed, "Yeah, you are such a goody-goody."

"You're always sucking up to Mom and Mrs. Random," Molly said hastily.

Both of them were astonished at the amazing detail of the dreary dugout their brother had made. In about a week, they were expecting the Big Bad Wolf to arrive...

Unfortunately, this story has to come to an end because the Big Bad Wolf took a wrong turn at Albuquerque. (Whoops)

Anyway, the three little moles lived happily ever after for about 10 years. That's when the Wolf came back (he finally found his way) but that's another story.

Lacie proves to be surprisingly able to assist in pulling the huge radish from the ground. Celebration occurs as the family has "radish stew, radish cup cakes, and radish cake." Note the adequate sequence of events and the use of quotations. Developmentally, Courtney's use of character quotes is advanced, but the literature model provided a template that she followed in her own writing.

A sixth-grade example of narrative writing that is achieved through writing a fairy tale variant is shown in Student Sample 9.4. Mrs. Larson has asked her students to identify story elements in an original fairy tale and then to identify the elements in their proposed modern version. Character names, new settings, three new roadblocks, and a new solution are options provided by the students for their own versions. Blair fashions her tale, "The Three Little Moles," from "The Three Little Pigs," but changes the characters and the nature of their dugouts, and slips in a surprise ending. Prior to the writing assignment, this insightful teacher set specific criteria based on fairy tale elements and suggested character conversation as well. A rubric with specific components, style, and mechanics was distributed and discussed with the students prior to beginning their writing. This raised the expectations while providing a flexible framework for achieving their goals. The results are a testimony to the role of guided responsibility transmitted from teacher to young writers.

All of these narrative writing examples show the developmental scope and potential of narrative writing in the classroom. Variety, personality, voice, imagination, and experience pervade the young authors' writing samples. Realizing the importance of planning, high expectations, the literature model, and the writing process suggests the key to the success of these narrative writing samples.

Poetry Writing

Poetry matters (Fletcher, 2002). Poems are personal; they come from the heart, overflow with emotions, and brim with magical words. Some poems make us laugh and some open the world of fantasy for us. Poems economize on length—usually being short and to the point but powerful because of their well-selected language. Poetry brings the music of words to light and conveys sensory, emotional, and personal insights. Writing poetry for children is all about the joy of choosing the right topic and the best word, on the lengthy revision road to the perfect poem.

Ralph Fletcher (2002) in *Poetry Matters* recognizes that "The three pillars of poetry are emotion, image, and music" (p. 10). In *A Jar of Tiny Stars,* edited by Bernice Cullinan (1996), Karla Kuskin describes the ingredients in a recipe for a poem: "word sounds, rhythm, description, feeling, memory, rhyme, and imagination" (p. 17). In the same collection, Lillian Moore states that "Poetry should be like fireworks, packed carefully and artfully, ready to explode with unpredictable effects" (p. 47). Learning more about the foundation of poetry entices the young writer—the prospective poet—to learn the variety of poetic forms, the importance of word choice, and the power of a poem to say what no one else may be able to say. This section of the chapter invites teachers and students inside the poetry genre to explore the possibilities of the power of poetry and the way to make poetry "an X-ray of what is going inside of you" (Fletcher, 2002, p. 14).

Literature Cluster

CLASSIC AND CONTEMPORARY POETRY TO READ ALOUD IN PREPARATION FOR WRITING

Classic Poetry

Ciardi, John (1962). *You read to me, I'll read to you.* Illus. by Edward Gorey. Philadelphia: Lippincott.

Cole, William (Ed.) (1966). *Oh, what nonsense!* Illus. by Tomi Ungerer. New York: Viking.

Fisher, Aileen (1969). *In one door and out the other: A book of poems.* Illus. by Lillian Hoban. New York: Crowell.

Fleischmann, Paul (1988). *Joyful noise: Poems for two voices.* Illus. by Eric Beddows. New York: Harper.

Fyleman, Rose (2004). *Mary Middling and other silly folk: Nursery rhymes and nonsense poems.* Selected by Neil Philip. Illus. by Katja Bandlow. New York: Clarion.

Kuskin, Karla (1972). *Any me I want to be.* New York: Harper & Row.

Larrick, Nancy (1968/1985). *Piping down the valleys wild.* Illus. by Ellen Raskin. New York: Delacorte.

Livingston, Myra Cohn (1982). *A circle of seasons.* Illus. by Leonard Everett Fisher. New York: Holiday House.

McCord, David (1977). *One at a time: Collected poems for the young.* Illus. by Henry B. Kane. Boston: Little, Brown.

Merriam, Eve (1964). *It doesn't always have to rhyme.* Illus. by Malcolm Spooner. New York: Atheneum.

Moore, Lillian (1982). *Something new begins: New and selected poems.* Illus. by Mary Jane Dutton. New York: Atheneum.

O'Neill, Mary (1961/1989). *Hailstones and halibut bones.* Illus. by Leonard Weisgard. New York: Doubleday.

Prelutsky, Jack (1984). *The new kid on the block.* Illus. by James Stevenson. New York: Greenwillow.

Silverstein, Shel (1974). *Where the sidewalk ends.* New York: Harper & Row.

Untermeyer, Louie (Ed.) (1985). *Rainbow in the sky.* Illus. by Reginald Birch. San Diego: Harcourt Brace.

Viorst, Judith (1982). *If I were in charge of the world and other worries: Poems for children and their parents.* Illus. by Lynne Cherry. New York: Atheneum.

Willard, Nancy (1981). *A visit to William Blake's Inn: Poems for innocent and experienced travelers.* Illus. by Alice and Martin Provensen. San Diego: Harcourt Brace.

Worth, Valerie (1972). *Small poems.* Illus. by Natalie Babbitt. New York: Farrar, Straus & Giroux.

Contemporary Poetry

Florian, Douglas (2003). *Autumnblings.* New York: Greenwillow.

Florian, Douglas (2005). *Zoo's who.* San Diego: Harcourt.

George, Kristine O'Connell (2001). *Toasting marshmallows.* Illus. by Kate Kiesler. New York: Clarion.

Hopkins, Lee Bennett (2002). *Hoofbeats, claws & rippled fins: Creature poems.* Illus. by Stephen Alcorn. New York: HarperCollins.

Kiesler, Kate (Selecter) (2002). *Wings on the wind: Bird poems.* New York: Clarion.

Levy, Constance (2002). *SPLASH! Poems of our watery world.* Illus. by David Soman. New York: Orchard.

Lewis, J. Patrick (2002). *A world of wonders: Geographic travels in verse and rhyme.* Illus. by Allison Jay. New York: Dial.

Moore, Lilliam (2005). *Mural on Second Avenue: And other city poems.* Illus. by Roma Karas. Cambridge, MA: Candlewick.

Pollock Penny (2001). *When the moon is full: A lunar year.* Illus. by Mary Azarian. Boston: Little, Brown.

Prelutsky, Jack (2004). *If not for the cat.* Illus. by Ted Rand. New York: Greenwillow.

Rosenthal, Betsy R. (2004). *My house is singing.* Illus. by Margaret Chodow-Irvine. San Diego: Harcourt.

Silverstein, Shel (2005). *Runny Babbit: A billy sook.* New York: HarperCollins.

Soto, Gary (2005). *Worlds apart: Traveling with Fernie and me.* Illus. by Greg Clarke. New York: Putnam.

Stevenson, James (2003). *Corn chowder: Poems by James Stevenson.* New York: Greenwillow.

Wong, Janet (2003). *Knock on wood: Poems about superstitions.* Illus. by Julie Paschkis. New York: McElderry.

Immersing Children in the Poetic Genre

Myra Cohn Livingston (1990), renowned children's poet, states that, "There is no poem that can live, come alive, without a reader. The reader, the listener, breathes into each work of art his own experience, his own sensitivity, and re-creates it in meaningful terms" (p. 207). And so begins the process of immersing prospective young poets into this magical genre. The initial step in preparation for writing poetry in the elementary and middle grades is to immerse students in the genre itself (Glover, 1999; Graves, 1992; Heard, 1998; McClure, Harrison, & Reed, 1990). Start with teacher read-alouds of poetry. Start with award-winning poets—David McCord, Aileen Fisher, Karla Kuskin, Myra Cohn Livingston, Eve Merriam, John Ciardi, Lillian Moore, Arnold Adoff, Valerie Worth, Barbara Esbensen, and Mary Ann Hoberman. Move on to popular poetry books by Kristine O'Connell George, J. Patrick Lewis, and Alice Schertle. The Literature Cluster here provides a list of outstanding poetry books for sharing aloud. Explore the multiethnic nature of poetry through the works of Eloise Greenfield, Naomi Shahib Nye, Gary Soto, and Janet Wong. The Literature Cluster

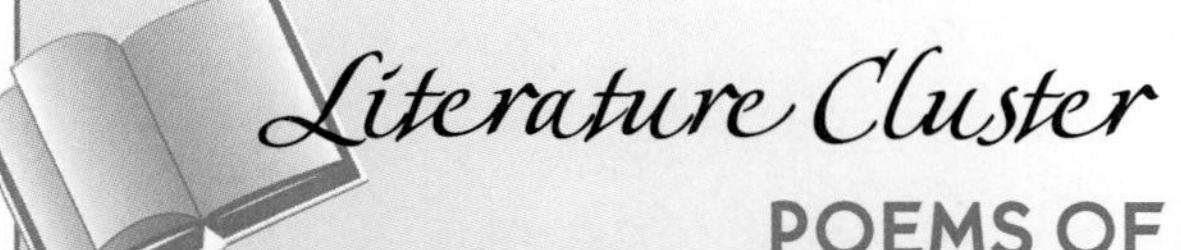

POEMS OF ALL CULTURES

Adoff, Arnold (2000). *Touch the poem*. Illus. by Lisa Desamini. New York: Scholastic.

Alarcon, F. X. (1998). *From the bellybutton of the moon and other summer poems/Del ombligo de la luna y otros poemas de verano*. San Francisco: Children's Book Press.

Alarcon, F. X. (2001). *Iguanas in the snow and other winter poems/Iguanas en la Nieve y otros poemas de invierno*. Illus. by Maya Christina Gonzales. San Francisco: Children's Book Press.

Carlson, L. M. (Ed.) (1998). *Sol a sol: Bilingual poems*. New York: Holt.

Delacre, Lulu (Selector) (2004). *Arrorro, mi nino: Latino lullabies and gentle games*. Musical arrangements by Cecilia Esquivel and Diana Saez. New York: Lee & Low.

Dunbar, Paul Lawrence (2000). *Jump back, home*. Illus. by A. Bryan et al. New York: Hyperion.

Gollub, M. (1998). *Cool melons—turn to frogs! The life and poems of Issa*. Illus. by Kazuko G. Stone. New York: Lee & Low.

Greenfield, Eloise (1978). *Honey, I love and other love poems*. Illus. by Leo & Diane Dillon. New York: Crowell.

Herrera, J. F. (1998). *Laughing out loud, I fly*. New York: HarperCollins.

Hughes, Langston (1994). *The dream keeper and other poems*. New York: Knopf.

Mak, Kam (2002). *My Chinatown: One year in poems*. New York: HarperCollins.

Medina, T. (2002). *Love to Langston*. New York: Lee & Low.

Myer, Walter Dean (2003). *blues journey*. Illus. by Christopher Myers. New York: Holiday House.

Nye, Naomi Shahib (1995). *The tree is older than you are*. New York: Simon & Schuster.

Steptoe, Javaka (1997). *In Daddy's arms, I am tall: African Americans celebrating fathers*. New York: Lee & Low.

Swann, Brian (1998). *Touching the distance: Native American riddle poems*. Illus. by Marian Rendon. San Diego: Harcourt Brace.

Wong, Janet (1996). *A suitcase of seaweed and other poems*. New York: McElderry.

Giggle Poetry is a user-friendly resource for budding poets. Students of all ages can read hundreds of poems, learn how to write a wide variety of poetry, and participate in poetry contests. The "Ask the Poet" section invites students to read interviews with favorite poets and submit their own questions via e-mail. **www.gigglepoetry.com**

Visit Jack Prelutsky's interactive Internet workshop to learn more about turning your ideas and words into powerful poems. *Poetry Writing with Jack Prelutsky* offers students writing tips, ideas for revisions, and a place for students to publish their finished poems online. **teacher.scholastic.com/writewit/poetry/jack_home.htm**

Rhyming is hard! *A Time for Rhyme* shows teachers and students how to compose great rhyming poems. **www.grandpatucker.com/rhyme-time1.html-ssi**

Stone Soup is a magazine for children made up entirely of the creative work of children. View a sample issue and learn how students can publish their poems and stories on the Stone Soup Web site. **www.stonesoup.com/index.html**

To look more closely at these materials and others related to "Narrative and Poetic Writing," visit the Companion Website at www.prenhall.com/hancock.

below presents multicultural poetry books that span the international perspective. Discover the themed anthologies of Lee Bennett Hopkins and Paul Janeczko. These books echo the sounds of poetry, the taste of words, and the images of potential poetic topics.

Next, invite students to explore the large numbers of poetry books available for convenient use in the classroom. Have them read and mark favorites with name-labeled colored adhesive notes. Circulate the books around tables or poetry groups. Ask students to copy, in their own handwriting, some of their favorite poems on colored and framed paper. As they experience the movement of their own manuscript or cursive writing, they will likely grasp the rhythm and music of the poetry itself. Additional resources for budding poets may be accessed through the quality poetry-based Web sites in the Tech Tip included here.

Invite children to create a classroom anthology of favorite poems, accurately documenting the poet and the collection from which each poem was selected. Spiral bind a class book of poetic favorites, long before students are invited to write poetry of their own. Internalizing the sounds, the language, the rhythm, and the images of poetry of recognized children's and young adult poets will prepare students for the eventual writing of their own poems.

Starting with the Senses

One of the best ways to begin young poets' quests for poetic success in writing is to help them to utilize the power of the senses. Describing something in a fresh way, painting a verbal image of a familiar object, and conveying emotion within the poem is the beginning of desired poetic success. Ralph Fletcher (2002) inspires a list of sensory experience to enhance the quality of student poetry:

- ***Look closely.*** Start by putting a new lens on your view of ordinary things. For example, look closely at a pansy and see the smiling face that looks back. Observe the beauty of nature in the wing pattern of a monarch butterfly. Watch a sunset and the play of the last rays on the window pane, the forest floor, or the shadows of the backyard trees.

A strand of light peers through the window
Lighting up my beloved vase. (Christine, Grade 5)

- ***Listen carefully.*** Tune into the sounds of the early morning, focus on the distant train whistle, or capture the interplay of the car horns and the ambulance siren. Listen to the buzz of chatter at a sports event or the drone of 300 students at noon recess.

  The ice storm speaks to me from the icicles.
  I walk on the ice.
  It sounds like glass breaking. (Kristine, Grade 3)

- ***Smell deeply.*** Inhale the scent of newly sharpened pencils, the aroma of banana bread baking in the oven, or the familiar smells of the zoo. Linger over the daily smell of the school cafeteria or the crisp odor of burning autumn leaves. Reflect on the blended aroma of the restaurants in an ethnic neighborhood or the appetizing scent of your grandmother's apple pie.

  The fresh scent of falling rain,
  The smell of new-mown grass,
  Inhale the lilacs that smell purple. (Kayla, Grade 4)

- ***Experiment with touch.*** Let your fingers investigate the texture of tree bark, the wood grain of an antique desk, or the intricate symbols of braille. Finger the petals of a daisy, the fur of the neighborhood cat, or the imprint of an old book cover.

  I trace the carvings with my finger
  Gazing at its soft sky-blue. (Christine, Grade 5)

- ***Explore tastes.*** Savor the cool tartness of strawberry ice cream, the bittersweet flavor of smooth chocolate, or the slow, minty-green melting of a spearmint life-saver. Enjoy the crunch of a fresh-picked garden carrot, the stickiness of a hot slice of pizza, or the smoothness of classic cheesecake.

  Salty popcorn
  Buttered popcorn
  Cheese popcorn
  Caramel popcorn
  Lemon popcorn
  I like popcorn. (Title 1 kindergarten students)

Observations such as these can inspire the young poet to focus on details and descriptive word choice. Finding a way to create a single snapshot of a common image through word choice with just a bit of poetic surprise provides students with a successful entrance into the poetic realm.

The Language of Poetry

The language of poetry is reminiscent of music as it attempts to capture the rhythm and sometimes the rhyme of words. When read aloud, even an unrhymed poem exudes the rhythm of well-chosen language. Poets carefully select their words, but they also employ repetition, alliteration, onomatopoeia, and other poetic devices into their pieces. As young poets witness, define, and build on examples and models of these devices, their own poetry writing becomes a richer literacy experience. The following poetic devices illustrate the power of language in writing poems.

Comparisons: Similes and Metaphors. Poetry often compares images, feelings, and actions. The poetic devices used to forge these comparisons are similes and metaphors. A simile is an explicit comparison between two persons, places, or things signaled by the use of *like* or *as*. A child writes, "A bully is like a large pot of water about to bubble and boil." A metaphor is an implied comparison between two persons, places, or things *without* the use of *like* or *as*. A child writes, "A bully is a bubbling kettle of boiling water."

Berries frame the forest path as a wooden
square would frame a painting.
So beautiful. (Anthony, Grade 5)

Alliteration. The repetition of initial sounds in consecutive or ongoing words exemplifies alliteration. Such repetitions make poetry fun to read and provide the rhythmic characteristics of the poetic genre. Marcia O'Shell's *Alphabet Annie Announces on All American Album* invites readers to practice sound repetition by modeling alliterative statements:

Brainstorming Betty builds better bicycles in bustling Boston.

Children then follow the pattern as they create simple alliterations. Eventually, this skill becomes a strategy as they apply alliteration in their own poems.

Onomatopoeia. Onomatopoeia is a poetic device in which poets bring life to their poems through the use of sound words such as *gobble, crash, slurp,* and *buzz*. This poetic device expands word choice into a sensory experience allowing readers to hear the word as well as visualize it:

The breeze whistles with the trees.
The butterflies sneeze with the buzzing bees. (Jerod, Grade 3)

Repetition. Repetition becomes a simple poetic device when words, phrases, or entire lines are repeated to add interest or dramatic impact to a poem:

In December snow starts to fall.
It covers the ground like a fuzzy white blanket.
When it falls on you it is like confetti.
In December snow starts to fall. (Ry Ann, Grade 6)

Syllable and Word Count Poems

One of the most effective ways to generate initial success with writing poetry is to explore the use of prescribed formats. In doing so, the framework and "rules" of the poetic form are provided while the topic and the word choice comes from within the young poet. A good place to began is with the creation of haikus.

Originating in Japan almost 800 years ago, the *haiku* consists of three unrhymed lines of five, seven, and five syllables, with the entire poem totaling only seventeen syllables. Haiku typically describes a scene from nature and may include a reference to a season.

Because haiku shares complex ideas for deeper reflection, this abstract form of poetry should be reserved for intermediate and middle-school poets.

Storm clouds move slowly
Gray and silent in the wind
Like smoke in the sky. (Joshua, Grade 2)

A similar format is used by the *cinquain,* a five-line poem containing a total of twenty-two syllables. The per line syllable count of 2-4-6-8-2 creates a flow tying all five lines together:

Soft cats
Cuddly creatures
Bundles of shiny, sleek fur
Long bushy tails and piercing eyes
Whiskers. (Elizabeth, Grade 6)

The *diamante* is a seven-line poem that takes the shape of a diamond by using a formula for word selection that assumes a knowledge of opposites and parts of speech. The following structure can he used to create the peom:

Line 1: The subject (one noun)
Line 2: Description of the subject (two adjectives)
Line 3: Description of the subject (three *–ing* participles)
Line 4: Two nouns related to the subject and two nouns related to the opposite
Line 5: Description of the opposite (three *–ing* participles)
Line 6: Description of the opposite (two adjectives)
Line 7: The opposite of the subject (one noun)

Snow
Sparkling, white
Soft, flaky, cool
Fun, icy, wet, muddy
Dirty, yucky, oozing
Brown, sticky
Mud. (Hannah, Grade 3)

Rhymed Verse Poems

The *couplet* is a grouping of two lines of poetry that go together, usually rhyming and expressing a complete thought.

The razor runs sharply through the overgrown beard
While the barber reflects on the smooth image mirrored. (Patrick, Grade 4)

The *quatrain* is a grouping of four lines of poetry typically following an *abab* or *abba* rhyme pattern:

The sky is not so far away
It looms above the field in bloom
The horizon meets between sky and hay
I linger there as harvest comes soon. (Sara, Grade 5)

The *limerick* is a well-recognized five-line form of poetry originally made famous by Edmund Lear and more recently by X. J. Kennedy. Lines 1, 2, and 5 have three accented

STUDENT SAMPLE 9.5
A third grader's acrostic poem.

syllables while lines 3 and 4 are shorter with two accented syllables. When read aloud, a limerick bounces along with its humor and rhythm:

There once was a brown raccoon.
She liked to sleep until noon.
She was never at school
She broke every rule.
She won't be seeing third grade soon. (Melissa, Grade 2)

Free Form Poems

Free form poems express ideas and emotions without restrictions of rhyme or number of words per line. The *acrostic* is a poem that forms a selected topic word with the first letter of each line. The lines expand from each letter with a word or phrase that forms the lines of the poem. Student Sample 9.5 illustrates an acrostic based on the word "Panda."

Lesson Plan 9.1 details the modeling, process writing, and technology-enhanced presentation of acrostic poems.

LESSON PLAN 9.1

TITLE: Celebrate the Seasons with Acrostic Poems

Grade Level: 3–6

Time Frame: Two 45-minute sessions

Standards

IRA/NCTE Standards: 4, 6, 8

NETS for Students: 1, 3

Objectives

- Students will learn the structure of acrostic poetry by viewing examples in literature.
- Students will utilize word processing or publishing software to create an acrostic poem about a season or seasonal event.

Materials

- Literature:

  Schnur, Steven, (2002). *Winter: An Alphabet Acrostic*. Illus. by Leslie Evans. Clarion.
  Schnur, Steven, (1999). *Spring: An Alphabet Acrostic*. Illus. by Leslie Evans. Clarion.
  Schnur, Steven, (2001). *Summer: An Alphabet Acrostic*. Illus. by Leslie Evans. Clarion.
  Schnur, Steven, (1997). *Autumn: An Alphabet Acrostic*. Illus. by Leslie Evans. Clarion.
- Computers with word processing and/or publishing software

Motivation

- Read one or more of Steven Schnur's books aloud to your students. Invite students to comment on what they notice about the book's illustrations and text. Point out that the author uses a style of poetry called *acrostic poetry*.

Procedures

Day1

- Explain that acrostic poems read downward with the first letter of each line being part of a topic word. Each letter expands with a word or short phrase that describes the original word. Point out that the topic word is generally written in colorful capital letters. Emphasize that the acrostic poem is not a rhyming poem, but rather focuses on meaning and content.
- Invite students to compose their own seasonal acrostic poem. (Some students may choose to write about a particular holiday or event that occurs within a particular season.) Students should select a topic word and brainstorm lists of descriptive words or phrases to describe the topic word.

Day 2

- Allow students time to draft, revise, and edit their acrostic poems.
- Demonstrate how to publish an acrostic poem using word processing or publishing software. Include instruction on using different fonts, changing font size and color, inserting illustrations (from file or clip art), and adding a page border. Encourage students to be creative while maintaining the format of an acrostic poem.

Assessment

- Teacher-developed rubric or checklist to assess students' understanding of acrostic poems and the use of relevant software applications.

Accommodation/Modification

- Vary the length of words/phrases used to describe the topic word in the acrostic poem to suit needs of individual students.
- Students who will might benefit from viewing additional examples of acrostic poems may visit Acrostic Poems for Children (http://www.holycross.edu/departments/socant/dhummon/acrostics/acrostics.html). This site also contains excellent resources for teachers.

Visit the Meeting the Standards module in Chapter 9 of the Companion Website at www.prenhall.com/hancock to adapt this lesson to meet your state's standards.

A *concrete poem,* also known as a *shape poem,* arranges the words of a poem to mimic the shape of a selected topic. A concrete poem is therefore both a visual and textual portrait. Student Sample 9.6 presents a basketball as a concrete poem.

Free verse is another example of free form poetry that has no restriction of rhyme or line length. It is a particularly popular form of poetry in the intermediate and middle-level grades. Despite the fact that free verse does not have to rhyme, the placement and flow of the words on the page are key to conveying the images, emotions, and language of this poetic format.

To help students explore the free verse format, teachers may begin with asking their students to write a descriptive paragraph about a topic (e.g., nature, an embarrassing episode, an inspiration, a hobby or pastime). If the paragraph is written on a computer through word processing, the possibilities for formatting are endless. The following list suggests ways to create highly effective free verse poems:

- *Experiment with line breaks.* The use of word processing allows students to explore a variety of line breaks in free verse poems. Simply moving a single word to a separate line or making that word a part of the next line can make a visual and an emotional difference to the reader. Similarly, the stanza break can also have an impact. Experiment, print out, read, and explore the possibilities.
- *Utilize the white space of the page.* White space can be a line space that builds in a moment of silence or reflection, or a single word on a line that requires slow reading and a moment to pause, to take a breath, before moving on to the rest of the poem. Use these spaces wisely to create the desired impact.
- *Create a powerful ending.* The ending of a poem matters greatly. The final image is the one that stays with the reader long after the words have finished conveying their meaning. A young poet may recognize the "best" line to place in the ending of a poem.

Additional names of poetic forms are defined and exemplified in Paul Janeczko's *A Kick in the Head: An Everyday Guide to Poetic Forms.* The Literature Cluster below presents a list of poetry books that provide varied structured poetic models.

STUDENT SAMPLE 9.6
A fourth grader's concrete poem.

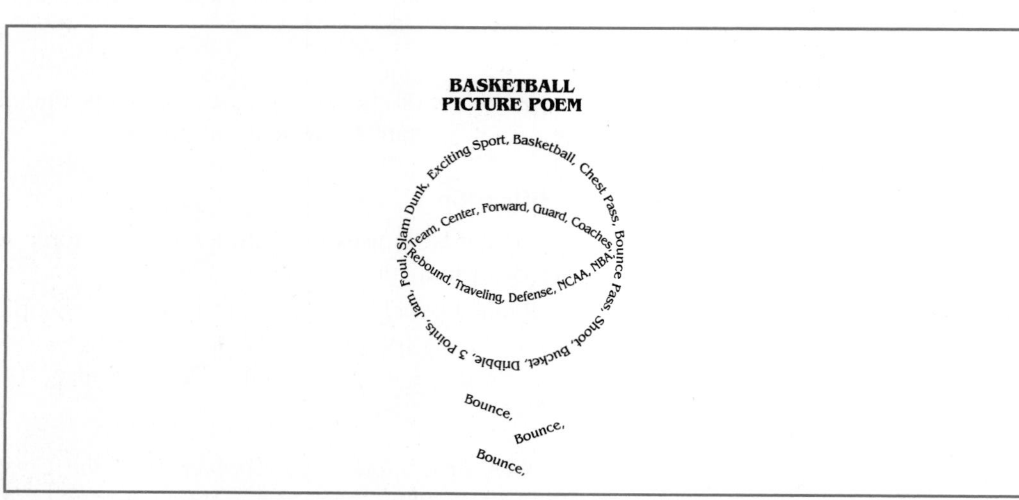

STRUCTURED POETRY MODELS THROUGH LITERATURE

Concrete Poetry

Franco, Betsy (2003). *Mathematickles!* Illus. by Steven Salerno. McElderry.

Graham, Joan Bransfield (1994). *Splish splash*. Illus. by Steve Scott. Boston: Houghton Mifflin.

Graham, Joan Bransfield (1999). *Flicker flash*. Illus. by Nancy Davis. Boston: Houghton Mifflin.

Grandits, John (2004). *Technically, it's not my fault: Concrete poems*. New York: Clarion.

Janezcko (2002). *A poke in the I: A collection of concrete poems*. Illus. by Chris Raschka. New York: Candlewick.

Lewis, J. Patrick (1998). *Doodle dandies: Poems that take shape*. Illus. by Lisa Desamini. New York: Atheneum.

Roemer, Heidi B. (2004). *Come to my party and other shape poems*. Illus. by Hideko Takahashi. New York: Holt.

Soto, Gary (1992). *Neighborhood odes*. San Diego: Harcourt.

Free Verse

Esbensen, Barbara (2000). *Echoes for the eye: Poems to celebrate patterns in nature*. Illus. by Helen K. Davie. New York: HarperCollins.

Sidman, Joyce (2005). *Song of the water boatman & other pond poems*. Illus. by Beckie Prange. Boston: Houghton Mifflin.

Haiku

Lewis, J. Patrick (1995). *Black swan white crows*. Illus. with woodcuts by Chris Manson. New York: Atheneum.

Prelutsky, Jack (2004). *If not for the cat*. Illus. by Ted Rand. New York: Greenwillow.

Shannon, C. (1996). *Spring: A haiku story*. New York: Greenwillow.

Limericks

Kennedy, X. J. (1986). *Brats*. Illus. by James Watts. New York: Atheneum.

Lear, Edmund (1995). *Daffy down dillies: Silly limericks by Edmund Lear*. Honesdale, PA: Boyds Mills Press/Wordsong.

Lobel, Arnold (1983). *The book of pigericks*. New York: Harper & Row.

Combinations of Poetic Forms

Katz, Susan (2005). *Looking for jaguar: And other rain forest poems*. Illus. by Lee Christiansen. New York: Greenwillow.

Janeczko, Paul (2005). *A kick in the head: An everyday guide to poetic forms*. Illus. by Chris Raschka. Cambridge, MA: Candlewick.

Poetry and the Writing Process

There is a distinct parallel between the writing process—rehearsal, drafting, revising, editing, publishing—and the creation of poetry. The rehearsal stage involves considering topics, generating a list of descriptive words, and considering several appropriate formats for the topic. Determining what to write about is critical to the art of writing poetry. Fletcher (2002) has identified the following topics as springboards for poetry: concerns of the heart (feelings about family, friends, and loved ones); what you see (observations of mundane objects seen through a fresh lens); what you wonder about (haunting questions to which there is no answer); and concerns of the world (overpopulation, peace, and human injustice). A passionate topic ensures an optimal poem writing experience.

Preparing the first draft of a poem may take only a short time. Getting ideas down on paper for a poem is less labor intensive than most writing genres, but the work lies ahead in revision.

All poets recognize both the art and the critical nature of revision in the creation of poetry. John Ciardi suggests getting a big wastebasket and keeping it full. If you want to be a writer, you first must agree to be a rewriter. Janet Wong claims to have written ten to fifty drafts for each of her published poems. Eve Merriam reveals spending weeks looking for just the right word. So the novice poet, too, must be willing to spend the time perfecting the format, selecting powerful word choice, mastering the spacing, constructing the title, painting the images through the senses, and relaying passion through poetic form.

Editing poetry looks a bit different than editing other types of writing as "poetic license" may allow for suspending conventional rules for capitalization and punctuation. Editing poetry certainly addresses spelling, but it may bypass conventional correctness for impact and effectiveness of formatting and style.

Publishing poetry usually involves the use of word processing, including selection of font, size of font, placement on the page, effective use of white space, and final impact on the reader's eye and the listener's ear. The flow of words on and off the page are particularly important in the final draft of a poem.

Children's Poetry—A Developmental Perspective

By viewing and analyzing a variety of poetic formats, children will quickly find that their poetry writing evidences growth over time. While young children may dabble with some uncertainty in this genre, older students are likely to show confidence and personality within their poems. A discussion of the assignments and the resulting student poetry provides guidelines for quality instruction as well as anticipation of and expectations for work products.

Young poets brainstorm word choice for their acrostic poem.

STUDENT SAMPLE 9.7 A second grader's poem.

Younger students love poetry but may appreciate a framework in developing their own poetic writing. Student Sample 9.7 reveals how a wise teacher provided a visual format for an initial poetry attempt by her second graders. Maria captures the texture, color, and shape of a Thanksgiving turkey, while Mitchell (Student Sample 9.8) provides further sensory words to describe a favorite holiday meal. The teacher preceded the writing with a model of the format and generated a whole class poem prior to releasing children to write their own. Free choice writing under the Thanksgiving theme included turkey, ham, cranberry, apples, and stuffing. The day before Thanksgiving all children shared their final products in the author's chair.

Another group of second graders responded positively to some initial guidance in writing poetry using the "If I Could . . . I Would" format. Student Sample 9.9 illustrates how this technique provided the impetus for a free verse poem by Sharon entitled "If I Could Change." Note how this young poet actually wrote a series of six poems as she had many ideas she desired to share. Also note how the use of word processing assisted Sharon with her final product.

Sixth-grade poetry radiates more confidence, voice, and risk taking. Maturity soars to a new level in Jason's "The Eagle" (Student Sample 9.10), which reflects the power of emotion in free verse format. Finally, "literary borrowing" from a Shel Silverstein poem provides the backdrop for Kendra's "The Day I Cleaned My Desk Out" (Student Sample 9.11). The objects in her desk form a poem that is an extension of her personality.

Some sixth graders still love the security of the formatted poem that provides the framework for their experiences and imaginations. The bio-poem format (a line-by-line description of the character's likes, fears, and hopes) provided Paul the opportunity to give poetic life to the Cowardly Lion from Frank Baum's *Wizard of Oz* (Student Sample 9.12). Paul utilizes the guidelines of the bio-poem to showcase his own understanding of this unique character.

STUDENT SAMPLE 9.8
A second grader's poem.

All of these poetry writing samples show the scope and promise of formats for young poets. Word choice, topic variety, and individual personalities shine through in each example. Once again, literature models, high teacher expectations, and the writing process gradually build toward success in poetry writing experiences.

Assessing Children's Poetry

Joan Glazer (1997) cites several basic criteria that distinguish great poems from good poems, both in published and novice poets:

- A fresh and original view of the subject is presented.
- Insight or emotion is shown or felt.
- Poetic devices are used effectively
- Language (word choice) is used effectively.
- The voice within the poem is distinctive and sincere.
- The poem follows the format of the prescribed poetic form including syllables, format, and/or shape (if applicable).

STUDENT SAMPLE 9.9
A second grader's poem.

IF I COULD CHANGE

If I could change,
I'd change into an elephant.
I'd be fat and hairy.

And if I were a ladybug,
I'd fly everywhere until I got tired.

If I were a giant,
I'd go to a city.
I'd smash the cookie place
and eat the cookies.

If I were a pear, or apple,
I'd be yummy and juicy.

If I were a rubber ducky,
I'd squeak until I felt water.

And if I were a tiger,
I'd roar a big rooaarr!!!

by Sharon

STUDENT SAMPLE 9.10
A second grader's poem.

The Eagle

The eagle soured up above.
It's wings spread out so gracefully.
A symbol of peace and love.
The nations symbol.
It cries out
We are the brave, the proud

STUDENT SAMPLE 9.11
A third grader's poem.

The Day I Cleaned My Desk Out

The dreaded day arrived and Mrs. Hessenflow proclaimed, "it's time to clean desk out." When I opened the lid I found....
12 paper clips
11 broken pencils
10 earring pieces
9 old assignments
8 notes from friends
7 wads of gums
6 candy wrappers
5 chewed erasers
4 past due library books
3 pairs of scissors
2 stale potatochips
1 lost retainer............ so that's where my retainer has been!

STUDENT SAMPLE 9.12 A third grader's poem.

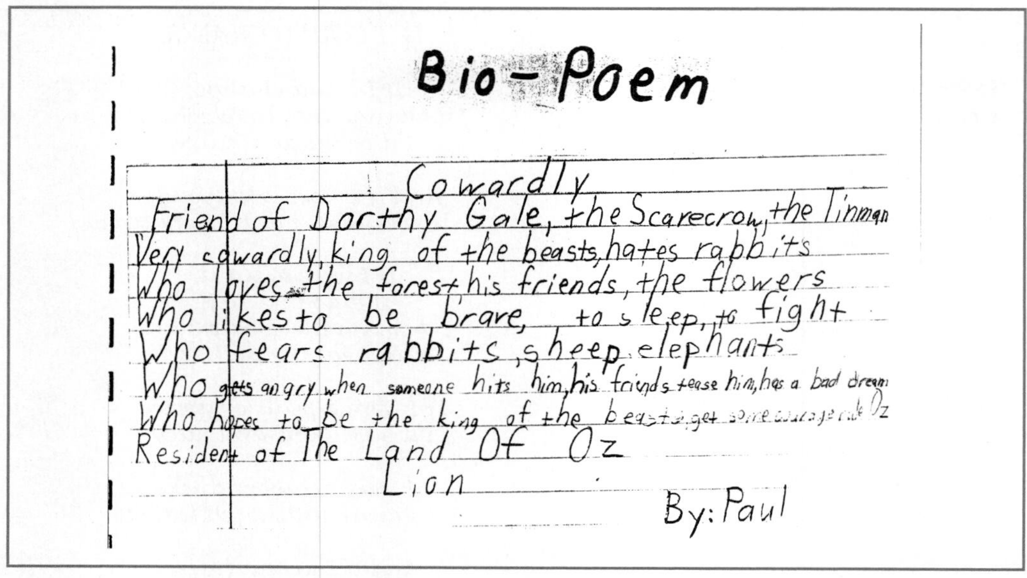

These criteria can assist in creating a broader list of expectations for most types of poetry that children will write. Creating a rubric or a checklist of criteria prior to a poetry writing aligns the ability of the poet with the selected developmental standards. Early attempts at writing poetry may focus on the prescribed format. Later attempts should focus on the importance of word choice. With more practice and instruction, the use of literary devices become an expectation. As comfort and confidence build, the voice and emotion of the poet will emerge. Keeping track and documenting poetry over time provides evidence of ongoing growth in the poetic realm. A poetry folder, file, or personal anthology provides an optimal way to house these personal poetic efforts. Writing across poetic types, following growing knowledge of poetic devices, and hearing the emergence of voice and personality in each poem provides motivation and satisfaction in poetic writing.

Visit the Companion Website at www.prenhall.com/hancock and gauge your understanding of Chapter 9 concepts with the self-assessments.

Closing Thoughts

The seemingly best writing is that which springs from personal experience and imagination. Narrative and poetic writing provides opportunities to share experience, emotions, and creative thoughts. With literature as a springboard, with a teacher who writes as a model, and with time and opportunities for practice, children gain confidence and evidence growth in the narrative and poetic writing genres. Mary Ann Hoberman (2002), children's book author and poet-recipient of the 2004 National Council of Teachers of English Poetry Award, offers the following observation:

> I think of our English language as a vast treasure, free for the taking . . . Each time you discover the perfect word for your purpose, each time you shape a fine sentence, each time you awaken a reader's imagination, you will feel fulfilled. . . . I wish you a wonderful lifetime of writing. (pp. 48–49)

With encouragement and gradual, modeled writing instruction, your students can be motivated to capture the essence of writing and the fulfillment that it brings to the mind and heart. Narrative and poetic text forms seem to be an effective springboard to early writing, building confidence for future writing experiences across a variety of writing genres.

References

Applebee, A. (1978). *The child's concept of story: Ages 2 to 17.* Chicago, IL: University of Chicago Press.

DiCamillo, K. (2005). Character is the engine. In Nancy L. Roser & Miriam Martinez (Eds.), *What a Character! Character study as a guide to literary meaning making in Grades K–8* (pp. 26–35). Newark, DE: International Reading Association.

Dressel, J. H. (1990). The effects of listening to and discussing different qualities of children's literature on the narrative writing of fifth graders. *Research in the Teaching of English, 24,* 397–414.

Fletcher, R. (2002). *Poetry matters: Writing a poem from the inside out.* New York: HarperCollins.

Glazer, J. (1997). *Introduction to children's literature* (2nd ed.). Upper Saddle River, NJ: Merrill/Prentice Hall.

Glover, M. K. (1999). *A garden of poets: Poetry writing in the elementary classroom.* Urbana, IL: National Council of Teachers of English.

Graves, D. H. (1989). *Experiment with fiction.* Portsmouth, NH: Heinemann.

Graves, D. H. (1992). *Explore poetry.* Portsmouth, NH: Heinemann.

Hancock, M. R. (2004). *Celebrating literature and response: Children, books, and teachers in K–8 classrooms* (2nd ed.). Upper Saddle River, NJ: Merrill/ Prentice Hall.

Heard, G. (1998). *Awakening the heart: Exploring poetry in elementary and middle school.* Portsmouth, NH: Heinemann.

Hoberman, M. A. (2002). Dear young poet. In P. B. Janeczko, *Seeing the blue between: Advice and inspiration for young poets* (pp. 48–49). Cambridge, MA: Candlewick.

Livingston, M. C. (1990). *Climb into the bell tower.* New York: Harper & Row

Martinez, M. G., & Roser, N. L. (2005). Students developing understanding of character. In N. L. Roser & M. G. Martinez (Eds.), *What a character! Character study as a guide to literary meaning making in Grades K–8* (pp. 6–12). Newark, DE: International Reading Association.

McClure, A., Harrison, P., & Reed, S. (1990). *Sunrises and songs: Reading and writing poetry in an elementary language classroom.* Portsmouth, NH: Heinemann.

Roser, N. L, & Martinez, M. G. (2005). *What a character! Character study as a guide to literary meaning making in Grades K–8.* Newark, DE: International Reading Association.

Tompkins, G. E. (2005). *Language arts: Patterns of practice* (6th ed.). Upper Saddle River, NJ: Merrill/ Prentice Hall.

Children's Books Cited

Avi (2002). *Crispin: The Cross of lead.* New York: Hyperion

Aylesworth, Jim (2001). *The burger and the hot dog.* Illus. by Stephen Gammell. New York: Atheneum.

Clements, Andrew (1996). *Frindle.* Illus. by Brian Selznick. New York: Simon & Schuster.

Cooney, Barbera (1982). *Miss Rumphius.* New York: Viking.

Cooper, Susan (1993). *The boggart.* New York: McElderry.

Cullinan, Bernice E. (Ed.) (1996). *A jar of tiny stars: Poems by NCTE award-winning poets.* Honesdale, PA: Wordsong/Boyds Mills Press & National Council of Teachers of English.

DiCamillo, Kate (2000). *Because of Winn-Dixie.* Cambridge, MA: Candlewick.

DiCamillo, Kate (2003). *The tale of Despereaux.* Illus. by Timothy Basil Ering. Cambridge, MA: Candlewick.

Florian, Douglas (1998). *Insectlopedia.* San Diego: Harcourt Brace.

Florian, Douglas (2002). *Summersaults.* New York: Greenwillow.

Heard, Georgia (Selector) (2002). *This place I know: Poems of comfort.* Illus. by 18 renowned illustrators. Cambridge, MA: Candlewick.

Henkes, Kevin (2004). *Kitten's first full moon.* New York: Greenwillow.

Janeczko, Paul B. (2005). *A kick in the head: An everyday guide to poetic forms.* Cambridge, MA: Candlewick Press.

Kennedy, X. J. (2002). *Exploding gravy: Poems to make you laugh.* Illus. by Joy Allen. Boston: Little, Brown.

Lear, Edward (1991). *The owl and the pussycat.* Illus. by Jan Brett. New York: Putnam.

Naylor, Phyllis Reynolds (1996). *The bomb in the Bessledorf bus depot.* New York: Atheneum.

O'Shell, Marcia (1988). *Alphabet Annie announces an all-American album.* New York: Houghton Mifflin.

Paterson, Katherine (1991). *Lyddie.* New York: Lodestar.

Polacco, Patricia (1990). *Thundercake.* New York: Philomel.

Prelutsky, Jack (2002). *Scranimals.* New York: Scholastic.

Rylant, Cynthia (1982). *When I was young in the mountains.* Illus. by Diane Goode. New York: Dutton.

Schertle, Alice (1996). *Keepers.* Illus. by Ted Rand. New York: Lothrop, Lee & Shepard.

Spinelli, Jerry (1990). *Maniac Magee.* New York: HarperCollins.

Silverstein, Shel (1996). *Falling up.* New York: HarperCollins.

Soto, Gary (1997). *Snapshots from the wedding.* Illus. by Stephanie Garcia. New York: Putnam.

Tolstoy, Aleksei (1998). *The gigantic turnip.* Illus. by Niamh Shartey. Brooklyn, NY: Barefoot Books.

Williams, Vera B. (1982). *A chair for my mother.* New York: Greenwillow.

Wong, Janet (2002). *You have to write.* Illus. by Teresa Flavin. New York: McElderry.

Woodson, Jacqueline (1997). *We had a picnic this Sunday past.* Illus. by Diane Greenseid. New York: Hyperion.

Chapter 10

EXPOSITORY WRITING

Sharing Information in a Literary Mode

No one noticed that the church bells were tolling more often than usual to announce one death, then another. . . . No one knew that a killer was already moving through their streets with them, an invisible stalker that would go house to house until it had touched everyone, rich or poor, in some terrible way.

FROM *AN AMERICAN PLAGUE* BY JIM MURPHY

Expository writing is a means of sharing information with readers, providing a dramatic focus on lesser-known topics from the ever-evolving broad world of facts. The best of expository texts is typified by powerful writing, expressive voice, and sometimes specialized vocabulary steering engaged readers toward this increasingly popular genre. The information shared through expository trade books might include a harrowing approach and description of a long-forgotten epidemic described in Jim Murphy's *An American Plague: The True and Terrifying Story of the Yellow Fever Epidemic of 1793*. It might include a discussion of the similarities and differences between alligators and crocodiles, as articulated by Seymour Simon in *Crocodiles and Alligators*. Informational text might focus on the meteorological causes and devastating effects of the Gulf Coast hurricanes as described in Patricia Lauber's *Hurricane: Earth's Mightiest Storms*. Children have a natural affinity for information that might begin with an interest in natural disasters, a curiosity for spiders, or an appreciation for art or ballet. Expository text provides a surprisingly motivating tool to attract readers and writers to their craft through the power and lure of information.

Common myths surround nonfiction writing, which has unjustifiably been characterized as dry, impersonal, long, encyclopedia-like, and formula-driven (Harvey, 1998). Teachers need to debunk these myths. Nonfiction can move beyond the transmittal of information and become energetic, action-filled, and passionate. This chapter attempts to bring life and energy to expository writing for both teachers and students. Writing will always be hard work, but literary models of quality nonfiction writing provide prototypes and exemplary patterns while setting expectations higher than they have been set in the past. Teachers are constantly growing in their knowledge of and ability to teach expository writing. Guidelines in this chapter will make the task of teaching nonfiction writing more comfortable, more literary, and more productive and satisfying for both teachers as sharers of expository models and students as writers of expository text.

Most children encounter expository writing for the first time when asked to do a "report," perhaps on an animal, a famous person, or a state. But expository writing extends far beyond this archaic parameter. Informational writing may also include personal notes or business letters, and autobiographical or biographical vignettes. For many years, elementary teachers shied away from all expository text—in both reading and writing—assuming that the story form was the favorite venue and level of accomplishment of young readers and writers (Duke, 2000). Researchers and practitioners have provided intriguing input on the value and utilization of expository text and writing with primary students (Duthie, 1996; Guillaume, 1998; Palmer & Stewart, 2003; Yopp & Yopp, 2000), and intermediate and middle-level students (Graves, 1989; Hoyt, 2002; Kristo & Bamford, 2004). This chapter highlights a fresh view of the literary model and its impact on expository writing. By presenting quality nonfiction trade books as models of literary writing, by discerning and graphically representing their text structure, by showcasing the literary elements of strong nonfiction writing, and by building an awareness of varied access features, teachers provide higher expectations and introduce replicable prototypes that ensure ongoing growth and success in the expository realm.

The most effective way to learn about expository writing is to witness it modeled in children's informational books. These books also lead apprentice writers toward an understanding of expository text structure and the organization of informational writing. The foundation of this chapter is the use of quality nonfiction literature for children as a model, framework, and prototype for teaching expository writing to emerging informational authors.

Objectives

- To showcase the importance of reading aloud nonfiction as students internalize expository text structure.
- To build an awareness of the literature model of the five types of expository text structure.
- To model incorporating the elements of literary nonfiction in writing from a world of facts.

- To build an awareness of the possible access features to enhance the visual presentation of expository writing.
- To model the underpinnings of the inquiry process by guiding primary grade apprentices into the nonfiction realm.
- To provide a framework for the inquiry process of independent topic selection, resource collection, information gathering, literary writing, selection of visual access features, and sound presentation of information with intermediate and middle-level students.

Reading Aloud Nonfiction

Because children typically are less familiar with how expository reading and writing "work," reading informational nonfiction should be a mandatory precursor to attempting to write expository text (Raphael, Kirschner, & Englert, 1988). Literature serves as an ideal model of text structure and a framework for writing. Anyone who still believes the notion that nonfiction reading and writing are boring has not witnessed the increasing quality of published trade books that not only inform, but challenge, motivate, and entice the reader to read more about a subject.

Most recommendations for reading fiction aloud apply to reading nonfiction aloud. But there are several points to remember, as suggested by Doiron (1994):

- Begin with nonfiction books that you enjoy. As with any read-aloud, your own investment and enthusiasm for a nonfiction read-aloud are quickly detected by students. You might select a title related to a content area topic, an award-winning recommendation, or a book that inspires response on a timely area of interest.
- Read the book before reading it aloud. Being familiar with the content and preparing ways to make the read-aloud effective and interesting are prerequisites for the nonfiction read-aloud.
- Provide background information on the topic. This allows students to activate prior knowledge or devise questions for further inquiry. Sharing an artifact or a news story, conducting an experiment, or dramatizing a historical event pave the way to a meaningful informational read-aloud.
- Share the "great gift of the genre" (Vardell & Copland, 1992). Nonfiction has the power to develop critical thinking as students become active listeners as they process and challenge new information. The discussion surrounding nonfiction involves higher-level thinking and stimulates further inquiry.
- Highlight the authors, illustrators, and book features of nonfiction. Comment on the date of publication for accuracy and the research background of the writer as authority. Discuss the format, organization, and access features of the textual layout.
- Read only portions of nonfiction. Unlike narrative, which generally needs to be read aloud cover to cover, nonfiction permits the reading of a single chapter, a brief selection, or several short excerpts from the book. Just enough to capture the reader's desire to connect with the book seems to be the right recipe for informational text.
- Read a variety of nonfiction—from science to history, from the arts to current events. Nonfiction is not only found in literature. It can assume many forms and formats that deserve to be shared—from a newspaper or magazine article to a favorite recipe or a simple or complex set of directions.
- Showcase quality writing in nonfiction text. Pointing out techniques of good writing that move nonfiction from boring to energized forms an important

The Teacher Prep Web site will help you become a better teacher by linking you to classroom videos, student artifacts, teaching strategies, lesson plans, relevant education leadership articles, and practical information on licensing, creating a portfolio, implementing standards, and being successful in field experiences. Visit this resource at www.prenhall.com/teacherprep.

lesson as students transition from reading expository text to writing it. Discovering the elements of strong nonfiction writing identifies those traits to be carried out in their own informational organization and text.

Reading a balance of both narrative and expository text helps children experience two ways of knowing how literature works (Crook & Lehman, 1991). Caswell and Duke (1998) identified nonnarrative writing as a "way in" to the world of literacy for emergent readers. "More experience with nonnarrative texts in the early grades may help mitigate the difficulties many students encounter with these texts later in schooling" (p. 108). As children internalize the style, language, and organization of nonfiction, they are better prepared to identify and follow expository text structure in their own informational writing.

Expository Text Structure

When authors write to share information, they organize different kinds of topics in different ways. These expository text structures provide the framework for both reading and writing expository text with children (McGee & Richgels, 1985; Moss, 2004; Piccolo, 1987). There are five commonly used structures in the elementary and middle school include: (a) description; (b) sequence; (c) comparison and contrast; (d) cause and effect; and (e) problem and solution (Tompkins, 2004). Stretching across curricular areas and among diverse topics, these patterns consistently occur and provide a structured means for gathering or sharing information in a meaningful way.

Description

A writer can structure expository writing by describing the particular characteristics, examples, or features of a topic—for example, marsupials, the Australian outback, earthquakes, a planet, New York City, China, or the space shuttle. Gail Gibbons does a masterful job of description in *The Honey Makers* and *Soaring with the Wind: The Bald Eagle.* A descriptive paragraph on manatees written by a second-grade student reflects the beginnings of expository writing (Student Sample 10.1) A list of facts about manatees expands to sentences that describe the age, predators, habitat, size and shape, and migration of this creature.

Alphabet books, often seen as only a primary writing venue, provide an ideal format for descriptive writing. The Literature Cluster on page 295 provides a list of alphabet books to inspire both text and format for an alphabetical book on animals, states, countries, or plants. While much of Keeley's's third-grade Kansas ABC book (Student Sample 10.2) comes from prior knowledge, she has read and researched lesser-known facts to include new information for more challenging letters.

Sequence

An expository writer might share a topic through a numerical or chronological list of facts. Directions, step-by-step instructions, historical events, or biographical facts can be shared sequentially. For example, a writer may tell how to construct a home aquarium, sequence the accomplishments of U.S. presidents, or share the major events in the life of Lou Gehrig. Jim Murphy shares sequenced, historical events in *The Great Fire* and *Blizzard* while Diane Stanley chronicles the lives of *Leonardo daVinci* and *Saladin: Noble Prince of Islam.* Both biographical information and chronological data blend logically and seamlessly into the sequential text structure format.

STUDENT SAMPLE 10.1 Second grader's expository writing.

I learned a lot of things about
manatees. I learnd that they can
live to 50 to 60. I also learned that
manatees can only stay under
water for 5 minutes. I also
learnd that alligators and sharks
awont atack all the time on
manatees. I also learnd that
boats can kill manatees. I
learnd they live in Florida.
Their skin is smooth and soft.
Their legs are small. Their body
is shaped like a pear. Their
body is all gray with wiskers
on its chin. I also learnd
that they move to wormer
waters in the winter.

Name: Lauren
Grade: 2

Literature Cluster

ALPHABET BOOKS FOR EARLY INFORMATIONAL WRITING

Cheney, L. (2004). *A is for Abigail: An almanac of amazing American women*. Illus. by Robin Preiss Glasser. New York: Simon & Schuster.

Chin-Lee, C. (1997). *A is for Asia*. New York: Orchard.

Ehlert, L. (1989). *Eating the alphabet: Fruits and vegetables from A to Z*. New York: San Diego: Harcourt Brace.

Grodin, E. (2004). *D is for democracy: A citizen's alphabet*. Illus. by Victor Juhasz. Chelsea, MI: Sleeping Bear Press.

Jordan, M., & Jordan, T. (1996). *Amazon alphabet*. New York: Kingfisher.

Knowlton, J. (1988). *Geography from A to Z: A picture glossary*. New York: HarperCollins.

Kratter, Paul (2004). *The living rain forest: An animal alphabet*. Watertown, MA: Charlesbridge.

McCurdy, M. (1998). *The sailor's alphabet*. Boston: Houghton Mifflin.

McPhail, D. (1989). *Animals A to Z*. New York: Scholastic.

Mullins, P. (1993). *V for vanishing: An alphabet of endangered animals*. New York: HarperCollins.

Onyefulu, I (1993). *A is for Africa*. New York: Cobblehill.

Palotta, J. (1986). *The icky bug alphabet book*. Watertown, MA: Charlesbridge.

Rice, J. (1990). *Cowboy alphabet*. Gretna, LA: Pelican.

Rose, D. L. (2000). *Into the A, B, Sea*. Illus by Steve Jenkins. New York: Scholastic.

Wargin, K. J. (2004). *M is for melody: A music alphabet*. Illus. by Katherine Larson. Chelsea, MI: Sleeping Bear Press.

Wormell, C. (2004). *Teeth, tails, & tentacles: An animal counting book*. Philadelphia: Running Press.

STUDENT SAMPLE 10.2 Third grader's ABC expository writing.

Comparison and Contrast

When writers use a compare/contrast format for expository writing, they explain the similarities and differences between two or more things. Topics for comparison (How are they alike?) and contrast (How are they different?) include people, places, animals, historical events, or natural phenomenon. For example, a writer may compare and contrast hurricanes and tornadoes, grizzly bears and koalas, or the Greeks and the Romans. Seymour Simon compares and contrasts celestial bodies in the solar system in *The Universe* while David Macauley compares mechanical operations in *The New Way Things Work.* Comparative and contrasting paragraphs provide excellent practice in pointing out similarities and differences between two or more people, places, or things.

Cause and Effect

Using this structure, an expository writer explains the causes and ultimate effects of scientific phenomenon or historical events. For example, writers may discuss why leaves change color, the tragedy of the vanishing ozone layer, or the causes and implications of the Great Depression. Patricia Lauber examines nature's devastation through a cause and effect structure in *Flood: Wrestling with the Mississippi,* while Laurence Pringle explains environmental rejuvenation in *Fire in the Forest: A Cycle of Growth and Renewal.* Paragraphs of cause and effect capture higher level thinking through the writing process.

Problem and Solution

A writer can explore an expository topic by stating a problem and providing probable solutions to it. For example, the oil spills in the Alaskan waterway, global warming, or feeding the growing world population are topics aligned with this text structure. Dorothy Henshaw Patent's *Children Save the Rain Forest* and Andrea Warren's *Orphan Train Rider:*

One Boy's True Story explain scientific and historical problems that resulted in useful solutions. Inventions, for example, might provide ideal formats for writing paragraphs of problem and solution. Informational or biographical books provide the foundational background for composing this higher-level composition.

Combination Text Structure

In addition to these five basic expository text structures, writers may also combine more than one text structure to share information. Laurence Pringle both describes and sequences in *Extraordinary Life: The Story of a Monarch Butterfly* and Jennifer Armstrong describes, chronicles, and explains the incredible challenge encountered by *Shipwreck at the Bottom of the World: The Extraordinary True Story of Shackleton and the Endurance* and the ultimate escape of its crew from its Antarctic imprisonment.

Graphic organizers which provide visual formats to record information, for each of the five expository text structures are presented in Figure 10.1. They provide several

FIGURE 10.1 Graphic organizers for the five expository text structures.

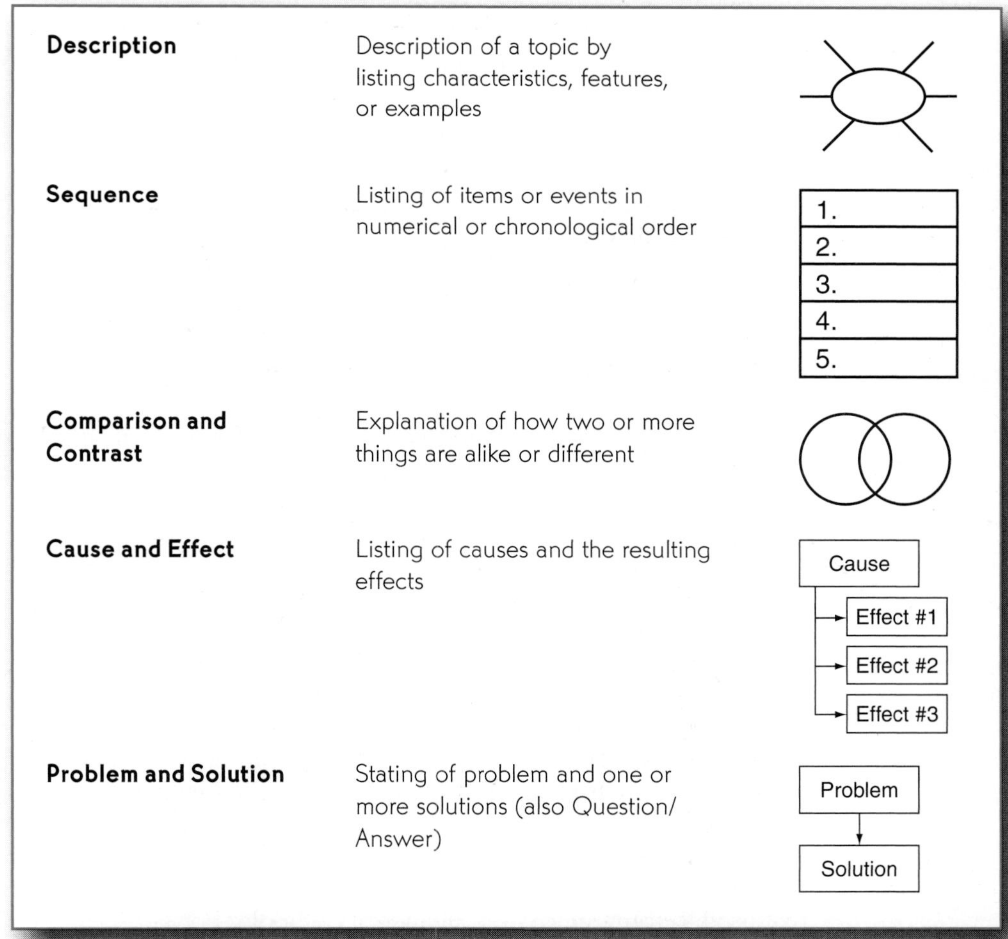

Source: Gail E. Tompkins, Language Arts: Patterns in Practice, *6th ed. © 2005. Adapted by permission of Pearson Education, Inc., Upper Saddle River, NJ.*

organizational uses for both reading and writing. The graphic organizers can be used for recording or brainstorming researched information for student-generated expository text. Animal reports, for example, readily fit into the descriptive format as modeled by Jim Arnosky's *All About Turtles*. A biographical account of a famous American might fit into the sequential format of David Adler's *Lou Gehrig: The Luckiest Man*. A scientific compare/contrast of high and low weather fronts might mirror Jack Challoner's *Hurricane and Tornado*. The causes and effects of the water cycle might pattern with the format of Betsy Maestro's *Why Do Leaves Change Color?* A problem/solution structure from Joseph Wallace's *The Lightbulb* might provide the framework for a report on Henry Ford's invention of the automobile. Quality literature provides the framework, pattern, and organizational scheme for turning facts into well-written texts.

The student Venn diagram based on comparing and contrasting the ancient city-states of Sparta and Athens, for example, leads to the organization of a expository report showcasing similarities and differences (Student Sample 10.3). As readers select an appropriate text structure for delivering their own self-selected topic or information to their audience, the text structure graphic organizer model further helps them internalize their information in a meaningful format as they attempt to replicate the text structure in their own writing. The graphic organizer provides the framework or outline for the related written text. While expository text structure provides a framework for the beginnings of an informational report, the literary elements of expository text and techniques for enhancing informational formats (e.g., dynamic titles, effective word choice, sentence flow, compelling voice) provide more ways to entice the reader of a nonfiction report by incorporating these elements of nonfiction literature.

The Literature Cluster on page 300 presents an extensive list of quality books that assume and model the five expository text structures. As teachers read these (or portions of them) aloud, students might chart new information into the selected web formats suggested above helping readers and writers internalize the options of expository text structure.

Creating Literary Nonfiction from Factual Information

Literary nonfiction delivers informational text written in a style that incorporates the magic of language and characteristics of quality narrative text while effectively engaging the reader in factual information in both the aesthetic and efferent realms. In other words, literary nonfiction transfers facts through a creative writing style and captures the reader's curiosity and personal interaction with the text. A vivid example of literary nonfiction is Louise Borden and Mary Kay Kroeger's *Fly High! The Story of Bessie Coleman*. Written in a free verse format, simple, carefully selected words flow into sentences that range between the short and direct to the long and involved. Born in rural Texas in 1892, Bessie loved school, yet she was forced to work in the cotton fields, making her even more determined to be somebody when she grew up—the first African American woman to earn a pilot's license. The story is filled not only with facts but with emotion as readers feel admiration reading about Bessie's dedication to her goal and sadness learning about her early death. What the reader experiences is fact woven with an emotional thread that engages the reader's mind (efferent) and heart (aesthetic). This type of writing sets high expectations for students today and moves them away from the dull, encyclopedic entries that used to form the basis of elementary school reports.

As children become more aware readers of literary nonfiction, they focus more on both the language and the writing techniques of quality authors, transfering these nonfiction elements to their own expository writing (Hancock, 2004). The writing power of

STUDENT SAMPLE 10.3 Sixth grader's comparison/contrast graphic organizer and expository essay.

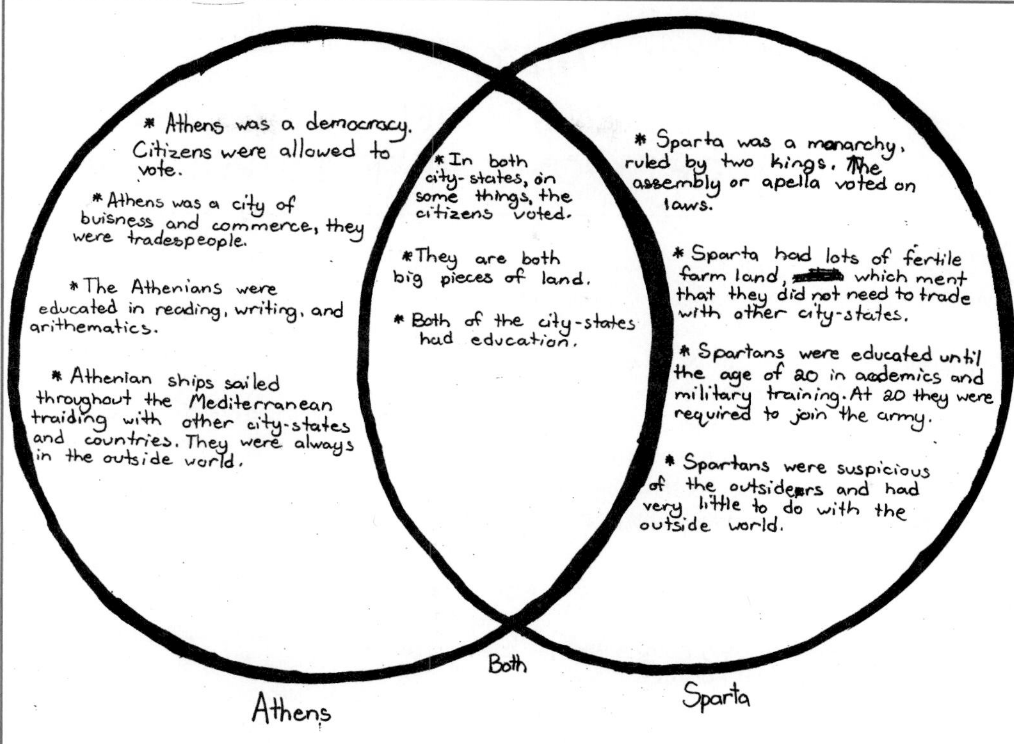

ATHENS & SPARTA

City-states in Ancient Greece are like small countries. They were made small enough so that every citizen would know each other. Greeks made city-states because Greece was so mountainous that they could not travel to different places. They made small city states for groups of people. Athens and Sparta were the most important city-states. There aren't many things Athens and Sparta have in common, but they are two very different places.

In Athens and Sparta the citizens would vote the majority of the time. Both of them are very large pieces of land. The city-states had education too, but learned many different things. Athens and Sparta do have similarities, but few.

Athens was a democracy. The citizens there were allowed to vote. Sparta was a monarchy, ruled by two kings. The assembly or apella voted on laws. Athens was a city of business and commerce, they were trades people. They went to different places to trade with each other. Sparta had a lot of fertile farmland, which meant that they didn't have a reason to trade with other city-states. The Athenians were educated in reading, writing, and arithmetic. They valued their knowledge. Spartans were educated until the age of twenty in academics and military training. At twenty they were required to got to the army. They had to have very strong bodies. Athenian ships sailed throughout the Mediterranean trading with other city-states and countries. They were in the outside world. Spartans were suspicious of the outsiders and had very little to do with the outside world.

Athens and Sparta as you read are very important, but in their own way. They had different ways of doing things. The life in Greece is so different to America. It is interesting to learn what it would be like.

By: Brenna

CHILDREN'S NONFICTION AS A MODEL OF EXPOSITORY TEXT STRUCTURE

Description

Arnosky, Jim (2000). *A manatee morning.* New York: Simon & Schuster.

Brandenburg, Jim (1996). *Scruffy: A wolf finds his place in the pack.* New York: Walker.

Darling, Kathy (1997). *Chameleons on location.* Photographs by Tara Darling. New York: Lothrop, Lee & Shepard.

Gibbons, Gail (1998). *Penguins!* New York: Holiday House.

Halls, Kelly Milner (2004). *Albino animals.* Plain City, OH: Darby Creek Publishers.

Osborne, Mary Pope (1996). *One world, many religions.* New York: Knopf.

Patent, Dorothy Hinshaw (1997). *Flashy fantastic rain forest frogs.* Illus by K. J. Jubb. New York: Walker.

Penny, Malcolm (1997). *How bats "see" in the dark.* New York: Benchmark.

Sis, Peter (2004). *The train of states.* New York: Greenwillow.

Swinburne, S. R. (1999). *Unbeatable beaks.* Illus. by J. Paley. New York: Holt.

West, D. C., & West, J. M. (2000). *Uncle Sam and Old Glory.* Woodcuts by C. Manson. New York: Atheneum.

Sequence

Adler, David (1997). *Lou Gehrig: The luckiest man.* Illus. by T. Widener. San Diego: Harcourt Brace.

Ammon, Richard (2000). *An Amish year.* Illus. by P. Patrick. New York: Atheneum.

Bial, Raymond (1997). *Where Lincoln walked.* New York: Walker.

Blumberg, Rhoda (2004). *York's adventures with Lewis and Clark: An African American's part in the great expedition.* New York: HarperCollins.

Cowley, Joy (1999). *Red-eyed tree frog.* Photographs by N. Bishop. New York: Scholastic.

Locker, Thomas (1995). *Sky tree.* New York: HarperCollins.

Matthews, Tom L. (1998). *Light shining through the mist.* Washington, DC: National Geographic.

McWhorter, Diane (2004). *A dream of freedom: The civil rights movement from 1954–1968.* New York: Scholastic.

O'Conner, Jane (2004). *If the walls could talk: Family life at the White House.* Illus. by Gary Hovland. New York: Simon & Schuster.

Schmandt-Besserat, Denise (1999). *The history of counting.* Illus. by M. Hays. New York: Morrow.

Smith, Roland (1996). *Journey of the red wolf.* New York: Cobblehill/Dutton.

Compare and Contrast

Budhos, Marina (1999). *Conversations with immigrant teenagers.* New York: Holt.

Challoner, Jack (2000). *Hurricane & tornado.* New York: Dorling Kindersley.

Crews, Nina (1999). *A high, low, near, far, loud, quiet story.* New York: Greenwillow.

Dewey, Jennifer Owings (1991). *A night and day in the desert.* New York: Little, Brown.

Harness, Cheryl (2004). *Franklin & Eleanor.* New York: Dutton.

King, Elizabeth (1992). *Chile fever: Celebration of peppers.* New York: Dutton.

Lankford, Mary D. (1998). *Dominoes around the world.* Illus. by K. Dugan. New York: Morrow.

Lauber, Patricia (1999). *What you never knew about fingers, forks, & chopsticks.* Illus. by J. Manders. New York: Simon & Schuster.

Markle, Sandra (2004). *Outside and inside killer bees.* New York: Walker.

Markle, Sandra (2004). *Spiders: Biggest! Littlest.* Photographs by Simon Pollard. Horesdale, PA: Boyds Mills Press.

McKissack, P. C., & McKissack, F. L. (1994). *Christmas in the big house, Christmas in the quarters.* Illus. by John Thompson. New York: Scholastic.

McMillan, Bruce (1995). *Puffins climb, penguins rhyme.* New York: Gulliver.

Patent, Dorothy Henshaw (1994). *Deer and elk.* Photographs by William Munoz. New York: Clarion.

Pearce, Q. L. (1997). *Why is a frog not a toad?* Illus. by Ron Mazellan. Los Angeles, CA: Lowell.

Schanzer, Rosalyn (2004). *George vs. George: The American Revolution seen from both sides.* Washington, DC: National Geographic.

Scott, Elaine (2004). *Poles apart: Why penguins and polar bears will never be neighbors.* New York: Viking.

Singer, Marilyn (2000). *On the same day in March: A tour of the world's weather.* Illus. by F. Lessac. New York: HarperCollins.

Cause and Effect

Berger, M., & Berger, G. (1998). *Why don't haircuts hurt?* Illus. by K. Barnes. New York: Scholastic.

Ferrie, Richard (1999). *The world turned upside down.* New York: Holiday House.

Kramer, Stephen (1997). *Eye of the storm: Chasing storms with Warren Faidley.* Photographs by Warren Faidley. New York: Putnam.

Martin, Terry (1996). *Why do sunflowers face the sun?* New York: Dorling Kindersley.

Miller, Debbie (1997). *Disappearing lake: Nature's magic in Denali National Park.* Illus. by Jon Van Zyle. New York: Walker.

Murphy, Jim (2000). *Blizzard: The storm that changed America.* New York: Scholastic.

Pfeffer, Wendy (1997). *A log's life.* Illus. by R. Brickman. New York: Simon & Schuster.

Platt, Richard (1999). *Castle diary: The journal of Tobias Burgess, page.* Illus. by Chris Riddell. Cambridge, MA: Candlewick.

Simon, Seymour (1997). *Lightning.* New York: Morrow Junior Books.

Simon, Seymour (1999).*Tornadoes.* New York: Morrow Junior Books.

Tunnell, Michael O. & Chilcoat, George W. (1996). *The children of Topaz: The story of a Japanese-American internment camp.* New York: Holiday House.

Problem and Solution

Freedman, Russell (1994). *Kids at work.* New York: Clarion.

Fry, Annette R. (1994). *The orphan trains.* New York: New Discovery Books.

Harness, Cheryl (1995). *The amazing impossible Erie Canal.* New York: Simon & Schuster.

Kuhn, Betsy (1999). *Angels of mercy: The army nurses of World War II.* New York: Atheneum.

Lerner, Carol (1998). *Backyard garden.* New York: Morrow.

Mallory, Kenneth (1998). *A home by the sea: Protecting coastal wildlife.* San Diego: Harcourt Brace.

Patent, Dorothy Henshaw (1996). *Children save the rainforest.* Photographs by D. Perlman. New York: Cobblehill/Dutton.

Reinhard, Johan (1999). *Discovering the Inca ice maiden.* Photographs by J. Reinhard & S. Alvarez. Washington, DC: National Geographic Society.

Robinson, Sharon (2004). *Promises to keep: How Jackie Robinson changed America.* New York: Scholastic.

Stanley, Jerry (1996). *Children of the dust bowl: The story of the school at Weedpatch Camp.* New York: Crown.

Swain, Gwenyth (1999). *Carrying.* (Small World series). Minneapolis, MN: Carolrhoda.

Thimmesh, Catherine (2000). *Girls think of everything: Stories of ingenious Inventions by women.* Illus. by M. Sweet. Boston: Houghton Mifflin.

Combination

Armstrong, Jennifer (1998). *Shipwreck at the bottom of the world. The extraordinary true story of Shackleton and the Endurance.* New York: Crown. (Description; Sequence; Problem/solution)

George, Lindsay B. (1999). *Around the world: Who's been here?* New York: Greenwillow. (Sequence; Description)

Goodman, Susan E. (2000). *Ultimate field trip 4: A week in the 1800s.* Photographs by M. J. Doolittle. New York: Atheneum.

Harness, Cheryl (1998). *Ghosts of the White House.* New York: Simon & Schuster. (Description; Sequence)

Hooper, Meredith (1998). *The drop in my drink.* Illus. by C. Coady. New York: Viking. (Cause/effect; Sequence)

Lauber, Patricia (1996). *Hurricanes: Earth's mightiest storms.* New York: Scholastic. (Description; Cause/effect)

Lewin, Ted (1996). *Market.* New York: Lothrop, Lee & Shepard. (Compare/contrast; Description)

Miller, Debbie S. (1994). *A caribou journey.* Illus. by Jon Van Zyle. Boston: Little, Brown. (Sequence; Description)

Sandler, Martin (1996). *Inventors.* New York: HarperCollins. (Cause/effect; Problem/solution)

Williams, Jean K. (1996). *The Amish.* New York: Franklin Watts. (Description; Problem/solution) nonfiction can be modeled by teachers who identify these nonfiction elements, discuss literary examples, and offer suggestions to evolving nonfiction writers in the classroom.

Literary Nonfiction Techniques

The following literary nonfiction techniques provide guidelines for the young nonfiction writer. While they should be featured one at a time, several techniques can eventually be showcased and blended into nonfiction writing. As children grow in their experiences with nonfiction, more aspects of literary nonfiction become the means of expanding expository writing.

Dynamic Titles. The best expository writers are skilled in drawing readers into a web of information that is enhanced by the creative use of enticing titles, both of a book (or project) and its chapters (or sections). Doug Wechsler's *Bizarre Birds* contains a chapter titled "Strange Looks" that is followed by unique subtitles of "Gaudy Feathers" and "Hairless Hairdos." Another chapter is called "Birds Eat What?" with subtitles of "Candlelight Dinners" and "Bottomless Pits." Encouraging children to notice the intriguing titles of nonfiction will broaden their understanding of audience appeal and meaningful organization in expository text.

Invested Interest in the Topic. If an author of nonfiction conveys an underlying reason for extensive investigation, the reader is exposed to a commitment to the research process and a passion for the topic. As children self-select topics for research, they need to realize the commitment and sense of inquiry that accompanies genuine research. Children quickly learn that they write best about what they know or about topics in which they have a deep interest. Children who bring passion to the topic of their research will bring excitement to their writing. A good literature model for students to follow is Ted Lewin and Betsy Lewin's *Gorilla Walk,* which describes the authors' own real-life adventures in the forests of Uganda, meeting the mountain gorilla face to face. Spending much of their lives intrigued by gorillas, they were able to share an informative experience with their readers.

Meaningful Focus. Strong nonfiction authors know how to limit or organize their topics to bring focused information to the reader. Instead of telling readers everything about the Gold Rush, Jerry Stanley focuses on the impact of a single African American—Mifflin Gibbs—on the Gold Rush, creating an absorbing civil rights story in *Hurry Freedom: African Americans in Gold Rush California*. Too often children choose a topic that is too broad—Kansas, China, weather, seasons. Too much information can overwhelm and discourage young writers. Focusing on a particular aspect of Kansas (forts), a city in China (Beijing), a weather phenomenon (tornadoes), or a single season (winter) limits the research quest and results in effective, targeted information.

Effective Word Choice. The magic of language in literary nonfiction breathes life into facts as well-chosen words blend into visual images and memorable expository text. Jonathan London's *Panther: Shadow of the Swamp* reveals how the power of words generate description and action. "The blinding heat of summer quivers above the swamp. A long, thick tail twitches in the saw grass. A shadow flows. It is panther." Rich, carefully chosen nouns, adjectives, and verbs bring to life facts and images related to the panther. Teachers need to surround children with this type of quality literature and to point out effective word choice within an expository context. These models of powerful language eventually bring a spark to the informational writing of students, particularly during revisions.

Fresh Vocabulary. The presentation of distinctive vocabulary based on sound research and defining words within the context of writing provides a memorable way to share information with the readers. George Ancona's *Charro: The Mexican Cowboy* embeds Spanish words such as *hacienda, mariachis,* and *sombrero* in the context of English informational text. The use of the words in context assists in internalizing the definitions of new words. When a child writes a report on alligators or hurricanes or ostriches, the unique vocabulary specific to the topic needs to be strategically incorporated into the text to both define and inform. Italicizing or boldfacing can highlight the use of these terms for the reader, drawing special attention to new terminology that expands understanding of the topic.

Sentence Flow. Expository writing requires the use of a variety of sentence patterns to engage the reader and to capture the aesthetic tone of the information. In Anne Rockwell's simple primary trade book, *One Bean,* the author skillfully expands sentences as the book evolves, mirroring the growth of a bean from seed to plant. The first sentences of the book are simply stated: "I had one bean. It was dry and smooth and hard." As the seed grows into a blossoming plant, Rockwell expands sentences: "The buds burst open and lots of white flowers blossomed among the green, green leaves." Variety of sentences in informational writing allows readers to process and reflect on evolving information. The teacher who points this out in literature becomes a model for writing and for showing students how short statements as well as long and informative ones serve a purpose in expository writing.

Compelling Voice. The voice of the author provides authority and strength to the facts and convinces readers about the authenticity of the topic itself. Ruby Bridges's *Through My Eyes* captures the authentic voice of the author who as a six-year-old student was isolated despite segregation orders at William Franz Elementary School in New Orleans in 1960. Ruby offers her reflections as a child forced to eat lunch alone:

> It was a lonely time . . . As time went on, I couldn't eat . . . I began hiding my uneaten sandwiches in a storage cabinet in the classroom. I poured my carton of milk into the big jar of paste we had in the room . . . After that she [Mrs. Henry] usually ate with me so I wouldn't be lonely. (p. 48)

The use of direct quotations in biography or real voices in face-to-face interviews brings events and people to life. As children grow as expository writers, the technique of capturing the compelling voice of an authentic person brings information to life.

Inviting Leads. A well-written introduction or opening paragraph of a nonfiction book or an expository report immediately captures the curiosity of readers and entices them to want to know more about a topic. Jim Arnosky's *All About Turtles* begins with a series of compelling questions to be answered as the text unfolds. "Have you ever wondered about turtles? . . . Why do turtles have shells? What do turtles eat? How old can turtles live to be?" In *Thunder on the Plains: The Story of the American Buffalo* Ken Robbins chooses dramatic words and powerful numbers to depict the travesty of the wasteful slaughter of the buffalo. "This is the story of a great shaggy creature, a very American beast, one found here and nowhere else . . . In 1875 there were perhaps fifty million of them. Just twenty-five years later nearly every one of them was gone." Noting how nonfiction authors open their books provides a variety of literary devices with which children can open their own expository reports.

Literature Cluster
ELEMENTS AND TECHNIQUES OF LITERARY NONFICTION

Dynamic Titles

Ketchum, Liza (2000). *Into a new country: Eight remarkable women of the West*. Boston: Little, Brown.

Murphy, Jim (2000). *Blizzard! The storm that changed America*. New York: Scholastic.

Settel, Joanne (1999). *Exploding ants: Amazing facts about how animals adapt*. New York: Atheneum.

Wechsler, Doug (1999). *Bizarre birds*. Photographs by the author and Vireo. Honesdale, PA: Boyds Mills Press.

Invested Interest in the Topic

Allen, Thomas B. (2004). *George Washington, spymaster: How the Americans outspied the British and won the Revolutionary War*. Illus. by Cheryl Harness. Washington, DC: National Geographic.

Lewin, Ted & Lewin, Betsy (1999). *Gorilla walk*. New York: Lothrop, Lee & Shepard.

Myers, Walter Dean (2001). *The greatest: Mohammed Ali*. New York: Scholastic.

Meaningful Focus

Orgill, Roxane (2001). *Shout, sister, shout! Ten girl singers who shaped a century*. New York: McElderry Books.

Stanley, Jerry (2000). *Hurry freedom: African Americans in Gold Rush California*. New York: Crown.

St. George, Judith (2004). *You're on your way, Teddy Roosevelt*. Illus. by Matt Faulkner. New York: Philomel.

Thimmesh, Catherine (2000). *Girls think of everything: Stories of ingenious inventions by women*. Illus. by Melissa Sweet. Boston: Houghton Mifflin.

Effective Word Choice

London, Jonathan (2000). *Panther: Shadow of the swamp*. Illus. by P. Morin. Cambridge, MA: Candlewick Press.

Miller, Debbie S. (2000). *River of life*. Illus. by J. Van Zyle. New York: Clarion.

Myers, Walter Dean (1998). *At Her Majesty's request: An African princess in Victorian England*. New York: Scholastic.

Thought-Provoking Conclusions. Final paragraphs leave a reader with lingering thoughts and inquiries and often inspire continuing discussion or investigation. Lynn Curlee's *Liberty* shares an inspiring visual and textual account of the Statue of Liberty's history and the promise that the light of liberty will continue to enlighten the world. Her final sentence inspires both reflection and discussion: "As long as she lives in our hearts and our minds, Liberty will enlighten the world." While most of the book overflows with engineering details and statistical facts about the construction of the statue, this conclusion leaves the reader with an aesthetic response that goes beyond the end of the book. As children learn how to conclude their reports, they will discover that it is best to leave the reader not with another fact, but perhaps with a thought that inspires heartfelt feeling, ongoing curiosity, or further research.

Revelation of the Lesser-Known Fact. In the deluge of information gathered for a book or a student report, the lesser-known fact may become one that is savored and remembered as it is strategically implanted in the text. For example, Judith St. George's

Fresh Vocabulary

Ancona, George (1999). *Charro: The Mexican cowboy.* San Diego: Harcourt Brace.

Dash, Joan (2000). *The longitude prize.* Illus. by D. Petricic. New York: Frances Foster Books/Farrar, Straus & Giroux.

Simon, Seymoar (1999). *Crocodiles and alligators.* New York: HarperColllins.

Sentence Flow

Borden, Louise & Kroeger, Mary Kay (2001). *Fly high! The story of Bessie Coleman.* Illus. by T. Flavin. New York: McElderry Books.

Burleigh, Robert (1998). *Black whiteness: Admiral Byrd in the Antarctic.* Illus. by W. L. Krudop. New York: Atheneum.

Rockwell, Anne (1998). *One bean.* Illus. by M. Halsey. San Diego: Silver Whistle/Harcourt Brace.

Compelling Voice

Bridges, Ruby (1999). *Through my eyes.* Articles and interviews compiled and edited by Margo Lundell. New York: Scholastic.

Montgomery, Sy (2001). *The man-eating tigers of Sunbardans.* Illus Photographs by Eleanor Briggs. Boston: Houghton Mifflin.

Philip, Neil (2000). *A braid of lives: Native American childhood.* Clarion.

Inviting Leads

Armstrong, Jennifer (1998). *Shipwreck at the bottom of the world: The extraordinary true story of Shackleton and the Endurance.* New York: Crown.

Arnosky, Jim (2000). *All about turtles.* New York: Scholastic.

Robbins, Ken (2001). *Thunder on the Plains: The story of the American buffalo.* New York: Atheneum.

Thought-Provoking Conclusions

Bial, Raymond (1999). *One-room school.* Boston: Houghton Mifflin.

Curlee, Lynn (2000). *Liberty.* New York: Atheneum.

Revelation of the Lesser-Known Fact

Fisher, Leonard Everett (1999). *Alexander Graham Bell.* New York: Atheneum.

Montgomery, Sy (2004). *Search for the Golden Moon Bear: Science and adventure in the Asian tropics.* Boston: Houghton Mifflin.

Stanley, Diane (2000). *Michelangelo.* New York: HarperCollins.

St. George, Judith (2000). *So you want to be President.* Illus. by David Small. New York: Philomel.

So You Want to Be President? shares little known facts and comical anecdotes about our former presidents amidst a backdrop of Caldecott winning political cartoon-like art by David Small. Did you know that "Andrew Johnson once served his guests turtle soup, oysters, fish, beef, turkey, mutton chops, chicken, mushrooms, string beans, partridges, duck, pudding, jellies, and lots of wine. All at one dinner!"? Pointing out the enticing power of the lesser-known fact will cause children to locate one such item in their own research. Placed strategically and cleverly within a factual text, the lesser-known fact can provide a relaxed moment in an otherwise serious report.

The techniques of literary nonfiction suggest strategies for building student awareness and for transferring these elements into their own expository writing. Although no writer should include all of them in any one nonfiction piece, they do provide a repertoire of techniques of the expository writing craft that can be used when appropriate. The Literature Cluster above extends the list of examples of other trade books that provide models of quality nonfiction at primary, intermediate, and middle-levels. Teachers need to gradually transition their writers toward literary nonfiction by incorporating the elements and techniques exemplified in these books.

Access Features: Visually Enhancing Expository Text

As respected authors of children's nonfiction submit quality nonfiction trade books to their publishers, they find that some information lends itself particularly well to access features—visual and textual elements such as maps, glossaries, photographs, and indexes (Bamford & Kristo, 2002). Children who write expository text need to utilize the same features when they share factual information with a reader. Learning how to select from one or more of the suggested access features of nonfiction can add meaningful visual information when used as an effective presentation technique. Such options will inspire young writers to share information through both textual and visual means in an expository report.

Bibliography. A bibliography of resources includes documented evidence of information shared through expository text. As student's informational resources creatively expand to include interviews, Internet sites, museum Web sites, diaries, music lyrics, videotapes, original documents, and, of course, books, a bibliography becomes an important showcase of the authenticity and authority of information. Locating bibliographies that go beyond books in their listing widens the possibilities of resources for investigative research. An extensive bibliography of books, periodicals, sources, and Web sites accompanies Walter Dean Myer's *USS Constellation: Pride of the American Navy,* modeling the extensive possibilities of varied resources in the research process.

Books for Further Reading. While teachers generally require a bibliography of resources used for gaining information for an expository report, children typically locate many more resources than the ones they actually use to compose their reports. Some titles may be more advanced while some may be written at a primary level. Recording these additional resources in a "For Further Reading" section recognizes an apparent audience of skilled and unskilled readers who may have interest in reading more about a topic. Well-known children's authors often include a recommended list of additional readings for their audience. For example, Diane Stanley includes both her bibliography of resources as well as titles "Recommended for Younger Readers" in her picture book biography of *Joan of Arc.* This access feature invites readers to further pursue an interesting topic.

Photographs. Both archival and new photographs can be incorporated into expository text to visually enhance textual information. Sandra Markle's use of striking color photographs in *Growing Up Wild: Wolves* capture wolf cubs as they explore, play, hunt, and learn the rules of growing up in the wild. Photographs coordinate with the text, bringing visual images that aid informational comprehension. With digital cameras, even primary age children are able to photographically document the growing of a plant, the changing colors of leaves, or the metamorphosis of a butterfly. The complimentary power of text and visual features evidences itself as words and images blend together.

Captions. While some photographs speak for themselves by coordinating with text, others require a caption that expands information beyond the text. Jim Murphy provides captions alongside archival photographs in *Blizzard: The Storm that Changed America* that contain new information and incorporate human interest. A photograph from the Connecticut Historical Society, for example, projects the impact and severity of the Great Blizzard of 1888 on the East Coast. The caption reads: "This resident of Danbury, Connecticut, pauses for a moment before digging his way through a daunting pile of snow outside his home" (p. 109). The photograph of a real person (and others like it) bring the reality of the blizzard of the century to life. While words do much to convey this information in the text, pictures and descriptive captions add a visual dimension to this incredible storm. Children can readily write single sentences that expand textual material beyond words to visual portrayals and accompanying informational captions.

Glossary. While vocabulary is best introduced when it is embedded in the context of textual information, glossaries can provide an additional review of new words discovered and defined within an expository report. Sandra Markle's *Outside and Inside Kangaroos* includes a glossary with dictionary pronunciations defining words like *embryo, joey, marsupial,* and *tendon* with references to the pages on which the words appeared. The glossary feature provides an effective accounting and review of fresh vocabulary learned in the context of the topical report. Written in the children's own words, the definitions reflect the level of understanding that the individual learner gained from his or her research.

Index. Longer reports and books lend themselves to creating an index of vocabulary, people, places, and things related to a selected topic. An index can be as simple as the one that appears in Martin Jenkins's *The Emperor's Egg* or as complex as the three-page index in Jennifer Armstrong's *Shipwreck at the Bottom of the World*. The index serves as a guide to finding information in expository text. Since nonfiction is not meant to necessarily be read from cover to cover, an index signals a means to find the name of a particular crew member, the role of icebergs in the wreck, and so forth. An index exemplifies "how nonfiction works" and provides an access feature that children actually enjoy creating. Since they know their report better than anyone else, their decisions on words for indexing reveal commitment, knowledge, and passion for the topic.

Map. The visual information in a map works best when it accompanies textual information and enables the reader to understand where an event occurred. Diane Stanley's *Michelangelo* begins with an Author's Note and an accompanying map of Italy during the Renaissance. The map reflects that Italy was a peninsula carved into many republics or independent states and a caption verifies that Italy did not become a unified country until 1870. This background information aids readers as they consider the various locations and church leaders under whom Michelangelo created his most famous masterpieces. In student reports maps can serve the reader in many ways and provide another visual access feature. Biographical accounts and historical topics in particular provide opportunities for map inclusion.

Sidebars. Charts, lists, and diagrams that serve informational text can be featured in a marginal drawing or textual display. S. D. Schindler's sketches in the margins of Arthur Dorros's *A Tree Is Growing* stretch the reader beyond the text to additional information. For example, colored sketches of springtails, nematodes, mites, fungi, and bacteria are presented in the right-hand margin of an illustrated page on natural forest floor decay. Stephen Swinburne's *Coyote: North America's Dog* features additional textual information in a sidebar format. For children with artistic, visual learning styles, these options provide a means of simplifying the amount of text while effectively sharing information in presentation margins.

Timelines/Chronologies. The sequence of biographies and historical events lend themselves to chronological summaries through timelines. Timelines may highlight ongoing progress through years in the building of a national monument as in Lynn Curlee's *Rushmore* or they may showcase specific days, months, and years from the life of a great stateman as in James Cross Giblin's *The Amazing Life of Benjamin Franklin*. These visual features provide an overview or summary of information revealed in the expository text, that is brought together in a meaningful sequential form. Children find sequence as an appealing organizational aspect of history and biography and readily prepare this access feature either before or after writing their text.

Literature Cluster

ACCESS FEATURES FOR ENHANCING EXPOSITORY TEXT

Bibliography/Further Reading/ Websites/Discography

Bachrach, Susan D. (2000). *The Nazi Olympics: Berlin 1936*. Boston: Little, Brown.

Freedman, Russell (2004). *The voice that challenged a nation: Marian Anderson and the struggle for equal rights*. New York: Clarion.

Lasky, Kathryn (1998). *A brilliant streak: The making of Mark Twain*. Illus. by Barry Moser. San Diego: Harcourt Brace.

Captions

Bial, Raymond (2004). *Where Washington walked*. New York: Walker.

Goodman, Susan E. (1999). *Ultimate field trip 3: Wading into marine biology*. Photographs by M. J. Doolittle. New York: Atheneum.

Montgomery, Sy (2004). *The tarantula scientist*. Photographs by Nic Bishop. Boston: Houghton Mifflin.

Diagrams/Documentation

Blacklock , Dyan (2004). *The Roman army*. Illus. by David Kennett. New York: Walker.

Fisher, Leonard Everett (1999). *Alexander Graham Bell*. New York: Atheneum.

Jenkins, Steve (2004). *Actual size*. Houghton Mifflin.

Myers, Walter Dean (1999). *At Her Majesty's request: An African princess in Victorian England*. New York: Scholastic.

Glossary

Ancona, George (1999). *Charro: The Mexican cowboy*. San Diego: Harcourt Brace.

Bobrick, Benson (2004). *Fight for freedom: The American Revolutionary War*. New York: Atheneum.

Burleigh, Robert (2004). *Seurat and la Grande Jatte*. New York: Abrams.

Markle, Sandra (2000). *Outside and inside dinosaurs*. New York: Atheneum.

Index

Bausum, Ann (2004). *With courage and cloth: Winning the fight for a woman's right to vote*. Washington, DC: National Geographic.

Jenkins, Martin (1999). *The emperor's egg*. Illus. by Jane Chapman. Cambridge, MA: Candlewick.

Visual Vignettes. When a writer shares important additional information and facts in language-rich charts, tables, and notes, they are often called *visual vignettes*, a powerful combination of textual display and visual literacy as sources for transferring information. Unlike sidebars, they find a home across an entire page, not just in the margins. For example, journal text blends with both photographs and sketches in Jennifer Owings Dewey's *Antarctic Journal: Four months at the bottom of the world*. Funded by the National Science Foundation, the author ventured to this remote environment to capture the world's last great wilderness through both text and art—from sketches, photographs and journal entries to letters home. Children with visual talents and learning styles might seek this type of access feature in both their reading and their expository presentation style.

Of course, no one book or expository report could effectively employ all of these suggested access features. Yet teachers should share the benefits of each using quality nonfiction literature as a model. The Literature Cluster above presents quality literature that models each type of access feature.

Lewin, Ted & Betsy (1999). *Gorilla walk*. New York: Lothrop, Lee & Shepard.

Maps

Morrison, Taylor (2004). *The coast mappers*. Boston: Houghton Mifflin.

Parker, Nancy Winslow (1996). *Locks crocs, & skeeters: The story of the Panama Canal*. New York: Greenwillow.

Stanley, Diane (2000). *Michelangelo*. New York: HarperCollins.

Webb, Sophie (2004). *Looking for seabirds: Journal from an Alaskan voyage*. Boston: Houghton Mifflin.

Photographs

Day, Trevor (2000). *Youch! It bites!: Real-life monsters, up close*. Designed by Mike Jolley. New York: Simon & Schuster.

Horenstein, Henry (1999). *A is for . . . ?* New York: Gulliver Books/Harcourt Brace.

Jackson, Robert (2004). *Meet me in St. Louis: A trip to the 1904 World's Fair*. New York: HarperCollins.

Myers, Walter Dean (2004). *USS Constellation: Pride of the American Navy*. New York: Holiday House.

Partridge, Elizabeth (1998). *Restless spirit: The life and work of Dorothea Lange*. New York: Viking.

Sidebars

Brimmer, Larry Dane (2004). *Subway: The story of tunnels, tubes, and tracks*. Honesdale, PA: Boyds Mills Press.

Dorros, Arthur (1997). *A tree is growing*. Illus. by S. D. Schindler. New York: Scholastic.

Swinburne, Stephen R. (1999). *Coyote: North. America's dog*. Honesdale, PA: Boyds Mills Press.

Timeline/Chronology

Aliki (1999). *William Shakespeare & the Globe*. New York: HarperCollins.

Curlee, Lynn (2000). *Liberty*. New York: Atheneum.

Giblin, James Cross (2000). *The amazing life of Benjamin Franklin*. Illus. by M. Dooling. New York: Scholastic.

Hoose, Phillip (2004). *The race to save the lord God bird*. New York: Farrar. Straus & Giroux.

Visual Vignettes

Arnosky, Jim (2004). *Following the coast*. New York: HarperCollins.

Dewey, Jennifer O. (2001). *Antarctic journal: Four months at the bottom of the world*. New York: HarperCollins.

Harness, Cheryl (2001). *Remember the ladies: 100 great American women*. New York: HarperCollins.

Rector, Anne Elizabeth (2004). *Anne Elizabeth's diary: A young artist's true story*. With additional text by Kathleen Krull. Boston: Little, Brown.

Technology also serves a powerful role in designing and enhancing the access features that may become integral to a student's report. The Tech Tip (on page 310) highlights several resources to support the researcher and report writer. Selectively incorporating two or three access features to well-written expository text adds to the presentation and pride of an informational topic. Having this large repertoire of access features at hand adds higher-level thinking to planning and presenting an effective expository report.

Putting It All Together: The Early Inquiry Process

Sharing informational text with young children paves the road toward independent research and expository writing as children pass through the elementary grades. Yopp & Yopp (2000) suggest several ways to introduce expository text to young children:

- Choosing nonfiction as a read-aloud option opens the genre to primary grade students.

Tech TIP

Using Technology to Enhance Research Reports

Designed for young writers and researchers, *NoodleBib MLA Starter* is a free web-based tool designed to aid students in finding relevant sources, citing those sources, and creating a bibliography. **www.noodletools.com/**

Digital cameras allow students to preview and edit their photographs prior to printing their favorite snapshots. Students may prefer to insert digital photographs directly into their word-processed research reports. Visit *National Geographic Traveler Magazine* **www.nationalgeographic.com/traveler/photos/phototips0507/pt.html** for learning about the benefits of digital photography and professional tips on taking great photographs.

User-friendly software products such as *TimeLiner* or *Timeline Maker* **www.timelinemaker.com/overview.html** allow students to enhance their nonfiction reports or slide shows by visually organizing information on a chronological time line. Students can even add graphics, sound, video clips, and extensive notes to the time lines. **http://www.tomsnyder.com**

To look more closely at these materials and others related to "Expository Writing," visit the Companion Website at www.prenhall.com/hancock.

- Pairing informational text with narrative selections sets fact and fiction side by side for young children. For example, Jane Yolen's *Owl Moon* and Barbara Esbensen's *Tiger with Wings: The Great Horned Owl* pair as nonfiction enriches the understanding and appreciation for fiction.
- Informational trade books can be paired with textbooks or curricular-mandated topics. Students studying weather may read Seymour Simon's books on storms, lightning, tornadoes, and hurricanes. Children studying the planets can read Simon's series on each planet and celestial body.
- Informational trade books might be used for direct instruction in reading. Several researchers (Chaney, 1993; Yopp & Yopp, 2000) recommend alphabet books for phonemic awareness, contextual knowledge, comprehension building, and structure for framing a class informational book. For example, Christopher Wormell's *Teeth, Tails, and Tentacles: An Alphabet Counting Book* provides simple reading experiences (e.g., 5 five starfish arms; 6 six frog eyes) enhanced by a more challenging paragraph in the back of the book (e.g., Ochre Starfish; American Bullfrog).
- Classroom libraries should offer nonfiction as a choice for free reading. Rather than isolating nonfiction for report research, the informational bookshelves should provide an open invitation for self-selected reading options.

Writing expository text reflects a developmental process. Simple reports in a second grade might begin with a topic sentence about koala bears, generate three statements about what koala bears eat, when they sleep, where they live, and a final sentence sharing one's feelings about this animal. The K-W-L chart (Ogle, 1986) outlines what children

KNOW, information they WANT TO KNOW, and information they LEARN by doing their research. While this seems quite simple and uncomplicated, the K-W-L approach lays the groundwork for the developmental steps in the inquiry process. Children need to know how to generate meaningful questions as teachers prepare them for the inquiry process.

Steps in the Early Inquiry Process

Tower (2000) effectively breaks the inquiry process into steps that must be modeled by a teacher if students are destined to become young researchers. Teachers tend to thrust research into the hands of children too quickly, resulting in student, teacher, and parental frustrations. Learning the stages of the inquiry process, introducing them to the class one-at-a-time, and building a foundation for inquiry are preliminary steps to creating writers of expository reports.

Planning Time for Question Development. Generating questions is a difficult task for students. While K-W-L charts document what a child Knows, what a child Wants to know, and what he or she has Learned, the questions generated in the W column tend to be factual questions to which children already know the answers. The ultimate goal involves getting children to move beyond superficial inquiry to generate bigger questions—those that have no single right answer but inspire further investigation. For example, instead of "What do elephants eat?" children might broaden their inquiry to determine "Should elephants be kept in confinement in zoos?" School tends to provide practice in asking and answering the simple questions but does little to help model or generate the bigger questions. Short, Harste, & Burke (1996) suggest giving students time to explore their topics long before narrowing their search to specific questions.

Determining Whether Inquiry Topics Should Be Whole Class or Individual. Early in the school year, teachers might find confidence in working with a whole-class inquiry. Gathering plentiful resources, building from the school curriculum, working together on a common goal, and teaching modeling of carrying out inquiry while scaffolding student learning provide many reasons for taking the whole-class approach (Calkins, 1994). Individually selected topics, on the other hand, engage children in their passions, make questioning easier as materials hold relevance for each child, provide student choice under a general curricular umbrella, and encourage a wider range of topics (Harvey, 1998).

Providing Experience with Nonfiction Books. If nonfiction and expository text appears unfamiliar to children, they must engage with it as readers before tackling it as writers. The tips for reading nonfiction aloud in the previous section are a beginning for this informational immersion. Bamford and Kristo (2002) suggest several ways in which children can explore nonfiction: cover-to-cover read-alouds; participatory read-alouds; chapter read-alouds; caption reading; browsing; and believe-ot-or-not sharing. Natural enjoyment of nonfiction topics seems to fuel this initial immersion in the nonfiction genre and provides the prior genre knowledge needed to investigate and share acquired information.

Developing an Ongoing List of Resources. Books come to mind as the most abundant resource of which teachers need to be aware. The Orbis Pictus Award for Outstanding Nonfiction for Children issued by the National Council of Teachers of English honors the best of nonfiction trade books based on criteria of authenticity, documentation, accuracy, engaging writing and illustration, and appropriateness to the curriculum. Figure 10.2 lists the winners of this prestigious award since its inception in 1990. In addition, other quality resources are available including the Internet, human and community

FIGURE 10.2 Orbis Pictus Award for Outstanding Nonfiction for Children.

2006	*Children of the Great Depression* by Russell Freedman (Clarion)
2005	*York's Adventures with Lewis and Clark: An African American's Part in the Great Expedition* by Rhoda Blumberg (Scholastic)
2004	*American Plague: The True and Terrifying Story of the Yellow Fever Epidemic of 1793* by Jim Murphy (Clarion)
2003	*When Marian Sang: The True Recital of Marian Anderson: The Voice of a Century* by Pam Muñoz Ryan (Scholastic)
2002	*Black Potatoes: The Story of the Great Irish Famine* by Susan Campbell Bartoletti (Houghton Mifflin)
2001	*Hurry Freedom: African Americans in Gold Rush California* by Jerry Stanley (Crown)
2000	*Through My Eyes* by Ruby Bridges and Margo Lundell (Scholastic)
1999	*Shipwreck at the Bottom of the World: The extraordinary True Story of Shackleton and the Endurance* by Jennifer Armstrong (Crown)
1998	*An Extraordinary Life: The Story of a Monarch Butterfly* by Laurence Pringle, illus. by Ron Marstall (Orchard)
1997	*Leonardo daVinci* by Diane Stanley (Morrow)
1996	*The Great Fire* by Jim Murphy (Scholastic)
1995	*Safari Beneath the Sea: The Wonder of the North Pacific Coast* by Diane Swanson (Sierra Club)
1994	*Across America on an Emigrant Train* by Jim Murphy (Clarion)
1993	*Children of the Dust Bowl: The True Story of the School at Weedpatch Camp* by Jerry Stanley (Crown)
1992	*Flight: The Journey of Charles Lindbergh* by Robert Burleigh, with illus. by Mike Wimmer (Philomel)
1991	*Franklin Delano Roosevelt* by Russell Freedman (Clarion)
1990	*The Great Little Madison* by Jean Fritz (Putnam)

resources, and e-mail communication. Keeping track of these resources for curricular topics provides quick contact sources for student investigations.

Providing an Environment for Inquiry and Talk. Students are quick to share knowledge, facts, and information on real topics. Talk can even identify misconceptions in a risk-free learning setting. From student talk comes brainstorming sessions, graphic webs, K-W-L charts, and visual representations of emerging knowledge. Modeling higher-level questions, accepting plausible answers to those questions, and encouraging risk taking as a thinker and researcher have far-reaching implications.

Modeling Teacher Research on a Topic of Self-Interest. If teachers walk children through the research process on a passionate topic (traveling to a foreign country, rose gardening, building a bluebird house), they will incorporate books, Internet sites,

STUDENT SAMPLE 10.4
A second-grade expository report.

WHAT'S IN A RAIN FOREST?
by Shelly

Inside a rain forest that's in Whashington, there is stuff like birds, snakes, frogs, dragonfly's, and butterfly's. It has to rain more for thier to be a rain forest.

After raining there may be a puddle so big you can swim in it. It's a beatiful place to visit someday.

There's vines, trees, and bushes everywhere. Everything in thier is all green.

Some of the animals are green, too. Like the frogs, dragonfly's and butterfly's. Sometimes snakes!

Sometimimes, thier's little ponds or lakes. You can see deer around those area's.

Rain forest are very beatiful places. Theyre filled with lots of neat animals.

interviews with specialists, and even visits to community locations. Modeling how an adult captures information through a variety of resources sets the pattern for children conducting their own research. Just as reading and writing are processes, so, too, is research a process with before, during, and after steps resulting in a final product. Taking children on that investigative journey through the step-by-step process allows them to witness the stages of research that include generating questions on a focused topic, gathering data, organizing information, analyzing and evaluating facts, and presenting the information in a useful format.

Student Sample 10.4 illustrates how the inquiry process and immersion in nonfiction results in the written expository report, "What's in a Rain Forest?" by a second grader. Focusing on a single research question, Shelly draws from her own experience of living in Washington state and information from nonfiction trade books to compose her own informational text. Teacher reading of nonfiction, modeling of research questions, and organization of information have provided the practice to put each step to work in the expository composing process.

Putting It All Together: Progressing to an Informational Report

As children enter the intermediate grades, their expository reports build on individual research skills introduced and practiced in the primary grades (as discussed in the previous section). Reports may find focus in both content areas and personal interest domains.

While the steps for writing an informational report parallel early stages of expository writing, they move beyond to teacher guidance while fostering independence in gathering, organizing, and presenting information.

There are seven steps in intermediate and middle-level report writing:

1. Selecting and narrowing a topic
2. Formulating research questions
3. Gathering information from a variety of sources
4. Determining text structure for optimal dissemination of the information
5. Drafting, revising, and editing the report
6. Selecting appropriate access features to enhance informational delivery
7. Presenting the report in a format useful to the reading audience.

Discussing each of these steps in detail provides the needed guidance and the optimal model in report writing in the intermediate and middle grades. Each step can easily become a full-day lesson as teacher guidance and modeling leads to independent researching.

Selecting and Narrowing a Topic

Because a writer will be invested in researching and authoring a report over a period of several weeks, the importance of topic selection and personal investment cannot be overemphasized. The tendency for most young writers is to choose too broad of a topic—one on which there is too much information available. Teacher modeling of nonfiction book topics can assist in narrowing the topic to a reasonable size. For example, the Revolutionary War is far too large for a fifth-grade writer, but the uniforms of soldiers of the American Revolution will focus the research and provide both a written and visual presentation format. By middle school, the uniforms of the British soldiers in the Battle of Concord might bring even further focus to the report. The topic of weather is far too broad as a science topic, but a focus on tornadoes brings the topic down to reasonable size for a successful report for an intermediate writer. By middle-school, that topic might even be further focused to the tornado that hit Andover, Kansas, in the 1980s. Passionate interest and a narrowing of the topic are essential first steps in ensuring that successful research and writing accompanies the topic.

Formulating Research Questions

"What do I want to learn about this topic and share with my audience?" should be the starting point of constructing three research questions. These questions can be factual or they can incorporate higher level thinking that investigates deeper levels of a topic. For example, "How did the uniforms of the British and American Revolutionary soldiers differ?" "What colors, materials, and distinctive features characterized the uniforms of the American soldiers?" "How did the quality (or lack of quality) of the uniforms impact the performance of the soldiers?" Questions for a weather-related topic might include "What conditions are necessary for the formation of a tornado?" "What are the recorded wind forces and estimated damages of tornadoes?" and "What warning systems can be activated to prevent the loss of human life during a tornado?" Brainstorming and clarifying these questions are key to the success and focus of a report.

Gathering Information from a Variety of Sources

As the grade level grows, so too do the number and type of sources for information gathering. While encyclopedia research is a beginning, quality trade books, especially those with authentic research themselves, provide an incredible source for information. Learning to accurately record that information, cite precise quotations, and reword facts in one's own words accompany that task. At least three trade books on a topic should be accessed to verify and confirm accuracy of information. In addition, quality Web sites should be consulted to provide an enhanced perspective on the topic. Lesson Plan 10.1 exemplifies the research process by focusing on information and fact gathering.

LESSON PLAN 10.1

TITLE: Researching American Presidents

Grade Level: 4–8

Time Frame: 3–5 45-minute sessions

Standards

IRA/NCTE Standards: 1, 7, 8

NETS for Students: 3, 5

Objectives

- Students will use a variety of resources (Internet and literature) to conduct research on presidents of the United States.
- Students will utilize computer technology to communicate their findings to suit their purpose and audience.

Materials

- Assortment of literature about U.S. presidents

  Harris, Benjamin (2005/2006). *Getting to Know the U.S. Presidents* (series). Children's Press.

  Whitney, David (2001). *The American Presidents: Biographies of the Chief Executives from George Washington to George W. Bush* (9th ed.). Reader's Digest.

  Rubel, David (2005). *Scholastic Encyclopedia of the Presidents and Their Times.* Scholastic.
- Computers with Internet for student use
- Word processing programs to create bibliography
- *Inspiration* or other software to create graphic organizers
- Computer, projector, and large screen for teacher demonstration of Web sites and software

Motivation

- Using a projector, screen, and computer, introduce the class to the Internet Public Library site POTUS: Presidents of the United States (www.ipl.org/div/potus). Discuss the features of the Web site and show students how to access information and links.

Procedures

Session 1

- Explain to the students that they will use literature and the POTUS Web site to conduct research on a president of their choice.
- As a class, view *NoodleBib MLA Starter* (www.noodletools.com/) and discuss the importance of creating a bibliography when conducting research. Discuss the features of the Web site and model how to create a bibliography. Remind students that they need to keep an updated bibliography as they gather facts and images from the Internet and literature.
- In addition to biographical information (date of birth, home state, family information, etc.), students should gather and organize facts into the following (or similar) categories:
    1. Important world events that took place during the presidency
    2. Ways this president made a difference in the United States and the world
    3. Fun facts/trivia about the president

Sessions 2–4

- Allow students time to gather facts and information, organize the information into categories, and keep an updated bibliography.
- Using a projector, screen, and computer, model how students can use *Inspiration* software to create a graphic organizer to showcase their facts. For example, students may choose to create a graphic organizer with color-coded bubbles or fonts to emphasize the different categories of facts and information.
- Students who are already familiar with *Inspiration* may import pictures and illustrations to enhance their graphic organizers. Advanced students may add additional information to their graphic organizers by inserting hyperlinks to the POTUS Web site. Creativity should be encouraged.

Session 5

- Students may share their graphic organizers by projecting them on a screen or by printing them out.

Assessment

- Teacher-developed rubric or checklist is used to assess students' ability to research, gather facts, and create a graphic organizer and bibliography.

Accommodation/Modification

- *Kidspiration* (a version of *Inspiration* designed for primary students) may be used with students who are novice technology users.
- To differentiate instruction, the teacher may increase/reduce the number of facts each student is expected to find.

Visit the Meeting the Standards module in Chapter 10 of the Companion Website at www.prenhall.com/hancock to adapt this lesson to meet your state's standards.

Although the Internet provides a plethora of Web sites for information gathering, teachers must model the process of verifying online sources. While National Geographic

Evaluating Web Pages and Web Resources

Kathy Schrock's *Teacher Helpers: Critical Evaluation Information* is a free resource containing print-friendly evaluation surveys that will assist students of all ages to evaluate the content of Web pages. **school.discovery.com/schrockguide/eval.html**

Evaluate Web Pages is an online module through which students and teachers can learn more about evaluating web resources, including a ready-to-use PowerPoint presentation. www.widener.edu/Tools_Resources/Libraries/Wolfgram_Memorial_Library/Evaluate_Web_Pages/659

To look more closely at these materials and others related to "Expository Writing," visit the Companion Website at www.prenhall.com/hancock.

or PBS Web sites are credible, a personal Web site created by a history buff or a weather fanatic may be less accurate. An entire lesson on credibility of information on the Internet should be modeled prior to using it as a source for research. The Tech Tip included here explains how to do this.

Student researchers must also be made aware of the importance of recording bibliographic citations as a source of information. Once again, nonfiction books with bibliographies provide an excellent model for this format for both books and Web sites. Students should realize the importance of using a variety of sources in their information gathering. Some of the greatest learning takes place as students discover how authorities in a field contradict, overlap, and recognize each other.

Determining Text Structure

As discussed earlier in the chapter, the recognition and determination of the proper text structures through which to share acquired information is important. While description or compare and contrast are the likely modes for intermediate students, increasingly higher-level questions can lead middle-level students into the realm of problem and solution or cause and effect. Utilizing the appropriate graphic organizer as a framework or outline for a report assists in both written and visual presentation.

Drafting, Revising, and Editing the Report

The writing process takes front and center during the drafting stage of the expository report. The importance of focus, organization, word choice, voice, sentence fluency, and conventions must be considered of prime importance in the expository writing mode. Information delivered must captivate the reader, answer the research questions, and provide accurate details delivered in a passionate voice. Vocabulary words must be introduced in context while sequential order guides the reader through new concepts and intriguing facts. The writing process honored in narrative writing is no less important in expository composition. In fact, the task of writing factual information in a literary mode is perhaps twice the challenge for an expository writer. Yet the background of nonfiction read-alouds, the exposure to quality nonfiction trade books in self-selected reading, and directed instruction in this mode of writing provides the necessary background to meet this challenge over time.

The same writing workshop format with peer revision and peer editing holds true for expository writing. Perhaps the peer review takes on an even more important role as the reader must absorb and comprehend new information. Clarity of delivery, use of technical vocabulary, and the retention of the author's voice must make sense to the peer reader. While the types of feedback may differ from a narrative writing workshop, the importance and the suggestions are equally important in expository format.

Selecting Appropriate Access Features

As the writing unfolds, as the revisions are made, and as the editing occurs, the writer of expository text retains a visual image of the evolving presentation of the report. That evolving image includes the types of access features that will enhance the presentation of the report. For example, the diagram and labeling of the Revolutionary soldier uniform or the parts of a tornado aid and assist the reader in understanding the text. A sidebar on the most devastating tornadoes or a timeline of battles of the Revolutionary War also enhance and add to the written text. A glossary of terms or an index might further guide the reader through the report. Teachers may even suggest a certain number of well-selected access features to supplement the written parts of the report.

In the textual and visual world of nonfiction, it is important to realize the value of both words and images. Making these an important part of the expository report itself assists writers as they realize that some information is best delivered in writing while other information is best shared through a visual image. Awareness of potential access features and planning for these alongside writing leads toward the optimal presentation of the final project.

Presentation of the Expository Report

With the use of word processing and visual images achieved through technology, the final expository report may exhibit fresh character, visual enhancement, and bibliographic

Second graders practice sharing their expository report in a PowerPoint format.

STUDENT SAMPLE 10.5
A fourth-grade expository draft.

IMMIGRANTS
by Ashley

Many immigrants came from 1820–1925! When the immigrants came on the boats the poor ones didn't get first class. Most of immigrants got killed by Shipwreck or diseases. Then they finally landed at Ellis Island. When they got there the first thing they saw was the Statue of Liberty. Some of them worked in the town but the other people didn't want to. Lots of them were very poor and couldn't pay the rent so they got kicked out of their home. In the spring the kids were so hot so they broke open the fire hydrant and played in the water. Almost all of the food they had like bread, fish, fruit, and veggies are in crates out in the streets. All the kids and grownups, go to school at night. Lots of the men go to work, in the day. Some of the jobs they might have are factory men, fire men, and miners. Over thousands of trees in the forest had been taken down for houses. If the immigrants didn't have enough money to work in the city they had to become a farmer and maybe live there life in the west. They started making there own things you could use on the crops. Soon they became pioneers. The most frightning thing on the prairie was prairie fires. In the winter there would be mounts of snow. The prairie life wasn't so bad. They were very lonely. The closest nieghborhood was about 90 miles away.

authenticity. Quality trade books, especially those of Orbis Pictus Award quality, provide high expectations for the blending of expository text and visual image. Design and organization add to the written text as the audience can both read and view the final product of the investigative research efforts.

Ashley's draft fourth-grade report on immigrants contains the beginning signs of internalizing portions of the inquiry process (Student Sample 10.5). Her topic is rather broad, so she might be urged to focus on Italian-American or German-American immigrants. Immigration discussion progresses from the treacherous overseas voyage to the emotional landing at Ellis Island to the crowded challenges of the tenements to the ultimate movement west toward open land and fresh opportunities. Ashley utilized a sequence format for data gathering and utilized several nonfiction trade books in gathering authentic information to put in her own words. As she continues work on this expository writing, a teacher or peer may guide her toward including a stronger ending and access features (e.g., a sidebar, timeline, or number graph) that enable her to share visual information beyond the text with her audience.

Visit the Companion Website at www.prenhall.com/hancock and gauge your understanding of Chapter 10 concepts with the self-assessments.

Closing Thoughts

Expository writing is interdisciplinary by nature and implies connections with informational books and content area learning (Freeman & Person, 1998). With greater demands on time in the elementary and middle-level classroom, expository reports incorporating a plethora of language arts skills seems to provide learning across the curriculum—literacy and topical knowledge. Students often recall their "reports" from their K–8 classrooms as a most positive writing experience. If teachers can further enhance that experience through reading aloud nonfiction books, teaching expository text structure, building awareness of access features, and blending written text and visual image as part of the presentation of a report, then expository writing will grow in its fulfilling sense of achievement to young authors.

Teachers quickly realize that they must teach the expository writing process step by step while holding the hands of their students. Writing expository texts does not come as naturally as narrative writing. By utilizing literature models and by modeling techniques and features of expository text, they can gradually guide students toward effective delivery of informational text through both textual and visual means. The goal of expository writing is to blend both textual and visual information into a comfortable format for an audience of interested readers who stand to learn new information on a topic of interest to both reader and writer.

References

Bamford, R. A., & Kristo, J. V. (Eds.) (2002). *Making facts come alive: Choosing quality nonfiction literature* (2nd ed.). Norwood, MA: Christopher-Gordon.

Calkins, L. M. (1994). *The art of teaching writing* (2nd ed.). Portsmouth, NH: Heinemann.

Caswell, L., & Duke, N. (1998). Non-narrative as a catalyst for literacy development. *Language Arts, 75,* 108–117.

Chaney, J. A. (1993). Alphabet books: Resources for learning. *The Reading Teacher, 47,* 96–104.

Crook, P. R., & Lehman, B. (1991). Themes for two voices: Children's fiction and Nonfiction as "whole literature." *Language Arts, 68,* 34–41.

Doiron, R. (1994). Using nonfiction in a read-aloud program. Letting the facts speak for themselves. *The Reading Teacher, 47,* 616–624,

Duke, N. K. (2000). 3.6 minutes per day: The scarcity of informational texts in first grade. *Reading Research Quarterly, 35,* 202–224.

Duthie, C. (1996). *True stories: Nonfiction literacy in the primary classroom.* York, ME: Stenhouse.

Flood, J., Lapp, D., & Farnan, N. (1986). A reading-writing procedure that teaches expository paragraph structure. *The Reading Teacher, 39,* 556–562.

Freeman, E., & Person, D. (1998). *Connecting informational children's books with content area learning.* Needham Heights, MA: Allyn & Bacon.

Graves, D. H. (1989). *Investigate nonfiction: The reading/writing teacher's companion.* Portsmouth, NH: Heinemann.

Guillaume, A. (1998). Learning with text in the primary grades. *The Reading Teacher, 51,* 476–486.

Hancock, M. R. (2004). *A celebration of literature and response: Children, books, and teachers in K–8 classrooms* (2nd ed.). Upper Saddle River, NJ: Merrill/Prentice Hall.

Harvey, S. (1998). *Nonfiction matters: Reading, writing, and research in grades* 3–8. York, ME: Stenhouse.

Hoyt, L. (2002). *Make it real: Strategies for success with informational texts.* Portsmouth, NH: Heinemann.

Kristo, J., & Bamford, R. (2004). *Nonfiction in focus: A comprehensive framework for helping students become independent readers and writers of nonfiction, K–6.* New York: Scholastic Professional Books.

McGee, L. M., & Richgels, D. J. (1985). Teaching expository text structure to elementary students. *The Reading Teacher, 38,* 739–748.

Moss, B. (2004). Teaching expository text structures through information trade book retellings. *The Reading Teacher, 57 (8),* 710–718.

Ogle, D. (1986). K-W-L: A teaching model that develops active reading of expository text. *The Reading Teacher, 39,* 564–570.

Palmer, R. G., & Stewart, R. A. (2003). Nonfiction trade book use in primary grades. *The Reading Teacher, 57,* 38–48.

Piccolo, J. A. (1987). Expository text structure: Teaching and learning strategies. *The Reading Teacher, 40,* 838–847.

Raphael, T. E., Kirschner, B. W., & Englert, C. S. (1988). Expository writing programs: Making connections between reading and writing. *The Reading Teacher, 41,* 790–795.

Short, K., Harste, J., & Burke, C. (1996). *Creating classrooms for authors and inquirers* (2nd ed.). Portsmouth, NH: Heinemann.

Tompkins, G. E. (2005). *Language Arts: Patterns in practice* (6th ed.). Upper Saddle River, NJ: Merrill/Prentice Hall.

Tower, C. (2000). Questions that matter: Preparing elementary students for the inquiry process. *The Reading Teacher, 53,* 550–557.

Vardell, S., & Copland, K. A. (1992). Reading aloud and responding to nonfiction: Let's talk about it. In E. B. Freeman & D. G. Person (Eds.), *Using nonfiction trade books in the elementary classroom: From ants to zeppelins* (pp. 76–85). Urbana, IL: National Council of Teachers of English.

Yopp, R. H., & Yopp, H. K. (2000). Sharing informational text with young children. *The Reading Teacher, 53,* 410–423.

Children's Books Cited

Adler, David (1997). *Lou Gherig: The luckiest man.* Illus. by Terry Widener. San Diego: Harcourt.

Ancona, George (1999). *Charro: The Mexican cowboy.* San Diego: Harcourt.

Armstrong, Jennifer (1998). *Shipwreck at the bottom of the world: The extraordinary true story of Shackleton and the Endurance.* New York: Crown.

Arnosky, Jim (2000). *All about turtles.* New York: Scholastic.

Borden, Louise, & Kroeger, Mary Kay (2001). *Fly high! The story of Bessie Coleman.* Illus. by Teresa Flavin. New York: McElderry.

Bridges, Ruby (1999). *Through my eyes.* Articles and interviews compiled and edited by Margo Lundell. New York: Scholastic.

Challoner, Jack (2000). *Hurricane and tornado.* New York: Dorling Kindersley.

Curlee, Lynn (1999). *Rushmore.* New York: Atheneum.

Curlee, Lynn (2000). *Liberty.* New York: Atheneum.

Dewey, Jennifer Owings (2001). *Antarctic journal: Four months at the bottom of the world.* New York: HarperCollins.

Esbensen, Barbara (1996). *Tiger with wings: The great horned owl.* Illus. by Mary Barrett Brown. New York: Orchard.

Giblin, James Cross (2000). *The amazing life of Benjamin Franklin.* Illus. by M. Dooling. New York: Scholastic.

Gibbons, Gail (1997). *The honey makers.* New York: Morrow Junior Books.

Gibbons, Gail (1998). *Soaring with the wind: The bald eagle.* New York: HarperCollins.

Jenkins, Martin (1999). *The emperor's egg.* Illus. by Jane Chapman. Cambridge, MA: Candlewick.

Lauber, Patricia (1996). *Flood: Wrestling with the Mississippi.* Washington, DC: National Geographic.

Lauber, Patricia (1996). *Hurricanes: Earth's mightiest storms.* New York: Scholastic.

Lewin, Ted, & Lewin, Betsy (1999). *Gorilla walk.* New York: Lothrop, Lee & Shepard.

London, Jonathan (2000). *Panther: Shadow of the swamp.* Illus. by P. Morin. Cambridge, MA: Candlewick Press.

Macauley, David (1998). *The new way things work.* Boston: Houghton Mifflin.

Markle, Sandra (1999). *Outside and inside kangaroos.* New York: Atheneum.

Markle, Sandra (2001). *Growing up wild: Wolves.* New York: Atheneum.

Murphy, Jim (1995). *The great fire.* New York: Scholastic.

Murphy, Jim (2000). *Blizzard: The storm that changed America.* New York: Scholastic.

Murphy, Jim (2003). *An American plague: The true and terrifying story of the yellow fever epidemic of 1793.* New York: Clarion.

Myers, Walter Dean (2004). *USS Constellation: Pride of the American Navy.* New York: Holiday House.

Patent, Dorothy Henshaw (1996). *Children save the rain forest.* New York: Dutton.

Pringle, Laurence (1996). *An extraordinary life: The story of a monarch butterfly.* Illus. by Bob Marstall. New York: Orchard.

Robbins, Ken (2001). *Thunder on the plains: The story of the American buffalo.* New York: Atheneum.

Rockwell, Anne (1998). *One bean.* Illus. by M. Halsey. San Diego: Harcourt.

St. George, Judith (2000). *So you want to be President?* Illus. by David Small. New York: Philomel.

Simon, Seymour (1999). *Crocodiles and alligators.* New York: HarperCollins.

Simon, Seymour (1998). *The universe.* New York: HarperCollins.

Stanley, Diane (1996). *Leonardo da Vinci.* New York: Morrow.

Stanley, Diane (1998). *Joan of Arc.* New York: Morrow.

Stanley, Diane (2000). *Michelangelo.* New York: HarperCollins.

Stanley, Diane (2002). *Saladin: Noble prince of Islam.* New York: HarperCollins.

Stanley, Jerry (2000). *Hurry freedom: African Americans in Gold Rush California.* New York: Crown.

Swinburne, Stephen R. (1999). *Coyote: North America's dog.* Honesdale, PA: Boyds Mills Press.

Wallace, Joseph (1999). *The lightbulb.* New York: Atheneum.

Warren Andrea (1996). *Orphan train rider: One boy's true story.* New York: Houghton Mifflin.

Wechsler, Doug (1999). *Bizarre birds.* Honesdale PA: Boyds Mills Press.

Wormell, Christopher (2004). *Teeth, tails, and tentacles: An animal counting book.* Philadelphia: Running Press.

Yolen, Jane (1987). *Owl moon.* Illus. by John Schoenherr. New York: Philomel.

Chapter 11

VIEWING AND VISUAL REPRESENTATION

Extending the Language Arts

Each day she saw the kids in the first grade across the hall reading, and before the year was over, some of the kids in her own class began to read. Not Trisha. Still, she loved being at school because she could draw.

FROM *THANK YOU, MR. FALKER* BY PATRICIA POLACCO

Not all children thrive on reading and writing as their primary modes of reception and communication in the language arts. Trisha, in *Thank you, Mr. Falker,* struggles in school and bears up under the teasing of peers before her fifth-grade teacher helps her overcome her dyslexia. Yet classmates surround Trisha to watch her work creative magic with crayons. Her drawing continuously revealed a gift and eventually an acceptable mode of communication that helped her achieve status as a revered children's author and illustrator. The visual representations of Trisha, Patricia Polacco, and the viewing of her illustrations by children of all ages have helped her overcome the devastating stigma of her childhood and has inspired others to accept their individual talents and diverse modes of communication.

As educators realize that writing is not the only medium of communication, they are openly accepting visual representation as an alternate, valued form of disseminating ideas and knowledge. Viewing and interpreting graphic representations, artwork, tables or figures, photographs, and other visual models is actually being taught as an information-gathering skill and reading strategy. As technology enhances the visual nature of our world, the language arts have expanded to fulfill the needs and options of new forms of communicating and receiving information. Viewing and visual representation acknowledge the expanding role of the language arts in a technological society.

A reconceptualization of literacy defines the myriad ways that learners gain and exhibit knowledge and skills beyond the traditional language arts of reading and writing. An expanded view of literacy seems limitless as we begin to explore the possibilities of all the ways in which learners interact with and through our growing visual world (Albers, 1997; Piazza, 1999; Rief, 1999). Figure 11.1 enumerates the breadth of resources for acquiring knowledge and representing learning that have contributed to the complex expansion of the definition of literacy.

FIGURE 11.1 **Visual viewing and representation: Sources and formats.**

Viewing	Visual Representation
Illustrations in children's books	Maps
Technology/computers	Charts/tables
World Wide Web	Diagrams
Moving images	Photographs
Sound effects	Posters
Television	Video productions (VCRs)
MTV	Technology productions
CNN	Digital photographs
Weather Channel	Web pages
Video arcade games	PowerPoint presentations
CD-ROMs	Digital art
Magazines	Artwork
Films	Graphs
Photographs	Story illustration
Newspapers	Timelines
Comic books	Graphic organizers
Art/museums	Journal entries
Advertisements	Sketch to stretch
Greeting cards	Visual dictionaries
Travel brochures	Logos
Bookmarks	Concrete poetry
Pamphlets	Story quilts
	Picture books

If schools are to continue to see themselves linked to the real world of work and leisure, literacy education must then reflect the technological reality of these worlds. Current educational systems typically stress a limited range of visual literacy, opting instead for the printed word over the visual image as a medium for and a documentation of learning. Yet everywhere outside of the classroom, the layering of information, multiple types of viewing, and visual representation, as well as documentation through various artistic forms predominate (Flood, Heath, & Lapp, 1997).

The visual arts encompass everything from dramatic performances to television and video games (reading, listening, viewing) while the communication arts (writing, speaking, visually representing) exist both independently and as integral elements of the visual arts. Children's ability to focus on several things simultaneously (channel surfing, video games, cell phones) receives little notice in the classroom. As teachers, we seem to hold on to an irrational loyalty to reading and writing. An excuse for omitting visual arts from the classroom is simply the fear that time spent with media is time taken away from traditional receptive and communicative arts.

Literacy education requires that teachers move toward blending traditional communication of information with the visual forms of display that our society currently embraces (Fox, 1999). Video productions, photographic projects, and the creation of graphs, diagrams, and charts showcase individual abilities of students. In classrooms with a broad view of literacy, the talented illustrator and the creative photographer receive as much praise as the report writer and the formal lecturer. This new view of literacy invites educators to stretch the possibilities for the representation of knowledge and skills beyond the printed word to both artistic and electronic displays of visual information. An expanded view of representing knowledge can only result in all educational partners—teachers, students, parents, administrators, teacher educators, and educational researchers—learning more.

Differences between a traditional and an expanded definition of literacy appear to lie somewhere between traditional print (text) and nonprint (nontext) materials. Hence, educators are likely to claim that a difference does exist between print literacy (textbooks, trade books) and visual literacy (art, technology, film, televisions, videos, etc.). Yet, in simple terms, parallels do exist between words and pictures. Actually, a reciprocal relationship may exist between the two as evidenced by the following example.

Marc Brown, the author/illustrator of picture books beginning with the classic *Arthur's Nose* (1976/2001), has successfully adapted his visual character, Arthur, to both the television screen and interactive CDs. Arthur in aardvark guise faces the same kind of childhood problems that a human child faces, constantly surrounded by emotional and social turmoil. Arthur serves as a means for children to identify and face their own childhood problems, and viewing the television series and the CDs has likely caused them to read the books (and vice versa). The same phenomenon holds true for the *Reading Rainbow* television series, which has adapted high quality children's literature to the television screen. The series has had a dramatic positive impact on children as readers.

A similar relationship exists between the world of art (images) and language (words). A trip to an art museum or the viewing of art slides in the classroom results in a discussion of the masterpieces viewed. Language (print/talk) serves as the vehicle for transmitting the critical thoughts and ideas inspired by the artwork (nonprint) (Frei, 1999). Similarly, the message of musical lyrics (print) and the complementary music video (nonprint) merge into a meaningful whole. In fact, we often come away from an encounter with illustrated literature, a discussion of art, and a music video with a clearer understanding than if the visual element were omitted and language was the sole vehicle for transmission.

Definitions distinguish the two new, emerging language arts concepts suggested by national standards (IRA/NCTE, 1996). "Viewing" includes the receptive language arts that allow the learner to acquire knowledge. Viewing is a process that includes perceiving, listening, thinking, evaluating, connecting, and responding. Viewing is the "neglected communication process" (Flood, Lapp, & Wood, 1998, p. 300) as meager information is available to assist teachers and students in learning material they view in a variety of formats. "Visual representation" includes the communicative means of documenting knowledge through a nonprint or visual mode. Visual representing may occur on a canvas, poster, or computer screen, and it may take the form of an artwork, a map, a diagram, a chart, or any visual construct that transmits information. Since these two components of visual literacy are so intricately connected, dividing this chapter into two sections would prove misleading. Therefore, this chapter addresses the language arts components that integrate viewing and visual representation as essentials of making and communicating meaning.

Objectives

- To understand the language arts of viewing children's book illustrations and visually representing story through art.
- To experience viewing graphic organizers to make meaning or provide a framework for learning and to examine visually representing knowledge through a graphic organizer.
- To participate in viewing illustrated journals through literary examples while authentically representing thought and emotions through illustrations in response to literature.
- To expand the role of language arts by viewing films, DVDs, videotapes, CDs, and CD-ROMs to determine how they visually represent knowledge through the new literacies.
- To understand the integrated nature of viewing and visual representation just as reading/writing and listening/speaking are naturally linked.
- To appreciate the blended visual and textual nature of Internet Web sites as potential resources of credible information.

The Picture Book and Visual Literacy

Children today grow up in a visual world surrounded by a barrage of images on computer monitors, across Internet sites, on television and movie screens, and throughout their home and school environments. The term "visual literacy" implies a level of discrimination that can sort through this deluge of visual images in an attempt to develop a personal sense of discretionary viewing and judgment. Because teachers readily accept the illustrations in children's books as a resource in the construction of meaning, it seems appropriate that the discussion of visual literacy beginning with picture book illustration may be the most comfortable start for an introduction to the mutual nature of viewing and visual representation. The illustrations in picture books naturally invite active participation in viewing and can provide a knowledge base for the visual representation of story through artistic response (Hubbard, 1996). Today, teachers are challenged to consider the natural link between the visual literacy of picture book illustration and the aesthetic understanding that derives from a total encounter with an illustrated book. With the abundance of picture books available to children at home, school, bookstores, and libraries, it becomes increasingly important for children to develop a sense for judging quality and establishing personal taste in book illustration.

Teacher Prep

The Teacher Prep Web site will help you become a better teacher by linking you to classroom videos, student artifacts, teaching strategies, lesson plans, relevant education leadership articles, and practical information on licensing, creating a portfolio, implementing standards, and being successful in field experiences. Visit this resource at www.prenhall.com/teacherprep.

A picture book is a celebration of both text and art. The words that tell a story enhanced by artful illustrations possess the potential to blend into magical reading and response experiences and even viewing and visual representation experiences. Children are more drawn to detail in art and more aware of their personal artistic perceptions than adults give them credit. Unfortunately, as children get older they tend to be "dulled by overload or by the real and imagined expectations our educational system have imposed on us which alter the way we view images" (Tunnell & Jacobs, 2004, p. 36). Children often learn to ignore their personal reactions to and the details in illustrations as they struggle to fulfill narrowly focused views of learning—closed-ended questions or fill in the blank activities. In becoming less aware of detail and personal meaning, they become less sensitive to the differences in the art of the picture book and less discriminating in the process of developing personal tastes.

The recognition of viewing and visual representation as authentic language arts causes us to readjust our judgmental lens toward the value of art. In *The Potential of Picture Books,* Barbara Kiefer (1994) describes visual literacy for children as the ability to "discriminate and interpret what they see. This process involves their attention, recognition, and finally their understanding" (p. 8). Teachers, parents, and librarians play a crucial role in helping children develop the ability to "see" through picture book illustrations. By enriching discriminatory abilities and encouraging the development of personal taste in visual imagery in picture books, children can attain independence of expression and response. To accomplish this, however, teachers must learn much more about children's book illustrations, including style, medium, and design, as well as more about the illustrators themselves. Yet it is not necessary for teachers to become experts in art appreciation to inspire aesthetic responses to art in children. Teachers can help children respond more fully to picture book art through discussion and related classroom activities. Enhancing visual literacy through picture books begins with a fresh view of illustrations through a child's eyes (Kiefer, 1995).

If a knowledgeable teacher attends to the choices, comments, and exuberance students exhibit toward a variety of illustrations, individual tastes and responses can be cultivated. Teachers have long recognized the potential of picture books to develop reading and writing literacy. Now picture books stand poised to elicit the intellectual, emotional, and visual response of children to art. Picture books provide an exceptional means of nurturing visual literacy and artistic appreciation in an increasingly visual world by focusing on the selection of high quality illustrated books for children, the elements of artistic design and the variety of artistic style in these books, media choices and applications, and the graphic techniques incorporated. Following the viewing of illustrated children's books, teachers are encouraged to invite children to visually represent the art of the picture book either by making one's own "book" or by exhibiting an artistic response to literature through a drawing, watercolor, or collage.

Selecting Picture Books

Picture books are a child's first invitation into the world of literature and the potential start of a lifelong adventure with reading. Quality time spent with literature should be accompanied by the highest quality text and illustration. While children's choices of books must be honored, adults must be responsible for selecting a pool of quality literature from which endearing favorites may grow. The following criteria adapted from John Stewig's *Looking at Picture Books* (1995) will assist teachers, librarians, and parents in identifying quality visual experiences:

- The artist uses an original idea that allows the viewer to see something familiar in a new way or to introduce something not ever seen before.

- The art captivates the viewer because of style, medium, sequence, or placement on the page.
- The art enhances or extends the text, creating a greater understanding of the words through artistic images or additional details not mentioned in the text.
- The art invites viewer response through noticing, discussing, pointing, relating to text, discovering details, and expressing feelings.

Although art seems the dominant focus in visual literacy, the language of the book must contain rich familiar and unfamiliar words, include a variety of sentence structures, use literary devices that captivate the reader and listener, and invite reader/viewer response. Only when quality art and text combine does a quality experience ensue.

A variety of prestigious awards reflect the highest standards of illustration and text. Established in 1938, the Caldecott Medal is presented annually to the illustrator of the most distinguished picture book for children for the preceding year. A number of honor books are also named each year by the selection committee of the American Library Association. In addition, the Coretta Scott King Award (established 1974) and the Pura Belpé Award (established 1996) for illustrations highlight quality multicultural picture books for children. These award-winning titles can be shared with children of appropriate age levels as exemplary picture books, thus exposing them to the highest standards for quality.

Artistic Design in Picture Books

While the interplay of a picture book's text and illustration blends key literacy components, visual literacy is extended to another dimension through book design—the book's size and shape, the book cover, the endpapers, the title page, the lettering, and the spacing of art and text on the page. Reaching beyond the standard visual and verbal aspects of a book, the design is often what intrigues children about a book in the first place. An attractive cover in compelling color with unique lettering draws children into a book to explore both pictures and story. The blend of a picture book's text, illustrations, and design elements results in a greater overall effect than any one of these components can achieve separately.

Book Size and Shape. Why do picture books vary in size? How do the text and illustrations often lend themselves to special formats? Answering these questions and speculation about design decisions help children become higher level thinkers and problem solvers.

Some books require a larger than usual format for presenting their compelling artwork. Some notable oversized formats include Lois Ehlert's *Cuckoo/Cucú: A Mexican Folktale;* Janet Steven's *Tops and Bottoms,* and Paul Zelinsky's *Rapunzel.* Undersized formats are less usual but include an updated version of Helen Bannerman's *The Story of Little Babaji* illustrated by Fred Marcellino. Special sizes include the postcard format of Vera B. Williams and Jennifer Williams's *Stringbean's Trip to the Shining Sea,* the narrow vertical format housing Janice May Udry's *A Tree is Nice,* and the natural shape of Lois Ehlert's *Hands.* After sharing these titles with children, speculate the rationale for selecting these formats.

Book Jackets. The illustration on the front cover of a book serves as an invitation to explore further. A teacher might begin a lesson in visual literacy by showing the cover and asking the question, "What do you think this book is about?" The illustration on the back cover may offer students a reason to reflect, relive, or relate the book to their own experience. As children get their initial reading cues from a book's cover, engagement in literature is ignited.

The art on many book covers wraps around from front to back, providing a poster-like scene. Make children aware of this quality in books such as Will Hillenbrand's humorous illustration on Phyllis Root's *Kiss the Cow* or the Italian flair of Diane Stanley's *Michelangelo,* which blends authentic Renaissance and illustrator art. Other book jackets have separate but related illustrations on the front and back covers. Explore D. B. Johnson's *Henry Hikes to Fitchburg* and E. B. Lewis's illustration for Elizabeth Fitzgerald Howard's *Virgie Goes to School with us Boys* as examples of this design. Encourage children to enter and revisit the text through these visual invitations to read, respond, and reflect.

Endpapers. The end papers of a book often go unnoticed by hurried readers. An astute teacher, however, can open children's eyes to these effective connecting links between a book's front and back covers and the pages within. The color and art of a book's endpapers provide an interesting transition from the exterior to the interior of the book. In their simplest form, endpapers are colored but illustration free. Even then, their colors are chosen carefully to enhance the book cover, to convey information, or to express a mood or feeling. Open Seymour Simon's *Crocodiles and Alligators* and note the reptile skin texture on the dark green pages. Observe the choice of plain, smoky-blue endpapers to compliment the limited pastel tones in Brock Cole's original tale, *Buttons.*

Many illustrators plan for endpapers that visually complement the story or the artwork of the book's interior. Diana Pomeroy's (1997) *Wildflower ABC* is an alphabet book of potato prints. Its endpapers are a shower of repeated patterns of golden poppies, purple asters, and wild roses, all created with the potato print motif that graces the book. S. D. Nelson uses mural-like replication of the battle of the Little Big Horn on the endpapers of Joseph Bruchac's *Crazy Horse's Vision.* Note the varied skin tones of the children's hands that decorate the endpapers of Karen Katz's *The Colors of Us.* The meaningful connections between story and endpapers make them worth noting, sharing, and responding to prior to or following a book experience. Once children are made aware of these special connections, they are certain to stop and note them independently as they begin their own journeys through a book.

Title Page. The title page introduces readers to publication details about a book—its complete title as well as the names of the author, illustrator, and publisher. The title page can be housed on a single page, but often extends across two pages. Insights into the story can be gleaned by examining the illustration accompanying the title page. A double-page spread by James Ransome invites the reader into the simple cabin and fenced-in yard of the slave quarters in Tony Johnston's *The Wagon.* While the bright sunlight and blooming sunflowers give the impression of impending joy, the dark, sullen cabin, absence of people, and shadowed fenceposts temper the mood. The open gate invites the reader/viewer to turn the page and become part of this moment in history when the emancipation of slaves had become a reality. In Sarah Stewart's *The Journey,* David Small illustrates the double title page with an Amish horse-drawn cart that seems to be moving across the page, causing the viewer to turn the page to see where this vehicle may be headed. An awareness of the visual possibilities of the title page can aid in building comprehension, set story mood and tone, and provide an appreciation for the ability of art to capture the attention of readers.

Borders. Some illustrators choose to use borders around their illustrations to artistically complement the main illustrations. Others incorporate borders to predict forthcoming events or to reveal a story-within-a-story. The creative use of borders enhances artistic presentation, but also extends meaning beyond the text. The masterful crafting of border is synonymous with the work of Jan Brett. Her classic retelling of *The Mitten* exemplifies the artistic use of borders to enrich the unfolding story. The story's animals are cleverly packed in the mitten one by one, while mitten-shaped cutouts in the right and left borders of double-page spreads review and preview mitten inhabitants. Jan Brett has continued her border art in *Comet's Nine Lives* with frames made of shells, rope, and sealife and with needlepoint creations in *Hedgie's Surprise*. This consistent visual feature in Brett's work lends itself to children's natural inclinations to take the time to notice far more details than adults.

Lettering and Type. Lettering and type selection requires three decisions for the book designer or illustrator (a) font selection, (b) type size, and (c) color. Font selection must match a story genre, reflect a historical period, or suit a mood or setting. Shana Corey's *You Forgot Your Skirt, Amelia Bloomer* incorporates hand lettering by illustrator Chesley McClaren and a Victorian-like font to reflect the fashionable setting of the story in mid-eighteenth-century America. The size of type should consider the age of audience, the book size, and the message of the author. Jon Scieszka's *The Stinky Cheese Man and Other Fairly Stupid Tales* is a classic example of both reducing and enlarging text, even on the same page. In Doreen Cronin's *Click, Clack, Moo: Cows that Type,* illustrator Betsy Lewin uses a dual font to differentiate story text from typewriter produced letters. Choosing color—perhaps black type on light background or white type on dark background—is another decision the designer must make. In *More than Anything Else,* a childhood biography of Booker T. Washington, Marie Bradby's text meshes with Chris Soentpiet's art. From sunup to sundown, the type is black set on the pure white background of the salt works where Booker and his Papa arduously labor. Most of the book, however, is presented in yellow type with dark backgrounds reflecting the light of the kerosene lantern, candles, or fireplace by which Booker learned to read. These types of design decisions combine to blend a picture book into a visual work of art.

Space. The arrangement of text in relation to illustrations is another aspect of book design to be noted. Text can appear consistently on the same side of the page as in *Tea with Milk* by Allen Say or it can be alternated from right side to left side intermittently as the text is integrated with the artwork itself. Lisa Campbell Ernst's *Stella Louella's Runaway Book,* for example, cleverly reflects this technique as text appears on the refrigerator door at the diner, on mattresses at the Bed Bazaar, and on the librarian's desk. This seems to occur most often when a book is written and illustrated by the same person.

No single design element alone guarantees a successful picture book. It is the effective blending of all design elements with exquisite illustrations (and powerful text) that creates a cohesive whole. Only then does the picture book appeal to the eye and stir the visual imagination of the reader/viewer. Open any book that has won a Caldecott Medal and note the blending of design elements into an integrated and captivating picture book. As teachers and students open their eyes to the intricacies of book design, they grow in their appreciation of artistic qualities and often incorporate them as they write, draw, and design their own picture books.

Artistic Style in Picture Books

The artistic style of an illustration is revealed in the way in which the artist uses the elements of art and the chosen media to create a visual image. Style is a result of all the decisions an illustrator makes regarding the right blend of color, line, and shape in producing a final product, like placing a signature on a work of art. As children are immersed in literature as art, they easily begin to recognize the "style" of the artist through the somewhat predictable nature of their work (think about the distinctive styles of Patricia Polacco, Tomie dePaola, Steven Kellogg, and Floyd Cooper).

Six basic styles of art are recognized in children's book illustrations:

- ***Realism.*** A style that depicts people, nature, and objects as they might actually appear in the real world. Ruth Sanderson's oils render a Russian tale as lifelike people and animals form the images in *The Golden Mare, the Firebird, and the Magic Ring*.
- ***Surrealism.*** A style that skews realism in its attempts to represent a mingling of the unconcious with the dreamlike qualities of imagination. David Weisner's wordless art in *Sector 7* allows the reader's mind to take flight as the story unfurls through a fantasy-like world.
- ***Expressionism.*** A style that gives form to strong inner feelings through the use of bright colors and figures that are a bit modified or distorted. D. B. Johnson's *Henry Hikes to Fitchburg* projects a somewhat geometric style that brings angles and sharp edges to the characters and natural setting.
- ***Impressionism.*** A style that uses the movement of light and color to define shape. Emily Arnold McCully, a Caldecott award–winning artist, captures distinct images of water and light through her pastel watercolors in *Mirette and Bellini Cross Niagara Falls*.
- ***Cartoon art.*** A style that uses bright colors and stark pen and ink outlines to focus viewer attention and convey the essence of characters and objects that have been simplified in appearance. Steven Kellogg's retold folktale of *The Three Sillies* incorporates outrageous comedy through his ink and watercolor cartoonlike characters and backgrounds.

Although children do not need to apply these terms to illustrator styles, teachers need to be aware of them as they discuss the characteristics of an illustrator's style. The Literature Cluster on page 331 lists a number of illustrators and books that exemplify each style.

Artistic Media in Picture Books

Examining the artistic media that illustrators select to create their works of art can help children understand and appreciate picture books while encouraging them to respond by using these media in their own artistic expressions. Information on media may be located in small print on the copyright page of a book or on the cover where information about the illustrator is given. Children should be encouraged to reflect on why an illustrator choose a particular medium and what effect it achieved. They can compare several books by the same illustrator to see what media were used.

Six common art media are used in children's book illustrations: (a) oil paints, (b) watercolors, (c) graphite/colored pencils, (d) pastels/chalk, (e) acrylics, and (f) mixed media. Mixed media refers to the blending of several art media for a special, unique effect. Oil paints dominate the deep, rich illustrations of Thomas Locker in more than twenty picture books. *Water Dance* and *Sky Tree: Seeing Science Through Art* portray the changes in nature influenced by the water cycle and the seasons. Because children are rarely exposed to oils, Locker's artwork can also serve as an introduction to the art of the great masters. Watercolor has the power to portray a variety of moods from whimsical and lighthearted to serious and downcast. Illustrator Jerry Pinkney reveals his artistic magic as he presents visual images of the racing tigers as "they melted into a pool of butter as golden as a dream come true" in *Sam and the Tigers* by Julius Lester.

Literature Cluster

ARTISTIC STYLES IN PICTURE BOOKS

Note: The illustrator's name is indicated in **boldface.**

Realism

Lewin, Ted (1998). *The storytellers.* New York: Lothrop, Lee, & Shepard.

Sanderson, Ruth (2002). *Cinderella.* New York: Little, Brown.

Say, Allen (1993). *Grandfather's journey.* Boston: Houghton Mifflin.

Schroeder, Alan (1996). *Minty: A story of young Harriet Tubman.* Illus. by **Jerry Pinkney.** New York: Dial.

Woodson, Jacqueline (2001). *The other side.* Illus. by **E. B. Lewis.** New York: Putnam.

Zelinsky, Paul (1997). *Rapunzel.* New York: Dutton.

Surrealism

Gruen, John (1996). *Flowers and fables.* Illus. by **Rafal Obinski.** San Diego: Harcourt.

Sis, Peter (1996). *Starry messenger: Galileo Galilei.* New York: Farrar, Straus & Giroux.

Weisner, David (1991). *Tuesday.* New York: Clarion.

Wood, Audrey (2000). *Jubal's wish.* Illus. by **Don Wood.** New York: Scholastic.

Expressionism

Best, Cari (1999). *Three cheers for Catherine the great.* Illus. by **Giselle Potter.** New York: Dorling Kindersley.

Bunting, Eve (1994). *Smoky night.* Illus. by **David Diaz.** San Diego: Harcourt.

Myers, Christopher (1999). *Black cat.* New York: Scholastic.

Ringgold, Faith (1991). *Tar beach.* New York: Crown.

Soto, Gary (1995). *Chato's kitchen.* Illus. by **Susan Guevara.** New York: Putnam.

Impressionism

McCully, Emily Arnold (1992). *Mirette on the high wire.* New York: Putnam.

Stevenson, James (1995). *Sweet corn: Poems.* New York: Greenwillow.

Yolen, Jane (1987). *Owl moon.* Illus. by **John Schoenherr.** New York: Philomel.

Young, Ed (1989). *Lon Po Po.* New York: Philomel.

Cartoon Art

Ernst, Lisa Campbell (1998). *Stella Louella's runaway book.* New York: Simon & Schuster.

Henkes, Kevin (1991). *Chrysanthemum.* New York: Greenwillow.

Moss, Lloyd (1995). *Zin! Zin! Zin! A violin.* Illus. by **Marjorie Priceman.** New York: Simon & Schuster.

Rothman, Peggy (1995). *Officer Buckle and Gloria.* New York: Putnam.

Yorinks, Arthur (1996). *Hey, Al.* Illus. by **Richard Egielski.** New York: Farrar, Straus & Giroux.

Graphite pencils define the shades of night in John Coy's (1996) *Night Driving* illustrated by Peter McCarty. Black, gray, and white cafes, gas pumps, and truck stops give striking realism to this nostalgic driving experience. Chris Van Allsburg's graphite drawings for *The Mysteries of Harris Burdick* (1984) often come to mind when teachers and children explore this medium. Lisa Campbell Ernst incorporates an ink outline to complement the pastel drawings used to illustrate *Stella Louella's Runaway Book.* Thomas B. Allen also uses pastels to color his charcoal-drawn illustrations in George Shannon's *Climbing Kansas Mountains.* More artists are introducing acrylics and mixed media or experimenting with new media to bring rich color, texture, and dimension to children's books. Teachers can help children explore media through illustrator studies that use viewing and visual representation to enhance visual literacy. The Literature Cluster on page 332 lists a variety of books that reflect common media choices in children's books.

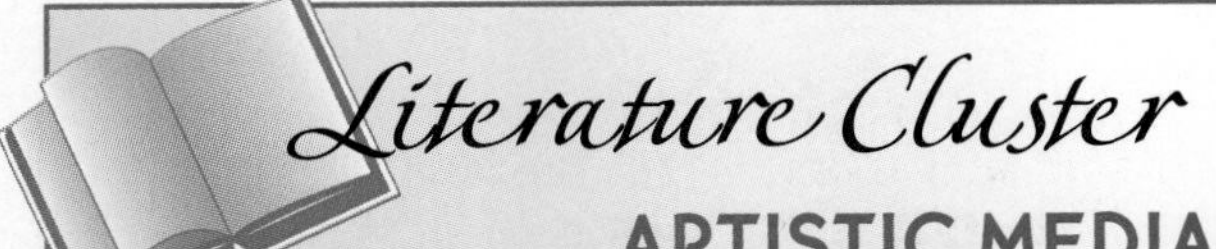

Literature Cluster

ARTISTIC MEDIA IN PICTURE BOOKS

Oil

Cline-Ransome, Lesa (2000). *Satchel Paige.* Illus. by James E. Ransome. New York: Simon & Schuster.

Locker, Thomas (with Candace Christiansen) (1995). *Sky tree: Seeing science through art.* New York: HarperCollins.

Zelinsky, Paul (1997). *Rapunzel.* New York: Dutton.

Graphite/Colored Pencil

Aylesworth, Jim. (1999). *The full belly bowl.* Illus. by Wendy Anderson Halperin. New York: Atheneum.

Benet, Rosemary, & Benet, Stephen Vincent (2001). *Johnny Appleseed.* Illus. by S. D. Schindler. New York: McElderry Books.

Pastels

Ammon, Richard (2001). *Amish horses.* Illus. by Pamela Patrick. New York: Atheneum.

Ernst, Lisa Campbell (1998). *Stella Louella's runaway book.* New York: Simon & Schuster.

Mollel, Tolowa M. (2000). *Subira Subira.* Illus. by Linda Sapport. New York: Clarion.

Watercolor

Arnold, Marsha D. (2000). *The bravest of us all.* Illus. by Brad Sneed. New York: Dial.

DeFelice, Cynthia (2000). *Cold feet.* Illus. by Robert Andrew Parker. New York: DK Ink.

Florian, Douglas (1998). *Insectlopedia.* San Diego: Harcourt Brace.

Lewin, Ted & Betsy (2000). *Elephant walk.* Illus. by Ted Lewin. New York: Lothrop, Lee & Shepard.

McCully, Emily Arnold (2000). *Mirette & Bellini cross Niagara Falls.* New York: Putnam.

Stevenson, James (1998). *Popcorn.* New York: Greenwillow.

Tunnell, Michael O. (1997). *Mailing May.* Illus. by Ted Rand. New York: Greenwillow.

Wiesner, David (1999). *Sector 7.* New York: Clarion.

Acrylic Paints

Curlee, Lynn (2000). *Liberty.* Atheneum.

Edwards, Pamela Duncan (1997). *Dinorella: A prehistoric fairy tale.* Illus. by Henry Cole. New York: Hyperion.

Fisher, Leonard Everett (1999). *Alexander Graham Bell.* New York: Atheneum.

Howe, James (1999). *Horace & Morris, but mostly Dolores.* Illus. by AmyWalrod. New York: Atheneum.

Stanley, Diane (1998). *Joan of Arc.* New York: Morrow.

Mixed Media

Krull, Kathleen (1996). *Wilma unlimited: How Wilma Rudolph became the world's fastest woman.* Illus. by David Diaz. San Diego: Harcourt Brace.

McKissack Patricia (2000). *The honest-to-goodness truth.* Illus. by Giselle Potter. New York: Simon & Schuster. (pencil, ink, gouache, gesso, watercolor)

Root, Phyllis (2000). *Kiss the cow!* Illus. by Will Hillebrand. Cambridge, MA: Candlewick (on vellum)

St. George, Judith (2000). *So you want to be President.* Illus. by David Small. New York: Philomel. (ink, watercolor, pastel, chalk)

Stevens, Janet, & Crummel, Susan Stevens (1999). *Cook-a-doodle-do.* Illus. by Janet Stevens. San Diego: Harcourt Brace. (watercolor, colored pencil, gesso, & photographic and digital elements)

Graphic Techniques in Picture Books

Beyond selecting media with which to present images, illustrators choose creative graphic techniques to transmit the visions carried in their minds. Woodcuts give a strong, bold, powerful impression. An image is drawn on a woodblock, and the wood is cut away with special knives until only the lines of the drawing remain above the surface. Ink is rolled on the lines and the wood is pressed onto paper to print the image. Mary Azarian, the 1999 Caldecott recipient, skillfully used tinted woodcuts to capture the rural Vermont landscape and the rugged characters in Jacqueline Briggs Martin's *Snowflake Bentley*. The bold and colorful linoleum-cut prints of Mary Wormell in *Bernard the Angry Rooster* prove to be an effective choice for sharing nostalgic memories of childhood and home. Although these techniques may be far too intricate for children to create in their own art, they easily recognize them in children's book illustrations and an art teacher may even demonstrate each technique for further understanding.

Scratchboard—a white board covered with black ink into which a drawing is scratched with a sharp tool—has become the technique of choice for Brian Pinkney, the illustrator of Andrea Pinkney's *Duke Ellington* and *Bill Pickett: Rodeo Ridin' Cowboy*. Pinkney adds color with oils or pastels, wiping away the excess. Children can be shown how to informally explore this technique in school by covering pieces of paper with crayon colors hidden with black crayon and scratching out a drawing with a sharp object.

Collage is an artistic composition made by gluing different materials onto a surface. The master of paper collage is Eric Carle, whose twenty-five years of book illustrating reflect his ability to bring paper to life. Carle's animals are particularly impressive as overlapped tissue paper giraffes, elephants, and roosters fill the page. Carle's insect quintet employs this technique with *The Very Hungry Caterpillar, The Very Busy Spider, The Very Quiet Cricket, The Very Lonely Firefly,* and *The Very Clumsy Click Beetle*. As this technique has become the hallmark of Carle's work, his illustrations are perhaps the most recognizable by young children.

Cut paper layering is related to collage but requires an even sharper eye and hand for defining detail. David Wisniewski has been honored for this technique for *Golem,* the 1997 Caldecott Medal book. This artist uses colored paper for his cut illustrations that are held together with double-stick photo mounts. He uses a precise bladed knife—often as many as a thousand blades to complete sixteen illustrations in a single book—to cut the paper in a way that is so acute that one can almost feel its sharpness. Older children appreciate the accuracy and challenge of this time-consuming technique.

Photography is another technique used to create the foundation for text or as a building block for additional media. Bruce McMillan uses nostalgic black and white photos and tints them with oil colors, a process used at the turn of the century. Pure photography is the hallmark of many well-honored informational books. Children can learn much from the photography and selections of George Ancona, Christopher Knight, Tana Hoban, and Ken Robbins. Students can take their disposable cameras on a field trip and then use their photographs in a book of their own.

Digitally illustrated books are appearing frequently on the market as the new technology of computer-generated art lures book illustrators and publishing houses. Audrey Wood's *The Red Racer* and Don Wood's art in *Jubal's Wish* were drawn with a digital pen on a digital tablet by hand. Children are drawn to the vivid color, sharp images, and cartoonlike design of this technique. Dan Yaccarino's digitally rendered character of *Oswald,* a bold, blue octopus, extends a *Nick Jr.* television series to the world of books. The potential of software to contribute to children's own book illustrating attempts (*Kid Pix Deluxe*) provides an artistic and technology-based medium for illustration.

The more teachers know about and appreciate the design of a picture book, the artistic styles, the media choices, the graphic techniques, and specific children's book illustrators, the more they open the world of visual literacy to children. With proper modeling through discussion and visual attention, children soon differentiate between illustrators, techniques, and media. They naturally begin to notice distinct endpapers, full-spread book covers, and font selections. The picture book provides an excellent model for visual literacy and serves as an important first step into the world of art.

As children learn about the art of the picture book, they become ready and eager to explore art in a more global context. Illustrations in children's books can prepare youth for trips to local and big city art museums and inspire them to perhaps explore the lives and work of renowned artists. Children's book illustrations can comfortably and confidently open the world of art to a child at an impressionable age and further the potential impact of art in that lifelong learner.

Viewing/Visual Representation as a Complement to Writing

"I see, and write what I see, and what is written tells me what I did not know and what I need to know. The line, written and drawn, instructs as I practice the visual art of writing" (Murray, 1996, p. 3). Donald Murray, contemplating the relationship between drawing and writing, believes that writers observe, then write what they observe; thus, writing exists as a visual art. A good writer brings a visualization to the reader through well-chosen words and created images making the written word a work of art in the mind's eye. For example, Pam Conrad's *Prairie Song* and Patricia MacLachlan's *Sarah, Plain and Tall* paint a portrait with words of the tallgrass prairie, the early homesteads, the devastating drought, and the steadfast pioneers who settled the Great Plains. As a reader absorbs the descriptive language of quality literature, words create an image of the setting, the characters, and episodes that fill the pages of a book. Words paint pictures, pictures tell stories.

In exploring visual literacy, it is critical to consider the mutual relationship between writing and the visual image. While the power of words paints visual images in the mind of the reader, the visual image can also serve as an inspiration for the words that eventually become the stories, poems, and reports of children. The relationship between artistic drawing and writing in the elementary classroom occurs in several valuable contexts:

- Drawing/art serves as a catalyst for writing. (Rehearsal stage)
- Drawing/art reflects comprehension. (Sketch-to-stretch strategy)
- Drawing/art expands the aesthetic realm in journals. (Sketchbook journals)
- Drawing/art enhances learning in the content areas. (Learning logs)

Art as Rehearsal for Writing

The impressive link between art and writing begins early in a child's life as drawing becomes a rehearsal for oral story and, eventually, the written word. The brainstorming and rehearsal stage of the writing process for young children typically includes a drawing that inspires emergent words, sentences, and stories. Too often teachers demand the written product first, while utilizing visual image through drawing as a reward for completing the writing. Yet early drawings of kindergarten children often reveal the beginnings of literacy as *X*s, *O*s, and *T*s find their way into their unique visual images. And almost every child has a story to tell when asked to "Tell me about what you have drawn." The visual

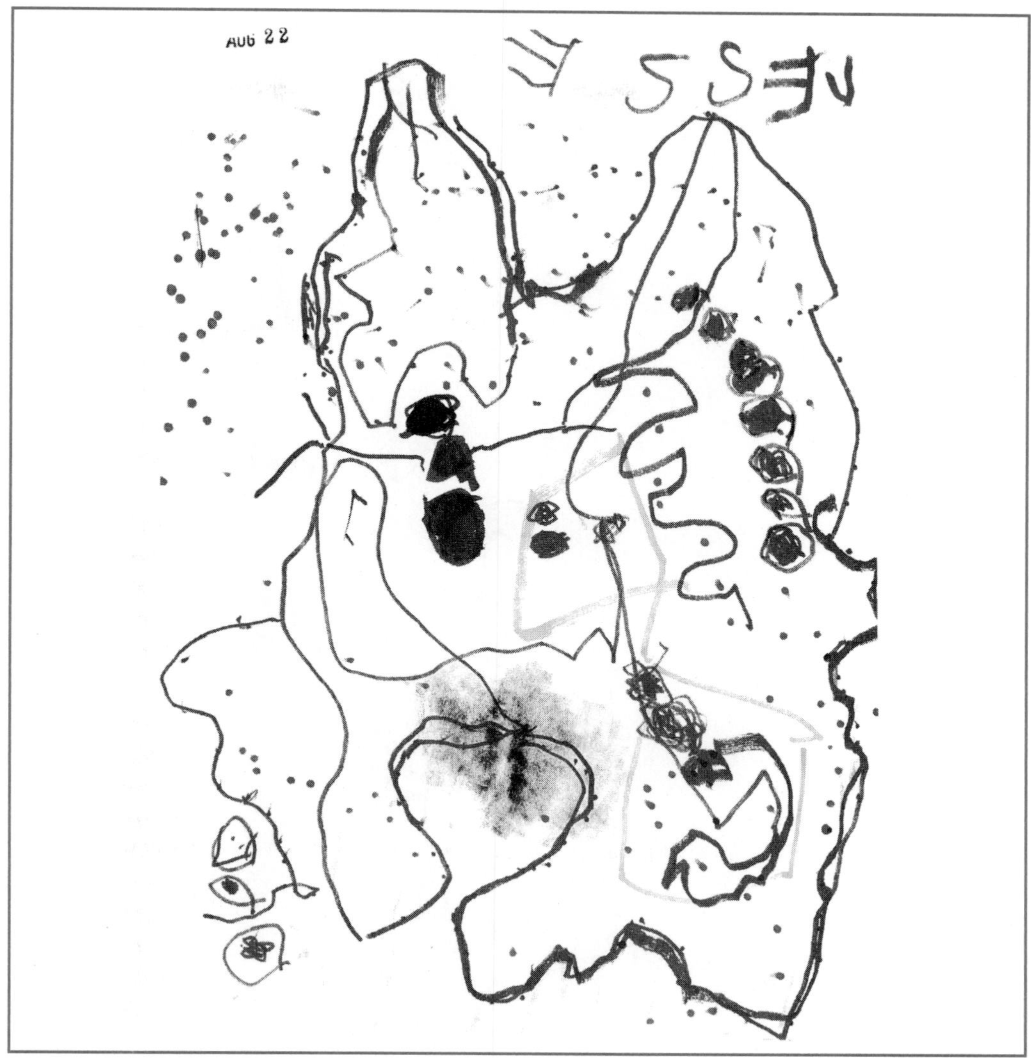

STUDENT SAMPLE 11.1 Jesse's kindergarten journal.

image is indeed rehearsal and practice for the stories young writers want to share. Perhaps teachers should reconsider the potential of art as a catalyst for writing at all age levels.

Although children do not have the ability to put a story into conventional print text, they are more than delighted to "tell" a bystander their story as reflected in their art. The accompanying drawings from kindergarten journals overflow with story. Throughout the school year, five-year-old Jesse is filled with artistic expression, although few letters or words appear in his daily journal (see Student Sample 11.1). Jesse's mind is undoubtedly filled with imaginative stories, however, as his intricate drawings may reveal action and adventure when he "tells" his drawing to the teacher. Five-year-old Jacob, on the other hand, provides some risk taking as he uses some letters to "tell his story" (see Student Sample 11.2). Note the "story" in the teacher's print below Jacob's drawing as children elaborate on their artistic rehearsal for story. Five-year-old Andrea reveals some story risk taking as she "reads" her story to her teacher: "There are 13 chicks and they hatched and we are going to play with them" (see Student Sample 11.3).

STUDENT SAMPLE 11.2 Jacob's kindergarten journal.

As teachers begin to see the potential of art to reveal story and to encourage writing, they are more likely to realize the importance of art as a rehearsal, as a visual representation of ideas, and as a springboard for both children's writing and reading of their own text. Daily journals in kindergarten, first grade, and even second grade might begin with a visual representation and then move on to written text in the student's constructed form.

Sketch-to-Stretch Strategy

The sketch-to-stretch instructional strategy (Whitin, 1996b) serves as response to literature in a visual format. The strategy is described as sketching what a story means to the reader. As children listen or read a story, they share their interpretations through drawing or the use of artistic media. The relationship of sketch-to-stretch to the writing process reveals

STUDENT SAMPLE 11.3 Andrea's kindergarten journal.

itself as students sketch, revise, reshape, and share their visual interpretations of literature. Sketching challenges readers and teachers to see things in new ways, to grow continuously, and to appreciate unexpected outcomes. Phyllis Whitin's (1996a) study of seventh-graders revealed several benefits of the sketch-to-stretch strategy in response to a chapter book, Wilson Rawls's *Summer of the Monkeys:*

- Sketching provides an avenue for writing. If students sketch to express thoughts, the sketch becomes a detailed expression of feelings. A sketch provides a visual from which to write an effective commentary. Sketching helps foster detailed writing; it does not duplicate it.
- Sketching links experiences. Sketches foster connections between and among texts. Informal talk built around sketches can actually provide links between characters, settings, episodes, and reactions. Response moves from visual images to expanded talk to higher-level intertextual connections.
- Sharing sketches generates new ideas. Community plays a role in expanding ideas and multiple interpretations. Sketches serve as works in progress as peer talk generates fresh ideas for enhancing, detailing, and depicting new versions of revised thoughts. Listening and viewing are active processes that lead to further clarification through writing.

Sketch-to-stretch provides a means to explore ideas through visual symbols so they may be later conveyed through clear, concise, language through talk or writing.

An adaptation of the sketch-to-stretch strategy can be seen in Ashley's third-grade visual representation of her favorite part of Sid Fleischman's *The Whipping Boy*

STUDENT SAMPLE 11.4 A third grader's sketch-to-stretch for Sid Fleischman's *The Whipping Boy*.

(Student Sample 11.4). Ashley draws Prince Brat and Jemmy in the rat-infested underground sewers. Details reveal specific aspects of the text. In comparing Ashley's generic written response to her personal artistic response, it appears that her artwork reveals an even greater understanding of the story than her words are able to share.

Sketchbook Journals

Integrated writing and art journals—sketchbook journals—provide opportunities for students to record verbal and artistic images as they express their thoughts and emotions. Teachers invite their students to capture a special experience by both writing and drawing about it. For example, field trips provide a venue for collecting visual images and thoughts away from the classroom. Whether venturing with primary students to the zoo, or hunting with fifth graders for fossils in an abandoned quarry, the sketchbook journal provides an outlet for information and images. Virginia Wright Frierson's *A Desert Scrapbook: Dawn to Dusk in the Sonoran Desert* and *An Island Scrapbook: Dawn to Dusk on a Barrier Island* model the interplay of nature art and journal writing as observation and words work together to share images and thoughts. Using a journal for field notes and sketches allows children to find poetry in a twisted tree trunk, words in a giant sunflower, or a story in a grove of oak trees. The value of the sketchbook journal goes beyond the simple act of observation. The sketches and written notes set the stage for additional writing upon return to the classroom (Chancer & Rester-Zodrow, 1997).

The creation of an electronic school scrapbook moves beyond handwritten text and hand-drawn illustrations to the realm of technology. Digital photos, news clippings, artifacts, and memorabilia become the means of creating visual representations of the school experience. Lesson Plan 11.1 details and sequences the steps involved in engaging students in such a visual project.

LESSON PLAN 11.1

TITLE: Creating an Electronic School Scrapbook

Grade Level: 5–8

Time Frame: Ongoing throughout the school year (project should be introduced at the beginning of the school year)

Standards

IRA/NCTE Standards: 1, 7, 8

NETS for Students: 3, 5

Objectives

- Students will utilize technology (digital camera, scanners, colored printer, presentation software, computer, etc.) to create a visual representation of their favorite school memories.
- Students will write personal narratives and/or picture captions to describe school events and projects.

Materials

- Computers with presentation software (such as PowerPoint) for student use.
- Digital photographs, pictures, ticket stubs, invitations, news clipping, artifacts, and other memorabilia that represent the current school year or a specific school event (will be collected throughout the school year).
- Literature *A North American Rainforest Scrapbook* (1999) and *An Island Scrapbook* (1998) by Virginia Wright Frierson.

Motivation

- Show students some yearbooks from previous school years and discuss common features and purposes of yearbooks.
- Explain to students that they will create an electronic yearbook (or scrapbook) filled with favorite pictures and memorabilia to represent the current school year.

Procedures

- As a class, brainstorm ideas of features and events that should be included in the electronic scrapbook. Students may suggest special celebrations, field trips, contests, etc. Assign pairs of students to be in charge of certain events. Emphasize that the tentative plan may change as the school year progresses. It is difficult to project what will happen during the upcoming year.
- Demonstrate how to use a digital camera, scanner, and presentation software (such as PowerPoint). It is also important that students learn how and where they should save digital pictures. Consider creating special computer files for the purpose of the yearbook. Designate the role(s) of official class photographer(s). Other students

may be in charge of collecting programs, tickets, or other keepsakes. Such mementos may be scanned and inserted into the electronic scrapbook.

- Throughout the year, students will work on the electronic yearbook by creating slides with pictures and written accounts of the school year. Students may want to add music, animation, video clips, hyperlinks, etc. The possibilities are endless!
- At the end of the school year, provide all students with copies of the electronic scrapbook (burn to CDs or DVDs). Consider posting a copy on the Internet (ask for parental permission).

Assessment

- Teacher-created checklist or rubric reflecting lesson objectives

Accommodation/Modification

- Assign specific tasks to suit individual students' needs, strengths, and interests.

Visit the Meeting the Standards module in Chapter 11 of the Companion Website at www.prenhall.com/hancock to adapt this lesson to meet your state's standards.

A number of quality children's books reinforce the effectiveness of combining art and writing in journals. The Literature Cluster below lists several titles that retain a journal format but are enhanced by art that accompanies words. These serve as models and

Literature Cluster

JOURNAL FORMATS

Words and Sketches: Journal Formats with Visual Representations

Moss, Marisa (1996). *Amelia writes again.* Berkeley, CA: Tricycle Press.

Moss, Marisa (1998). *Rachel's journal: The story of a pioneer girl.* San Diego, CA: Harcourt Brace.

Rocklin, Joanne (1997). *For your eyes only! (FYEO).* New York: Scholastic.

Stewart, Sarah (2001). *The journey.* Illus. by David Small. New York: Farrar, Straus and Giroux.

Turner, Ann (1997). *Mississippi mud: Three prairie journals.* Illus. by Robert Blake. New York: HarperCollins.

Williams, Vera B. (1981). *Three days on a river in a red canoe.* New York: Greenwillow.

Words Awaiting Sketches: Journal Formats Inviting Visual Representation

Blos, Joan (1979). *A gathering of days: A New England girl's journal.* New York: Scribner's.

Cushman, Karen (1994). *Catherine, called Birdy.* Boston: Clarion.

George, Jean Craighead (1959/1988). *My side of the mountain.* New York: Dutton.

Heinrich, Bernd (1990). *An owl in the house: A naturalist's diary.* New York: Little, Brown

Hesse, Karen (2000). *Stowaway.* New York: Margaret K. McElderry Books.

Lyons, Mary E. (1995), *Keeping secrets: The girlhood diaries of seven women writers.* New York: Holt.

springboards for the art and writing connection that is an important component of visual literacy.

Learning Logs and Visual Representation

Art also enhances learning in the content areas of science, social studies, and mathematics. Learning logs imply a consistent notebook in which to record ongoing knowledge and understanding in content area study.

Math journals invite children to write or draw whatever they need to explain how they solved a problem. A third-grader's drawing (Student Sample 11.5) shows how visual representation assists in determining "How many wheels in all?" Note how the drawn images enhance John's understanding of multiplication and how his creative mind finds the final answer to the query.

Social studies invites visual timelines, detailed maps, and sketches of historical artifacts. Fourth graders Danita and Ally merge information and art to produce a visual representation of the Blackfoot Indians of the Great Plains. Their rough drafts from a learning log eventually evolve into a PowerPoint presentation (Student Sample 11.6) blending texts, clipart graphics, and their growing knowledge of Native Americans from a historical perspective.

Science lends itself to labeled diagrams, life-cycle charts, and patterns in nature to enhance learning. Brooke, an enthusiastic fourth grader, records her bone observations

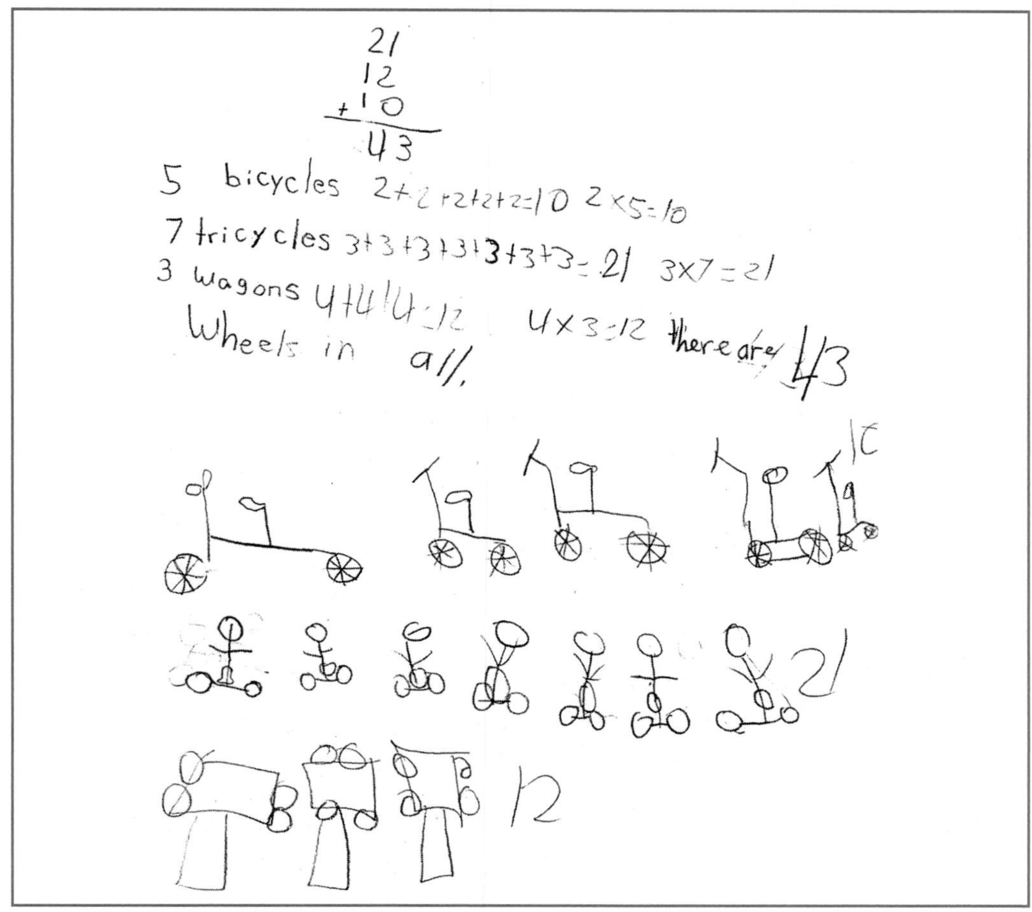

STUDENT SAMPLE 11.5 A third grader's mathematical visual representation.

STUDENT SAMPLE 11.6 A Fourth-Grade Social Studies PowerPoint as Visual Representation.

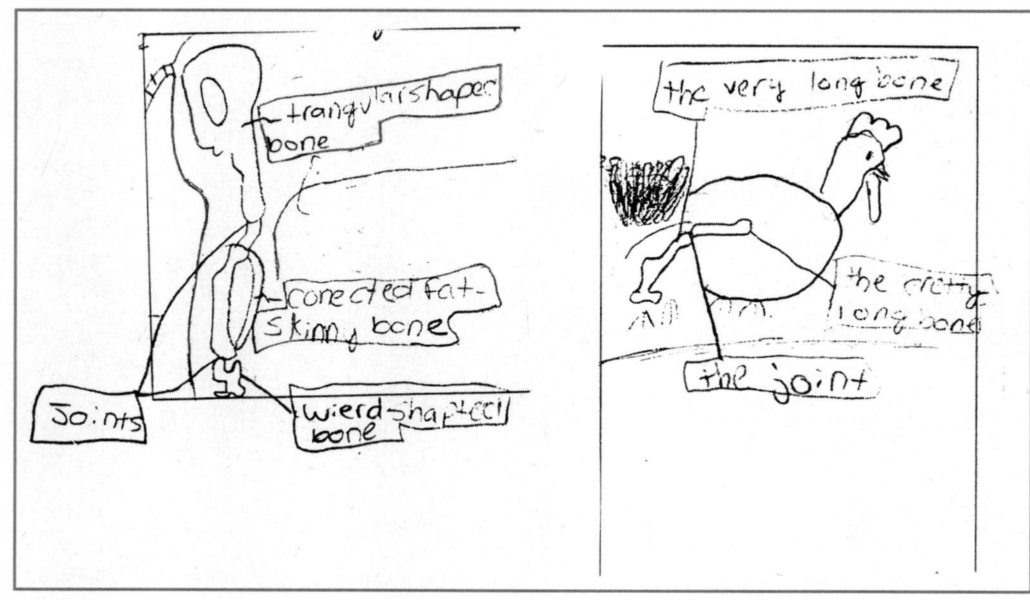

STUDENT SAMPLE 11.7 A Fourth-Grade Science Diagram as Visual Representation.

through a sketch with labels and then draws and labels bones as they might appear in a chicken (Student Sample 11.7). The blending of art and text in a learning log format contributes to greater flexibility in documentation of learning. Rather than knowledge being dependent on writing alone, the visual representation brings memorable images to the learner and assists in grasping and recalling scientific information.

Chapter 14, which discusses interdisciplinary instruction, provides further evidence of the potential of drawing as performance assessment and as a means to enhance conceptual understandings. The realization that the writing and art connection involves visual literacy is important as teachers look for ways to incorporate viewing and visual representation into literacy learning experiences.

Art as Response to Literature

The primary means to enhance visual literacy in the classroom, lies in art enhancement meaningfully designed by the teacher. These activities extensions lie in the literature itself rather than being artificially attached to a book. For example, Diana Pomeroy's *One Potato* and *Wildflower ABC* illustrate various colorful quantities of vegetables and wildflowers created though potato printing. A natural, authentic connection includes potato prints in counting patterns or ABC shapes. The final two pages of these books actually provide suggestions for using the procedure with children. Another example can be found in the three-dimensional collages Molly Bang uses to illustrate Sylvia Cassedy's haiku translations in *Red Dragonfly on My Shoulder*. Screws, safety pins, feathers, keys, clothespins, and chocolate-covered almonds provide inspiration for an art activity related to the book. Art extensions are misused in the classroom context if they are distanced from the book itself and used only as an extension activity. The artistic response to literature has unfortunately been devalued because of this overuse in some literature connections that do not justify art as a medium of interpretation. Many quality titles provide valid art enhancements that extend the message and relive the memory of the reading and viewing experience.

Illustrator Studies

As children have been supported in literature-based classrooms throughs the study of authors, so too does visual literacy support the study of those who illustrate books, both story and information (Madura, 1995). Gathering as many books by an illustrator as possible, setting up a classroom display, visiting an illustrator Web site, and valuing distinctive characteristics of an artist provides a framework for visual literacy through illustration. In addition to lingering over an illustrator's books, viewing videos of illustrators (for example, Patricia Polacco or Eric Carle) brings artists to life as real persons and artistic creators. The Literature Cluster on page 344 presents a list of picture book and informational picture book illustrators that make ideal illustrator studies at primary and intermediate levels. Immersing children in the illustrations, styles, techniques, media, and design choices of these illustrators makes for visual awareness and illustrator appreciation.

Art Elements as Response

The high quality of artwork represented by the work of children's book illustrators deserves and demands both attention and response. Both classroom and art teachers are

Literature Cluster
ILLUSTRATOR STUDIES AND BOOK EXAMPLES

Mary Azarian
Martin, Jacqueline Briggs (1998). *Snowflake Bentley.* Illus. by M. Azarian. Boston: Houghton Mifflin.

David Diaz
Bunting, Eve (1994). *Smoky night.* Illus. by David Diaz. San Diego: Harcourt Brace.

Leo & Diane Dillon
Musgrove, Margaret (1976). *Ashanti to Zulu: African traditions.* Illus. by Leo & Diane Dillon. New York: Dial.

Lois Ehlert
Ehlert, Lois (1989). *Color zoo.* New York: Lippincott.

Tom Feelings
Feelings, Tom (1993). *Soul looks back in wonder.* New York: Dial.

Denise Fleming
Fleming, Denise (1993). *In a small, small pond.* New York: Holt.

Kevin Henkes
Henkes, Kevin (1996). *Lily's purple plastic purse.* New York: Greenwillow.

E. B. Lewis
Howard, Elizabeth Fitzgerald (2000). *Virgie goes to school with us boys.* Illus. by E. B. Lewis. New York: Simon & Schuster.

Emily Arnold McCully
McCully, E. A. (1992). *Mirette on the high wire.* New York: Putnam.

Brian Pinkney
Pinkney, Andrea Davis (1998). *Duke Ellington.* Illus. by Brian Pinkney. New York: Hyperion.

Jerry Pinkney
Schroeder, Alan (1996). *Minty: A story of young Harriet Tubman.* Illus. by J. Pinkney. New York: Dial.

Marjorie Priceman
Moss, L. (1995). *Zin! Zin! Zin! A violin.* Illus. by Marjorie Priceman. New York: Simon & Schuster.

Peggy Rathman
Rathman, Peggy (1995). *Officer Buckle and Gloria.* New York: Putnam.

Faith Ringgold
Ringgold, Faith (1991). *Tar beach.* New York: Crown.

Allen Say
Say, Allen (1993). *Grandfather's journey.* Boston: Houghton Mifflin.

Peter Sis
Sis, Peter (1996). *Starry messenger: Galileo Galilei.* New York: Farrar, Straus & Giroux.

David Small
St. George, Judith (2000). *So you want to be President.* Illus. by David Small. New York: Philomel.

Diane Stanley
Stanley, Diane (2000). *Michelangelo.* New York: HarperCollins.

beginning to teach art elements through the work of award-winning illustrators. As studies of an illustrator's works are displayed and their stories read to children, elements of art are showcased and discussed. A directed response invites each child to incorporate an art element in a student-created work (Hancock, 2004). Figure 11.2 presents sample illustrators and art elements across grade levels. These art element connections provide masters of children's book illustration as models for artistic response. Teachers assume reading of text and viewing and discussion of illustration before artistic expression. The artistic response to the art of the picture book brings individual interpretation of art forms to life. Children learn more about observation of art and become keener in their encounters with illustration, a step toward visual literacy.

FIGURE 11.2 Art elements and visual representation.

Grade 1: Leo Lionni

Lesson focus: Lionni's mice collage
Media: Torn/cut paper
Art concepts: Collage; overlapping; paper techniques and usage
Illustrator models:

Lionni, Leo (1967). *Frederick.* New York: Pantheon.
Lionni, Leo (1969). *Alexander and the wind-up mouse.* New York: Pantheon.
Lionni, Leo (1971). *Theodore and the talking mushroon.* New York: Pantheon.
Lionni, Leo (1981). *Mouse days.* New York: Pantheon.
Lionni, Leo (1992). *Mr. McMouse.* New York: Knopf.

Grade 2: Eric Carle

Lesson focus: Carle's animal train using simple shapes
Media: Printed paper/tissue paper
Art concepts: Mixed media; using shapes to create form; texture
Illustrator models:

Carle, Eric (1968). *1, 2, 3 to the zoo.* New York: Philomel.
Carle, Eric (1971). *Do you want to be my friend?* New York: Crowell/HarperCollins.
Carle, Eric (1987). *Have you seen my cat?* New York: Picture Book Studio/S & S.
Carle, Eric (1989). *Animals, animals.* New York: Philomel.

Grade 3: Paul Goble

Lesson focus: Goble's Native American teepee with skies showing value
Media: Crayons/watercolors
Art concepts: Color value; tint and shade; patterns
Illustrator models:

Goble, Paul (1983). *Star boy.* New York: Bradbury Press.
Goble, Paul (1988). *Her seven brothers.* New York: Bradbury Press.
Goble, Paul (1990). *Dream wolf.* New York: Bradbury Press.
Goble, Paul (1992). *Love flute.* New York: Bradbury Press.

Grade 4: Peter Parnall

Lesson focus: Parnall's trees
Media: Pencil/colored pencil
Art concepts: Lines; linear quality; contour; restricted palette
Illustrator models:

Baylor, Byrd (1986). *I'm in charge of celebrations.* Illus. by Peter Parnall. New York: Scribner's
Parnall, Peter (1988). *Apple tree.* New York: Macmillan.
Parnall, Peter (1990). *Woodpile.* New York: Macmillan.
Parnall, Peter (1991). *The rock.* New York: Macmillan.

Grade 5: Patricia Polacco

Lesson focus: Polacco's people
Media: Pencils, colored pencils, acrylic markers

Source: From M. R. Hancock, (2004). A celebration of literature and response: Children, books, and teachers in K–8 classrooms (2nd ed.). *Upper Saddle River, NJ: Merrill/Prentice Hall, pp. 265–266.*

FIGURE 11.2 (Continued)

Art concepts: Contrasting elements; facial proportions; pattern repetition
Illustrator models:

Polacco, Patricia (1988). *Rechenka's eggs.* New York: Philomel
Polacco, Patricia (1990). *Babushka's doll.* New York: Simon & Schuster.
Polacco, Patricia (1990). *Thunder cake.* New York: Philomel.
Polacco, Patricia (1992). *Mrs. Katz and Tush.* New York: Philomel.

Grades 6–8: Jerry Pinkney

Lesson focus: Pinkney's watercolor flowers
Media: Watercolor
Art concepts: Watercolor techniques—transparent overlays; light to dark
Illustrator models:

Carlstrom, Nancy (1987). *Wild, wild sunflower child, Anna.* Illus. by Jerry Pinkney. New York: Macmillan.
Lester, Julius (1988). *More tales of Uncle Remus.* Illus. by Jerry Pinkney. New York: Dial Books.
McKissack, Patricia (1988). *Mirandy and Brother Wind.* Illus. by Jerry Pinkney. New York: Knopf.
Pinkney, Gloria (1992). *Back home.* Illus. by Jerry Pinkney. New York: Dial Books.

Viewing and Visual Representation Through Webbing

Webbing is a visual strategy for representing and organizing information and ideas. In the classroom setting, a web is a visual display of categories of information and of their relationships created by teachers and students to structure ideas and aid learning. Webbing is the process of constructing a web, or visual representation, of organized relationships among ideas or categories of information (Bromley, 1996). Because of their usefulness across disciplines, webs can also be referred to as semantic maps, concept maps, networks, or graphic organizers. A web usually contains a core concept surrounded by various aspects of related information. Webbing is an effective way of both viewing and representing knowledge in a conceptual pattern at all grade levels (Bromley, Irwin-DeVitis, & Modlo, 1995). In a teacher education classroom, a web can be used to model an instructional, literature-based unit on the environment, the Middle Ages, or mammals. In a fifth-grade classroom, a web can be used to differentiate the varied causes of the Civil War. In a third-grade classroom, a teacher can generate topics about deserts (names, locations, characteristics) as children brainstorm possible reports. In a first-grade classroom, a teacher follows the reading of Eric Carle's *The Very Hungry Caterpillar* with a simple web of the stages in the life of a butterfly.

Visually organized ideas and information aid the development of vocabulary, comprehension, and learning (Flood, Lapp, & Wood, 1998). Studies indicate that visual representation comprehension effects appear greatest when student are guided in their use and are actively engaged in constructing webs themselves (Reutzel, 1985). Much collaboration utilizing the integrated language arts occurs during a webbing activity (talking, listening, reading, writing, viewing, visually representing) as students share information, analyze ideas and relationships, and construct knowledge in a visual form. While webbing can occur across the entire curriculum, the focus of this discussion is webbing with children's literature in a language arts context. Bromley (1996) identifies the benefits of webbing, in this case, webbing with children's literature:

- Webbing encourages response to literature. Rather than focusing on closed-ended questions, webbing utilizes open-ended prompts that encourage rich response and varied perspectives on literature.
- Webbing extends comprehension. New information is related to prior knowledge through a visual schema. Before a lesson, webs organize prior knowledge in preparation for reading. After a lesson, new information can be added to the existing web as documentation of learning.
- Webbing builds literacy. The integration of reading, writing, listening, speaking, viewing, and visual representing dominate web creation. Language is used in authentic ways to reflect knowledge. Webs provide formats for discussion, retellings, literary analysis, or brainstorming mechanisms to organize writing.
- Webbing enhances learning. The visual enhancement of recording information on a web is an aid to learning and retention of information. Student involvement through active learning provide rich and varied responses and insights.

Figure 11.3 visually represents these four benefits.

A pair of sixth-grade examples illustrate the connection between webbing of information and enhanced understanding. Lauren's visual and textual character web of Brian, the main character in Gary Paulsen's *Hatchet* (Student Sample 11.8) reveals varied perspectives on dimensional aspects of his appearance, qualities of friendship, interests, abilities,

FIGURE 11.3 Webbing with literature possibilities.

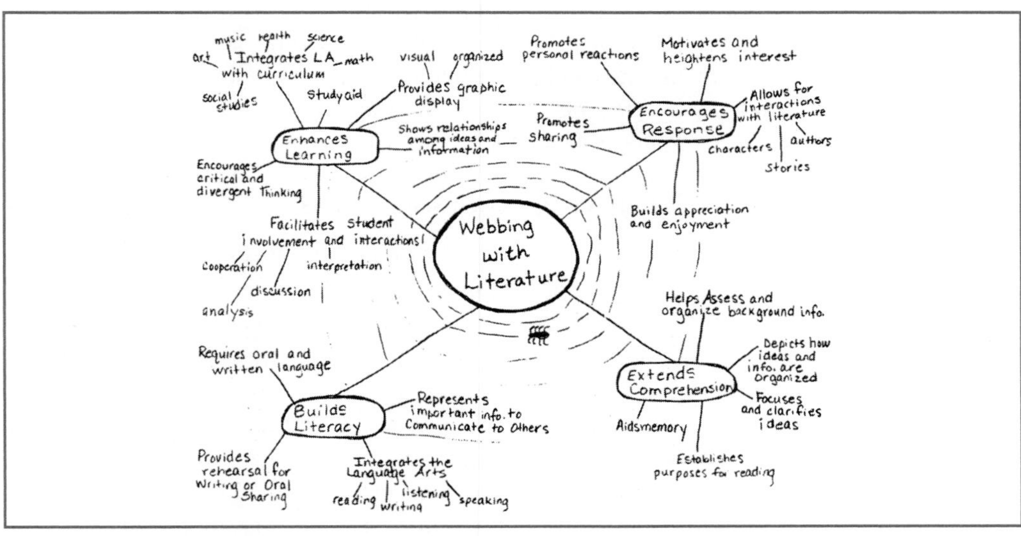

Source: K. D. Bromley (1996). Webbing with Literature: Creating Story Maps with Children's Books *(2nd ed., p. 5). Published by Allyn & Bacon, Boston, MA. Copyright © 1996 by Pearson Education. Reprinted by permission of the publisher.*

Fourth graders display their graphic web for their collaborative science report on manatees.

and outlook on life. Each portion of the character web contrasts the "old" Brian with the "new." Karl's reading of Elizabeth Yate's *Amos Fortune, Free Man* resulted in a sequential retelling of major events in the biography (Student Sample 11.9). The blend of detailed art and text jointly reveal the emotional events in Amos's life as they blend to reflect reader comprehension and personal impressions.

Many teachers utilize webs as a planning tool to organize thematic instruction or interdisciplinary curriculum. While webbing brings structure and order to thinking, it invites flexibility as new ideas occur while providing an overview of an entire unit of study. Teachers also use webs in language arts to develop background knowledge, to organize new knowledge, and as a brainstorming tool for writing.

Both teachers and children are capable of creating formats for webs to suit curricular needs. Today, however, computer software for webbing produces customized webs for the individual needs of students and teachers.

- *KidPix* allows even the youngest child to experience webbing. Students can visualize a concept in a web format, label parts of the web, and outline information, while easily moving back and forth between the two formats.
- *The Literary Mapper* focuses on literature-based webbing. Predeveloped maps contain character, setting, and action that can be filled in by the reader. Brainstorming, listing, and editing can change the existing webs for individual needs and books.
- *The Semantic Mapper* allows students to create their own webs and labels. Students conducting research can readily see visual representation of their inquiry process.
- *Inspiration,* typically used by Grade 4–8 teachers, and *Kidspiration,* a K–3 primary version, model the thinking process through brainstorming ideas, creating webs, and writing an outline. Quick movement between the two formats is possible, and changes made in one appear in the other.

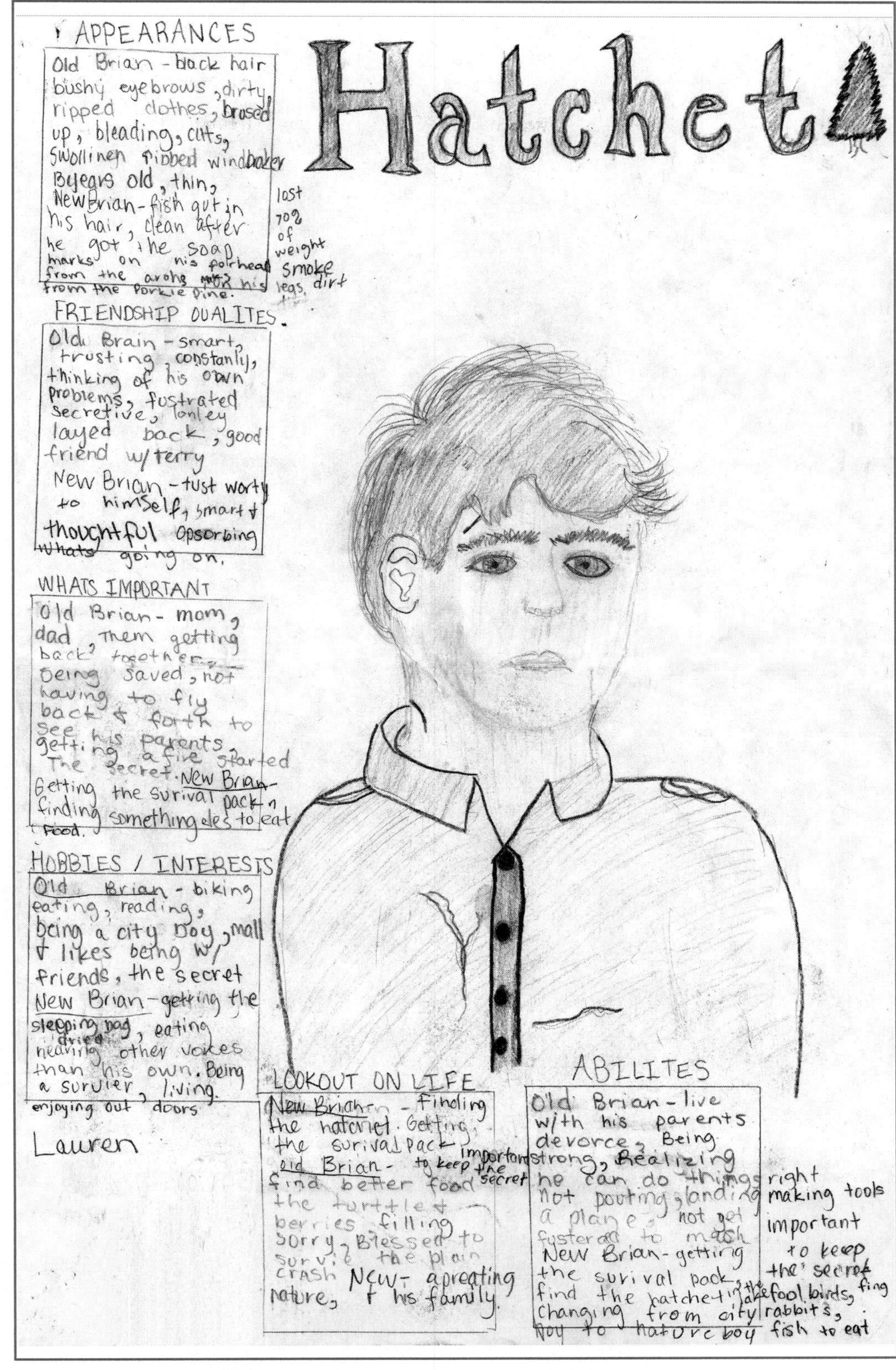

STUDENT SAMPLE 11.8 A Sixth-Grade Character Web of Brian in Gary Paulsen's *Hatchet*.

STUDENT SAMPLE 11.9 Sixth-Grader's Visual Depiction of Major Plot Events in Elizabeth Yates' *Amos Fortune, Free Man.*

STUDENT SAMPLE 11.10 A Fifth-Grade PowerPoint Character Map for Ralph Fletcher's *Flying Solo.*

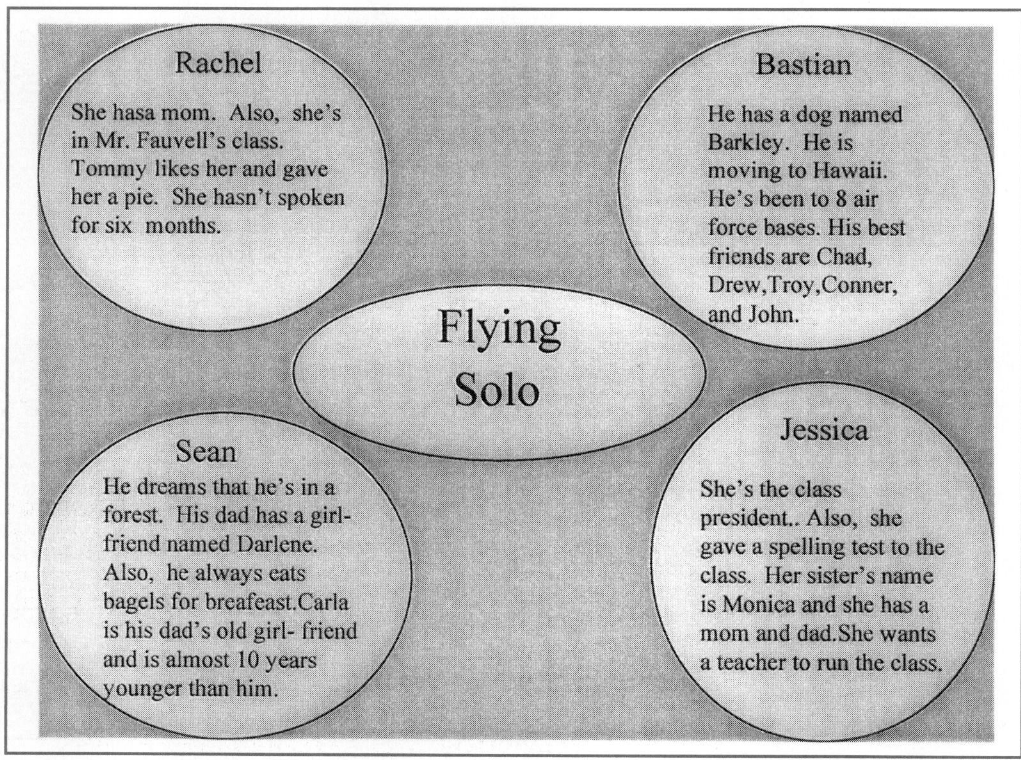

Software creates shortcuts for the visualization of thoughts in creating literature webs. Kristofer's fifth-grade representation of a character map for Ralph Fletcher's *Flying Solo* (Student Sample 11.10) reveals a well-organized description of four characters from the book. Often reluctant to write in traditional formats or reports, Kristofer is motivated by this format of webbing via technology to complete the assignment with neatness and pride while revealing his comprehension of the characters in the book.

Webbing therefore appears to be a powerful learning tool both for organizing comprehension of reading and for preparation for writing. The varied web formats provide the foundation for recording reading and rehearsing writing that leads to deeper understanding and clearer communication of thought.

The Tech Tip below reviews the many ways in which viewing and visual representation enhance the language arts through videos, picture book illustration, and graphic organizers.

Visual Connections: Technology and Literacy

Encourage your students to adapt their own stories into movies with the help of user-friendly software applications such as iMovie (Mac OS) or Movie Maker (Windows). Students can create, edit, and share their movies right on the computer or turn them into DVDs.

Visit the *Caldecott Medal Home Page* (American Library Association) to learn more about Caldecott Medal winners and honor books, from 1938 to the present. **www.ala.org/ala/alsc/awardsscholarships/literaryawds/caldecottmedal/caldecottmedal.htm**

Picturing Books: A Website About Picture Books is a fun location where students can explore elements, types, and genres of picture books. There is also a section about evaluating picture books, and the anatomy of a picture book (such as borders and the copyright page). Examples from authentic literature are provided. **picturingbooks.imaginarylands.org/**

Students can write and illustrate their own nonfiction picture books about field trips, favorite recess activities, etc., with the help of technology commonly available at schools, such as computers, scanners, digital cameras, color printers.

Many well-known illustrators, such as Eric Carle and Jan Brett, have developed extensive Web sites including samples of their art and ideas for student-friendly art activities. These sites enhance the reading experience by bringing the artist and his/her work to life! Visit the Web site for this book for a list of children's illustrator sites. **www.prenhall.com/hancock**

The software product *Inspiration* (Inspiration, Inc.) allows students to visually arrange their ideas in the form of graphic organizers. Students illustrate their ideas and convey meaning by inserting graphics or importing their own digital images. With the click of a button, students can transform the web into a traditional outline. *Kidspiration* is a simpler version designed for primary-grade students.

To look more closely at these materials and others related to "Viewing and Visual Representation", visit the Companion Website at www.prenhall.com/hancock.

Viewing Films, Videos, DVDs, and CD-ROMs

In the past, film has rarely been approached as serious material for literacy instruction. Frequently used as a supplemental resource, follow-up activity, reward initiative, or filler for a substitute teacher, film has played a less dominant role in the elementary classroom than other instructional materials. Without teacher direction, video viewing can deteriorate into a passive activity. Yet film can be "an accessible and engaging material which can bind children together and bring validation to their varied home and school literacy experiences" (Whipple, 1998).

Film viewing plays a major role in popular culture and in the daily lives of students. Teachers often become resentful and judgmental about frequent home viewing practices as choices over printed text. Yet students' video experiences and collective knowledge of films can actually provide an opportunity to support literacy development and to make connections with printed text.

Students' growing understanding and use of film and other forms of nonprint text is often referred to as "media literacy"—composing, comprehending, interpreting, analyzing, and appreciating the language and texts of print and nonprint text. While print media includes books, magazines, and newspaper, nonprint media includes film, television, videotape, video games, and Internet. Cox (1998) clearly points out the primary benefit of recognizing film viewing as valid instruction. Recognition and use of student knowledge of film can provide an equal playing field for students who have traditionally been thought to be at-risk literacy learners. Validation of alternates to printed text including film and videotape, television, or photographs, opens doors to classroom discussion and inclusion in the classroom community of learners for all students.

For example, only a few second-grade students may have read Sarah MacLachlan's *Sarah, Plain and Tall,* but many more may have rented the film version from the video store or viewed it on television. Children may also be able to make connections between other texts or films on pioneers, courage, struggles, or westward movement creating a dynamic classroom conversation. In a classroom which acknowledges visual literacy, "intertextual connections" (Short, 1993) expand to "intermedia connections" as print text and nonprint text merge as a source of background knowledge.

Literature-Based Opportunities Through Film

For years, children have attempted to naturally and genuinely infuse discussion of film into their responses to literature. While teachers attempt to prompt text-to-text connections, children have consistently drawn from their own experiences and persisted with text-to-film connections. Children repeatedly talk about the relationships that exist for them between written texts and films of the same name (for example, *Babe: The Gallant Pig,* 1985/1995; *Harry Potter and the Sorcerer's Stone,* 1998/2001). In general, most teachers have missed opportunities to acknowledge the film references made by students during class discussion and, in many cases, have actually devalued them in relation to connections to related printed text.

As teachers begin to acknowledge the instructional value of nonprint text, the transfer of reader response theory (Rosenblatt, 1938, 1978) from written text to film text takes a somewhat natural leap. The premises of reader response theory (recall the discussion in Chapter 1) suggest that readers are actively engaged in the reading process and that they construct meaning from their prior knowledge and personal experiences. Meaning does not lie within the text, but in what happens between each reader and the text. A student's individual thoughts and reflections create the personal response to literature. In offering quality literature and a wide variety of response activities, teachers promote personal risk taking as individuals share personal responses to literature.

In recent years, some connections have been made between "reader response to literature" and "viewer response to film" (Whipple, 1998). Fehlman (1994) and Cox (1989) parallel the viewer (reader) watching the film (the text) in the classroom environment (context) to the reader response experience. Following this comparison, the viewer brings as much, or even more, to the visual literacy event than the film itself. Just as the reader fluctuates between the efferent (informational) and aesthetic (feeling) stance throughout a book, so too does the viewer alternate between information and emotion in the viewing of a film. The viewer breathes life into the film, making it his or her own by connecting it to personal feelings, experiences, values, and thoughts. The goal of finding the "right" interpretation to film becomes as remote as finding the "right" interpretation to literature.

After children view a film for the first time, they should engage in a whole-class response to share overall impressions. Like a literary response, a whole-class sharing opportunity provides a chance to interact and interpret the experienced visual event. Children naturally share likes and dislikes, favorite and least favorite parts, favorite and least favorite characters. The following experiential, aesthetic, cognitive, and interpretive prompts (Hancock, 2004) for literature provide parallel guidelines for teachers who initiate response-based discussion to film or choose to have students individually respond to the film in journal formats:

- ***Experiential prompts.*** Focus on what the viewer brings to the film experience.
  How do you relate this film to your own life?
  Does [name of character] remind you of someone you know?
  Does [name of character] remind you of some other character you've met in a book or film?
- ***Aesthetic prompts.*** Focus on promoting emotional interactions with the film characters and circumstances.
  How did this film make you feel?
  How would you feel if you were [name of character] in this situation?
  How would you feel if you were [name another character]?
- ***Cognitive prompts.*** Focus on problem solving, making predictions, and making inferences about characters and circumstances.
  What do you think will happen to [name of character] in the future?
  If you were [name a character], what would you have done in this situation?
  What advice would you give [name a character] in this situation?
- ***Interpretive prompts.*** Focus on meaning, message, theme, values, and personal judgment of characters.
  What meaning or message does this film have for you?
  Why do you believe [name of character] did or did not make the right choice?
  What to you think the following words meant? [Quote from film]
  What kind of person do you think [name of character] is? How do you know?

Piazza (1999) suggests that film literacy must move beyond these personal responses to an analytic and evaluative response dealing with detailed aspects of content, technical qualities, format, and acting. This may occur on a repeated brief viewing of teacher-selected portions to further engage viewers. A simplied version of Piazza's response prompts include the following:

- Content

  How was this story made compelling on film?

  How were you drawn into the film?

  How satisfied were you with the story's organization?

  How was the dialogue made effective?

  From whose point of view was the story told? Why?

  Was the story well-edited to cut out unnecessary parts? What would you edit out or add in?

  How was the film fair in its portrayal of characters and events?
- Technical production

  How did lighting affect the interpretation of the story?

  How did the musical soundtrack add to or detract from the story?

  How did camera angles create interesting effects?

  What special effects aroused emotional responses?

  How effective was the length of the film? How would you make it longer or shorter?
- Acting

  Which characters did you really care about? Why?

  Which characters were appropriately or inappropriately portrayed?

  How well did the characters deliver their lines?

Response prompts to film, like response prompts to literature, will need to be modeled and practiced, and growth over time will be expected. Since most children have only viewed, but never responded to films, guidance, support, and acceptance of thoughts provide a foundation for more mature responses.

Of particular importance today are the number of films that are based on actual pieces of quality children's literature. Interrelationships exist, but they are not the same experience at all. A film is not a replication of the printed text, although the story may stay true to the book. Films are multisensory and engage our minds differently than books. Books force the reader to use the mind's eye and imagination by creating pictures in our heads. Films, however, fill in the gaps for us by showing rather than merely telling. Comparing and contrasting the "reader" version of a book and the "viewer" version of the film fosters the connections that are a part of higher order critical thinking. Piazza (1999) suggests the following critical thinking prompts to discern differences and similarities between children's books and film versions of those books:

How are the characters the same? Different?

How has the film updated material in the book?

How has the film changed the point of view of the book?

How did the film create a new emphasis for the story?

How did the filmmaker organize the events for the viewing audience?

How is the chronology of events presented in the book? In the film?

Which scenes from the book are not in the film and vice versa?

How are scenes from the book changed?

How are the endings the same? Different?

Literature Cluster

BOOKS INTO FILMS (AND FILMS INTO BOOKS)

DiCamillo, Kate (2000). *Because of Winn-Dixie.* Cambridge, MA: Candlewick.

[Film] (2005). *Because of Winn-Dixie.* Beverly Hills, CA: Twentieth Century Fox Home Entertainment.

King-Smith, Dick (1985). *Babe, the gallant pig.* Illus. by Mary Rayner. New York: Crown.

[Film] (1996). *Babe.* Hollywood, CA: Universal Pictures.

Lewis, C. S. (2004/c1950). *The chronicles of Narnia.* New York: HarperCollins.

[Film] (2002). *The chronicles of Narnia* (BBC production). Los Angeles: Home Vision Entertainment.

MacLachlan, Patricia (1985). *Sarah, plain and tall.* New York: HarperCollins.

[Film] (1990). *Sarah, plain and tall.* Los Angeles: Hallmark Home Entertainment.

MacLachlan, Patricia (1994). *Skylark.* New York: HarperCollins.

[Film] (1992). *Skylark.* Los Angeles: Hallmark Home Entertainment.

Rowling, J. K. (1997). *Harry Potter and the sorcerer's stone.* New York: Arthur A. Levine/ Scholastic.

[Film] (2002). *Harry Potter and the sorcerer's stone.* Burbank, CA: Warner Home Video.

Rowling, J. K. (1999). *Harry Potter and the prisoner of Azkaban.* New York: Arthur A. Levine/ Scholastic.

[Film] (2004). *Harry Potter and the prisoner of Azkaban.* Burbank, CA: Warner Home Video.

The Literature Cluster above presents a few popular books that have recently been adapted to film or DVD and video formats. Obviously, it is preferable that the reading of the book occurs prior to the viewing of the film, but teachers are likely to find that children have already seen the video version, with only a few having read the book. Yet children inspired by a film will likely choose to read the book of the same title if made readily accessible following the viewing of a film.

Viewing Content Area Information Through Videos and DVDs

Many quality videos present information in the content areas through effective, visual means. Those issued by *National Geographic,* PBS, and many other educationally oriented foundations provide quality viewing for learning experiences. *Bowker's Complete Video Directory* (1996) and the *Video Sourcebook* (1996) contain comprehensive listings of videos for all purposes. Yet active engagement in watching an informational video can be better ensured through a teaching strategy designed specifically for video observation—the Collaborative Listening-Viewing Guide (Flood, Lapp, & Wood, 1990; Wood, 1990). The CLVG provides a template for taking notes as students receive, record, and process viewed information with the aid of their peers. There are five specific phases in the Collaborative Listening-Viewing Guide:

- ***Preview/review information*** (Pre-viewing stage). The preview shares the coming attraction of the video to prepare students for what is to follow. The preview might contain a list of terms, names, or places presented as a graphic organizer to better prepare the student for the video. The review consists of eliciting information on the topic which students already know.

- ***Record*** (During-viewing stage). Students individually record significant ideas, concepts, phrases, names, or events on the left side of their form. Writing should be brief and even incorporate abbreviations so that writing does not interfere with viewing. Teachers may need to model a think-aloud during a short video to indicate what is significant and how brief notes are critical to this viewing process.
- ***Elaborate*** (Post-viewing stage). After viewing the video, students meet in small groups to discuss their transcripts. Students recall details, extend ideas, add personal anecdotes, draw analogies, and elaborate on their abbreviated notes. Students then record extended information on the right side of the form. If possible, this phase should take place immediately following video viewing.
- ***Synthesize*** (Post-viewing stage). All groups contribute their elaborated knowledge to the whole class. As groups share, the teacher might record major ideas, synthesize information, and make generalizations about the content while avoiding unimportant details.
- ***Extend*** (Post-viewing stage). Students work in pairs to design a project related to the topic, write a paragraph synthesizing the information, develop a chart or map of key concepts, or research an aspect of the topic in more detail.

When teachers structure the presentation of visual information in this way, there is likely to be a greater match between what students see and the information they retrieve as active, engaged viewers. Figure 11.4 presents student notes when following the five phases of the Collaborative Listening—Viewing Guide.

FIGURE 11.4
Excerpt from a Collaborative Listening-Viewing Guide.

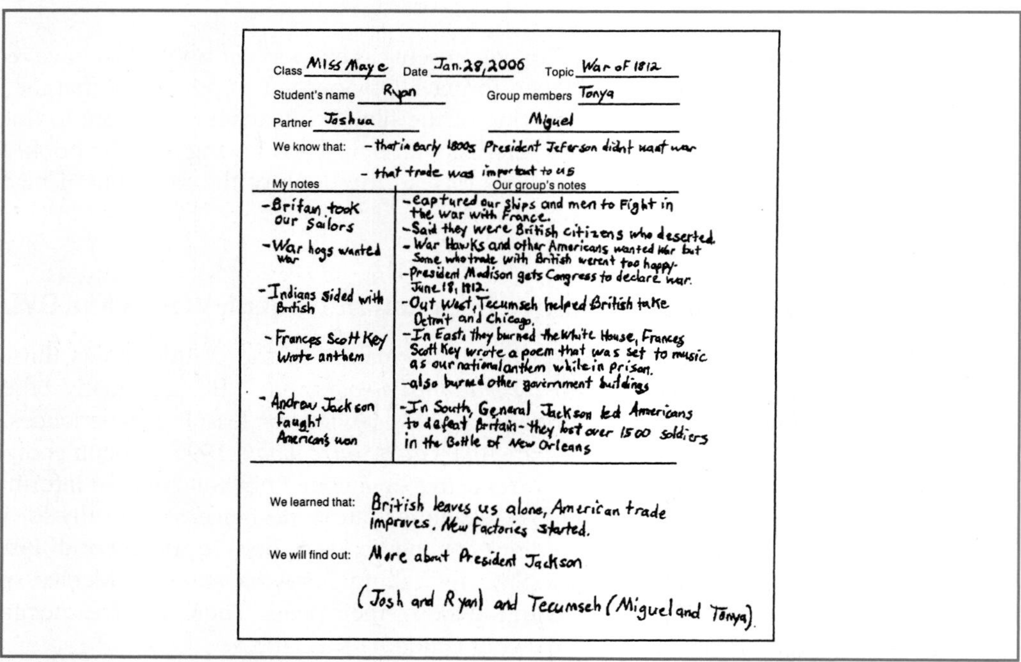

Class Miss Maye Date Jan. 28, 2006 Topic War of 1812
Student's name Ryan Group members Tonya
Partner Joshua Miguel
We know that: – that in early 1800s President Jeferson didn't want war
– that trade was important to us

My notes	Our group's notes
-Britain took our Sailors	-captured our ships and men to Fight in the war with France. -Said they were British citizens who deserted.
-War hogs wanted war	-War Hawks and other Americans wanted War but Some who trade with British werent too happy. -President Madison gets Congress to declare war. June 18, 1812.
-Indians sided with British	-Out West, Tecumseh helped British take Detroit and Chicago.
-Frances Scott Key Wrote anthem	-In East, they burned the White House, Frances Scott Key wrote a poem that was set to music as our national anthem while in prison. -also burned other government buildings
-Andrew Jackson faught American's won	-In South, General Jackson led Americans to defeat Britain - they lost over 1500 soldiers in the Battle of New Orleans

We learned that: British leaves us alone, American trade improves. New Factories started.

We will find out: More about President Jackson (Josh and Ryan) and Tecumseh (Miguel and Tonya)

Source: From J. Lapp, D. Lapp, & K. Wood (1998). Viewing: The Neglected Communication Process or "When What You See Isn't What You Get." The Reading Teacher, *52, 300–304. Reprinted with permission of James Flood and the International Reading Association.*

Viewing the Internet

A discussion of visual literacy would not be complete without establishing the importance of the visual nature of the Internet and its role in the new literacies. Never before has such a powerful technology for literacy entered so many classrooms in such a short period of time (Leu, 2002). The Internet is a vehicle for a host of new technologies that require a fresh look at making sense of online text and the visual accompaniments that enhance its presentation.

Text and visual representation merge to create motivating home pages for content exploration. A growing collection of research suggests that "reading" the Internet requires new comprehension skills and strategies (Coiro, 2005; Schmar-Dobler, 2003; Sutherland-Smith, 2002). Reading online is a complex process that requires knowledge of search engines and how information is organized within Web sites. While Internet Web sites demand new navigational skills, the blend of text and visual representations (lists, tables, charts, links) propose a new literacy that extends beyond traditional informational reading.

Navigating and viewing an Internet Web site is a challenge that begins upon arrival at the site. Scanning for titles, headings, diagrams, boldface words, and visual cues is part of an initial preview. Previewing the homepage also gives the viewer a sense of site organization, breadth of information, and connections among included concepts. Skimming text is not enough to ascertain the amount and kinds of information included. The overview must include a strategic thought process of how the information is aligned and leveled with purposeful information.

Coiro (2005) provides a seven-step process for previewing the visual and textual nature of a Web site:

- Read the title of the homepage and Web site. These are often presented in a visual context that can overpower the text itself.
- Scan menu choices. Amidst the color and visuals on the homepage, locate the menus that appear on the left side or across the top of the window. This provides the big picture of Web site content.
- Make predictions about where the links may lead. Because Web sites have multiple levels of information, it is critical to realize this complex path. In addition, links lead to varied visual venues that familiarize the user with varied levels of the site.
- Explore interactive functions that contain additional levels of information. Highly visual in nature, animated images, pop-up menus, and scroll bars are common means to levels of related information available on the site.
- Check for the name of the Web site author and the last date it was updated. Click on the "About This Site" button to access this information. While it is easy to be attracted by visual appeal of color and animation, remember that the authenticity, credibility, and current features of information are most important.
- Try out the site map or internal search engine of the site. This exploration leads you visually to navigate the breadth and depth of the site information.
- Make a judgment about the usability of the site. Don't be influenced entirely by the visual nature of a site. While such visual aspects of information may attract users initially, it is the information itself that will provide the needed material.

By utilizing these steps, students may move away from the typical random clicking that often characterizes online Internet experiences (Sutherland-Smith, 2002). More information on the textual and visual nature of the Internet and its role in the new literacies of our society are presented in Chapter 13.

This process helps viewers stop, think, and anticipate the location of where sought-after information might be found. This process discourages disorientation among paths of irrelevant information and encourages deeper engagement with relevant visual and textual features that lead to the targeted information.

Teacher modeling of these steps while thinking aloud to articulate the navigating process is essential. While the text and visual nature of literacy work in conjunction with each other on Internet Web sites, consider both dimensions of this navigational process.

Visit the Companion Website at www.prenhall.com/hancock and gauge your understanding of Chapter 11 concepts with the self-assessments.

Closing Thoughts

Visual literacy is about encouraging students to observe and view, interpret, brainstorm, and represent their understandings of the world through more than words. It is about teaching students to use visual images, in addition to words, to help them make sense of information, emotions, and literature. Perhaps this chapter has convinced you that students can read and write with more than words and can actually become more aesthetic readers and better writers by becoming close observers and users of language. Students who normally do not experience success through the written word can often meet expected outcomes through visual representations of what they know, think, and learn.

Visual literacy actually expands the meaning-making process in the classroom and extends the literacy spectrum to include drawing and art on a daily rather than an intermittent basis. Visual literacy is not a replacement for the traditional reading and writing of a language arts classroom. It is simply an alternative means to construct meaning and communicate understanding. Despite ongoing pressures to economize on time factors in the ever-expanding curriculum, teachers must envision visual literacy not as an add-on, but as an integrated, alternative means to capture, enhance, and exhibit learning through multiple ways.

References

Albers, P. (1997). Art as literacy. *Language Arts, 74,* 338–356.

Bromley, K. D. (1996). *Webbing with literature: Creating story maps with children's books.* Boston: Allyn & Bacon.

Bromley, K., Irwin-DeVitis, L., & Modlo, M. (1995). *Graphic organizers: Visual strategies for active learning.* New York: Scholastic.

Chancer, J., & Rester-Zodrow, C. (1997). *Moon journals: Writing, art, and inquiry through focused nature study.* Portsmouth, NH: Heinemann.

Coiro, J. (2005). Making sense of online text. *Educational Leadership, 63,* 30–35.

Cox, C. (1998). *Media literacy: Classroom practices in the teaching of the English language arts.* Urbana, IL: National Council of Teachers of English.

Cox, C., & Many, J. (1989). Worlds of possibilities in response to literature, film, and life. *Language Arts, 66,* 287–294.

Fehlman, R. H. (1994). Teaching film in the 1990's. *English Journal, 83,* 39–46.

Flood, J., Heath, S. B., & Lapp, D. (Eds.) (1997). *Handbook of research on teaching literacy through the communicative and visual arts.* New York: Macmillan.

Flood, J., Lapp, D., & Wood, K. (1998). Viewing: The neglected communication process or "When what you see isn't what you get." *The Reading Teacher, 52,* 300–304.

Fox, R. F. (1999). Beating the moon: A reflection on media and literacy. *Language Arts, 76,* 479–482.

Frei, R. I. (1999). Making meaning with art: Children's stories. *Language Arts, 76,* 386–392.

Hancock, M. R. (2004). *A celebration of literature and response: Children, books, and teachers in K–8 classrooms* (2nd ed.). Upper Saddle River, NJ: Merrill/Prentice Hall.

Hubbard, R. S. (1996). Visual responses to literature: Imagination through images. *The New Advocate, 9,* 309–323.

International Reading Association and National Council of Teachers of English (1996). *Standards for the English Language Arts*. Newark, DE/Urbana, IL: IRA/NCTE.

Kiefer, B. Z. (1994). *The potential of picture books: From visual literacy to aesthetic understanding*. Upper Saddle River, NJ: Merrill/Prentice Hall.

Kiefer, B. Z. (1995). Responding to literature as art in picture books. In N. L. Roser & M. G. Martinez (Eds.), *Book talk and beyond: Children and teachers respond to literature* (pp. 191–200). Newark, DE: International Reading Association.

Leu, D. J. (2002). The new literacies: Research on reading instruction with the Internet. In A. E. Farnstrup & S. J. Samuels (Eds.), *What research has to say about reading instruction* (pp. 310–336). Newark, DE: International Reading Association.

Madura, R. S. (1995). The line and texture of aesthetic response: Primary children study authors and illustrators. *The Reading Teacher, 49,* 110–118.

Murray, D. H. (1996). *Crafting a life in essay, story, and poem*. Portsmouth, NH: Heinemann.

Piazza, C. L. (1999). *Multiple forms of literacy: Teaching literacy and the arts*. Upper Saddle River, NJ: Merrill/ Prentice Hall.

Reutzel, D. R. (1985). Story maps improve comprehension. *The Reading Teacher, 38,* 400–404.

Rief, L. (1999). *Vision and voice: Extending the literacy spectrum*. Portsmouth, NH: Heinemann.

Rosenblatt, L. M. (1938/1995). *Literature as exploration*. New York: Modern Language Association.

Rosenblatt, L. M. (1978). *The reader, the text, the poem: The transactional theory of the literary work*. Carbondale: Southern Illinois University Press.

Schmar-Dobler, E. (2003). Reading on the Internet: The link between literacy and technology. *Journal of Adolescent and Adult Literacy,* 47, 80–85.

Short, K. (1993). Making connections across literature and life. In K. Holland, R. Hungerford, & S. Ernst (Eds.), *Journeying: Children responding to literature* (pp. 284–301). Portsmouth, NH: Heinemann.

Stewig, J. W. (1995). *Looking at picture books*. Fort Atkinson, WI: Highsmith Press.

Sutherland-Smith, W. (2002). Weaving the literacy web: Changes in reading from page to screen. *The Reading Teacher, 55,* 662–669.

Tunnell, M. O., & Jacobs, J. S. (2004). *Children's literature, briefly* (3rd ed.). Upper Saddle River, NJ: Merrill/ Prentice Hall.

Whipple, M. (1998). Let's go to the movies: Rethinking the role of film in the elementary classroom. *Language Arts,* 76, 144–150.

Whitin, P. (1996a). Exploring visual response to literature. *Research in the Teaching of English, 30,* 114–140.

Whitin, P. (1996b). *Sketching stories, stretching minds*. Portsmouth, NH: Heinemann.

Wood, K. D. (1990). The collaborative listening-viewing guide: An aid for note taking. *Middle School Journal, 22,* 53–56.

Children's Books Cited

Bannerman, Helen (1898/1996). *The story of Little Babaji*. Illus. by Fred Marcellino. New York: HarperCollins.

Bradby, Marie (1995). *More than anything else*. Illus. by Chris Soentpiet. New York: Orchard Books.

Brett, Jan (1989). *The mitten*. New York: Putnam.

Brett, Jan (1996). *Comet's nine lives*. New York: Putnam.

Brett, Jan (2000). *Hedgie's surprise*. New York: Putnam.

Brown, Marc (1976/2001). *Arthur's nose* (25th Anniversary Edition). Boston: Little, Brown.

Bruchac, Joseph (2000). Crazy *Horse's vision*. Illus. by S. D. Nelson. New York: Lee & Low.

Carle, Eric (1968). *The very hungry caterpillar*. New York: Philomel.

Carle, Eric (1984). *The very busy spider*. New York: Philomel.

Carle, Eric (1990). *The very quiet cricket*. New York: Philomel.

Carle, Eric (1995). *The very lonely firefly*. New York: Philomel.

Carle, Eric (1999). *The very clumsy click beetle*. New York: Philomel.

Cassedy, Sylvia (translator) (1992). *Red dragonfly on my shoulder*. Illus. by Molly Bang. New York: HarperCollins.

Cole, Brock (2000). *Buttons*. New York: Farrar, Straus and Giroux.

Conrad, Pam (1985). *Prairie song*. New York: HarperCollins.

Corey, Shana (2000). *You forgot your skirt, Amelia Bloomer*. Illus. by Chesley McClaren. New York: Scholastic.

Coy, John (1996). *Night driving*. Illus. by Peter McCarty. New York: Holt.

Cronin, Doreen (2000). *Click clack moo: Cows that type*. Illus. by Betsy Lewin. New York: Simon & Schuster.

Ehlert, Lois (1997). *Cuckoo/Cucú: A Mexican folktale*. San Diego: Harcourt Brace.

Ehlert, Lois (1997). *Hands*. San Diego: Harcourt Brace.

Ernst, Lisa Campbell (1998). *Stella Louella's runaway book*. New York: Simon & Schuster.

Fleischman, Sid (1986). *The whipping boy*. New York: Greenwillow.

Fletcher, Ralph (1998). *Flying solo*. New York: Clarion.
Howard, Elizabeth Fitzgerald (2001). *Virgie goes to school with us boys*. Illus. by E. B. Lewis. New York: Simon & Schuster.
Johnson, D. B. (2000). *Henry hikes to Fitchburg*. Boston: Houghton Mifflin.
Johnston, Tony (1996). *The wagon*. Illus. by James Ransome. New York: Tambourine.
Katz, Karen (1999). *The colors of us*. New York: Holt.
Kellogg, Steven (1999). *The three sillies*. Cambridge, MA: Candlewick.
King-Smith, Dick (1985). *Babe: The gallant pig*. Illus. by Mary Rayner. New York: Crown.
Lester, Julius (1996). *Sam and the tigers*. Illus. by Jerry Pinkney. New York: Dial.
Locker, Thomas (1997). *Water dance*. San Diego: Harcourt Brace.
Locker, Thomas (with Candace Christiansen) (1995). *Sky tree: Seeing science through art*. New York: HarperCollins.
MacLachlan, Patricia (1985). *Sarah, plain and tall*. New York: Harper & Row.
Martin, Jacqueline Briggs (1998). *Snowflake Bentley*. Illus. by Mary Azarian. Boston: Houghton Mifflin.
McCully, Emily Arnold (2000). *Mirette and Bellini cross Niagara Falls*. New York: Putnam.
Paulsen, Gary (1987). *Hatchet*. New York: Bradbury.
Pinkney, Andrea Davis (1996). *Bill Pickett: Rodeo ridin' cowboy*. Illus. by Brian Pinkney. New York: Four Winds Press.
Pinkney, Andrea Davis (1998). *Duke Ellington*. Illus. by Brian Pinkney. New York: Hyperion.
Polacco, Patricia (1998). *Thank you, Mr. Falker*. New York: Philomel.
Pomeroy, Diana (1996). *One potato*. San Diego: Harcourt Brace.
Pomeroy, Diana (1997). *Wildflower ABC*. San Diego: Harcourt Brace.
Rawls, Wilson (1976). *Summer of the monkeys*. Garden City. NY: Doubleday.
Root Phyllis (2000). *Kiss the cow*. Illus. by Will Hildebrand. Cambridge, MA: Candlewick.
Sanderson, Ruth (2001). *The golden mare, the firebird, and the magic ring*. Boston: Little, Brown.
Say, Allen (1999). *Tea with milk*. Boston: Houghton Mifflin.
Scieszka, Jon (1992). *The stinky cheese man and other fairly stupid tales*. Illus. by Lane Smith. New York: Viking.
Shannon, George (1993). *Climbing Kansas mountains*. Illus. by Thomas B. Allen. New York: Bradbury.
Simon, Seymour (1999). *Crocodiles and alligators*. New York: Morrow.
Stanley, Diane (2000). *Michelangelo*. New York: Morrow.
Stewart, Sarah (2001). *The journey*. Illus. by David Small. New York: Farrar, Straus and Giroux.
Van Allsburg, Chris (1984). *The mysteries of Harris Burdick*. Boston: Houghton Mifflin.
Weisner, David (1999). *Sector 7*. New York: Clarion.
Williams, Vera B., & Williams, Jennifer (1988). *Stringbean's trip to the shining sea*. New York: Greenwillow.
Wisniewski, David (1996). *Golem*. New York: Clarion.
Wood, Audrey (1996). *The red racer*. New York: Simon & Schuster.
Wormell, Mary (2001). *Bernard, the angry rooster*. New York: Farrar, Straus and Giroux.
Wright Frierson, Virginia (1996). *A desert scrapbook: Dawn to dusk in the Sonoran desert*. New York: Simon & Schuster.
Wright Frierson, Virginia (1998). *An Island scrapbook: Dawn to dusk on a barrier island*. New York: Simon & Schuster.
Yaccarino, Dan (2001). *Oswald*. New York: Atheneum.
Yates, Elizabeth (1950). *Amos Fortune, free man*. New York: Dutton.

Software Cited

Inspiration. Portland, OR: Inspiration Software (Grades 4–12).
Kidspiration. Portland, OR: Inspiration Software (Grades K–3).
Kid Pix. San Rafael, CA: Broderbund Software.
The Literary Mapper. Gainesville, FL: Teacher Support Software.
The Semantic Mapper. Gainesville, FL: Teacher Support Software.
Thinking Networks for Reading and Writing. New York: Thinking Networks.

Chapter 12

SUPPORTIVE TOOLS FOR WRITING

Spelling, Grammar, Mechanics, Handwriting, and Word Processing

When should you say [write] whom, *and when . . .*
should you say [write] who?
Whom *is the one to* whom *something is done,*
and who *is the one* who *does it.*
She is the one who *was dressed in red*
to whom *the carnivorous grandmother said,*
"The better to eat you with, my dear."

FROM *MINE, ALL MINE: A BOOK ABOUT PRONOUNS* BY RUTH HELLER*

Ruth Heller's whimsical example of the proper use of pronouns reflects a distinct departure from the drill and practice of parts of speech that typified our own years as students in elementary classrooms. Today's more casual approach to language, however, has not undermined the need and respect for accuracy of spelling, grammar and mechanics (punctuation, capitalization) as well as handwriting and word processing in students' written products that are shared with a wider audience.

Even the best writers require a repertoire of tools to polish their written products and prepare them for their reading audience. If the momentum of a piece of writing is disrupted by inaccurate spelling, incorrect grammar, lack of punctuation and capitalization, or indecipherable handwriting, the reader is likely to lose interest and abandon even a great piece of writing in frustration.

To ensure that all writers and readers will share a well-written product, teachers introduce, practice, and help students master the tools of spelling, grammar, mechanics, and handwriting/word processing in their writing. Society understandably requires, and will continue to require, accuracy, attention to detail, and precision in written communication skills. The impressions of a writer are often based not on the content quality of his or her writing but on the delivery of the message to the reader. Therefore, all students should strive for accuracy and proficiency in using the polishing tools that are integral to good writing (Invernizzi, Abouzeid, & Bloodgood, 1997).

The purpose of this chapter is to take a balanced view of teaching students to not only practice and utilize supportive writing tools in traditional contexts, but to master and apply them in the authentic context of their writing. Alternating between times when accuracy counts and times when risk taking takes precedence over accuracy means differentiating purposes for students. Journal writing, brainstorming webs, first drafts, and informal writing encourage the free, spontaneous recording of thoughts. This spontaneity should never be discouraged, particularly with emergent writers. On the other hand, final drafts of formal written pieces and letters as well as writing that will be scrutinized by others require accurate spelling, grammar, mechanics, and handwriting or word processing. These essential tools must be internalized by emerging students as they begin the process of becoming lifelong writers who will use writing as a communication skill throughout their daily lives.

These tools help writers express more precisely what they mean. They offer an opportunity to more clearly state a message, tell a story, state a poetic theme, or convey information. If the writing tools are viewed as aids to communication and understanding, rather than as errors to be corrected in red ink, they become more meaningful as teachers help students to learn about them and to see them in a positive rather than negative light. The writer who maintains control of writing tools will convey meaning clearly to an interested, motivated reader.

Traditionally, departures from adult standards have been viewed as "errors." Unfortunately, we have forgotten that children learn written language just as they do oral language—not through direct instruction but through discovery and the formulation of increasingly sophisticated hypotheses. "Errors" should more accurately be viewed and

*From *Mine, All Mine: A Book About Pronouns* by Ruth Heller, copyright © 1997 by The Ruth Heller Trust. Used by permission of Grosset & Dunlap, A Division of Penguin Young Readers Group, A Member of Penguin Group (USA) Inc., 345 Hudson Street, New York, NY 10014. All rights reserved.

referred to as "approximations" (Cambourne, 1988) of learning. Teachers need to learn to deal effectively with "approximations" that are actually reflective of the writer's thinking and, in some cases, evidence of the writer's growth toward mastering the structures and conventions of written English. In the past, language arts teachers have been encouraged and even trained to look for errors in students' papers. The reading of student work turns into an "error hunt" (Weaver, 1996), not an attempt to appreciate what the writers have said, how they have said it, or how much they have exhibited learning about conventions. Perfection is most likely to be an unattainable goal, little more than a theoretical ideal. In reading this chapter, keep a reasonable perspective on "error" as "approximation" and realize that the outcome is to gradually equip young writers with strategies for using writing tools to improve their final drafts. Writing is a developmental process that evidences itself in continuous growth in accurate spelling, conventional grammar and mechanics, and audience-focused presentation.

Objectives

- To understand the developmental perspectives of spelling as a means to guide and direct instruction.
- To recognize the classroom environment that balances conventional spelling with the risk-taking aspects of developmental writing.
- To enumerate spelling strategies and recognize their importance in creating independent spellers.
- To recognize and respect the role of conventional grammar and mechanics as editing tools in the writing process.
- To understand the importance of both handwriting and word processing as tools to support the final stage of the writing process.

Spelling

The first tool that supports the writing process is spelling. Often children and parents alike enjoy the togetherness of practicing for the weekly twenty-word spelling practice. The real "test" of spelling, however, lies in a child's ability to apply common spelling words and learned spelling rules in the embedded context of real writing. Although spelling may be the least challenging of school subjects to many children, it can be quite complex when considered at its deeper application levels. Spelling will be explored through a developmental lens with attention to setting the optimal environment for its inclusion in authentic writing. Spelling strategies, the heartbeat of independent spelling, will also be explored to provide the rich background needed by teachers to provide the most appropriate and effective embedded spelling instruction in the writing classroom.

Teacher Prep

The Teacher Prep Web site will help you become a better teacher by linking you to classroom videos, student artifacts, teaching strategies, lesson plans, relevant education leadership articles, and practical information on licensing, creating a portfolio, implementing standards, and being successful in field experiences. Visit this resource at www.prenhall.com/teacherprep.

A Developmental Perspective on Spelling

The developmental perspective that pervades this textbook also applies to the individual emergence of conventional spelling in children. Gentry (1981; 1987), Henderson (1981), and Read (1986) have all identified five

FIGURE 12.1 Developmental stages of spelling: Characteristics and instructional insights.

Stage 1: Precommunicative Spelling (Preschool and Beginning Kindergarten)

Characteristics

Use of scribbles, drawings, letterlike forms, uppercase and lowercase letters, and numbers to represent words.
Symbols written top to bottom, left to right, or placed randomly on the page.
No indication of sound/symbol relationships.
Examples: XT5STP 5TTTSB

Instructional Insights

Provide many opportunities to "write" on paper.
Use a pencil for writing and crayons for drawing.
Provide an effective writing model on chart paper, overhead, or chalkboard.
Demonstrate directionality in big books by pointing top to bottom and left to right.
Ask child to tell you what he or she has written and record it in manuscript below his/her writing.

Stage 2: Semiphonetic Spelling (Kindergarten and Beginning First Grade)

Characteristics

Awareness of the sound/symbol relationship in words.
Use of one-, two-, or three-letter spellings designating words.
Use of letter-name strategy
Examples: rkt mtr bd lrn

Instructional Insights

Pronounce words slowly to hear all sounds, especially consonants or letter-name vowels.
Work with the alphabet and letter sounds.
Locate objects that begin with designated sounds.
Ask child to read what he or she has written and record in manuscript below the writing.

Stage 3: Phonetic Spelling (Beginning First Grade—End First Grade)

Characteristics

Represents beginning, middle, and end sound features in a word.
Overemphasizes the use sounds over standard letter combinations and endings.
Attempts long and short vowels, plurals, and past tense, but with a degree of inaccuracy.
Examples: monstr kidz

Source: Adapted from G. Tompkins (1998). Language Arts: Content and Teaching Strategies. *4th ed. Upper Saddle River, NJ: Merrill/Prentice Hall.*

developmental stages of spelling through which all children pass to becoming conventional spellers:

1. Precommunicative spelling
2. Semiphonetic spelling
3. Phonetic spelling
4. Transitional spelling
5. Conventional spelling

FIGURE 12.1 (Continued)

Instructional Insights

Model phonetic writing with beginning, middle, and end sounds.
Include lessons on long and short vowels sounds.
Use rhyming words to teach vowel sounds.
Teach endings such as *-s, -es, -ed, -ing.*
Invite children to participate in interactive writing experiences.

Stage 4: Transitional Spelling (Second Through Third Grade)

Characteristics

Visual memory becomes an important aspect of spelling.
Includes correct letters, but often reverses them.
Uses a variety of strategies to locate or create conventional spelling.
Uses a high percentage of correctly spelled words.

Examples: figuer thare

Instructional Insights

Teach consonant and vowel digraphs and other essential spelling patterns (*oo, oy, oi*).
Showcase silent letters in words (*gh, kn*, final *e*).
Teach strategy of visualizing a word and determining if it looks right.
Internalize common sight/functional words that defy phonics (*what, were, was*).
Model proofreading to locate and correct misspelled words.

Stage 5: Conventional/Standard Spelling (Third Grade and Beyond)

Characteristics

Knows how to spell a large number of words conventionally.
Knows how to apply some spelling strategies to locate and produce correct spellings.
Internalizes rules that govern difficult vowel and constant combinations.
Learns to spell words that do not follow the "rules" of spelling.
Uses silent letters and applies consistent spelling rules.
Determines a word is incorrectly spelled and writes alternatives to locate correct spelling.

Examples: monster figure

Instructional Insights

Teach root words, prefixes, and suffixes.
Teach syllabication of longer words to assist in spelling.
Teach homonyms, contractions, irregular spellings.
Practice proofreading to locate and correct misspelled words.
Expect proofreading on all final drafts.
Keep a personal spelling dictionary of challenging words used in the context of writing.

While all children go through these stages, some travel through them at a fast pace, seemingly bypassing certain stages. Others travel through slowly, lingering in one stage until truly ready to move on to the next. Documentation of each student's developmental spelling stages is essential for a teacher to show evidence of some growth over time. Figure 12.1 lists five developmental spelling stages and enumerates characteristics that distinguish one stage from the other. Teachers who work with young children (K–3) will particularly begin to note characteristics of these stages in their students' writing. There is no timetable or definite ages or grade levels during which students pass through these stages. A teacher who is aware of these stages, however, typically notes distinct changes and growth over time and applies instructional techniques to nudge students ahead to the oncoming stage.

The terms "invented spelling" or "kid spelling" have previously been used to designate the movement of a child through these developmental spelling stages toward conventional spelling. However, these terms tend to ignore the thought process that accompanies the complex development of spelling. Therefore, the terms "constructed spelling" or "developmental spelling" seem to more accurately describe the critical thinking, problem solving, and decision making that are a part of transferring a word from the mind into symbols on a piece of paper. Constructed spellings, the reasoned approximations and strategies students use as they write, are based on what learners know about words—the rules, patterns, sounds, visual configurations, meanings, and word origins of language.

Student journals are an excellent means to gather and discern the various stages of constructed spelling (Bear & Templeton, 1998). The student samples presented over the next few pages provide examples of each stage of development. Note these examples carefully, compare them to the characteristics in Figure 12.1, and begin to internalize the sequence of the stages. The more experience you have with young children's writing, the more competent you will become in determining a child's developmental spelling stage. Often children show characteristics of more than one stage at a time—another indication of forward developmental movement.

Stage 1: Precommunicative Spelling. This first developmental stage is often referred to as the babbling stage of spelling. You are likely to note uppercase and lowercase letters, numbers, and even drawn symbols randomly strung together. The distinguishing characteristic of this stage is that there is *no* sound/symbol relationship between the symbols on the page and the sounds of the words. Although children will "read" what they wrote, there is no phonetic means to accurately decipher the text. Yet this stage is important as it designates knowledge of the printed marks on the page and their ability to convey a message—a first step toward being a reader, writer, and speller. Student Sample 12.1 is from Jesse's kindergarten journal in which he literally throws letters on the page. There is no sound/symbol relationship between the letters and the proposed message Jesse intends to convey.

Stage 2: Semiphonetic Spelling. This stage implies growth into a sound/symbol relationship between the letters on the page and the actual sounds in the words. A distinguishing feature of this stage is that not all sounds are represented by symbols. While the initial or final consonant might be in place, vowel sounds and even consonant blends are not evidenced. The positiveness of this stage is the recognition of phonemic awareness as a resource for placing printed symbols on the page. At this stage, a teacher (with the use of picture cues) can begin to decipher some of the words, while the child can actually begin to "read" what they have written, even if all words and sounds are not present on the page. Student Sample 12.2 shows the constructed spelling of "I played in the leaves" written by a kindergarten student on a fall day. Note the beginning appearance of vowels, but only those long vowel sounds that actually mirror the vowel's letter name.

Stage 3: Phonetic Spelling. This stage evidences itself as words begin to be spelled as they sound out. All phonemes (word segments/syllables) are represented by at least a single letter, although the letters may be unconventional. Teachers find it quite

STUDENT SAMPLE 12.1 A kindergarten journal depicts precommunicative spelling.

easy to decipher words, sentences, and entire stories that reflect the connection between sounds and symbols for each segment of each word recorded on paper. Student Sample 12.3 shows the sentence "He [the cat] is sticking his tongue out." The writer succeeds in using some sight words (*he, is*) while sounding out the rest of the sentence. Note the presence of correct consonant sounds and an attempt at including vowels, even if approximations.

STUDENT SAMPLE 12.2 A kindergarten journal depicting semiphonetic spelling.

STUDENT SAMPLE 12.3
A first-grade journal depicting phonetic spelling.

Children in the phonetic stage actively contruct spellings. Student Sample 12.4 illustrates Hilary's first grade journal, which relies heavily on phonics and little on visual memory. "Spiders make webs and with the webs they catch flies. So many kids run and are scared of spiders." Most vowels and some consonants are misrepresented. However, all syllables/phonemes are represented by one or more characters. These two phonetic examples illustrate the developmental continuum of "sounding out" during the phonetic stage.

Stage 4: Transitional Spelling. This stage indicates growth as vowels become placeholders in every syllable of a word. Although the correct vowel may not be present, some vowel will always be used to represent a missing sound. A distinct characteristic of this stage is the apparent use of visual memory in attempts to spell words correctly. Because children are typically readers at this stage, they can actually close their eyes and recall a word they have previously seen in print. Although the results are not always accurate, the transitional speller manages to represent even difficult words quite accurately. Student Sample 12.5 represents Kurt's second-grade retelling of Trinka Noble's *The Day Jimmy's*

STUDENT SAMPLE 12.4
A first-grade journal depicting phonetic spelling.

Siydrs make weps and with
the weps thay cec flis
Somy Kis and ronp aor Serd
ove Siydrs.

Hilary

STUDENT SAMPLE 12.5 A second-grade journal depicting transitional spelling.

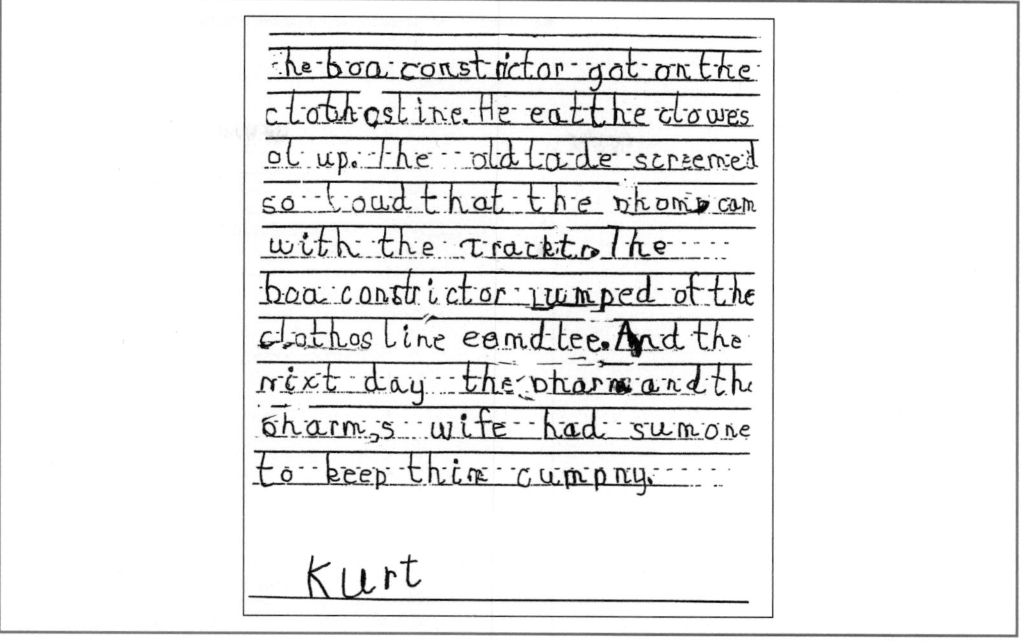

The boa constrictor got on the
clothsline. He eat the clowes
ol up. The old lade screemed
so loud that the phoms cam
with the tracktr. The
boa constrictor jumped of the
clothos line eemdtee. And the
nixt day the pharm and th
pharm's wife had sumone
to keep thim cumpny.

Kurt

Boa Ate the Wash. All words are decipherable, although many are spelled phonetically. Note the additional attempts at including vowels, even if incorrect, and the risk taking of words like "immediately."

Stage 5: Conventional/Standard Spelling. This final stage marks the attainment of conventional spelling. Although all individuals confront spelling challenges throughout their lives, the conventional speller gets most words correct or at least is aware of strategies that assist in determining the correct spelling of a word. The most often asked question in a discussion of developmental spelling is when children should be expected to reach this stage. Typically, third to fourth grade is a time to suspect learning difficulties or just plain laziness if spelling has not reached the standards expected at this stage. Student Sample 12.6 illustrates how Greg, a fourth grader, was inspired by Chris Van Allsburg's *The Mysteries of Harris Burdick.* Although there are a few spelling errors, none are so blatant that they disrupt the drama of this story. Even the misspellings provide reasoned attempts at the intended words. Perfection is not the hallmark of conventional spelling, but a high percentage of correctness is expected.

An Environment for Teaching Spelling

Just as language arts educators view reading and writing as processes, so too do they view spelling as a developmental process. Just as reading and writing are facilitated by skills applied as strategies, so too does spelling apply skills and rules that convert to spelling strategies. How then should you teach spelling? Routman (1996) offers the following suggestions about spelling strategies that can provide the basis for a sound spelling program.

- *Set up a classroom environment that encourages children to become good spellers.* Balancing the encouragement of risk taking with a respect for accurate spelling conveys the idea that writing is important but that accuracy polishes writing for its

STUDENT SAMPLE 12.6 Fourth-grade writing depicting conventional spelling.

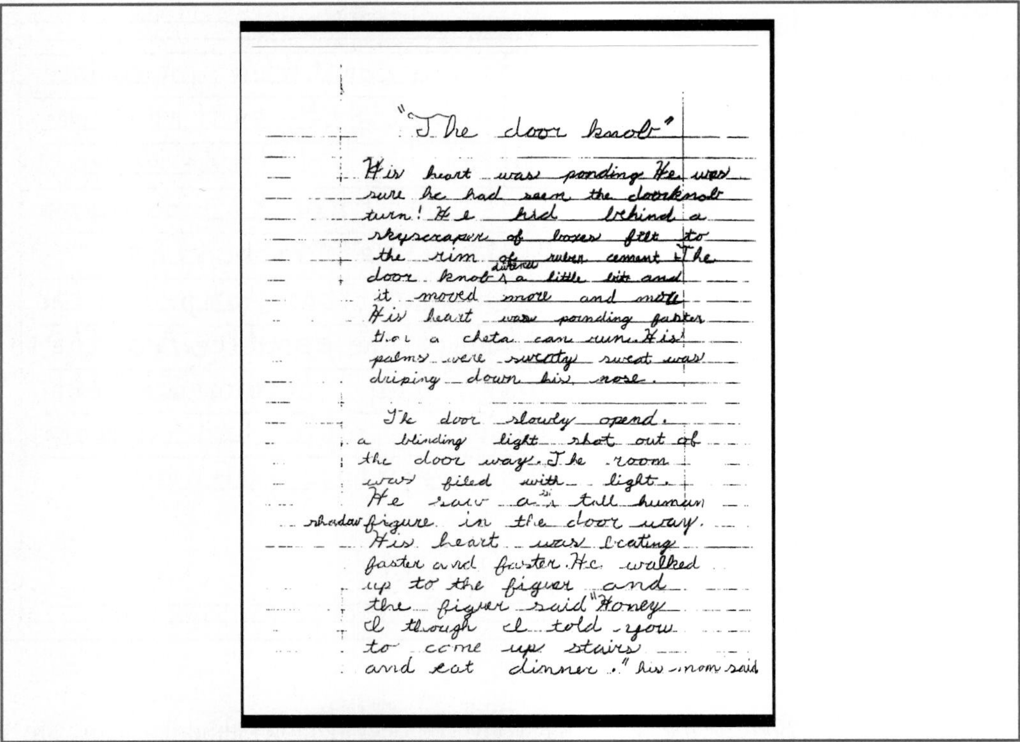

"The door knob"

His heart was ponding He was
sure he had seen the doorknob
turn! He hid behind a
skyscraper of boxes felt to
the rim of ruber cement The
door knob [twisted] a little bit and
it moved more and more
His heart was pounding faster
than a cheta can run. His
palms were sweaty sweat was
driping down his nose.

The door slowly opend.
a blinding light shot out of
the door way. The room
was filed with light.
He saw a tall human
shadow figure in the door way.
His heart was beating
faster and faster. He walked
up to the figuer and
the figuer said "Honey
I though I told you
to come up stairs
and eat dinner." his mom said

audience. The presence of a word wall, use of individual spelling dictionaries, and teaching of spelling strategies sends the message that good spelling is valued. Readers typically become better spellers. Students should be given many opportunities to read, both for the love of reading and its secondary impact on spelling acquisition.

- *Become an accurate spelling model for your students.* All words displayed on bulletin boards, morning messages, and demonstrations should be spelled correctly. In modeling final draft writing, teachers can verbalize the application of spelling strategies to discover the correct spelling of troublesome words.
- *Become more knowledgeable about the teaching of spelling.* Often teachers think that spelling is the easiest subject to teach. If they really knew more about it, they would know there is much more to teaching spelling than providing a weekly routine of spelling activities. Learning more about spelling from this chapter is a beginning for an expansion of your spelling knowledge.
- *Raise your expectations for good (not perfect) spelling.* Knowing the difference between sloppiness and laziness and developmental spelling ability is where this premise takes hold. Striking a balance between developmental ability and conventional spelling for each child is a professional decision. Individual tracking of spelling development is critical to knowing the difference between spelling challenges and frustrations. By fourth grade, however, most children should have achieved spelling competence with common words. New words will always be a challenge, but striving toward the use of strategies to confront these challenges provides an additional level of spelling instruction.
- *Help students produce final copies with correct spellings.* A multiple perspective for identifying words that need correction (self-edited, peer-edited, teacher-edited)

and the incorporation of a variety of strategies to correct misspellings must be guided by a knowledgeable teacher. Demonstrating strategies to confront spelling challenges is an instructional model that helps children move toward accuracy. Internalizing these strategies moves the student along to success as a lifelong speller. But students cannot be left on their own; they must be guided by a teacher who models how to utilize a variety of tools to seek out the accurate spelling of challenging words.

- *Demonstrate, model, and apply proofreading in the context of real writing.* In order for students to develop a "spelling conscience" (Turbill, 2000), they need to become effective proofreaders from the time they learn to read and write. Proofreading workshop and overhead demonstrations provide the model for applying these skills in their daily writing. Proofreading actually translates to the way many standardized tests evaluate spelling ability.
- *Realize that spelling is important but it reflects only a limited aspect of writing ability.* Writing needs to be evaluated on more than spelling accuracy, although correct spelling must be emphasized in final drafts.

In addition to articulating a well-defined philosophy to students that supports correct spelling, a teacher must communicate that committed philosophy to parents as well. A teacher can convey messages to parents through the things he or she does related to accurate spelling:

- Send student writing home in a final copy on a regular basis. While parents need to see daily efforts at writing/spelling, they also need to see final products that reflect high spelling expectations.
- Be sure spelling is correct on all writing for public display or reading—on every thing from writing that is submitted for contests to bulletin board displays to newspaper publication. Accuracy reflects on the school, the teacher, and the student. Explain to your students the importance of accuracy to the reading audience.
- Inform parents about the developmental levels of spelling and how they impact the spelling abilities of young children. Reinforce the message that too much emphasis on accuracy can result in a breakdown in risk taking that is a part of real writing. Use open house or parent night to showcase research and information on these levels for emergent learners. Use parent conferences to document the growth of spelling over time for K–2 students.
- Keep parents updated on your spelling program through newsletters. Send home weekly lists, but also emphasize the responsibility of the speller to utilize correct spelling in the context of writing. Hopefully, the report card will reflect both traditional and embedded spelling instruction, but portfolios of student writing will document the latter.

Moving parents beyond traditional spelling knowledge and practice while striking a balance between risk taking, developmental spelling ability, and correctness is a challenge for even the best teachers.

An Instructional Plan for Teaching Spelling

A balanced plan for spelling instruction blends some traditional spelling methods with current embedded spelling philosophies. A comprehensive view of spelling instruction implies that spelling should be taught and evaluated through both the traditional testing of relevant words and the application of spelling in the natural context of writing. The emphasis on spelling strategies is also a component of this balanced perspective. Under the blended philosophy, the "correctness" of spelling must be extended beyond "right" and "wrong" to an analytical evaluation by an informed teacher. This balanced philosophical stance can result in quality spelling instruction through both a traditional and a contextual stance.

Weekly Spelling Tests. Think back to your days as an elementary school student and the weekly list of twenty new words that you hoped to learn to spell correctly. The typical spelling textbook reinforced a pattern through a list of related words—for example, *-ing* words, *-ed* words, *ie* and *ei* words, and long *a* words. Remember the seemingly effective tests and exercises: writing each word ten times, writing each word in a sentence or story, taking the pretest and doing the workbook pages, correcting the workbook pages, taking the final test (which included a surprise bonus word). As a result of repetition and parental assistance, you and most of your classmates probably received an A. However, your teacher seldom checked to see whether you remembered those words the following Monday. In fact, most teachers often overlooked the misspelling of a previous spelling word in the context of writing as the focus stayed on "this week's" list of spelling words.

Hopefully, research and common sense have moved educators beyond these practices. How can we retain the nostalgia of this practice, yet realize that words learned in isolation have little to no carryover to real writing? A recent survey revealed that parents remain staunch supporters of the direct teaching of spelling as a separate subject (Chandler, 2000). In fact, even in today's hectic world, parents will take the time to help their children practice the coveted weekly spelling list. A carryover from their own education, they tend to pride themselves and their child on weekly achievement in spelling. In maintaining a balanced spelling program, support exists to retain this practice, but to acquire the list of spelling words from a variety of relevant sources rather than a rule-dominated spelling textbook. Where then can a teacher acquire a list of twenty weekly spelling words?

- Words that the teacher knows the student *must know* at the assigned grade level. Grade-level lists of common words abound and should provide a guideline for five words per week that ensure that students are mastering common grade-level words.
- Words that a teacher notices the students *need*. An astute teacher will recognize patterns in errors of several students in the classroom. The misspelling of *ie* and *ei* words, for example, might draw attention to a need for five words that replicate this pattern. In this way the pattern/rule becomes a part of the spelling curriculum out of need rather than because of its placement in a textbook.
- Words that are being meaningfully used *in the classroom context*. Seasonal words and curricular themes guide selection of five words per week that are relevant to classroom study. *October, pumpkin, mammal, ocean,* and *pioneer* might be appropriate for a third-grade classroom while *autumn, weather, hurricane, Atlantic Ocean,* and *recycle* might appear on a fifth-grade list.
- Words that each student *wants to know* how to spell. Selected from the context of writing needs for each week, five words are self-selected by the speller. Recorded on an index card, these are the only words that vary for each student. Rymer and Williams (2000), in fact, suggest an important relationship between explicit spelling

instruction, weekly spelling tests, and the spelling used in children's self-selected writing.

While the traditional spelling practice and list can be mastered, the teacher/student selected words and context for those words carry greater relevancy to the speller's lives. Teachers can still send a list home (including the 15 standard and 5 individualized words) and a test can be given (15 words by the teacher and 5 words by spelling partners). In this way, educators may preserve the treasured practice of weekly spelling tests while maintaining a philosophy that demands a meaning-centered approach to learning.

Spelling in the Context of Writing. The most meaningful way to assess authentic spelling ability is the application of spelling strategies in the context of real writing (Hughes & Searles, 2000). The active construction of spelling over time provides documentation of spelling growth. Young children do not need to exhibit perfect spelling to evidence growth over time—they just need to keep writing. Teachers must foster the idea that correct spelling in a writing context does matter. With too much emphasis on correct spelling in the early stages of writing, children can lose their natural, genuine spontaneity as writers. Journals and first drafts should be safe territory for getting thoughts on paper rather than focusing on accuracy.

The embedded teaching of spelling requires teachers to use meaningful opportunities to teach spelling in the context of daily writing opportunities. Whether as a minilesson in a writing workshop or as a necessary step during the editing (proofreading) stage of the writing process, the context of authentic writing creates many learning opportunities for becoming a better speller.

Writing workshop or daily and weekly writing assignments provide the essential format for teaching spelling words and spelling strategies when students need them. Proofreading at the editing stage of the writing process in which misspellings are indicated by the writer, a peer editor, or the teacher provide effective practice in locating and correcting spelling miscues. High expectations for locating and correcting misspellings must be communicated and modeled by the teacher. In fact, the teacher actually needs to use a transparency of student writing to demonstrate locating and indicating misspelled words and then verbally strategizing ways to reach conventional spelling in a writing piece. Teachers must constantly speak openly and honestly to students about the importance of presenting themselves as competent spellers on final writing drafts.

A personal spelling dictionary—a spiral notebook in which the student designates pages from A to Z—provides a permanent record of words that were misspelled in the context of real writing. Such a dictionary becomes an excellent resource for locating the correct spelling of words confronted in the past. An ongoing list in the spelling dictionary provides documented evidence of challenging words to which the speller has gained ownership.

Spelling can be challenging to many students. Teachers should provide strategies and coping mechanisms to deal with struggling spellers rather than demean them because of spelling difficulties. All children need to be valued as learners, and spelling should not be a deterrent to recognizing a child's worth as a writer in his or her expression of fresh, unique ideas.

Teaching Spelling Strategies. An effective way to become a competent speller is to employ a repertoire of spelling strategies that can be accessed during spelling challenges.

What do good spellers do when they come to a word they cannot spell? Wilde (1992) found that children used several techniques: placeholding (just writing a word any way and moving on); human resource (asking an adult or a peer how to spell the word); textual resource (using a dictionary or another book to find the word); generate, monitor, and revise (writing a word until it looks correct); and ownership (using words writers that the student knows how to spell). Recognizing those spelling strategies, modeling them, valuing them when you see their use, and teaching them to spellers provides a critical portion of the spelling curriculum. Moving beyond twenty words per week, the learning and internalization of spelling strategies provides tools for success as a lifelong speller.

As discussed in earlier chapters, a strategy is a skill that is learned and then applied in a meaningful context. Spelling strategies imply the ability to confront a challenging spelling word in the context of authentic writing by using one or more ways to accurately spell the word. One of the most effective ways of enumerating these strategies is by asking spellers what they do when they do not know how to spell a word. A study by Bouffler (1984) enumerated ten strategies of spellers. As you read through these, think of incidents and words in which you (or your students) have survived a spelling challenge by applying one or more of the following real actions that learners take:

- *Spelling a word as it sounds.* Known as phonetic spelling, this often results in inaccuracies such as *stashion* (station) or *sisers* (scissors).
- *Spelling a word as it sounds out.* This technique exaggerates, and stretches out words so all phonetic sounds can be heard. Often results in inaccuracies such as *huwah* (who) or *hafah* (half).
- *Spelling a word as it articulates.* Sounds are represented by where they are articulated in the word. Also leads to inaccuracies as in *chridagen* (tried again) or *jress* (dress).
- *Spelling a word as it means.* Spellers can locate known words within more difficult related words (for example, *sign* within *signal, nation* within *nationality*).
- *Spelling a word as it looks.* Visual memory carries important implications for spelling, although reversal errors are possible (for example, *shcool* for *school* and *nigt* for night).
- *Spelling a word by analogy.* Spellers overapply what they already know about correct spelling to new words—for example, *fantastick* (fantastic) and *reskyou* (rescue).
- *Spelling a word by linguistic content.* The proximity of a word to another word in the writing can unintentionally influence the spelling of the word. For example, *any envelope* might be spelled *eny envelope* because of the closeness of the two words.
- *Spelling a word by reference to authority.* The writer looks to more proficient spellers or convenient print sources (classmates, adults, books, other materials) to assist with correct spelling.
- *Opting for an alternative word choice.* If spellers do not know how to spell a word, they choose a word they do know how to spell. This is an unfortunate result of too much emphasis on correct spelling (especially in first draft writing). It negatively influences simple word choice and eliminates the use of powerful vocabulary words in the context of writing. Try to encourage risk taking in your spellers.
- *Leaving the spelling of a word up to the reader.* This strategy often makes a teacher smile during proofreading. The writer makes the handwriting unclear or traces

FIGURE 12.2
Simple spelling strategies for the primary level.

- What does the word look like when you close your eyes?
- Is the word a long word or a short word?
- Is the word like any word you know?
- Is the word written nearby?
- What sounds do you hear in the word?

over letters and leaves it up to the reader to determine if the spelling is correct. Especially true for the vowels *i* and *e* and for vowel combinations like *ie* and *ei*.

Students benefit most when spelling strategies are demonstrated, displayed, and applied in the context of real writing. Spelling strategy minilessons, teacher modeling, and continuous application in authentic writing create writers with tools to become lifelong spellers. While many of these strategies are sound techniques for acquiring conventional spelling, many still lead to a misspelling. Yet they provide students with an arsenal of techniques to apply when they do not know how to spell a word.

Figures 12.2 and 12.3 present compilations of spelling strategies from research by Marinelli (1996) for primary spellers and by Wilde (1992) for intermediate and middle-level spellers. Teachers need to do the following:

- Model these strategies verbally on a daily basis in the context authentic writing in front of children.
- Post these strategies on a bulletin board so students can readily access a variety of means to discover the accurate spelling of a word.
- Point out these strategies on a daily basis in guiding individual children in their goal to reach spelling accuracy.

FIGURE 12.3
Intermediate and middle level spelling strategies.

- Use the word wall. Alphabetical lists of words added throughout the year by teacher and students providing word relevance and ownership while providing a ready reference for correct spelling of popular and commonly used words.
- Use people as resources. Good spellers become a resource to other spellers through word ownership.
- Use other print resources. Remember where you might have seen a difficult word in print. It could be on a bulletin board, in a textbook, in a report, or in a library book.
- Write the word three times. Try spelling the word three times as you visualize it in your mind and select the most visually correct form. Confirm the correct spelling with the written form.
- Stretch the word by slowly sounding it out so you can hear and represent each sound.
- Look for small words that might appear within a larger word.
- Use a dictionary or thesaurus as a printed spelling resource.
- Use a personal dictionary to locate words you have previously spelled. You once owned these words, so now locate them in your dictionary to correctly spell them again.

- Include these strategies as the basis of a portion of spelling instruction.
- Emphasize the use of spelling strategies in the editing stage of the writing process. De-emphasize the need to apply them in writing first drafts; emphasizing correct spelling in a first draft can inhibit risk taking, natural flow, and the quality word choice of the writer.

Final Thoughts on Spelling

As a new teacher, you will face some important decisions on how to teach spelling. Your district or school may have an existing spelling program in place that you may need to follow. Although a spelling textbook provides a secure framework for spelling instruction, try to apply what you have learned in this chapter on developmental spelling, spelling strategies, and spelling in the context of student writing. In addition to these new options, technology also invites spellers to explore interactive options on a variety of Web sites (see the Tech Tip included on page 377). Providing a mix of instructional spelling options is likely the most effective way to practice spelling both in isolated lists and in the context of writing.

An ultimate spelling goal should be to guide students to become lifelong spellers who possess the strategies to spell challenging words they wish to use in their writing. While textbook lists and instruction provide a single perspective on spelling instruction, you will want to move your students beyond that view to include the importance of being able to apply independent spelling strategies in the context of authentic writing.

Grammar and Mechanics

Just as conventional spelling imposes a cultural judgment on writing, so too does the proper use of writing conventions. What are the conventions of writing? Writing conventions are tools to help the writer and the reader who will read the text and understand

The morning message encourages close observation for accurate capitalization and punctuation.

Technology-Based Spelling and Grammar

Spelling Software

A variety of spelling software is available for students of all ages and spelling abilities. *JumpStart Spelling* (Knowledge Adventure) and *Curious George Reads, Writes, & Spells* (Simon & Schuster) are just two examples of spelling software programs that come in CD-ROM format. Other titles, such as *iSpellWell* (Voelker Software) may be downloaded from the Internet and can be accessed both from school and home (there is often a trial period followed by user license fee). Some software offers mostly drill and practice with limited options for customizing lessons or spelling words, but some does allow students and teachers to enter their weekly spelling list and customize the activities. **www.ispellwell.com/documentation/index.htm**

Web-Based Spelling Activities

The Internet offers a plethora of spelling-related activities and lesson ideas for both teachers and students.

ESL Interlink offers many free online spelling lessons ranging from level 1 (primary sight words) to level 5 (advanced spelling word). Students actively participate by listening to words, typing words, or identifying misspelled words. The computer provides instant feedback. **eslus.com/LESSONS/SPELL/SPELL.HTM**

Discovery School's *Puzzle Maker* is a puzzle generation tool for teachers and students. Using the weekly spelling list, the user can create and print customized word searches, crosswords, and many other puzzles. **www.puzzlemaker.com/**

Spellbound (BBC Education) provides the student with a correctly spelled word then scrambles the letters and the student puts them back in order. Best for primary students. **www.bbc.co.uk/education/dynamo/den/spelling/index.htm**

Alien Scavenger Hunt: Letter Bugs and *Alien Scavenger Hunt: Space Trash* (Game Goo) are interactive games where students use the mouse to click on letters that make up a word. Cartoonlike "aliens" provide instructions and feedback. **www.cogcon.com/gamegoo/gooey.html**

Spelling/Grammar Check

Word-processing instruction should address editing and spelling tools included in most word-processing programs. It is important to truly *teach* students how to use such electronic editing tools to improve their writing. Common problems include confusion over the application of similar-sounding words (*there* and *their*) or words with similar spelling patterns (*college* and *collage*), and misuse of apostrophes (*its* and *it's*). The spell/grammar-check user is likely requested to select one of several proposed words, which can often be challenging for student authors. A strong sense of word recognition and understanding of basic grammar rules are required to make an appropriate choice.

To look more closely at these materials and others related to "Supportive Tools for Writing", visit the Companion Website at www.prenhall.com/hancock.

FIGURE 12.4
Grammar to be taught incidentally, in the course of reading and writing.

- Parts of speech (noun, pronoun, verb, adjective, adverb, preposition, conjunction, interjection)
- Subject/predicate
- Subject-verb agreement
- Main verb/auxiliary verb
- Verb tense (present, past, future, present perfect, past perfect)
- Pronoun-antecedent agreement
- Phrases and clauses
- Connecting clauses (*and, but, or*)

what the writer is trying to say (Graves, 1994). In reality, they are every mark that a writer puts on the paper—the uppercase and lowercase letters, the words and spaces between them, the punctuation marks that complete every sentence. In this textbook, specific aspects of grammar, punctuation, and capitalization are considered conventions. Figures 12.4, 12.5, and 12.6 present examples of conventions (grammar, punctuation, capitalization) that provide the focus on "correctness" in writing in the elementary and middle-level classroom.

As in spelling, blatant errors in grammar, punctuation, and capitalization detract from the quality of writing. Expectations for the use of conventional grammar and mechanics today are as valued as they have been in the past. However, the context for teaching conventions has dramatically changed. Drill-and-practice textbook pages and worksheets have been traded for minilessons and applications in the context of real writing during the editing stage of the writing process. As students are given the chance to identify and rectify grammatical and mechanical errors in the context of their own writing, they will discover the relevance of the rules and expectations of standard conventions.

Remember copying ten sentences and capitalizing the first word in each sentence? This was more an exercise in copying than in rule application. Today students might be asked to scrutinize their own well-written paragraph through an *editing workshop* to make certain that each sentence begins with a capital letter. Remember following the isolated, sequential order of skill practice in a language arts textbook? Today an effective teacher will conduct a *convention minilesson* focusing on a need that is exhibiting itself in several students' writing—for example, remembering to enclose dialogue in quotation marks. Remember copying ten sentences and inserting commas in a series where needed? Today students may be introduced to the rule of commas in a series from *a model of literature,* then asked to locate (or to incorporate) series words in their own writing and punctuate accordingly. Good teachers have never stopped teaching conventions. They are simply teaching them when the student indicates he or she needs a rule rather than when a textbook designates the learning of a particular skill to take place. Teachers exercise professional judgments as they move simple conventions toward becoming internalized, lifelong writing strategies.

Reconceptualizing the teaching of grammar and other conventions is necessary if students are to become writers. Hillocks (1987) has found that a comprehensive review of research studies provides *no* support for teaching grammar as a means to improving composition skills. This finding implies that conventions taught in isolated contexts have no carryover to authentic needs for conventional grammar in writers. There are

FIGURE 12.5 Punctuation marks and common uses.

Punctuation	Uses and Examples
Period	At the end of a statement or request sentence: *The President took the oath of office.* *Please pass the ketchup.* After abbreviations: *U.K.* *Dr.* *Mrs.* *Mr.* *Ms.* *Ave.* After initials: *Marjorie R. Hancock* *John F. Kennedy*
Question Mark	At the end of a sentence that asks a question: *What time does the party begin?*
Comma	To separate Items in a series: *The buffet featured beef, chicken, and fish.* To separate numbers in dates: *November 7, 2002* To separate two independent clauses joined by a conjunction: *We rode the train, and we ate in the dining car.* To set off clauses within a sentence: *In spite of the large crowd, the Wildcats lost the homecoming game.* In quotations: *"You must get to school on time," said Mother.* *"I really hope," begged Anna, "that you will stay."* To set off appositives: *My, what a busy day it has been!* To follow the greeting in a letter: *Dearest Grandma,* To follow the closing of a letter: *Sincerely yours,*
Apostrophe	In contractions: *don't* *wouldn't* *can't* *we're* In possessives: *my friend's house* *her mother's car*
Exclamation Point	At the end of a sentence expressing strong feeling: *That was the best pie I ever ate!*
Quotation Mark	To set off the words of a speaker: *"I will arrive before five," promised Jacob.* *"I imagine," pondered Anna, "that you will be the queen."*
Colon	To introduce a list: *The suitcase contained the following: pajamas, bathrobe, slippers, and toothbrush.* Between numbers in time: *11:45* *2:00*
Semicolon	To separate independent clauses (can be used instead of a period): *We enjoyed the theater; we were sorry to see the play end.* To separate phrases that already contain commas: *We made a list of fruits, vegetables, and relishes; meats, fish, and cheeses; and soft drinks and other liquid refreshments.*

FIGURE 12.6 Capitalization rules and examples.

- Use capital letters at the beginning of a sentence: *The grocery store is only two blocks away from the school.*
- Use capital letters for proper nouns including the following:

  Names of people: *Marjorie Hancock* *David Letterman*
  Titles: *Dr.* *Mr.* *Mrs.* *Ms.* *Colonel*
  Cities and states: *Milwaukee* *Wisconsin*
  Countries and nationalities: *Ireland* *Irish*
  Book and magazine titles (the first and most important words):
  Bud, not Buddy *National Geographic Traveler*
  Days and months: *Monday* *Tuesday* *October* *December*
  Holidays: *Fourth of July* *Thanksgiving* *Veterans Day*
  Names of places: *Great Salt Lake* *National Gallery* *Grand Teton*
  Rocky Mountain National Park
  Names of streets: *Plymouth Road* *Pennsylvania Avenue*

several reasons why a formal study of grammar does not transfer to student writing (Weaver, 1996):

- Much of what is taught (parts of speech, subject-verb agreement, etc.) has little relevance to writing itself. A student's ability to analyze existing sentences is not as powerful as writing his or her own sentences.
- Grammar is so complex and abstract that it is not easily learned or well-learned in the elementary and middle-level stage of development.
- Students find grammar boring and do not really learn it. Students going through the motion of grammar exercises may appear to have learned a concept, but such exercises do not transfer to their real writing.
- Even when grammar is learned, it is not applied in appropriate writing situations. In many cases, more time is spent on grammar practice than on authentic writing.
- Traditional grammar reflects a behavioral philosophy in which learning is equated with practice and habit (e.g., performance on standardized tests). The application of grammar concepts requires cognitive understanding not gained through practice exercises.

Whatever the reasons, research does not support the belief that teaching grammar or conventions in isolation will typically improve writing.

The implication, therefore, is that grammar and conventions taught in the context of a child's own writing (or in a child's own language acquisition) are more likely to be meaningful, become internalized, and be more consistently applied in subsequent writing than rules and standards learned through isolated drill and practice. Figure 12.7 summarizes guidelines that teachers can follow.

In spite of the research, some teachers continue to teach grammar and conventions in traditional ways. Perhaps that is because it is easier to assign exercises and grade them with an answer key than to lead students through the complex process of producing effective pieces of writing. This chapter shows teachers how to take the new road—"the one less traveled by"—that can make all the difference for young writers. Lesson Plan 12.1, "Wacky Tales and Parts of Speech" exemplifies this fresh idea for teaching skills in a dynamic, interactive mode.

FIGURE 12.7
Guidelines for teaching grammar and writing conventions in the context of writing.

- Engage students in writing, writing, and more writing.
- Immerse students in the reading of good literature.
- Teach all aspects of grammar and writing conventions within the context of student writing.
- Introduce only a minimum of terminology that tends to confuse rather than clarify.
- Emphasize those aspects of grammar that are particularly useful in helping writers revise sentences to make them more effective:

  Variety in sentence structure
  Reordering sentence elements
  Expanding and combining sentences
- Emphasize those aspects of grammar that are particularly useful in helping writers edit sentences for conventions.
- Teach terms, structures, and skills when writers need them—ideally, when they are ready to revise or edit.
- Explore grammatical patterns of ethnic and community dialects via film, audiotape, or literature, and contrast them with accepted communication dialect.
- Become a teacher-researcher to determine the effects of your teaching of selected aspects of grammar or conventions on individual student writing.

Source: Adapted from Constance Weaver (1996). Teaching grammar in context. *Portsmouth, NH; Boynton/Cook Publishers.*

LESSON PLAN 12.1

TITLE: Wacky Tales and Parts of Speech

Grade Level: 3–6

Time Frame: 45–60 minutes

Standards

IRA/NCTE Standards: 6, 8

NETS for Students: 1, 3

Objectives

- Students will identify parts of speech in text during shared reading experience.
- Students will apply their understanding of parts of speech while writing a Wacky Web Tale.

Materials

- Computers with Internet access for student use.
- Computer, projector and large screen for teacher demonstration of Web site.
- An assortment of children's literature about parts of speech:

  Cleary, Brian, P. (1999). *A Mink, a Fink, a Skating Rink: What Is a Noun?* (*Words Are Categorical* series)

  Heller, Ruth (1997). *Merry-Go-Round* (*World of Language* series).

Motivation

- Read one or more of the children's books about parts of speech.
- Depending on students' prior knowledge of parts of speech, discuss, define, or review the meaning of adjectives, nouns, verbs, etc. Provide examples from children's literature.

Procedures

- Distribute copies of children's literature about parts of speech to pairs of students. (The two series listed above include several titles in each series.)
- In pairs, students read and discuss the story, define their assigned part(s) of speech, and apply their understanding by writing a few sentences including their assigned part of speech.
- Allow time for students to share their findings with the class. Encourage discussion and refer to the literature for further examples.
- Using a projector and large screen, introduce students to the *Wacky Web Tales* Web site (www.eduplace.com/tales/). Discuss the features of the Web site. Direct the students' attention to the "help" section.
- Explain to students that they will create their own wacky stories (similar to MadLibs) while applying what they have learned about parts of speech. Students may choose from the many tales featured on the Web site.
- Allow time for printing stories and sharing with peers.

Assessment

- Teacher may check the printed out stories for completion and accurate use of parts of speech.

Accommodation/Modification

- Encourage struggling students to consult the "help" feature on the *Wacky Web Tales* Web site for further clarification of particular parts of speech.
- Students may work in small groups. Each group member may be assigned the responsibility to come up with only adjectives, for example. Another group member may be responsible for verbs or nouns.

Visit the Meeting the Standards module in Chapter 12 of the Companion Website at www.prenhall.com/hancock to adapt this lesson to meet your state's standards.

This next three sections of the chapter discuss three instructional components for modeling, demonstrating, and teaching convention instruction and the accompanying application of these writing conventions as they grow into lifelong writing strategies: (a) literature as the model of writing conventions, (b) using minilessons to teach writing conventions, and (c) editing and proofreading workshop. A discussion of each of these demonstrates just how conventions might effectively be taught and emphasized.

Literature as the Model of Writing Conventions

From the day a child begins reading engagement, he or she is introduced to the conventions of writing. Capital letters identify the months in *Chicken Soup with Rice* by Maurice Sendak; quotation marks designate characters speaking in *Watch Out! Big Bro's Coming!* by Jez Alborough. Commas provide the rhythm and space between "One, two, buckle my shoe . . . Three, four, shut the door" in Iona Opie and Rosemary Wells's *Here Comes*

Mother Goose. Awareness of conventions begins through literature long before children use them in their own writing.

Trade books provide an excellent resource for locating and discussing conventions. Children's authors use conventions to enhance and convey the meaning of their text. Make a transparency of a page from a picture book or chapter book and ask the children to examine the page for the use of one or more conventional elements of grammar, punctuation, or capitalization. Donald Graves (1994) suggests pursuing the following aspects of writing conventions:

- Kinds of punctuation marks
- Use of nouns, verbs, pronouns in relation to nouns, adjectives in relation to nouns, or adverbs in relation to verbs
- How each convention clarifies the author's meaning
- What might be misunderstood if the convention were omitted
- The advantages of use of well-chosen language, such as strong verbs, snappy adjectives, or timely adverbs

The Literature Cluster on page 384 lists a number of children's books and the focus of conventions of writing for each. Using literature as conventional models of use of parts of speech, correct grammar, precise punctuation, and accurate capitalization may be the most effective means of "teaching" these conventions. Opening children's eyes to the use of conventions in the context of real writing sends the message of their importance to both the writer and the reader.

Using Minilessons to Teach Writing Conventions

A main format for the instruction of conventions is the minilesson, a crucial aspect of the writing workshop in which a skill is introduced and immediately applied whenever students exhibit a need for it in the context of their authentic writing. The concept of the minilesson was originally introduced by Lucy Calkins (1986) and further elaborated by Nancie Atwell (1987). Not only are minilessons taught on various aspects of the writing craft but also on writing conventions. The sheer number of writing conventions to be taught at various grade levels seems overwhelming, but brief lessons of five to ten minutes of direct instruction taught to whole class, small groups, or individual learners seem to have impact on the use of conventions in the students' writing.

Teachers should not assume that everyone will or should learn the convention and immediately be able to apply it in writing. They will have to guide students in the application of the convention in the context of their own writing and to teach additional minilessons as more students demonstrate a need for the convention throughout their writing.

An excellent example might be a sixth-grade minilesson on the use of quotation marks, capital letters, and commas in dialogue. Through kidwatching and constant monitoring of writing folders, Mrs. Larson noted that a recent pattern of including dialogue in stories has taken place among many students as they attempted to write fairy tale variants. Andrew, in particular, was using a great deal of dialogue in his Gingerbread Boy variant. An overhead transparency of the traditional *The Gingerbread Man* retold by Jim Aylesworth demonstrated to Andrew (and others) how these authors designate a character speaking.

> One day, the little old woman said, "Let's make a gingerbread man!"
> "Yes, let's do!" said the little old man, and they did.

The students also looked at transparencies of Richard Egielski's *The Gingerbread Boy* (set in New York's Central Park) and Mirra Ginsburg's *Clay Boy* (another variant). They noted

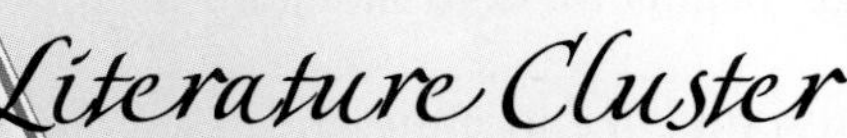

Literature Cluster

LITERATURE AS A MODEL OF PARTS OF SPEECH AND CONVENTIONS

Parts of Speech

Base, Graham (1986). *Animalia*. New York: Abrams.

Cleary, Brian P. (1999). *A mink, a fink, a skating rink. What is a noun?* Illus. by Jenya Prosmitsky. Minneapolis, MN: Carolrhoda.

Cleary, Brian P. (2000). *Hairy, scary, ordinary. What is an adjective?* Illus. by Jenya Prosmitsky. Minneapolis, MN: Carolrhoda.

Cleary, Brian P. (2001). *To root, to toot, to parachute. What is a verb?* Illus. by Jenya Prosmitsky. Minneapolis, MN: Carolrhoda.

Cleary, Brian P. (2002). *Under, over, by the clover: What is a preposition?* Illus. by Brian Gable. Minneapolis, MN: Carolrhoda.

Cleary, Brian P. (2003). *Dearly, nearly, insincerely: What is an adverb?* Illus. by Brian Gable. Minneapolis, MN: Carolrhoda.

Cleary, Brian P. (2004). *I and you and don't forget who: What is a pronoun?* Illus. by Brian Gable. Minneapolis, MN: Carolrhoda.

Heller, Ruth (1988). *Kites sail high: A book about verbs.* New York: Grosset & Dunlap.

Heller, Ruth (1989). *A cache of jewels and other collective nouns.* New York: Grosset & Dunlap.

Heller, Ruth (1989). *Many luscious lollipops: A book about adjectives.* New York: Grosset & Dunlap.

Heller, Ruth (1990). *Merry-go-round: A book about nouns.* New York: Grosset & Dunlap.

Heller, Ruth (1991). *Up, up and away: A book about adverbs.* New York: Grosset & Dunlap.

Heller, Ruth (1995). *Behind the mask: A book about prepositions.* New York: Grosset & Dunlap.

Heller, Ruth (1998). *Fantastic! Wow! and Unreal! A book about interjections and conjunctions.* New York: Grosset & Dunlap.

Conventions

Alborough, Jez (2005). *Tall.* Cambridge, MA: Candlewick.

Cronin, Doreen (2003). *Duck for President.* Illus. by Betsy Lewin. New York: Simon and Schuster.

Hindley, Judy (2002). *Do like a duck does!* Illus. by Ivan Bates. Cambridge, MA: Candlewick.

O'Conner, George (2004). *Kapow!* New York: Simon & Schuster.

Palatini, Margie (2001). *The web files.* Illus. by Richard Egileski. New York: Hyperion.

Pulver, Robin (2003). *Punctuation takes a vacation.* Illus. by Lynn Rowe Reed. New York: Holiday House.

Raschka, Chris (1993). *Yo! Yes?* New York: Scholastic.

Raschka, Chris (2000). *Ring! Yo?* New York: Dorling Kindersley.

beginning and ending quotations marks at first, and Mrs. Larson also pointed out the use of a comma (or an ending mark) to separate the speaker from the words spoken. Some students began to notice split quotations, all in the context of real literature written by real authors whose goal was to employ accurate conventions.

With student permission, Mrs. Larson also created a transparency of a Andrew's first-draft story using dialogue. The class community of writers attempted to apply what they had learned from the literature examples to their own classmate's piece—"The Gingerbread Boy and His Dog Ginger." Mrs. Larson knew that the complex nature of quotation marks required additional guided application during the editing portion of the writing workshop, but this introductory lesson had made students aware of the conventional skill used to denote conversation in writing. Student Sample 12.7 presents Andrew's final draft of his retold tale. Although his quotations might not be perfect, Andrew and his classmates

STUDENT SAMPLE 12.7 Sixth-grade final draft of a retold tale depicting the developing use of conventions.

THE GINGERBREAD BOY AND HIS DOG GINGER
by Andrew

Once upon a time in a little house in a valley, there was a little girl making a sugar boy cookie and a sugar dog cookie for a baking contest. The little girl thought she was adding sugar, but she realized that she had added ginger. "Oh, no!" screamed the little girl, "My kooky, cool, cookies are ruined!" She decided to bake them anyway.

Then she opened the oven and out leaped the Gingerbread Boy and his dog Ginger. The Gingerbread Boy rode like the wind on Ginger. The little girl hurried after them. "Hey, I haven't had a chance to taste you!" bellowed the little girl.

"Catch me if you can!" yelled the Gingerbread Boy.

"Ruff ruff!" barked Ginger. The Gingerbread Boy came across a rat. "Hey, Gingerbread Boy and Ginger slow down so I can nibble on your heads!" squealed the rat.

"Catch me if you can!" exclaimed the Gingerbread Boy, "I left the little girl behind and I'm going to leave you!"

"Bark ruff bark!" howled Ginger. They rode until they came upon a road.

"How are we going to get across?" questioned the Gingerbread Boy, "There are too many cars." Out of nowhere a weasel appeared.

"Can I be of any assistance?" asked the weasel.

"Yes, can you get us across this road safely?" replied the Gingerbread Boy.

"Certainly, just climb on my back and we'll be on our way." So, as they went the weasel told them to get closer to his head.

When the weasel was about to eat them, Ginger barked and vaulted off with the Gingerbread Boy. Weasel got hit by a semi.

In the afternoon it hot like an oven. It was so hot that the Gingerbread boy and Ginger dried up and couldn't move. The little girl and the rat caught up with them but they were too hard to eat. "I can't nibble on their heads!" whined the ragged and rough rat.

"Now, I won't be able to taste them!" cried the little girl. The rat and the little girl left the Gingerbread Boy and Ginger. Later the weasel came along and ate them. "Mmmm, crunchy!" weasel said excitedly. Happily the wild and worn out weasel ran away.

have had an impressive learning experience through a literature model and a teacher-initiated minlesson introduced at the right moment in an authentic writing context.

As these young writers return to their desks, some will immediately apply the dialogue conventions, others will need guidance in using them, and others may not even be concerned with them since conversation is not included in their current piece. Yet Mrs. Larson makes a note in her plan book of tentative additional lessons for those who need more guidance and for those who are just beginning to use dialogue in their writing.

Keeping track of conventions taught in minilessons is an important aspect of this teaching process (Graves, 1994). A three-ring binder should house materials (literature and writing samples) used in minilessons, and a list of children who attended them. In addition, a master list of conventions demonstrated and dates of minilessons are important as teachers must be able to document the teaching of grammar, mechanics, and capitalization skills. The notebook can become a resource for individual lessons or serve as a reminder about a particular lesson. Young writers, too, should keep track of the conventions they use either through a checklist or an ongoing list.

How do you know when to teach a convention minilesson? First and foremost, plan a minilesson when student writers ask for one. When sixth graders note the use of the ellipses in Gary Paulsen's *Hatchet,* they ask about this literary device and want to utilize it in their own writing. Curiosity and need designate the time for a convention minilesson. Second, look through student writing folders at least once a week to self-determine the overall convention needs of your writers. Look for the range of conventions they are using as well as the accuracy of those conventions. Determine the topics (specific grammar, punctuation, capitalization skills) for which you will prepare minilessons the next week and post them for the class. Finally, especially as a new teacher, check a scope and sequence chart from a textbook series or a recommended grammar text or reference book to ascertain that you are teaching minilessons for which writers at your grade level will be responsible for on state or national tests. This technique will guide a new teacher in a grade-level curriculum and address the reality of classroom teaching. Standardized tests often designate conventional usage, punctuation, capitalization, and spelling as "language arts," lacking authentic reflection of the real writing occurring in your classroom. Thus, you must be certain that you mesh your constructivist writing philosophy with the requirements of your district so students and teachers can survive standardized tests in a holistic teaching environment.

Editing and Proofreading Workshop

The main format for demonstrating the application of conventions as a writing and proofreading strategy occurs during the editing workshop portion of the writing workshop. The fourth stage of the writing process encourages editing, the locating and correction of spelling, capitalization, punctuation, grammar, and sentence structure errors. Teachers can demonstrate the proofreading and problem-solving aspects of the editing process by asking permission to use a student sample of writing on a transparency (or a draft copy on a projected computer screen).

Using standard editing marks (Figure 12.8), class members designate what changes would make the message clearer to the reader. Some teachers guide discussion sentence

FIGURE 12.8
Editing Marks for Proofreading.

Function	*Mark*	*Example*
Delete	ℯ	Brachiosaurus liked eating plants in at the swamp.
Insert	^	No one knows ^for sure why the dinosaurs died out.
Indent paragraph	¶	¶ Dinosaurs lived millions and millions of years ago. Some were very large and some were small.
Capitalize	≡	Tyrannosaurus rex was the most terrible dinosaur.
Change to lowercase	/	Scientists who study dinosaurs are called Paleontologists.
Add period	⊙	All the dinosaurs are extinct ⊙
Add comma	^,	Some dinosaurs lived on land, some in water and some in the air.
Add apostrophe	✓'	Tyrannosaurus Rex's teeth were 6 inches long!

Source: G. E. Tompkins, Language Arts Patterns in Practice, *6th edition. © 2005. Adapted by permission of Pearson Education, Inc., Upper Saddle River, NJ.*

FIGURE 12.9
Third-grade editing checklist.

The title of my writing is ______________________
My editing partner is ______________________
I read my story to a friend and STOPPED for
Periods ____________
Question marks ____________
Exclamation points ____________
I took out extra words that I didn't need ____________
I added words that I did need ____________
I checked for capital letters ____________
At the beginning of each sentence ____________
For the first letter of a name ____________
For the word "I" ____________
I circled words that may be misspelled ____________
Correct spellings: ________ ____________
________ ____________
________ ____________

by sentence. Others designate only specific focused skills for editing attention rather than overwhelming students in an attempt to correct all conventional errors.

As children return to their desks or writing tables, each child should at first *self-edit* his or her own writing piece. Next, partners should *peer-edit* their work. Finally, the *teacher-edit* is essential, especially if the writing will be scrutinized by the public eye. Each of the three stages of editing should use a different color marker or pencil so the writer can differentiate between the three editors. While perfection is not the goal, correct conventions serve as signposts to the reader so the focus of reading can be information rather than distractions. Checklists also provide guidelines for editing at the self-editing and peer-editing stages. Examples are shown in Figures 12.9 and 12.10. The fifth and final

FIGURE 12.10
Fifth-grade proofreading checklist.

________ **Spelling:** Read your writing and circle all the words you think are misspelled.
________ Self-edited
________ Peer-edited
________ Teacher-edited
________ **Punctuation:** Put correct punctuation at the end of each sentence (period, question mark, exclamation point).
________ **Capitalization:** Put a capital letter at the beginning of each sentence.
________ Keep margins on both sides of your paper.
________ Check for commas in a list.
________ Put a capital letter for the name of a person or place.
________ Capitalize the word "I."
________ Use apostrophe ('s or s') to show ownership.
________ Check for quotation marks for speaker's words.
________ Check for comma to separate speaker's words from the speaker.
________ Other personal proofreading skills.

stage of the writing process, publishing, includes the accurate application of edited conventions into the piece so the writing readily conveys the message the writer intends for the reader. The final draft should be virtually free of spelling errors and conventional inaccuracies so that meaning will flow without distractions to the reader.

Handwriting and Word Processing

In a world laden with technology, the teaching of the art of handwriting faces extinction. Yet everyday a worker, a parent, a child picks up a pencil or a pen and performs some meaningful task with traditional manuscript or cursive handwriting. Just as books will never be totally replaced by e-books, so too will handwriting never be totally replaced by word processing. There are just too many opportunities during the course of a single day that warrant conventional handwriting. In addition, society judges a person by the appearance of his or her writing. Sloppy writing reflects poor judgment while neat writing receives praise. Handwriting provides the vehicle for carrying a message to others.

Yet how much time should be spent in schools, burdened by an overflowing curriculum, teaching handwriting, either in manuscript or cursive form? Word processing has changed our lives, our productivity, and our display of written language. Inexpensive printers and programs with dozens of fonts provide the means to create an admirable product while simultaneously showcasing technology skills through keyboarding and word processing.

This section of the chapter speaks to both worlds—traditional handwriting and keyboarding. Primary teachers (K–3), in particular, need to know about conventional handwriting (Farris, 1991), while intermediate and middle-level teachers need to be aware of the power of word processing to showcase learning products. Being aware of both worlds ensures that teachers strike an appropriate balance between them. Indeed, there are mixed views on this topic, but being prepared for both worlds seems to best prepare the teacher. The best way to introduce the debate (and debates within the debate) is through a historical perspective.

Manuscript and Cursive Handwriting

Manuscript writing, known commonly as printing, was brought to the United States in the early 1920s. Manuscript print describes the simple stroked letters easiest for young children to recognize and to reproduce in print. Manuscript writing quickly became the most widely taught method in the primary grades. The great popularity is most attributed to the connection between a relatively easily learned system and the type of print used in textbooks and trade books. Figure 12.11 illustrates a popular manuscript model. Advocates of manuscript letter forms enumerate their strengths:

- Simple strokes allow children to master all letter forms and use them in emergent writing tasks.
- The physical movement for each stroke is shorter because each letter is made up of separate strokes.
- Block letter forms are less fatiguing to young children (than sustained motion due to letter joinings).
- Manuscript is more easily read than other forms of writing, thus aiding in comprehension and reading rate.

As children use manuscript print to emerge as readers and writers, they are anxious to learn the adult style of writing—cursive letters. Cursive writing proponents advocate cursive as a more rapid means of writing. Typically at the end of second grade or the beginning of third grade, teachers helped children make the transition from the block

FIGURE 12.11 The Zaner-Bloser manuscript alphabet.

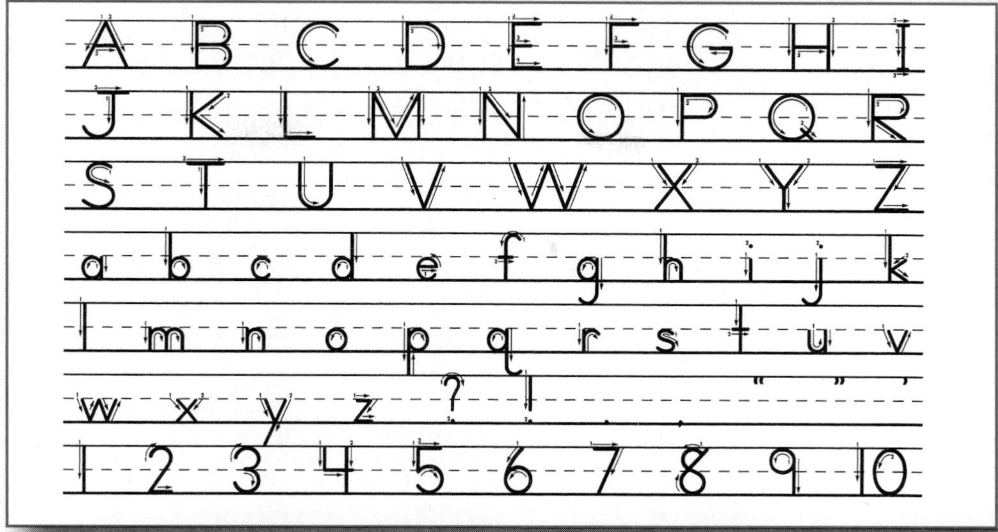

Source: *From Zaner-Bloser Handwriting, © Zaner-Bloser, Inc. Used with permission from Zaner-Bloser, Inc. All rights reserved.*

formed manuscript to the connected, slanted units of cursive writing. Hours were often spent in perfecting movements, strokes, and slants in striving for the perfect letter formation. Figure 12.12 presents a popular model of cursive writing. Advocates cite the following benefits of cursive writing:

- Cursive writing increases the speed at which ideas can be reproduced in print.
- Cursive writing is the written standard of the adult world.

FIGURE 12.12 The Zaner-Bloser cursive alphabet.

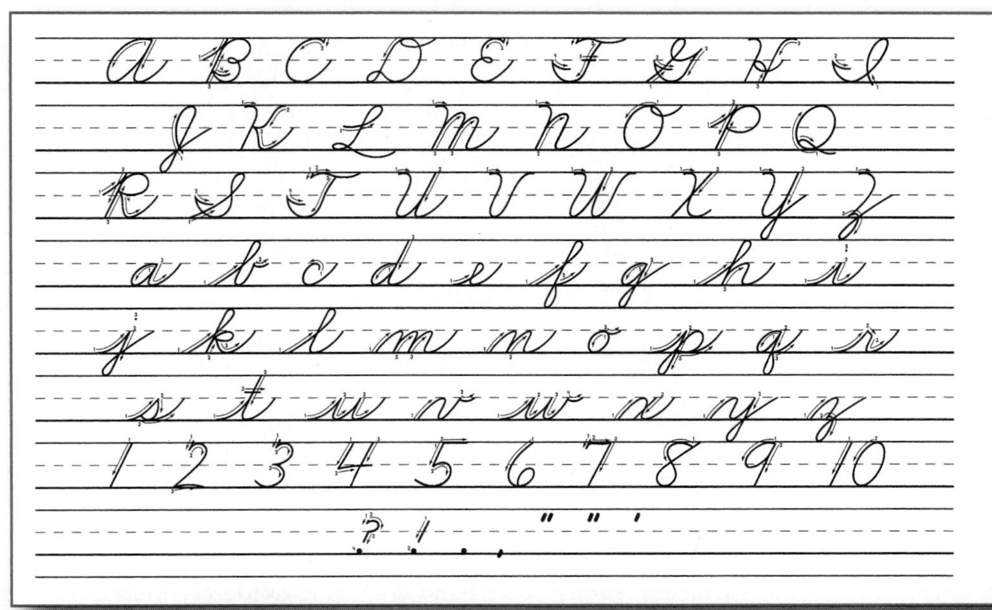

Source: *From Zaner-Bloser Handwriting, © Zaner-Bloser, Inc. Used with permission from Zaner-Bloser, Inc. All rights reserved.*

FIGURE 12.13 D'Nealian manuscript and cursive handwriting forms.

Source: D'Nealian manuscript and cursive alphabet from D'Nealian Handwriting Grade I *by Donald Neal Thurber. Copyright © 1999 by Addison-Wesley Educational Publishers, Inc. Reprinted by permission of Pearson Education, Inc. D'Nealian Handwriting is a registered trademark of Donald Neal Thurber.*

So for several decades in American education, manuscript became the hallmark of the early primary grades, while cursive writing became the dominant print choice of third grade and up.

In the 1970s a modified slanted alphabet called D'Nealian was developed by Donald Neal Thurber, a Michigan teacher, and introduced to American schools (Figure 12.13). D'Nealian is characterized by a slanted manuscript that more easily transitions into a cursive format. Instead of block letter formations, D'Nealian manuscript contains ending movements that may make hooking letters together at the cursive stage more feasible. Proponents cite the following benefits for D'Nealian writing:

- The letters are simplified without the flourishes of traditional cursive.
- Initial instruction facilitates the transition from manuscript to cursive writing as students only need to learn to connect strokes to most letters.
- Only five letters (*f*, *r*, *s*, *v*, and *z*) are different in the cursive form.

The main argument of D'Nealian opponents is that the introduction of a style different than early print in children's books may actually hamper emergent reading ability, especially if introduced too early.

Handwriting Instruction

Both manuscript and cursive handwriting are used in schools today. An awareness of both methods seems necessary to be prepared for teaching. Yet how much handwriting instruction is necessary in today's world? Regardless of method, handwriting instruction is essential, even in today's technological world. However, handwriting instruction has moved from a drill-and-practice task to a more meaningful writing context. This is the main difference between today's instruction and how students were exposed to handwriting in the past.

There are a few firm rules for today's limited but meaningful manuscript and cursive handwriting instruction:

- Follow one method of handwriting instruction consistently in a school or school district.
- Present a constant model of quality handwriting for children.
- Display a model of the handwriting being taught in the classroom both in the front of the room and on each child's desk.
- Emphasize real writing tasks for practice (see examples below).

The direct teaching of handwriting today involves demonstrating, modeling, and practicing within the context of meaningful language arts activities rather than the drill-and-practice of the past. The following contextual activities are frequently used for handwriting practice:

- ***Morning message.*** The message written on the board should provide the best model, manuscript or cursive, of the classroom teacher. It must align with the handwriting program supported by the school. If children copy a morning message, then that becomes their handwriting practice for the day.
- ***Language experience story.*** The story, dictated to the teacher by the children, should be written in standard manuscript writing and provide a model for reading and copying. Even copying or creating a recipe used for a class cooking experience might be reproduced in authentic handwriting.
- ***Poetry.*** Poetry initially chanted can become an opportunity for recording in print in a poetry booklet. A poem-of-the-day can become handwriting practice as the movement inspired by the words becomes the movement that creates the print.
- ***Letters and notes.*** Writing letters reminds children that legibility is key to communication. Writing a reminder or invitation to a parent provides an authentic task in which good handwriting can be practiced.
- ***Final draft copies/publishing.*** At the upper primary, intermediate, and middle levels of instruction, handwriting practice takes place within the final stage of writing workshop as final draft copies are published. Showcasing best handwriting in the context of a student's own work reinforces ownership and pride in a final writing product.

The evaluative elements of handwriting, both manuscript and cursive, focus on legibility. So regardless of the method, the following characteristics should be considered as children develop their writing skills:

- ***Letter formation.*** Are the letters formed correctly and the strokes made in order?
- ***Size and proportion.*** Are uppercase letters twice as large as lowercase in manuscript writing? Are uppercase letters three times as large as lower case in cursive?
- ***Spacing.*** Is there one letter space between words and two letter spaces between sentences? Is the spacing consistent within words?
- ***Slant.*** Is it consistent? Is it slanted to the right for cursive?
- ***Alignment.*** Are letters sitting on the lines? Are uppercase letters all the same size and lowercase letters all the same size?
- ***Line quality.*** Is the thickness, darkness, and direction of the lines consistent? Are there even, fluid, uniform strokes evident in the handwriting?

Many report cards still have an entry for a handwriting grade as part of language arts. Documentation of dated handwriting pieces over time is even more indicative of progressive growth in mastering the art of handwriting. Since less time is used for handwriting instruction, perfection seems unrealistic. Legibility seems to be the highest priority as a handwriting outcome. Handwriting varies developmentally from grade level to grade level and from individual to individual.

Word Processing

Technology has placed word processing programs literally at the fingertips of students today. Classroom computers and computer labs provide the opportunity for children to utilize word processing programs to present writing products in all forms—projects, reports, poems, and letters—in a legible format. But the availability of word processing also demands instruction in keyboarding skills. School districts are trading handwriting time for keyboarding exercises as education prepares students for the workplace. Virtually all jobs today include aspects of word processing, and the skill of keyboarding must be recognized and attended to in the elementary and middle-school curriculum. But the "when" and "what" of keyboarding has raised interesting issues.

If educators acknowledge that computers and related word-processing applications have a place in the writing curriculum, then educators must acknowledge that keyboarding instruction belongs there as well (Sullivan & Sharp, 2000). The first question that arises concerns the age at which correct keyboarding skills should be introduced. Most educators believe that formal keyboard instruction should begin at the fourth or fifth-grade level. In the primary grades, the focus should be on overall familiarity with the letters, the return key, the space bar, and the home row. Actual touch typing (the ability to type without looking at the keys) should not begin until at least fourth grade. Letter position should be emphasized in the primary grades, with the introduction and focus changing to touch typing as students gain the dexterity and finger span required for that technique.

The second question related to keyboarding concerns the content—what to teach. Keyboarding instruction focuses on technique, accuracy, and speed. Keyboarding techniques means more than correct placement of fingers on home keys. Other habits that must be considered include straight posture, positioning wrists above the keyboard, and looking at the text being entered rather than the monitor or the keys themselves. Once technique has been established, the emphasis can shift to speed and accuracy, but that is likely to be reserved for middle-school instruction. Once keyboarding is mastered, adeptness allows students to focus on the writing itself.

Real examples of children's use of word processing to produce quality writing products are evidenced at all grade levels and seen throughout this text. Student Sample 12.8 highlights Megan's second-grade PowerPoint presentation on her chosen career, although the task of typing this piece involved much time, Megan expressed delight in its presentation. Student Sample 12.9 showcases how Carl, a fifth-grade, self-created and word processed directions for new students to check out a school library book.

Much more will be shared about the implications of technology for the writing and presentation of projects and products in Chapter 13, which focuses on technology and the language arts. These initial examples across grade levels provide a sense of the importance of facilitating keyboarding at approximately the fourth- or fifth-grade level. While handwriting (manuscript and cursive) should be modeled, demonstrated, and practiced in daily authentic writing contexts, keyboarding and word processing carries equal weight as a means of communication in an electronic age. The more time students

STUDENT SAMPLE 12.8
A Second-Grade Word-Processed PowerPoint Slide.

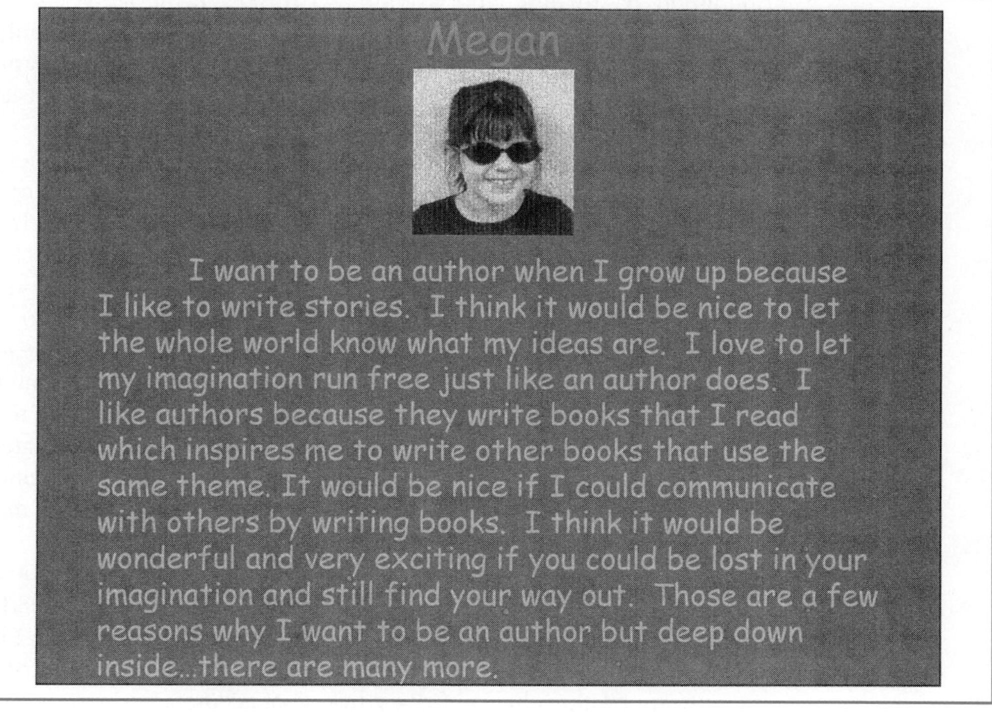

STUDENT SAMPLE 12.9
A Fifth Grader's Word-Processed Technical Directions.

Before you go the library , get your card from your teacher. Next , go to the library. Once you get in, go get a bookstick. Fourth, put your card in the card holder with your teacher's name on it. Then, look on the computer and find what you want. Sometimes they will have something to color. Also, there are rules. Number one is don't talk loudly. Number two is *NO RUNNING!!!!!!* Once you get your book, then chek out and read silently.

THE END

spend at a computer keyboard, the greater the need to devote time to keyboarding instruction.

Visit the Companion Website at www.prenhall.com/hancock and gauge your understanding of Chapter 12 concepts with the self-assessments.

Closing Thoughts

While holding on to the traditional writing conventions related to spelling, grammar, mechanics, and handwriting remains unquestionable, the means to achieving this conventionality requires reconsideration. The same developmental perspective that applies to oral language, reading, and writing also applies to the literacy learner's ongoing journey toward correctness in writing conventions. Developmental spelling, the gradual internalization of correct grammar, the ongoing application of the mechanics of punctuation and capitalization, and the legibility of a student's handwriting and mastery of word processing must be viewed from a developmental perspective.

Rather than demanding emergent, risk-taking writers to achieve presentation perfection, teachers must use the developmental opportunity to monitor, analyze, instruct, and track ongoing skills in spelling, grammar, mechanics, and handwriting—the supportive tools of the language arts. These skills cannot be ignored and teachers cannot expect children to master them on their own. Direct modeling and instruction with constant application within authentic writing contexts provides the balanced approach toward internalizing skills as they emerge as the strategies of an independent learner. Teachers must know more about recognizing the stages of developmental spelling, discerning the ongoing grammatical and mechanical needs of the emergent writer, and blending the skills of handwriting and word processing in order to individualize instruction and create writers who move toward accepted writing conventions. This formidable task requires knowledge of conventions, timing of interventions, insightful recognition of needs, and repeated revisiting of the supportive writing tools throughout the elementary and middle-level curriculum.

Correct spelling, grammar, mechanics, and handwriting is not an end in itself—there must be some purpose to it. Accuracy in these areas helps a child's voice be heard. For children to truly care about accurate spelling, grammar, mechanics, handwriting, and word processing, they must truly care about the writing itself. Writing practice does not ensure accurate supporting skills nor does the use of accurate supporting tools ensure quality writing. Yet if a teacher does not have a strong writing program, the supportive tools become isolated, meaningless, and ineffective. These supportive tools must be accurately applied to a simple goal: helping a child's writing voice to reach its intended audience.

References

Atwell, Nancy (1987/1998). *In the middle: New understandings about writing, reading, and learning*. Portsmouth, NH: Boynton/Cook/Heinemann.

Bear, D. R., & Templeton, S. (1998). Explorations in developmental spelling: Foundations for learning and teaching phonics, spelling, and vocabulary. *The Reading Teacher, 52,* 222–242.

Bouffler, C. (1984). Spelling as a language process. In L. Unsworth (Ed.), *Reading, writing, and spelling—Proceedings of the Fifth Macarthur Reading/Language Symposium,* Sydney, Australia. Quoted in B. Cambourne & J. Turbill, (1991). *Coping with chaos* (pp. 24–25). Portsmouth, NH: Heinemann.

Calkins, L. M. (1986/1994). *The art of teaching writing*. Portsmouth, NH: Heinemann.

Cambourne, B. (1988). *The whole story: Natural learning and the acquisition of literacy in the classroom*. New York: Scholastic.

Chandler, K., and the Mapleton Teacher-Research Group. (2000). Squaring up to spelling: A teacher-research group surveys parents. *Language Arts, 77,* 224–231.

Farris, P. J. (1991). Handwriting instruction should not become extinct. *Language Arts, 68,* 312–314.

Gentry, J. (1981). Learning to spell developmentally. *The Reading Teacher, 34,* 378–381.

Gentry, J. R. (1987). *Spel . . . is a four-letter word*. Portsmouth, NH: Heinemann.

Gill, C. H., & Scharer, P. (1996). "Why do they get it on Friday and misspell it on Monday?" Teachers inquiring about their students as spellers. *Language Arts, 73,* 89–96.

Graves, D. (1994). *A fresh look at writing*. Portsmouth, NH: Heinemann.

Henderson, E. H. (1981). *Learning to read and spell*. DeKalb, IL: Northern Illinois University Press.

Hillocks, G., Jr. (1987). *Research on written composition: New directions for teaching*. Urbana, IL: National Conference on Research in English and the ERIC Clearinghouse on Reading and Communication Skills.

Hughes, M., & Searles, D. (2000). Spelling and "the second R." *Language Arts, 77,* 203–208.

Invernizzi, M. A., Abouzeid, M. P., & Bloodgood, J. W. (1997). Spelling, grammar, and meaning in the language arts classroom. *Language Arts, 74,* 184–192.

Laminack, L. L., & Wood, K. (1996). *Spelling in use: Looking closely at spelling in whole language classrooms.* Portsmouth, NH: Heinemann.

Marinelli, S. (1996). Integrated spelling in the classroom. *Primary Voices K–6, 4,* 11–13.

Read, C. (1986). *Children's creative spelling.* London: Routledge & Kegan Paul.

Rosencrans, G. (1998). *The spelling book: Teaching children how to spell, not what to spell.* Newark, DE: International Reading Association.

Routman, R. (1996). *Literacy at the crossroads.* Portsmouth, NH: Heinemann.

Rymer, R., & Williams, C. (2000). "Wasn't that a spelling word?": Spelling instruction and young children's writing. *Language Arts, 77,* 241–249.

Turbill, J. (2000). Developing a spelling conscience. *Language Arts, 77,* 209–217.

Weaver, C. (1996). *Teaching grammar in context.* Portsmouth, NH: Heinemann.

Wilde, S. (1992). *You kan red this! Spelling and punctuation for whole language classrooms, K–6.* Portsmouth, NH: Heinemann.

Children's Books Cited

Alborough, Jez (1997). *Watch out! Big Bro's coming!* Cambridge, MA: Candlewick Press.

Aylesworth, Jim (Reteller) (1998). *The gingerbread man.* Illus. by Barbara McClintock. New York: Scholastic.

Egielski, Richard (1997). *The gingerbread boy.* New York: Laura Geringer/HarperCollins.

Ginsburg, Mirra (1997). *Clay boy.* Illus. by Jos. A. Smith. New York: Greenwillow.

Heller, Ruth (1997). *Mine, all mine: A book about pronouns.* New York: Grosset & Dunlap.

Noble, Trinka (1980). *The day Jimmy's boa ate the wash.* Illus. by Steven Kellogg. New York: Dial.

Opie, Iona (1999). *Here comes Mother Goose.* Illus. by Rosemary Wells. Cambridge, MA: Candlewick.

Paulsen, Gary (1987). *Hatchet.* New York: Bradbury.

Sendak, Maurice (1962). *Chicken soup with rice.* New York: Harper.

Van Allsburg, Chris (1984). *The mysteries of Harris Burdick.* Boston: Houghton Mifflin.

Chapter 13

TECHNOLOGY AND THE LANGUAGE ARTS

Exploring the New Literacies

All that summer Miss Rumphius, her pockets full of seeds, wandered over fields and headlands, sowing lupines . . .
The next spring there were lupines everywhere. . . .
"You must do something to make the world more beautiful."

FROM *MISS RUMPHIUS* BY BARBARA COONEY

The "*Miss Rumphius* Effect" is a term originated by Donald J. Leu Jr. (1999) to describe the vast sharing and exchange of technological "envisionments" via Internet project Web sites occurring in classrooms across the globe. In Barbara Cooney's picture book, *Miss Rumphius,* the main character, travels the world experiencing many adventures. When she returns home, she sets out to make the world a better place by planting lupines wherever she goes. From fields to highways, from highways to county roads, she scattered her seeds. The next spring, blue and purple and rose-colored lupines appeared on hillsides everywhere. This classic picture book theme reflects how an individual can create a vision of a better world and act on it through sharing. In today's technology-based classrooms, teachers and children exist "who are enriching our instructional worlds by planting new visions for literacy and learning on the Internet, transforming the nature of this new technology" (Leu, Leu, & Coiro, 2004, p. 187). Other classrooms use these new visions as resources, making children's worlds richer and more meaningful in a technological age.

Teachers sharing their successes are making valuable technological connections for more children. Imagining new possibilities for literacy and learning, implementing them through technology, and sharing their work with others develop curriculum networks that extend materials for curricular instruction. New technologies can break down classroom walls inviting effective teaching and learning to be immediately accessible to other classrooms. Instead of viewing technological innovation as a threat, an infringement, or a competition to teaching as we know it, educators need to view technology as an opportunity to renew the spirit of learning and as a dynamic means to extend knowledge (Hancock, 2000).

Technology is radically changing education and the teaching profession. Whether educators applaud or oppose this ongoing development, the nature of literacy and learning is being redefined by the digital technologies that are quickly becoming a part of the information age in which we live (Karchmer, Mallette, Kara-Soterious, & Leu, 2005). Today's language arts teachers still engage students in comprehension, process writing, critical thinking skills, and other tasks as they have in the past. Today's students, however, access and apply these skills through electronic books, electronic mail, and a plethora of online resources. Just as the content of the language arts has dynamically expanded to meet the needs of a changing world, the way in which the language arts are delivered, produced, and disseminated in the classroom and beyond have also changed.

Technology will not replace the human side of teaching nor will it operate without the command of language. Frank Smith (1999) recognizes that people and technology remain inseparable—they coexist and each helps determine the role of the other. He views language as an "internal technology" or a "tool" that originates deep inside the human brain allowing people to share feelings, communicate thoughts, and express ideas. In fact, language has been continuously adapted to describe technological terms (*memory, surfing*), to convey visual images (*icon, Web site*), and to enumerate the power of the computer (*bit, byte, RAM*).

Technology will not solve all the problems related to teaching and learning that exist as part of the language arts community. Learning is natural, continuous, and social, taking place in the company of other learners. Human learning is characterized by imagination, identification, and social interaction. Teaching depends on relationships between people and it is teachers who ignite the imagination of students, facilitate identification of learner strengths, and promote social interaction among peers. Once teachers stop fretting about being replaced by a computer or being pressured by the demands technology creates for them, they may realize that teaching and technology can mutually exist in a changing world and that each can be enhanced by the other.

If teachers hope to prepare children for the futures they deserve and require, they must expand their vision of literacy beyond books (Leu, 2000). The future demands that students be prepared for much more than book literacies. The rapid appearance of networked information and communication technology—the Internet—requires a fundamental redefining of the literacy curriculum. Teachers need to include the use of the Internet in their preparation for teaching and their delivery of instruction. As a classroom teacher, you cannot afford to leave the work to the technology teacher, just as a teacher educator cannot afford to leave this responsibility to a required technology course.

The purpose of this chapter is to introduce teachers to the technology resources that exist in the language arts domain. The purpose is not to turn every teacher into a technological expert, but to open opportunities for acquiring teaching ideas, accessing knowledge and information, and inviting communication with other educators who have found success in applying technology in the language arts curriculum. The chapter will also explore presentation possibilities, meaningful software, and useful Internet resources that can be used to support children on their literacy journeys.

As you read this chapter, consider the high expectations set for "tomorrow's teachers" and "today's students" as literacy and technology blend into meaningful planning and instruction.

Objectives

- To provide a rationale for blending technology and the *new literacies* as an approach to enhance both language arts instruction and learning.
- To share the possibilities of a variety of technology presentation tools to enhance the delivery of language arts instruction.
- To share popular reading software while considering quality and meaningful use of student time and effort.
- To share popular writing software while considering quality and meaningful use of student time and effort.
- To delineate learning objectives in students' effective and productive use of the Internet.
- To provide examples of the use of the Internet for teacher planning of literacy instruction.
- To explore the possibilities for using the Internet for visual exploration with primary students.
- To provide examples of using the Internet for exploration for research, problem solving, and collecting data.
- To explore the possibilities of using the Internet for communication and publication.

Technology, Language Arts, and the New Literacies

Teacher Prep

The Teacher Prep Web site will help you become a better teacher by linking you to classroom videos, student artifacts, teaching strategies, lesson plans, relevant education leadership articles, and practical information on licensing, creating a portfolio, implementing standards, and being successful in field experiences. Visit this resource at www.prenhall.com/teacherprep.

Whether a teacher is reluctant to try new technology or energized by it, the nature of literacy and learning are being redefined and "the times they are a'changing" (Gambrell, 2005). The World Wide Web, e-mail, digitalized children's literature, electronic chat rooms, and classroom home pages reflect only the beginning of ongoing, continuous expansion into the new literacies from traditional language arts experiences.

In initially exploring the possibilities of blending the language arts with technology, it is imperative to begin by examining the standards issued by the International Society for Technology in Education (2002). Figure 13.1 presents the ISTE *National Educational Technology Standards for Teachers* (NETS*T) (2000b). These standards provide a sense of what teachers must prepare students

FIGURE 13.1 ISTE National Educational Technology Standards for Teachers.

NETS for Teachers

Educational Technology Standards and Performance Indicators for All Teachers

Building on the NETS for Students, the ISTE NETS for Teachers (NETS•T), which focus on preservice teacher education, define the fundamental concepts, knowledge, skills, and attitudes for applying technology in educational settings. All candidates seeking certification or endorsements in teacher preparation should meet these educational technology standards. It is the responsibility of faculty across the university and at cooperating schools to provide opportunities for teacher candidates to meet these standards.

The six standards areas with performance indicators listed below are designed to be general enough to be customized to fit state, university, or district guidelines and yet specific enough to define the scope of the topic. Performance indicators for each standard provide specific outcomes to be measured when developing a set of assessment tools. The standards and the performance indicators also provide guidelines for teachers currently in the classroom.

1. TECHNOLOGY OPERATIONS AND CONCEPTS

   Teachers demonstrate a sound understanding of technology operations and concepts. Teachers:
   - demonstrate introductory knowledge, skills, and understanding of concepts related to technology (as described in the ISTE National Education Technology Standards for Students).
   - demonstrate continual growth in technology knowledge and skills to stay abreast of current and emerging technologies.

2. PLANNING AND DESIGNING LEARNING ENVIRONMENTS AND EXPERIENCES

   Teachers plan and design effective learning environments and experiences supported by technology. Teachers:
   - design developmentally appropriate learning opportunities that apply technology-enhanced instructional strategies to support the diverse needs of learners.
   - apply current research on teaching and learning with technology when planning learning environments and experiences.
   - identify and locate technology resources and evaluate them for accuracy and suitability.
   - plan for the management of technology resources within the context of learning activities.
   - plan strategies to manage student learning in a technology-enhanced environment.

3. TEACHING, LEARNING, AND THE CURRICULUM

   Teachers implement curriculum plans that include methods and strategies for applying technology to maximize student learning. Teachers:
   - facilitate technology-enhanced experiences that address content standards and student technology standards.
   - use technology to support learner-centered strategies that address the diverse needs of students.
   - apply technology to develop students' higher order skills and creativity.
   - manage student learning activities in a technology-enhanced environment.

4. ASSESSMENT AND EVALUATION

   Teachers apply technology to facilitate a variety of effective assessment and evaluation strategies. Teachers:
   - apply technology in assessing student learning of subject matter using a variety of assessment techniques.
   - use technology resources to collect and analyze data, interpret results, and communicate findings to improve instructional practice and maximize student learning.
   - apply multiple methods of evaluation to determine students' appropriate use of technology resources for learning, communication, and productivity.

Source: Reprinted with permission from National Educational Technology Standards for Teachers—Connecting Curriculum and Technology, *published by the International Society for Technology in Education (ISTE) NETS Project.*

FIGURE 13.1 (Continued)

5. PRODUCTIVITY AND PROFESSIONAL PRACTICE

Teachers use technology to enhance their productivity and professional practice. Teachers:

- use technology resources to engage in ongoing professional development and lifelong learning.
- continually evaluate and reflect on professional practice to make informed decisions regarding the use of technology in support of student learning.
- apply technology to increase productivity.
- use technology to communicate and collaborate with peers, parents, and the larger community in order to nurture student learning.

6. SOCIAL, ETHICAL, LEGAL, AND HUMAN ISSUES

Teachers understand the social, ethical, legal, and human issues surrounding the use of technology in PK-12 schools and apply those principles in practice. Teachers:

- model and teach legal and ethical practice related to technology use.
- apply technology resources to enable and empower learners with diverse backgrounds, characteristics, and abilities.
- identify and use technology resources that affirm diversity.
- promote safe and healthy use of technology resources.
- facilitate equitable access to technology resources for all students.

to be able to do with technology. Being prepared to use technology and knowing how that technology can support students language arts learning must become integral skills in every teacher's professional repertoire. Teachers must create learning experiences that enable students to achieve technology competencies in a meaningful way.

The technology standards also move beyond teacher's responsibilities to those of students, as shown in Figure 13.2, which features the ISTE *National Educational Technology Standards for Students* (NETS*S) (2000a). Since our society demands that technology-capable citizens learn to live in an increasingly complex world, students must be able to use technology effectively. The standards issued for students focus on the students' perspective through specific grade levels and curricular areas, including the language arts, for learning outcomes blending curriculum and technology. Internalizing these student-based standards can assist teachers in recognizing the potential of technology for student learning, both in the classroom and in their futures.

Leu (2002) defines the *new literacies* as "skills, strategies, and insights necessary to successfully exploit the rapidly changing information and communication technologies that continuously emerge in our world" (p. 313). The new literacies include the need for strategies for preparation for constant change, critical evaluation, strategic knowledge, social learning, and cultural context engagement. While these emerging new literacies provide an adequate rationale for incorporating technology in our language arts classrooms, several additional thought-provoking reasons illustrate why teachers need to enthusiastically, although cautiously, enter the technological domain (Balajthy, 2000):

- ***Technology improves instruction.*** Research studies are gradually reporting evidence of achievement gains in students due to computer use (Bowman, 1998;

FIGURE 13.2 ISTE National Educational Technology Standards for Students (NETS*S).

NETS for Students

Technology Foundation Standards for All Students

The technology foundation standards for students are divided into six broad categories. Standards within each category are to be introduced, reinforced, and mastered by students. These categories provide a framework for linking performance indicators within the Profiles for Technology Literate Students to the standards. Teachers can use these standards and profiles as guidelines for planning technology-based activities in which students achieve success in learning, communication, and life skills.

Technology Foundation Standards for Students

1. Basic operations and concepts
   - Students demonstrate a sound understanding of the nature and operation of technology systems.
   - Students are proficient in the use of technology.
2. Social, ethical, and human issues
   - Students understand the ethical, cultural, and societal issues related to technology.
   - Students practice responsible use of technology systems, information, and software.
   - Students develop positive attitudes toward technology uses that support lifelong learning, collaboration, personal pursuits, and productivity.
3. Technology productivity tools
   - Students use technology tools to enhance learning, increase productivity, and promote creativity.
   - Students use productivity tools to collaborate in constructing technology-enhanced models, prepare publications, and produce other creative works.
4. Technology communications tools
   - Students use telecommunications to collaborate, publish, and interact with peers, experts, and other audiences.
   - Students use a variety of media and formats to communicate information and ideas effectively to multiple audiences.
5. Technology research tools
   - Students use technology to locate, evaluate, and collect information from a variety of sources.
   - Students use technology tools to process data and report results.
   - Students evaluate and select new information resources and technological innovations based on the appropriateness for specific tasks.
6. Technology problem-solving and decision-making tools
   - Students use technology resources for solving problems and making informed decisions.
   - Students employ technology in the development of strategies for solving problems in the real world.

Source: Reprinted with permission from National Educational Technology Standards for Students—Connecting Curriculum and Technology, *published by the International Society for Technology in Education (ISTE) NETS Project.*

DeJong & Bus, 2004; Leu, 2002; Wood, 2005). To obtain the professed achievement accredited to technology, however, teachers must consider the following:

Computer applications must reflect the *best practices* in teaching reading and literacy. Reading materials must be high-quality authentic texts reflecting both narrative and expository writing across genres. Writing assignments must be authentic, based on student experience and choice, and process-based. Direct instruction of strategies should be motivating and designed with feedback to the learner.

Computer software must be monitored for *appropriate level of instruction* for individuals. Teaching skills that have already been mastered, or frustrating students with skills that are too advanced makes no sense. Just as teachers monitor the ongoing needs of the learner in effective literacy practice, so too must software precisely target the changing needs of the student using it.

Computer use should be prioritized to *expand the expectations of the learner*. Technology should not simply replace existing literacy activities with computer-based activities. Using computers to add to the richness and rigor of the classroom literacy curriculum should be the highest priority for planning and implementation.

- ***Technology fosters higher-level thinking.*** Lifelong learners in the 21st century will be challenged to think critically, analytically, and creatively. They will need to be decision makers, problem solvers, and design developers to achieve goals and create new products. While these have been the declared goals of education, they have become inescapable as the need to analyze and synthesize, evaluate, connect ideas, and envision new options becomes inevitable. Technology can transform teaching and learning for creating critical thinkers.

Computer application software can be used for *high level activities*. Moving away from rote learning of inferior software to applications such as word processing, databases, and spreadsheets provides practice in recognizing trends and patterns, and in comparing and contrasting information. Using authentic data from the class or the Internet provides additional experiences for authentic thinking situations.

Children can be guided through *modeling* to make well-organized searches of the Internet. Provide modeled guidelines for critically analyzing the accessed information. Gradually lead toward independent research that employs informed ways of sorting through and analyzing the vast amount of information available for authentic decision making.

The new applications of technology can be viewed as simply small steps toward their *implications for the future*. The time and effort in creating a novice class Web page simply provides basic foundations for future projects. The reading, writing, and collaboration in such a project has a substantial impact on learning and offers authentic "how-to" experiences that can be built upon in the future.

- ***Technology challenges teachers to rethink teaching/learning.*** The advent of the vast, global information network of the Internet demands that teachers rethink what is important in learning. A fresh goal of creating literate, spirited, critical thinkers for the future must surround instructional planning. Jonassen, Peck, and Wilson (1999) have identified five terms necessary for learning in the future: (a) active, (b) constructive, (c) intentional, (d) authentic, and (e) cooperative. These learning characteristics imply different types of instruction, activities, and assignments than those demanded by an isolated, "right answer" learning perspective.

- ***Technology meets students at their learning levels.*** Teachers must be given the time to prepare Web searches, technology-based projects, and even Internet researched instruction that meet the interests and reading abilities of students.

Since this is a new venture for most teachers, this takes additional time than does traditional planning. In order to match Web-based curriculum and learning levels, teachers need planning time to explore, locate, analyze, and bookmark new Web sites. Classroom Web sites that display student work are effective connections between learners of similar ages and interests.

- ***Technology provides vast information to utilize research skills.*** Rather than being mere consumers of information, students must be taught to analyze and select the information that best meets their needs. Teaching students to do basic research on the Web parallels some of the same research skills used in the print-based library. Developing research questions, researching a question, organizing the information, and presenting the information keep the research process intact. However, the impact of technology has enriched the way in which we research, write, and share.
- ***Technology allows all students to succeed.*** The federal government's legislative initiative to support use of the Internet has impacted equal, quality education in schools throughout the United States. In 2000, 77% of classrooms had an Internet-connected computer. It is quite possible that this phenomenon has extended to almost all classrooms today, both urban and rural in both advantaged and disadvantaged communities. Multicultural electronic books and specialized software support students whose first language is not English. While socioeconomic conditions will continue to be an issue in equal access to technology, federal funding of technology has provided adequate resources, at least through Internet access, to most children.

Although the above list of advantages is convincing, teachers may look toward less idealistic and more concrete ideas to persuade them to incorporate technology in their classrooms. *Technology needs to be considered a tool to enhance teaching and learning—not an end in itself.* This statement should guide teachers as they make decisions about what kinds of technologies and what types of activities will enhance their instruction and bring about greater student learning. Figure 13.3 provides a list of technology terms related to presentation tools, instructional strategies, and communication modes. A familiarity with these terms will provide teachers with a foundation for embracing the technology possibilities connected to the language arts.

Language Arts Software

Today's students have been learning through technology long before they enter the elementary classroom. Long before their school experience, many children have been glued to monitors and have watched thousands of hours of visual images, operated VCR/DVD players and cell phones, played countless electronic games, accessed information on home computers, and utilized other high-tech devices.

Technology today challenges the teacher to think differently about meeting the literacy and developmental needs of individual learners. While each student brings a unique blend of prior knowledge, language, cultural background, and personal characteristics to a learning task, not every student needs to learn every bit of knowledge in the same way, in the same sequence, or at the same moment (Fox & Mitchell, 2000). Quality educational software provides a means of motivating, capturing interest, and individualizing literacy instruction, built on the foundations of quality instruction.

Three different types of educational software foster literacy skill and strategy development:

- ***Computer-assisted instruction.*** Computer-assisted instruction (CAI) was the first type of software to be used in schools, yet still remains a mainstay of basic

FIGURE 13.3 **A Brief Technology Glossary for the Language Arts Classroom.**

- **Blogging:** A blog (web log) is a Web site in which journal entries are posted on a regular basis. Authoring a blog or contributing to an existing blog is called "blogging." A blog commonly consists of hypertext, images, and links (to other Web sites, audio, video, etc.) and uses a conversational style of communication. In the language arts classroom, students may create their own blogs to respond to literature or document experiences. Teachers may create a blog to serve as a discussion forum for a current topic or a particular book.
- **Digital camera:** A camera that takes digital photographs and stores them as digital files. The pictures can then be incorporated into multimedia projects. The latest digital cameras often have many functions and the same device can capture photographs, video, and sound.
- **Digital projector:** This type of projector is an electro-optical machine that converts data from a computer or video source (such as a DVD/VCR player or visual presenter) to a bright image that is then projected on a distant wall or projection screen using a lens system. In the language arts classroom, the digital presenter is a necessary tool that serves many purposes: It makes computer images (such as Web sites and PowerPoint presentations) accessible to a large group of students. If used in combination with an interactive whiteboard, it replaces the need for chalkboards or dry-erase boards. When connected to a VCR/DVD player, moving images may be displayed on a large projection screen rather than a television screen.
- **Document cameras and visual presenters:** More advanced than a traditional overhead projector, the document cameras and visual presenters allow teachers to show three-dimensional objects or texts and colorful images from literature or sheets of paper to large audiences. In contrast to a traditional overhead projector, the document camera or visual presenter must be connected to a separate projector or TV monitor. Teachers in the language arts classroom use such devices to present literature during a shared reading experience or to teach writing lessons while projecting student-written writing samples on a large screen.
- **Instant messaging:** Instant messaging (IM) is one type of Internet communication. Instant messaging differs from e-mail in that conversations happen in real time (messages are sent instantly, much like a telephone conversation but with text). IMs are often live but may be left as messages to be read and responded to later. It is common for IMers to use abbreviations and emoticons. It is important for the language arts teacher to be aware of students' frequent use of this versatile communication tool and perhaps think of ways to make use of instant messaging as an instructional tool.
- **Interactive storybooks/electronic texts:** Targeting primarily younger children, interactive storybooks are on-screen books read by narrators as words are highlighted on screen. Clicking on words with the mouse activates the audio so students can listen to the words multiple times. Many electronic books are interactive in nature, allowing students to activate animations and choose the path of the story (such as alternative plots or endings). Electronic books are available for purchase on CDs or as downloads from the Internet.
- **Interactive whiteboard:** This is a dry-erase whiteboard writing surface that can electronically capture notes written on the surface using dry-erase markers. The interactive whiteboard can also be used to control computer-generated images projected on the whiteboard. Creative software (commonly included with the interactive whiteboard) offers myriad possibilities. The use of an interactive whiteboard requires a computer and a digital projector.
- **Interactive wireless pad:** Functioning much like an interactive whiteboard, the interactive wireless pad is a small whiteboard (about the size of a notebook) that is completely wireless and allows teachers to teach from anywhere in the classroom. The pad(s) can be passed out to students who can contribute from their desks. The interactive wireless pad is most effective if used in conjunction with the interactive whiteboard, classroom computer, and projector.

FIGURE 13.3 (Continued)

- **Keypals (electronic penpals):** This is the e-mail equivalent of a penpal. In the language arts classroom, e-mail correspondence may motivate students to write more frequently and improve their communication skills. Students may exchange emails with authors, illustrators, family members, or students from across the globe.
- **Personal response system:** Also referred to as electronic response system this combines interaction and assessment to enhance classroom productivity. Using remote controls, students can answer questions with a simple click of a button. Results are instantly charted and displayed for real-time student feedback and lesson refinement. Software offers the teacher (or students) opportunities to create gamelike, interactive activities.
- **Podcasting:** This consists of audio or video files placed on the Internet to which anyone to subscribe. In the language arts classroom, podcasting may function as an exciting communication tool with unlimited listening options and student-produced podcasts. The following books provide more information:

  Cochrane, Todd (2005). *Podcasting: Do It Yourself Guide.* Indianapolis, IN: Wiley.

  Geoghegan, Michael, & Klass, Dan (2005). *Podcast Solutions: The Complete Guide to Podcasting.* Berkeley, CA: Friends of ED.
- **Scanner:** This is a device that analyzes a physical image (such as a photograph, printed text, or handwriting) and converts it to a digital image. In the language arts classroom, students often use scanners to insert photographs or student-generated artwork into their word-processed stories or multimedia presentations.
- **WebQuest:** This is a research activity in which students collect information primarily from the World Wide Web. First invented by Bernie Dodge in 1995, WebQuest was defined as "an inquiry-oriented activity in which some or all of the information that learners interact with comes from resources on the Internet, optionally supplemented with videoconferencing." (See webquest.sdsu.edu/ for more information). Students typically complete WebQuests in groups. Each student typically has a "role" or specific area to research. In the language arts classroom, WebQuests can serve as a foundation for students' research papers, nonfiction reports, and multimedia presentations.

school-based computer curriculum. It provides teachers with ready-made access to the following software products:

Drill-and-practice software that provides for the practice of content that has already been taught.

Tutorial software that teaches new information and principles as well as providing for practice.

Learning game software, including drill-and-practice in a format that incorporates a challenge specifically designed to motivate students and capture their interest in learning.

While tutorials can be used for individualized instruction, drill-and-practice and learning games software should follow classroom instruction. All types serve a role in today's classrooms and contribute to ongoing skill and strategy development and application by meeting individual and small group needs. Computer-assisted instruction cannot replace the direct, well-planned instruction of an effective teacher, but it can provide an extension for extended practice, revisiting a skill, or mastering a concept.

- ***Electronic storybooks.*** This category includes CD-ROM talking books, which are interactive, digital versions of stories that employ multimedia features such as

Labeling, visual representation, and explanation extend computer graphing into the language arts.

animation, music, sound effects, highlighted text, and modeled fluency reading (Labbo, 2000). Many talking book screens are interactive because the software allows children to use the mouse to access words that are pronounced, passages that are reread, illustrations that become animated, and special effects that produce visual or auditory responses. The interactive nature of these CD-ROM talking books create the potential for supporting young children's literacy development as the talking books model phonemic awareness, encourage repeated readings, and develop a sense of story to influence positive reading behaviors (Lefever-Davis & Pearman, 2005).

- ***Computer application/presentation software.*** In addition to educational software, computer application software consisting of word processing, spreadsheet, database, and presentation programs (e.g., Microsoft Office, Microsoft Word, Excel, Access, and PowerPoint) is now considered essential as workplace technology demands mastery of basic computer applications to obtain jobs. Students use these applications to assemble information into research findings and reports. Elementary school versions of application software (e.g., Kid Pix Studio Deluxe, Storybook Weaver, and Hyperstudio) nurture reading, writing, and research sharing at even early primary levels. Preparing to share researched topics through visual enhancement and text font selection motivates most students beyond the traditional copying of the final draft of a report.

Prior to selecting or utilizing any software with children in a literacy context, teachers should know what skills and strategies each child needs, how students need to apply those skills and strategies in authentic contexts, and which software would be most beneficial in matching those needs. Fox and Mitchell (2000) have suggested guidelines for evaluating skill-development software (Figure 13.4) including freedom of movement among activities, skill levels within a program, and branching or Web-designed options allowing direct access to teaching or drill-and-practice activities. Examination of specific examples of reading and writing software will further enhance a teacher's knowledge of software possibilities in the classroom.

Software for Reading Development

Emerging technologies challenge the traditional view of reading as interacting with text in a sequential, linear style. Reading via technology challenges students to navigate through

FIGURE 13.4 Guidelines for Evaluating Skill-Development Software.

Ask the following questions to determine whether the software will meaningfully enhance instruction and learning:

- Are children practicing skills they have already mastered?
- Are voices clear and precise?
- Are skills sequenced from easy to difficult?
- Are allowances made to bypass lengthy introductions after a student is familiar with the program?
- Are different levels of difficulty within skills present?
- Are pictures easy to identify?
- Are opportunities to apply skills within authentic reading available?
- Are management tools to help the teacher keep track of skill practice included?
- Are explanations of principles clear and at a level the students can understand?
- Are students given access to a dictionary to help with writing and spelling?
- Are opportunities to apply skills within authentic reading/writing available?

Source: Adapted from B. J. Fox & M. J. Mitchell (2000). Using technology to support word recognition, spelling, and vocabulary acquisition. In S. B. Wepner, W. J. Valmont, & R. Thurlow, Linking literacy and technology: A guide for K–8 classrooms *(p. 45). Newark, DE: National Council of Teachers of English.*

information and ideas in a recursive fashion, moving back and forth between screens and Web site options. Access to information through icons, images, animation, voice, and sound supports comprehension and extends meaning beyond a text. While reading software has gained popularity, it is only valuable for instructional purposes when it fits within the larger context of the curriculum and provides a way of interactive learning not already available through other media (Wepner & Ray, 2000).

Three types of educational software have been recognized for stretching reading development and enhancing comprehension: (a) electronic books, (b) learning adventures, and (c) reading comprehension and assessment software. The levels of this technology range from emergent literacy to developing readers and beyond to independent readers.

Electronic books use children's literature in multimedia formats with original illustrations. Not only do they share a rich blend of literature with children, but they include imagination and pleasure as part of the reading process. The animation of narrative texts heightens attention to the characters, plot, and setting. The use of electronic books has shown benefits to reading skills and development (Labbo & Reinking, 1999; Lefever-Davis & Pearman, 2005). Lesson Plan 13.1 models the use of electronic storybooks in conjunction with reading children's literature.

LESSON PLAN 13.1

TITLE: Interacting with Books

Grade Level: K–3

Time Frame: Two of 30-minute sessions

Standards

IRA/NCTE Standards: 1, 3

NETS for Students: 1, 3, 4

Objectives

- Students will read print and electronic texts to build an understanding of plot, setting, and character development.
- Students will apply a range of strategies to comprehend, interpret, evaluate, and appreciate texts.

Materials

- Sets of interactive storybook and corresponding literature:

  Rainbow Fish Interactive Storybook CD-ROM (Dorling Kindersley Ltd.) and Marcus Pfister (1992) *The Rainbow Fish*. North South Books.

  The Cat in the Hat CD-ROM (Living Books) and Dr. Seuss (1957) *The Cat in the Hat* (Random House).
- Literature response journals (or drawing paper) for student use.
- Computers with headphones for individual student use (or one classroom computer connected to digital projector and large screen).

Motivation

- Introduce one of the print books to the class and read aloud. Discuss plot, setting, and character development as needed.

Procedures

Day 1

- Ask students to respond to the story in their literature response journals by writing and/or drawing about favorite parts of the story.
- Encourage students to share their responses and interpretations with the class.

Day 2

- Explain to students that stories can be told in many different ways. For example, they may read stories in books, watch stories or movies on television or DVD, or just listen to someone retell a story without using any pictures or words. Introduce students to the electronic storybook (if possible, show them the CD-ROM) and explain that this is a different version of the same story they heard yesterday.
- Allow students time to explore the electronic storybook. Use headphones if students are working individually. After a while, ask students to share some of the features that they have discovered with the class (animations, rereading of text, etc.). Ask students if they notice any differences between the print book version and the interactive version.
- After students have had ample time to read the electronic version, ask them to revisit their response journals from yesterday. Encourage students to add ideas or pictures based on their interaction with the electronic text.

Assessment

- As a class, discuss any differences between the plot, setting, and character development in the print book and electronic book. What did students enjoy most about the different versions?
- Review students' literature response journals to check for story understanding. Notice what additions students may have added to their journals after interacting with the electronic version of the story.

Accommodation/Modification

- A wide range of literature/electronic storybooks are available to suit the needs and reading levels of individual students.

Visit the Meeting the Standards module in Chapter 13 of the Companion Website at www.prenhall.com/hancock to adapt this lesson to meet your state's standards.

Marc Brown's *Arthur's Teacher's Trouble,* for example, contains 24 screens, each with story text displayed and read aloud in the presence of an authentic illustration. Clicking a word results in pronunciation while clicking on an illustration feature results in animation. Characters provide additional dialogue or perform actions, while other objects come alive. Other types of electronic books and some audiobooks on CDs across many reading levels are listed in the Literature Cluster below.

Linda Labbo (2000) offers a list of 12 suggestions as teachers model (demonstrate), mentor (ongoing support), and manage (state outcomes, set time limits, make assignments) the use of CD-ROM storybooks. Figure 13.5 lists these suggestions with a brief rationale for each activity. The list assumes children will have access to the CD-ROM books for multiple readings and readings over time.

Learning adventures offer opportunities for vocabulary and comprehension development as students problem solve their way through a variety of decision-making challenges.

SAMPLES OF ELECTRONIC AND AUDIO BOOKS

E-Books

Brown, Marc (2004). Arthur's birthday deluxe [Computer software]. San Francisco: Broderbund/The Learning Company.

Brown, Marc (2004). Arthur's computer adventure [Computer software]. San Francisco: Broderbund/The Learning Company.

Cannon, Janelle (2004). Stellaluna [Computer software]. San Francisco: Broderbund/The Learning Company.

Geisel, Theodor (2004). The cat in the hat [Computer software]. San Francisco: Broderbund/The Learning Company.

Henkes, Kevin (2005). Shiela Rae, the brave [Computer software]. San Francisco: Broderbund/The Learning Company.

Osborne, Mary Pope (2005). Favorite Greek myths [Computer software]. New York: Scholastic.

Audiobooks (available as CS or CD)

Creech, Sharon (2005). *Replay.* Read by Christopher Burns. New York: Harper Recorded Books.

Curtis, Christopher Paul (2005). *Bucking the Sarge.* Read by Michael Boatman. Danbury, CT: Listening Library.

Danziger, Paula (2005). *The cat ate my gymsuit.* Read by a full cast. Syracuse, NY: Full Cast Audio.

Fleischman, Sid (2004). *By the great horn spoon.* Read by a full cast. Syracuse, NY: Full Cast Audio.

Funke, Cornelia (2005). *Inkspell.* Read by Brendan Fraser. Danbury, CT: Listening Library.

Rowling, J. K. (2005). *Harry Potter and the half-blood prince.* Read by Jim Dale. Danbury, CT: Listening Library.

Ryan, Pam Muñoz (2004). *When Marian sang.* Read by Gail Nelson. Palo Alto, CA: Live Oak.

FIGURE 13.5
Twelve Things to do with a Talking Book in a Computer Center.

Initial Interactive Level

1. *Listen to the story first.* Enjoy the features of multimedia technology and appreciate the literature. Point out the print aspects of the presentation.

Fluency and Comprehension Level

2. *Read along with the story.* Digital choral reading of a section of the story assists sight word recognition and enhances fluency.
3. *Echo read the story.* Children repeat words or phrases as they are read aloud to them on the screen allowing them to recognize sight words in context.
4. *Read it first, then listen.* Attempt to read the phrases on the screen first, then listen to the text read aloud on the screen allowing students to benefit from immediate feedback.
5. *Partner read in a digital readers theatre.* Assign a small group individual character roles to foster expressive reading, peer collaboration, reluctant reader support, and more fluent reading.

Word Level

6. *Look for words you know.* Pointing out words they know provides immediate feedback as they locate a word, read it aloud, and check accuracy by accessing the talking book pronunciation.
7. *Select words with the same sounds.* Select and sort out words with the same beginning sound, vowel pattern, or syllable structure.
8. *Select rhyming words.* Point out rhyming pattern words in text, highlight them, and get feedback from the narrator's pronunciation.

Metacognitive and Story Response Level

9. *Read along with a book copy.* Compare the digital version with the book version in formatting, illustrations, and arrangement of text.
10. *Describe how one screen fits with other screens.* Encourage children to make higher-level connections (inferences, conclusions, sequence of events, cause/effect) as they engage in meaning-making across different sections of the story.
11. *Explain how special effects fit the story.* Discuss how music, color tones, sound effects, or animation affect the story to appreciate aesthetic qualities of the multimedia enhancements.
12. *Discuss similar stories.* Intertextual connections link this story to others or to personal experiences to encourage enhanced comprehension.

Source: Adapted from L. D. Labbo (2000). 12 things young children can do with a talking book in a classroom computer center. The Reading Teacher, *53, 542–546.*

Particularly useful for older readers, *Where in the World is Carmen Santiago?* and other software titles from that series engage students in Grades 3 through 8 in detective adventures while the titles in the *Oregon Trail* series engage students in simulation activities. Reading, strategic thinking, planning, and problem solving mentally enrich these adventures. Multimedia learning adventures also offer opportunities for collaboration as pairs or small teams work together, interactively discuss, debate, and agree on strategies.

Much reading comprehension and assessment software is authentically literature-based and intended to lead students to read entire books on their own. The CD-ROM format of *M-ss-ng L-nks*, for example, includes passages from 13 award-winning children's books while challenging students to use structural cues to interpret passages. Purposes include increasing comprehension, using context clues, appreciating quality writing, building vocabulary, and improving spelling. *Reading Galaxy* provides passages from 30 popular books, sharing just enough about setting, situation, and character to whet a reader's appetite to read the trade book independently. *Accelerated Reader* appears extremely popular in schools because it tracks students' reading and comprehension of 22,000 trade books. However, quizzes track recall of lower-level comprehension through multiple choice questions and children are limited to selecting literature included in the program.

Reading software must be aligned with reading standards and outcomes, teaching philosophy, and the needs of individual students in order for it to be an effective instructional strategy. Figure 13.6 provides a sound list of features to consider when determining

FIGURE 13.6 Evaluating Reading Software for Instructional Needs.

Considerations for Software Design

- Compelling activities and tasks that hold student interest.
- Clear, concise, and easy to follow directions requiring minimal adult help.
- High-quality graphics and sounds, integral to the content, and age-appropriate.
- Related content that fits into or expands the curriculum.
- Inspires student imagination and creativity beyond traditional instruction.
- Significant practice on important concepts for skill building.
- Interactive and cooperative aspects between and among students.
- Narrated text so students can read passages independently and/or highlighted text so readers can follow along.
- Accommodation of differing age and ability levels.
- Built-in record keeping or assessment features to provide accountability for technology.
- Availability of teacher's guide, instructional introduction, and handout materials.
- Availability of printed copy of text on screen for children.

Considerations for Planning

- Prior to use, develop skills and confidence with the software.
- Read the manual to familiarize oneself with features and practical connections.
- Consult the teacher's guide for lesson plans and tips to integrate the program.
- Check the publisher Web site for additional assistance and ideas.
- Consult other teachers who are using the software.
- Distinguish what the software can do that traditional instruction cannot.

Considerations for Management

- Try the program with students to determine how varying abilities interact with it.
- Model the program for optimal use by students.
- Create a computer schedule and rules to assist with appropriate and efficient use.
- Pair students so at least one has some computer skills.
- Challenge children to verbalize what they are experiencing through the software.

Adapted from S. B. Wepner, & L. C. Ray (2000). Using technology for reading development. In S. B. Wepner, W. J. Valmont, & R. Thurlow (Eds.), Linking literacy and technology *(pp. 91, 93). Newark, DE: International Reading Association.*

value of software for instruction (Wepner & Ray, 2000). All considerations must also pass three overarching standards:

- The software offers something special that cannot be offered with traditional instruction.
- The software actually accomplishes what it professes to accomplish.
- The software content is accurate, developmentally appropriate, and sensitive to race, age, gender, ethnicity, and disabilities.

Integrating technology into instruction demands a significant investment of money, time, and effort, so teachers are encouraged to choose wisely, selectively, and responsibly from a limited number of quality software packages.

Software for Writing Development

Integrated as a tool in the writing classroom, technology holds great promise as a means of crafting, presenting, and sharing writing products with a broader audience than traditional writing. Technology, however, must build on the writing instruction findings that have emerged from two decades of writing research. Through the teacher action research of Nancie Atwell (1987), Lucy Calkins (1986), Donald Graves (1983), and Donald Murray (1982), teachers have learned much about the writing process. Techniques such as writing workshop, the five stages of the writing process, focus on writing traits, and the variety of narrative, expository, and poetic writing formats must be the foundation of technology integration. Such integration is meant to enhance the quality of student writing, improve the appearance of presentation, and broaden the audience of the writing piece.

The extensiveness of software programs designed for writers can be overwhelming to teachers as they focus on age-appropriate programs with varied presentation options for their students. To bring some order to the vast number of writing programs for K–8 students, Sullivan and Sharp (2000) suggest three categories to differentiate the types, features, and capabilities of each program: (a) word-processing programs, (b) creative word-processing programs, and (c) production word-processing programs.

Word-processing programs incorporate basic text entry, formatting, and editing. While enhancements such as graphics exist, their primary purpose is to enter and format text. Today's word-processing programs invite students to enter text and customize font, style, and size. *Microsoft Word* and *WordPerfect* contain sophisticated formatting that meets the needs of the writer. After mastering basic word-processing fundamentals, students choose from an array of choices to manipulate their text. These programs provide a variety of formats, allow for insertion of tables or graphics, and supply features that expand to meet the growing needs of the writer.

Creative word-processing programs foster creativity in students through the integration of text and visuals. Programs that combine a visual environment with a writing platform encourage student visual and written creativity. An added emphasis on illustration as an integral part of the story-writing process provides for graphic features including clip art, drawing, and painting tools. Students have the opportunity to not only write but illustrate their work. The story can be creatively designed with textual captions and printed out in the format of a book. *Storybook Weaver Deluxe* combines child-friendly word processing with a library of graphics and sounds that breathe life into stories. Students can hear their stories read by their own voices or by the computer's text-to-speech feature. Features include a spell-check, thesaurus, story starters, and dual-language option. *Kid*

Works Deluxe, Imagination Express (including background music), and *Easy Book Deluxe* provide other examples for blending art and text in picture book-like formats.

Production word-processing programs allow students to produce a finished product as a multimedia presentation whose capabilities move far beyond writing into the problem-solving and decision-making domain. The end result of production programs move beyond text to visual and audio enhancement. Often referred to as "desktop publishing," these programs can print signs, banners, letterheads, greeting cards, newsletters, and original drawings, as well as import photographs or scanned images. Packages that add sound and motion allow users to create multimedia environments for more creative presentations. The *Print Shop Deluxe* puts thousands of graphics and photos, layouts and templates, and photo-editing capabilities at the hands of students. They can easily enhance home-school connections through invitations, classroom newsletters, and student-of-the-week features. *Framemaker* includes a word processor, page designer, graphics editor, and book-building features to prepare documents for publication. *Writers Studio* guides students through the five stages of the writing process. The package includes graphic organizers, lists of topics, student-generated spelling lists, and evaluation checklists. Although learning the nuances of each production program takes time, students quickly move from a tool that must be learned to a tool to assist learning.

The move to a multimedia environment is most apparent in a program such as *Power Point*, designed to create visual presentations. Students enter the textual focus of their reports on slides. Soon they learn to animate their presentations, bringing each point into view at the click of the mouse. Sounds can then be introduced to accompany each slide and clip art or photos can be inserted. Finally, sound effects can accompany the slides as they appear on the screen. Presentation programs instantly integrate writing and speaking with the visual arts. In a simpler form, *Kid Pix Studio Deluxe* offers younger computer users opportunities to create in a multimedia environment. Students may build a series of animated pictures with creative backgrounds enhanced by text of varied fonts and sizes. A student PowerPoint presentation in Student Sample 13.1 showcases a fifth-grade student's ability to present textual and visual information via technology.

HyperStudio is another multimedia package that uses "cards" (pages) and "stacks" (files) to branch into different cards through "buttons" (links). Sounds, videoclips, photos, graphics, and clip art make this program highly appealing to students. Teachers can use this program to scan their students' class photos to identify the author of student-generated stories.

Students take extreme pride in their work when they know that technology allows them to share with others within and beyond their own classrooms—even with writers in other states or countries. Besides providing quality presentation, word-processing programs prepare stories, poems, essays, and informational reports to be shared with an even wider global audience.

The Internet: Pathway to Teaching and Learning

The Internet is a global computer network capable of quickly exchanging vast amounts of information. One site on the Internet may lead to millions of others, many of which contain additional media resources such as video, audio, animation, and e-mail (Leu, 1997). The Internet is the most efficient way to store, access, and communicate large amounts of information to vast numbers of people interested in identifying and solving problems. To prepare our students for the challenges of the future, the Internet must be central to the teaching mission. The Internet provides new technologies to classrooms, thus redefining literacy, learning, and teaching.

STUDENT SAMPLE 13.1 Fifth-Grade Power-Point Blending Textual and Visual Literacy.

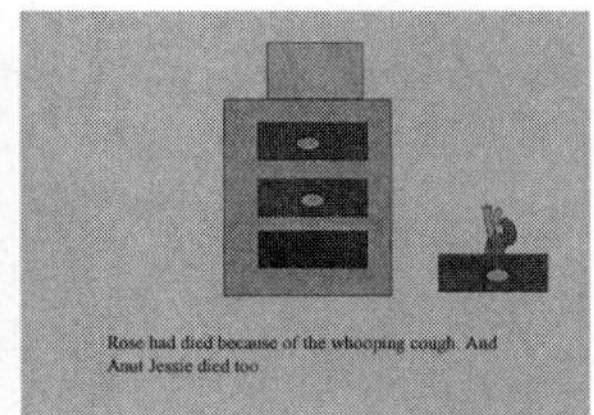

The Internet is clearly changing what it means to be literate. While traditional reading and writing remain constant even on a computer monitor, Leu (1997; 2002) describes five important changes taking place as children interact with Internet text:

- *Students need to acquire new and increasingly sophisticated navigational strategies.* Because so much information is available, students must learn not only how to navigate search engines and browsers used to explore the Web, but also how to effectively navigate each Web site that they encounter. Each site exhibits information in a unique manner, thus creating new forms of text organization. Traditional narrative and expository text format knowledge may not be sufficient to unpack the meaning of text.
- *Students continually need to update their ability to communicate within new technologies.* Literacy today may not be literacy tomorrow as being literate implies a continuous developmental process paralleling the demands of technology. New versions of web browsers and updated Web sites demand continuous strategic reading contexts.
- *Students require high level critical thinking and reasoning about the information appearing on the Internet.* Because anyone can publish anything on the Internet, teachers must scrutinize Web sites and evaluate the accuracy of information. Textbook and book publishers have traditionally maintained standards of accuracy, philosophical stance, etc., but the Internet leaves discretion to the user.
- *Students must be supported in an awareness of the variety of meanings in multiple media forms in which messages appear.* While text has been accepted as having multiple meanings, video, audio, and animation may also be interpreted in a variety of ways. Students must develop new composing, comprehension, and response capabilities that result from encountering a variety of media within a single source.
- *Students learn on the Internet through socially mediated learning with others, even more so than in traditional learning environments.* Facilitating social learning opportunities through workshop and cooperative learning activities may carry over to listservs, chat rooms, collaborative Internet projects, and teleconferences.

For the purposes of this chapter, the use of the Internet has been divided into four areas for discussion:

1. ***Using the Internet to plan literacy instruction.*** This includes teacher accessing Web sites to plan and enhance language arts teaching and learning.
2. ***Using the Internet for visual exploration (Grades K–2).*** This includes teacher accessing and building visual lessons and visual representation assignments for hands-on participation by young literacy learners.
3. ***Using the Internet for student exploration (Grades 3–8).*** This includes the power of Web sites for research, problem solving, and collecting and sharing data.
4. ***Using the Internet for communication and publishing.*** This includes the possibilities and potential of e-mail and Web site publication sites allowing for a global audience for communicating thoughts and sharing written products.

Using the Internet to Plan Literacy Instruction

If teachers are to prepare students for the future, they need to embrace the ideas afforded by the Internet. Using the Internet as a resource for teaching provides materials and ideas for enhanced delivery of instruction. Knowledge of the effective access of the Internet requires recognition of the different types of sites available to teachers to support instruction (Karchmer, 2000). Keep in mind that *searching,* rather than *browsing,* assists in efficiently accessing relevant curricular content. There are six types of Internet planning sites available to teachers: (a) central sites/language arts, (b) central sites/literature-based language arts, (c) teacher-created children's projects, (d) author/illustrator Web sites, (e) online communities, and (f) online journals.

Central Sites/Language Arts. As teachers seek ways in which the Internet can help with curricular planning, they will find that a few central sites share enormous amounts of useful lesson ideas. While the sites share ideas across the curriculum, most of the lessons and ideas naturally incorporate the integrated language arts as a vehicle for learning.

Read, Write, Think, sponsored by the International Reading Association, National Council of Teachers of English, and Marco Polo, guides teachers to a current list of standards-based lesson plans for all areas of language arts and reading instruction. Teachers are encouraged to submit their own quality lesson plans to add to the already substantive ones that overflow this site. **Literacy Web** was created at the University of Connecticut to promote the use of the Internet as a tool to assist teachers in searching best practices in literacy instruction. Featuring the new literacies (Leu, 2002), the information can be sorted by grade level, literacy topic, and level of research. **TALK: Technology Assisting Literacy Knowledge** accesses model lessons that integrate software, the Internet, and the best literacy practices. A special link to the language arts content area lessons provides a great place to begin a search for the ideal lesson.

Blue Web'n contains carefully reviewed and screened curricular ideas that receive a site Blue Ribbon. Easy to locate because of a searchable database, teachers can quickly find materials related to their grade-level standards and curricular topics. **The New York Times Learning Network** is sectioned for teachers, students, and parents. This site shares great lesson plans coordinated with free *New York Times* articles, current events, lesson plan archives, and links to curriculum resources in all areas. **Yahooligans Teachers' Guide** provides useful materials for elementary and middle level teachers. Although the site contains only a limited number of curriculum resources, those available are very good.

Central Sites/Literature-Based Language Arts. These sites compile information on many different areas of language arts, children's literature, and teacher resources, organizing this information within directories to make location easy. Often an effective place to start a search, central sites are more efficient than a search engine. These sites are ideal for creating literature-based instructional plans or for locating literature-related resources for engagement or extended activities for students before, during, or after a literature-based experience.

The Children's Literature Web Guide, created by David K. Brown of the University of Calgary, incorporates comprehensive links to literature-based resources including award-winning books, author/illustrator sites, journal reviews, discussion groups about literature, and additional public library Web sites. **Carol Hurst's Children's Literature Site** posts original book reviews, author studies, and lesson plans by an expert in children's literature. Abundant lists also link children's literature to content and curricular areas to support literature-based instruction across the curriculum. **Project Gutenberg** is a useful site for downloading poetry, fables and myths, famous speeches, and classic literature. The **Jan Brett Home Page** invites children to read one of the author's many outstanding picture books to learn more about the author, to engage in one of its many literature-related activities, or to share their own projects related to Brett's many books. Specific author and illustrator sites have become plentiful and masterfully designed and can easily be located through a search engine.

Teacher-Created Children's Projects. Teachers post instructional ideas, strategies, and questions over the Internet through Web sites created specifically to showcase ideas and practices being implemented in real classrooms. Based on the premise of "sharing the beauty" as supported by Miss Rumphius, many sites also invite other classrooms to join in on these projects. **Global SchoolNet's Internet Project Registry** provides a search engine that permits teachers to review a rich set of upcoming projects often seeking classrooms for collaboration. Similarly, the **Global Schoolhouse Projects and Registry** provides a site for permanent, ongoing classroom projects. Hundreds of examples like these exist on the Internet and are worthy of access and consideration. Teachers should even consider personal Web sites to post individual projects to the world of classrooms across the globe.

Author/Illustrator Web Sites. There are several types of sites related to authors and illustrators that have been developed by authors, publishers, and admirers of the author's work. Sites developed by the authors provide the most authentic insights into their lives and may include resources for teachers to download. On many of these sites, e-mail may be sent directly to the book creator and replies can be expected in a timely manner. Jan Brett, Patricia Polacco, Eric Carle, Dave Pilkey, and Audrey Wood are among the authors and illustrators represented.

As teachers bookmark these Web sites, students learn not only about authors, illustrators, and books but also about technology through hands-on practice (McNair, 2000). The information on these Web sites is usually quite current and often result in students accessing literature on the library shelves that they have discovered on the author site.

Literature series sites developed by publishers may post answers to most frequently asked questions, conduct online interviews, or post lesson plans and links related to publications. Scholastic's **Harry Potter** site and Random House's **Magic Treehouse Homepage** provide book summaries and teacher's guides while motivating students to read further books in the series. Sites for C. S. Lewis, L. M. Montgomery, and Laura Ingalls Wilder also provide motivation to read both Internet information and more books by these classic authors.

Further listing of Internet Web sites related to award-winning children's literature can be found by accessing books devoted to listings on this topic. R. Story-Huffman's (2002) *Newbery on the Net* and *Caldecott on the Net* provide extensive Web site listings. M. D. Newman's (2004) *Cyberlit* supplies ample online connections to children's literature for the primary grades.

Online Communities. Commonly known as listservs, these sites provide environments for teachers with similar interests to discuss important topics. Several have subscription addresses so a member automatically receives important announcements and releases. Electronic discussions support the exchange of ideas and viewpoints. The potential exists for questions or responses to reach thousands of people, providing a supportive environment for both preservice and practicing teachers.

RTEACHER provides a forum for conversations about literacy through a group of diverse educators interested in using the Internet for literacy education. The **American Association of School Librarians** has several electronic discussion lists to support the exchange of ideas and resources with library media specialists. **CHILDLIT** and **KIDLIT-L** both provide an outlet for discussion and critical analysis of children's literature.

Online Journals. A limited number of journals are published online and are available at no cost to the reader, particularly in archived, previously published form. **ReadingOnline,** the free electronic journal of the International Reading Association, contains great resources, including sections on electronic classrooms and new literacies. Features include the use of multimedia resources and discussion forums for articles read online. Many other journals to which teachers subscribe now have online versions with archival accessibility to almost any article previously published. A wealth of research-based and practical information lies at the fingertips of teachers through online journals.

Using the Internet for Visual Exploration: Primary Grades (K–2)

The primary grades (K–2) provide literacy experiences to enhance the early reading, writing, viewing, and learning of young children. Primary teachers are rightfully concerned with limited instructional time for providing the foundations of these important lifelong skills. The Internet provides many fine resources for the very youngest learners to enhance important experiences with stories, letters, sounds, writing, and listening. These classrooms demand the inclusion of multimedia computers to support animation, sound, and other technologies that require memory and speed.

Issues directly related to the primary grades include ensuring child safety, supporting emergent navigational skills, and seeking out supportive technologies. An important suggestion may be to limit primary children's use of Internet sites to those bookmarked by the teacher. Teacher use of several sources assist in locating child-safe Web sites. **Yahooligans** is one of the largest collections of useful sites for children with links that are screened for child safety. **Great Sites** has been developed by the American Library Association and includes over 700 outstanding sites for children.

Ask Jeeves for Kids is a popular search engine that allows children to ask questions directly in the search window box instead of using the keyword strategy. Demonstrated by a teacher on a projection system, this process can provide a home-school connection. **KidsClick,** a lesser-known search engine, actually provides the reading level of each resource and indicates whether it contains illustrations. Because the search results come from a smaller database, this might be a sound first-time search engine at the primary level.

Teachers might also be cautioned to channel all children's e-mail through the teacher's e-mail address, including author communication or electronic key pals. The technology curriculum for primary students might include teaching children simple navigational skills such as bookmarks, mouse movements and clicks, hyperlinks. Teachers may choose to introduce an in-class Internet workshop, but they should strive to keep it simple. Basic reading, writing, and drawing connections at established Web sites ensure success.

Some specific examples of quality sites for primary students address both literacy and technology standards. **Alex's Scribbles-Koala Trouble** contains wonderful stories about Max the koala bear, written by a 5-year-old boy and his dad in Australia. Hyperlinks require children to click on illustrations to move the story ahead. Emergent readers not only build confidence in their own reading but can draw their own pictures and write a sentence or story after reading one of Max's adventures. **Boowa and Kwala** visit different countries through songs and interactive games. Sites are filled with music, sounds, and animation that may assist with phonemic awareness.

Internet Coloring Books encourage children to print out their work and write about their pictures, thus reinforcing the reading, writing, and visual representation connection. **DrawYourOwnPicture, FEMA's Coloring Book,** and **Smokey Bear's Official Home Page** provide three resources of this integrative nature.

The scientific visual images are featured at **Nanoworld Image Gallery,** where students can find images taken by an electron microscope, copy the label (or predict the image), and write a sentence describing the picture. At **The Mind's Eye Monster Exchange Project,** children draw a picture of a monster then write a description of it. Paired classes exchange descriptions and attempt to draw a picture of what they think their partner's monster looks like. Images are posted on the Web site so classes can see the originals and compare them with their counterparts.

Other popular visual websites that align with the primary curriculum include **Online Autumn, Pumpkin Patch,** and **An Apple A Day. Stage Hands Puppets Activity Page** provides outstanding puppet activities that support oral language while **Billy Bear's Internet Post Office** provides a great writing activity to introduce students to safe electronic forms of communication through e-cards to which they can add music, and a message and stamp. In addition to exposing young children to visual literacy, they will be learning some of the preliminary navigating, typing, and accessing skills necessary to be technologically literate in a changing world.

Using the Internet for Student Exploration (Grades 3–8)

While teacher planning is a single first-step in melding instruction and technology, the richest connections may be those in which teachers prepare and model assignments that require active engagement by students with the Internet. Leu, Leu, & Coiro (2004) suggest four instructional models that incorporate direct facilitation and meaningful connections to the language arts via the Internet:

- Internet Workshop
- Internet Project
- Internet Inquiry
- WebQuests

Each of these strategies is built on the concept of distributed learning. Since no single person can be expected to know everything on or about the rich and complex world of the Internet, it is best for both students and teachers to learn from one another, sharing content knowledge, navigational skills, and critical analysis of Web site information. Discussing each of these instructional strategies in sequence provides an ongoing plan for developmental growth in incorporating the Internet in varied layers of learning the language arts through a meaningful content context throughout the elementary and middle level.

Internet Workshop. Internet Workshop (Leu, Leu, & Coiro, 2004) provides a comfortable way for teachers to get started with using the Internet for instruction. The use of the term "workshop" reflects similarities with the reading workshop and writing workshop process approach supported by this textbook. The purposes of the Internet Workshop include developing students' ability to access information from the Internet, to learn about the topic to be studied, and to think critically about the information being read.

The workshop format implies cooperation, sharing, discussion, and learning over time. It typically requires four steps in planning and implementation:

1. Locating and bookmarking a quality site with content related to the curriculum (e.g., dinosaurs, deserts, Underground Railroad, Depression, Dust Bowl). Visit a central site, locate a specialized Web site, and bookmark it for students.

2. Developing an activity requiring each student to navigate and use the information from the site. Prepare an open-ended activity page that requires students to read various portions of the Web site, fill in open-ended responses to queries, and bring to the scheduled workshop.
3. Assigning an activity to be completed during a one-week period. If there is only one Internet-connected computer in a classroom, students may work in scheduled pairs to complete the assignment. If a computer lab is available, students can complete it during scheduled lab time.
4. Sharing information, questions, and new insights during a scheduled, whole-class or small-group workshop session. Workshop takes place during a scheduled time period during which content information and navigational skills are discussed. In addition, cooperative sharing and critical analysis skills are modeled. During the session, students share what they have learned, what they do not understand, and what they want to learn next.

Even teachers with little Internet experience can provide the planning, guidance, and modeling needed to accomplish the stages of these relatively simple Internet Workshop tasks. Examples of Internet Workshops developed by teachers are available at **Internet Workshop.** An example of an Internet Workshop about the Titanic is showcased in Figure 13.7 and reveals the possibilities of linking literacy and content through navigational Internet use.

Internet Project. Collaboration on a common classroom project with other students around the world is the key component of Internet Project. Two approaches to an Internet Project direct this instructional strategy. The first approach is a Web Site Internet Project, a permanent project that is coordinated by an individual at a common Web site. To participate, the teacher simply needs to visit the site and follow the directions for becoming involved. Currently, there are various Web sites on which these projects can be registered and posted. **The Internet Projects Registry** of the Global Schoolhouse and **Collaborative Learning Project Center** display a wide array of projects putting teachers and students in touch with classrooms around the world.

The second approach to Internet Project, intended for the more technology-based teacher, is to initiate a fresh project with another interested teacher located through the Internet. These spontaneous Internet Projects, inspired by a teacher, then seek interested classrooms for collaboration. As teachers express interest through e-mail, students in various classrooms complete the project and share their findings. The following procedures for developing and implementing a spontaneous Internet Project should be followed:

- Write a collaborative project description for an upcoming unit (at least several months in advance) and include a summary of the project, a precise list of goals or outcomes, a list of expectations for participating classrooms, and a time line for starting and ending the project.
- Post the information several months in advance at a variety of Internet Project sites including **Global SchoolNet's Internet Project Registry. SchoolNet's Grassroots Project Gallery,** or **Intercultural E-Mail Classroom Connections.**
- Arrange operational details with teachers from other classrooms who choose to collaborate. This requires specific guidelines and time frames.
- Complete the project, sharing information with collaborating classrooms. Reading, writing, and evaluating information become key components of the project.

FIGURE 13.7 Internet Workshop: Stories from the Titanic.

Stories from the Titanic

In this activity you will do the following:

- Conduct research on the Internet and discover information about people who were on the Titanic.
- Read and take notes about people on the Titanic.
- Try and learn the complete story about these people.
- When you are ready, you will be called as a witness to the U.S. Senate Hearings on the Titanic Disaster. You will take the part of the person(s) you have studied and tell your story about what happened.
- You will be asked to respond to questions as if you were this person.

Research Projects (Choose 1)

Project 1: Ruth Dodge

You are Mrs. Washington Dodge (Ruth Vidaver), from San Francisco, California, who boarded the Titanic at Southampton with your husband Dr. Washington Dodge and your son Washington Dodge Jr. Learn all you can about Ruth Dodge's experiences in preparation for the Senate hearings. You will find these resources useful:

Encyclopedia Titanica: Search this site using Ruth Dodge's last name. You will find lots of great resources.
Dr. Dodge's Wife Tells Story of Titanic Wreck

Project 2: Dr. Washington Dodge

You are Dr. Washington Dodge, one of the surviving men from the Titanic. You boarded the Titanic at Southampton with your wife, Ruth Dodge, and your son Washington Dodge Jr. Learn all you can about

Source: Internet Workshop Web site (http://web.syr.edu/djleu/workshop.html). Text courtesy Donald J. Leu.

FIGURE 13.7 (Continued)

Dr. Washington Dodge's experiences in preparation for the Senate hearings. You will find these resources useful:

Union Democrat

R.M.S. Titanic Survivors Describe Awful Scene 1912

Titanic Rescue Described by San Francisco Survivor

Washington Dodge Tells of Titanic Sinking

Encyclopedia Titanica: Search this site using Washington Dodge's last name. You will find lots of great resources.

Project 3: A Reporter Discovers the Tragedy of the Third Class Passengers

You are a newspaper reporter for the New York Herald. No one is reporting on the tragedy suffered by the 3rd class, or steerage passengers. While most of the first class passengers were saved, most of the poorer, third class passengers died. Your job is to testify about how the third class passengers were ignored in this tragedy. You are the only reporter who can tell this important story during the Senate hearings. Use these important resources:

The Unsung Heroes of the Titanic

The Charts and Maps Room

Encyclopedia Titanica

Project 4: Stories from Third Class Passengers

You are one of the few third class passengers who survived. You have been asked to report to the Senate Committee about your experiences on the Titanic. Visit Encyclopedia Titanica and select one of the third class passengers.

(Select "Third Class Passengers" from the Passenger List and look for the names of survivors. These are in italics.)

You may wish to select from one of these survivors:

Mrs. Stanton Abbott

Margaret Devaney

Amy Zillah Elsie Stanley

August "Wennerström" (Andersson)

Eugene Patrick Daly

Edward Arthur Dorking

Ernst Ulrik Persson

Learn as much as you can about one of these third class passengers. Then, read about the tragedy of the third class passengers at The Unsung Heroes of the Titanic. Be prepared to tell the stories you discovered.

Project 5: The Unsinkable Molly Brown

You are Mrs. James Joseph Brown (Margaret Tobin), sometimes called "The Unsinkable Molly Brown." Study your history and be prepared to tell your story about what happened on the Titanic. Use this resource:

The Heroines of the Titanic

Project 6: A Newspaper Reporter Discovers Survivor Stories

You are a newspaper reporter for The Chicago Tribune who is in New York when the survivors return. You interview as many as you can. The Senate Committee wants to hear the stories you have learned.

FIGURE 13.7 (Continued)

Be prepared to tell the stories of at least two different survivors you have interviewed. Use these resources:

Encyclopedia Titanica
Stories

Project 7: A Newspaper Reporter Discovers Stories from First Class Passengers

You are a newspaper reporter for The New York Post Dispatch. You have been assigned to interview the first class passengers who survived as they arrive at the docks. You interview as many as you can. The Senate Committee wants to hear the stories you have learned. Be prepared to tell the stories of at least two first-class survivors you have interviewed. Use these resources:

Encyclopedia Titanica
Stories

Figure 13.8 provides several examples of language arts project descriptions posted at Global School Net's Internet Projects registry.

Benefits of a worldwide Internet Project reach far beyond the project itself. First, interacting electronically with students from another culture develops a greater appreciation for diversity—the hallmark of a global perspective on the world. Second, communication skills are developed as writing must be clear, precise, and accurate for others to understand and make meaning from messages. Finally, reading information from all over the world provides a dynamic way to learn. Curricular content takes on life when information is shared with students in different locations with common interests.

Internet Inquiry. As students (and teachers) become more adept at locating Internet resources, Internet Inquiry becomes a useful instructional strategy to develop independent research and new literacy skills (reading, writing, inquiry, searching, analysis) while reaching across the disciplines for self-generated content exploration. The key component of Internet Inquiry is that the research questions originate with a child's individual interests. Internet Inquiry consists of five phases (Leu & Leu, 2000):

1. ***Question.*** Students identify and phrase an important question they wish to explore. Brainstorming sessions and teacher modeling of writing research questions become an important part of this process. Questions can be generated on any topic (Why have dinosaurs become extinct?), on any topic within a curricular area (How do weather fronts influence local weather conditions?), or more specifically on any topic in a particular aspect of the curriculum (What were the living conditions of slaves prior to the Civil War?).
2. ***Search.*** Students conduct an Internet search to explore their topic. The search engines that should be used for child-appropriate sites include **Yahooligans, Ask Jeeves for Kids,** and the **American Library Association's 700+ Sites** (Amazing, Spectacular, Mysterious, Colorful Web Sites for Kids and the Adults Who Care About Them).
3. ***Analyze.*** Students should think critically and focus on the information they have located as they target an answer to their research question.

FIGURE 13.8 Internet Projects Registry: Sample K–8 Projects.

1. ELWOOD, THE WORLD'S MOST TRAVELED DOLL (#562) by Dough Hand (#73155)
   Dates: 01/15/06 to 05/15/06
   Ages: 6 to 11
   Project Level: Basic Project
   Curriculum Areas: Arts; Community Interest; Information Technology; Language; Mathematics; Science; Social Studies; Technology;
   Technology Types: Email, List server;
   Collaboration Types: Travel Buddy;
   Project Summary: ELWOOD IS A LIFE SIZE II YEAR OLD BOY DOLL THAT HAS TRAVELED TO ALL 50 STATES, 5 CONTINENTS, AND 17 COUNTRIES. HE ALLOWS MY CLASS ROOM TO LIVE A VICARIOUS LIFE LINE TO THEIR DREAMS AND TO THEIR EDUCATION. TO THE CLASSES HE MEETS HE OPENS UP THEIR IMAGINATIONS TO DISCOVER THEIR DREAMS.
2. Exchange students between differents countries (#2959) by Josep Lluis Asensio (#79712)
   Dates: 01/09/06 to 06/23/06
   Ages: 7 to 21
   Project Level: Basic Project
   Curriculum Areas: Language;
   Technology Types: Audio: files, clips, CDs, tapes; Email, List server;
   Graphics: photo, draw, paint; Postal Mail; Text: stories, essays, letters;
   Collaboration Types: Information Exchange; Global Classroom; Keypais; Virtual Meeting or Gathering;
   Project Summary: We are a little school of foreigners languages in Barcelona. We have groups of English, German, French, Spanish and Catalan. We are looking for others school which want join their students with ours. Our basic wishes are that our students use the language which are learning and over more that they know others cultures and traditions from others countries. We want exchange information and experiences by e-mail. If you have some questions, you can send me email to jlluis.asensio@e-comunicat.com. Thanks
3. Famous Stories Travel around the World (#2440) by Mihaela Andreea Silter (#71910)
   Dates: 09/01/06 to 12/28/06
   Ages: 9 to 17
   Project Level: Basic Project
   Curriculum Areas: Arts; Community Interest; Information Technology; Language; Social Studies;
   Technology Types: Email, List server;
   Collaboration Types: Electronic Publishing; Information Exchange; Global Classroom; Intercultural Exchange; Global Classroom; Intercultural Exchange;
   Project Summary: This project gives our students the opportunity to read, summarize and illustrate (drawings/artworks) stories for children written by famous writers from their countries.
4. Groundhog Day Weather (#2978) by Kathleen Hartman (#74485)
   Dates: 01/08/06 to 02/07/06
   Ages: 5 to 14
   Project Level: Basic Project
   Curriculum Areas: Language; Mathematics; Science; Technology;
   Technology Types: Email, List server; Spreadsheet: data, analysis;
   Collaboration Types: Information Exchange;
   Project Summary: Our 4th grade students would like participants to record their weather conditions for Groundhog Day. On Thursday, February 2, 2006 we would like you to collect data on the weather conditions in your town at noon.

Source: Global Schoolhouse Internet Projects Registry (http://www.gsn.org/pr/index.html). Copyright © GlobalSchoolNet.org. Reprinted with permission.

FIGURE 13.8 (Continued)

5. Mouse Tales (#2964) by Susan Silverman (#74050)
   Dates: 01/01/06 to 02/14/06 Registration is Closed!
   Ages: 6 to 11
   Project Level: Basic Project
   Curriculum Areas: Language; Multicultural Studies; Social Studies;
   Technology Types: Email, List server; Graphics: photo, draw, paint;
   Text: stories, essays, letters; Video: files, clips, CDs, tapes;
   Collaboration Types: Electronic Publishing;
   Project Summary: Classes will read a "mouse" book as a springboard for a response activity of their choice. Participants are welcome to suggest resources. After reading the story students will engage in language arts, math, science or social studies activities that will be showcased on a web site.

6. Newsday 2005 Jan–May (#2662) by Al Rogers (#4)
   Dates: 02/13/06 to 05/26/06
   Ages: 10 to 16
   Project Level: Basic Project
   Curriculum Areas: Arts; Business; Community Interest; English as Foreign Language; Information Technology; International Relations; Language; Multicultural Studies; Social Studies; Technology;
   Technology Types: Email, List server; Postal Mail; Web-published; Text: stories, essays, letters; Discussion Forum;
   Collaboration Types: Electronic Publishing; Information Exchange; Peer Feedback;
   Project Summary: Your students write news articles and then submit them to the "Newsday" newswire on March 27–April 21, 2006. Then they produce their own newspaper based on the articles submitted by all of the participating classes. You send a copy of your newspaper to all other participants. You then receive copies of newspapers published by the other classes. It's a wonderful literacy project.

7. Stately Postcards (#2987) by Cynthia Gray (#78547)
   Dates: 02/01/06 to 05/30/06
   Ages: 12 to 14
   Project Level: Basic Project
   Curriculum Areas: History; Social Studies;
   Technology Types: Email, List server; Desktop Document Sharing;
   Text: stories, essays, letters; Discussion Forum;
   Collaboration Types: Information Exchange; Information Search; Virtual Meeting or Gathering;
   Project Summary: Each participating class is asked to submit a postcard describing their State & Capital along with some important demographic facts. We would also like to know what was going on in your state during important times in our nation's history. What was your state like in 1492, 1607, 1676, 1776, 1812, 1831 and in 1850? What are some other important dates or events that happened in your state like, when was your state admitted into statehood? We would also like to hear what you think about living in your state. You are invited to join in our discussion threads to answer questions about your state or ask others about their state.

8. The Day I Was Born project Now Allows Your Students to Become Authors of an Online History Book (#564) by Catherine Campanella (#39)
   Dates: 01/01/06 to 12/31/09
   Ages: 9 to 19
   Project Level: Basic Project

FIGURE 13.8 (Continued)

Curriculum Areas: Arts; History; Information Technology; Language; Mathematics; Science; Social Studies; Technology;
Technology Types: Audio: files, clips, CDs, tapes; Student created Webs; Digital Portfolios; Web-published; Video: files, clips, CDs, tapes;
Collaboration Types: Electronic Publishing; Information Exchange; Information Search;
Project Summary: Students are guided through the Internet to find out what was happening in the world on the day they were born. If teachers are interested, student results may be included in "The Day I Was Born Online History Book." Please see Full Project Description for more details about the project.

9. To a New Life (#2982) by Larry Olinger (#80098)
Dates: 01/20/06 to 01/01/07
Ages: 11 to 16
Project Level: Basic Project
Curriculum Areas: Engish as Foreign Language; Language; Multicultural Studies;
Technology Types: Graphics: photo, draw, paint; Web-published; Text: stories, essays, letters; Video: files, clips, CDs, tapes; Discussion Forum;
Collaboration Types: Information Exchange; Global Classroom; Intercultural Exchange;
Project Summary: Moving can be an exciting, and sometimes trying time. There are so many new things to see and adapt to, it is easy to become overwhelmed. This project is a forum in which students can share the experiences they had while moving. It can be a move across town, or around the world, either way sharing experiences can bring comfort to those who will move soon, and offer a sense of common experience to those who have already moved.

10. Virtual Village (#2983) by Theresa Takahashi (#80103)
Dates: 01/01/06 to 12/01/06
Ages: 10 to 21
Project Level: Basic Project
Curriculum Areas: Language; Social Studies;
Technology Types: Email, List server; Graphics: photo, draw, paint; Web-published; Spreadsheet: data, analysis;
Collaboration Types: Electronic Publishing; Information Exchange;
Project Summary: This project was created to give students a chance to learn about the culture of the Native Americans before Columbus arrived in North America. This project aligns with numerous California state standards in the Language Arts area and the Social Studies area.

4. ***Compose.*** Students provide a written and/or visual presentation of their findings. While this could be a traditional report, it might also be a PowerPoint presentation or a poster presentation.
5. ***Share.*** Students share their questions and answers with others at a special time and in a special format.

Internet Inquiry requires students to utilize all aspects of the language arts allowing them to read, write, listen, speak, view, and visually represent across the entire curriculum. The meaningful focus on self-generated inquiry enhanced by technological research and resulting in visual and oral or written presentations provides a brilliant blend of integrating research strategies, Internet research, and presentation skills.

WebQuests. A final instructional framework is called a WebQuest (Leu & Leu, 2000), which is typically a research project developed by teachers on a Web site for students to follow in pursuing a learning experience using the Internet. Because WebQuests are located on Web pages, they are available to other teachers. WebQuest pages usually contain the following sections:

- ***Introduction.*** A description of the learning activity in a brief paragraph.
- ***Task description.*** A list of each of the tasks each student must complete.
- ***Process description.*** A description of how each task should be completed.
- ***Information resources.*** Links to the information resources on the Internet that will be required to complete the activity.
- ***Organizing acquired information.*** Directs students to answer questions, fill in a concept map, or complete a time line or other organizational framework.
- ***Concluding remark.*** Reminds students about what they have learned and often offers the opportunity to explore related topics.
- ***Evaluation.*** A scoring chart or rubric that asks for student evaluation.

Teachers can find out more information about the WebQuest model across grade levels at **The WebQuest Page.** Many WebQuests tend to focus on specific learning tasks and do not ask the student to evaluate information or do any problem solving. However, their availability assists teachers who are yet unfamiliar with constructing their own WebQuest but are seeking a model for their students. Accessing the WebQuest Page Web site resulted in the WebQuests built on fables, fairy tales, poetry, and Eric Carle's *The Grouchy Ladybug.* One WebQuest Page model titled "A Moment in Time" invites fourth- through seventh-grade students to choose a poem, picture book, and novel to create a time capsule. Examples abound and provide outstanding models for creating one's own WebQuest to post for other teachers.

Plentiful Internet Web sites stretch the limits of a teacher's time and help to locate those that most effectively link with a school's literacy and interdisciplinary curriculum. The *Miss Rumphius* Award is presented by members of the RTEACHER listserv to educators who develop and share exceptional Internet resources for literacy and learning. The award honors teachers who "make the world a more beautiful place" by spreading technology successes. The list can be located online at the Web site for the International Reading Association Figure 13.9 showcases that Web site and the abundant, quality links that await your access and instructional planning at all grade levels.

Internet Sites for Electronic Communication and Publishing

E-mail and online publishing have introduced an unprecedented opportunity for writing instruction, the craft of writing, and dissemination of writing to a wide audience. The Internet has opened possibilities for communicating with students in classrooms around the world and for polishing and publishing writing to share with the global community.

E-mail as a communication tool offers outstanding potential for the reading and writing program, allowing innovative teachers to enhance the curriculum through interactive writing with other classrooms (Larson, 2002). E-mail projects between and among classes not only promote authentic writing skills but provide opportunities for students to learn firsthand about other cultures.

Teachers may locate key pal partnerships (e-mail pen pals) with classrooms in other states or countries. Teachers can pair students to discuss common areas of study or topics of common interest. E-mail exchanges can also be conceptualized between an expert in an area of study (zoologist, author, poet) and the class. Professors can even pair language

FIGURE 13.9 Winners of the Miss Rumphius Award, given Annually by the International Reading Association to Teachers who Develop and Share Exceptional Internet Resources for Literacy and Learning.

Elementary Sites

Apple Bytes

That Susan Silverman strikes again with a collaborative celebration of fall apples. Perfect for a primary grade classroom and a great model for what all of us can do with the Internet in our classroom.

Benjamin Franklin: A Man of Many Talents

Everything you ever wanted to know about the great writer and inventor can be found at this informative site, which includes quizzes, experiments, and a list of Franklin-related links.

Bunny Readers

This is an excellent example of how to connect and collaborate with classrooms around the country. The student illustrations and stories are a treat.

Charlotte's Web

This delightful site has quizzes, puzzles, and chapter summaries for E. B. White's story *Charlotte's Web*. The site was developed by Mrs. Taverna's second grade class at Pocantico Hills Elementary School.

Children's Encyclopedia of Women

An interesting site featuring profiles of many famous women, written by third- and fourth-grade students.

Cinco de Mayo

Explore Hispanic culture through children's literature, important historical events, music, cultural traditions, and even a cooking adventure and fiesta at the end of the unit.

Creation Stories and Myths

An outstanding resource for explanatory myths from a wide variety of cultures.

Earth Day Groceries Project

A project to encourage other classrooms to decorate paper grocery bags with environmental messages and distribute these to stores for Earth Day.

Fall Internet Poetry Project—Mrs. McGowan's First Grade

Join in on a fall poetry project or see what collaborative work between classrooms can accomplish by visiting this site and having your students enjoy the pleasure of fall poetry created by primary grade children.

Fall Is Here! We Love It!

Inspired by Elaine Good's autumn book, *Fall is Here! I Love It!*, this collaborative literacy project provides a forum for students to share signs of autumn in their different communities through writings and illustrations.

Mr. Fontanella's Kindergarten Class

This site is a wonderful resource model for all kindergarten classes. It contains a useful parent page, class news, permission forms, informational articles for parents, as well as a school calendar.

Gander Academy's Theme-Related Resources on the WWW

Nicely organized curriculum resources used at this school organized by topic or theme.

FIGURE 13.9 (Continued)

Mrs. Hall's First Grade Classroom

If you are a first grade teacher interested in integrating the Internet into your classroom reading program, here's the place for you. Take a look at the first grade Web ring Sharon Hall has developed and the many resources for parents.

Harriet Tubman and the Underground Railroad

A remarkable location for the study of this important American.

Hazel's Home Page

A wonderfully comprehensive location with many valuable resources. A great resource for teachers new to the Internet seeking instructional ideas.

Hobart-Malang Electronic Mail Project

A wonderful example of a cross-cultural curriculum project.

The Home of the Looneys: The Traveling Lobster Buddies

The classroom home page of Marjorie Duby's fifth graders with many outstanding resources for reading. The Looney Lobster project is a wonderful model for a travel-buddy project that integrates the reading of children's literature and writing.

Mr. Leahy's Class: Greenway Elementary School

This well organized web site does a great job of showcasing student's work. The site includes links to forms used in the classroom and award-winning projects from past years.

Logootee Elementary West

The home page for this school in Indiana, USA with great support for teachers beginning their Internet journeys.

The North Star Navigators

This exciting location takes your children on a journey to discover their own "North Star." Many exciting activities in this very creative curriculum project. Many children have found their own "North Star" with these experiences.

Online Autumn

An interactive site filled with original student poems, stories, and graphic organizers about different aspects of autumn. It shows how many teachers can share their students' work, providing important resources for all our classrooms. A great model!

Mr. Roemer's Fifth Grade Polar Bears

This Web site is a great example of how Web site can be used to build a sense of school community. The site includes several student activities, projects, and educational resources.

Room 100, Buckman Elementary School

A wealth of resources can be found at this one site. Listen to children reading, view images in the classroom microscope cam, study Dr. Martin Luther King, Jr.'s time line.

The Three R's of Our Fight For Freedom

Using the theme of the American Revolution, this site is chock-full of creative games, dioramas, slide shows, poetry and pictures, as well as links to interactive games, puzzles and more.

FIGURE 13.9 (Continued)

Tunia's Travels

Follow along with Tunia, a plush ladybug toy, as she travels the world. This site also offers excellent ladybug-related resources, including information on ladybug books, ladybug habitats, and ladybug food, and an invitation to write to Tunia.

Vietnam

A tremendous resource for students and teachers learning about Vietnam. The site includes picture books, quizzes, photos, and excellent teacher resources with Web links.

Middle School Sites

Mrs. DeCosa's School Web Page

Created for a seventh-grade English class, this site features classroom curricula such as assignments, topics, resource tools, and student work. Of special interest is a parents' page, with tips to help parents help their children become better students.

Ms. Smith's English Page

This classroom Web site combines a useful mix of fun and information. Featured student articles and topics change monthly. Teachers interested in starting to use technology in their own classroom will find this Web page a true resource.

Source: http://www.reading.org/resources/community/links_rumphius_links.html. Reprinted with permission of the International Reading Association. All rights reserved.

arts methods students in teacher education with elementary students to discuss award-winning literature, the writing process, or reading strategies. Some collaborative email generation sites include **Teaching.Com** where individual keypals, a partner class, or volunteers 50+ years of age for an intergenerational experience could be located. A teacher may also subscribe to a K–12 e-mail list at **Intercultural Email Classroom Connections.** A message posted at this site will link partners in a particular country or state.

Writing becomes even more exhilarating when guided by creative ideas and mentoring from Web sites. **Writer's Window** features a writing workshop that guides students through the writing of stories, poems, reviews, and essays with exercises and writing tips. Writing from students ages 5 to 18 is showcased to inspire creativity. **Poetry Express** walks students through the poetry writing process and provides guidelines for 15 different types of poetry. **Biography Maker** provides writing guides for questioning, learning, synthesis, and story telling as the stages of writing an inviting biography. The Internet thus provides guidance for writing across literary genres.

Publication is the final stage of the writing process. With the incorporation of technology, not only is the format of this stage more professional, but young writers have new and exciting opportunities to publish their work because of the Internet.

KidPub is a well-organized Web site that has already provided 4,2000 students opportunities to see their writing published on the Internet. Students can submit poems and stories using a form provided at the site. Maintained by a parent in Massachusetts, stories are posted within three days of being received and feedback is provided as to why the piece was selected. Students can keep track of how many readers have read their work. **International Kids' Space** is a site for sharing works of art, short stories, and even music with others. **Cyberkids** is a quarterly online magazine inviting submissions from students ages 7 to 11. After a preliminary screening, readers vote for winning entries, which are subsequently published.

Several book dealer sites like **amazon.com** or **barnesandnoble.com** provide opportunities for students to write and post reviews of children's books. Students use a search engine to locate the Web site and post their revised reviews. Using the school name and initials provides the necessary precaution in posting.

The Internet opens new doors to authentic writing experiences as students communicate with other students from around the world and publish their own works to a wider audience. Although a teacher must supervise and scrutinize these opportunities very carefully, the rewards for communicating with a global audience appear endless.

Visit the Companion Website at www.prenhall.com/hancock and gauge your understanding of Chapter 13 concepts with the self-assessments.

Closing Thoughts

Technology has provided language arts educators a boon for teaching. School districts across the nation hold high expectations that teachers utilize technology and discover new and enriching ways to benefit from this educational opportunity. Although blending technology and the language arts is surrounded by risk taking and challenge, this chapter provides a first step in exploring the many avenues and creative possibilities created by technology and the Internet. When teachers reach out to other teachers and share ideas like *Miss Rumphius,* educators enhance their effectiveness and touch the lives of countless students. Educational technology exists not in a vacuum but in a complex network of teachers of varying technological knowledge. Sharing the joys, frustrations, and successes of technology in the language arts classroom with others new to the realm of technology may be the most efficient and effective way of spreading the best of language arts instruction and learning to the largest number of teachers and students.

Issues and tentative barriers to utilizing technology to enhance teaching and learning abound (Rhodes, 2000). Educators are constantly joining in on the negative chorus: *Not enough computers available to the children. Not enough time for teachers to scrutinize materials or learn to use software programs. Not enough technical support in the schools. Not enough time devoted to technology staff development. Not enough time in light of standards-based testing and national testing mandates.* Comments like these seem to point to the fact that most teachers do not really understand how to integrate technology into instruction and how to have students use it effectively. As this chapter has illustrated, technology provides a means to actually integrate the language arts among themselves and among other curricular areas. Educators should thus be asking different questions: *How can technology effectively enhance the teaching and learning of literacy in my classroom? What can technology do to make literacy teaching and literacy learning more effective? How can technology assist in integrating the language arts within themselves and across the curriculum for effective, efficient instruction?*

The best practices in teaching, whether online or offline, engage students in active learning. Students should be participants who are actively engaged in literacy events, not sideline spectators. Technology offers an opportunity for educators to reach the students who will live in a dynamic future. Technology will neither replace the human side of teaching, nor will it be a panacea for all problems related to teaching and learning. Since the ultimate goal of language arts educators is to help students become independent and thoughtful lifelong readers and writers, listeners and speakers, viewers and visual representatives of learning, then technology stands at the forefront of changing teaching and learning in the new millennium.

References

Atwell, N. (1987). *In the middle: Reading, writing, and learning with adolescents.* Portsmouth, NH: Heinemann.

Balajthy, E. (2000). Is technology worth my professional time, resources, and effort? In S. B. Wepner, W. J. Valmont, & R. Thurlow, *Linking literacy and technology* (pp. 203–217). Newark, DE: International Reading Association.

Bowman, J. (1998). Technology, tutoring and improved reading. *English Update: Newsletter from the Center on English Learning and Achievement, 3,* 2–3.

Calkins, L. M. (1986). *The art of teaching writing.* Portsmouth, NH: Heinemann.

DeJong, M. T., & Bus, A. G. (2004). The efficacy of electronic books in fostering kindergarten children's emergent story understanding. *Reading Research Quarterly, 39,* 378–393.

Fox, B. J., & Mitchell, M. J. (2000). Using technology to support word recognition, spelling, and vocabulary acquisition. In S. B. Wepner, W. J. Valmont, & R. Thurlow (Eds.), *Linking literacy and technology: A guide for K–8 classrooms* (pp. 42–75). Newark, DE: International Reading Association.

Gambrell, L. B. (2005). Reading literature, reading text, reading the Internet: The times they are a'changing. *The Reading Teacher, 58,* 588–591.

Graves, D. H. (1983). *Writing: Teachers and children at work.* Portsmouth, NH: Heinemann.

Hancock, M. (2000). The survival of the book in a megabyte world: Children's literature in the new millennium. *Journal of Children's Literature, 26,* 8–16.

International Reading Association (2002). *Integrating literacy and technology into the curriculum: A position statement of the International Reading Association.* Newark, DE: Author.

International Society for Technology in Education (2000a). *National Educational Technology Standards for Students: Connecting Curriculum and Technology.* Eugene, OR: ISTE/U.S. Department of Education.

International Society for Technology in Education (2000b). *National Educational Technology Standards for Teachers.* Eugene, OR: ISTE/U.S. Department of Education.

International Society for Technology in Education (2002). *National Educational Technology Standards.* Retrieved March 21, 2006, from http://cnets.iste.org

Jonassen, D. H., Peck, K. L., & Wilson, B. G. (1999). *Learning with technology: A constructivist approach.* Upper Saddle River, NJ: Merrill.

Karchmer, R. A. (2000). Understanding teachers' perspectives of Internet use in the classroom: Implications for teacher education and staff development. *Reading and Writing Quarterly, 16,* 81–85.

Karchmer, R. A. (2001). The journey ahead: Thirteen teachers report how the Internet influences literacy and literacy instruction in their K–12 classrooms. *Reading Research Quarterly, 36,* 442–466.

Karchmer, R. A., Mallette, M. H., Kara-Soterious, J., & Leu, D.J. (Eds.) (2005). *Innovative approaches to literacy education.* Newark, DE: International Reading Association.

Labbo, L. D. (2000). 12 things young children can do with a talking book in a classroom computer center. *The Reading Teacher, 53,* 542–546.

Labbo, L. D., & Reinking, D. (1999). Negotiating the multiple realities of technology in literacy research and instruction. *Reading Research Quarterly, 34,* 478–493.

Larson, L. C. (2002). The keypal project: Integrating literature response and technology. *Kansas Journal of Reading, 18,* 57–62.

Lefever-Davis, S., & Pearman, C. (2005). Early readers and electronic texts: CD-ROM storybook features that influence reading behaviors. *The Reading Teacher, 58,* 446–454.

Leu, D. J. (1997). Caity's question: Literacy as deixis on the Internet. *The Reading Teacher, 51,* 62–67.

Leu, D. J. (1999). The Miss Rumphius effect: Envisionments for literacy and learning that transform the Internet. *The Reading Teacher, 52,* 636–642.

Leu, D. J. (2000). Our children's future: Changing the focus of literacy and literacy instruction. *The Reading Teacher, 53,* 424–429.

Leu, D. J. (2002). The new literacies: Research on reading instruction with the Internet. In A. E. Farnstrup & S. J. Samules (Eds.), *What research has to say about reading instruction* (pp. 310–336). Newark, DE: International Reading Association.

Leu, D. J., & Leu, D. D. (2000). *Teaching with the Internet: Lessons from the classroom* (3rd ed.). Norwood, MA: Christopher-Gordon.

Leu, D. J., Leu, D. D., & Coiro, J. (2004). *Teaching with the Internet K–12: New literacies for new times* (4th ed.). Norwood, MA: Christopher-Gordon.

McNair, J. C. (2000). Using the Internet to acquaint children with authors and illustrators of children's literature. *The Dragon Lode, 19,* 11–14.

Murray, D. H. (1982). *Learning by teaching*. Montclair, NJ: Boynton/Cook.

Newman, M. D. (2004). *Cyberlit: Online connections to children's literature for the primary grades*. Lanham, MD: Scarecrow Press.

Reinking, D. (1995). Reading and writing with computers: Literacy research in a post-typographic world. In K. A. Hinchman, D. J. Leu Jr., & C. K. Kinzer (Eds.), *Perspectives on literacy research and practice* (pp. 17–33). Chicago: National Reading Conference.

Reinking, D., Labbo, L., & McKenna, M. (1997). Navigating the changing landscape of literacy: Current research in computer-based reading and writing. In J. Flood, S. B. Heath, & D. Lapp (Eds.), *Handbook of research on teaching literacy through the communicative and visual arts* (pp. 77–92). New York: Macmillan.

Rhodes, C. S. (2000). Literacy and technology: Vital connections. *The Dragon Lode, 19,* 15–17.

Smith, F. (1999). When irresistible technology meets irreplaceable teachers. *Language Arts, 76,* 414–421.

Story-Huffman, R. (2002). *Caldecott on the net* (2nd ed.). Fort Atkinson, WI: Alleyside Press.

Story-Huffman, R. (2002). *Newbery on the net* (2nd ed.). Fort Atkinson, WI: Alleyside Press.

Sullivan, J. E., & Sharp, J. (2000). Using technology for writing development. In S. B. Wepner, W. J. Valmont, & R. Thurlow (Eds.), *Linking literacy and technology: A guide for K–8 classrooms* (pp. 106–132). Newark, DE: International Reading Association.

Wepner, S. B., & Ray, L. C. (2000). Using technology for reading development. In S. B. Wepner, W. J. Valmont, & R. Thurlow (Eds.), *Linking literacy and technology: A guide for K–8 classrooms* (pp. 76–105). Newark, DE: International Reading Association.

Wood, C. (2005). Beginning readers' use of "talking books" software can affect their reading strategies. *Journal of Research in Reading, 28,* 170–182.

Children's Books Cited

Carle, Eric (1977). *The grouchy ladybug*. New York: HarperCollins.

Cooney, Barbara (1982). *Miss Rumphius*. New York: Viking Press.

Software Cited

Accelerated Reader (1999). [Computer software]. Wisconsin Rapids, WI: Advantage Learning Systems.

Arthur's Teacher Trouble (1993). [Computer software]. Cambridge, MA: Broderbund/The Learning Company.

Easy Book Deluxe (1998). [Computer software]. Pleasantville, NY: Sunburst Communications.

FrameMaker (1995). [Computer software]. San Jose, CA: Adobe Systems.

HyperStudio (1996). [Computer software]. El Cajon, CA: Roger Wagner Publishing.

Imagination Express (1994). [Computer software]. Redmond, WA: Edmark.

Kid Pix Studio Deluxe (1998). [Computer software]. Cambridge, MA: Broderbund/The Learning Company.

M-ss-ng L-nks (1998). [Computer software]. Pleasantville, NY: Sunburst Communications.

Oregon Trail (1999). [Computer software]. Cambridge, MA: The Learning Company.

The Print Shop Deluxe (1996). [Computer software]. Cambridge, MA: Broderbund/The Learning Company.

Reading Galaxy (1996). [Computer software]. Cambridge, MA: Broderbund/The Learning Company.

Storybook Weaver Deluxe (1996). [Computer software]. Cambridge, MA: The Learning Company.

Where in the World Is Carmen Santiago? (1998). [Computer software]. Cambridge, MA: Broderbund/The Learning Company.

Writers Studio (1998). [Computer software]. Sunnyvale, CA: Computer Curriculum Corporation.

Chapter 14

INTERDISCIPLINARY INSTRUCTION

Language Arts Connections to the Content Areas

Prairie winds swept down on this loose, dry soil, scooped it up, and carried it into the air as enormous choking clouds of dust.

FROM *CHILDREN OF THE GREAT DEPRESSION,* BY RUSSELL FREEDMAN

The dirt blew down so thick
it scratched my eyes
and stung my tender skin,
it plugged my nose and filled inside my mouth.

FROM *OUT OF THE DUST* BY KAREN HESSE

The overburdened curriculum has necessitated the inclusion of the language arts across the curriculum in the elementary and middle-level classroom. Intuitive teachers find ways to blend the topics of similar content areas with literature. The mathematics, science, and social studies curricula naturally link to literacy through reading, writing, listening, speaking, viewing, and visual representation, particularly through the creative literature connection. The quotes above show how a nonfiction account of the Great Depression era can be introduced through the blending of the accuracy and documented details of Russell Freedman's research with the voice and emotions of Karen Hesse's Billie Jo struggling to survive in Dust Bowl Oklahoma during the same period. In this opening example, nonfiction and fiction literature have the power to bring history to life. In the same spirit, the language arts hold promise to enhance mathematics and science understanding as students "write" their own subtraction problems, "visually represent" an atom, "view" a film on tornadoes, or "read" Shel Silverstein poems (*Where the Sidewalk Ends*) that invite mathematical calculations.

The natural integration of language arts is critical for all content areas. No longer can language arts be isolated to a 40-minute period per day. Such limited exposure to key receptive and communicative skills does not provide enough time or practice for growth as a literate individual. Nor does language arts in isolation truly reflect the ways in which they are used in a real-life setting. Therefore, the solution realistically lies in naturally infusing the language arts into the content areas of social studies, mathematics, and science.

Effective blending and "blurring the edges" (Chatton & Collins, 1999) integrates the curriculum through the language arts and the content areas. *Reading* Patricia Beatty's. *Charley Skedaddle* during a fifth-grade study of the Civil War, *writing* one's own life-based subtraction story problems, *visually representing* a graph and list of findings from a science experiment on weather, *speaking* about one-side of a debatable current event issue, *viewing* a *National Geographic* Web site on the underground railroad, or *listening* to John Lithgow reading *The Carnival of the Animals* on a CD accompanied by classical music have always made sense as quality instruction. Yet educators have just begun to explore and appreciate the varied possibilities of learning language and constructing meaning through the language arts in content area instruction.

The term *content area literacy* has come to mean more than simply learning to read and write through textbooks. It refers to learning through all the literacies that surround today's students—from textbooks to trade books, from e-mail to instant messaging, from encyclopedias to Internet Web sites (Moss, 2005). Thinking beyond the textbook encourages the most meaningful effects of interdisciplinary instruction.

Social studies, science, and mathematics are the academic subject areas in which students can effectively learn about and use all the language arts—reading, writing, listening, speaking, viewing, and visual representation. Integrating the language arts and the content areas requires that students perform language arts activities within the various content areas.

The objectives of this chapter attempt to convince the teacher that an interdisciplinary approach is a natural, effective, meaningful form of instruction that efficiently blends the language arts with content area knowledge.

Objectives

- To explore the language arts and their relationship to teaching and learning across curricular areas.
- To clarify the roles of literature, language, and language arts activities as a door into the realm of integration.
- To establish clear social studies and language arts connections through effective lessons and thematic units.

- To explore both mathematics and language arts as related communication disciplines.
- To parallel science inquiry with language arts strategies that establish higher-level thinking processes.
- To invite teachers to efficiently plan cross-curricular teaching for accountability in infusing the language arts meaningfully into social studies, mathematics, and science instruction.

Language Arts Across the Disciplines

The goal of integrating the language arts into the content areas is "to make learning in prescribed curricular areas meaningful, connected, and less fragmented" (Maxim & Five, 1998, p. 1). Reading, writing, listening, speaking, viewing, and visual representation should be used to learn content information as well as literacy skills. Isolating the language arts to a literacy block is not simply unrealistic—it is impossible. Language skills inevitably pervade the content areas in a natural, relevant, meaningful way and must be practiced, articulated, and expressed within those content areas.

Teachers who want to integrate the language arts across the curriculum should begin to do the following early in the school year:

- Examine the district curriculum at your grade level in the content areas.
- Visit the library/media center and locate resources for the units to be studied—books, videos, posters, Internet sites.
- Locate themed literature across the genres—fiction, nonfiction, poetry, historical fiction—to enhance the curricular study.
- Check resources in your own classroom and match them with units of study.
- Place all resources in special crates, bookcases, or displays so they are easily accessible to students.
- Create bibliographies of both student and teacher resources.
- Read and become familiar with the new literature and resources you have discovered.
- Create opportunities for collaborative group inquiry and study of various aspects of a unit of study.
- Use reading, writing, viewing and visual representation as vehicles for gaining and sharing knowledge on a topic.
- Create opportunities for presenting research in a variety of genres.

For most teachers literature provides the initial link to interdisciplinary instruction. Initial integration typically begins with a trickle of children's books that are read aloud to enhance instruction as literature breathes life into elementary social studies, mathematics, science, and the arts. A teacher read-aloud of Karen Cushman's *Catherine, Called Birdy* enhances a sixth-grade study of life in the Middle Ages. Robert E. Wells's *What's Faster than a Speeding Cheetah?* serves as a humorous, fact-based introduction to a fourth-grade unit on graphing. Meredith Hooper's *The Drop in my Drink: The Story of Water and Our Planet* verbally and visually clarifies an understanding of the water cycle and water pollution for third-grade students. Diane Stanley's *Michelangelo* clarifies the lifelong efforts of the Renaissance artist. Each of these books reveal how the creative and relevant utilization of quality literature can provide a natural link with interdisciplinary instruction.

The Teacher Prep Web site will help you become a better teacher by linking you to classroom videos, student artifacts, teaching strategies, lesson plans, relevant education leadership articles, and practical information on licensing, creating a portfolio, implementing standards, and being successful in field experiences. Visit this resource at www.prenhall.com/teacherprep.

Language itself provides the second link to interdisciplinary instruction. Information builds on the ability to use and understand the language of content area information. Language pervades discussion of social studies (*colonization, electoral college, cultural diversity, continent, bartering, industrialization, legislature*), mathematics (*subtraction, integer, problem solving, probability, fractions, decimal, equivalent*), science (*hurricane, mammal, camouflage, chemical reaction, metamorphosis, molecule, mitosis*), and or the arts (*perspective, concerto, pirouette, Byzantine, classical, cello, cadence*). So teachers quickly note that the vocabulary of the content areas is yet another way in which language naturally pervades instruction. Learning the language of the disciplines is a fundamental step toward learning in the discipline.

A third link for infusing the language arts across the disciplines involves the many language arts-based activities that naturally include reading, writing, listening, speaking, viewing, and visual representation within and across each area of study. Each of the six language arts provides common links to each of the content areas. Figure 14.1 provides

FIGURE 14.1 Language Arts Related to Content Areas.

Social Studies

Reading: Read a book picture book on immigration.
Writing: Write a bio-poem of a famous American.
Listening: Listen to a readers theatre about Thanksgiving.
Speaking: Dramatize hearing the news of emancipation.
Viewing: Observe Americana through the art of Norman Rockwell.
Visual Representation: Draw a time line of the Revolutionary War. Label each important event with a date and a drawing to depict the event.

Science

Reading: Read an informational book to find more about the planets.
Writing: Write a prediction for your science lab on chemical reactions.
Listening: Listen to the CD-ROM of Thomas Edison's first transmission of his voice by telephone.
Speaking: Give an oral report on Isaac Newton's theory of gravity.
Viewing: Observe and record the growth of a bean seed over a two-week period.
Visual Representation: Replicate and label the sequence of events in the formation of warm and cold fronts.

Mathematics

Reading: Read Denise Schmandt-Besserat's *The History of Counting* to determine the varied counting systems across human civilization.
Writing: Write a story in which your main character is one centimeter tall.
Listening: Count to 100 on the 100th day of school and bring in 100 of some object.
Speaking: Explain double-digit division to your math partner.
Viewing: Observe the use of measurement in everyday life (shoe size, liters, pounds, inches, degrees).
Visual Representation: Draw a diagram to illustrate your understanding of 100 divided by 4.

The Arts

Reading: Read a book from the series *A Weekend with the Artist.*
Writing: Create the lyrics to a song based on a favorite book character.
Listening: Enjoy Mozart while writing in your journal.
Speaking: Take part in a class play.
Viewing: Attend a performance of a musical performed by a local arts council.
Visual Representation: Replicate the media and style of a distinctive children's book illustrator.

simple ways, even through single activities, in which the language arts naturally provide effective instruction in surrounding content area instruction. Teachers of content, therefore, are indeed teachers of the language arts as reading, writing, listening, speaking, viewing, and visual representation become vehicles for receiving new information and sharing acquired knowledge.

Literature Across the Disciplines

Quality children's literature lies at the heart of the integrated curriculum. Learning to match literature to the content areas requires both a knowledge of the grade-level curriculum and a knowledge of children's literature. Teachers must be aware of the curricular content they are required to teach—community in second grade, fractions in fourth grade, magnets and electricity in sixth grade. At the same time, teachers must also be knowledgeable about children's books so they can select quality titles across a variety of genres (from poetry to folktales, nonfiction to historical fiction) to share in their content area instruction. Teachers who know both areas well can make the matches necessary for both curricular enhancement and meaningful language arts connections. They can implement this dual knowledge of content and literature as follows:

- Match literature to a related topic.
- Introduce new genres to explore in the content areas.
- Make certain that books with a variety of reading levels are available as resources to all students.
- Match books with individual student interests and inquiries.
- Select related read-alouds that capture a common experience and focus on the language and vocabulary of a particular unit of study.
- Form literature groups to read and discuss titles of similar interests.
- Connect reading, writing, listening, speaking, viewing, and visual representation activities and assignments to the content areas.
- Help students gather, organize, and express their ideas through the help of literature resources.
- Encourage writing in new modes (plays, journals, interviews, poster sessions).
- Share literature in a variety of models of writing for sharing information (ABC books).
- Utilize background knowledge from literature to inspire questioning and inquiry.

Language as Communication Across the Disciplines

Social studies, science, mathematics, and the arts, while predominantly based on knowledge, are indeed language-based. Figure 14.2 demonstrates a pyramid hierarchy and distribution of language in our world. A learner's vocabulary begins on a foundation of *real-world language* that pervades a child's life on a daily basis. Everyday language provides most of the words children use to survive on a personal level. The *language of the classroom* provides a more specialized vocabulary of respect, politeness, courtesy, permission, sharing, and collaborating. Specific language of the classroom can even point to concrete words such as *easel, listening center, computer lab, media center,* or *principal's office.*

The *disciplinary components* of language form an even more specific vocabulary for the content areas. Social studies, science, mathematics, and the arts have a vocabulary of

FIGURE 14.2 A Pyramid of Language Across the Disciplines.

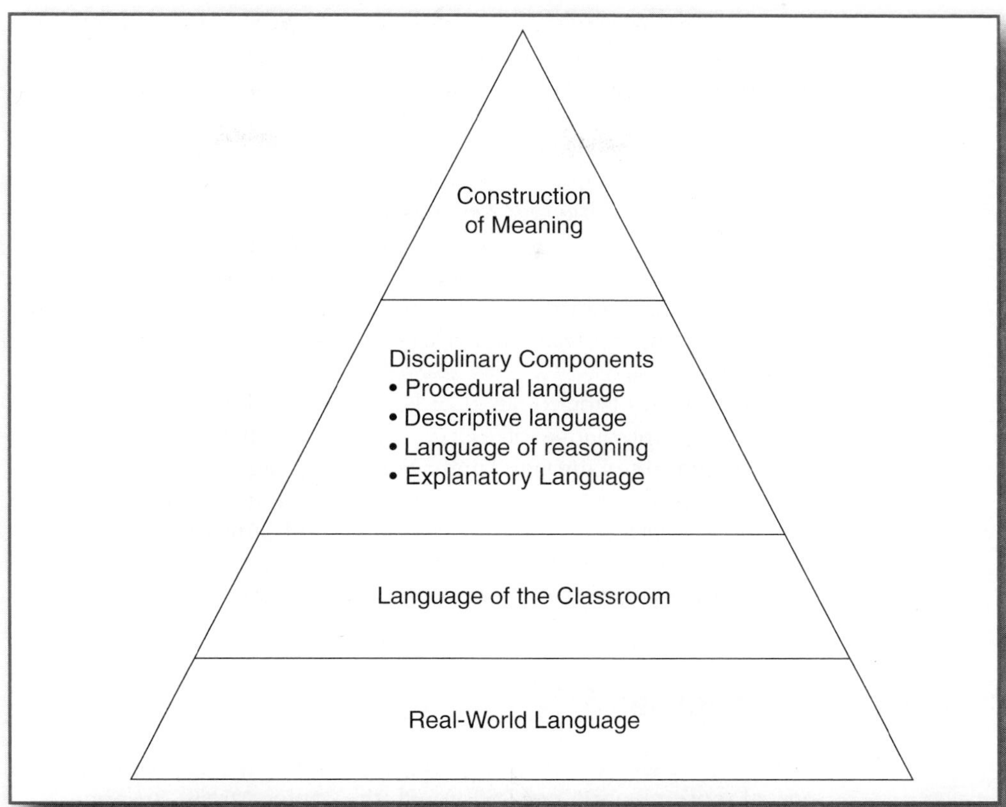

their own with curriculum-specific words that are understood and employed to demonstrate learning in each area. For example, the terms *desert, rain forest, mountain, tundra,* and *grasslands* describe various geographic features of the environment. In order to differentiate and discuss, common ground knowledge of this content-specific language is necessary. Beyond the vocabulary of the discipline, learners need activity-specific language to negotiate meaning within each content area. There are four types of activity-specific language: (a) procedural language, (b) descriptive language, (c) the language of reasoning, and (d) explanatory language.

Procedural language reflects the sequencing of intentions according to both order and time. Procedural language might be utilized to construct time lines representing the battles of the Civil War, the nature of the water cycle, the steps in two-digit division, or the process of using oil paints. Words that denote order, time sequence, and relationships form the vocabulary of procedural language.

Descriptive language clarifies more specific components of learning. The Battle of Gettysburg, evaporation, 27 remainder 16, or impressionism more specifically point the learner toward knowledge. Part of descriptive language is reflective language, which includes the thinking, wondering, and imagining that are a part of the reflective process of learning. A student might wonder what might have happened if the South had won the Civil War, why we know evaporation occurs if we can't see it happening, how many 1-inch cubes would fill a 10-inch by 10-inch cube, what type of strokes and pastel colors can be identified in a Monet masterpiece. Introspective reflections during learning can be articulated through descriptive and reflective language leading toward the construction of meaning.

The *language of reasoning* causes the learner to operate through higher level thinking. A child might compare the fragile landscape of the desert to the lush growth of a tropical rain forest. Learners might predict the outcome of boiling a pot of water. Young mathematicians might infer the relationship of equivalent fractions through visual models. Words like *might, maybe, if . . . then,* and *suppose* recur throughout the language of reasoning as learners use language to "figure out" how our world operates.

Explanatory language recounts, describes, and justifies the findings and outcomes of learning that have taken place. Explaining the impact of the defeat at Gettysburg, reporting the outcome of an experiment, articulating the outcome of a problem-solving situation in mathematics, and discussing the impact of impressionism on the art world requires definitive language that summarizes, generalizes, and pulls the threads of understanding together.

At the top of the pyramid of language learning lies the *construction of meaning* that reflects the knowledge of the content areas. That knowledge can be documented, assessed, performed through language and language-based activities and projects that reflect learning. As understanding evidences itself as knowledge, language plays a key role in elevating the learner from novice to expert and in moving from speculation to knowledge. Language surrounds learning in all the content areas and provides the scaffolding support needed to negotiate the channels of learning in social studies, science, and mathematics.

Interdisciplinary Language Arts

Language-based activities involving reading, writing, listening, speaking, viewing, and visual representation weave through the content areas. Response journals to Christopher Paul Curtis's *The Watsons Go to Birmingham—1963,* reflections on the poems in Joan Bransfield Graham's *Flicker Flash* that visually enhance the understanding of light, and problem solving one's way through Jon Sczieska's *Math Curse* or *Science Verse* provide literature-based and language-based learning across the curriculum. The K-W-L Chart (what I know; what I want to find out; what I learned) provides an organizational framework for inquiry in all content areas. Figure 14.1 listed several examples of language arts activities that meaningfully find their way into content area instruction. These practices can "count" as language arts in the context of interdisciplinary learning. For teachers pressured by the demands of the curriculum and the pressures of assessment, the content areas related to social studies, science, mathematics, and the arts can become content-embedded arenas for well-connected language arts activities. The basic principles of learning that hold true for language development should guide the curricular and instructional decisions teachers make in the content areas.

Social Studies and Language Arts Connections

What is the best way for teachers to pinpoint specific language arts activities that creatively and meaningfully link to the social studies curriculum? Because the connections are quite clear (Farris, 2004), because the possibilities are seemingly endless (Cordeiro, 1995), and because teachers typically have confidence in teaching the social studies, this content area is strongly suggested as the first to fully integrate with the language arts (Roser & Keehn, 2002). There are six social studies that constitute this curricular area at the elementary and middle levels: (a) anthropology, (b) economics, (c) history, (d) geography, (e) political

Fourth graders draw and label a mural for a social studies project.

science and civics education, and (f) sociology. These areas are fully integrated and supported by the *Curriculum Standards for the Social Studies* (National Council for the Social Studies, 1994).

Across the Country (and Around the World) Through Picture Books

Picture books provide an excellent means of conveying an understanding of social studies. Although textbooks contain factual information and explanation, literature can make geographic concepts come to life for children (Louie, 1993). The integration of reading, writing, and social studies is effectively accomplished through a classroom journey in which picture books transport students to another time, place, or culture while providing standards-based learning about the United States and the world today.

Start with a large outline map of the United States or the world. Throughout the unit, add names and symbols from books as it evolves into a class mural. Use Sharon Purviance and Marcia O'Shell's *Alphabet Annie Announces an All-American Alphabet* and write alliterative sentences related to states that include the names of cities, products, and traits—for example, "Susie Strauss skis, sings, and strums on the slopes of Sun Valley."

Read aloud general books such as Woody Guthrie's *This Land is Your Land,* which paints a visual image of "the redwood forests," to "the wheat fields waving" to "the diamond desert." Read aloud specific titles for each section of the country to enhance the journey. The Literature Cluster on page 442 provides some guidelines. Culminate the experience with Amy Cohn's *From Sea to Shining Sea: A Treasury of American Folklore and Folk Songs* or Barbara Younger's *Purple Mountains Majesty: The Story of Katharine Lee Bates and "America the Beautiful."* Discovering the regions and history of America can carry a class for a few weeks or might even weave a weekly web throughout the entire school year.

Teachers can easily adapt strategies and locate literature to move beyond their borders to discover the world. Anita Lobel's *Away from Home* takes an alphabetical journey to the corners of the world as the alliterative pattern becomes a model for a class journey. Marjorie Priceman's *How to Make an Apple Pie and See the World* whisks the readers across the globe to access first-class ingredients for a sumptuous apple pie. The classroom becomes a collage of language-based activities that expand global understandings.

PICTURE BOOKS ACROSS THE COUNTRY (AND AROUND THE WORLD)

The Northeast

Bial, Raymond (1993). *Amish home.* Boston: Houghton Mifflin.

Hendershot, (1987). *In coal country.* Illus. by Thomas B. Allen. New York: Knopf.

Lasky, Kathryn (1983). *Sugaring time.* Illus. by C. G. Knight. New York: Macmillan.

Mitchell, Barbara (1997). *Waterman's child.* Illus. by Daniel San Souci. New York: HarperCollins.

Parnell, Peter (1986). *Winter barn.* New York: Macmillan.

Van Leeuwen, Jane (1998). *Nothing here but trees.* New York: Dial.

Yolen, Jane (1998). *Raising Yoder's barn.* Illus. by Bernie Fuchs. Boston: Little, Brown.

The Southeast

Allen, Thomas B (1989). *On granddaddy's farm.* New York: Knopf.

Asch, Frank (1997). *Sawgrass poems: A view of the Everglades.* Illus. by Ted Levin. San Diego: Harcourt.

George, Jean C. (1995). *Everglades.* Illus. by Wendell Minor. New York: HarperCollins.

Milnes, Gerald (1990). *Granny will your dog bite? And other mountain rhymes.* Illus. by K. Root. New York: Knopf.

Rylant, Cynthia (1991). *Appalachia: The voice of sleeping birds.* San Diego: Harcourt.

Wells, Rosemary (1998). *Mary on horseback: Three mountain stories.* Illus. by Peter McCarty. New York: Dial.

The Midwest and Great Plains

Sandburg, Carl (1998). *Grassroots.* Illus. by Wendell Minor. New York: HarperCollins.

Thomas, Joyce Carol (1998). *I have heard of a land.* Illus. by Floyd Cooper. New York: HarperCollins.

Turner, Ann (1997). *Mississippi mud:* Three prairie journals. Illus. by Robert J. Bloke. New York: HarperCollins.

Williams, David (1993). *Grandma Essie's covered wagon.* Illus. by W. Sadowski. New York: Knopf.

The Southwest

Baylor, Byrd (1983). *The best town in the world.* Illus. by Ron Himler. New York: Scribner.

DePaola, Tomie (1983). *The tale of the bluebonnet: An old tale of Texas.* New York: Putnam.

Kellogg, Steven (1986). *Pecos Bill.* New York: Morrow.

Lesser, Carolyn (1997). *Storm in the desert.* Illus. by Ted Rand. San Diego: Harcourt.

Wright-Frierson, Virginia (1997). *Desert scrapbook: Dawn to dusk in the Sonoran Desert.* New York: Simon & Schuster.

The Far West

Ada, Alma Flor (1997). *Gathering the sun: An alphabet in Spanish and English.* Illus. by Simon Silva. New York: Scholastic.

DePaola, Tomie (1988). *The legend of the Indian paintbrush.* New York: Putnam.

Goble, Paul (1985). *The great race of the birds and animals.* New York: Bradbury.

Lewis, Claudia (1987). *Long ago in Oregon.* Illus. by J. Fontaine. New York: Harper & Row.

Service, Robert (1987). *The cremation of Sam McGee.* New York: Greenwillow.

Around the World

Chin-Lee Cynthia (1987). *A is for Asia.* Illus. by Yumi Heo. New York: Scholastic.

Dooley, Norah (1996). *Everybody bakes bread.* Illus. by Peter J. Thornton. Minneapolis, MN: Carolrhoda.

Knight, Margy Burns (1996). *Talking walls.* Illus. by Anne S. O'Brien. Gardiner, ME: Tilbury House.

Lewin, Ted (1996). *Market!* New York: Lothrop, Lee, & Shepard.

Sturges, Philemon (1998). *Bridges are to cross.* Illus. by Giles Laroche. New York: Putnam.

Wells, Ruth (1992). *A to zen: A book of Japanese culture.* Illus. by Yoshi. Saxonville, MA: Picture Book Studio.

Reflecting on History Through Readers Theatre, Drama, and First-Hand Accounts

Readers theatre provides a motivating format for blending oral language, dramatic reading, careful listening, and quality literature, particularly from a historical perspective (Young & Vardell, 1993). Readers theatre not only improves reading fluency but it enhances understanding of historical contexts and attitudes. Whether reading from a prepared script or altering the text to fit a readers theatre format, the value of this engaged activity spans both language arts and social studies.

Katie's Trunk by Ann Turner contains a blend of both narrative and dialogue by several characters. A script can easily be prepared giving the reader a glimpse into the beginnings of the American Revolution. History can be brought to life in a dramatic reading of the words of common people who witnessed the disagreements leading to the fight for America's freedom. Similarly, *Bull Run* by Paul Fleischman presents a ready-made dramatic reading for up to sixteen students. The text provides two-page reflections by eight Northern and eight Southern characters of different stature and backgrounds before, during, and after the historic battle of Bull Run. The perspective of soldiers, common folk, and leaders reflects the changing thoughts and view about war itself. The words are powerful and capture the dialect and reality of the Civil War period. The performance read from the text will blend the powerful voices that occur intermittently throughout the book. This book places the reader in the role of a historical character while reading fluency, articulation, and expression abound. Because such books can be easily converted to scripts, even a single chapter from a historical fiction title will provide varied script-writing opportunities in the middle school.

Kornfeld & Leyden (2005) suggest that drama provides a way to link the present to a historical past that seems unrelated to a child's own life. Books such as Jeanette Winter's *Follow the Drinking Gourd* and Deborah Hopkinson's *Sweet Clara and the Freedom Quilt* can be acted out to gain a better understanding of the Underground Railroad. Reading Rosa Park and Jim Haskins's *I am Rosa Parks* and Eloise Greenfield's Y*oung Rosa Parks: Civil Rights Heroine* combined with dramatic reenactments provide richer understanding of the power of individual stands during the Civil Rights movement. Integrating literature, drama, and history offers students vital comprehensive learning experiences as they experience the joy of learning through collaborative efforts.

Lesson Plan 14.1 invites students to take on the role of a young Civil War soldier who is writing heartfelt letters from the war front. Blending the emotions of first-hand accounts of the personal aspects of history with historical facts and relevant information provide a meaningful historical experience through writing.

LESSON PLAN 14.1

TITLE: **Writing Letters Home**

Grade Level: 5–8

Time Frame: Three or four 45-minute sessions

Standards

IRA/NCTE Standards: 1, 5, 12

NETS for Students: 5

Objectives

- Students will access their prior knowledge of the Civil War to simulate first-hand accounts (letters) from the war front.
- Students will demonstrate their understanding of the events and circumstances of the Civil War by including historically accurate and/or relevant facts and details in their letters to the homefront.

Materials

- Assortment of books about the Civil War with primary accounts:

  Armstrong, Jennifer (2005). *Photo by Brady: A Picture of the Civil War*. Atheneum Books for Young Readers.

  Gragg, Rod, ed. (2001). *From Fields of Fire and Glory: Letters of the Civil War*. Chronicle Books.

  Murphy, Jim (1990). *The Boys' War*. Clarion Books.
- Computers with Internet for student use
- Word-processing programs and/or paper and pens for publishing letters

Motivation

- Share teacher-selected excerpts from the literature. Emphasize the books' authentic photographs and primary accounts (letters, quotations, etc.). Discuss the importance of the Civil War letters (primary accounts of the war, often written by young soldiers) and what it must have been like to receive such letters.

Procedures

Day 1

- Explain to students that they will access their prior knowledge of the Civil War to write a letter from the point of view of a young soldier (or nurse, civilian, etc.). Review several examples of letters from *The Boys' War* and *From Fields of Fire and Glory: Letters of the Civil War* (or similar books) and discuss common features of the letters. Emphasize that the students' letters should be personal and heartfelt, yet historically accurate.
- Explain to students what they should include in their letters. You may suggest the following:

  Reference to foods or food shortages

  Reference to historically accurate battles, geographic locations, and events

  Description of conditions at the camps

  Historically accurate dates

  Personal thoughts about the war, family conflicts or circumstances, or future dreams and plans
- Emphasize that letters should be written in first person, from the point of view of a soldier (or nurse, civilian, etc.).
- Allow students time to gather facts and information, organize the information, and begin their first drafts.

Days 2–4

- Continue to share and discuss photographs and letters from the literature. Introduce the PBS Web site *Images of the Civil War* (www.pbs.org/civilwar/cwimages) as an additional resource for visual images.
- In writing workshop, provide students time to draft, revise, edit, and publish their letters.
- Final copies may be word processed or written in neat handwriting. (For an authentic touch, use parchment paper and encourage students to use cursive font.)
- Students may share their letters with the class by reading them aloud, posting them on a bulletin board, and/or publishing a class book.

Assessment

- Teacher-developed rubric or checklist to assess students' ability to write with an authentic voice from a soldier's point of view and incorporate historically accurate and relevant facts and details.

Accommodation/Modification

- Use additional literature (of various reading levels) and online resources to suit students' reading abilities and interests.
- To differentiate instruction, increase (or reduce) the number of facts each student is expected to include in his or her letter.

Visit the Meeting the Standards module in Chapter 14 of the Companion Website at www.prenhall.com/hancock to adapt this lesson to meet your state's standards.

From Picture Book Biographies to Bio-Poems

There is a vast assortment of simple biographies that combine picture books with historical data on famous persons. Encouraging students to read these biographies, learn the historical background surrounding a famous person, and incorporate a related writing activity is both efficient and effective. The Literature Cluster on page 446 features picture book biographies of famous Americans across disciplines as well as notable world figures.

A related writing activity which emerges naturally from a study of historical figures involves composing a nine-line "bio-poem" (Danielson, 1989) about those individuals portrayed in picture book biographies. The format consists of nine lines of biographical information:

Line 1: First name of a biographical subject
Line 2: Four adjectives describing the subject
Line 3: Husband, wife, sibling, etc. of. . .
Line 4: Who loves . . . (three people, places, or things)
Line 5: Who feels . . . (three emotional phrases)
Line 6: Who fears . . . (three things)
Line 7: Who would like to see . . . (three dreams)
Line 8: Resident of . . . (country, city, state)
Line 9: Last name of biographical subject

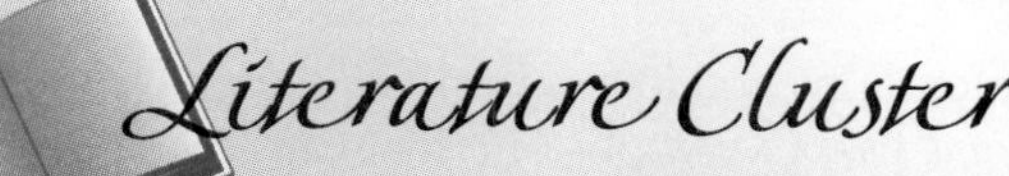

PICTURE BOOK BIOGRAPHIES FOR CREATING BIO-POEMS

Adler, David A. (2005). *Joe Louis*. Illus. by M. Widener. New York: Atheneum.

Brighton, Catherine (1990). *Mozart: Scenes from the childhood of the great composer*. New York: Doubleday.

Bruchac, Joseph (2004). *Jim Thorpe's bright path*. Illus. by S. D. Nelson. New York: Lee & Low.

Cooper, Floyd (1994). *Coming home: From the life of Langston Hughes*. New York: Philomel.

Corey, Shana (2000). *You forgot your skirt, Amelia Bloomer!* Illus. by Chesley McLaren. New York: Scholastic.

Farris, Christine King (2003). *My brother, Martin: A sister remembers growing up wth Rev. Dr. Martin Luther King Jr.* Illus. by Chris Soentpiet. New York: Simon & Schuster.

Krensky, Stephen (2001). *Shooting for the moon: The amazing life and times of Annie Oakley*. Illus. by Bernie Fuchs. New York: Farrar, Straus & Giroux.

Littlesugar, Amy (1998). *Shake Rag: From the life of Elvis Presley*. Illus. by Floyd Cooper. New York: Philomel.

McDonough, Yona Zeldis (1997). *Anne Frank*. Illus. by Malcah Zeldis. New York: Holt.

Osborne, Mary Pope (2002). *New York's bravest*. Illus. by Steve Johnson & Lou Fancher. New York: Knopf.

Following the reading of Stephen Krensky's *Shooting for the Moon: The Amazing Life and Times of Annie Oakley*, two preservice teachers served as models by composing the bio-poem shown in Student Sample 14.1, which highlights the personality and achievements of Annie Oakley.

This bio-poem became a model for a display of fifth-grade bio-poems on a "Who's Who?" bio-poem bulletin board inspired by picture book biographies featuring famous people across all disciplines.

STUDENT SAMPLE 14.1 A Preservice Teacher Model of a Bio-Poem.*

Annie (Phoebe Ann)
Sister to six brothers and sisters
Daughter to loving mother and hardworking father
Committed, determined, giving
Who loves to shoot, perform and walk in the woods
Who likes practice, hard work and success
Who fears being poor again, being alone and the death of a family member or friend
Who gets angry when people use her, over hunt and take things for granted
Who hopes to continue performing in the Wild West Show, aim
high to hit her mark and continue to shoot for the moon
Resident of Ohio
Oakley (Mozee)

**Based on biographical information in Stephen Krensky (2001).* Shooting for the moon: The amazing life and times of Annie Oakley. *Illus. by Bernie Fuchs. New York: Atheneum.*

Using Historical Fiction as a Basis for Response and Character Journals

A response journal is a place for students to express their thoughts, insights, feeling, reactions, questions, connections, and opinions while reading a book (Hancock, 2004). Written response to literature is a powerful means of capturing special transactions with books that make reading a rewarding journey. Historical fiction, in particular, invites students to record individual thoughts while reading a book about a specific period in American or world history.

The resulting journal entries require a transfer of the reader to another time and place. Readers bring life to historical fictional characters and find themselves immersed in historical context and events. Historical facts, figures, and names weave themselves into journal entries. For teachers desiring to offer some guidelines to students writing journal responses, the following questions may serve as response prompts to connect history and language arts:

- What historical facts are mentioned in the book that you already knew from our study of this historical period?
- What new and interesting facts were presented?
- How does the life of the main character fit into the historical period (in terms of dress, education, societal expectations, etc.)?
- How do the actions of the main character fit into the standards for the historical period?
- What impression of life during this historical period are projected?

Literature response journals must always capture a student's thoughts spontaneously during reading rather than retrospectively after completion of the novel. A growing understanding of a historical period will emerge through the unfolding reactions of the reader during the reading process.

Another means of extending response to historical fiction is to have students write in a character journal—a journal in which the student becomes the main character by writing in his or her voice (Hancock, 1993). Karen Hesse's *Letters from Rifka,* for example, models a character journal as it is written in first-person narrative style and presents a series of journal entries written by Rifka in the margins of a book of Pushkin poetry as she emigrates from Russia to America. The type of historical fiction that best lends itself to character journals must have a strong character with whom the reader can identify blended with the presence of a strong sense of a historical period. Student Sample 14.2 illustrates an entry from a character journal entry prepared by Rebecca, who writes in the voice of Rifka as the soldiers question her at the train station. The Literature Cluster on page 448 presents a list of historical fiction that might be used with a literature response or character journal.

Putting It All Together: Thematic Social Studies Unit

Because interdisciplinary instruction advocates the teaching of integrated rather than isolated bits of information, the thematic unit becomes an essential component of social studies and language arts teaching. The selection and elaboration of a social studies theme or concept through literature and literacy reflect the synthesis of integrated instruction. Well-conceived thematic units that are built on a blend of content and literacy can lead students beyond facts and dates to a deeper understanding of concept (Shanahan, Robinson, & Schneider, 1995).

Designing thematic instruction and planning an array of literacy-based activities associated with them provides a solid base for effective teaching (Pappas, Kiefer, and

STUDENT SAMPLE 14.2
A Third-Grade Character Journal: Language Arts and Social Studies.

The gcards looked at me. I didn't know what to do. One of them came over, "What are you doing here?" "I'm looking for my ring." I said. The other one was looking in the train. He had found my knapsack and had threw it on the ground. "Whats this" he said looking at me and why is it a so heavy bag. It is my landrey, I am taking to the pond to wash. I should go now, running to the trian. Stop! he yelled. The train whistel she Jumped into the trian, then it left. They were out of sight.

Literature Cluster

HISTORICAL FICTION FOR LITERATURE RESPONSE OR CHARACTER JOURNALS

Avi (1990). *The true confessions of Charlotte Doyle*. New York: Orchard.

Collier, James Lincoln, & Collier, Christopher (1974). *My brother Sam is dead*. New York: Four Winds Press.

Curtis, Christopher Paul (1996). *The Watsons go to Birmingham—1963*. New York: Delacorte.

Cushman, Karen (1996). *The ballad of Lucy Whipple*. New York: Clarion.

DeFelice, Cynthia (1996). *The apprenticeship of Lucas Whitaker*. New York: Farrar Straus & Giroux.

Draper, Sharon (1997). *Forged by fire*. New York: Atheneum.

Hesse, Karen (1997). *Out of the dust*. New York: Scholastic.

Hom, Jennifer (2001). *Boston Jane*. New York: HarperCollins.

Lowry, Lois (1989). *Number the stars*. Boston: Houghton Mifflin.

MacLachlan, Patricia (1985). *Sarah, plain and tall*. New York: Harper & Row.

Paterson, Katherine (1990). *Lyddie*. New York: Dutton.

Paterson, Katherine (1996). *Jip*. New York: Lodestar.

Peck, Richard (2000). *A year down under*. New York: Dial/Penguin Putnam.

Reeder, Carolyn (1989). *Shades of gray*. New York: Macmillan.

Salisbury, Graham (1994). *Under the blood red sun*. New York: Delacorte.

Taylor, Mildred (1987). *The friendship*. New York: Dial.

Whelan, Gloria (2002). *Angel on the square*. New York: HarperCollins.

Levstik, 1996). Hancock (2004) suggests the following five steps for planning a thematic unit:

- Choose a broad-based theme and title.
- Brainstorm titles of related children's literature.
- Locate additional children's picture books and chapter books through library searches or Internet Web sites.
- Create a graphic web or organizer reflecting the connections between the literature and the subthemes.
- Plan meaningful literacy activities for whole-class, small-group, and individual participation.

Figures 14.3 (The Dirty Thirties) and 14.4 (The Freedom Struggle), two quality samples of thematic units, illustrate this literacy-based process and showcase the literature that surrounds effective social studies and literacy integration.

An excellent resource that encourages teachers to blend literature and the language arts into social studies curriculum is the annual list generated by the National Council for the Social Studies (NCSS) and the Children's Book Council (CBC), entitled *Notable Social Studies Trade Books for Young People.* These listings are organized by the thematic strands of the *Curriculum Standards for Social Studies.* Teachers will find it useful to print this list and highlight titles related to their grade-level curriculum. Another useful resource is the American Library Association journal, *Book Links,* which devotes at least one themed issue each year to topics related to social studies.

Language arts and social studies widen a student's world by providing the opportunity to participate in new experiences, visit new places, and become a genuine part of the past. The rich resources of literature blended with worthy language arts activities brings social studies to life in a way that offers meaningful links to each child's own life.

Mathematics and Language Arts: From Story Problems to Problem Solving

Many teachers are faced with finding new ways to effectively and meaningfully weave the language arts into mathematical learning. The use of reading, writing, listening, speaking, viewing, and visual representation in mathematics leads to greater understanding and learning for students. Many useful written media from the language arts domain become a means of documenting mathematical thought and understanding. From math journals to discussions about math, communicating through the language arts in mathematics is an essential means toward understanding (Whitin & Whitin, 2000). When students communicate mathematical information, they remember it, understand it, and use it to uncover even more information. Teachers must be cognizant of the powerful link between mathematics and the language arts.

- Teachers need to know how to help students grow into accomplished communicators of mathematics who can describe their thought processes clearly.
- Teachers must help children make their thinking visible to others by encouraging them to talk and write about the process they use to problem solve.
- Teachers must naturally embed speaking, writing, and visual representation into daily mathematics learning.

FIGURE 14.3 Thematic social studies unit: The Dirty Thirties (A Better Life's A Comin').

Trials and Tribulations (Dust Bowl)

Booth, David. (1997). *The dust bowl*
Slade, Arthur. (2003). *Dust*
Stanley, Jerry. (1992). *Children of the dust bowl: the true story of the school at Weedpatch camp*
Turner, Ann. (1995). *Dust for dinner*
Yancey, Diane. (2004). *Life during the dust bowl*

Riches to Rags (The Great Depression)

Adler, David. (1999). *The Babe and I*
Brown, Harriet. (2002). *Welcome to Kit's world, 1934: Growing up during America's Great Depression*
Lied, Kate. (1997). *Potato: A tale from the Great Depression*
Munoz Ryan, Pam. (2000). *Esperenza rising*
Taylor, Mildred D. (1976). *Roll of thunder, hear my cry*

Making Do (Life in the 1930's)

Curtis, Christopher Paul. (1999). *Bud, not Buddy*
Friedrich, Elizabeth. (1996). *Leah's pony*
Peck, Richard. (2000). *A year down yonder*
Stewart, Sarah. (1997). *The gardener*

Experiences and Memories (People of the Era)

Durbin, william. (2002). *The journal of C. J. Jackson: a Dust Bowl migrant*
Hesse, Karen. (1997). *Out of the dust.*
Low, Ann Marie. (1984). *Dust bowl diary*
MacLachlan, patricia. (1995). *What you know first*
Moss, Marissa. (2001). *Rosie's journal: A story of a girl in the Great Depression*

There are many communication techniques that can be used to incorporate the language arts as a means of making and communicating mathematical understanding.

Math Journals

The math journal is an effective means of revealing mathematical understanding (or misunderstanding) through writing and visual representation. Writing about mathematics, such as describing how a problem is solved, helps children clarify their thinking and

FIGURE 14.4 Thematic social studies unit: The Freedom Struggle: Freedom For Us All.

A Place Called Freedom (Sander, 1997)

The Fight for Freedom
(The American Revolution, The Civil War)

The Blue and the Gray (Bunting, 1996)
The Hatmaker's Sign: A Story by Benjamin Franklin (Fleming, 1998)
Give Me Liberty: The Story of the Declaration of Independence (Freedman, 2000)
The Amazing Life of Benjamin Franklin (Cross, 2000)
Across Five Aprils (Hunt, 1964)
Charlotte (Deines, 1998)
Dear Ellen Bee: A Civil War Scrapbook of Two Union Spies (Lyons, 2000)
The Boy's War: Confederate and Union Soldiers Talk About the Civil War (Murphy, 1990)
A Young Patriot (Murphy, 1996)
The Revolutionary War (Stewart, 1991)
The Drummer Boy of Vicksburg (Wisler, 1997)

Guaranteed Freedoms
(The Bill of Rights)

An Amish Year (Ammon, 2000)
Nothing But the Truth (Avi, 1991)
The True Confessions of Charlotte Doyle (Avi, 1990)
Toliver's Secret (Brady, 1976)
Sleds on Boston Common (Borden, 2000)
The Landry News (Clements, 1999)
1791–1991 The Bill of Rights and Beyond (1991)
Thunder at Gettysburg (Gauch, 1975)
A Long Way to Go: A Story of Women's Right to vote (Oneal, 1990)
Freedom of Worship (Sherrow, 1997)
The Gold Cadillac (Taylor, 1987)

Let Freedom Ring
(Symbols of Freedom)

A Memorial for Mr. Lincoln (Ashabranner, 1992)
Fireworks, Picnics, and Flags (Giblin, 1983)
Honey, I Love and other Poems (Greenfield, 1972)
Sweet Clara and the Freedom Quilt (Hopkinson, 1993)
The Wagon (Johnston, 1996)
Famous Illustrated Speeches and Documents: The Pledge of Allegiance (Kallen, 1994)
The Story of the Star-Spangled Banner: By the Dawn's Early Light (Kroll, 1994)
The Gettysburg Address (Lincoln, 1995)
The Flag We Love (Ryan, 1996)
Country Road (Souci, 1993)
The Memory Coat (Woodruff, 1999)

Individual Freedom
(Equal for All)

More Than Anything Else (Bradley, 1995)
Through My Eyes (Bridges, 1999)
White Socks Only (Coleman, 1996)
Paperboy (Holland, 1999)
Virgie Goes to School With Us Boys (Howard, 2000)
Run Away Home (McKassack, 1997)
Caterina: The Clever Farm Girl (Peterson, 1996)
My Dream of Martin Luther King (Ringgold, 1995)
Amelia and Eleanor Go For a Ride (Ryan, 1999)
Journey to Freedom: A story of the Underground Railroad (Wright, 1994)

Personal Freedom
(Choices)

The Bravest of Us All (Arnold, 2000)
Train to Somewhere (Bunting, 1996)
Because of Winn Dixie (DiCamillo, 2000)
Grandmother's Pigeon (Erdich, 1996)
Out of the Dust (Hesse, 1997)
Amber on the Mountain (Johnston, 1994)
Boom Town (Levitin, 1998)
Holes (Sachar, 1998)
Maniac Magee (Spinelli, 1990)
The Other Side (Woodson 2001)

Pink and Say (Polacco, 1994)

develop deeper understanding (National Council of Teachers of Mathematics, 1996). Such writing or drawing about mathematics has several objectives:

- Encourages learners to reflect on what they know.
- Gives learners a new perspective on a mathematical concept.
- Provides an individual record of mathematical understandings.

A daily math journal might be initiated with various prompts that accompany a problem-solving situation:

- To explain your reasoning, use words, numbers, and, and if you like, pictures.
- Write or draw in your journal whatever will help you think about solving the problem.
- I think the answer is ____________. I think this because ___________.
- I figured out the answer by ____________________. The answer is _________.
- Today I learned ____.
- I'm not sure about _______________________________________.
- I'm wondering about ______________________________________.

The individual nature of journals in math parallel the uniqueness of the language arts learner. All children vary in the way they use their math journals. With risk-taking encouragement, they develop a unique style that conveys developing conceptual understanding or misunderstanding.

Another way of using the math journal is to use writing and visual representation to represent mathematical ideas. Children can be encouraged to explain subtraction or demonstrate equivalent fractions through drawings and words.

Authoring Mathematics

Student-authored math problems are a popular means of creating a deeper application of mathematical concepts. Using student names, incorporating real-life or classroom situations, and creating and graphing class surveys are just some ways in which children become authors of their own mathematical examples for class problem solving. A "mathematician's chair" parallels the "author's chair" as talking the language of math enhances learning. The following probes serve as examples of student reaction to self-created mathematical problems:

- What did you like about the problem?
- Do you agree or disagree with the solution?
- How could the author improve the problem or solution?
- How could the author change the problem to create a new problem or change the solution to arrive at a new way to solve the problem?

By "talking the language of mathematics," children's communication may lead toward greater understanding. By "writing or visually representing the language of mathematics," students also indicate their personal level of mathematical understanding. Student Sample 14.3 reflects a third grader's composition of a word problem and a visual representation of its solution. Student Sample 14.4 provides a bar graph that visually represents class data collection and analysis of second graders' favorite soft drinks. Both examples mirror the power of both writing and visual representation in making mathematical understanding visible through words or pictures.

STUDENT SAMPLE 14.3 A Student-Created Word Problem and Solution.

Literature and Mathematics

Whitin & Whitin (2001) elaborate on "what counts" in math-related books for children. From number sense to counting, from mathematical operations to pattern recognition, from geometric shapes to problem solving, children's literature provides a means of linking language and mathematics. Matching literature to the curricular goals of your grade-level in mathematics provides motivation, clarity, visual aids, and verbal reinforcement of mathematical concepts. Literature-based activities can facilitate many goals related to mathematical concepts:

- Inspire and motivate learners to view their surroundings from a mathematical perspective.
- Demonstrate mathematical concepts in a supportive context.
- Offer a range of genre options for exploring a mathematical concept.

STUDENT SAMPLE 14.4 Second-Grade Favorite "Pop" Survey: Data Collection and Graphic Analysis.

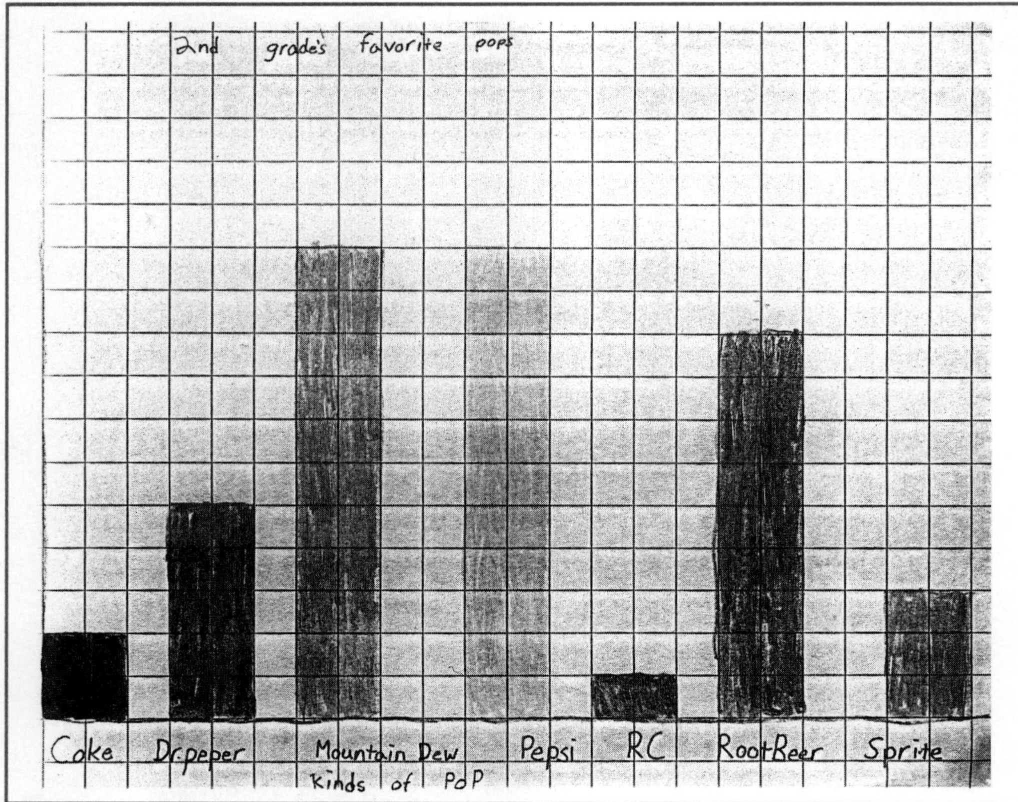

- Invite students to make personal connections with mathematical ideas, thus seeing the relevance of mathematics in their own lives.

Patricia Hunsader (2004) created a mathematics trade book evaluation rubric that evaluates both mathematical and literary standards. The following are some of the questions she considers in selecting relevant mathematics literature:

> Is the book's mathematical content (text, computation, scale, vocabulary, and graphics) correct and accurate?
>
> Is the book's mathematics content visible and effectively presented?
>
> Is the book's mathematics content intellectually and developmentally appropriate for its audience?
>
> Does the book facilitate the reader's involvement in, and use and transfer of, its mathematics?
>
> Do the book's mathematics and story complement each other?
>
> How great are the resources needed to help readers benefit from the book's mathematics? (p. 623)

Given the multiple benefits to students of using appropriate literature in mathematics, the extra effort in answering these questions is most certainly warranted.

The clear, crisp, color photographs in Tana Hoban's picture books invite young children from pre-kindergarten to Grade 1 to observe and discuss the shapes and patterns that make up our everyday world. Books like *Shapes, Shapes, Shapes* and *Round, Round,*

Round also become the model for patterned books created by the children themselves. For example, after reading *Circles, Triangles, and Squares,* children can take a community or playground walk to observe those shapes in their local environment. A photograph captures their shape and they return to the classroom to create a book page for a class book of shapes. A story frame of "I saw a __________." accompanied by a shape drawing and the photograph documents the observation of shapes in the environment. The pages can be laminated and bound into a class book that emergent readers can read and enjoy over and over again.

Other books such as Suzanne Aker's *What Comes in 2s, 3s,* and *4s?* and Diane Hamm's *How Many Feet in the Bed?* provide additional models for creating page-by-page patterned books based on simple mathematical concepts such as pattern, ratios and counting. Arlene Alda's paintings inspire children to view artwork with a mathematical eye in *Arlene Alda's ABC* and Arlene Alda's *1, 2, 3, What Do You See?* Even young children can begin to warm to mathematics through literature, language, and language arts connections.

Perhaps the most common children's literature based in mathematical concepts are the counting books. While many view counting books as simple sequences of the numbers 1 through 10, the astute teacher will note that the numerical concepts have become more intricate in recent years. Counting books emphasize some of the simplest to some of the more complex mathematical counting. Each can become the prototype for the creation of class counting books and accelerated or decelerated to the developmental level of the math learner.

Literature and mathematics have become "best friends" as books inspire and translate math into a rich experience. Stories actually enable students to make personal connections to mathematical ideas and see the relevance of mathematics in their lives. Not all books that attest to combine mathematical concept with story are effective, however. The Literature Cluster on page 456 suggests books that will enhance mathematical understandings through well-written text and visual, illustrative accuracy.

Writing with a Mathematical Focus

Many children thrive on the opportunity to integrate their narrative storytelling abilities with mathematical situations. Writing about the adventures in a garden from the perspective of a 3-centimeter bug gets the creative juices flowing and provides a comparative model for measurement. Dayle Ann Dodds's *Minnie's Diner: A Multiplying Menu* provides a template for children to write their own story on the power of exponential values. Even Sarah Weeks *Two Eggs, Please* provides a backdrop for explaining a concept as simple as *same and different.* Mathematical poetry used as motivation for lessons can begin with several by Shel Silverstein. "Band-Aids" or "The Monkey" from *Where the Sidewalk Ends* both provide an imaginative language link to mathematics.

Expository writing with a mathematical focus might be perceived through *Liberty* or *Rushmore* by Lynn Curlee, which focus on mathematical dimensions of these national treasures while also providing comparative dates of completion, costs, and length of construction.

Using student writing to assess understanding of mathematics is a viable means of evaluation. Writing about mathematics will reveal what a student has learned, the level of reasoning applied to the concept, and noticeable gaps in understanding or information. Writing is important for learning about individual understanding and skills and providing beneficial experiences to particular students. Writing also provides an excellent vehicle for communicating with parents about what their children are learning and the progress they are making. Hence, language arts provides a meaningful link for documenting mathematical understandings.

Literature Cluster

MATHEMATICAL TITLES WITH A MEANINGFUL BLEND

Anno, Masaichiro, and Mitsumasa, Anno (1983). *Anno's mysterious multiplying jar*. Putnam. (factorials)

Anno, Mitsumasa (1995). *Anno's magic seeds*. New York: Philomel. (grouping)

Brooks, Bruce (1997). *NBA by the numbers*. New York: Scholastic. (counting by 10s)

Demi (1997). *One grain of rice: A mathematical folktale*. New York: Scholastic. (progressions)

Fleming, Denise (1992). *Count!* New York: Holt. (counting by 10s)

Franco, Betsy (2004). *Mathematickles!* Illus. by Steven Salerno. New York: McElderry. (math + language equations)

Friedman, Ailenn (1994). *The king's commissioners*. Illus. by Susan Guevara. New York: Scholastic. (counting large numbers)

Hopkins, Lee Bennett (Ed.) (1997). *Marvelous math: A book of poems*. Illus. by Karen Barbour. New York: Simon & Schuster.

Leedy, Loreen (1998). *Measuring Penny*. New York: Holt. (measurement)

Leedy, Loreen (2005). *The great graph contest*. New York: Holiday House. (graphing)

McKissack, Patricia (1992). *A million fish . . . . more or less*. Illus. by Dena Schutzer. New York: Knopf. (numbers integral to a tale)

Milich, Zoran (2005). *City 1 2 3*. Toronto: Kids Can Press. (observation/counting)

Nagda, Ann Whitehead (2005). *Panda math: Learning about subtraction from Hua Mei and Mei Sheng*. In collaboration with the San Diego Zoo. New York: Holt. (subtraction)

Neuschwander, Cindy (2005). *Mummy math: An adventure in geometry*. Illus. by Bryan Langdo. New York: Holt. (geometry)

Schmandt-Besserat, Denise (1999). *The history of counting*. Illus. by Michael Hays. New York: Morrow.

Schwartz, David M. (1985). *How much is a million?* Illus. by Steven Kellogg. New York: Lothrop, Lee & Shepard. (large numbers)

Schwartz, David M. (1989). *If you made a million*. Illus. by Steven Kellogg. New York: Lothrop, Lee, & Shepard.

Schwartz, David M. (1999). *If you hopped like a frog*. Illus. by James Warhola. New York: Scholastic. (ratio/proportion)

Schwartz, David M. (1999). *On beyond a million:* An amazing math journey. Illus. by Paul Meisel. New York: Random House. (larger numbers)

Scieszka, Jon (1995). *Math curse*. Illus. by Lane Smith. New York: Viking. (problem solving)

Sierra, Judy (1997). *Counting crocodiles*. Illus. by Will Hildebrand. San Diego: Harcourt.

Language Arts and Science: From Observation to Data Analysis

How do children learn science? Remarkably, learning in science incorporates some of the same principles for effective instruction in which children learn the language arts. Observe the links between parallel terminology and philosophy that pervade both science and language arts learning:

- Actively engaging in learning through hands-on activities
- Constructing knowledge through collaboration
- Providing both time and opportunities to engage with material
- Utilizing familiar, everyday phenomena as a rich focus for study

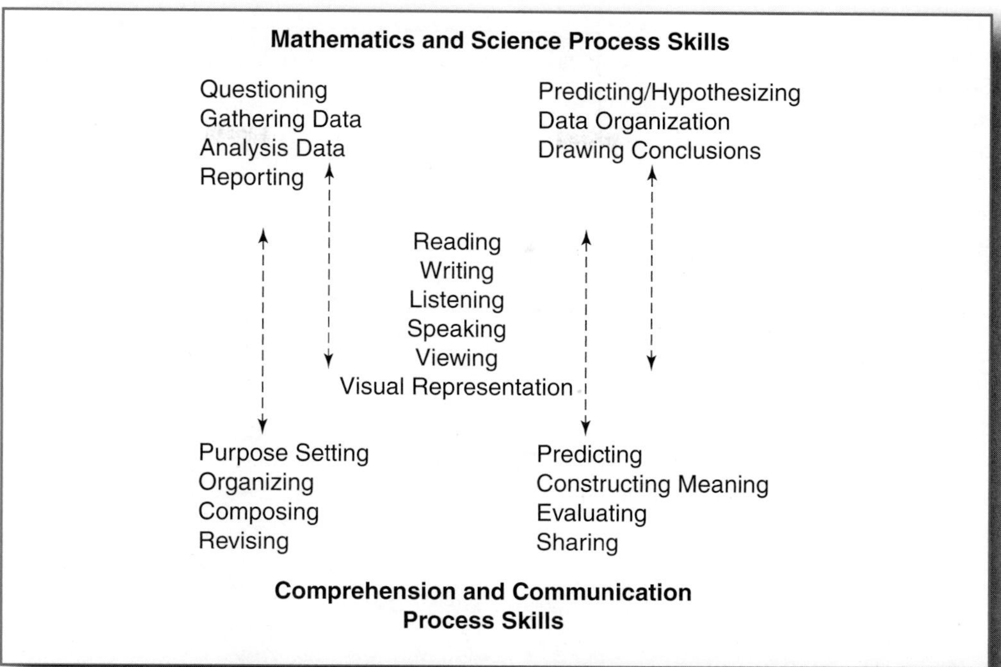

FIGURE 14.5 The Reciprocal Nature of Literacy Processes and Mathematics and Science Understanding.

- Capturing both the wonder and inquiry of science as part of learning
- Feeling (aesthetic response) as well as knowing (efferent response) as essential parts of science learning
- Continual revision of their understanding of the world parallel developmental levels of the learner

These instructional principles for science indeed parallel the instructional principles of language arts presented in Chapter 1.

The reciprocal nature of literacy processes and mathematics and science understanding is shown in Figure 14.5, lists both the process skills of science (questioning, predicting/hypothesizing, data gathering, data organization, data analysis, drawing conclusions, reporting) and the parallel processes of literacy comprehension and communication (purpose setting, predicting, organizing, constructing meaning, composing, evaluating, revising, sharing). Both the science and the literacy process skills are activated through the language arts (reading, writing, listening, speaking, viewing, and visual representation). The goals of both literacy and science are meaning-centered. Thus, the process skills necessary for constructing meaning and communicating understanding are integrated through the language arts.

Science Logs

As is the case in mathematics, the use of writing and visual representation become key vehicles for promoting observations and predictions (Doris, 1991). A science log invites the young scientist to record observations through visual representation and words. Even with very young children, the power of observation through art and language becomes a powerful tool for learning. Two examples are shown in Student Samples 14.5 and 14.6—David's observations of a baby chick and Jennifer's observations of a plant.

Name of Scientist David

I looked at A Babby chiK

A picture of what I saw

I noticed The chik are 2 wecks old and They are grew ther first fedrs. They git skair and they are changing culer.

STUDENT SAMPLE 14.5 A Second-Grade Animal Observation: Language and Visual Representation.

As children's observation increases, so too do the properties they may observe and record in any given experiment. Figure 14.6 presents an example of an observation recording form (Fisher, 1995), which provides an upper primary template for visual representation and textual evidence of understanding for comparative observational skills. As intermediate students transition to spiral notebooks or science logs, their data collection still supports the visual and textual focus of the language arts.

Science and Literature

Literature provides scientific information to promote the higher-level thinking skills that are a part of expository and informational reading. Expository skills such as description, compare/contrast, cause/effect, classification, and sequence can be utilized in the reading of scientific informational text. For example, Seymour Simon's *Crocodiles and Alligators* provides the scientific content for a Venn diagram.

Author studies of science trade books provide models for the scientific process. Patricia Lauber, Sandra Markle, Laurence Pringle, and Seymour Simon all have ample books that reveal their scientific process of inquiry, data collection, and data analysis. Authors do bring scientific expertise and process to the development of their trade books.

Challenging students to read science-based informational books provides them with an opportunity to learn more about a self-selected science topic. After locating interesting

STUDENT SAMPLE 14.6 A Second-Grade Plant Observation: Language and Visual Representation.

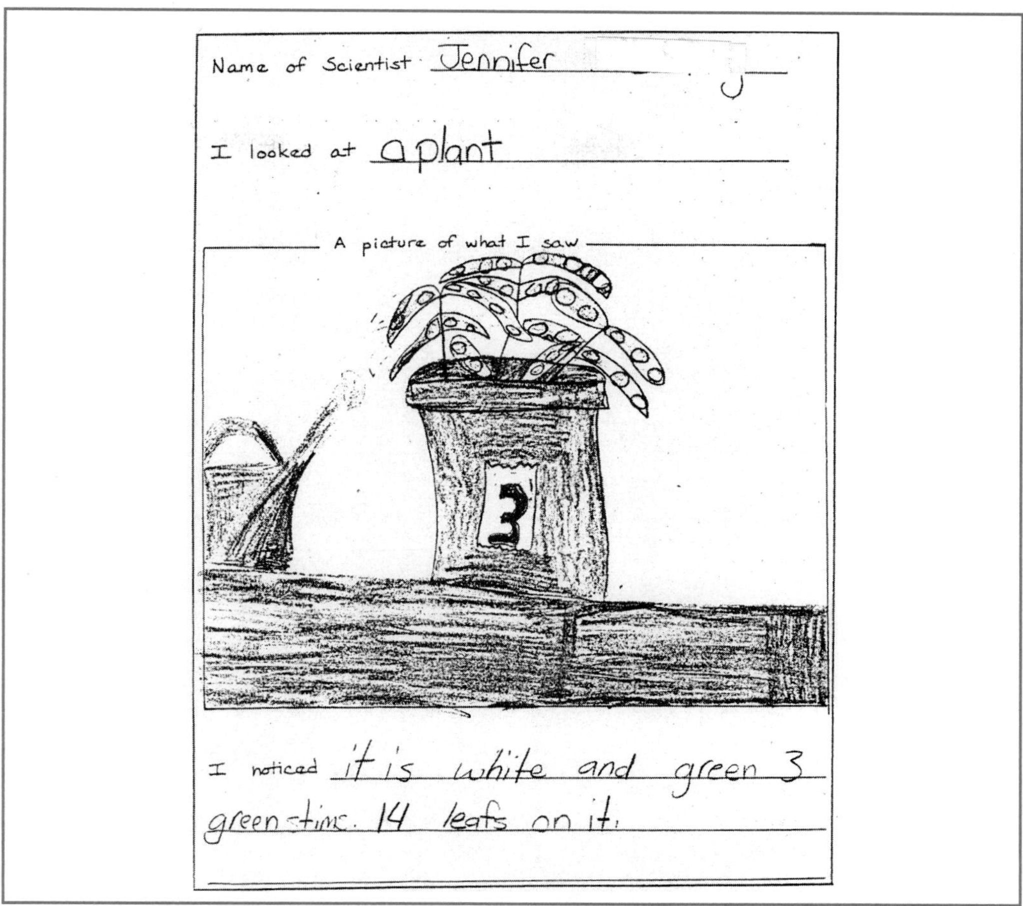

scientific facts and marking them with a post-it tag, they can share them with an informational literature circle. They can also compile an informational chart alongside their reading, or may even write a daily response that states and provides a personal response to the most interesting fact read that day.

Expository and Narrative Science Writing

Side-by-side expository animal reports and related, imaginative porquoi animal tales are examples of how informational and story writing can blend science and language arts. Melissa's fourth-grade report on meadowlarks (Student Sample 14.7) and her creative pourquoi story (Student Sample 14.8) illustrate how students can build on their knowledge of animal and bird topics. The contrast of informational and narrative writing in the context of science provides a dual perspective on writing on a single topic.

Putting It All Together: Science-Based Thematic Units

Science concepts provide a natural link to language arts and literature. From weather, planets, or animals in the primary grades to electricity/magnetism, anatomy, or natural disasters in the intermediate grades, thematic units extend the possibilities for linking language arts, literature, and science concepts (Kaser, 2001; Rice, 2002).

FIGURE 14.6
An Example of a Recording Form for Science Experiments.

EXPERIMENT RECORDING FORM

SCIENTIST: ______________________ DATE: ______________________

My question: ______________________

____

____

Materials:

1. ______________________
2. ______________________
3. ______________________
4. ______________________
5. ______________________

What we will do: ______________________

____

____

What we will learn: ______________________

____

____

Picture of my experiment: ______________________

Source: B. Fisher, (1995). Thinking and learning together: Curriculum and community in a primary classroom. *Portsmouth, NH: Heinemann, p. 330.*

STUDENT SAMPLE 14.7
A Fourth-Grade Informational Report.

THE MEADOWLARK
by Melissa

Do you know what bird is the state bird of Kansas, Montana, Nebraska, North Dakota, Oregon, and Wyoming? The answer is the Western Meadowlark.

Meadowlarks are about the size of a robin, but have a heavier body, a shorter tail, and a longer bill. The back, wings, and tail are brownish, streaked with black. The throat and under parts are bright yellow with a large, black V-shaped band on the breast.

Their yellow throats are 8½ to 11 inches long. Its feathers are brown streaked with black. Its breast is a bright, black-spotted yellow, adorned with a striking crescent of glossy black feathers just below the throat. The tail has white outer feathers. The bill is straight and pointed. The female bird is a bit smaller than her mate, and her plumage is a shade paler.

It eats insects and seeds on the ground. It sits on a fence post. The meadowlark makes the nest on the ground hidden in the grass. They lay five eggs in the nest. They lay 3–7 white eggs speckled with reddish-brown. The nest is cleverly hidden in the______. The mother bird may wait until an intruder is almost on her before she flies away.

The Kansas boys and girls chose the meadowlark to be the state bird.

STUDENT SAMPLE 14.8
A Fourth-Grade Pourquoi Story.

HOW THE MEADOWLARK GOT ITS YELLOW CHEST
by Melissa

There were some yellow leaves and Jenny, a meadowlark, rubbed up against the leaves. There was something black and she rubbed up against it and it made a V-shape on her chest and on the other feathers. She went back to the leaves and rubbed up against them. She has some black feathers on her back.

Jenny saw a cloud above her. She went to rub up against it. So she has a little white on her back.

She was proud the way she was. Her friends thought she was beautiful. And that is how the meadowlark got its yellow chest.

FIGURE 14.7 Language-Based Activities in a Science Thematic Unit.

A model unit, "This is the Forest Primeval" (Figure 14.7), serves as a strong example of interdisciplinary links. The natural environment of the forest served as a backdrop for locating both literature and language-based activities steeped in a science unit. Note both the various genres included in the Literature Cluster on page 462 and the variety of language-based activities that surround the topic. In fact, you may even note the natural infusion of social studies and mathematics in addressing the topic. Letter writing, literature study, and a guest speaker blend with leaf classification, planting trees, and photosynthesis study.

An excellent resource for literature and language arts connections to science is the annual list *Outstanding Science Trade Books for Students K–12* published by the National Science Teachers Association. After printing the list, highlight the selections that relate to your grade-level science curriculum. In addition, the American Library Association's journal, *Book Links,* provides science-related themed issues that blend literature and language arts for curricular science concepts. The use of these resources invites teachers to readily create instructional units that promote inquiry through both science and the language arts.

Teachers striving to integrate technology and the language arts across disciplines should consider the social studies, mathematics, and science connections offered through the Internet. The Tech Tip included here provides inspiration and a springboard for the types of interdisciplinary possibilities that result when these domains are blended into quality instruction.

Visit the Companion Website at www.prenhall.com/hancock and gauge your understanding of Chapter 14 concepts with the self-assessments.

Literature Cluster

LITERATURE ACROSS GENRES FOR SCIENCE THEMATIC UNIT: THIS IS THE FOREST PRIMEVAL

The Life and Legends of Trees

Avi (1995). *Poppy.* Orchard. ANIMAL FANTASY/ Chapter Book

Behn, H. (1992). *Trees: A Poem.* Henry Holt. POEM PICTURE BOOK

Cohen, B. (1995). *Robin Hood and Little John.* Philomel. EPIC TALE.

Daugherty, J. (1939). *Daniel Boone.* Viking. LITERATURE CLASSIC

Douglas, W. (1994). *Muir of the Mountains.* San Francisco: Sierra Club. BIOGRAPHY

Kellogg, S. (1984). *Paul Bunyan: A Tall Tale.* Morrow. FOLKTALE

Lesser, R. (1984). *Hansel & Gretel.* Illus by P. Zelinsky. Dodd. FAIRYTALE

Levy, C. (1994). *A Tree Place and other poems.* McElderry. POETRY

Lindbergh, R. (1990). *Johnny Applessed.* Little, Brown. POEM PICTURE BOOK

Wood, A. (1996). *The Bunyans.* Scholastic. FOLKTALE

Yarbrough, C. (1996). *Little Tree Growin' in the Shade.* Putnam. MULTICULTURAL

A Walk Through the Deciduous Forest

Burnie, D et. al. (1988). *Tree* (Eyewitness Guide). Knopf. INFORMATIONAL

George, J. C. (1988). *One Day in the Woods.* Crowell. INFORMATIONAL NARRATIVE

Lyon, G. E. (1989). *A B Cedar.* ABC PICTURE BOOK: An alphabet of trees, Orchard.

Pine, J. (1995). *Trees: A Nature Study Book.* Harper-Collins. INFORMATIONAL

Sayre, A. P. (1994). *Temperate Deciduous Forest.* 21st Century Books INFORMATIONAL

——— (1996). *Trees and Forests.* Scholastic (Voyages of Discovery). INFORMATIONAL

Watts, M. T. (1963). *Master Tree Finder: A Manual for the Identification of Trees by their Leaves.* Nature Study Guild. INFORMATIONAL

Zim, H. S. (1956). *Trees: A Guide to Familiar American Trees.* Golden Press. INFORMATIONAL

Friend or Foe of the Forest

Bunting, Eve (1993). *Someday a Tree.* Clarion. PICTURE STORYBOOK

Jaspersohn, W. (1996). *Timber! From Trees to Wood Products.* Little, Brown. INFORMATIONAL

Lauber, P. (1991). *Summer of Fire: Yellowstone 1988.* Orchard. INFORMATIONAL

Levine, E. (1995). *The Tree that Would Not Die.* Scholastic. HISTORICAL FICTION

Pringle, L. (1995). *Fire in the Forest.* Atheneum. INFORMATIONAL

Winslow, M. (1995). *Loggers and Railroad Workers.* 21st Century Books. INFORMATIONAL

Growth and Change in the Life Cycle of a Tree

Arnosky, J. (1992). *Crinkleroot's Guide to Knowing the Trees.* Bradbury. INFORMATIONAL

Butterfield, M (1995). *Richard Orr's Nature Cross Section.* Dorling Kindersley. INFO PICTURE BK

Ehlert, L. (1991). *Read Leaf, Yellow Leaf.* Harcourt. PICTURE BOOK

Locker, T & Christiansen, C. (1995). *Sky Tree: Seeing Science through Art.* Harper. PICTURE BOOK

Maestro, B. (1994). *Why Do Leaves Change Color?* Harper Collins. INFO PICTURE BOOK

Markle, S. (1993). *Outside and Inside Trees.* Bradbury. INFORMATIONAL

Romanova, N. (1985). *Once there was a Tree.* Dial. PICTURE STORYBOOK

Simon, S. (1993). *Autumn across America.* Hyperion. INFORMATIONAL

Van Allsburg, C. (1986). *The Stranger.* Houghton Mifflin. PICTURE BOOK/FANTASY

Interdisciplinary Technology Links

Social Studies

The Internet is an excellent resource for enhancing your integrated social studies lessons. *The Internet Public Library, The Library of Congress* home page, and *National Geographic Online* are good starting points inviting your students to access primary source documents and experience cultures from all over the world. **www.ipl.org/** **www.loc.gov/** **www.nationalgeographic.com/**

A virtual tour is an economical and practical alternative to traditional field trips. "Travel" with your students as they explore history, geography, and cultures from across the globe. *Virtual Tours* lists hundreds of tours of museums, exhibits, points of interests, and the U.S. government. This is a commercial site (with banners and some advertisement) but a great source for teachers planning Internet journeys. **www.virtualfreesites.com/tours.html**

Math

The Math Forum is an outstanding site sponsored by Drexel University. It offers links to chat areas and listservs so students from across the globe can communicate about math. In addition, students will benefit from Internet activities and projects, math problem of the week, a "reference shelf," and numerous links to useful math sites on the web. **mathforum.org/**

Biographies of Women Mathematicians is a developing site where students can read about women mathematicians. Students can also research and write about additional female mathematicians and submit their biographies to this site. **www.agnesscott.edu/lriddle/women/women.htm**

Fruit Game is a fun, interactive math game where students play against the computer. Invite your students to play the game and explain in writing the steps necessary for winning. **www.2020tech.com/fruit/index.html**

Science

Science NetLinks and *Science Learning Network* offer students a wealth of resources to spark interest in scientific reading and writing. **www.sciencenetlinks.com/**

Kinetic City: Mission to Vearth is an interactive science game produced by the American Association for the Advancement of Science. The students participate in activities involving hands-on experiments, visual arts, writing, and an online science simulation. **www.kcmtv.com/**

Ask an Expert, Ask a Mad Scientist, and *Ask the Experts at Scientific American Magazine* invite students to communicate with science experts from around the world. Students formulate and submit their own questions or obtain answers by exploring previously submitted inquiries. **www.askanexpert.com/**
www.madsci.org/
www.sciam.com/askexpert

To look more closely at these materials and others related to "Interdisciplinary Instruction," visit the Companion Website at www.prenhall.com/hancock.

Closing Thoughts

When seeking a reason for incorporating literature, language, and language arts across the entire content area curriculum, Rachel Carson's *The Sense of Wonder* (1956/1998) provides a sensitive and realistic rationale for the classroom teacher:

> *I sincerely believe that for the child . . . it is not half so important to know as to feel. If facts are the seeds that later produce knowledge and wisdom, then the emotions and the impressions of the senses are the fertile soil in which the seeds must grow. The years of early childhood are the time to prepare the soil. Once the emotions have been aroused—a sense of the beautiful, the excitement of the new and the unknown, a feeling of sympathy, pity, admiration, or love—then we wish for knowledge about the object of our emotional response. Once found, it has lasting meaning. It is more important to pave the way for the child to want to know than to put him on a diet of facts he is not ready to assimilate.* (p. 45)

Perhaps the integration of literature, language, and language arts will provide an aesthetic incentive for developing a natural sense of the wonder of knowledge and learning meant to last throughout a child's entire life. Language arts and literature provide a natural doorway to introduce children to the content areas while savoring the wonder and wisdom that resides within their individual realms.

Teachers are encouraged to consider the possibilities that interdisciplinary integration can bring to teaching and learning. The authentic blend of the language arts with social studies, science, and mathematics actually provides a more authentic scenario for the presentation of instructional concepts. A curriculum that has been invigorated by the infusion of language and literature will provide a stronger link to the instructional outcomes related to both content area and communication arts standards.

References

Carson, Rachel (1956/1998). *The sense of wonder.* Photographs by Nick Kelsh. New York: Harper-Collins.

Chatton, B., & Collins, N. L. D. (1999). *Blurring the edges: Integrated curriculum through writing and children's literature.* Portsmouth, NH: Heinemann.

Cordeiro, P. (Ed.) (1995). *Endless possibilities: Generating curriculum in social studies and literacy.* Portsmouth, NH: Heinemann.

Danielson, K. E. (1989). Helping history come alive with literature. *Social Studies, 80,* 65–68.

Doris, E. (1991). *Doing what scientists do: Children learn to investigate their world.* Portsmouth, NH: Heinemann.

Farris, P. J. (2004). *Elementary and middle school social studies: An interdisciplinary instructional approach* (4th ed.). New York: McGraw-Hill.

Fisher, B. (1995). *Thinking and learning together: Curriculum and community in a primary classroom.* Portsmouth, NH: Heinemann.

Hancock, M. R. (1993). Character journals: Initiating involvement and identification through literature. *Journal of Reading, 37,* 42–50.

Hancock, M. R. (2004). *A celebration of literature and response: Children, books, and teachers in K–8 classrooms* (2nd ed.). Upper Saddle River, NJ: Merrill/Prentice Hall.

Hunsader, P. D. (2004). Mathematics trade books: Establishing their value and assessing their quality. *The Reading Teacher, 57,* 618–629.

Kaser, S. (2001). Searching the heavens with children's literature: A design for teaching science. *Language Arts, 78,* 348–356.

Kornfeld, J., & Leyden, G. (2005). Acting out: Literature, drama, and connecting with history. *The Reading Teacher, 59,* 230–238.

Louie, B. Y. (1993). Using literature to teach location. *Social Studies and the Young Learner, 5,* 17–18, 22.

Maxim, D., & Five, C. L. (1998). Making meaningful connections to content areas. *School Talk, 3,* 1–2.

Moss, B. (2005). Making a case and a place for effective content area literacy instruction in the elementary grades. *The Reading Teacher, 59,* 46–55.

National Council for Teachers of Mathematics (1996). *Principles and standards for school mathematics.* Reston, VA: Author.

National Council for the Social Studies (1994). *Curriculum standards for social studies: Expectations of excellence.* Washington, DC: Author.

Pappas, C., Kiefer, B., & Levstik, L. (1996). *An integrated language perspective in the elementary school: Theory in action* (2nd ed.). New York: Longman.

Rice, D. C. (2002). Using trade books in teaching elementary science: Facts and fallacies. *The Reading Teacher, 55,* 552–565.

Roser, N., & Keehn, S. (2002). Fostering thought, talk, and inquiry: Linking literature and the social studies. *The Reading Teacher, 55,* 416–426.

Shanahan, T., Robinson, B., & Schneider, M. (1995). Integrating curriculum: Avoiding some of the pitfalls of thematic units. *The Reading Teacher, 48,* 718–719.

Whitin, D., & Whitin, P. (2001). What counts in math-related books for children. *Journal of Children's Literature, 27,* 49–55.

Whitin, P., & Whitin, D. J. (2000). *Math is language, too: Talking and writing in the mathematics classroom.* Urbana, IL: National Council of Teachers of English; Reston, VA: National Council of Teachers of Mathematics.

Young, T., & Vardell, S. M. (1993). Weaving readers theater and nonfiction into curriculum. *The Reading Teacher, 46,* 396–409.

Children's Books Cited

Aker, Suzanne (1990). *What comes in 2's, 3's, & 4's?* New York: Simon & Schuster.

Alda, Arlene (1993). *Arlene Alda's ABC: What do you see?* Berkeley, CA: Tricycle Press.

Alda, Arlene (1998). *Arlene Alda's 1, 2, 3: What do you see?* Berkeley, CA: Tricycle Press.

Beatty, Patricia (1987). *Charley Skedaddle.* New York: Morrow.

Benjamin, Anne (1996). *Young Rosa Parks: Civil Rights Heroine.* New York: Troll.

Cohn, Amy L. (Compiler) (1993). *From sea to shining sea: A treasury of American folklore and folk songs.* New York: Scholastic.

Curlee, Lynn (1999). *Rushmore.* New York: Atheneum.

Curlee, Lynn (2000). *Liberty.* New York: Atheneum.

Curtis, Christopher Paul (1996). *The Watsons go to Birmingham—1963.* New York: Delacorte.

Cushman, Karen (1994). *Catherine, called Birdy.* Clarion.

Dodds, Dayle Ann (2004). *Minnie's diner.* Illus. by John Manders. Cambridge, MA: Candlewick.

Fleischman, Paul (1993). *Bull Run.* Illus. by David Frampton. New York: HarperCollins.

Freedman, Russell (2005). *Children of the Great Depression.* New York: Clarion.

Graham, Joan Bransfield (1999). *Flicker flash.* Illus. by Nancy Davis. Boston: Houghton Mifflin.

Guthrie, Woody (1998). *This land is your land.* Illus. by K. Jakobsen. Boston: Little, Brown.

Hamm, Diane (1991). *How many feet in the bed?* Illus. by Kate Salley Palmer. New York: Simon & Schuster.

Hesse, Karen (1992). *Letters from Rifka.* New York: Scholastic.

Hesse, Karen (1997). *Out of the dust.* New York: Scholastic.

Hoban, Tana (1974). *Circles, triangles, and squares.* New York: Simon & Schuster.

Hoban, Tana (1983). *Round and round and round.* New York: Morrow.

Hoban, Tana (1986). *Shapes, shapes, shapes.* New York: Greenwillow.

Hooper, Meredith (1996). *The drop in my drink: The story of water and our planet.* Illus. by Chris Coady. New York: Putnam.

Hopkinson, Deborah (1993). *Sweet Clara and the freedom quilt.* Illus. by James Ransome. New York: Knopf.

Krensky, Stephen (2001). *Shooting for the moon: The amazing life and times of Annie Oakley.* Illus. by Bernie Fuchs. New York: Atheneum.

Lithgow, John (2004). *Carnival of the animals.* Illus. by Boris Kulikov. [Book & CD] New York: Simon & Schuster.

Lobel, Anita (1994). *Away from home.* New York: Greenwillow.

Parks, Rosa, & Haskins, Jim (1997). *I am Rosa Parks.* New York: Dial.

Priceman, Marjorie (1994). *How to make an apple pie and see the world.* New York: Knopf.

Purviance, Sharon & O'Shell, Marcia (1988). *Alphabet Annie announces an all-American alphabet.* Boston: Houghton Mifflin.

Scieszka, Jon (1995). *Math curse.* Illus. by Lane Smith. New York: Viking.

Sczieska, Jon (2004). *Science verse.* Illus. by Lane Smith. New York: Viking.

Silverstein, Shel (1974). *Where the sidewalk ends.* New York: Harper & Row.

Simon, Seymour (1999). *Crocodiles and Alligators.* New York: HarperCollins.

Stanley, Diane (2000). *Michelangelo.* New York: HarperCollins.

Turner, Ann (1992). *Katie's trunk.* Illus. by Ron Himler. New York: Macmillan.

Weeks, Sarah (2003). *Two eggs, please.* Illus. by Betsy Lewin. New York: Atheneum.

Wells, Robert E. (1997). *What's faster than a speeding cheetah?* New York: Whitman.

Winter, Jeanette (1988). *Follow the drinking gourd.* New York: Holiday House.

Younger, Barbara (1998). *Purple mountains majesty: The story of Katharine Lee Bates and "America the Beautiful."* Illus. by S. Schuett. New York: Dutton.

Chapter 15

LITERACY ASSESSMENT

Monitoring Ongoing Growth and Progress

Miss Malarkey is a good teacher. Usually she's really nice. But a couple of weeks ago she started acting a little weird. She started talking about THE TEST: The Instructional Performance Through Understanding Test . . .

FROM *TESTING MISS MALARKEY* BY JUDY FINCHLER

In this humorous picture book, Miss Malarkey is on edge as she prepares her elementary class for the annual standardized test. Drill and practice replaces the normal learning activities of the school day. Students are even served fish (brain food) at lunch and taught stress-reducing yoga in gym class. While this tale pokes fun at standardized testing, it reminds us of the reality of constant pressure on teachers to prepare students for testing and on students to perform on these one-time, often high-stakes, measurements of learning.

Fortunately, most teachers still base overall analysis of growth and progress in learning the language arts on authentic assessments collected continuously over an entire school year. While standardized tests have become an accepted reality driven by national and state mandates, teachers still know that the most accurate evaluation of language learning is based on assessment of tasks students perform on a daily basis in the classroom. Assessment and evaluation may be the most difficult tasks performed by a teacher as they impact both judgment of a student's capabilities and of the process of teaching itself. This chapter will focus on how teachers can teach literacy within high-stakes accountability systems while still remaining true to authentic assessment linked to literacy instruction (Wolf & Wolf, 2002). Teachers can avoid the "Miss Malarkey complex" and still produce professional accountability in a test-laden society.

Assessment has aptly been described as a "puzzle" (Hill & Ruptic, 1994) with many pieces that must fit together to provide a variety of information to meet the needs of different audiences. Politicians and the public clamor for statistical numbers that reflect traditional accountability and effectiveness of schools. School administrators crave evidence of "adequate yearly progress," the effectiveness of the curriculum, instructional materials, and talented teachers to meet state standards. Parents want to know that their child is making continuous progress and that instruction is effective in making that happen. Teachers desire data that will assist them in planning instruction and activities that nudge and challenge, but not frustrate, the individual learner. Students seek to emphasize their strengths and define their areas for continued growth. With so many assessment needs, there is certainly no one test and no single answer to the assessment puzzle. Assessment must serve more purposes than school accountability. Assessment must be more than a numerical score on a test. Assessment must go beyond a single test to truly serve its many purposes and constituencies.

The most effective practices in literacy assessment happen when decision makers, teachers, parents, and students work side by side in trusting relationships focusing on growth, nurturing, and self-evaluation (Hansen, 1998). These individualized assessments provide descriptive evidence of a student's literacy understandings and progress over time, but they do not classify children as winners and losers. In reality, however, society demands additional accountability through high-stakes testing that pits and measures individual against individual, classroom against classroom, teacher against teacher, school against school, district against district, and state against state, even at the elementary and middle-levels of education. National standardized testing and state testing based on state standards have become, to varying extents, a mandated portion of the overall assessment process.

In the midst of the demands for accountability, the effective language arts teacher learns to *balance* the rigorous demands of a number-conscious society with professional know-how to achieve the best practices in literacy assessment (Calkins, Montgomery, Santman, & Falk, 1998). While accommodating and respecting the goals of national and state testing, effective teachers judiciously include some of the best strategies for literacy assessment in their own yearlong assessment program. They can honor national and state mandates while still being true to a philosophy that focuses on a child-centered view of assessment.

This chapter addresses all aspects of the assessment spectrum—observation, performance checklists, self-evaluation, portfolios, conferences, prescribed reading assessments, and even standardized tests. As you work toward becoming a well-rounded language arts professional, you will learn to mix, match, balance, and blend a variety of valuable assessment tools in an effort to address various perspectives on the growth and progress of each child for whom you share responsibility.

This chapter strives to build an awareness of many assessment options in language arts so you, as the well-informed language arts teacher, can pick and choose from a repertoire that brings fresh, positive perspectives to the value of each student in your classroom.

Objectives

- To build an understanding that the purpose of assessment is to evaluate an individual's literacy as well as a teacher's instructional effectiveness.
- To grasp the importance of both formal and informal authentic assessment tools to paint a portrait of the literacy learner.
- To realize the importance of observation strategies in focusing on the individual learner.
- To assist in facilitating the organization of literacy collections for reflection and goal setting in the language arts.
- To grasp the reality of prescribed testing, particularly in reading, to document ongoing literacy progress.
- To realize the importance of reporting individual literacy progress through both traditional progress reports and reflective conferences.
- To appreciate and address the implications of high stakes testing in the reality of teaching.
- To create a balanced approach to assessment that blends the requirements of mandated testing with the effectiveness of individualized authentic assessment.

The Purposes of Literacy Assessment

Teacher Prep

The Teacher Prep Web site will help you become a better teacher by linking you to classroom videos, artifacts, strategies, lesson relevant education leadership articles, and practical information on licensing, creating a portfolio, implementing standards, and being successful in field experiences. Visit this resources at www.prenhall.com/teacherprep.

A natural, reciprocal relationship exists between the literacy curriculum, literacy assessment, and literacy instruction (Cobb, 2003). *Curriculum* guides the teacher toward student achievement of content standards, local benchmarks, and daily learning. *Assessment* provides the students multiple opportunities to show they "know" the curriculum. *Instruction* defines the planned teaching and learning experiences that address the curriculum. In inverse order, instruction also informs assessment as literacy outcomes guide the content of assessment tools. Assessment then informs teachers of the level of curricular understanding and whether their instruction is effectively impacting learning. Curriculum, assessment, and instruction work in tandem to provide ongoing effective learning in the classroom.

There are three major purposes for putting professional time and effort into the assessment of the language arts in the classroom (International Reading Association & National Council of Teachers of English, 1994):

1. ***For the guidance and improvement of learning.*** Teachers must be aware of the literacy development of each child that is occurring over time in the classroom context. Individual student's strengths and weaknesses must be identified so that a teacher can plan for increased learning in areas that need support. If the goal is to help children learn more, both quantitatively and qualitatively, teachers must be aware of a baseline of learning performance in reading, writing, listening, speaking, viewing, and visual representation. Gathering information early and often on the current status of the learner provides a continuous basis for

guiding and improving the learning of each child throughout the academic year. *Assessment impacts language arts learning.*

2. ***For the guidance and improvement of instruction.*** Assessment that focuses only on student learning ensures that the difficulties are "in" the student. Literacy acquisition, however, occurs as a result of a complex set of dynamics, including instruction. Teachers are empowered to make a difference for each child through the detailed lesson planning and appropriate instructional methodology they share in the classroom. By keeping a thumb on the pulse of the literacy abilities of each child in the classroom, teachers are able to improve their own teaching by targeting areas in which students need additional support. For example, if children have mastered a particular reading strategy (such as picture cues), there is no need to re-teach that skill. Instructional time can best be served by teaching a new strategy (such as visualization) that can be applied in the context of reading. If the new reading strategy does not take hold, teachers must revise their teaching by trying another presentation method or suggesting additional practice to help children internalize the strategy. A teacher must be constantly aware of the progress of each child so appropriate instruction can be aligned with individual literacy needs. Therefore, continuous assessment of discrete skills, strategies, and processes as well as overall performance must be monitored to determine if instruction has been effective. *Assessment informs language arts instruction.*

3. ***To monitor the outcomes of instruction.*** Teachers need both qualitative (authentic work samples) and quantitative (numerical scores, checklists) documentation of student performance to be able to document learning (or lack of it) to parents and administrators. Information must be readily available to determine the capabilities of each student in all areas of the language arts. The outcomes of instruction must, in most cases, be currently aligned with state standards (for example, "By the end of third grade, the student will . . ."). As accountable professionals, teachers must be able to document that each child has mastered predetermined outcomes with both physical documentation and numerical evidence. Outcomes that are reached imply effective teaching, effective programs, or effective staff development. Outcomes that remain underaccomplished imply a need for improved instruction, improved programs or materials, or additional staff development. As educators, teachers must find feasible means to reach learners, not place the blame for the learning deficits on the learners themselves. Therefore, the third purpose of assessment is to keep a close watch on learning to determine the need for schoolwide, districtwide, or statewide reform. *Assessment aligns with stated language arts outcomes.*

Rhodes and Shanklin (1993) list several principles that exemplify these three purposes of assessment. As you read each, envision a classroom context from previous chapters for addressing each principle.

- Assess authentic literacy.
- Assess literacy in a variety of contexts.
- Assess the literacy environment, instruction, and students.
- Assess processes as well as products.
- Analyze error patterns as they impact ongoing instruction.
- Consider prior knowledge in the assessment of literacy.
- Base assessment on developmental patterns in literacy.
- Use standards in the assessment of literacy.

- Use multiple forms of data collection to make decisions.
- Involve students, parents, and other school personnel in the assessment process.
- Make assessment an ongoing part of everyday literacy leaning and instruction.

The most important thought to carry away from this discussion of why we assess literacy and the language arts is that *"meaningful assessment interacts and aligns with instruction and has value for student, teacher, and parent"* (Routman, 2000). Assessment must promote learning, not just measure it. Assessment must move beyond its role as an indicator of a child's performance to a role of improving instruction. Assessment must be fair to the learner by showing both strengths and weaknesses. While assessment monitors the performance of children, it also provides useful information to teachers about the effectiveness of their instruction.

The Assessment Cycle

Where does assessment fit in the overall schema of our educational system? Figure 15.1 provides an effective model of the essential educational components surrounding assessment. The model indicates the foundational components of assessment—national standards, state

FIGURE 15.1 The Assessment Cycle.

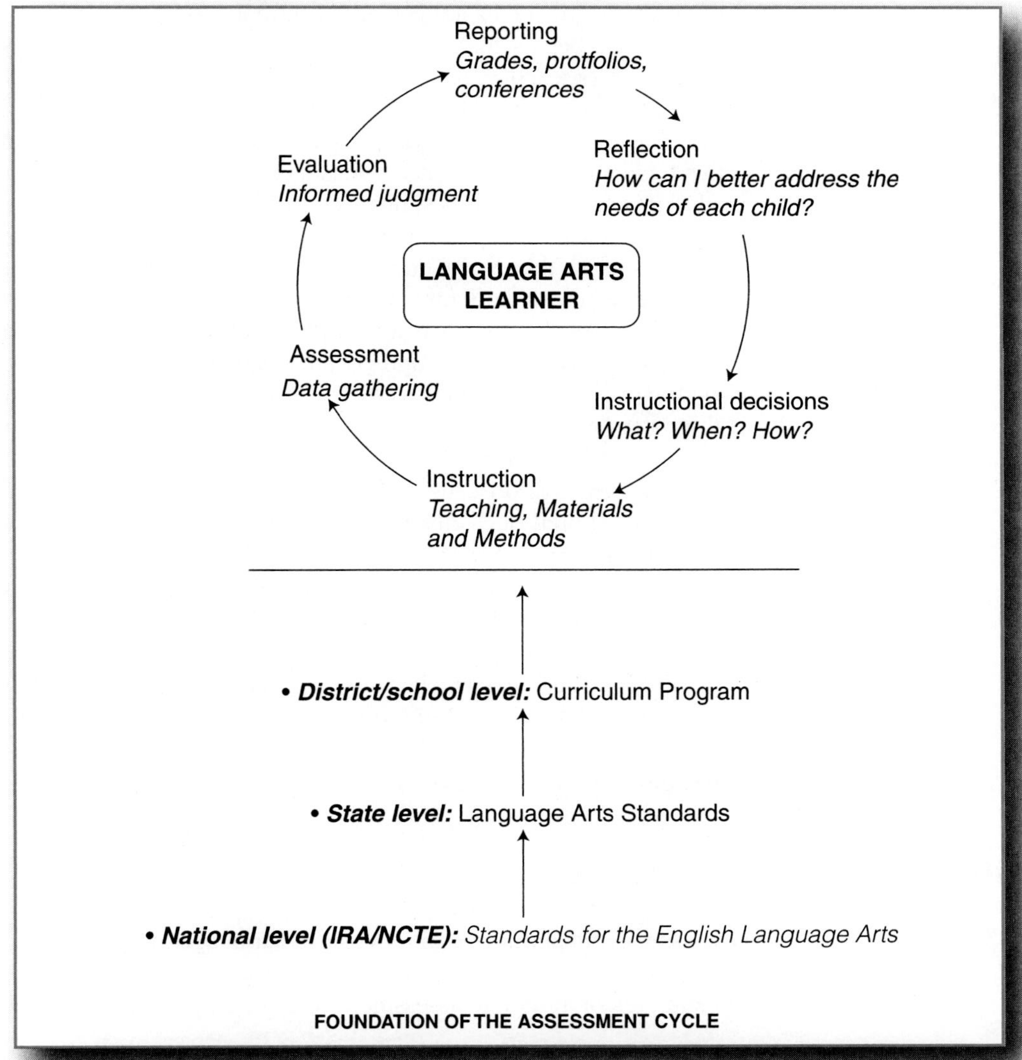

standards, and curriculum or program directives. The assessment cycle itself incorporates (a) instruction, (b) assessment, (c) evaluation, (d) reporting, and (e) reflection, and instructional decisions.

The foundational components of the assessment cycle begin with the *national standards* of each curricular area a teacher will teach. For language arts, the *Standards for the English Language Arts* (IRA/NCTE, 1996) enumerate general national standards for optimal outcomes as a literate citizen. These national standards then inform *state* language arts *standards,* goals, and outcomes. These are the learning outcomes designed to track learners at various levels of performance in the language arts. Districts align those state outcomes with a designed or selected *curriculum* that informs teachers *what* needs to be taught at various grade levels. Often a district will dictate a particular *program* (e.g., a basal reading series, a language arts textbook) to assist in addressing the prescribed curriculum.

Now the Assessment Cycle begins. Each teacher utilizes his or her own teaching philosophy, style, and methodology to design and deliver *instruction* to meet the curricular goal. Following instruction, *assessment* of individual learners (through a variety of techniques to be discussed in this chapter) takes place. Assessment involves collecting information and work samples as well as recording observations. Gathering evidence of learning (or lack of it) is the essential component of assessment.

When the assessment data are gathered (through testing, observation, performance, portfolios), the teacher begins the process of *evaluation*—one of the most critical and time-consuming aspects of teaching. During this stage, a teacher objectively interprets the evidence of learning and makes judgments or decisions based on that evidence. These can include the designation of an aligned reading group, a letter grade, or decisions regarding ongoing instruction. At this stage growth is celebrated, while lack of progress is addressed through a new instructional plan. Evaluation may be enhanced through student self-evaluation and goal-setting in an effort to bring ownership and personal investment into the learning process.

In order to share this evaluation information with others, it is necessary to facilitate *reporting* of the results to students, to parents, to school and/or district administrators, and even to state entities. Reporting is accomplished at the local level through report cards and permanent records, and through parent, teacher, and student conferences. Building principals then report local results to their district offices while superintendents report results to their state educational authorities. State educational departments in turn report to the Department of Education.

Back in the real world of the classroom, the teacher begins a *reflection* process that encourages instructional decisions to better address the needs of individual students. On a broader scale, a school district may decide to purchase a new textbook, adopt a new program, or provide additional staff development that addresses more effective ways of addressing the literacy needs of learners. And so the cycle begins anew as teachers continuously address curriculum through revamped instruction and new materials to best impact the literacy learner. *Assessment not only serves to monitor student performance in the language arts but also informs language arts instruction.* The continuous cycle of assessment to inform a teacher's knowledge of both students and instruction occurs continuously throughout the entire school year.

Authentic Language Arts Assessment

Authentic assessment should be the focus of a language arts educator's overall assessment plan (Valencia, Hiebert, & Afflerbach, 1994). Throughout each chapter of this textbook, specific examples of authentic assessment have been presented in specific contexts of the language arts (e.g., retellings, literature circles, literature response journals, six-trait writing rubrics). Characteristics of authentic assessment better clarify the why and what of collecting data from these literacy experiences. These are several goals to keep in mind in order for authentic assessment to occur. Assessment should:

- ***Be ongoing.*** Learning data should be collected on a continuous basis, over time, so both small and large increments of growth can be detected.
- ***Be multidimensional.*** Data should be incorporated from a variety of sources (e.g., work samples, test scores, project rubrics, skill checklists) and represent the individual learner.
- ***Provide positive feedback.*** Teachers should show specific ways in which the child has grown as a literate individual, while encouraging renewed efforts toward further literacy progress.
- ***Allow for self-evaluation.*** Encouraging learners to make judgments and set goals for their own literacy learning provides initiative and incentive to focus on targeted areas for literacy growth (e.g., reading more books, increasing spelling proficiency, improving vocabulary in writing contexts).
- ***Value what students know.*** Building from learning strengths (rather than focusing on deficits), authentic assessment encourages growth from a baseline of what the child can do as a literate individual, not what he or she cannot do.
- ***Inform instruction.*** Student performance reflects the effectiveness of language arts instruction; lack of student performance should impact instructional change to better serve the needs of literacy learners.

The opposing term of *inauthentic assessment* generally applies to high-stakes testing, one-time opportunities showing results that are used for making spontaneous judgments that can affect a child's educational future. Typically in the form of a standardized test, inauthentic assessment has several shortcomings: (a) it tends to measure one child against another (rather than valuing individual growth); (b) it focuses on what a child does not know (rather than what he or she does know); (c) it is usually a one-time shot (with no other authentic opportunity or means to reveal growth). Yet standardized testing is the reality of teaching—not its enemy. A special section later in this chapter explains how new teachers can meet the demands and reality of high-stakes testing while still remaining true to gathering authentic assessment on a daily basis in a valid classroom context.

The following sections focus on ways to collect assessment data in a meaningful, ongoing, purposeful way that will reveal the authentic strengths of the individual language arts learner. These types of authentic assessment include interest and attitude surveys and interviews, observational strategies, checklists, rubrics, and literacy portfolios and profiles.

Portrait of the Literacy Learner: Surveys and Interviews

Authentic assessment begins with information acquired about each student early in the school year. Taking the form of interest surveys, attitude surveys, and interviews, these data-gathering techniques provide information on the whole child that may impact effective instructional planning, deepen individual understandings, and expand teacher knowledge of talents, learning styles, and interests. Building from broad knowledge about a child certainly strengthens the growing bond and genuine concern that is essential to a trusting relationship between teacher and learner.

Even before the school year begins, many teachers will mail a letter of welcome to new students (and their parents) and include surveys for both the child and the parent.

Additional insights can be gained from interests, special talents, and out-of-school activities. Lists of books read or titles of pieces written provide opportunities not only to fit interests into the curriculum but to expand interests as well. In their haste to teach children language arts, teachers may not realize the importance of learning about the whole child and how home interests and habits impact school learning. A variety of student-centered questions (Hill & Ruptic, 1994) might be asked:

- What do you like [not like] about reading?
- What do you like [not like] about writing?
- What is the hardest [easiest] thing for you at school?
- What have you done at school that has made you very proud of yourself?
- What would you like to learn more about in reading and writing this year?
- What else would you like to tell me about you as a reader and writer?

Primary children can be asked to draw a self-portrait (see Figure 15.2) and fill in a basic information sheet. An "All About Me Book" is an appropriate means of gathering personal and academic information on favorite books, pastimes, games, friends, family members, and interests.

Parents are encouraged to take time to fill out informational surveys to help their child's teacher become better acquainted with the child as a reader, writer, and language arts learner. Interviews administered via phone or an online Web site can also provide a means of capturing interesting background on students. Asking a few, well-focused questions, can provide data to project interests, attitudes, and outcomes for the upcoming school year (Hill & Ruptic, 1994; Rhodes & Shanklin 1993). Parents or guardians might be asked the following questions:

- How does your child feel about going to school?
- What goals do you have for your child this school year?
- What are your child's interests and outside pastimes?
- What activities do you enjoy together as a family?

FIGURE 15.2 Self-Portrait of an Early Literacy Learner.

Source: B. C. Hill & C. Ruptic (1994). Practical aspects of authentic assessment: Putting the pieces together *(pp. 171 and 173). Norwood, MA: Christopher-Gordon.*

- Do you read together? What do you read? How often?
- What types of reading and writing does your child enjoy?
- Is there anything that might affect your child's reading and writing?
- What are some additional things that would be helpful for me to know about your child?

Attitudes about reading and writing also provide insights into setting goals for the new school year. In fact, students' attitudes and interests ultimately affect their engagement with literacy. "How students feel about reading [writing] is as important as whether they are able to read [write], for the value of reading [writing] lies in its use rather than its possession" (Estes, 1971). The *Reading Attitude Survey* (McKenna & Kear, 1990) and the *Writing Attitude Survey* (Kear, Coffman, McKenna, & Ambrosio, 2000) provide Garfield the cat illustrations indicating varying attitudes on aspects of reading—from ecstasy to boredom—or on writing—from "thumbs up" to frustration. These user-friendly surveys provide a delightful and valid experience for students with tremendous insights for the teacher. Children find these surveys easy to complete as teachers read aloud (Kindergarten–Grade 1), provide assistance with individual items (Grades 3–4), or allow independent completion (Grades 5–8). Group and individual analysis provides early insight into time spent on reading and writing, attitude toward reading and writing, and specific aspects and choices of the reading and writing processes. See article citations from *The Reading Teacher* (Kear & McKenna, 1990; Kear, Coffman, McKenna, Ambrosio, 2000) for accessing and duplicating these attitude surveys for classroom use (in the references at the end of this chapter).

Although such data collection instruments may provide valuable insights into the literacy flavor and fervor of individual students, it is best not to overuse them and to select wisely for your grade level and needs. Once collected, the data need to be evaluated and summarized to make the most effective use of these rich data resources. Highlighting key information and glancing at these surveys from time to time put the professional in direct touch with each child in the classroom. Place them in a three-ring binder or teacher folder divided with the names of each child for ongoing reference and information.

Observation Strategies

One of the most informal, yet effective ways for a teacher to keep a thumb on the literacy pulse of a child is through continuous, ongoing observation or "kidwatching," a term coined by Yetta Goodman (1985). Kidwatching includes direct, intentional, and systematic observations by teachers. It involves the process of learning to observe what is there and utilizing that information to make a better classroom. Although the simplicity of the term *kidwatching* implies that anyone can do it, a teacher quickly learns that there is much prowess to seeing and recording learning, interactions, and individual insights gathered through focused observations. Timothy O'Keefe (1997) captures the essence of this learned technique: "Kidwatching is not for the faint of heart. It requires commitment, risk taking, and valuing the good in each child. However, kidwatching is its own reward" (p. 5). While observations can be spontaneously stored in a teacher's mind, a permanent record of these learning and instructional insights can be recorded through anecdotal records, checklists, and a developmental continuum. As you read on, you will discover the art of observation and recording to be a meaningful yet challenging means of authentic assessment. Focused on the primary grades, the following three observational strategies are equally effective with older students as well.

Anecdotal Records. One of the most effective ways to assess student performance is through the recording of kidwatching observations through anecdotal records—brief but focused comments written by the teacher. Think of them as "snapshots of information" that reflect student progress or can be used to define future instruction (Rhodes & Nathenson-Meija, 1992). Anecdotal records should do the following:

- Accurately, immediately, and relevantly record and report to parents and students what a child can do.
- Value the oral, written, and visual contributions each child makes within the learning community.
- Give voice to students who otherwise are silenced on the fringes of the literacy learning experience.
- Identify emerging trends and patterns among students that inform instructional planning.
- Sensitize the teacher to the unique personal qualities and learning styles of each child.
- Track changes in attitude and behavior that might affect learning.
- Provide a permanent record of fleeting moments that blend into the total literacy environment of the classroom.

One of the most effective ways to begin anecdotal records is to write something, even a single thought, every day about every child. Observational focuses (e.g., reading strategies, oral responses) may become targeted and keener over time. Teachers use clipboards with mailing labels (with date and name) which they later transfer to individual file folders in chronological order. Others use flip index cards with student names to record reflective observations, while still others use a clipboard grid for each child for an ongoing record of observations. Others transfer informal notes into computer files and compile sequenced data sheets over the entire school year. Figure 15.3 presents some anecdotal

FIGURE 15.3 Anecdotal Records During First-Grade Independent Reading.

Anecdotal Records for: Independent Reading / First Grade

CRYSTAL	DANNY	JACOB	JESSE
Chose I Went Walking. Used this for a big book lesson last week. Confidence builder	Requests this morning's read aloud!		Brought a book from home
KYLIE	SHELBY	JAIRA	AUSTIN
Daydreaming Book open but no attention to it	Same book 4 days in a row	Mumble reading & finger pointing but really reading	Another nonfiction on animals He really loves them!
CHRIS	DANIEL	GRAYSON	JESSICA
Reading with Grayson ABC book	Wandering for 10 minutes to make a selection — Perhaps needs to have a book ready-to-go	Reading with Chris ABC Book	
TREVOR	REJOYCE	CODY	WILLIE
	Tells me the little girl in The Snowy Day is her!	Reminder: Forgets library books at home!	Trades books 4 times. Can't find one he likes. More likely too challenged

records in a single-page format with notes on first-grade students during a 20-minute independent reading time. The teacher used five focused questions on specific aspects of independent reading to target her observations:

- What book(s) are being self-selected?
- Does the child choose to read alone or with a partner (whom?)?
- What reading behaviors are evident?
- What evidence of comprehension/understanding is apparent?
- How well does the child stay focused on the reading task?

After school that day, the teacher dates and types the notes into a computer file designated for each child while reflecting on the attitudes, strategies, comprehension, and response of each individual. Tomorrow the teacher will observe those students missed today with a goal of at least a single anecdotal record each week of the school year for each child either during reading, writing, or related language arts activities. The focused anecdotal record can even provide authentic information related to content standards (Boyd-Batstone, 2004).

Regardless of the means of collection, a teacher's insightful comments can provide a more valid assessment than a test score or a letter grade elicited from certain tasks and assist effectively in reporting specific examples of progress to parents. Sitting with a child and watching or listening carefully is the best way to get to know students as readers and writers. Anecdotal records can be included at parent-teacher-student conferences and in summary at Individual Educational Progress (IEP) meetings, and they can serve as content for written narrative comments in descriptive evaluations. Although such records are time consuming, they record and organize data in a meaningful way for both teacher and student.

Developmental Continuum and Checklists. Because of their developmental nature, the language arts lend themselves to a developmental literacy continuum and literacy checklists for various aspects of language arts skills and strategies (Hill, 2001). These forms of assessment imply that children learn the same aspects of language but at different rates and at different times.

A continuum is a visual representation of literacy development using descriptors to depict the developmental stages of learning. This time line of literacy learning keeps track of abilities, accomplishments, and mastered skills and activities in a simple, understandable, and consistent format. The continuum provides a common language for teachers, parents, and students to talk about reading and writing development. A continuum tends to emphasize that learning is an ongoing a process that emphasizes individual progress rather than competition. Each continuum includes descriptors based on developmental stages. Typical descriptors include (in developmental order) preconventional, emergent, developing, beginning, Expanding, bridging, fluent, proficient, and independent. A continuum such as the one shown in Figure 15.4 requires highlighting as descriptive characteristics of a stage are achieved. This continuum model encourages ongoing assessment of particular skills and strategies. Even a quick glance at this informs and assures the teacher of gradual progress in literacy skills. If a child gets bogged down or takes a step backward, a teacher can readily address the problem that may be causing this lack of progress. On the other hand, a rapid jump on the continuum often denotes a rapid internalization of the reading process and gives reason to celebrate.

In a similar manner, the writing continuum checklist shown in Figure 15.5 suggests an ongoing listing of evidence on which the behavior, skill, or activity of writing are

FIGURE 15.4
Reading Continuum: K–8 Stages of Literacy Development.

Reading Continuum

Effort ☐☐☐

Preconventional	Emergent	Developing	Beginning	Expanding
• Holds book, correctly turns pages. • Chooses book and has favorites. • Shows start/end of book • Listens and responds to literature. • Knows some letter names. • Interested in environmental print.	• Pretends to read. • Uses illustrations to tell stories. • Participates in reading of familiar books. • Knows most letter sounds. • Recognizes names/words in context. • Memorizes pattern books and familiar books. • Rhymes and plays with words.	• Sees self as reader. • Reads books with word patterns. • Knows most letter sounds. • Retells main idea of text. • Recognizes simple words. • Relies on print and illustrations.	• Reads early-reader books. • Relies on print more than illustrations. • Uses sentence structure clues. • Uses meaning clues. • Uses phonetic clues. • Retells beginning, middle, end. • Recognize names/words by sight. • Begins to read silently. • Understands basic punctuation.	• Reads beginning chapter books. • Reads and finishes a variety of materials with frequent guidance. • Uses reading strategies appropriately. • Retells plot, characters, and events. • Recognizes different types of books. • Makes connections between reading, writing, and experiences. • Silent reads for short periods.

Effort ☐☐☐

Bridging	Fluent	Proficient	Independent
• Reads medium level chapter books. • Reads and finishes a variety of materials with guidance. • Reads and understands most new words. • Uses reference materials to locate information with guidance. • Increases knowledge of literary elements and genres. • Silent reads for extended periods	• Reads most young adult literature. • Selects, reads and finishes a wide variety of materials. • Uses reference materials independently. • Understands literary elements and genres. • Begins to interpret deeper meaning in young adult literature with frequent guidance. • Participates in guided literary discussions.	• Reads complex young adult literature. • Moves between many genres with case. • Integrates non-fiction information to develop a deeper understanding. • Interprets sophislicated meaning in young adult literature with guidance. • Participates in complex literary discussions.	• Voluntarily reads and understands a wide variety of complex and sophisticated materials with case. • Evaluates, Interprets and analyzes literary elements critically.

Source: B. C. Hill & C. Ruptic (1994). Practical aspects of authentic assessment: Putting the pieces together *(pp. 237–241). Norwood, MA: Christopher-Gordon.*

FIGURE 15.5 Writing Continuum Checklist: K–8 Stages of Literacy Development.

Preconventional

			Makes marks other than drawing on paper (scribble writing)
			Primarily relies on pictures to convey meaning
			Sometimes labels and adds "words" to pictures
			Tells about own writing
			Writes random recognizable letters

Emergent

			Sees self as writer
			Copies names and familiar words
			Uses pictures and print to convey meaning
			Pretends to read own writing
			Prints with uppercase letters
			Uses beginning/ending consonants to make words

Developing

			Takes risks with writing
			Begins to read own writing
			Writes names and favorite words
			Writing is from top–bottom, left–right, front–back
			May interchange uppercase and lowercase letters
			Begins to use spacing between words
			Uses beginning, middle, and ending sounds to make words
			Begins to write noun–verb phrases

Beginning

			Writes pieces that self and others can read
			Begins to write recognizable short sentences
			Writes about observations and experiences with some descriptive words
			Experiments with capitals and punctuation
			Forms many letters legibly
			Uses phonetic spelling to write independently
			Spells some words correctly
			Begins to revise by adding on

Expanding

			Begins to consider audience
			Writes pieces with beginning, middle, and end
			Revises by adding description and detail
			Listens to peers' writing and offers feedback
			Edits for punctuation and spelling
			Uses capital letters and periods
			Forms letters with ease
			Spells many common words correctly

FIGURE 15.5 **(Continued)**

Bridging

			Begins to write for various purposes
			Begins to organize ideas in logical sequence
			Begins to develop paragraphs
			Begins to revise by adding literary devices
			Develops editing and proofreading skills
			Employs strategies to spell difficult words correctly

Fluent

			Uses appropriate tone and mood for a variety of purposes
			Experiments with complex sentence structure
			Connects paragraphs in logical sequence
			Uses an increased repertoire of literary devices
			Revises for clarity by adding reasons and examples
			Includes deleting in revision strategies
			Edits with greater precision (spelling, grammar, punctuation, capitalization)

Proficient

			Adapts style for a wide range of purposes
			Varies sentence complexity naturally
			Uses literary devices effectively
			Integrates information from a variety of sources to increase power of writing
			Uses sophisticated descriptive language
			Uses many revision strategies effectively

Independent

			Writes cohesive in-depth pieces
			Internalizes writing process
			Analyzes and evaluates written material in-depth
			Perseveres through complex writing projects

Source: B. C. Hill, & C. Ruptic (1994). Practical aspects of authentic assessment: Putting the pieces together *(pp. 247–249). Norwood, MA: Christopher-Gordon.*

observed by the teacher. If little or no progress is observed, the teacher is responsible for remediation or a fresh instructional strategy to reach the learner. If progress is steady, however, the teacher validates the instruction as well as the efforts of the learner.

The checklist format can also be a quick but thorough list of skills and strategies to be learned and applied in reading and writing. Discrete items are checked or dated as each student incorporates them into his or her reading and writing repertoire. An example of this type of checklist is shown in Figure 15.6, which records intermediate reading strategies during independent reading (Keene & Zimmerman, 1997).

FIGURE 15.6 Reading Strategies Student Checklist.

Reading Strategies: I Use Checklist—4–8th Level

Name ______________________________ Date __________

Book Title ______________________________ Pages __________

Check those reading strategies you used in today's reading. Remember: Not all strategies are likely to be used in one reading period. Indicate with a check and the page number on which you used the strategy.

	YES	NO	COMMENT
Prior Knowledge *I think about what I already know before, during, and after reading.*			
Ideas and Theme *I am able to determine the main idea and theme of the story.*			
Asking Questions *I ask questions of myself, the author, and the text.*			
Creating Images *I create visual and sensory images during and after reading.*			
Drawing Inferences *I conclude, predict, and interpret While before, during, and after reading the text.*			
Retelling *I can retell and summarize what I have read.*			

Fix-Up Strategies
I use the following strategies when my understanding breaks down

Circle all those that apply

Using context
Word recognition
Word analysis
Rereading
Reading ahead
Decoding
Monitoring for meaning
Determining importance

Source: Adapted from E. O. Keene & S. Zimmerman (1997). Mosaic of thought: Teaching comprehension in a reader's workshop. *Portsmouth, NH: Heinemann.*

Anecdotal records, developmental continuums, and literacy checklists provide a quick and easy, yet effective, observational tool for keeping track of children's literacy development. Whether tallied during a current school year or placed in a permanent record for K–8 literacy development, these assessment tools provide a means of ensuring that literacy growth, confirmed by ongoing dates, is occurring within each individual learner. The advantage of these assessment instruments is that they help the teacher focus and assure the importance of even small steps toward success for each literacy learner.

Rubrics: Performance-Based Scoring Guides

A rubric is a scoring guide used to assess and evaluate the quality of a student's work against predetermined standards. This performance-based assessment tool identifies key elements of proficiency, typically in reading fluency and writing development, but also applicable in many areas of the language arts. A rubric has three essential features:

- ***Evaluative criteria.*** Statements used to distinguish acceptable from unacceptable responses.
- ***Qualitative definitions.*** Descriptions of each level of performance differentiating qualitative differences.
- ***Scoring strategy.*** The rules for scoring, either analytically (criterion scored separately) or holistically (overall quality judgment)

Three to five criteria constitute a good rubric, but the criteria must be teachable so the students can increase their ability to use the criteria in completing the task. The teacher must focus on the evaluative criteria during instruction. These criteria must be shared with the student prior to assignment of a learning task.

It is not easy for a teacher to write a good rubric, but a well-written one gives clarity and purpose to a task. Students realize the standard of performance and are prepared to work toward it. Reporting to the students through the use of the same criteria creates scoring that has real meaning. Not only do results indicate what students can do, but students can take part in assessing their own performance.

Figure 15.7 features Mrs. Larson's writing assignment and writing rubric created for her sixth-grade writing class as they wrote a simulated journal entry built on John Wesley Powell's journey down the Colorado River. Note the well-defined and specifically designated features of the varying levels of performance. Mrs. Larson shared these with her students *prior to* assigning the writing task so that students could internalize the criteria and strive to meet the designated level. Because a rubric models expectations, the final drafts of the journal entries often meet or exceed teacher expectations. Student Sample 15.1 reveals Ben's final draft, which he submitted after taking his piece through the writing process. As you read it, determine Ben's level of performance according to the rubric criteria.

Even more powerful is the option of student-generated rubrics that meaningfully share the assessment process with students. Built on the proposed outcomes of the lesson, a teacher and student together determine the qualities that differentiate varying levels of learning performance. Stiggins (1997) suggests that the true potential of classroom assessment is reached when teachers "open the assessment process up and welcome students into that process as full partners" (p. 18). Skillings and Ferrell (2000) included real students in establishing a rubric on the use of characterization.

FIGURE 15.7 Mrs. Larson's Sixth-Grade Simulated Journal Assignment and Rubric.

Name: Ben ______________________ Date: ______________________

"An Account of Exploration"

(based on the story *Conquering the Colorado* by Ramsey Ullman)

Situation:

In August of 1869, John Wesley Powell and his companions faced the great challenge of exploring the Great Canyon. Imagine yourself as a member of General Powell's expedition. In your quest to conquer the Colorado, you line, portage, run rapids, and leap falls. The weather is alternating from broiling heat to torrential downpours and cold nights. Every day, you are facing a shortage of food as well as other supplies. After overcoming wild rapids and cataracts for several weeks, you finally reach rapids that are too wild to ride, with no route for portaging. To run these rapids would be "sure destruction," according to Powell himself. The alternative, to abandon the boats and try to climb out of the canyon, is an equally risky option.

Here is what you will do:

Write a journal entry explaining in **detail** what your experience has been like so far. **Although you will mostly write about the big decision for how to go on (and if you can go on), you should also discuss your feelings about the expedition and your adventures.** You are writing this for others to read at the end of your journey. Use **descriptive** language to help the readers picture your experiences and the some scenery in their minds. Make sure you include an appropriate date. **Use your imagination!** However, make sure that your journal entry is **realistic** and **makes sense.**

Your journal entry will be graded based on the following scoring guide:

Exemplary:

- A realistic journal entry is written, including a date *(August 1869)*, by an imaginary member of Powell's expedition of the Grand Canyon in 1869.
- The entry describes the dilemma of deciding *how* and *if* the group should go on. Examples are given of route options, possible risks involved, and personal feelings and preferences. **The examples are very clearly written, make sense, and are historically and/or geographically accurate** (based on the information in *Conquering the Colorado*).
- There are no errors in spelling and/or conventions.
- The journal entry includes advanced work. Examples include (but are not limited to) vivid and detailed descriptions of experiences that you have had so far on the expedition. The writing is exceptional and it is easy for the reader to imagine your life as a adventurous explorer.

Proficient:

- A realistic journal entry is written, including a date *(August 1869)*, by an imaginary member of Powell's expedition of the Grand Canyon in 1869.
- The entry describes the dilemma of deciding *how* and *if* the group should go on. Examples are given of route options, possible risks involved, and personal feelings and preferences. **The examples are well-written, make sense, and are historically and/or geographically accurate** (based on the information in *Conquering the Colorado*).
- There are no errors in spelling and/or conventions.

Progressing:

- A realistic journal entry is written, including a date *(August 1869)*, by an imaginary member of Powell's expedition of the Grand Canyon in 1869.
- The entry describes the dilemma of deciding *how* and *if* the group should go on. Examples are given of route options, possible risks involved, and personal feelings and preferences. **Some examples are unclear and do not always make sense. The information is not always historically and/or geographically accurate** (based on the information in *Conquering the Colorado*).
- There are some errors in spelling and/or conventions.

Not meeting standards:

- The student has failed to write a realistic journal entry as an imaginary member of Powell's expedition, including a date of the journal entry.
- A journal entry is written but fails to describe the dilemma of *how* and *if* the group should go on.
- There are errors in spelling and/or conventions that make it difficult for the reader to understand the meaning of the composition.

STUDENT SAMPLE 15.1
Ben's Simulated Journal, Based on the Rubric Shown in Figure 15.7.

August/27/1869
Dear Journal,

It's been a drastic journey. We've been through the toil of rapids, cascades, venomous snakes, and shortage of food.

One day I was ravenously searching for food when we found an Indian garden. We were lucky we found it because we barely had any food left. The rapids had a strong hold on us. While we where running down the rapids Dwayne fell out. Billy Bob and Powell plunged into the water and hit each other. The two Howards plunged into the water and rescued Dwayne, Billy Bob, and Powell. Dwayne hurt his arm. Billy Bob and Powell's ribs where really roughed up! We rested for the night a few hours later. In the morning Dwayne, Billy Bob, Powell, and the Howards caught a cold because the water was freezing. We all recovered after a while.

Then one night, Powell told out crew that we had to make a choice. To keep on going down the rapids, or to climb out of the canyon? It is a very hard decision! If we go down the rapids, the boat could hit a rock and sink, or someone could fall out and get hurt. If we climb out of the canyon we good lose more energy fast and stare easier. I didn't come down here for nothing, I came down here to finish my journey and that's exactly what I am going to do! While I was going to tell Powell that I want to run the rapids, I fell into a cactus. I hurt my arm and leg a slight bit. I had Jade pull out a piece of cactus out of my arm. It was very painful!

Anyway I told Powell and my friends about my decision. Dwayne and Billy Bob are going down the rapids with me. The supper that we ate was delicious. It has recharged me for the end of the big journey. I was in a super condition after a while. I hope my gigantic choice was the wise one. I am going down the rapids.

Sincerely,
Butch Thompson

Figure 15.8 shows some of the elements of this rubric as a result of teacher-student collaboration in determining outcomes and assessment criteria. Rubrics cooperatively created by students and teachers may provide meaningful results based on student expectations for their own learning. A Web site (www.rubistar.com) provides a template for generating teacher-created or student-generated rubrics for classroom criterion-based assessments.

Self-Evaluation and Reflection

What children can do in the language arts varies tremendously. Students can and do know their literacy strengths and weaknesses, but teachers must help them find value in themselves if they are to further succeed as literacy learners. Students should consider the following questions in relation to reading, writing, listening, speaking, viewing, and visual representation (Hansen, 1998).

- ***What do I do well?*** Your task as a teacher is to help students find what they do well, celebrate their strengths, and challenge them to stretch toward a higher goal. Unfortunately, many children feel less value in themselves because of continued reminders of deficiencies in learning. Imagine hearing "Nothing. I'm nobody" in response to this first query. Every child has something they do well at in reading, writing, listening, speaking, viewing, or visual representation. Helping them identify and articulate that strength defines an important teaching role. Valuing oneself as a literate individual must precede the answer to this question. Teachers play a critical role in the self-esteem of the learner.

FIGURE 15.8 **Teacher and Student-Generated Rubrics.**

Structured Character Rubric/Teacher

3	2	1
• Choose a character • Write four things the character did • Write two reasons for character's actions • Illustrate character in appropriate setting with at least three details • Complete sentences • Proper heading • Neatly done	• Choose a character • Write two to three things the character did • Write one reason for character's actions • Illustrate character in appropriate setting with at least two details • Most sentences are complete • Heading complete • Not as neat	• Choose a character • Write one thing the character did • No reason given for the character's actions • Illustration wrong for setting—few details • Some sentences not complete • Heading incomplete • Paper is messy

Expanded Rubric/Students

3 Very best level	2 Okay level	1 Not so good level
• Shows clear understanding • Shows creativity • Illustrations colored with details • Correct spelling • Done on time • Neatly done • Proper heading	• Some understanding • A little creativity • A few colors and details • Some spelling errors • Done on time—1 day late • Not neatest work • Proper heading	• Not so clear understanding • Little or no creativity • Little coloring and details • Many spelling errors • More than 1 day late • Sloppy work • May have proper heading

Source: M. J. Skillings, & R. Ferrell (2000). Student-generated rubrics: Bringing students into the assessment process. The Reading Teacher, *53, 452–455.*

- ***What is the most recent thing I've learned to do?*** Knowing you do something well is just the beginning. Now the student must share his or her accomplishments while becoming aware of personal growth. Different responses, of course, occur across grade levels. "I learned to read this book," says Demetrius, a first grader, as he holds up Sue Williams's *I Went Walking*, while Kelsey, a sixth grader, states, "I learned to write a more interesting lead to my story." Although all responses are different, all portray children as learners and all are valued as steps in literacy growth.
- ***What do I want to learn next in order to grow?*** This question forces the learner to look ahead, articulate the next stage of learning, and actually set a goal This query builds momentum as the child learns that learning something new means there is another step to learning more. Lifelong learning works this way as there is truly no end to the cycle of learning. Initiating responsibility for their own growth, students quickly learn to respond by stating their next goal. "I want to learn to read another

Fourth graders work diligently to compose a self evaluative reflection on their performances on a language arts project.

book by that author," or "Now I want to learn to write a stronger ending to my story," become next steps in learning. If the child articulates the goal, it puts ownership and commitment to the goal in the hands of the learner, rather than in the agenda of the teacher. Nurturing children toward becoming independent learners is an important outcome of self-evaluation Yet the teacher stands by to temper realistic options and facilitate instruction and materials to help the child reach that goal.

- ***What will I do to accomplish this?*** This question leads the learner toward a plan of action. While having a goal is important, determining the small steps toward reaching that goal is critical. Several step-by-step tasks sets a plan in motion. For example, the student who wants to write a better story ending might (a) reread endings of books she has already read; (b) identify elements of the writing craft that authors use to write powerful endings; (c) reread her own previous endings to her stories; (d) apply the writer's craft to rewriting the endings of her own stories; (e) start a new story with the goal of writing a great ending.

  While intermediate and middle-level students can actually break their goal into learning elements, younger children need the guidance of the teacher who models how to break a task into smaller pieces. For example, reading Arnold Lobel's *Frog and Toad are Friends* independently might include (a) listening to an audiotape of the book and following along; (b) reading aloud with a partner who has already read the book; (c) reading one chapter independently; (d) reading the entire book independently. Somehow, the task seems more doable if it is broken into small steps that lead to the accomplishment.

- ***What might I use to document what I have learned?*** The need for tangible evidence to reflect learning is the focus of this inquiry. Documentation for the previous examples could include an audiotape of the student reading *Frog and Toad are Friends* or a before/after view of the rewriting of the ending of a story to indicate application of the writer's craft. If children can see a visual connection to learning that will be the "proof" of their learning, they are more likely to strive to achieve the goal. Dealing with the concrete (a list of books, a thank-you note) assists in reaching and "proving" that they have reached a goal.

An appropriate venue for responding to these reflective questions is the reading or writing conference (see previous chapters) that occurs in the context of the reading or writing workshop. Conferences become personal interviews by asking questions to bring out information that teachers could not know without getting inside students' minds (Fu & Lamme, 2002). A casual, conversational approach used in conferencing allows the teacher to focus on critical questions, yet adjust or build on responses as the conversation evolves. Active listening, flexibility in questioning, recording key information, keeping to a reflective framework, and showing genuine respect to the learner provide key points in getting genuine responses. Lesson Plan 15.1 models the process of reflection in the context of poetry writing. As children follow the progress of Jack, the main character of Sharon Creech's *Love That Dog,* they reflect on their own growth as poets.

LESSON PLAN 15.1

TITLE: **Reflecting on Poetry Writing**

Grade Level: 3–5

Time Frame: Three to five 30-minute sessions

Standards

IRA/NCTE Standards: 11, 12

NETS for Students: 5

Objectives

- Students will compare and contrast their personal progress as writers of poetry to that of Jack, the main character in *Love That Dog* by Sharon Creech.
- Students will realize the importance of self-reflection and revision as part of the poetry writing process.

Materials

- Creech, Sharon (2001). *Love That Dog*. Joanna Cotler Books.
- Response journals for students (writing paper or notebooks)
- Visual presenter (Elmo), projector (or overhead) and large screen
- Computer, projector, visual presenter (Elmo), and large screen for teacher demonstration of Web sites and literature

Motivation

- Using a projector, screen, and computer, introduce the class to Sharon Creech's Web site at www.sharoncreech.com/index.html. Read about *Love That Dog* and discuss how the author came up with ideas for the book.

Procedures

Day 1

- Begin reading *Love That Dog* aloud. Display the text on the visual presenter (or make overhead copies) to show the students how the words are printed on each page. Read aloud each of the referenced poems from the book before getting to the part where Jack comments on them. Encourage students to respond to each poem. After reading Jack's reactions, encourage class discussion. What did Jack think about the poems? Do you agree or disagree with his comments? How do think Jack feels about writing poetry? What are *your* feelings about writing poetry? Continue to read and discuss as time allows.

- Ask students to write their own poems (perhaps free-verse or formula poems) and reflect in a journal on their thoughts and feelings as they compose them.

Days 2–4

- Continue to read and discuss the book. After reading the part about Walter Dean Meyers (March 14), read the poem "Love That Boy" (reprinted in the back of *Love That Dog*) and visit Walter Dean Meyer's official Web site at www.harperchildrens.com/authorintro/index.asp?authorid=12522.
- Ask students to use a favorite poem as a model to write their own poems, just like Jack did with *Love That Boy*. In their journals, the students may discuss their favorite poems and the feelings these poems evoke in them.
- Emphasize how Jack is growing as a writer and overcoming many of his initial trepidations about writing poetry. Encourage students to make connections with their own progress as poets. Emphasize the importance of self-reflection and self-assessment of our own work.

Day 5

- Finish reading the book. Go back and review some of Jack's early journal entries and compare those with the end of the book. Encourage students to review their own responses to detect personal growth.
- Ask students to share some of their poems with the class.

Assessment

- Teacher-student conferences to monitor and discuss personal growth and changes in attitudes/perceptions toward poetry writing.

Accommodation/Modification

- Assist struggling students in selecting favorite poems and/or reading poems.
- Based on students' journal responses, the teacher may encourage students to write to the author of their favorite poem.

Visit the Meeting the Standards module in Chapter 15 of the Companion Website at www.prenhall.com/hancock to adapt this lesson to meet your state's standards.

The use of these five self-reflective questions over time become internalized and a natural part of everyday learning. Children begin to look ahead, to decide where they want to go next, and to plan how to reach that goal. This self-evaluative component parallels the process that is a critical part of portfolio assessment as self-reflection and goal-setting play key roles in the portfolio process. Post these questions in your classroom, ask them on a daily basis, model how you respond to them as an adult learner, and facilitate your students reaching their learning goals. The relationship between the self-evaluation process and one's journey as a lifelong learner make the time and the effort of this process in the classroom extremely worthwhile.

The Tech Tip included on page 489 highlights technology-based assessment tools. While some are mentioned in this section of the chapter, others provide new opportunities to offer authentic assessment to both students and teachers.

Assessment through Technology

Personal Digital Assistant

The personal digital assistant (PDA)—a small, handheld computer—can come in handy for teachers engaged in "kidwatching." Most PDAs are equipped with word-processing and spreadsheet software, allowing teachers to create simple assessment tools such as literacy checklists and anecdotal records. The collected assessment data can easily be transferred (hot synced) to the teacher's computer files or electronic grade book.

Rubrics

Kathy Schrock's Guide for Educators offers an extensive collection of assessment rubrics and graphic organizers that may be helpful as teachers begin to design their own content-specific rubrics. Links to related articles are also included. **http://school.discovery.com/schrockguide/assess.html#rubrics**

RubiStar is a free, web-based tool designed to help teachers who wants to use quality rubrics. Educators can choose from a wide range of templates, search for already-made rubrics, or develop their own from scratch. **http://rubistar.4teachers.org/index.php**

Electronic Literacy Portfolios

Similar in nature to traditional portfolios, *electronic literacy portfolios* (or *e-portfolios*) are becoming increasingly common in today's digital world. Electronic portfolios may include multimedia, sound files, active hyperlinks, and digital video and photography. Such portfolios may be stored on a computer's hard drive, a school's shared drive, or posted on the Internet. If stored on the web, such portfolios can be made accessible from remote locations (to be enjoyed by a child's grandparent for example). Instructional technology specialist Sandy Beck discusses the advantage of online portfolios and how to use them in her online article *Beck's Bits and Bytes.* **www.forsyth.k12.ga.us/sbeck/electronic_portfolios.htm**

Online Assessment Tools

QuizStar is a free web-based program where teachers can create and post their own online quizzes. This technology allows teachers and students to receive instant feedback (test scores), track, progress over time, and access the quizzes from remote locations (students may take a practice quiz from a home computer). *Quia* and *Quizlab* are examples of commercial Web sites with more advanced features.
http://quizstar.4teachers.org/ **www.quia.com** **www.quizlab.com**

To look more closely at these materials and others related to "Literacy Assessment," visit the Companion Website at www.prenhall.com/hancock.

Literacy Collections as Assessment

The assembling, organization, and presentation of student data are a complex part of assessment. Gathering data is only the initial portion of the process as effective presentation of data adds insight into the evaluative growth and progress of a learner. Two collection configurations for presenting ongoing data and work samples for elementary and middle-level students include literacy portfolios and literacy profiles. Each of these "literacy collections" provides an extensive array of detailed documentation of learning. While the literacy portfolio is student-centered and individual, the literacy profile is teacher-centered and professional. Both have important purposes in creating a genuine portrait of the literacy learner.

Literacy collections document a variety of literacy activities and accomplishments over time and across disciplines (Rhodes & Shanklin, 1993). They serve as an alternative to formal testing and focus on process as well as product while enabling reflection on accomplishments and goal setting for improvement. Literacy collections encourage communication at all levels (teacher-student; student-student; teacher-student-parent; teacher-teacher). The outcomes of collecting and presenting data as a literacy collection include the following:

- Student empowerment and appreciation of developing, sharing, and reflecting on his or her own literacy accomplishments
- Student ownership contributing to a sense of growth, progress, and goals across time
- Collaborative (rather than competitive) assessment involving student, teacher, and parents
- Parental engagement in first-hand documentation of achievement
- Teacher professionalism in the analysis, synthesis, and instructional decision making through a variety of data sources
- Teacher awareness of effectiveness of a blend of student-centered goal setting with teacher as professional decision maker, with both based on data relevant to each component of the learning team—student, teacher, and parent

Literacy Portfolios

The literacy portfolio provides documentation of student learning in all aspects of the language arts—reading, writing, listening, speaking, viewing, and visual representation. The variety of artifacts and uniqueness of each learner is showcased through a limited collection of literacy documentation collected over a period of time, selected by the student, reflected upon through oral or written means, and utilized as the basis of goal setting for future literacy growth (Tierney, Carter, & Desai, 1991).

The literacy portfolio is prepared through a four-stage process that is based on student-centered ownership and control:

- ***Collecting.*** Significant artifacts that represent elements of literacy are gathered over a period of time (grading period, quarter, school year). These artifacts represent limitless aspects of all the language arts. Figure 15.9 lists some of the many options available as evidence of learning in each of the six language arts. Note that the artifacts do not necessarily conform to a three-ring binder format. The multidimensions of learning inspire a variety of sizes and shapes in literacy performance.

FIGURE 15.9 Potential Literacy Portfolio Artifacts.

Reading
- Data list of books read
- Sustained silent reading record
- Response journal entries
- Written retellings
- Story maps
- Reading strategy checklist
- List of favorite books and authors

Writing
- Topics to write about list
- Lists of pieces written
- Drafts of a writing piece
- Analytic scoring of writing product
- Evidence of spelling strategies
- Author circle evaluation
- Self-assessments of writing
- Editing strategies checklist

Listening
- Response to teacher read-aloud
- List of PBS /Discovery Channel programs
- Response to visit of school author visit

Speaking
- Videotape of student play
- Videotape of oral report
- Audiotape of literature circle
- Self-evaluation of literature circle participation

Viewing
- List of videos adapted from literature
- Responses to videos viewed in class
- Photographs from field trips
- Documentation of plays or performances attended

Visual Representation
- Photographs of content area projects
- Graphic organizers
- Sketch to stretch activities
- PowerPoint presentation
- Word processing of a poem

Note to Student: Since the Language Arts are integrated, these artifacts could apply to more than one language arts category.

- ***Selecting.*** The student selects a limited number of literacy artifacts from the larger collection. The selected examples might be the student's best-liked, most important, or significant, or they may reflect acquisition of learning. The key is to limit the number to a few significant pieces that reflect reading, writing, listening, speaking, viewing, and visual representation. In fact, a single piece for each of the language arts forces the student to be highly selective with quality and significance taking precedence over quantity of work.
- ***Reflecting.*** The stage that distinguishes a literacy portfolio from a simple work folder is the element of reflection. Each student must write a reflection that includes (a) description/background of the artifact; (b) why it was selected; and (c) what it shows about the student as a literacy learner. The reflective portion of the portfolio is the most critical in thinking about the value and relevance of literacy to student lives.
- ***Projecting/goal setting.*** Following reflections on strengths, needs, and priorities in literacy learning, the student sets three to five specific goals to grow as a literate individual. These goals are typed on index cards and attached to a student's desk as a constant reminder of desired literacy priorities.

Throughout the school year, portfolios are continuously updated through ongoing collections, discriminate selections, insightful reflections, and new goal setting. Portfolios can be shared between peers, during teacher-student conferences, and as the basis of student-led parent conferences (see upcoming section of this chapter). They provide a dimension beyond test scores or report card grades and expand the vision of the child as a literacy learner. Portfolios celebrate the unique qualities and literacy accomplishments of each learner, without comparison or competition involved.

Literacy Profiles

A literacy profile is a verbal snapshot that captures the selection and analysis of a student's language arts performance by a teacher (Rhodes & Shanklin, 1993). Especially useful in parent conferences, staffings, and clinical placements, the literacy profile triangulates data (collects data from at least three sources) for optimal insights into the student as a literacy learner. The profile contains information not relevant and meaningful to students, but of high interest to teachers as professionals.

The profile for each student can be divided into three sections: (a) interests, (b) strategies, and (c) developmental level. Several data sources can be accumulated and synthesized for each section (Figure 15.10). In fact, the literacy profile is likely to carry all informative pieces about a child's literacy learning *except* the child's work itself. A narrative description emphasizes student strengths and explains areas for further growth. The profile concludes with a separate list of instructional recommendations for parents and for the current and additional teachers.

Used alongside a literacy portfolio (student ownership), it provides the broadest view of the child as a literacy learner. Literacy profiles showcase the professionalism of the teacher as a decision maker. Based on inventories, surveys, diagnostic tests, checklists, and standardized test scores (and furthered informed by documented student work in the literacy portfolio), a teaching professional is able to analyze the literacy strengths and needs and prioritize instructional decisions to assist the learner in further literacy growth.

Prescribed Literacy Assessment

Recent emphasis on performance on formal and informal tests has brought the requirement for continuous literacy testing, particularly in reading, to the language arts classroom (Barrentine & Stokes, 2005). Teachers are expected to use formal, published testing and informal recording to keep ongoing records of student performance. While it would take an entire textbook to describe the multiple factors of potential assessments in detail, this section provides an overview of the types of assessments that are typically prescribed by a school district to assess ongoing progress and placement in reading and writing.

A list of literacy assessment tools used by elementary and middle-level teachers can be provided by focusing on early, middle, and developed literacy. Each of these lists provides a generic test name, but specific, published tools are available through school districts. It is critical to realize that this dimension of assessment is expected and required in most schools as placement and instructional decision-making tools for individual students. The following are some of the currently mandated or teacher selected literacy assessments from a K–8 perspective:

- Concepts of print test
- Phonemic awareness evaluation
- Sound-letter association assessment
- Listening comprehension tests
- Running records with retelling guides

FIGURE 15.10 **Literacy Profiles—Reading and Writing Resources.**

	Reading Collection Resources
Interests:	Informal interest inventories Interest information from parents, teachers Classroom reading use Informal book selection activities
Strategies:	Reading interview Emergent reading/writing inventory Qualitative reading inventory Reading miscue inventory Assessments through instruction Parent and teacher interviews Anecdotal notes from classroom observations
Developmental Level:	Emergent reading/writing inventory Qualitative reading inventory Reading miscue inventory Assessments through instruction Parent and teacher interviews Anecdotal notes from classroom observations Standardized test scores
	Writing Collection Resources
Interests:	Informal interest inventories Interest information from parents, teachers Classroom writing use Lists of hot topics Pieces the student has already written
Strategies:	Writing interview Emergent reading/writing inventory Authoring cycle profile Assessments through instruction Parent and teacher interviews Anecdotal notes from classroom observations
Developmental Level:	Emergent reading/writing inventory Authoring cycle profile Holistic analysis of final products Assessments through instruction Parent and teacher interviews Anecdotal notes from classroom observations Standardized test scores

Source: L. K. Rhodes & N. L. Shanklin (1993). Windows into literacy: Assessing learners K–8. *Portsmouth, NH: Heinemann.*

FIGURE 15.11 Further Reading for Prescribed Literacy Assessments.

Clay, M. M. (2002). *An observation survey of early literacy achievement* (2nd ed.). Portsmouth, NH: Heinemann.

Clay, M. M. (2000). *Running records for classroom teachers*. Portsmouth, NH: Heinemann.

Filippo, R. F. (2003). *Assessing readers' qualitative diagnosis and instruction*. Portsmouth, NH: Heinemann.

Gunning, T. (2002). *Assessing and correcting reading and writing difficulties*. Boston: Allyn & Bacon.

Mariotti, A. S, & Homan, S. P. (Eds.) (2005). *Linking reading assessment to instruction: An application textbook for elementary classroom teachers* (4th ed.). Mahwah, NJ: Lawrence Erlbaum.

Reutzel, D. R., & Cooter, R. B. (2003). *Strategies for reading assessment and instruction: Helping every child succeed* (2nd ed.). Upper Saddle River, NJ: Merrill/Prentice Hall.

Rhodes, L. K. (1993). *Literacy assessment: A handbook of instruments*. Portsmouth, NH: Heinemann.

Silvaroli, N. J., & Wheelock, W. H. (2004). *Classroom reading inventory* (10th ed.). Boston: McGraw-Hill.

Spandell, V. (2001). *Creating writers: Through 6-trait writing assessment and instruction* (3rd ed.). New York: Addison-Wesley/Longman.

Wilde, S. (2000). *Miscue analysis made easy: Building on student strengths*. Portsmouth, NH: Heinemann.

Woods, M. L., & Moe, A. J. (2003). *Analytical reading inventory* (7th ed.). Upper Saddle River, NJ: Merrill/Prentice Hall.

- Miscue analysis
- Sight word lists
- Word analysis tests
- Decoding strategies inventory
- Comprehension strategy inventory
- Cloze tests
- Informal reading inventory
- Trait writing rubric
- Spelling stage identification test
- State-mandated tests

Figure 15.11 provides a list of professional books that will more deeply inform the teacher about the incorporation of several of these assessments into the literacy program and how resulting scores can inform literacy placements and individualized instruction. Results of these tests can effectively inform teacher decision making to guide instruction, group performance, or individualized learning.

Reporting Literacy Assessment to Parents

The reporting process in elementary and middle schools is constantly being revised as educators strive to match their reporting needs with the existing curriculum. Most schools are blending the traditional methods of reporting progress through report cards. However, a new, student-centered view of parent teacher conferences several times per year has invigorated and enhanced the authenticity of learning that goes beyond letter or numerical grades. Particularly in the language arts domain, evidence of student work alongside traditional grade report cards provides richer, deeper, and more informative monitoring of student progress. Considering both the sharing of "grades" and the documentation of authentic work samples during a conference provides two needed perspectives for discussing progress (or lack of it) with concerned parents.

Progress Reports: A Traditional Format

Most teachers are mandated to share grades, and the school progress report, in most cases, is the primary vehicle for sharing them with parents. Many report cards, however, have a new look as checklists, narratives, and child-composed self-evaluations are appended or constitute an integral part of the report card. These fresh evaluation tools more accurately reflect what and how children are being taught and the progress they are making in learning (Azwell & Schmar, 1995).

Parents have expressed a need for four types of information from report cards (Harste, 1996):

- Information about what was expected
- Information about what went on in the classroom
- Descriptions of how well their child did
- What they as parents can do to support learning

Because letter grades do not answer all of these inquiries, more teachers are adding a narrative letter to report cards to address these issues. That letter begins with specific activities that took place in language arts during the grading period. This section remains the same for each child. Next, teachers write a paragraph describing how each child did in relation to the curriculum, identifying strengths and weaknesses. Anecdotal records become an excellent resource for detailing these comments. Of course, this paragraph will be individualized for each child. Finally, teachers add comments of how parents may support classroom learning at home.

A self-evaluative letter written by the child may also be attached to the report card. To make this task manageable, students select a single project or product to talk about rather than trying to talk about all activities. Whether a few sentences (primary grades) or several paragraphs (intermediate/middle school), the voice of the child as learner finds its way into the evaluation process.

Most schools still incorporate traditional report cards. However, it seems impossible and improbable to translate a wealth of classroom experiences into a single letter grade, number, or check in a single box. As a professional, you should feel challenged to move beyond a required letter grade to provide additional narrative information on each child. Parents and guardians want to know that the classroom teacher cares about, understands, and appreciates the uniqueness of each child. Narrative comments communicate this kind of information.

Figure 15.12 focuses on two formats in which varied aspects of the language arts are reported through two different report card formats—primary and intermediate. Note the tendency to integrate reading, writing, and oral communication under the language arts heading. Some report cards reflect dual perspectives on language learning. For example, spelling may be assessed within the context of student authentic writing as well as on a weekly spelling list. Writing may be evaluated through both a process and a product approach. In some cases, report cards contain checklists of grade-level state standards. Report cards continue to evolve, but they should always align with the standards and the way the curriculum is taught in each classroom. If the printed report card fails to do this, the teacher must provide additional information to share the uniqueness and accomplishments of the learner with parents.

FIGURE 15.12 Language Arts Progress Reports.

PRIMARY (K–2) PROGRESS REPORT
SCHOOL YEAR ____ ____

STUDENT ______________________

SCHOOL ______________________

TEACHER ______________________

Attendance				
Days absent				
Days tardy				
School work is affected because of absences				

Beginning = Needs more time; Consistently = Almost always; Developing = Progressing satisfactorily; Blank = Not evaluated at this time

	1st Quarter			2nd Quarter			3rd Quarter			4th Quarter		
	Needs More Time	Progressing Satisfactorily	Almost Always	Needs More Time	Progressing Satisfactorily	Almost Always	Needs More Time	Progressing Satisfactorily	Almost Always	Needs More Time	Progressing Satisfactorily	Almost Always
COMMUNICATION ESSENTIAL OBJECTIVES												
Reading												
Reads for enjoyment												
Sequences pictures												
Sequences sentences												
Identifies letters												
Recognizes letter sounds												
Demonstrates comprehension in reading												
Knows and uses basic reading vocabulary												
Uses decoding skills (e.g., phonics and context clues)												
Speaking and Listening												
Uses oral language appropriately												
Listens attentively for short perods of time												
Follows oral instructions												
Writing												
Uses legible manuscript												
Uses inventive spelling												
Copies a given sentences												
Expresses ideas in writing												

1st Quarter Comments:	**2nd Quarter Comments:**
3rd Quarter Comments:	**4th Quarter Comments:** Grade Placement for Next Year_______

Conferences: A Reflective Experience

The most effective communication tool to showcase individual learning is the conference format. The conference can take place in a variety of formats—student-teacher; student-parent-teacher; student-parent—while it provides an opportunity for those who know the learner best to celebrate accomplishments, voice concerns, and set fresh

FIGURE 15.12 (Continued)

STUDENTS PROGRESS REPORT

Student ____________________ School ____________________

Teacher ____________________ Grade ______ Year ______ To ______

Principal ____________________

Cumulative Attendance by Reporting Periods →

Days Present	1.	2.	3.	4.	Total
Days Absent	1.	2.	3.	4.	Total
Times Tardy	1.	2.	3.	4.	Total

* Achievemant level and specific skills presented will be discussed at parent-teacher conferences.

Reporting Period	PROGRESS: Progress Satistactary for Ability	PROGRESS: Not Working Up to Ability	ACHIEVEMENT: Work Above Average	ACHIEVEMENT: Work Average	ACHIEVEMENT: Work Below Average	Level *: If other than Grade Assigned
READING						
1						
2						
3						
4						
LANGUAGE						
1						
2						
3						
4						
HANDWRITING						
1						
2						
3						
4						
SPELLING						
1						
2						
3						
4						

Any area not marked has not been stressed during this reporting period	1: Highly Satisfactory	1: Satisfactory	1: Improving	1: Needs to Improve	2: Highly Satisfactory	2: Satisfactory	2: Improving	2: Needs to Improve	3: Highly Satisfactory	3: Satisfactory	3: Improving	3: Needs to Improve	4: Highly Satisfactory	4: Satisfactory	4: Improving	4: Needs to Improve
READING																
Comprehends what is read																
Reads orally with expression																
Shows interest in independent reading																
Understands and retains concepts																
Learns and applies word attack skills																
LANGUAGE																
Uses correct grammar in speaking																
Uses correct grammar in written work																
Organizes and expresses ideas clearly																
Shows creative ability in language																
Uses proper capitalization and punctuation																
Learns and applies dictionary and other reference skills																
HANDWRITING																
Forms letters and numerals correctely																
Written neatly and legibly																
SPELLING																
Spells assigned words																
Spells correctly in written work																

COMMENTS

goals. Pride, purpose, and resolve surround each type of conference and showcase the child as a unique literacy learner. Jane Hansen (1998) stated, "When you listen, your students tell you what you have never heard. They help you understand what you never knew. They take you where you don't expect to go." The self-evaluative aspects of the conference format, particularly in language arts, provide an opportunity for learners to evaluate themselves, to bring meaning to their work, and to show commitment to and value growth.

Student-Teacher Conferences. While student-teacher interactions occur on a daily basis in the classroom, the focus of a one-on-one conference between student and teacher is essential several times per evaluation period. While the teacher serves as facilitator, it is the student who carries most of the discussion by talking about himself or herself as a literate person. Questions must be structured to encourage students to give extended answers that demonstrate personal reflection. Risk taking, sharing, and initiation of ideas are hallmarks of effective conferences. The literacy portfolio containing language arts artifacts becomes the focus of the conference, with the student explaining how each language arts piece reflects an aspect of his or her literacy. The tone of the conference remains positive, focusing on what the learner can do, but gradually leads toward reflection on what the learner wants to be able to do in the future.

Student-teacher conferences can last from 15 to 20 minutes with a set agenda: (a) student talks about literacy strengths; (b) student talks about literacy needs and priorities; (c) student, with the guidance of teacher, sets specific literacy goals. Goals are recorded and become a constant reminder of areas of emphasis in the coming weeks. A great variety of literacy goals exists that children may choose to pursue, but it is important for the child to set the goal and to state it in his or her own words. A written record of those goals placed on an index card on a desk or in a notebook provides a constant reminder of targeted literacy development.

Student-Parent-Teacher Conferences. For many decades, the learner was isolated from the conference between a parent and a teacher. Remember how you were forced to stay at home or sent to the library or playground, never allowed to hear the things that were said about you or your work. You received that information secondhand as your parent(s) exited the classroom and you begged to hear what had been said. Educators have finally realized the importance of the learner's role in the parent-teacher conference. While the teacher facilitates the agenda of the conference, the child is able to answer questions, show pride in work completed, admit areas that require additional attention, and respond to parental inquiries. Even young children delight in talking about what they can do as readers and writers. A report card is generally shared at these conferences, but showing portfolios alongside traditional grades provides a masterful means of showing a full perspective on the learner.

Some parents may desire time alone with the teacher to discuss behavior or specific problems. A child can be dismissed after 10 minutes of a conference and still feel he or she has played a contributory role. If your teaching philosophy is child-centered, it seems impossible to eliminate the child from playing a key role in the conference. Teachers are learning to balance the habits of the past with the effectiveness of student participation and find a way to effectively include all voices in a conference.

Student-Led Parent-Teacher Conferences. The purpose of the student-led parent-teacher conference is to help students accept the responsibility of reporting literacy progress to their parents. Successfully implemented in K–8 settings, this process enables students to interpret their own literacy growth (Cleland, 1999) as they learn accountability for work produced, improve communication skills, increase leadership skills, and develop problem-solving strategies and decision-making methods. The model of student-led parent-teacher conferences involves three phases of activities for parents, teachers, and students:

- ***Preparation phase.*** Parents must be prepared for this new type of conference setting. Through a letter home or introduction at a back-to-school night, parents can learn about the rationale for handing over leadership roles to students and the goals of increased accountability, involvement, and control. Students prepare invitations including suggested time, date, place, and purpose of the conference as well as interesting things parents will see. The preparation phase also includes role-playing and practice in communication skills. Students practice formal introductions, showing details of their work, and answering questions. Of course, portfolios, as mentioned earlier in the chapter, are prepared, organized, and scrutinized so each child will be in touch with his or her work. A format for a "Letter to Parents," placed in the portfolio, provides an outline or agenda for viewing and discussing the child's work. Finally, the teacher sets the final appointments and comfortably arranges the room for the conferences.
- ***Implementation phase.*** The teacher acts only as a facilitator by giving support and encouragement to students, intervening only if necessary. Some teachers prefer one family conference at a time, while others like three to four family conferences taking place simultaneously for 30 to 45 minutes as the teacher joins each group for 10 minutes. The student greets the parents, guides them to the conference center, and begins to follow the agenda prepared in the letter. The child reads, explains, talks, shows, directs, and informs. Some teachers actually prefer a checklist to make certain all important areas are covered. The parent has shown a commitment to the child by attending the conference but is asked to make a written comment about the child's work. Some parents will still request a traditional parent-teacher conference, and the teacher must be prepared to set up additional time for this to occur.
- ***Evaluation phase.*** The day following the completion of all conferences, the students and teacher need to discuss what worked well, identify any problems, and determine what changes could be made to improve the conferences. Parents often provide unsolicited input as they communicate through notes, e-mails, and phone calls the pride they felt in the presentation of their child. Children gain confidence through this experience and grow in their ability to share their work in subsequent conferences.

The student-led conference seems to be the ultimate exchange to which teachers strives in sharing assessment. While it takes much time and preparation, students become accountable to themselves and their parents for a display of their literacy strengths and areas for continued growth. More progress is likely to take place if students assume their responsibility as literacy learners.

The Issue of High-Stakes Testing

As this chapter concludes, the issue at the forefront of the educational arena concerns "teaching in a world focused on testing" (Buckner, 2002). The increase in the amount of testing, the number of students tested, and the decline in the age of students being tested across the nation characterize the current educational scenario. Public and political criticism of schools tends to lead to even more assessment. The No Child Left Behind legislation mandates testing for children throughout their academic K–12 careers and demands adequate yearly progress for each learner.

State and local districts are increasingly using test scores to make a variety of important decisions. The term "high-stakes testing" applies to critical decisions on student promotion or retention, teacher review and merit, and state or federal funding based on the results of targeted testing. The test is typically a single multiple-choice format that yields limited information upon which to make valid instructional decisions based on educational quality.

Testing students' skills and knowledge is an essential part of education and accountability is a professional responsibility. Yet testing provides only a single perspective on student learning. Most states have developed and adopted assessment tests aligned with their state standards. The positive aspect of these tests is that they are useful for making state-level decisions on education and they provide the public with some understanding of how well schools are doing.

On the other hand, reading test scores, for example, may show improvement, but these gains may be falsely attributed to effective instruction when they may likely be due to "teaching to the test." Teaching to the test implies that significant time is spent teaching not only the test content, but also test-taking strategies rather than focusing on the long-term outcomes implied by effective language arts instruction (Lawrence, 2002).

The negative side of high-stakes tests is that they do influence classroom instruction—the ways we teach reading and writing. Testing puts teachers in an ethical dilemma: effective instruction with long-range learning implications for children versus teaching to the test for short-term results. It is critical to remember it is not ethical to devote substantial instructional time to teaching to the test (International Reading Association, 1999). Professionalism requires an ethical view of testing as a mandate but not a driving force in what we teach. Yet America's love-hate relationship with testing and the nation's current emphasis on accountability often undermines the public's trust and confidence in teachers and public schools and may even dictate the way teachers teach (Winograd & Arrington, 1999).

Because tests are not perfect, no single test score can be considered a conclusive measure of a student's knowledge or ability. Any educational decision that will have a major impact on a child should not be made solely on the basis of a single test score, but on *multiple* measures of a child's performance. Teachers must inform parents of the many forms of performance-based assessment, used *in addition to* standardized tests, which can improve instruction and benefit students learning to read, write, and become literate citizens. Most of the lifelong literacy strategies taught in authentic reading and writing contexts cannot be adequately measured on a multiple-choice test. Yet these become the very strategies that receive less instructional attention in the classroom while teachers address items that can be tested in this limited, multiple-choice format. Just because a teacher is opposed to high-stakes testing does not mean she or he is opposed to assessment or accountability. Aligning teachers' purposes and goals of instruction with the type of assessments they use is key to the survival of literacy education (International Reading Association & National Council of Teachers of English, 1994).

Visit the Companion Website at www.prenhall.com/hancock and gauge your understanding of Chapter 15 concepts with the self-assessments.

Closing Thoughts

The complexity of the assessment puzzle may never completely be solved. But the potential solution is certainly not as simple as a single, standardized test that will do the whole job. The solution lies in piecing together the needs of decision makers, the knowledge of teachers, the aspirations of parents, and the goals of students by providing separate, but authentic pieces that reflect varying perspectives on authentic literacy learning. "Assessment should be viewed as ongoing and suggestive rather than fixed or definitive" (Tierney, 1998, p. 386). Highly individualized documentation of learning based in authentic classroom instruction with generous opportunities for self-assessment seem to provide the balanced pieces that will most effectively complete the literacy assessment puzzle.

Putting together the pieces of this literacy assessment puzzle requires the gathering of perspectives on each child from multiple data resources (surveys, interviews, checklists, continuums, rubrics, portfolio artifacts, and test scores) to provide an overall portrait of the individual learner over time. Teachers can be effective and remain true to teaching excellence despite the tug-of-war surrounding testing. Only the ongoing collecting of assessment data aligned with curriculum standards, the evaluation of that data to determine the needs of each individual student, and the use of the data to inform the instructional decision-making of a teacher will make a true difference in teaching and learning the language arts in our schools today.

References

Azwell, T., & Schmar, E. (Eds.) (1995). *Report card on report cards: Alternatives to consider*. Portsmouth, NH: Heinemann.

Barrentine, S. J., & Stokes, S. M. (Eds.) (2005). *Reading assessement: Principles and practices for elementary teachers* (2nd ed.). Newark, DE: International Reading Association.

Boyd-Batstone, P. (2004). Focused anecdotal records assessment: A tool for standards-based, authentic assessment. *The Reading Teacher, 58,* 230–239.

Buckner, A. (2002). Teaching in a world focused on testing. *Language Arts, 79,* 212–215.

Calkins, L., Montgomery, K., Santman, D., & Falk, B. (1998). *A teacher's guide to standardized reading tests: Knowledge is power*. Portsmouth, NH: Heinemann.

Cleland, J. V. (1999). We can charts: Building blocks for student-led conferences. *The Reading Teacher, 52,* 588–595.

Cobb, C. (2003). Effective instruction begins with purposeful assessments. *The Reading Teacher, 57,* 386–388.

Estes, T. H. (1971). A scale to measure attitudes toward reading. *Journal of Reading,* 15, 135–138.

Fu, D., & Lamme, L. L. (2002). Assessment through conversation. *Language Arts, 79,* 241–250.

Goodman, Y. (1985). Kidwatching: Observing children in the classroom. In A. Jagger & T. Smith-Burke (Eds.), *Observing the language learner* (pp. 9–18). Newark, DE: International Reading Association and National Council of Teachers of English.

Hansen, J. (1998). *When learners evaluate*. Portsmouth, NH: Heinemann.

Harste, J. (1996). Using a narrative report card. *School Talk, 2,* 3–4.

Hill, B. C. (2001). *Developmental continuums: A framework for literacy instruction and assessment, K–8*. Norwood, MA: Christopher-Gordon.

Hill, B. C., & Ruptic, C. (1994). *Practical aspects of authentic assessment: Putting the pieces together*. Norwood, MA: Christopher-Gordon.

Hill, B. C., Ruptic, C., & Norwick, L. (1998). *Classroom based assessment*. Norwood, MA: Christopher-Gordon.

International Reading Association (1999). High-stakes assessments in reading: A position statement of the International Reading Association. *The Reading Teacher, 53,* 257–264.

International Reading Association & National Council of Teachers of English (1994). *Standards for the assessment of reading and writing*. Prepared by the IRA/NCTE Joint Task Force on Assessment. Newark, DE: Author.

International Reading Association & National Council of Teachers of English (1996). *Standards for the English Language Arts*. Newark, DE: Author.

Kear, D. J., Coffman, G. A., McKenna, M. C., & Ambrosio, A. L. (2000). Measuring attitude toward writing: A new tool for teachers. *The Reading Teacher, 54,* 10–23.

Keene, E., & Zimmerman, S. (1997). *Mosaic of thought: Teaching comprehension in a reader's workshop*. Portsmouth, NH: Heinemann.

Lawrence, K. M. (2002). Red light, green light, 1-2-3: Tasks to prepare for standardized tests. *The Reading Teacher, 55,* 525–528.

McKenna, M. C., & Kear, D. (1990). Measuring attitude toward reading: A new tool for teachers. *The Reading Teacher, 43,* 626–639.

O'Keefe, T. (1997). The habit of kidwatching: Quality versus quantity. *School Talk, 3,* 4–5.

Rhodes, L. K., & Nathenson-Meija, S. (1992). Anecdotal records: A powerful tool for ongoing literacy assessment. *The Reading Teacher, 45,* 502–511.

Rhodes, L. K., & Shanklin, N. L. (1993). *Windows into literacy: Assessing learners K–8.* Portsmouth, NH: Heinemann.

Routman, R. (2000). *Conversations: Strategies for teaching, learning, and evaluating.* Portsmouth, NH: Heinemann.

Skillings, M. J. & Ferrell, R. (2000). Student-generated rubrics: Bringing students into the assessment process. *The Reading Teacher, 53,* 452–455.

Stiggins, R. (1997). *Student-centered classroom assessment.* Upper Saddle River, NJ: Merrill Prentice Hall.

Tierney, R. J. (1998). Literacy assessment reform: Shifting beliefs, principled possibilities, and emerging practices. *The Reading Teacher, 51,* 374–390.

Tierney, R. J., Carter, M., & Desai, L. (1991). *Portfolio assessment in the reading-writing classroom.* Norwood, MA: Christopher-Gordon.

Valencia, S. W., Hiebert, E. H., & Afflerbach, P. P. (1994). *Authentic reading assessment: Practices and possibilities.* Newark, DE: International Reading Association.

Winograd, P., & Arrington, H. J. (1999). Best practices in literacy assessment. In L. B. Gambrell, L. M. Morrow, S. B. Neuman, & M. Pressley (Eds.), *Best practices in literacy instruction* (pp. 210–241). New York: Guilford Press.

Wolf, S. A., & Wolf, K. P. (2002). Teaching *true* and *to* the test in writing. *Language Arts, 79,* 229–240.

Children's Books Cited

Creech, Sharon (2001). *Love that dog.* New York: HarperCollins.

Finchler, Judy (2000). *Testing Miss Malarkey.* Illus. by Kevin O'Malley. New York: Walker.

Lobel, Arnold (1970). *Frog and toad are friends.* New York: Harper & Row.

Williams, Sue (1990). I went walking. Illus. by Julie Vivas. San Diego: Harcourt.

Index

Note: Locators in italics indicate features.